October 22–23, 2011
Portland, Oregon, USA

**Association for
Computing Machinery**

Advancing Computing as a Science & Profession

GPCE'11

Proceedings of the Tenth International Conference on
Generative Programming and Component Engineering

Sponsored by:
ACM SIGPLAN

**Association for
Computing Machinery**

Advancing Computing as a Science & Profession

The Association for Computing Machinery
2 Penn Plaza, Suite 701
New York, New York 10121-0701

Notice to Past Authors of ACM-Published Articles
ACM intends to create a complete electronic archive of all articles and/or other material previously
published by ACM. If you have written a work that has been previously published by ACM in any journal
or conference proceedings prior to 1978, or any SIG Newsletter at any time, and you do NOT want this
work to appear in the ACM Digital Library, please inform permissions@acm.org, stating the title of the
work, the author(s), and where and when published.

ISBN: 978-1-4503-0689-8

Additional copies may be ordered prepaid from:

ACM Order Department
PO Box 11405
New York, NY 10286-1405

Phone: 1-800-342-6626 (USA and Canada)
    +1-212-626-0500 (all other countries)
Fax: +1-212-944-1318
E-mail: acmhelp@acm.org

ACM Order Number: 548112

Printed in the USA

Preface

These are the proceedings of the *10th ACM International Conference on Generative Programming and Component Engineering (GPCE'11)*, collocated with *Systems, Programming, Languages and Applications: Software for Humanity 2011 (SPLASH'11).* This year's conference continues its tradition of being the premier venue for researchers and practitioners interested in techniques that use program generation and component deployment to increase programmer productivity, improve software quality, and shorten the time-to-market of software products. In addition to exploring cutting-edge techniques of generative and component-based software, the goal of the conference is to foster further cross-fertilization between the software engineering and the programming languages research communities, a goal supported both by a strong technical program bringing in contributions and researchers from both research communities and from our collocation with *SPLASH.*

The call for papers attracted 55 submissions from Africa, Asia, Europe, and North and South America. The program committee accepted 18 papers that cover a variety of topics within the key areas of domain-specific languages, program generation and components, and also novel topics such as empirical studies of software product lines and model-based tool development for robotics. The program includes two keynotes: Matthias Felleisen from Northeastern University on *Multilingual Component Programming in Racket,* and Gary Shubert from Lockheed Martin Space Systems Company on the *Application of Model Based Development to Flexible Code Generation.* In addition, the program includes two technical talks that provide in-depth treatment of selected research results, namely inter-derivation of formal semantics and the industrial application of domain-specific languages to cryptography.

Putting together *GPCE'11* was a team effort. First of all, we would like to thank the authors, the keynote speakers, and the tech talk speakers for providing the content of the program. We would like to express our gratitude to the program committee and external reviewers, who worked very hard in reviewing papers and providing detailed suggestions for their improvements. We would also like to thank Chang Hwan Peter Kim, this year's Publicity Chair. Special thanks go to Yukki Wong for helping with the organization and to Vibeke Nielsen for designing an all-new graphical layout for the flyer, poster, and T-shirt. Finally, we would like to thank our sponsor, ACM SIGPLAN, for their continued support of these successful meetings.

We hope that you will find this program inspiring and compelling, and that the conference will provide you with a valuable opportunity to share ideas with other researchers and practitioners from institutions around the world.

Ewen Denney   **Ulrik Pagh Schultz**
GPCE'11 General Chair   *GPCE'11 Program Chair*
SGT/NASA Ames, USA   *University of Southern Denmark, Denmark*

Table of Contents

GPCE 2011 Conference Organization vii

Keynote Address 1
Session Chair: Ulrik P. Schultz *(University of Southern Denmark)*

- **Multilingual Component Programming in Racket**.. 1
  Matthias Felleisen *(Northeastern University)*

Session 1: Software Product Lines

- **Tailoring Dynamic Software Product Lines** 3
  Marko Rosenmüller, Norbert Siegmund, Mario Pukall *(University of Magdeburg)*,
  Sven Apel *(University of Passau)*

- **Feature Interactions, Products, and Composition** 13
  Don Batory *(University of Texas at Austin)*, Peter Höfner *(University of Augsburg)*,
  Jongwook Kim *(University of Texas at Austin)*

- **On the Impact of Feature Dependencies When Maintaining Preprocessor-Based Software
  Product Lines** 23
  Márcio Ribeiro, Felipe Queiroz, Paulo Borba, Társis Tolêdo *(Federal University of Pernambuco)*,
  Claus Brabrand *(IT University of Copenhagen)*, Sérgio Soares *(Federal University of Pernambuco)*

- **Investigating the Safe Evolution of Software Product Lines** 33
  Laís Neves, Leopoldo Teixeira, Paulo Borba *(Federal University of Pernambuco)*,
  Vander Alves *(University of Brasília)*,
  Demóstenes Sena, Uirá Kulezsa *(Federal University of Rio Grande do Norte)*

Session 2: Software Components

- **Static Analysis of Aspect Interaction and Composition in Component Models** 43
  Abdelhakim Hannousse *(Ascola, INRIA, EMN & Aelos, LINA)*, Rémi Douence *(LINA & INRIA)*,
  Gilles Ardourel *(Aelos, Université de Nantes, LINA)*

- **Infrastructure for Component-Based DDS Application Development** 53
  William R. Otte, Aniruddha Gokhale, Douglas C. Schmidt *(Vanderbilt University)*,
  Johnny Willemsen *(Remedy IT)*

Session 3: Applications

- **Generation of Geometric Programs Specified by Diagrams** 63
  Yulin Li *(Amazon Inc.)*, Gordon S. Novak, Jr. *(University of Texas at Austin)*

- **Model-Driven Engineering and Run-Time Model-Usage in Service Robotics**...................73
  Andreas Steck, Alex Lotz, Christian Schlegel *(University of Applied Sciences Ulm)*

- **Generating Database Migrations for Evolving Web Applications** 83
  Sander D. Vermolen, Guido Wachsmuth, Eelco Visser *(Delft University of Technology)*

Tech Talk 1
Session Chair: Ulrik P. Schultz *(University of Southern Denmark)*

- **Pragmatics for Formal Semantics** 93
  Olivier Danvy *(University of Aarhus)*

Keynote Address 2
Session Chair: Ewen Denney *(SGT/NASA Ames)*

- **Application of Model Based Development to Flexible Code Generation**.........................95
  Gary Shubert *(Lockheed Martin Space Systems)*

Session 4: Runtime

- **Reflection in Direct Style**..97
  Kenichi Asai *(Ochanomizu University)*

- **Firepile: Run-Time Compilation for GPUs in Scala**..107
  Nathaniel Nystrom *(University of Lugano)*, Derek White, Kishen Das *(University of Texas at Arlington)*

- **Monitoring Aspects for the Customization of Automatically Generated Code
  for Big-Step Models**...117
  Shahram Esmaeilsabzali, Bernd Fischer *(University of Southampton)*, Joanne M. Atlee *(University of Waterloo)*

- **Declaratively Defining Domain-Specific Language Debuggers**...........................127
  Ricky T. Lindeman, Lennart C. L. Kats, Eelco Visser *(Delft University of Technology)*

Session 5: Theory

- **Less is More: Unparser-completeness of Metalanguages for Template Engines**..............137
  B. J. Arnoldus, M. G. J. van den Brand, A. Serebrenik *(Eindhoven University of Technology)*

- **Towards Automatic Generation of Formal Specifications to Validate
  and Verify Reliable Distributed Systems**...147
  Vidar Slåtten, Frank Alexander Kraemer, Peter Herrmann *(Norwegian University of Science and Technology)*

Session 6: Programming

- **Comparing Complexity of API Designs:
  An Exploratory Experiment on DSL-based Framework Integration**..................157
  Stefan Sobernig *(WU Vienna)*, Patrick Gaubatz *(University of Vienna)*, Mark Strembeck *(WU Vienna)*,
  Uwe Zdun *(University of Vienna)*

- **Growing a Language Environment with Editor Libraries**...............................167
  Sebastian Erdweg *(University of Marburg)*, Lennart C. L. Kats *(Delft University of Technology)*,
  Tillmann Rendel, Christian Kästner, Klaus Ostermann *(University of Marburg)*,
  Eelco Visser *(Delft University of Technology)*

- **Helping Programmers Help Users**...177
  John Freeman, Jaakko Järvi, Wonseok Kim *(Texas A&M University)*,
  Mat Marcus *(Canyonlands Software Design)*, Sean Parent *(Adobe Systems, Inc.)*

Tech Talk 2
Session Chair: Ewen Denney *(SGT/NASA Ames)*,

- **Theorem-Based Circuit Derivation in Cryptol**..185
  John Launchbury *(Galois, Inc.)*

Author Index..186

GPCE 2011 Conference Organization

General Chair: Ewen Denney *(SGT/NASA Ames, USA)*

Program Chair: Ulrik Pagh Schultz *(University of Southern Denmark, Denmark)*

Publicity Chair: Chang Hwan Peter Kim *(University of Texas at Austin, USA)*

Steering Committee Chair: Charles Consel *(INRIA/University of Bordeaux, France)*

Steering Committee: Bernd Fischer *(University of Southampton, United Kingdom)*
Jaakko Järvi *(Texas A&M University, USA)*
Julia Lawall *(University of Copenhagen, Denmark)*
Jeremy Siek *(University of Colorado at Boulder, USA)*
Eelco Visser *(Delft University of Technology, The Netherlands)*

Program Committee: Don Batory *(University of Texas at Austin, USA)*
Walter Binder *(University of Lugano, Switzerland)*
Ras Bodik *(University of California at Berkeley, USA)*
Görel Hedin *(Lund University, Sweden)*
Bernd Fischer *(University of Southampton, UK)*
Tudor Girba *(netstyle.ch, Switzerland)*
Robert Glück *(University of Copenhagen, Denmark)*
Anirüddhā Gokhālé *(Vanderbilt University, USA)*
Christian Kästner *(Philipps Universität Marburg, Germany)*
Yanhong A. Liu *(State University of New York at Stony Brook, USA)*
Nicolas Loriant *(Imperial College, UK)*
Mat Marcus *(Canyonlands Software Design, USA)*
Marjan Mernik *(University of Maribor, Slovenia)*
Bruno C. d. S. Oliveira *(Seoul National University, Korea)*
Ina Schaefer *(TU Braunschweig, Germany)*
Lionel Seinturier *(University of Lille, France)*
Chung-chieh Shan *(Cornell University, USA)*
Jeremy Siek *(University of Colorado at Boulder, USA)*
Eric Tanter *(University of Chile, Chile)*
Eli Tilevich *(Virginia Tech, USA)*
Jurgen Vinju *(Centrum Wiskunde en Informatica, The Netherlands)*
Andrzej Wąsowski *(IT University of Copenhagen, Denmark)*
Jeremiah Willcock *(Indiana University, USA)*
Steffen Zschaler *(King's College London, UK)*

Additional reviewers:

Jesper Andersen	Torben Mogensen
Anya Helene Bagge	Adriaan Moors
Michael Becker	Philippe Moret
Thorsten Berger	Sebastien Mosser
Carl Friedrich Bolz	Alena Navahonskaya
Julien Bruneau	Cristobal Navarro
Deji Chen	Henrik Nilsson
Wontae Choi	Russel Nzekwa
Nathan Chong	Jason Perry
Giorgios Economopoulos	Rolf-Helge Pfeiffer
Sebastian Erdweg	Moss Prescott
Shahram Esmaeilsabzali	Thomas Pécseli
Niklas Fors	Tom Rothamel
Daniel Friedman	Francis Russell
Martin Gebauer	Aibek Sarimbekov
Sven Gestegard Robertz	Max Schaefer
Michael Gorbovitski	Steven She
Neville Grech	Erik Silkensen
Klaus Marius Hansen	Emma Soederberg
Yungbum Jung	Gabriel Tamura
Ingolf Krueger	Jonathan Turner
Wonchan Lee	Tijs Van Der Storm
Bo Lin	Alex Villazon
Frédéric Loiret	Joe Wegehaupt
Lukas Marek	Tetsuo Yokoyama

Sponsor:  SIGPLAN

Keynote

Multilingual Component Programming in Racket

Matthias Felleisen

PLT, Northeastern University

matthias @ ccs.neu.edu

Abstract

In the world of Racket, software systems consist of inter-operating components in different programming languages. A component's implementation language may provide the full functionality of Racket, or it may support a small domain-specific notation. Naturally, Racketeers construct languages as Racket components and compose them to create new languages. This talk will present the ideas behind Racket: language-specific components, the composition of components, and, most importantly, the rich support for building languages.

Categories and Subject Descriptors D.3.3 [*Programming Languages*]: Language Constructs and Features

General Terms Languages, Design

Keywords Multi-Lingual Component Programming

Recommended Readings

[1] R. K. Dybvig, R. Hieb, and C. Bruggeman. Syntactic abstraction in Scheme. *Lisp and Symbolic Computation*, 5(4):295–326, Dec. 1993.

Note: This paper establishes the foundations of the syntax system now used in Racket and Scheme. Its technical contributions are a syntax representation disjoint from existing data types and a computational, pattern-based syntax rewriting facility.

[2] R. Culpepper and M. Felleisen. Fortifying macros. In *ACM SIGPLAN International Conference on Functional Programming*, pages 235–246, 2010.

Note: This paper refines Dybvig et al.'s syntax system [1] so that programmers can declaratively specify constraints on new syntax. With this new mechanism, syntax extensions become features that are automatically (nearly) indistinguishable from built-in constructs.

[3] R. Culpepper and M. Felleisen. Debugging macros. In *Generative Programming and Component Engineering*, pages 135–144, 2007.

Note: This paper presents a strategy for implementing a macro debugger that correctly explains the hygienic expansions of macros [1, 2]. The debugger is a part of the Racket tool suite.

[4] M. Flatt. Composable and compilable macros: you want it when. In *ACM SIGPLAN International Conference on Functional Programming*, pages 72–83, 2002.

Note: This paper lifts the syntax system of Dybvig et al. [1] to the first-order module level. In this world, a module can export and import syntactic abstractions. At the same time, a strict separation between syntax elaboration and program execution enables the automatic and safe compilation of such modules.

[5] S. Krishnamurthi. *Linguistic Reuse*. PhD thesis, Rice University, 2001.

Note: This dissertation on syntactic extensions for first-class components inspired Flatt's development [4]. It also introduced the idea of *linguistic reuse*. To accommodate the existing tool chain, an embedded language should reuse the features of its host language.

[6] R. Culpepper, S. Owens, and M. Flatt. Syntactic abstraction in component interfaces. In *Generative Programming and Component Engineering*, pages 373–388, 2005.

Note: This paper proposes an alternative mechanism for sharing syntactic abstractions among first-class components.

[7] S. Tobin-Hochstadt, V. St-Amour, R. Culpepper, M. Flatt, and M. Felleisen. Languages as libraries. In *ACM SIGPLAN Conference on Programming Language Design and Implementation*, pages 132–141, 2011.

Note: This paper illustrates the idea of linguistic reuse via a comprehensive case study. It explains how linguistic reuse can happen during parsing, static analysis, code generation, and optimization. At the same time, it enumerates what the syntax system must provide in support of linguistic reuse beyond Flatt's syntax system [4] and Culpepper's fortified macros [2].

GPCE'11, October 22–23, 2011, Portland, Oregon, USA.
ACM 978-1-4503-0689-8/11/10.

Tailoring Dynamic Software Product Lines

Marko Rosenmüller, Norbert Siegmund,
Mario Pukall

University of Magdeburg, Germany

Sven Apel

University of Passau, Germany

Abstract

Software product lines (SPLs) and *adaptive systems* aim at variability to cope with changing requirements. Variability can be described in terms of *features*, which are central for development and configuration of SPLs. In traditional SPLs, features are bound statically before runtime. By contrast, adaptive systems support feature binding at runtime and are sometimes called *dynamic SPLs (DSPLs)*. DSPLs are usually built from coarse-grained components, which reduces the number of possible application scenarios. To overcome this limitation, we closely integrate static binding of traditional SPLs and runtime adaptation of DSPLs. We achieve this integration by statically generating a tailor-made DSPL from a highly customizable SPL. The generated DSPL provides only the runtime variability required by a particular application scenario and the execution environment. The DSPL supports self-configuration based on coarse-grained modules. We provide a feature-based adaptation mechanism that reduces the effort of computing an optimal configuration at runtime. In a case study, we demonstrate the practicability of our approach and show that a seamless integration of static binding and runtime adaptation reduces the complexity of the adaptation process.

Categories and Subject Descriptors D.2.13 [*Software Engineering*]: Reusable Software—Reusable libraries, Reuse models

General Terms Design, Languages

Keywords Software Product Lines, Dynamic Binding, Feature-oriented Programming

1. Introduction

Software product line (SPL) engineering aims at variable software by generating a set of tailor-made programs from a common code base (e.g., for different customers or application scenarios) [28]. SPL engineers consider *features* as central abstractions for configuration because they are implementation independent and map directly to user requirements. For example, a feature QUERYENGINE of an SPL for database management systems (DBMS) represents functionality to execute queries using the structured query language (SQL). In SPL engineering, features are usually *bound* statically. That is, a user selects the desired features and a generator creates

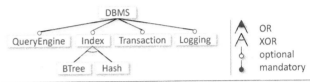

Figure 1. Feature model of a simple DBMS.

the corresponding software product containing exactly the needed features.

Valid feature combinations are often described in a *feature model* using a hierarchical representation of an SPL's features and constraints between them [12]. In Figure 1, we depict an example of the feature model of a *database management system (DBMS)*. Mandatory and optional features are denoted by filled and empty bullets. To specify invalid feature combinations, domain engineers define relations between features, such as OR and XOR, plus additional constraints such as *requires* (a feature requires another feature) or *excludes* (two features cannot be used in combination). In general, arbitrary propositional formulas can be used as constraints.

In contrast to an SPL, an adaptive system offers variability at runtime in order to adapt to changing requirements [18]. Approaches for runtime adaptation are often based on components and describe program adaptations at the architectural level [27]. They allow a programmer to specify adaptation rules for reconfiguring components and thereby abstract from the concrete implementation [14, 16, 20]. *Dynamic SPLs (DSPLs)* integrate concepts of SPLs and adaptive systems [1, 8]: The products of a DSPL can be reconfigured at runtime. In contrast to describing program adaptations using architectural models, there are DSPL approaches that support feature-based runtime adaptation. For example, some approaches use *feature models* to describe dependencies between features and to reason about runtime variability of DSPLs [10, 19, 21, 37]. Describing also program adaptations in terms of features abstracts from implementation details, simplifies reconfiguration of running programs, and allows for checking consistency of adaptations [10]. Such feature-based approaches use a mapping of DSPL features to the components that are used for implementation [21, 37]. However, components are usually coarse-grained and limit customizability of a DSPL. For example, it is imperative to customize components for embedded systems to remove unneeded functionality and to tailor the components with respect to the hardware [35]. Increasing customizability with small components is usually not an option due to an increasing communication overhead between the components [9].

We bridge the gap between feature-based variability modeling and component-based runtime adaptation, by integrating generative SPL engineering and DSPLs. In previous work, we have shown how to integrate static and dynamic feature binding by statically merging a set of features into a *dynamic binding unit* according

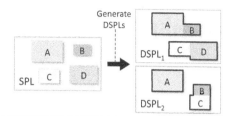

Figure 2. Generating tailor-made DSPLs from the features of an SPL (A–D): For $DSPL_1$ we generate two binding units (A, B) and (C, D); for $DSPL_2$ we generate binding units (A) and (B, C).

to the requirements of an application scenario [30]. At runtime, selected binding units are composed to derive a concrete program. In this paper, we extend our previous work to support runtime adaptation and self-configuration on top of binding units:

- We propose to generate tailor-made DSPLs: As illustrated in Figure 2, we implement an SPL with *feature-oriented software development (FOSD)* [2] and statically compose the required features to derive a DSPL. The DSPL supports reconfiguration at runtime based on coarse-grained dynamic binding units.
- We provide a feature-based approach for runtime adaptation and self-configuration.

In contrast to DSPLs that use components for dynamic binding, we generate tailored binding units from the SPL features (cf. Fig. 2). Due to this fine-grained static customization, we improve reuse and minimize resource requirements of DSPLs. We achieve runtime adaptation with a customizable adaptation framework, called *FeatureAce,* which we integrate into a generated DSPL. The framework supports autonomous self-configuration by using features for describing program adaptations and thus guarantees safety for modifications at runtime. By tailoring and minimizing the number of dynamically-bound modules, we reduce the effort for computing a configuration of a DSPL. We demonstrate practicability of our approach with a prototypical implementation of the adaptation framework and a case study. In summary, our contributions are:

- an approach of statically generating tailor-made DSPLs from SPL features, which improves software reuse (Section 3),
- a customizable adaptation framework including customization of adaptation rules and monitoring code (Section 3.1),
- a feature-based approach of adaptation and self-configuration (Section 4.1), which ensures composition safety (Section 4.2) by means of feature models while using coarse-grained binding units for adaptation,
- a case study that demonstrates practicability of our approach and illustrates the optimization capabilities with respect to reconfiguration and resource consumption (Section 5).

2. Feature-oriented Programming

Using components to implement variability is sometimes too restrictive because components are coarse-grained and thus limit customizability of an SPL. For example, many small features and cross-cutting functionality are hard to implement in individual components [17]. In contrast, *feature-oriented programming (FOP)* [6, 29] can be used to implement the features of an SPL in a modular way. With FOP, one can achieve the same variability in the implementation as it is described by the feature model. For example, we can modularize the transaction-management subsystem of a DBMS even though it affects many parts of the system. In FOP, features are implemented in *feature modules* as increments in functionality using a one-to-one mapping [6]. A user creates a

```
                                           CORE implementation
1  class DB {
2    bool Put(Key& key, Value& val) { ... }
3  };
```

```
                                             Feature QUERYENGINE
4  refines class DB {
5    QueryProcessor queryProc;
6    bool ProcessQuery(String& query) {
7      return queryProc.Execute(String& query);
8    }
9  };
```

```
                                             Feature TRANSACTION
10 refines class DB {
11   Txn* BeginTransaction() { ... }
12   bool Put(Key& key, Value& val) {
13     ... //transaction−specific code
14     return super::Put(key,val);
15   }
16 };
```

Figure 3. FeatureC++ code of class DB, decomposed along the CORE implementation and the features QUERYENGINE and TRANSACTION.

program (a *variant* of an SPL) by selecting features that satisfy requirements. Based on the feature selection (a.k.a., the *configuration*), a generator composes the corresponding feature modules to yield a concrete program.

FeatureC++. FeatureC++[1] is a language extension of C++ that supports FOP [4]. In Figure 3, we depict the FeatureC++ code of a class DB of a DBMS (cf. Fig. 1). A programmer typically decomposes a class into smaller class fragments called *base class* and *class refinements* according to the features of the SPL. A base class, such as class DB (Lines 1-3), implements basic functionality. For example, method Put (Line 2) stores data provided as key-value pairs. A class *refinement* is denoted by keyword **refines** and extends a base class to provide code required for a particular feature. The refinement in feature QUERYENGINE (Lines 4–9) introduces a new member queryProc and a new method ProcessQuery for processing SQL queries. Feature TRANSACTION overrides method Put (Line 12) and invokes the refined method using keyword super (Line 14). Based on the implementation shown in Figure 3, we can generate four different DBMS variants by composing different sets of feature modules: We can generate a simple DBMS consisting of CORE only, but we can also derive variants with any combination of the features QUERYENGINE and TRANSACTION.

Static and Dynamic Feature Binding. FeatureC++ supports static binding of features at compile-time and dynamic binding at load-time and runtime [30]. When binding all features of an SPL statically, a single binary is generated for the variant. At the class level, the FeatureC++ compiler merges the code of a base class and the refinements of selected features into a single class. For example, composing the CORE implementation and feature TRANSACTION of Figure 3 means to generate a single class DB that includes all code of the corresponding base class and its refinement in feature TRANSACTION.

For dynamic binding, FeatureC++ generates compound features, called *dynamic binding units*. A dynamic binding unit is tailored to an application scenario and consists of a set of statically merged features. It is similar to a component but it includes only required functionality. To yield a concrete program, a dynamic binding unit is bound as a whole with other dynamic binding units at runtime. At the class level, FeatureC++ supports dy-

[1] http://fosd.de/fcc

4

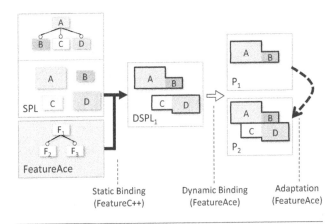

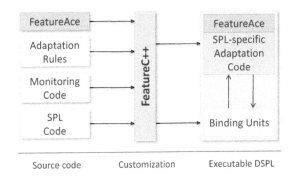

Figure 5. Generating a DSPL from FeatureAce, adaptation rules, monitoring code, and an SPL's implementation.

Figure 4. Static composition of an SPL and FeatureAce (➡) resulting in $DSPL_1$ and subsequent dynamic composition of binding units (⇒) resulting in adaptable programs P_1–P_4.

namic binding by generating dynamically composable class fragments. For example, to generate a binding unit that contains the features QUERYENGINE and TRANSACTION of Figure 3, the code of lines 4-16 is composed into a single class fragment. Multiple class fragments are dynamically composed using the *decorator* design pattern [15]. This allows us to change the configuration of a class at runtime, which is the basis for *generating* a DSPL from the features of an SPL. To enable dynamic loading, each binding unit is usually encapsulated in a separate dynamic link library (e.g. a Windows DLL). For a detailed description of dynamic binding units we refer to [30].

3. Generating Dynamic Software Product Lines

We generate a DSPL from an SPL by statically selecting the features required for dynamic binding and generating a set of dynamic binding units, as we illustrate in Figure 4 (cf. Fig 2). In $DSPL_1$, two binding units are generated: (A, B) and (C, D). The binding units are composed at runtime to yield the concrete program P_1 or P_2. One of the binding units (e.g., (A, B) in $DSPL_1$) usually acts as the base program, i.e., the part of the DSPL that provides basic functionality that is always needed. Hence, the base program is statically bound and is dynamically extended by additional binding units as required.

The transformation process from an SPL to a running program can be seen as a *staged configuration* [13]: In a first step, FeatureC++ statically merges a set of features into dynamic binding units (➡ in Figure 4). In a second step, the generated binding units are composed at runtime according to a dynamic feature selection (⇒ in Figure 4). Hence, a DSPL comprises a subset of the products of the SPL it was generated from. That is, a DSPL is a *specialization* of a corresponding SPL and provides dynamic variability only.

In contrast to our previous work [30], we support runtime adaptation of programs (i.e., reconfiguration) using a customizable framework, called FeatureAce. FeatureAce is included into a generated DSPL and is responsible for composing features and modifying a program's configuration at runtime. Reconfiguration of a program means to add and remove binding units dynamically. For example, program P_1 of Figure 4 can be reconfigured into P_2 by adding binding unit (C, D). FeatureAce computes the needed configuration changes using a SAT solver. Since FeatureAce itself is developed as an SPL, programmers can choose the required composition and adaptation mechanisms. In the following, we describe FeatureAce and the runtime adaptation process in detail.

3.1 FeatureAce: A Customizable Adaptation Framework

FeatureAce is an SPL-independent framework for (re)configuration of DSPLs at runtime. Based on a user-defined feature selection, the FeatureC++ compiler generates a tailor-made DSPL from SPL features and the features of FeatureAce (➡ in Figure 4). FeatureAce is statically bound using generated, SPL-specific glue code. In the executable DSPL, a generic metaprogram (part of FeatureAce) is responsible for controlling the dynamic composition of binding units (⇒ in Figure 4) and for self-adaptation at runtime (e.g., reconfiguring P_1 into P_2 in Figure 4). Programmers describe runtime adaptations with declarative adaptation rules. The execution of a rule is triggered by events spawned in monitoring code of the DSPL. To ensure correctness of program adaptations with respect to the feature model, FeatureAce computes a valid configuration by applying the adaptation rules to the feature model of the DSPL.

In Figure 5, we provide a more detailed view of the transformation process. A user selects the required features from FeatureAce, adaptation rules, monitoring code, and the SPL and the FeatureC++ compiler generates a customized DSPL:

- Users can customize FeatureAce to choose between manual and autonomous adaptation and to enable validation of adaptations if required.
- Adaptation rules are stored in separate feature modules to allow the programmer to choose actually required rules at deployment time, e.g., to choose between alternative adaptation rules.
- Monitoring code of the DSPL that triggers adaptation events is implemented in distinct feature modules. Hence, it is possible to use only required monitoring code and to choose between alternative implementations.

The customization of the adaptation infrastructure allows us to cope with changing requirements (e.g., to support different execution environments). In the following, we use static binding for customization of the adaptation infrastructure. In general, parts of this variability may also be needed at runtime, which requires dynamic binding of selected features of FeatureAce and adaptation code. This is beyond the scope of this paper but it illustrates that there are further challenges for improving the flexibility of our approach.

In Figure 6, we depict the feature diagram of FeatureAce. Feature AUTOINST encapsulates the functionality required for automated SPL instantiation using command-line arguments or a configuration file to provide an initial feature selection. Feature ADAPTATION enables modification of a running DSPL instance (i.e., the configured and running program) and feature SELF-CONFIG supports rule-based self-configuration. Feature VALIDATION checks the validity of an SPL variant before composing the binding units. For customization, a user defines the required adaptation facilities

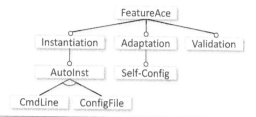

Figure 6. The feature model of FeatureAce. Customization of dynamic product instantiation and runtime adaptation capabilities is achieved by selecting the corresponding features.

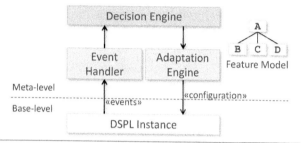

Figure 7. Architecture of a DSPL: Domain code is at the base-level and adaptation code is at the meta-level.

of FeatureAce and may even add user-defined extensions, such as special adaptation mechanisms. FeatureAce extensions are implemented as additional feature modules without the need for invasive modifications of the framework.

As shown in Figure 7, the adaptation metaprogram of FeatureAce provides a decision engine that uses the feature model of the DSPL to ensure validity of changes in the running program. Monitoring code for analyzing the context at runtime is located at the base-level. It is implemented in feature modules of the SPL because it is usually domain-specific. For example, code for monitoring DBMS queries may trigger an event for loading a feature that implements a special search index when a particular kind of query is detected. The events triggered by the monitoring code are captured by an event handler that activates the decision engine. Based on adaptation rules and the feature model, the decision engine computes a new configuration. The adaptation engine applies required configuration changes by loading and unloading binding units.

After generating a DSPL, there is an n-to-1 mapping of the original features to the dynamic binding units of the DSPL. For example, features A and B in Figure 4 map to binding unit (A,B) of $DSPL_1$. In the following, we call the binding units *features of the DSPL* and use a feature model to describe dynamic variability. The DSPL features are used for composition and adaptation at runtime, as we describe next.

3.2 Instantiation and Adaptation of DSPLs

FeatureAce supports a set of operations for instantiation and adaptation of a program from selected DSPL features at runtime:

Instantiation: A program is composed from multiple DSPL feature, implemented as binding units. The result is a stack of feature instances that represents a DSPL instance.

Adaptation: An already running DSPL instance can be modified by adding and removing features as well as activating and deactivating already loaded features.

Note that not every feature that can be bound at load-time can also be bound at runtime without further modification. For example,

```
1  void ConnectSQLite(string db) {
2    FeatureConfig::ActivateFeature("SQLite"); //activate feature SQLite
3    ConnectDB(db); //continue with activated feature
4  }
```

Figure 8. FeatureC++ source code for activating feature SQLITE from the base-level.

runtime adaptation requires to support consistent changes with respect to the state of objects. There are further issues, such as concurrency control and state transfer, that have to be considered for transition from an SPL to a DSPL [32]. As a solution, developers may provide special code for binding at runtime, such as *state transformer functions* [26]. Using FOP, this code can be separated in feature modules that are only included in a program when runtime adaptation is used. Implementation of such features is beyond the scope of this paper.

After composing a concrete DSPL instance, FeatureAce provides different adaptation mechanisms:

Add and remove features: A feature can be added to or removed from a running DSPL instance. A feature that is not part of any running DSPL instance can be deleted and unloaded.

Activate and deactivate features: A feature can be deactivated if it is temporarily not needed and can be reactivated later. This maintains the state of a feature while disabling its functionality.

The described operations are internally used by FeatureAce for runtime adaptation and can be accessed via an API from an external program or from the base-level of the DSPL itself.

Reflection vs. Rule-based Adaptation. There are two ways to use the adaptation mechanisms of FeatureAce. First, we support manual adaptation by external programs via the API of FeatureAce or by the DSPL itself using *reflection*. Second, we provide a rule-based adaptation mechanism. For manual adaptation, FeatureAce uses the feature model of the DSPL to validate a feature selection at runtime with a SAT solver.[2] When using the rule-based mechanism, we use a SAT solver to derive a valid configuration dynamically. To provide only the actually required variability at runtime, we transform the original SPL feature model according to the generated DSPL, as we describe in Section 4.

Via reflection, the base-level of a DSPL can access the adaptation meta-level for observing or modifying the current configuration. The reflection mechanism is sufficient for simple adaptations, e.g., when events can be directly mapped to a configuration change. In Figure 8, we depict an example of activating a feature for database access in a client by accessing the meta-level from the base-level (Line 2). This mechanism simplifies SPL development since no additional code for an adaptation metaprogram is needed. To separate domain implementation from adaptation mechanisms, programmers should implement such adaptation code in distinct feature modules.

4. Rule-based Program Adaptation

A more flexible mechanism that is independent of the implementation of an SPL is to describe adaptations in a declarative way using adaptation rules. An adaptation rule defines how a configuration of a DSPL must be changed when an event occurs. In contrast to many existing approaches, we use features to define adaptation rules. In particular, an adaptation rule describes constraints (e.g., required features) that the configuration of a program must satisfy after adaptation.

---

[2] Even though the SAT problem is NP-complete, it has been shown that validity of feature models can be efficiently checked [24].

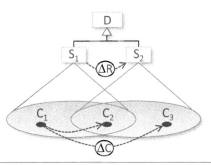

Figure 9. DSPL D with specializations S_1, S_2, configurations C_1–C_3, and adaptation from S_1 to S_2.

4.1 Feature-based Adaptation Rules

A configuration C of a program P of a DSPL is the set of features that is included in P. During adaptation, we derive a configuration C from a set of requirements R that define which features of the DSPL must be included in a valid program. In the simplest case, the requirements are defined by a set of required features (e.g., a user-defined feature selection). In general, however, a requirement may be an arbitrary *configuration constraint* (i.e., a propositional formula over the set of available features) that restricts the set of valid configurations [31]. A configuration constraint is not different from a domain constraint of a feature model but it is added to and removed from the model at runtime. For example, to express that a feature must be included in a program, we can define a *requires* constraint for that feature.

As an example consider the feature diagram of Figure 1 with an initial set of requirements R (e.g., defined by a user)[3]:

$$R = \{\text{QUERYENGINE}, \text{INDEX}\} \quad (1)$$

R defines that the features QUERYENGINE and INDEX must be included in a valid configuration. We can derive a valid configuration C that satisfies R:

$$C = \{\text{QUERYENGINE}, \text{INDEX}, \text{HASH}\}. \quad (2)$$

Because C must also satisfy the constraints defined in the feature model, such as the XOR constraint between HASH and BTREE (cf. Fig. 1), it must include one of the two features. In our example, we have chosen feature HASH. While C represents a single program, R defines a *specialization* S of our DSPL that represents multiple configurations, as illustrated in Figure 9. In this example, DSPL D has two specializations S_1 and S_2, which we denote with an empty arrowhead [31]. Each specialization represents multiple configurations (illustrated with a cone). For example, C_1 and C_2 are configurations of S_1. Each specialization represents a subset of the configurations of the unspecialized DSPL.

We can represent a set of requirements R as a single propositional formula using a conjunction of all requirements. For instance, R from equation (1) corresponds to the boolean constraint QUERYENGINE $\wedge$ INDEX. Since a feature model can also be translated into a propositional formula [5], we can check if a configuration C satisfies the requirements R for a feature model FM: If $FM \wedge R$ is `true` for configuration C, then C is valid with respect to R. Furthermore, we can use a SAT solver to test if R is a valid set of requirements with respect to FM. This can be done by checking whether we can derive at least a single valid configuration, i.e., $FM \wedge R$ must be satisfiable [36].

Adaptation Rules. The current configuration C of a running program of a DSPL is modified by a configuration change ΔC (i.e.,

a reconfiguration; cf. Fig. 9) that defines which features are added to C and which features are removed from C during adaptation. However, as we explain below, it is usually too restrictive to directly define configuration changes in an adaptation rule. Instead, an adaptation rule describes changes with respect to the active requirements R of a DSPL. We thus define an adaptation rule A as a pair $(E, \Delta R)$ where E is the event that triggers rule A and ΔR are modifications that must be applied to R when E is triggered. ΔR is a pair $(\Delta R_\oplus, \Delta R_\ominus)$ of added and removed requirements. We use operator $\bullet$ to denote adaptations (i.e., application of ΔR to R):

$$R' \;\; := \;\; \Delta R \bullet R \quad (3)$$
$$:= \;\; (R \setminus \Delta R_\ominus) \cup \Delta R_\oplus. \quad (4)$$

The modified requirements R' must be satisfied after applying rule A to a configuration C. That is, ΔR does *not* directly modify the configuration of a DSPL but it modifies a set of requirements R that correspond to a specialization of the DSPL. As illustrated in Figure 9, applying ΔR to S_1 results in specialization S_2.

From a modified set of requirements R', we derive a modified configuration C'. In Figure 9, we can derive two valid configurations C_2 or C_3 from S_2. For runtime adaptation, we have to choose one of these configurations. For example, we may choose the configuration with the smallest number of features. Finally, we derive the corresponding configuration change ΔC, which is a pair $(\Delta C_\oplus, \Delta C_\ominus)$. It defines the set of features that must be added $(\Delta C_\oplus)$ and removed $(\Delta C_\ominus)$ for adaptation. We compute it from the current configuration C and the target configuration C':

$$\Delta C \;\; := \;\; (\Delta C_\oplus, \Delta C_\ominus) \quad (5)$$
$$\Delta C_\oplus \;\; := \;\; C' \setminus C \quad (6)$$
$$\Delta C_\ominus \;\; := \;\; C \setminus C' \quad (7)$$

As a complete example, consider the DBMS from equations (1) and (2) with an adaptation rule A that is triggered on event E_{Range}, meaning that range queries are used:

$$A \;\; = \;\; (E_{Range}, (\{\text{BTREE}\}, \emptyset)) \quad (8)$$
$$R' \;\; = \;\; (\{\text{BTREE}\}, \emptyset)) \bullet R \quad (9)$$
$$= \;\; \{\text{QUERYENGINE}, \text{INDEX}, \text{BTREE}\} \quad (10)$$
$$C' \;\; = \;\; \{\text{QUERYENGINE}, \text{INDEX}, \text{BTREE}\} \quad (11)$$
$$\Delta C \;\; = \;\; (\{\text{BTREE}\}, \{\text{HASH}\}). \quad (12)$$

Rule A adds feature BTREE to R (i.e., BTREE must occur in a valid configuration), which results in the modified requirement R'. From R' we derive a new configuration C'. The required configuration change ΔC (adding feature BTREE and removing feature HASH) is derived from C and C' according to equations (5–7).

In contrast to modifying the set of requirements, a direct configuration change is too restrictive. For example, an adaptation rule that adds feature BTREE directly to configuration C violates the XOR constraint of the feature model (either BTREE or HASH must be selected). As another example, consider a rule that removes feature BTREE from a configuration because it is not required any longer. Such a rule causes a conflict if the feature to be removed is required by another constraint. With named requirements, we can simply remove the requirement that is not needed and the feature will only be removed from the configuration if not needed due to another requirement.

Specifying Adaptation Rules. We specify adaptation rules in a declarative language, as shown in the example in Figure 10; we depict the corresponding grammar in Figure 11. A rule consists of a name, a named adaptation event E (e.g., `OnTxn` in Line 2) that triggers adaptation, and actions ΔR, which describe the required configuration changes. Currently, we create adaptation events in mon-

---

[3] Users can provide an initial set of requirements in a configuration file using the declarative language VELVET [31]. The initial set can be empty.

```
1  //Load transaction management
2  BeginTxn : OnTxn => addReq(TX: Transaction);
3
4  //Process range queries
5  BeginRQ : OnRangeQuery => addReq(RQ: Btree);
6
7  //Remove constraint RQ
8  EndRQ : OnRangeQueryEnd => removeReq(RQ);
```

Figure 10. Two adaptation rules that add the named constraints TX and RQ (Lines 2 and 5) and a rule that removes constraint RQ (Line 8).

```
1   AdaptScript: Rule+ ;
2   Rule: RuleName ":" EventName "=>" Action+ ";" ;
3   RuleName: ID ;
4   EventName: ID ;
5   Action: AddReq | RemoveReq ;
6   AddReq: "addReq" "(" ReqName ":" Constraint ")" ;
7   RemoveReq: "removeReq" "(" ReqName ")" ;
8   ReqName: ID ;
9   Constraint: FeatureName | "(" Constraint ")" |
10     "!" Constraint | Constraint ConstrOp Constraint ;
11  ConstrOp: "&&" | "||" | "->" | "<->" ;
12  FeatureName: ID ;
```

Figure 11. Grammar of FeatureAce's adaptation rule specification language.

itoring code using the host language. For example, event `OnTxn` in Figure 10 is signaled when monitoring code observes a transaction query. The event triggers loading the transaction management feature as defined in rule `BeginTxn`. An action adds or removes named configuration constraints using keywords `addReq` and `removeReq` followed by a constraint definition (Line 5) or a constraint name respectively (Line 8). Each constraint has a name to be able to remove it from the requirements of a DSPL, as shown in Line 8.

Applying Adaptations. Before computing a new configuration when applying an adaptation rule, FeatureAce checks whether an adaptation is really needed: If a set of requirements R_i represent a specialized DSPL S_i (e.g., S_1 in Figure 9) then $R_{i+1} = \Delta R \bullet R_i$ corresponds to a new specialization S_{i+1} (e.g., S_2 in Figure 9). If S_i and S_{i+1} overlap then there are configurations that can be derived from both specializations (e.g., C_2 in Figure 9). Hence, if the current configuration of the DSPL is also a valid configuration of the new specialization, we do not have to adapt the running program. For example, adaptation of S_1 to S_2 in Figure 9 for configuration C_2 does not require a program adaptation. Hence, the decision engine of FeatureAce first checks whether the current configuration C_i already satisfies the new requirements R_{i+1}.

If this is not the case, we have to find a new configuration C_{i+1} that satisfies R_{i+1}. To test if there is at least one valid configuration that satisfies R_{i+1}, the decision engine checks satisfiability of the feature model including the new requirements. If there are multiple valid configurations, the decision algorithm has to choose the *best* one. Which configuration is the *best* depends on the domain, the application scenario, and the context at runtime [14, 38]. For example, we may choose the configuration with the smallest number of features or the smallest number of required adaptations. Other optimization goals are non-functional requirements [34], such as memory consumption, performance, or quality of service. We currently choose the configuration with the smallest number of configuration changes. For that reason, FeatureAce tries to keep already configured features to minimize changes. Features are removed when they violate a constraint. Hence, when an adaptation rule removes a con-

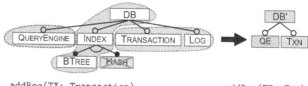

```
addReq(TX: Transaction)        addReq(TX: Txn)
addReq(RQ: Btree)              addReq(RQ: DB')
removeReq(RQ)                  removeReq(RQ)
```

Figure 12. Transformation of a feature model and the corresponding transformation of actions of adaptation rules (lower part) according to defined binding units. Transformed features in adaptation rules are underlined.

straint from requirements R, this does not always cause a reconfiguration. Furthermore, we remove features that are not required for a pre-defined time span to provide a simple mechanism for reducing resource consumption when features are not used anymore.

To reduce resource consumption, a configuration can also be explicitly minimized by rules, e.g., triggered by low working memory. In future work, we plan to use more sophisticated mechanisms to trigger unloading of features based on non-functional requirements. For example, we may remove unused features based on statistics and the workload of the system, or we may optimize a configuration using CSP[4] solvers [7, 38].

4.2 Safety of Runtime Adaptation

Since we merge multiple features of an SPL into a single binding unit of a generated DSPL, there is an n-to-1 mapping of SPL features to DSPL features. For safe adaptation at runtime, however, we have to reason about the dynamic variability provided by the generated DSPL, which represents a subset of the products that can be derived from the SPL. We thus transform the SPL's feature model according to the generated binding units and derive a special feature model of the DSPL. In the upper part of Figure 12, we show an example of such a feature model transformation. A detailed description of the transformation can be found in [30]. Since domain engineers define adaptation rules in terms of SPL features, we apply a corresponding transformation to the adaptation rules (lower part of Figure 12). This transformation is achieved by replacing each feature in the adaptation rules with the binding unit of the feature in the generated DSPL. For example, we have to replace all occurrences of feature TRANSACTION with its corresponding binding unit TXN (first action in Figure 12). After transforming all actions of Figure 12, requirement RQ (second action) is always satisfied because DB' is the root of the feature tree and included in every configuration. Hence, we can remove all actions that add or remove requirement RQ, such as the last two actions in Figure 12.

The correctness of an adaptation rule with respect to the SPL's feature model can be checked with a SAT solver already before runtime. Furthermore, we can check whether there are combinations of events that may result in configuration conflicts due to applying rules at the same time. For example, if two rules add conflicting requirements, only one adaptation would be possible. Unfortunately, this can only be checked for a small number of adaptation rules because there is an exponential number of combinations of adaptation rules and even the order of the adaptations matters. However, due to customization of the DSPL with a reduced number of features and adaptation rules, this may often be possible in practice.

After transforming the feature model including adaptation rules, we can validate the transformation by checking whether all transformed rules can be applied to the DSPL's feature model. For ex-

---
[4] Constraint satisfaction problem

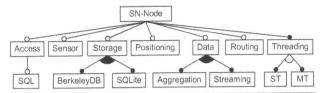

Figure 13. Feature diagram of an SPL for sensor network nodes.

ample, an adaptation rule that adds requirement ¬Btree is transformed into a rule with requirement ¬DB', which is not satisfiable since *DB'* is the root of the feature model and is always true. Such a rule is invalid with respect to the generated DSPL (i.e., with respect to the chosen binding units). As another example, consider the features TRANSACTION and LOG in Figure 12. Both features are part of binding unit TXN. Hence, both features are always present at the same time in the generated DSPL. Consequently, an adaptation rule that *requires* LOG and *excludes* TRANSACTION is invalid in this DSPL. Using a SAT solver, we can detect such invalid transformations before runtime.

Finally, the model transformation and the model-based runtime adaptation process guarantee that a new configuration is correct with respect to the original feature model. In combination with static type checking of the entire SPL [3], we can even ensure static type safety for runtime adaptations.

5. Case Study

By means of a case study, we demonstrate the practicability of our approach and show that binding units can reduce the time needed for runtime adaptation. We use an implementation of FeatureAce for FeatureC++, but the concept can be applied to other languages as well. As application scenario, we use a sensor network.

5.1 An SPL for Sensor Network Nodes

A sensor network (SN) is a network of interconnected embedded devices (e.g., via radio communication), which sense different kinds of information (temperature, light, etc.) [23]. There are different types of nodes in a sensor network. *Sensor nodes* measure data, store it locally, and send it to other nodes. *Aggregation nodes* aggregate data (e.g., computing the mean value) from other nodes. *Access nodes* provide access to clients that connect to the network.

With SPL technology, we can *generate* different program variants tailored to the different kinds of SN nodes. In Figure 13, we depict an excerpt of the feature diagram of an SPL for sensor nodes that we implemented in FeatureC++. Subfeatures of DATA are used for aggregation in aggregation nodes and streaming in access nodes. A node does not always play a single role (e.g., being a sensor node) but possibly multiple roles at the same time. For example, a node may aggregate data but may also be responsible for accessing the network. To compensate node failures and for efficiency, the role may change over the lifetime of a node. For example, if the access node fails due to exhausted battery power, a different node can reconfigure itself to provide this service. Due to hardware constraints, not all physical nodes can play every role. For example, only a node with sufficient storage capacity can be used for data aggregation. Such limitations influence the configuration process when defining binding units at deployment time:

1. *Static binding:* For embedded devices that do not allow dynamic changes to already loaded program code (because the executable code is stored in ROM), we do not support runtime adaptation and generate program variants statically.
2. *Runtime adaptation:* For all other nodes, we generate a DSPL using a subset of all features. We include only the features that

Hardware	Role	Binding Units
Simple	Sensor	StaticSense
Advanced	Positioning	Core, Positioning
	Sensor	Core, Sense
	DataAggregator	Core, QueryProc, Aggregation
	AccessNode	Core, QueryProc, Streaming

Table 1. Examples of different roles and their binding units for two kinds of devices.

Binding Unit	Features
StaticSense	Positioning, Routing, Sensor, Radio, ST
Core	Routing, Radio, Wi-Fi, MT
Positioning	Positioning
Sense	Sensor
QueryProc	Access, SQL, Data, Storage
Aggregation	Aggregation, SQLite
Streaming	Streaming, BerkeleyDB

Table 2. Sample configuration of different binding units.

are required for the used operating system, the hardware, and the roles a node can play.

3. *Binding units:* We reduce the overhead of dynamic binding and the number of possible variants by merging features into binding units when they are used always in combination.

For evaluation, we use a sensor network simulation, in which each node of the network is simulated by a separate process that communicates with other nodes. The nodes software can be deployed on embedded devices, but for simulation we use a desktop environment.

5.2 Defining Binding Units

In Table 1, we show a sample assignment of roles for two types of node hardware and the corresponding binding units. The binding units are composed from the features of Figure 13. We depict sample configurations in Table 2. In our example, simple node hardware (*Simple* in Table 1) with highly constrained resources does not support runtime adaptation and can only be used for sensor nodes. We use a statically composed variant for these nodes (binding unit STATICSENSE in Table 1).

Hardware with less resource constraints (*Advanced* in Table 1) that supports reconfiguration at runtime is used for different roles. An advanced node is deployed with role *Positioning*, for computing the relative position of the node. A node unloads the feature when the position has been determined. If a *sensor*, a *data aggregator*, or an *access node* is needed, an advanced node loads the required binding units. The node may also play different roles at the same time. For example, to process a streaming query, a DataAggregator additionally loads the STREAMING binding unit.

We observe that our approach provides a high flexibility with respect to possible deployment scenarios. We can define different feature configurations according to the used hardware at deployment time *and* according to required functionality at runtime. For example, a sensor node uses different binding units but a similar set of features depending on the used hardware (Simple or Advanced). We can also define completely different binding units and feature selections according to used hardware, application scenarios, etc.

The feature selection influences the binary size of the generated node software. A variant that uses only static binding (binding unit STATICSENSE in Table 1) does not include any code for runtime adaptation. It has a binary size of 48 KB, which is only half of the size of a runtime-adaptable variant with the same features and a size of 104 KB. This overhead mostly comes from code of the infrastructure for runtime adaptation (i.e., FeatureAce including a SAT-solver), which is independent of the number of features. As we observed in previous studies, the resource consumption increases with an increasing number of binding units [30]; it can be optimized by generating a DSPL that provides only required dynamic variability. The overhead is quite small compared to larger programs such as a node with stream processing, which has a binary size of 576 KB. Hence, our approach allows us to apply self-configuration also on resource-constrained devices. Nevertheless, on systems with highly limited resources only static binding is an option. With our approach, a user can choose at deployment time whether to use static binding or to support runtime adaptation.

5.3 Self-Adaptation

Adaptation Rules. We define adaptation rules within dedicated feature modules. For example, we place rules for activating and deactivating stream processing in feature STREAMING. The rules are thus included in a running program only if the corresponding feature is selected for dynamic binding. Based on the defined rules, a DSPL autonomously reconfigures itself according to the required features at runtime. In our scenario, a node loads the streaming binding unit when it receives a streaming query.

Reconfiguration of nodes is triggered by events spawned in monitoring code of the DSPL. We implement the monitorings in distinct feature modules that extend classes of the application SPL to separate adaptation code from the SPL's implementation. For example, to activate stream processing, the monitoring code captures incoming queries and triggers an adaptation when a streaming query is found. The corresponding rule adds a constraint for feature STREAMING (i.e., the feature must be included in a valid configuration). Another rule removes the constraint from the requirements after all streaming queries have been processed. We do not directly remove the feature because it would result in an unneeded reconfiguration when the feature is used again. A feature is only removed when it is excluded by other constraints or when other requirements such as limited working memory force to remove unneeded features. For example, we use a rule to unload the positioning feature when the position of a node has been determined.

Reconfiguration. In Figure 14, we depict evaluation results for the adaptation process.[5] We analyzed the time needed for computing whether an adaptation (using a SAT solver) is needed and the time for reconfiguration. To show the benefits of statically optimizing the feature model, we compared reconfiguration of the same sensor node (1) using the original feature model of the SPL including all 55 features and (2) using the transformed feature model of the DSPL with 6 features (i.e., one feature per binding unit; cf. Sec. 3.1). In the diagram, we depict the time a node requires to process queries that are sent every 300 ms.

Stream processing is triggered by incoming streaming queries (denoted with b in Fig. 14), which results in a runtime adaptation to load binding unit STREAMING. In our example, the adaptation must be finished before the query processing can continue. The first streaming query is detected after 5 s. Loading the STREAMING feature takes 20–60 ms (note that we use a logarithmic scale) and increases the response time because the execution is continued after reconfiguration. Computing the new configuration takes less than 1 ms. Assuming a minimal adaptation time of 20 ms, a node cannot reconfigure itself more than 50 times per second.

End of stream processing is denoted with (e). Instead of unloading the Streaming feature, a rule removes the constraint added be-

---

[5] For evaluation, we used an AMD 2.0 GHz CPU and Windows XP.

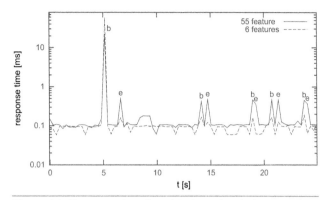

Figure 14. Response time (logarithmic scale) during reconfiguration of a query processing sensor network node using a feature model with 55 features and a simplified model with 6 features. Begin and end of stream processing are denoted with (b) and (e).

fore. Hence, all following adaptation events do not cause a reconfiguration. Nevertheless, the adaptation events increase the response time by about 0.32 ms when using the complete feature model with 55 features and 0.05 ms for the DSPL model with 6 features (with a 95 % confidence interval of ± 0.13 and ± 0.10 ms respectively). This computation time is required for checking whether the node has to be reconfigured due to the context change. Compared to a reconfiguration that takes 20-50 ms, 0.32 ms is a very small overhead. However, it means that the node cannot handle more than about 3000 changes of the adaptation context per second even though no adaptation is needed. On an embedded device this would be much less due to limited computing power. By contrast, the node with the simplified feature model with 6 features requires only 0.05 ms (i.e., 85 % less time) for checking whether an adaptation is needed. This demonstrates the importance of reducing the variability for runtime adaptation by optimizing the feature model.

5.4 Discussion

In our case study, we combined static feature binding with support for feature-based runtime adaptation. We have shown that we can achieve autonomous reconfiguration by including the adaptation mechanism and the feature model into the running DSPL. By generating binding units, we further optimize the runtime adaptation process, as we discuss next.

Implementation-independent Adaptations. Using features to describe adaptations, we provide an adaptation mechanism that abstracts from the modules actually used for dynamic binding. Hence, we can generate binding units that fit to an application scenario and the execution environment, while being able to reuse adaptation rules. As in component-based approaches, there is an m-to-n mapping of SPL features to dynamic binding units. At compile-time, we simplify this complex mapping by transforming the feature model and adaptation rules according to the generated binding units. The result is a simpler 1-to-1 or 1-to-n mapping of DSPL features to binary modules that must be considered during adaptation. We cannot always achieve a 1-to-1 mapping, because a compound feature may overlap with other compound features, which results in multiple code units per binding unit. These crosscutting modules correspond to *derivatives* known from feature-oriented software development [22].

Composition Safety. Using a feature model, we ensure that adaptations are correct with respect to domain constraints. As we have shown, this can be efficiently done at runtime before creating a variant by using a SAT solver. Furthermore, we can check if an adaptation rule is valid with respect to the feature model of the DSPL before runtime. Currently, we do not check whether a dynamically bound feature supports binding to an already running SPL instance (e.g., supporting state transfer; cf. Sec 3.2). This could be achieved with an extension of the feature model that allows for annotating such features.

Resource Consumption. We provide an adaptation mechanism with low resource requirements (e.g., binary size, computing power) due to (1) customization of the adaptation infrastructure and (2) customization of binding units by removing unused code. The flexible size of binding units minimizes dynamic binding and enables static optimizations, as we analyzed in previous work [30].

Computational Complexity. We have shown that we can reduce computations for reconfiguration at runtime in two ways: (1) by avoiding unneeded adaptations and (2) by simplifying the computations for checking satisfiability by transforming the feature model according to actually available variability. The time required for computing a valid configuration is small compared to an actual reconfiguration even when using a feature model with 55 features. However, frequently checking whether an adaptation is needed can easily require more computing power than available. Hence, it is important to simplify the feature model.

Including also non-functional requirements in these computations is a challenging task with respect to computational complexity [14]. Since the computation time to solve constraint satisfaction problems increases exponentially with the number of features [7, 38], it is even more important to reduce the number of binding units as far as possible. Our approach reduces the overall complexity and can be combined with CSP solvers to consider also numerical constraints (e.g., memory restrictions) when computing an optimal configuration at runtime [33]. Further simplification is possible by caching the results of a SAT or CSP solver.

6. Related Work

There are several approaches that use components and architecture-based runtime adaptation as proposed by Oreizy et al. [27]. We abstract from implementation details by using features for configuring a program at runtime. This allows us to reason about configuration changes at runtime at a conceptual level and to describe adaptation rules in a declarative way without taking the high-level architecture into account. There are also approaches that apply SPL concepts to develop adaptive systems, e.g., using feature-oriented concepts for modeling dynamic variability [10, 14, 19, 21, 37]. We aim at building a foundation for integrating existing approaches using features for SPL configuration *and* runtime adaptation. In the following, we compare our approach with respect to the most prominent related approaches.

Some approaches describe dynamic variability in terms of features [10, 21, 37]. Lee et al. use a feature model to describe static and dynamic variability of an SPL. They suggest to manually develop components (i.e., feature binding units) for implementing dynamic variability [21]. We decide *at build-time* which binding time to use and use features (i.e., not implementation units) for specifying adaptations and for validating a configuration. Furthermore, a component-based approach requires mapping features to components. We resolve the mapping before deployment by transforming the feature model and the adaptation rules accordingly.

Floch and Hallsteinsen et al. present with MADAM an approach for runtime adaptation that uses SPL techniques as well as architectural models [14, 19]. They propose to model variability using component-based SPL techniques [19]. We use features for modeling variability and runtime adaptation to further abstract from the underlying implementation and architecture.

Cetina et al. use feature models to describe the variability of an adaptive system [10]. To adapt a system, they modify a configura-

tion by adding or removing features. This results in the problems discussed in Section 5.4, which we solve by using constraints to describe current requirements on a system. Furthermore, we seamlessly integrate SPL engineering and runtime adaptation by applying SPL concepts to adaptation code (e.g., adaptation rules) and by supporting static binding of features and merging of features into binding units. The result is a transformed feature model for runtime adaptation that represents the required variability only.

Morin et al. describe variability with a feature model and realize variability of the component model of an adaptive system with aspect-oriented modeling (AOM) [25]. They use aspects to describe model adaptations and reconfigure the underlying program based on changes of the model. By contrast, we operate on features that are not only implementation independent but also independent of the component model of a system. Hence, our approach can be combined with an approach for model adaptation. This allows us to validate a configuration before adapting the component model.

Safe composition is important for component-based software development. For example, the Treaty framework combines verification of component assemblies using contracts and event-condition-action rules [11]. By contrast, we use feature models for validating configurations at runtime. Due to the use of FOP, we can furthermore check type-safety for an entire SPL before deployment [3]. In contrast to component-based approaches, we do not provide any means for verifying compositions based on contracts, but we think that approaches for verification are orthogonal to a feature-oriented approach for composition and can be integrated.

We use FOP for implementing adaptive systems, but our approach for feature-based adaptation may also be used with other implementation units such as aspects [10, 21, 25, 37]. In this case, we can still use features to describe adaptation changes. After a new configuration has been derived and validated, a corresponding set of components has to be determined. Some component approaches provide advanced capabilities for runtime adaptation not considered here (e.g., adaptation planning, state transfer, etc.). Such advanced mechanisms are complementary to a feature-based solution and features can be used to improve these mechanisms by abstracting from implementation details.

7. Summary

Current approaches for developing dynamic software product lines (DSPLs) commonly use coarse-grained components to implement variability. This reduces customizability and thus limits applicability of a DSPL. We presented an approach that allows us to tailor DSPLs by closely integrating traditional, static SPLs and DSPLs. Based on a feature-oriented implementation of an SPL and a customizable adaptation framework, we *generate tailor-made DSPLs* by using fine-grained features to statically generate coarse-grained *dynamic binding units*. As in traditional SPLs, we support fine-grained static customization for efficiency reasons; as in DSPLs, we provide adaptability at runtime by composing dynamic binding units at runtime. A dynamic binding unit is tailored to an application scenario by including only user-selected features.

For runtime adaptation, we describe adaptation rules in terms of features. We provide a feature-based adaptation mechanism by transforming the feature model of an SPL according to the binding units of the generated DSPL. By using a feature model to derive a valid configuration at runtime, our approach is independent of an SPL's implementation. Our integration of static binding and DSPLs reduces the overhead for dynamic binding, avoids unneeded dynamic variability, and simplifies computations at runtime.

In future work, we will integrate our work on optimizing non-functional properties of SPLs [33, 34]. This means to extend the dynamic variant selection process to optimize a variant with respect to non-functional constraints using CSP solvers.

Acknowledgments

We thank Thomas Thüm for comments on earlier drafts of this paper. Marko Rosenmüller and Mario Pukall are funded by German Research Foundation (DFG), project numbers SA 465/34-1 and SA 465/31-2. Norbert Siegmund is funded by German Ministry of Education and Research (BMBF), project number 01IM10002B. Sven Apel's work is supported by the German Research Foundation (DFG), project numbers AP 206/2 and AP 206/4.

References

[1] V. Alves, D. Schneider, M. Becker, N. Bencomo, and P. Grace. Comparitive Study of Variability Management in Software Product Lines and Runtime Adaptable Systems. In *Proc. Workshop on Variability Modelling of Software-intensive Systems (VaMoS)*, pages 9–17. University of Duisburg-Essen, 2009.

[2] S. Apel and C. Kästner. An Overview of Feature-Oriented Software Development. *Journal of Object Technology (JOT)*, 8(5):49–84, 2009.

[3] S. Apel, C. Kästner, A. Größlinger, and C. Lengauer. Type Safety for Feature-oriented Product Lines. *Automated Software Engineering*, 17(3):251–300, 2010.

[4] S. Apel, T. Leich, M. Rosenmüller, and G. Saake. FeatureC++: On the Symbiosis of Feature-Oriented and Aspect-Oriented Programming. In *Proc. Int'l. Conf. Generative Programming and Component Eng. (GPCE)*, volume 3676 of *LNCS*, pages 125–140. Springer, 2005.

[5] D. Batory. Feature Models, Grammars, and Propositional Formulas. In *Proc. Int'l. Software Product Line Conf. (SPLC)*, volume 3714 of *LNCS*, pages 7–20. Springer, 2005.

[6] D. Batory, J. N. Sarvela, and A. Rauschmayer. Scaling Step-Wise Refinement. *IEEE Trans. Softw. Eng. (TSE)*, 30(6):355–371, 2004.

[7] D. Benavides, A. Ruiz-Cortés, and P. Trinidad. Automated Reasoning on Feature Models. In *Proc. Int'l. Conf. Advanced Information Systems Engineering (CAiSE)*, volume 3520 of *LNCS*, pages 491–503. Springer, 2005.

[8] N. Bencomo, P. Sawyer, G. S. Blair, and P. Grace. Dynamically Adaptive Systems are Product Lines too: Using Model-Driven Techniques to Capture Dynamic Variability of Adaptive Systems. In *Proc. Int'l. Software Product Line Conf. (SPLC)*, pages 23–32. IEEE CS, 2008.

[9] T. J. Biggerstaff. A Perspective of Generative Reuse. *Annals of Software Engineering*, 5(1):169–226, 1998.

[10] C. Cetina, P. Giner, J. Fons, and V. Pelechano. Using Feature Models for Developing Self-Configuring Smart Homes. In *Proc. of Int'l. Conf. Autonomic and Autonomous Systems (ICAS)*, pages 179–188. IEEE CS, 2009.

[11] B. D. Claas Wilke, Jens Dietrich. Event-Driven Verification in Dynamic Component Models. In *Proc. Int'l. Workshop on Component-Oriented Programming (WCOP)*, pages 79–86. Karlsruher Institut für Technologie (KIT), 2010.

[12] K. Czarnecki and U. Eisenecker. *Generative Programming: Methods, Tools, and Applications*. Addison-Wesley, 2000.

[13] K. Czarnecki, S. Helsen, and U. Eisenecker. Staged Configuration Using Feature Models. In *Proc. Int'l. Software Product Line Conf. (SPLC)*, volume 3154 of *LNCS*, pages 266–283. Springer, 2004.

[14] J. Floch, S. Hallsteinsen, E. Stav, F. Eliassen, K. Lund, and E. Gjorven. Using Architecture Models for Runtime Adaptability. *IEEE Software*, 23(2):62–70, 2006.

[15] E. Gamma, R. Helm, R. Johnson, and J. Vlissides. *Design Patterns: Elements of Reusable Object-Oriented Software*. Addison-Wesley, 1995.

[16] D. Garlan, S.-W. Cheng, A.-C. Huang, B. Schmerl, and P. Steenkiste. Rainbow: Architecture-Based Self Adaptation with Reusable Infrastructure. *Computer*, 37(10):46–54, 2004.

[17] M. L. Griss. Implementing Product-Line Features with Component Reuse. In *Proc. Int'l. Conf. Software Reuse (ICSR)*, volume 1844 of *LNCS*, pages 137–152. Springer, 2000.

[18] S. Hallsteinsen, M. Hinchey, S. Park, and K. Schmid. Dynamic Software Product Lines. *Computer*, 41(4):93–95, 2008.

[19] S. Hallsteinsen, E. Stav, A. Solberg, and J. Floch. Using Product Line Techniques to Build Adaptive Systems. In *Proc. Int'l. Software Product Line Conf. (SPLC)*, pages 141–150. IEEE CS, 2006.

[20] H. Härtig, S. Zschaler, M. Pohlack, R. Aigner, S. Göbel, C. Pohl, and S. Röttger. Enforceable Component-based Realtime Contracts. *Real-Time Systems*, 35(1):1–31, 2007.

[21] J. Lee and K. C. Kang. A Feature-Oriented Approach to Developing Dynamically Reconfigurable Products in Product Line Engineering. In *Proc. Int'l. Software Product Line Conf. (SPLC)*, pages 131–140. IEEE CS, 2006.

[22] J. Liu, D. Batory, and C. Lengauer. Feature-Oriented Refactoring of Legacy Applications. In *Proc. Int'l. Conf. Software Engineering (ICSE)*, pages 112–121. ACM Press, 2006.

[23] I. Mahgoub and M. Ilyas. *Smart Dust: Sensor Network Applications, Architecture, and Design*. CRC Press, 2006.

[24] M. Mendonca, A. Wasowski, and K. Czarnecki. SAT-based Analysis of Feature Models is Easy. In *Proc. Int'l. Software Product Line Conf. (SPLC)*, pages 231–240. Software Engineering Institute, 2009.

[25] B. Morin, O. Barais, J.-M. Jezequel, F. Fleurey, and A. Solberg. Models at Runtime to Support Dynamic Adaptation. *Computer*, 42(10):44–51, 2009.

[26] I. Neamtiu, M. Hicks, G. Stoyle, and M. Oriol. Practical Dynamic Software Updating for C. In *Proc. Int'l. Conf. Programming Language Design and Implementation (PLDI)*, pages 72–83. ACM Press, 2006.

[27] P. Oreizy, M. M. Gorlick, R. N. Taylor, D. Heimbigner, G. Johnson, N. Medvidovic, A. Quilici, D. S. Rosenblum, and A. L. Wolf. An Architecture-based Approach to Self-adaptive Software. *IEEE Intelligent Systems*, 14(3):54–62, 1999.

[28] K. Pohl, G. Böckle, and F. van der Linden. *Software Product Line Engineering: Foundations, Principles and Techniques*. Springer, 2005.

[29] C. Prehofer. Feature-Oriented Programming: A Fresh Look at Objects. In *Proc. Europ. Conf. Object-Oriented Programming (ECOOP)*, volume 1241 of *LNCS*, pages 419–443. Springer, 1997.

[30] M. Rosenmüller, N. Siegmund, S. Apel, and G. Saake. Flexible Feature Binding in Software Product Lines. *Automated Software Engineering*, 18(2):163–197, 2011.

[31] M. Rosenmüller, N. Siegmund, T. Thüm, and G. Saake. Multi-Dimensional Variability Modeling. In *Proc. Workshop on Variability Modelling of Software-intensive Systems (VaMoS)*, pages 11–20. ACM Press, 2011.

[32] K. Schmid and H. Eichelberger. From Static to Dynamic Software Product Lines. In *Int'l. Workshop on Dynamic Software Product Lines (DSPL)*, pages 33–38. IEEE CS, 2008.

[33] N. Siegmund, M. Rosenmüller, C. Kästner, P. Giarrusso, S. Apel, and S. Kolesnikov. Scalable Prediction of Non-functional Properties in Software Product Lines. In *Proc. of Int'l. Software Product Lines Conf. (SPLC)*, 2011. to appear.

[34] N. Siegmund, M. Rosenmüller, M. Kuhlemann, C. Kästner, S. Apel, and G. Saake. SPL Conqueror: Toward Optimization of Non-functional Properties in Software Product Lines. *Software Quality Journal*, to appear, 2011.

[35] A. Tešanović, K. Sheng, and J. Hansson. Application-Tailored Database Systems: A Case of Aspects in an Embedded Database. In *Proc. of Int'l. Database Engineering and Applications Symposium (IDEAS)*, pages 291–301. IEEE CS, 2004.

[36] T. Thüm, D. Batory, and C. Kästner. Reasoning about Edits to Feature Models. In *Proc. Int'l. Conf. Software Engineering (ICSE)*, pages 254–264. IEEE CS, 2009.

[37] P. Trinidad, A. Ruiz-Cortés, and J. Peña. Mapping Feature Models onto Component Models to Build Dynamic Software Product Lines. In *Int'l. Workshop on Dynamic Software Product Lines (DSPL)*, pages 51–56. Kindai Kagaku Sha Co. Ltd., 2007.

[38] J. White, B. Dougherty, and D. C. Schmidt. Selecting Highly Optimal Architectural Feature Sets with Filtered Cartesian Flattening. *Journal of Systems and Software*, 82(8):1268–1284, 2009.

Feature Interactions, Products, and Composition

Don Batory

University of Texas at Austin
Austin, TX 78712 USA
batory@cs.utexas.edu

Peter Höfner

University of Augsburg, Germany
NICTA, Australia
peter.hoefner@nicta.com.au

Jongwook Kim

University of Texas at Austin
Austin, TX 78712 USA
jongwook@cs.utexas.edu

Abstract

The relationship between feature modules and feature interactions is not well-understood. To explain classic examples of feature interaction, we show that features are not only composed sequentially, but also by cross-product and interaction operations that heretofore were implicit in the literature. Using the CIDE tool as our starting point, we (a) present a formal model of these operations, (b) show how it connects and explains previously unrelated results in *Feature Oriented Software Development (FOSD)*, and (c) describe a tool, based on our formalism, that demonstrates how changes in composed documents can be back-propagated to their original feature module definitions, thereby improving FOSD tooling.

Categories and Subject Descriptors D.2.2 [*Design Tools and Techniques*]; F.3.2 [*Semantics of Programming Languages*]: Algebraic Approaches to Semantics; F.3.3 [*Studies of Program Constructs*]

General Terms Design, Theory

Keywords FOSD, CIDE, back-propagation, feature interactions, feature products

1. Introduction

Feature Oriented Software Development (FOSD) is the study of modularizing features (increments in program functionality), feature composition, and the use of features to synthesize programs of *software product lines (SPLs)* [2].

In FOSD, a *feature module* encapsulates changes that are made to a program in order to add a new capability or functionality. Such modules (often interpreted as transformations) are composed sequentially: if f and g are feature modules, their composition $f \cdot g$ represents the combined set of changes made by f and g. Not all compositions of features – called *expressions* – are meaningful: *feature models* define all legal expressions [8, 20]. Each expression, when evaluated, synthesizes a distinct program in an SPL. Each program in an SPL has an expression [4, 9, 34].

Features are the building blocks of programs. But what are the building blocks of features? In this paper, we present an algebra that shows modules called *colors* to be their building blocks. Just as programs are compositions of features, features are compositions

of colors. Our research extends a long line of prior work [3, 6, 23, 24, 26, 27, 30, 34].

The novelty and significance of our work is recognizing additional operations on features that are implicit in the literature, but never before made explicit. Besides sequential ($\cdot$) composition, there is also cross-product ($\times$) and interaction ($\#$) composition. In brief, when architects want both features f and g, they are asking for their cross-product, $f \times g$, which is governed by the following axiom:

$$f \times g = (f \# g) \cdot g \cdot f \qquad (1)$$

That is, architects want not only the composition of feature modules f and g, *but also a module* ($f \# g$) *that modifies and/or integrates f and g so that they work correctly together*. Modules f, g, and $f \# g$ are colors.

We explore feature products and feature interactions in this paper, spelling out the implications of (1). We review classic examples of feature interactions and introduce a formal model (coloring algebra) that was inspired by Kästner's CIDE [21] and that defines the sequential, cross-product, and interaction composition operations to be consistent with these examples. Our algebra unifies previously unrelated results in FOSD and reveals how changes in composed documents can be back-propagated to their original feature module definitions, thereby improving FOSD tooling. Lastly, we present a tool to create product lines of MS Word documents that supports this back-propagation idea.

2. Motivating Examples

We start with examples that lead us to postulate (1). Although taken from different domains, readers will recognize their underlying similarity.

2.1 Fire-and-Flood Control

A classic example of feature interactions is fire-and-flood control [19]. Adding fire control to a building requires fire sensors to be placed on every ceiling. When a sensor detects a fire, sprinklers are activated. Adding flood control is similar: water sensors are placed on every floor. When standing water is detected, the water main is turned off.

Constructing a building with either flood control or fire control is straightforward. Problems arise when both features are present: suppose a fire is detected at time i. Fire control activates sprinklers at time $i + 1$, standing water is detected by flood control at time $i + 2$, the water main is turned off at time $i + 3$, and the building burns down. *The solution is to modify the fire and flood modules so that they work together correctly.* From an architect's perspective, we want the cross-product of `fire` and `flood`:

$$\texttt{fire} \times \texttt{flood} = (\texttt{fire}\#\texttt{flood}) \cdot \texttt{fire} \cdot \texttt{flood}$$

Namely `fire` and `flood` are composed, followed by module (`flood`#`fire`) that modifies the `floor` and `fire` modules to correctly coordinate their behavior, typically by giving one feature priority over another [18].

Note: A common definition of *module* is a unit of code that may be linked with other modules but otherwise remains *unmodified* [1, 16]. In this paper, we assume (color) modules are documents and/or document fragments that "fit-together". More on this in Section 2.3.

2.2 Call Waiting and Call Forwarding

Another classic example is the call waiting `CW` and call fowarding `CF` features in telephony [6, 10, 18]. `CF` enables a customer to specify a secondary phone number to which additional calls are forwarded when a phone is busy. `CW` allows one call to be suspended while another call is answered. If both features are present and a call comes in while another is active, the phone system must decide whether the call should be forwarded or the user should be notified that another call has arrived. The resolution is defined by module `CW#CF`. Without a resolution, the phone system may behave erroneously.

Call waiting and call forwarding is similar to fire-and-flood control in that # defines a priority. In a phone system with both call waiting and call forwarding, we want the product `CW` × `CF` to include an appropriate resolution `CW#CF`.

Note: The Feature Interaction community uses the term "feature interaction" to mean a change in behavior when features are composed [10]. Formal analyses are used to detect such interactions. "Resolution" is a term indicating the changes needed to get the desired behavior; these changes are color modules called *interaction* modules. Henceforth, the name of a module `A#B` indicates the *interaction* of features `A` and `B`, and the module contents is the *resolution* of their interaction.

2.3 CIDE

CIDE is an advance in FOSD tooling that reduces the granularity of feature modules [22]. A source document is painted in different colors, one color per feature. All source that is painted "red" belongs to the `Red` feature, all source that is painted "green" belongs to the `Green` feature, etc. Red that appears inside green indicates an interaction – how the `Red` feature changes the source of the `Green` feature. Symmetrically, green that appears inside red indicates how the `Green` feature changes the source of the `Red` feature. We assume that colors only nest and otherwise do not overlap.

```
class stack {
  int ctr = 0;
  int size() {
    return ctr;
  }

  String s = new String();
  void empty() {
    ctr = 0;
    s = "";
  }
  void push(char a) {
    ctr++;
    s = String.valueOf(a)
        .concat(s);
  }
  void pop() {
    ctr--;
    s = s.substring(1);
  }
  char top() {
    return s.charAt(0);
  }
}
```

Figure 1: The Counted Stack (`Counter` × `Stack` × `Base`)

Consider a counted character stack [26], where characters are pushed and popped from a String and the number of characters on the stack are counted (Figure 1). There are three features: `Base`, `Stack`, and `Counter`. The `Base` feature is clear and represents an empty stack class. The `Stack` feature is green and contains the standard push, pop, empty, and top methods, along with a String that encodes the character stack. The `Counter` feature is red and contains an integer counter and size method. `Stack` and `Counter` interactions are red inside green, which reset, increment, and decrement the counter variable.

CIDE has preprocessor semantics, where the code of a feature `F` is effectively surrounded by `#ifdef F` – `#endif` statements. (CIDE differs from traditional preprocessors as it uses ASTs, rather than text, and is integrated with feature models [22]). Programs in CIDE can be "developed" incrementally by exposing features one at a time; this is how cross-products of features are simulated. Initially, the `Base` feature exposes only an empty stack class (Figure 2a). When the `Stack` feature is added, green and clear code is visible (Figure 2b). And when the `Counter` feature is added, all code is exposed (Figure 1).

Alternatively, we could expose or compose features in a different order: after `Base`, we could expose `Counter` (Figure 2c), which shows only the `Counter` introductions. Exposing `Stack` reveals the remaining code (Figure 1). Each of these "progressions" corresponds to a particular cross-product of features, as indicated in the subtitles of Figures 1 and 2. We return to this example later.

```
class stack {
}
```

(a) Base

```
class stack {
  int ctr = 0;
  int size() {
    return ctr;
  }
}
```

(c) `Counter` × `Base`

```
class stack {

  String s = new String();
  void empty() {
    s = "";
  }
  void push(char a) {
    s = String.valueOf(a)
        .concat(s);
  }
  void pop() {
    s = s.substring(1);
  }
  char top() {
    return s.charAt(0);
  }
}
```

(b) `Stack` × `Base`

Figure 2: Stepwise Developments of Counted Stack

CIDE offers a visually simple way to recognize n-way (or n^{th}-order) interactions by the nesting of n colors. So an interaction module `f#g#h` would be the set of all fragments that are nested 3-deep using any permutation of colors/features `f`, `g`, and `h`. In practice, 2-way interactions are common. 3-way interactions arise occasionally. 4-way or higher-order interactions seem rare. In any case, a formal model must be able to express arbitrary-order interactions.

2.4 Interaction of Language Features

The Feature Interaction community focusses on finding semantic interactions of features [10]. We do not dispute the importance of semantic interactions, but we note that interaction modules also arise in semantic documents. Here is a recent example [13].

Programming languages evolve through the addition of features, which may include new control structures, abstractions, or typing constructs. Each feature changes the syntax and semantics of a language.

Consider adding `Generics` to the calculus of *Featherweight Java (FJ)* to produce the calculus of *Generic Featherweight Java (GFJ)*. The required changes are woven throughout the syntax and semantics of FJ. The left-hand column of Figure 3 presents a subset of the syntax of FJ, the rules which formalize the subtyping relation that establish the inheritance hierarchy, and the typing rule that ensures expressions for object creation are well-formed. The corresponding definitions for GFJ = `Generics` × `FJ` appear in

Figure 3 table:

FJ Expression Syntax	FJ • Generic Expression Syntax
$e ::= x$ $\mid\ e.f$ $\mid\ e.m\ (\bar{e})$ $\mid\ new\ C(\bar{e})$ $\mid\ (C)\ e$	$e ::= x$ $\mid\ e.f$ $\mid\ e.m\ \langle\bar{T}\rangle\ (\bar{e})$ $\mid\ new\ C\ \langle\bar{T}\rangle\ (\bar{e})$ $\mid\ (C\ \langle\bar{T}\rangle)\ e$

FJ Subtyping	$T <: T$	GFJ Subtyping	$\Delta \vdash T <: T$

FJ	GFJ
	$\Delta \vdash X <: \Delta(X)$ (GS-Var)
$\dfrac{S<:T \quad T<:V}{S<:V}$ (S-Trans)	$\dfrac{\Delta \vdash S<:T \quad \Delta \vdash T<:V}{\Delta \vdash S<:V}$ (GS-Trans)
$T<:T$ (S-Refl)	$\Delta \vdash T<:T$ (GS-Refl)
$\dfrac{class\ C\ extends\ D\ \{\ldots\}}{C<:D}$ (S-Dir)	$\dfrac{class\ C\ \langle\overline{X \triangleright N}\rangle\ extends\ D\ \langle\bar{V}\rangle\ \{\ldots\}}{\Delta \vdash C\ \langle\bar{T}\rangle <: [\bar{T}/\bar{X}]\ D\ \langle\bar{V}\rangle}$ (GS-Dir)

FJ New Typing	$\Gamma \vdash e : T$	GFJ New Typing	$\Delta; \Gamma \vdash e : T$

FJ	GFJ
$\dfrac{fields(C) = \bar{D}\ \bar{f} \quad \Gamma \vdash \bar{e} : \bar{C} \quad \bar{C}<:\bar{D}}{\Gamma \vdash new\ C(\bar{e}) : C}$ (T-New)	$\dfrac{\Delta \vdash C\langle\bar{T}\rangle \quad fields(C\langle\bar{T}\rangle) = \bar{V}\ \bar{f} \quad \Delta;\Gamma \vdash \bar{e} : \bar{U} \quad \Delta \vdash \bar{U}<:\bar{V}}{\Delta;\Gamma \vdash new\ C\ \langle\bar{T}\rangle\ (\bar{e}) : C}$ (GT-New)

Figure 3: Selected FJ Definitions with GFJ Changes

the right-hand column where CIDE-shading indicates differences. As in CIDE, when the Generics feature is removed, the right-hand column simplifies to the left-hand column. These highlighted changes are the introductions and fragment definitions that belong to the Generics#FJ color.

The same holds for proofs of type soundness, the guarantee that the desired run-time behavior of a language, typically preservation and progress, is enforced. That is, proofs of type soundness for FJ are altered when the Generics feature is added: new proof cases are added and existing lemmas may be altered. The changes to the FJ proofs are also contained in the Generics#FJ color.

2.5 Recap

The sequential, cross-product, and interaction composition of features are pervasive in FOSD. A formal model is needed to define their properties precisely. Doing so axiomatizes the concepts in CIDE and our motivating examples.

3. A Coloring Algebra

We now develop an algebra for coloring where all colors are treated identically. Our model of FOSD is rooted in the way CIDE expresses features and their compositions. For exposition reasons, however, we motivate two types of colors: base and interaction.

A *base color* represents an individual feature whose module is a collection of one or more documents. When a base is added to a program, its documents are added; when the base is removed, its documents are removed. Base colors are denoted by individual letters (R, S, T). A dot-composition of base colors is the disjoint union of their documents.

A document can have any number of labeled *variation points (VPs)*, i.e. points at which a document fragment can be inserted. An *interaction color* is a #-expression (e.g. R#S, S#T, R#S#T) whose module consists of zero or more documents and document fragments that are to be inserted or *installed* at VPs. It is possible for some fragments to remain uninstalled after composition, as they may be installed later when another color module adds the required

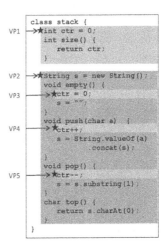

Figure 4: The Counted Stack With Variation Points

VPs. Think of a base color as an interaction color without document fragments.

Recall the counted stack. Figure 4 shows its five variation points indicated by ⋆. Each VP is associated with precisely one fragment. Base is a single document (an empty stack class) with two variation points VP1 and VP2. The Counter#Base module (red inside clear) contains the fragment that is installed at VP1. The Stack#Base module (green inside clear) contains the fragment that is installed at VP2. This fragment has three variation points VP3, VP4, and VP5. The Counter#Stack#Base module contains the three fragments that are installed at these points.

Figure 4 exhibits a key property of CIDE: VPs and fragments are *always* in 1-to-1 correspondence [7]. It is not possible for multiple fragments to be installed at the same variation point. (VPs could be placed next to each other to give the appearance that multiple fragments are installed at the same VP).

The next sections give our axiomatization of CIDE. We start with dot(·)-composition. We use 1 to denote the *empty color* or *empty module*. 1 contains no documents or fragments.

3.1 Dot Composition

Let R, S, and T be colors. The dot-composition R · S is the operation that (a) forms the disjoint union of their documents and (b) installs their document fragments, if possible. R · S represents a composite color. Three axioms of · are:

Identity :	$R \cdot 1 = R$	(2)
Commutativity :	$R \cdot S = S \cdot R$	(3)
Associativity :	$R \cdot (S \cdot T) = (R \cdot S) \cdot T$	(4)

Axioms (2) and (4) are standard for FOSD. Unlike traditional models (such as AHEAD [9], FeatureHouse [4], and DOP [11]), feature composition in CIDE is commutative (3) – the order in which a set of colors are dot-composed (a.k.a. "turned on") does not matter because the order in which fragments are installed at their VPs does not matter. Moreover, as we will see, commutativity follows from another axiom we define later.

3.2 Interaction Composition

R#S is the color that defines how R and S interact—it is the set of changes that are needed to make R and S work together correctly.

Three axioms of # are:

$$No\ Interaction: \qquad R\#1 = 1 \qquad\qquad (5)$$

$$Commutativity: \qquad R\#S = S\#R \qquad\qquad (6)$$

$$Associativity: \qquad R\#(S\#T) = (R\#S)\#T \qquad (7)$$

(5) states the elementary fact that that 1 cannot be changed and that it does not change other colors. As with sequential (dot) composition, the order in which features are #-composed in CIDE does not matter. An interaction module $R\#S\#T$ represents the set of changes for all permutations of colors R, S, and T. This justifies (6) and (7).

For the remainder of the paper we assume that interaction composition ($\#$) binds stronger than dot-composition ($\cdot$). These operations are related by a distributivity law [26]:

$$Distributivity\ I: \qquad R\#(S \cdot T) = (R\#S) \cdot (R\#T) \qquad (8)$$

That is, the interaction of R with $S \cdot T$ is the dot-composition of interactions $R\#S$ and $R\#T$. By commutativity of $\#$ (6), we can immediately derive the second distributivity law:

$$Distributivity\ II: \qquad (S \cdot T)\#R = (S\#R) \cdot (T\#R) \qquad (9)$$

Intuitively, these distributivity laws state that the interaction between a color R and a composed color $S \cdot T$ can be described by the composition of the interaction of R with S and T separately. From a practical point of view, defining interaction on base colors is sufficient.

3.3 Product Composition

$R \times S$ is the color that represents the product of R and S: as discussed earlier, it is the dot-composition of R and S with their interaction resolution $R\#S$:

$$Product: \qquad R \times S = R\#S \cdot R \cdot S \qquad (10)$$

The following theorems of $\times$ can be proven given the previous axioms (see Appendix):

$$Identity: \qquad R \times 1 = R \qquad\qquad (11)$$

$$Commutativity: \qquad R \times S = S \times R \qquad\qquad (12)$$

$$Associativity: \qquad (R \times S) \times T = R \times (S \times T) \qquad (13)$$

The meaning of these theorems should be self-evident.

3.4 Involution Axioms of CIDE

So far, our axioms are standard and the algebraic structures are well-known. Now we consider two basic behaviors of CIDE. In doing so, we are confronted by fundamental questions that lurk in a dark corner of classical feature modeling:

- What are the semantics of replicated features? What is $R \cdot R$ and $R \times R$ and $R\#R$?

- Can a feature interact with itself? What is $R\#R$?

- Do features have inverses?

As we will see, their answers depend on each other.

Consider the first question on replicated features. In classical feature models, a feature is either selected or it is not; feature replication *never* occurs. So color expressions like $R\#R$, $R \cdot R$, and $R \times R$ never arise. But CIDE raises the question of feature replication in an unusual way by nesting colors, forcing us to address replication.

Consider $R\#R$. Red inside red is indistinguishable from red. If R denotes red, this reads as:

$$(R\#R) \cdot R = R$$

Let B be blue. A more complex example is red-inside-blue-inside-red, which is indistinguishable from blue-inside-red:

$$(R\#B\#R) \cdot (B\#R) \cdot R = (B\#R) \cdot R$$

In creating our algebra, we faced the following design decision: should we admit an infinite number of non-empty terms to which we can ascribe no useful meaning or distinction ($R\#R$, $R\#R\#R$, $R\#S\#R$, $R\#R\#R\#R$, ...)? Or do we eliminate them for a simpler explanation? We chose the latter, and assert that a feature does not interact with itself:

$$\#\text{-}Involution: \qquad R\#R = 1 \qquad\qquad (14)$$

Given (14), the equalities of the above examples follow.

Now consider the meaning of $R \cdot R$ and $R \times R$. We can proceed in two ways; both are equivalent. The first recognizes a surprising property of CIDE. Its colors are invertable as CIDE fragments never override other fragments. In other words, either the documents of a color are present or they are not. And a color's fragments are either installed or they are not. So colors have a binary behavior: If a color R is to be dot composed with some program T, R can check to see if it is already installed. If it was, R removes its documents and fragments. Otherwise, R installs its documents and fragments as usual. Involution captures this two state existence elegantly:

$$Dot\text{-}Involution: \qquad R \cdot R = 1 \qquad\qquad (15)$$

That is, *all* colors (base and interaction) are the inverses of themselves. This axiom does not hold for other FOSD models [4, 9, 11], but it does hold for CIDE. It immediately follows that:

$$Involution: \qquad R \times R = 1 \qquad\qquad (16)$$

That is, features toggle from on to off, and a feature is a $\times$-involution of itself.

Note: The meaning of sequential composition (dot) is now stronger than we informally described in the Introduction. Back then, R and S were implicitly distinct modules with disjoint contents. Now, dot-composition removes contents shared by R and S. When R and S have identical contents, $R \cdot S = 1$.

Here is the second way: Features in CIDE (or any FOSD model) are either selected or they are not. A feature toggles between on and off, which is expressed by (16). Given this, (15) is immediately derived.

Although (15) is surprising, it comes with useful benefit that has long been absent and needed in FOSD. Namely, the ability to solve dot-equations for unknowns. We explore the utility of this capability in Section 4.3.

There are also other, deeper reasons for (15). We know of only three possible ways to deal with replicated features: (a) disallow them, (b) assume involution, or (c) assume idempotence. We ruled out (a) above and presented the consequences of (b). The remaining alternative is idempotence [5]: there is only one copy of a feature (i.e. $R \cdot R = R$). As mentioned earlier, an algebra should provide inverses (either to solve dot-equations for unknowns or for "turning off" features). The problem here is profound: the existence of inverse and idempotence implies that the universe consists of only one color: $R = 1 \cdot R = (R^{-1} \cdot R) \cdot R = R^{-1} \cdot (R \cdot R) = R^{-1} \cdot R = 1$. Simply put: idempotence and inverses do not work together. This is yet another reason for asserting (15).

3.5 Axiom Consistency and Irredundancy

Our axioms are consistent, i.e. they do not contradict themselves and there exist models – color expression instances and deductions – that satisfy these axioms. We have sketched some models in this section and used Mace4 [29] to generate models with a finite number of elements.

We have also used Prover9 [29], an automated theorem prover, to prove that axioms (3) and (5) can be entailed from the other axioms, leaving (2), (4), (6)–(10) irredundant. This can be shown by removing one axiom from the set and adding its formula as goal. An example is given in the Appendix.

From our experience, defining a consistent set of axioms was not easy; a slight change in one exposed truly unexpected contradictions that only tools like Prover9/Mace4 could find. With this confidence, we can compute the interactions of interactions – the interaction of R#S and T#U is R#S#T#U – and the product of interactions, etc., should they ever be needed.

3.6 Open Problems

There are four axioms/theorems of CIDE that are not shared by other FOSD approaches, namely dot-commutativity (3), $\times$-commutativity (12), dot-involution (15), and $\times$-involution (16). We conjecture that there is a subset of coloring axioms that can be used to model feature interactions in non-CIDE approaches, but this task is beyond the scope of this paper. Further, exploring the role of inverses in non-CIDE approaches, perhaps combining results from this paper, would also be useful. We know, for example, that transformations (features) that override (delete, replace), rather than extend, are believed not to have inverses. But retaining the history of a derivation, as does the unmixin tool of [9], does permit inverses to be computed. Again, we leave this exploration for future work.

4. Observations and Implications

4.1 Altering Module Composition Order

Kästner and Apel observed that the order in which feature modules are composed can be changed, *but this requires an alteration of the contents of their modules* [3, 24]. It was conjectured that for all composable feature modules F and G, there exists modules F' and G' such that:

$$F \cdot G = G' \cdot F' \qquad (17)$$

where the informal meanings of F and F' (G and G') are essentially the same. That is both F and F' add the capabilities of feature F, but do so in different ways so that (17) holds. How F maps to F' (and G to G') is not fully understood.

The essence of the solution was first suggested in [3, 24] and is captured elegantly by (1). Suppose f and g are features to compose and let F, F', G, and G' be their modules. We want the cross-product $g \times f$, where we start with module F and then dot-compose module G:

$$g \times f = G \cdot F$$
$$(g\#f \cdot g) \cdot f = G \cdot F$$

Module F = f consists of a single color and module G = g#f · g is composite. If we reverse the product order of f and g, we have definitions for modules F' and G':

$$f \times g = F' \cdot G'$$
$$(f\#g \cdot f) \cdot g = F' \cdot G'$$

Module $G' = g$ and module $F' = f\#g \cdot f$. It is the color f#g that "migrates" from G to F' that explains why feature module contents must change when their composition order changes. (Note: if f#g = 1, modules F and G are commutative). Permuting the order in which features are $\times$-composed is a matter of migrating interaction modules.

Note: Readers can see in Figures 1-2 an example. For the composition Counter $\times$ Stack $\times$ Base, the Stack module is Stack#Base and the Counter is Counter#Stack#Base · Counter#Base. For the composition Stack $\times$ Counter $\times$ Base, the Counter module is Counter#Base and the Stack module is Counter#Stack#Base · Stack#Base.

4.2 Cross-Product Expression Evaluation

To select a target program in an SPL, architects select the set of features that they want, such as {F,G,H}. A tool based on the coloring algebra forms the cross-product of these features, yielding a dot-product of colors using the axioms above:

$$F \times G \times H = F\#G\#H \cdot F\#G \cdot F\#H \cdot G\#H \cdot F \cdot G \cdot H \qquad (18)$$

Color modules are then retrieved from a repository and composed, thereby synthesizing the target program.

Note that a cross-product of n features produces a dot-expression of $(2^n - 1)$ colors. Experience shows that a *vast* majority of colors equal 1; rough indications are that $O(n) - O(n^2)$ colors are non-identities [21, 26]. Owing to color naming conventions, expression expansion need not be exponential in complexity, but linear in the size of a document. Here's how: Only non-identity colors are stored in a repository. Instead of expanding $F \times G \times H$, a tool searches the repository for modules whose names reference only F, G, and H, and composes them. (Module T#H would not be retrieved as $T \notin \{F, G, H\}$, but F#H would be). This is a linear operation in the total number of colors in the entire document. Stated differently, this operation is as fast as searching the entire document once.

The reason why a coloring algebra produces an exponential number of terms is that it must account for *all* possible interactions of features, although in any practical setting, a vanishingly small percentage of colors are non-empty.

4.3 New Tool Technologies

The following situation can arise: The source of a program in an SPL is produced and given to a client. The client modifies the program (possibly to fix bugs, improve performance, etc.). Now the changes to this program must be back-propagated to the original feature modules to make the changes permanent. If the client has access to the source of the entire SPL, this can be done. But suppose the client does not, and herein lies a difficulty.

Our algebra suggests a solution. A client requests program P, which corresponds to the following composite color $P = T_1 \cdot \ldots \cdot T_n$. The client manually modifies P to produce program $Q = T_0 \cdot T'_1 \cdot \ldots \cdot T_n$. (The client still sees VPs although their fragments may have been removed. He could add new VPs and fragments, and could change or delete any fragment or VP present in the program). When the client submits the updated program Q, a tool would know the original expression for P and could solve for the changes ΔP that were made to it:

$$
\begin{array}{lll}
\Delta P \cdot P = & Q & // \text{ given} \\
\Delta P \cdot P \cdot P = & Q \cdot P & // \cdot P \text{ to both sides} \\
\Delta P = & Q \cdot P & // (15) \\
\Delta P = & T_0 \cdot T'_1 \cdot \ldots \cdot T_n \cdot & // \text{ substitution} \\
& T_1 \cdot \ldots \cdot T_n & \\
\Delta P = & T_0 \cdot T'_1 \cdot T_1 & // (3) \text{ and } (15)
\end{array}
$$

Solving for ΔP is what diff-based tools do: they ignore unchanged colors and expose colors that were changed, added, or deleted. ΔP shows that color T_0 was added and T_1 was changed, where $T'_1 \cdot T_1$ is difference between the updated and original T_1 color.

Differencing leads to the possibility of a shredding tool, that takes a program with variation points as input and shreds it into colors. Only those colors that are new or that have changed must be updated in the color repository. In the next section, we describe a tool based on these ideas.

5. The Paan Tool

Office Open XML is an open standard of XML schemas adopted by Microsoft Office for its default file format. It specifies a compressed, XML-based encoding of Microsoft Office 2007 and 2010 documents, where different XML formats are used for Word, Visio, Excel, and InfoPath [17]. This allows non-Microsoft tools to extract and manipulate Office documents. By changing a .docx file to .zip and unzipping, the contents of a Word document (consisting of multiple XML files and directories) becomes visible.

We created a tool, called *Paan* — Korean for 'version', that enables us to explore a new implementation of CIDE concepts, but using the coloring algebra as its inspiration [25]. Specifically Paan works with MS Word documents, where it relies on the Custom XML Markup facility of MS Word to define nested regions of color and variation points. A markup *tag* is used to assign a feature name to a region (a.k.a. fragment) of a Word document. A fragment is identified by enclosing start and end tags. In Figure 5a, a pair of tags named blue surrounds a "Hello World" fragment; its XML representation is shown in Figure 5b.

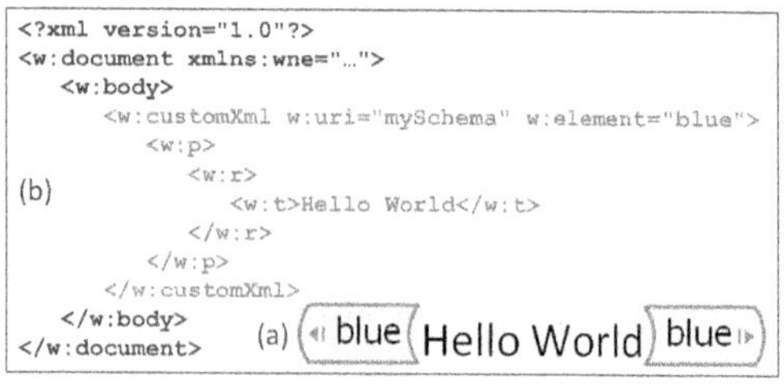

Figure 5: MS Word Custom Markup Tags and its XML

In CIDE, colors are nested like preprocessor #ifdef-#endif declarations. An inner color appears only if all of its enclosing colors (features) have been selected. Paan works the same way. In Figure 6a, red tags wrap vowels. Being surrounded by a blue tag, vowels appear only when both the blue and red features are selected.

The removal of unwanted features from a colored document is called *projection*. For implementation reasons, when a feature is projected (removed), a variation point is marked by an additional tag named _reserved_. Figure 6b shows the removal of the blue feature from Figure 6a; Figure 6c shows the removal of the red feature, exposing only blue.

Paan differs from CIDE in several ways. One, obviously, is the colorability of Word documents. More importantly, Paan was designed for the following scenario. Imagine documents where some features encompass proprietary or sensitive data that can only be exposed to certain communities. The full Word document, in such cases, could not be distributed. Instead, *only document projections are distributed*. Further, each community could *edit* their projected documents. Paan can automatically back-propagate these changes into the Paan repository, following the diffing concepts described in Section 4.3. The novelty of Paan is (a) it demonstrates how this scenario can be addressed, (b) it strictly follows the laws (axioms, theorems, . . .) of the coloring algebra (Section 5.3), and (c) works with MS Word documents.

5.1 Back-Propagation of Changes

Let W be a colored Word document and let W_p be a projection of W, where p is the set of features that have been retained. A user can now modify W_p at will, adding new VPs (that are instantiated with

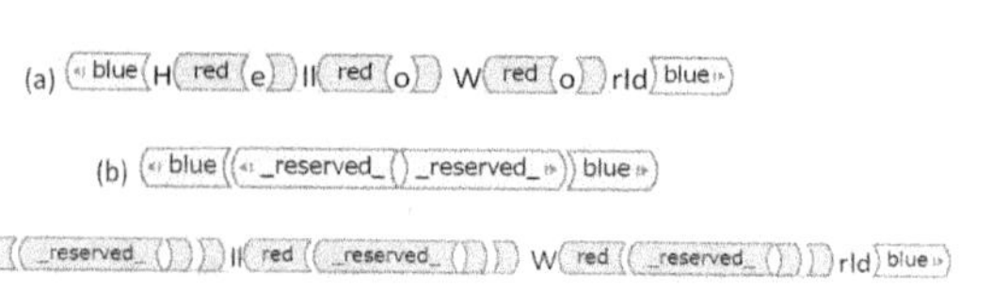

Figure 6: Nesting and Projection of Tags

their text fragments), modifying visible fragments, and deleting existing VPs (including VPs whose text has been projected).

To back-propagate the changes in W_p to W, Paan does the following. First, it maintains a copy of W in its repository that existed prior to projection. It then traverses W_p to locate VPs whose fragments were projected (removed). For each such VP i, it finds fragment i in W and restores that fragment in W_p. At the end, fragments of W that were removed to produce W_p have been restored. Paan then discards the original copy W and replaces it with W_p. The projection-back-propagate cycle continues.

Note: The restoration of projected VPs can be accomplished in linear time: a single pass through W to find all (VP,fragment) pairs and a single pass through W_p to restore projected VPs.

Paan's back-propagation implements the ideas of Section 4.3: A Paan repository can consist of multiple Word documents and directories. If a Word document has not been changed (which Paan knows by examining a Word document's revision number and comparing it to the revision number in the repository), Paan does not update the repository's copy. When updating individual Word documents, Paan simply assumes that all fragments in W_p have been modified, and proceeds to update its repository copy on this conservative (and functionally equivalent) basis.

5.2 Wrappers

Although CIDE supports wrappers [21], we need a more general support for wrappers in Word documents. A *wrapper* is a fragment that surrounds another fragment. Wrappers occur in FOSD languages as method extensions and in AOP as around advice of execution pointcuts of individual methods. Figure 7a shows a base method m() of class C. Figure 7b shows an extension of m() in AHEAD syntax that wraps m(). Figure 7c shows the identical extension of m() in AspectJ syntax. Figure 7d is the result of this extension. Figure 7e is how the extension and base is colored in Paan. Wrapper tags (BASE and RED) are in upper-case to distinguish them from non-wrappers (base) which are in lower-case.

An interesting property of wrappers is that they have exactly the opposite semantics of color nesting in CIDE. Let B be a base fragment and W be a wrapper of B. If B and W are also the names of their respective features, B belongs to the B module and wrapper W belongs to the interaction module W#B. Unlike nesting, where an interaction module T#B that modifies B is fully inside B, wrapping reverses the roles where the wrapped module B is fully inside W#B.

Note: Wrappers and non-wrappers are both colors, and their distinction is irrelevant to the coloring algebra. Stated differently, wrappers and non-wrappers are just different ways of implementing colors.

To understand how wrappers are projected, we generalize the nesting-only projection algorithm. Associated with every color module is a propositional formula whose terms are non-negated feature variables. As a first approximation, module F has the formula (F) and the interaction module $F_1\#...\#F_n$ represents the conjunction $(F_1 \wedge ... \wedge F_n)$.

```
(a)    void m() { counter++; }

(b)    void m() { print("before" + counter);
                  if (condition) Super.m();
                  print("after" + counter);
       }

(c)    void around() : execution(void C.m())
                { print("before" + counter);
                  if (condition) proceed();
                  print("after" + counter);
       }

(d)    void m() { print("before" + counter);
                  if (condition) counter++;
                  print("after" + counter);
       }

(e)    void m() { RED print("before" + counter);

                  if (condition) BASE counter++;

                  print("after" + counter);
       }
```

Figure 7: Wrappers

Projection of wrappers is accomplished in the following way: Paan traverses the Word document W in its repository in its entirety. Let p denote the set of features that were selected (meaning that their fragments are to remain after projection). The traversal of W encounters a sequence of fragments. Let T be a fragment and T(x) be its propositional formula. If T(p) is true, T is present in W_p. Otherwise, T is not included, and the traversal of T to the next fragment inside T continues. This is different than a document without wrappers, as once a fragment is eliminated, there is no need to search inside the fragment further.

To illustrate, Figure 8a shows a BASE fragment wrapped by a BLUE and GREEN fragment. Figure 8b shows only the BASE feature. Figure 8c shows only the BASE and GREEN features, and Figure 8d only the BASE and BLUE features.

Figure 8: Projecting Wrappers

Paan enables arbitrary higher-order wrappers by allowing users to define the predicate (and hence the interaction module) of a wrapper, so that all interactions permitted by the coloring algebra can be expressed.

In summary, wrappers slightly increase the complexity of the projection algorithm. Interestingly, the back-propagation algorithm for transferring edits of color modules back to the repository is uneffected.

5.3   Paan's Support of the Coloring Algebra

Paan supports the coloring algebra several visible ways. First is the non-involution axioms of # and dot that define the nesting or wrapping hierarchical coloring structure that is imposed on Word documents. Second is its enforcement of #-involution, which requires

special support. Figure 9a shows an edited document containing interaction R#B#R (red-inside-blue-inside-red). When this change is back-propagated, Paan moves the contents of R#B#R into B#R (Figure 9b), therefore enforcing (14). Doing so shows that Paan makes use of commutativity and involution to simplify interaction colors. The same applies to wrappers.

(a)   «red»This is a red region (blue this is a blue region (red this is a red region))). red»

(b)   «red»This is a red region (blue this is a blue region (this is a red region))). red»

Figure 9: Paan's Support for Axiom (14)

The third way is allowing users to select features in arbitrary orders, upholding the cross-product commutativity and associativity axioms. Cross-product involution asserts that a feature is either selected or deselected. The dot-involution axiom is essential to back-propagation.

Having said the above, it is possible that a tool like Paan could have been developed without a coloring algebra. The basic ideas of back-propagation are conceptually straightforward. But there are certain design decisions – such as involution – whose implications are not obvious, nor are they obviously consistent. Our formalization provides a confidence in this approach that an implementation could never provide or guarantee.

6.   Experience and Lessons Learned

Paan was evaluated on several SPLs [25]. One experiment converted an AHEAD SPL with nine Java classes into nine MS Word files, one per class. This SPL had 25 features; each of the MS Word files were colored accordingly. Three separate projections (configurations) were tested; the resulting Word files were converted into text files and then into Java files for compilation and subsequent execution (to verify that the Paan projections were correct). Another experiment converted HTML documentation for another AHEAD SPL, which included graphics, into a single MS Word file, from which different projections (documentation for specific SPL members) were produced. Back-propagation was tested by manually editing the above projected documents. Although more sophisticated and thorough testing was possible, manual comparisons were sufficient for our goals.

Word documents must conform to an Office Open XML schema. A straight-forward implementation of projection (leaving customized XML nodes indicating a projected VP) can invalidate schema conformity. So too can the restoration of a fragment at a VP during back-propagation invalidate schema conformity, if not done carefully.

An example is that `<paragraph>` structures in Office Open XML cannot be nested. Figure 10a shows "Hello world" enclosed in a blue region. Figure 10b shows a projection of blue. A string "abc" is appended before the projected VP (Figure 10c).

(a)   «blue»Hello world blue»

(b)   «blue» « _reserved_) _reserved_ » blue»

(c)   abc blue (_reserved_)

(d)   abc blue Hello world

Figure 10: Back-Propagation Error

We expect that back-propagation restores the "Hello world" fragment at the VP to produce Figure 10d. Unfortunately, the resulting Word file invalidates schema conformity. The reason is that the "abc" text is a `<paragraph>` that includes the VP. The fragment at the VP is also a `<paragraph>`, leading to nested `<paragraph>`s, which is an illegal structure.

Our solution was to recognize the errors that resulted in projection and/or back-propagation, and to apply local transformations that repaired the structure. From this we learned an important lesson: *Coloring is a functionality that should be an integral part of a tool's design: it should not be an after-thought, or be implemented as an after-thought, as we have done. The semantics of marking and coloring should be aligned from the beginning, thereby simplifying tool development.*

7. Related Work

Coloring can be traced to [12] where elements of UML models could be tagged with feature predicates. Given a set of selected features, an element would be removed from a model if its predicate is false. Modularizing elements that share the same predicate is the essence of coloring.

The coloring algebra is a descendant of [24, 26, 27]. *Derivatives* were the first identified building blocks of feature modules.[1] Unfortunately, the mathematics of derivatives was incomplete as compositions of derivatives were not fully associative, but only right-associative. This made it impossible to algebraically calculate the results of feature splitting (replacing T with R × S if T is split into features R and S) and feature merging (replacing R × S with T). CIDE showed a simple way to visualize features and their interactions, resulting in the coloring algebra, which does support splitting and merging.

Other algebras for feature-based composition, such as [5, 28], focus on the internal structure of color modules, rather than feature interactions. [5] is the first algebra (to our knowledge) that dealt with feature replication. Their solution uses *distance idempotence* (a form of idempotence where adjacency of identical features is not required). Feature composition was not commutative and feature modules (called feature structure trees) do not have inverses.

AHEAD [9] and FeatureHouse [4] are compositional approaches to FOSD where only dot-composition is supported. There is no notion of interaction modules, cross-product, and #-product operations. The distinctions of cross-products and #-products could be layered onto AHEAD and FeatureHouse as all expressions with cross-products can be reduced to dot-products of modules (where each color module can be encoded as an AHEAD or FeatureHouse module). Back-propagation of edits in composed modules is supported by the AHEAD tool called 'unmixin'. However, there was no formalization of back-propagation in AHEAD.

Delta-oriented Programming (DOP) [11, 34] is another compositional approach to FOSD which has a module structure similar to colors. DOP does permit features (or colors) to override (replace, delete) existing modules, so a restriction of our algebra (as discussed in Section 3.6) may be needed to describe it. DOP does not support cross-products or interaction operations (although it could, just like AHEAD and FeatureHouse). The main advance of our work is the axiomatization of coloring.

Aspect-oriented Programming (AOP) is related to colors in the following way. Base colors contain only introductions. AOP pointcuts designate join-points, which are implicit variation points. AOP advice designates code fragments to be inserted at join-points (or rather join-point shadows). The primary distinction between AOP and FOSD (and our work) is that aspects do not have simple composition semantics (e.g. they cannot always be expressed as a composition of simpler aspects [28]). Consequently the mathematics behind aspects is complicated.

Others have created similar tools to Paan although none support back-propagation. Rabiser et al. describe a tool that adopts DocBook for variability modeling [32]. Although the tool does not support wrappers, it uses generative techniques that are more powerful than coloring to produce customized documents for SPL members. Pure::Systems uses tagging (like Paan) to create a product line of Word documents [31]. Other than available web videos, little more is known about this tool.

Finally, there is a connection between back-propagation and maintaining the consistency of pairs of models [14, 15], one of which is derived from the other and the derived one is updated. Our work is a special case of this more general problem.

8. Conclusions

The relationship between features and feature interactions has long been a subject of interest. FOSD brings a twist in its focus on feature modularity and the composition of feature modules to build programs of product lines. Interactions occur when the behavior of a feature changes in the presence of another feature. Interaction modules contain the changes (a.k.a. resolution) to existing modules so that their features work correctly together.

We reviewed classical examples of feature interactions and presented a formalism (the coloring algebra) that (a) is based on Kästner's CIDE, (b) faithfully captures these examples and (c) provides a general framework in which to understand feature modules and feature interactions. The essence of our approach is recognizing the product ($\times$) and interaction ($\#$) operations besides sequential (dot) composition. Our algebra spells out the properties of these operations and their interrelationships. By doing so, we have shown how prior and unconnected results in FOSD can be unified. Further, our algebra suggested a more general way to support coloring, so that documents of a product line that were synthesized could be modified, and that these modifications could subsequently be back-propagated to their original feature-based product line representations. We presented a tool, Paan, that (a) implemented our algebra, (b) demonstrated the feasibility of back-propagation as we described it, and (c) worked with MS Word documents, all of which we believe are novel.

Our work advances the state of the art in understanding the integration of feature composition and feature interactions, and improved tooling for FOSD.

Acknowledgments. We thank J. Atlee, K. Czarnecki, and C. Kästner for their comments on an earlier version of this work. We are grateful to the GPCE referees for their helpful comments. Batory and Kim are supported by the NSF's Science of Design Project CCF 0724979. Höfner was partially supported by the DFG grant #MO 690/7.

References

[1] A. Aho, M. S. Lam, R. Sethi, and J. D. Ullman. *Compilers: Principles, Techniques, and Tools Second Edition.* pearson Education, 2006.

[2] S. Apel and C. Kästner. An overview of feature-oriented software development. *Journal of Object Technology*, July-August 2009.

[3] S. Apel, C. Kästner, and D. Batory. Aspectual feature modules. *ACM TSE*, 2008.

[4] S. Apel, C. Kästner, and C. Lengauer. Featurehouse: Language-independent, automated software composition. In *ICSE*, 2009.

[5] S. Apel, C. Lengauer, B. Möller, and C. Kästner. An algebraic foundation for automatic feature-based program synthesis. *Science of Computer Programming*, pages 1022–1047, 2010.

[6] S. Apel, W. Scholz, C. Lengauer, and C. Kästner. Detecting dependences and interactions in feature-oriented design. In *ISSRE*, 2010.

---

[1] The essential idea is this: Let F|G denote the changes made by F to G. Symmetrically, G|F denotes the changes made by G to F. Our interaction module F#G equals the dot composition of these two derivatives (F#G = F|G · G|F). And in general, an n-th order interaction $A_1 \# \ldots \# A_n$ corresponds to a dot composition of all n! permutations of these features as derivatives ($A_1 | \ldots | A_n \cdot A_n | \ldots | A_1 \cdot \ldots$). In short, derivatives are the building blocks of colors.

[7] P. Bassett. Frame-based software engineering. *IEEE Software*, 4(4), 1987.

[8] D. Batory. Feature Models, Grammars, and Propositional Formulas. In *SPLC*, Sept. 2005.

[9] D. Batory, J. Sarvela, and A. Rauschmayer. Scaling Step-Wise Refinement. *IEEE TSE*, June 2004.

[10] M. Calder, M. Kolberg, E. H. Magill, and S. Reiff-Marganiec. Feature interaction: A critical review and considered forecast. In *Computer Networks*, 2002.

[11] D. Clarke, M. Helvensteijn, and I. Schaefer. Abstract delta modeling. In *GPCE*, 2010.

[12] K. Czarnecki and M. Antkiewicz. Mapping features to models: A template approach based on superimposed variants. In *GPCE*, 2005.

[13] B. Delaware, W. Cook, and D. Batory. Theorem proving for product lines. In *OOPSLA/SPLASH*, 2011.

[14] Z. Diskin. Algebraic models for bidirectional model synchronization. In *MoDELS*, 2008.

[15] J. N. Foster, M. Greenwald, J. T. Moore, B. C. Pierce, and A. Schmitt. Combinators for bi-directional tree transformations: a linguistic approach to the view update problem. In *POPL*, 2005.

[16] C. Ghezzi, M. Jazayeri, and D. Mandrioli. *Fundamentals of Software Engineering*. Prentice Hall, 2002.

[17] E. International. Office open XML file formats, 2nd Edition. `http://www.ecma-international.org/publications/standards/Ecma-376.htm`, 2008.

[18] M. Jackson and P. Zave. Distributed feature composition: A virtual architecture for telecommunications services. *IEEE TSE*, Oct 1998.

[19] K. Kang. Private Correspondence, Oct. 2003.

[20] K. Kang, S. Cohen, J. Hess, W. Novak, and A. Peterson. Feature-oriented domain analysis (foda) feasibility study. CMU/SEI-90-TR-021, 1990.

[21] C. Kästner. *Virtual Separation of Concerns: Toward Preprocessors 2.0*. PhD thesis, University of Magdeburg, 2010.

[22] C. Kästner, S. Apel, and M. Kuhlemann. Granularity in software product lines. In *ICSE*, 2008.

[23] C. Kästner and et al. On the impact of the optional feature problem: Analysis and case studies. In *SPLC*, 2009.

[24] C. H. P. Kim, C. Kästner, and D. Batory. On the modularity of feature interactions. In *GPCE*, 2008.

[25] J. Kim. Paan: A Tool for Back-Propagating Changes to Projected Documents. M.Sc. Thesis, The University of Texas at Austin, 2011.

[26] J. Liu, D. Batory, and C. Lengauer. Feature Oriented Refactoring of Legacy Applications. In *ICSE*, 2006.

[27] J. Liu, D. Batory, and S. Nedunuri. Modeling interactions in feature oriented designs. In *Int. Conf. on Feature Interactions*, 2005.

[28] R. Lopez-Herrejon, D. Batory, and C. Lengauer. A Disciplined Approach to Aspect Composition. In *PEPM*, 2006.

[29] W. McCune. Prover9 and Mace4. `http://www.cs.unm.edu/~mccune/prover9/`, 2010.

[30] C. Prehofer. Feature Oriented Programming: A Fresh Look at Objects. In *ECOOP*, 1997.

[31] Automatic generation of word document variants. `http://www.pure-systems.com/flash/pv-wordintegration/flash.html`, 2010.

[32] R. Rabiser and et al. A Flexible Approach for Generating Product-Specific Documents in Product Lines. In *SPLC*, 2010.

[33] D. Roundy. Darcs: Distributed version management in haskell. In *Workshop on Haskell*, 2005.

[34] I. Schaefer, L. Bettini, F. Damiani, and N. Tanzarella. Delta-oriented programming of software product lines. In *SPLC*, 2010.

A. Deferred Proofs and Properties

This appendix gives more details about properties of our algebra. Specifically, we list proofs that were skipped.

LEMMA A.1. *The identity tile* 1 *is a left unit:*

$$1 \cdot R = R$$

PROOF. The claim follows immediately from (right) identity (2), involution (15), associativity (4) and involution again:

$$R = R \cdot 1 = R \cdot (R \cdot R) = (R \cdot R) \cdot R = 1 \cdot R \qquad \square$$

LEMMA A.2. *Dot-composition is commutative:*

$$R \cdot S = S \cdot R$$

PROOF. By involution (15), we get:

$$(S \cdot R) \cdot (S \cdot R) = 1$$

From this we can show the claim:

$$R \cdot S \overset{(2)}{=} (R \cdot S) \cdot 1 \overset{(15)}{=} (R \cdot S) \cdot (S \cdot R) \cdot (S \cdot R)$$
$$\overset{(4)}{=} (R \cdot (S \cdot S) \cdot R) \cdot (S \cdot R) \overset{(15)}{=} (R \cdot 1 \cdot R) \cdot (S \cdot R)$$
$$\overset{(2)}{=} (R \cdot R) \cdot (S \cdot R) \overset{(15)}{=} 1 \cdot (S \cdot R) \overset{(A.1)}{=} S \cdot R \qquad \square$$

LEMMA A.3. *The identity tile* 1 *does not interact with any tile, i.e.,* $R\#1 = 1$.

PROOF. The claim follows from involution (15), distributivity (8) and involution again:

$$R\#1 = R\#(S \cdot S) = R\#S \cdot R\#S = 1 \qquad \square$$

LEMMA A.4. *Product composition satisfies the following laws:*

(a) $R \times 1 = R$

(b) $R \times S = S \times R$

(c) $(R \times S) \times T = R \times (S \times T)$

(d) $R \times R = 1$

PROOF.

(a) Neutrality of 1 follows from the definition of product (10), Lemma A.3, and identity (2) and Lemma A.1:

$$R \times 1 = R\#1 \cdot R \cdot 1 = 1 \cdot R \cdot 1 = R$$

The remaining claims (Parts (b)–(d)) follow from the corresponding properties of dot- and interaction-composition. we only give references to the corresponding axioms and theorems.

(b) $R \times S \overset{(10)}{=} R\#S \cdot R \cdot S \overset{(3)}{=} S\#R \cdot S \cdot R \overset{(6)}{=} S \times R$

(c)
$$(R \times S) \times T \overset{(10)}{=} (R\#S \cdot R \cdot S) \times T$$
$$\overset{(10)}{=} (R\#S \cdot R \cdot S)\#T \cdot (R\#S \cdot R \cdot S) \cdot T$$
$$\overset{(9),(4)}{=} R\#S\#T \cdot R\#T \cdot S\#T \cdot R\#S \cdot R \cdot S \cdot T$$
$$\overset{(3)}{=} R\#S\#T \cdot R\#S \cdot R\#T \cdot R \cdot S\#T \cdot S \cdot T$$
$$\overset{(9),(4)}{=} R\#(S\#T \cdot S \cdot T) \cdot R \cdot (S\#T \cdot S \cdot T)$$
$$\overset{(10)}{=} R \times (S\#T \cdot S \cdot T)$$
$$\overset{(10)}{=} R \times (S \times T)$$

(d) $R \times R \overset{(10)}{=} R\#R \cdot R \cdot R \overset{(14)}{=} 1 \cdot R \cdot R \overset{(15)}{=} 1 \cdot 1 \overset{(2)}{=} 1 \qquad \square$

B. Prover9 and Mace4

Below we list an input template for the paramodulation-based theorem prover Prover9 [29]. It encodes the axioms of the presented algebra in an intuitive way, i.e., it accepts operators in infix, prefix and postfix notation; hence it is easy to use. Moreover, a quantification of the variables involved is often not necessary.

The same input file is accepted by the model generation tool Mace4—which complements Prover9. It can be used to detect non-theorems. All theorems of this paper can be proved fully automatically, Prover9 needs less than a second to prove each of them.

```
% LANGUAGE SPECIFICATION
  op(500, infix, ";").     % dot-composition (·)
  op(490, infix, "+").     % interaction-composition (#)
  op(500, infix, "X").     % product-composition (×)

% AXIOMS
  formulas(sos).
    % dot-composition
      x;1=x.
      x;(y;z) = (x;y);z.
      x;x =1.
    % interaction-composition
      x+y = y+x.
      x+(y+z) = (x+y)+z.
      x+x = 1.
      x+(y;z) = (x+y);(x+z).
    % product-composition
      x X y=(x+y);(x;y).
  end_of_list.

% CONJECTURE
  formulas(goals).
    % lemma to be proved, e.g.,
    x X y = y X x.
  end_of_list.
```

C. Irredundancy Example

We illustrate irredundancy by an example. Assume that we want to show that identity (2) does not follow from the other axioms. For that we feed Mace4 with axioms (4), (15), (6), (7), (14), (8), (10) and set (2) as goal. The tool immediately returns a model that satisfies these axioms, but violates (2) (where R below denotes an arbitrary tile):

#	R	1
R	1	1
1	1	1

·	R	1
R	1	1
1	1	1

×	R	1
R	1	1
1	1	1

This model shows that $R \cdot 1 = 1$ and hence identity (2) does not hold and cannot be inferred from the other axioms.

On the Impact of Feature Dependencies when Maintaining Preprocessor-based Software Product Lines

Márcio Ribeiro

Informatics Center
Federal University of Pernambuco
50740-540, Recife – PE – Brazil
mmr3@cin.ufpe.br

Felipe Queiroz

Informatics Center
Federal University of Pernambuco
50740-540, Recife – PE – Brazil
fbq@cin.ufpe.br

Paulo Borba

Informatics Center
Federal University of Pernambuco
50740-540, Recife – PE – Brazil
phmb@cin.ufpe.br

Társis Tolêdo

Informatics Center
Federal University of Pernambuco
50740-540, Recife – PE – Brazil
twt@cin.ufpe.br

Claus Brabrand

IT University of Copenhagen (ITU)
DK-2300, Copenhagen – Denmark
brabrand@itu.dk

Sérgio Soares

Informatics Center
Federal University of Pernambuco
50740-540, Recife – PE – Brazil
scbs@cin.ufpe.br

Abstract

During Software Product Line (SPL) maintenance tasks, Virtual Separation of Concerns (VSoC) allows the programmer to focus on one feature and hide the others. However, since features depend on each other through variables and control-flow, feature modularization is compromised since the maintenance of one feature may break another. In this context, *emergent interfaces* can capture dependencies between the feature we are maintaining and the others, making developers aware of dependencies. To better understand the impact of code level feature dependencies during SPL maintenance, we have investigated the following two questions: *how often methods with preprocessor directives contain feature dependencies? How feature dependencies impact maintenance effort when using VSoC and emergent interfaces?* Answering the former is important for assessing how often we may face feature dependency problems. Answering the latter is important to better understand to what extent emergent interfaces complement VSoC during maintenance tasks. To answer them, we analyze 43 SPLs of different domains, size, and languages. The data we collect from them complement previous work on preprocessor usage. They reveal that the feature dependencies we consider in this paper are reasonably common in practice; and that emergent interfaces can reduce maintenance effort during the SPL maintenance tasks we regard here.

Categories and Subject Descriptors D.2.8 [*Software Engineering*]: Metrics—Complexity measures ; D.3.3 [*Programming Languages*]: Language Constructs and Features—Patterns

General Terms Measurement, Design, Experimentation

Keywords Preprocessors, Software Product Lines, Modularity

GPCE'11, October 22–23, 2011, Portland, Oregon, USA.
Copyright © 2011 ACM 978-1-4503-0689-8/11/10... $10.00

1. Introduction

A Software Product Line (SPL) is a family of software systems developed from reusable assets. These systems share a common set of features that satisfy the needs of a particular market segment [3]. By reusing assets, it is possible to construct products through features defined according to customers' requirements [16]. In this context, features are the semantic units by which we can differentiate programs in a SPL [19].

To implement features, developers often use preprocessors [2, 7, 11] and associate conditional compilation directives like #ifdef and #endif to encompass feature code. Despite their widespread use, preprocessors have several drawbacks, including no support for separation of concerns [18]. To overcome this, researchers have proposed Virtual Separation of Concerns (VSoC) [7] as a way of allowing developers to hide feature code not relevant to the current task, reducing some of the preprocessor drawbacks. The main idea is to provide developers with a way of focusing on one feature implementation without being distracted by others [6]. However, VSoC is not enough to provide feature modularization, which aims at achieving comprehensibility and changeability [15].

In particular, these modularity problems arise because of shared elements among features such as variables and methods. In general this leads to subtle dependencies like when a feature assigns a value to a variable which is subsequently used by another feature. These code level feature dependencies might cause behavioral problems during SPL maintenance since the programmer may not be aware of them, as illustrated by two scenarios we cover in this paper: (i) maintenance of one feature only works for some products; and (ii) maintenance of one feature makes another not work.

To minimize these problems, we proposed the idea of *emergent interfaces* [17]. The idea is to capture dependencies between the feature a programmer is maintaining and the others. These interfaces emerge and give information about other features we might impact with our current maintenance task. Developers then become aware of the dependencies and, consequently, might avoid the maintainability problems described in the aforementioned scenarios. Notice that developers still have the VSoC benefits. Emergent interfaces complement VSoC in that in addition to hiding feature code, they provide dependency information.

Given the problem caused by code level feature dependencies and two approaches that provide benefits on feature modularity, we focus on the following research questions:

- **Question 1:** how often methods with preprocessor directives contain feature dependencies?
- **Question 2:** how feature dependencies impact maintenance effort when using VSoC and emergent interfaces?

Answering **Question 1** is important to assess to what extent dependencies is a problem in practice. In other words, how important this problem is. Answering **Question 2** is important to better understand to what extent emergent interfaces may complement VSoC during maintenance tasks.

Inspired by recent work [13, 14], we answer **Question 1** by analyzing 43 software product lines taken from different domains, size, and languages (C and Java). In particular, we built a tool — based on [13]— to compute data with respect to preprocessor usage and feature dependencies.

To answer **Question 2**, we use the same 43 product lines to investigate and compare maintenance effort when using VSoC and our emergent interface approach. For example, when the programmer changes the value of a variable, she needs to analyze whether or not the new value impacts other features. Thus, she should check each feature and determine possible dependencies. To perform this evaluation, we randomly select methods and variables from those SPLs. From one particular variable, we estimate the developer effort required to search for dependencies of the variable being maintained.

In Section 2, we present motivating examples to illustrate behavioral problems caused by feature dependencies. Then, in Section 3, we briefly introduce emergent interfaces. After that, we discuss the study settings in Section 4 and present the main contributions of this paper:

- data on preprocessor usage that reveals to what extent feature dependencies occur in practice (complementing previous work [13, 14]); and
- a comparison of VSoC and emergent interfaces in terms of maintenance effort.

The data we collect reveal that the code level feature dependencies we consider in this paper are reasonably common in practice. Regarding the effort evaluation, we observed effort reduction when using emergent interfaces during the SPL maintenance activities we tackle in this paper.

2. Motivating Examples

Virtual Separation of Concerns (VSoC) reduces some of the preprocessor drawbacks by allowing us to hide feature code not relevant to the current maintenance task [7]. Using this approach, developers can maintain a feature without being distracted by other features [6]. However, we show here that VSoC is not enough to provide feature modularization, which aims at achieving comprehensibility and changeability [15].

To illustrate the maintenance problems we mentioned in the introduction, we now discuss two scenarios likely to occur when using VSoC. Although we focus on VSoC, these scenarios can happen with simple preprocessor directives[1] like #ifdef.

Please note that the maintenance tasks we focus on here cause behavioral problems to the product line.

---

[1] In fact, such preprocessors problems are reported in bug tracking systems.

2.1 Scenario 1: Maintenance of one feature only works for some products

The first example comes from the *best lap*[2] product line. *Best lap* is a casual race game where the player tries to achieve the best time in one lap and qualify for the pole position. It is highly variant due to portability constraints: it needs to run on numerous platforms. In fact, the game is deployed on 65 devices [1].

In this game, there is a method responsible for computing the game score, as illustrated in Figure 1. The method contains a small rectangle at the end, representing a hidden feature that the developer is not concerned with and thus not seeing. Notice that there are no #ifdef statements. Instead, the VSoC approach relies on tools that use background colors to represent features, which helps on not polluting the code with preprocessors directives [7].

The hidden feature—in our example named *arena*—is an optional feature responsible for publishing the scores obtained by the player on the network. This way, players around the world are able to compare their results. All gray code in Figure 1 corresponds to such a feature. The method also contains a variable responsible for storing the player's total score (totalScore).

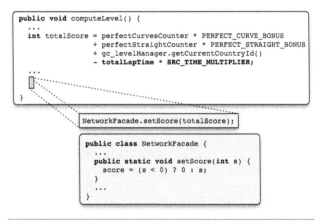

```
public void computeLevel() {
    ...
    int totalScore = perfectCurvesCounter * PERFECT_CURVE_BONUS
                   + perfectStraightCounter * PERFECT_STRAIGHT_BONUS
                   + gc_levelManager.getCurrentCountryId()
                   - totalLapTime * SRC_TIME_MULTIPLIER;
    ...
}

        NetworkFacade.setScore(totalScore);

        public class NetworkFacade {
            ...
            public static void setScore(int s) {
                score = (s < 0) ? 0 : s;
            }
            ...
        }
```

Figure 1. Maintenance only works for some products.

Now, suppose the developer were to implement the following new requirement in the (mandatory) *score* feature: let the game score be not only positive, but also negative. Also, suppose that the developer is using VSoC, so that there are hidden features throughout the code, including *arena*. The developer might well judge that they are not important for the current task. To accomplish the task, she localizes the *maintenance point* (the totalScore assignment) and changes its value (see the bold line in Figure 1). Building a product with the *arena* feature enabled and running it may make the developer incorrectly assume that everything is correct, since the negative total score correctly appears after the race. However, when publishing the score on the network, she notices that the negative score is in fact stored as zero (see the expanded *arena* code). Consequently, the maintenance was only correctly accomplished for products without *arena*.

Because there are hidden features, the developer might be unaware of another feature she is not maintaining uses totalScore and thus also needs to be changed accordingly to correctly complete the maintenance task. In fact, the impact on other features leads to two kinds of problems. The first one is **late error detection** [6], since we can only detect errors when we eventually happen to build and execute a product with the problematic feature combination (here, any product with *arena*). Second, devel-

---

[2] Best lap is a commercial product developed by Meantime Mobile Creations.

opers face **difficult navigation** throughout the code. Searching for uses of `totalScore` might increase developer effort. Depending on the number of hidden features, the developer needs to consider many locations to make sure the modification did not impact other features. However, it is possible that some—or even all—features might not need to be considered if they did not use the variables that were modified. Besides, some features are mutually exclusive in that, for instance, the presence of feature *A* prohibits the presence of feature *B*. In our particular case, if we are maintaining feature *A*, then there is no need for the developer to also consider feature *B*. Nevertheless, because this information might not be explicit in code, the developer is susceptible to consider code unnecessarily, increasing maintenance effort.

2.2 Scenario 2: Maintenance of one feature makes another not work

Our second scenario presents an example based on the *TaRGeT*[3] product line. By using *TaRGeT*, we can automatically generate test cases from use cases. So, we have a form in which users can edit use cases. Here, developers reported a bug at the editing use case screen: the system shows unconditionally an error message due to wrongly fulfillment of use case information (see the left side of Figure 2). In this context, a developer responsible for fixing the problem needs to implement the following new requirement: the system should point out which field of the use case screen the user need to fill in again due to validation errors. The idea is to paint the field (in red, for instance) so as to alert the user so that she can correct it.

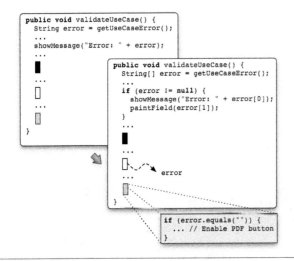

Figure 2. PDF feature does not work anymore.

To fix the bug, an `if` statement is enough. To implement the new requirement, she changed `String` to `String[]`, as illustrated at the right side of Figure 2. This way, she can use the array to store both the error message and the problematic field.

In the same method she is changing, however, there is an optional feature responsible for generating PDF files from the use case, in case no errors were found. From the GUI perspective, this feature consists of a small button at the top of the edit use case screen. The developer is unaware of this feature, so she did not realize that the maintenance introduced a problem in it. Since `error` is now an array, it will never be equal to the empty string, which means that the *PDF* button will never be enabled (see the *PDF*

---

[3] We do not use *TaRGeT* in our evaluation because very few features use preprocessors. The majority of the features are implemented with components and aspects.

feature code expanded in Figure 2). This now means that PDF documents will no longer be generated. Again, we have the **late error detection** problem. Besides, the **difficult navigation** problem occurs since the method contains three features. Navigating throughout them in search of dependencies may be time consuming. Further, developers are likely to analyze unnecessary features. For example, `error` is not used in the *black* feature.

3. Emergent Interfaces

The problems discussed so far occur when features *share* elements such as variables and methods. In this paper, whenever we have such sharing, we say that there is a *feature dependency* between the involved features. For instance, a mandatory feature might declare a variable subsequently used by an optional feature (see `totalScore` and `error` in Figures 1 and 2, respectively). We thus have a mandatory/optional feature dependency. We can also have feature dependencies like optional/optional and optional/mandatory.

Previously, we presented an approach named Emergent Interfaces [17] intended to help developers avoid the problems related to feature dependencies. The idea consists of determining, on demand, and according to a given maintenance task, interfaces for feature implementations. Such interfaces are neither predefined nor have a rigid structure. Instead, they **emerge** to provide information to the developer on feature dependencies, so she can avoid introducing problems to other features. Our idea complements VSoC in the sense that we still have the hiding benefits (which is important for comprehensibility), but at the same time we show the dependencies between features.

To do so, emergent interfaces capture dependencies between the feature we are maintaining and the remaining ones. In other words, when maintaining a feature, interfaces emerge to give information about other features we might impact with our maintenance. To consider features, emergent interfaces rely on feature code already annotated. We can, for example, use Colored IDE (CIDE) [7], a tool that enables feature annotations by using colors and implements the VSoC approach. To capture dependencies, emergent interfaces rely on feature-sensitive data-flow analysis [17]. In particular, we keep data-flow information for each possible product configuration. This means that our analyses take feature combinations into consideration.

To better illustrate how emergent interfaces work, consider **Scenario 1** of Section 2.1, where the developer is supposed to change the `totalScore` value. The first step when using our emergent approach consists of selecting the maintenance point. The developer is responsible for such a selection (see the dashed rectangle in Figure 3) which in this case is the `totalScore` assignment. Then, we perform code analysis based on data-flow analysis to capture the dependencies between the feature we are maintaining and the other ones. Finally, the interface emerges.

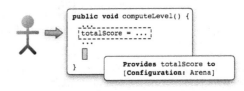

Figure 3. Emergent interface for Scenario 1.

The interface in Figure 3 states that maintenance may impact products containing the *arena* feature. In other words, we *provide* the actual `totalScore` value to the *arena* feature. The developer is now aware of the dependency. Reading the interface is important for **Scenario 1**, since the emerged information alerts the developer that she should also analyze the hidden *arena* feature. When investigating, she is likely to discover that she also needs to modify *arena*, and thus avoid the **late error detection** problem.

Note that the code might have many other hidden features with their own intricate dependencies, making code navigation difficult. In this context, consider **Scenario 2** presented in Section 2.2. In this scenario there are three features. So, we have the **difficult navigation** problem: searching for dependencies is time consuming. Emergent interfaces assist with this problem since they indicate precisely the product configurations the developer needs to analyze. Thus, our interfaces focus on the configurations we indeed might impact, avoiding developers from the task of analyzing unnecessary features, which is important to minimize the **difficult navigation** problem. As Figure 4 depicts, the interface focuses on the *white* and *gray* (*PDF*) features, since they use error. Now, the developer is aware of the error variable usage in both optional features. Again, the developer would probably discover she also needs to modify the *gray* (*PDF*) feature, thereby minimizing the **late error detection** problem.

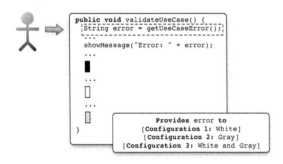

Figure 4. Emergent interface for Scenario 2.

Despite the aforementioned benefits, there is a risk associated with emergent interfaces. Depending on the data-flow analyses precision, some feature dependencies might not be captured. Then, developers who rely on interfaces cannot perceive these additional dependencies, which might lead to bugs after the maintenance task. To minimize such a risk, the tool responsible for computing emergent interfaces should consider data-flow analyses to catch feature dependencies as precisely as possible. However, there is a tradeoff: better precision; lower performance.

4. Study settings

After showing emergent interfaces and how they can deal with feature dependencies, we now present the details on how we performed our study to answer the two research questions we focus on this paper.

The study is based on 43 software product lines from different domains, sizes, and languages (C and Java). They range from simple product lines to complex ones such as linux. The majority is written in C and all of them contain several features implemented using conditional compilation directives.

We present the selected product lines in Table 1 (at the end of the paper). To compute feature dependencies, we built a tool based on a recent work [13]. We use this tool to compute metrics such as the *number of methods with preprocessor directives (MDi)* and the *number of methods with feature dependencies (MDe)*. Using these metrics, we are able to assess how often feature dependencies occur in the product lines investigated in this paper.

In particular, we compute the feature dependencies we illustrate in Figure 5. Each color corresponds to a feature. We represent feature nesting by putting one rectangle inside another. In addition, the alternative examples correspond to an #ifdef (light gray) followed

by an #else (dark gray) preprocessor directive. Each $\boxed{\text{x}}$ represents any use—inside if conditions, general expressions, method actual parameters etc—of the x variable. Although all examples show the variable x being declared and initialized, our tool is capable of detecting dependencies of declared but not initialized variables as well.

Given these feature dependencies we have in all of these product lines, we evaluate *how* they impact on maintenance effort when using VSoC and emergent interfaces. Our aim consists of understanding to what extent the latter may help complement the former.

Figure 6 shows how we perform our evaluation. The code presented in this figure is based on the *xterm* product line and we are using VSoC to hide features. In this particular case, we have four hidden code fragments[4], which consist of three features (*black*, *gray*, and *white*). The developer is supposed to maintain the screen variable (changing TScreen, changing the parameter xw etc). Notice that there is a fragment outside the screen scope. Thus, when maintaining such a variable, the developer does not need to analyze that fragment.

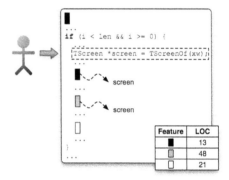

Figure 6. Maintaining the screen variable.

In this context, when using VSoC, the developer does not know anything about the hidden features. Hence, she might need to analyze each hidden fragment to be sure that the maintenance she performed does not impact them. For this particular example, she would analyze three fragments and three features that together correspond to 82 (13+48+21) source lines of code. On the other hand, emergent interfaces do not hide everything. They still use VSoC but at the same time provide information about dependencies among features, which might be valuable to decrease maintenance effort. For this example, the interface would point out that only two features (*black* and *gray*) use the screen variable. This information is important since the developer would then analyze only two fragments (instead of three) and two features (instead of three). This means that 21 source lines of code (*white* feature) can be discarded from this analysis. This way, our study covers the following three metrics: *source lines of code (SLoC)*, *number of fragments (NoFa)*, and *number of features (NoFe)*. We detail the results of our toy example in Table 2.

Approach	SLoC	NoFa	NoFe
VSoC	82	3	3
Emergent Interfaces	61	2	2

Table 2. VSoC *versus* Emergent Interfaces.

In this paper, we estimate maintenance effort by means of the number of source lines of code, fragments, and features we should

---
[4] We denote by *fragment*, any preprocessor directive such as #ifdef, #else, #elif, and so forth.

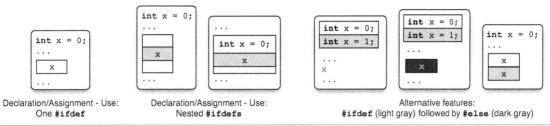

Declaration/Assignment - Use:
One `#ifdef`

Declaration/Assignment - Use:
Nested `#ifdefs`

Alternative features:
`#ifdef` (light gray) followed by `#else` (dark gray)

Figure 5. Feature dependencies we consider in our study.

analyze during a maintenance task. Therefore, the higher these metrics, the greater the maintenance effort. So, we use *SLoC*, *NoFa*, and *NoFe* to compare maintenance effort when using VSoC and emergent interfaces. Notice that the same effort can be observed regardless of the approach we choose. This happens when emergent interfaces point out feature dependencies in all fragments we indeed have to analyze. Emergent interfaces either reduce the maintenance effort or it remains the same as using VSoC. They decrease the effort when at least one fragment does not have dependencies with the feature we are maintaining.

To perform the effort study we propose, we randomly select methods with feature dependencies and then compute the aforementioned metrics for each approach. We select the methods from the 43 product lines presented in Table 1.

To have a representative study, we now need to tackle the problem of *which* methods we should select to perform the evaluation. On the one hand, we believe that if we select only methods with many fragments, we are favoring emergent interfaces, since the probability of finding at least one fragment with no feature dependency increases. On the other hand, if we select only methods with few fragments (one for instance), we cannot show differences between both approaches since the effort would often be the same. In this way, we need to select the methods carefully. To guarantee the selection of methods with both characteristics, we firstly divide them in two groups:

- **Group 1:** methods with 1 or 2 fragments; and
- **Group 2:** methods with more than 2 fragments.

We chose 2 as our threshold (to divide our groups) because the differences between both approaches appear from this value. In methods with feature dependencies, both approaches always have the same effort when we have only one fragment (same *SLoC*, $NoFa = 1$, and $NoFe = 1$).

Now that we have the groups defined, we randomly select methods accordingly. Firstly, we decided to pick three methods per product line. Since methods of **Group 1** are more common, we would have two methods of **Group 1** and only one of **Group 2**. However, depending on the product line, the quantity of methods of both groups varies significantly. For example, when considering the *libxml2*, we have 953 methods in **Group 1** and 125 methods in **Group 2**. So, we rather select the methods proportionally according to each product line (instead of three methods for all product lines). In this way, for *libxml2*, we select eight method of **Group 1** and one of **Group 2**.

So, the basic idea consists of selecting methods with feature dependencies to fit both groups proportionally according to each product line. Because a method may have more than one variable with dependency, we also randomly select one variable per method. Then, we start our effort evaluation from that variable taking its scope into consideration. Please, note we simulate a developer supposed to change a single variable. She can, for example, remove the variable declaration; change its value; change its type etc. From

this variable, we manually compute the metrics *SLoC*, *NoFa*, and *NoFe* to estimate the maintenance effort.

Last but not least, we also consider three replications. The idea consists of repeating the whole evaluation three times so that we can take the average of three independent observations.

We summarize how we perform our evaluation as an algorithm (see Algorithm 1).

Algorithm 1 General algorithm of our effort estimation.

---

  while we do not reach 3 replications **do**
    for each product line **do**
      - Randomly select methods with feature dependencies proportionally to fit the groups;
      for each method **do**
        - Randomly select a variable;
        - From this variable, compute the effort (*SLoC*, *NoFa*, and *NoFe*) of both approaches.
      end for
    end for
  end while

---

5. Results and Discussion

After discussing the study settings, in this section we answer the two research questions (Sections 5.1 and 5.2) based on the results obtained from our empirical study. Last but not least, we present in Section 5.3 the threats to validity.

5.1 Question 1

The first question we address in this paper is: *how often methods with preprocessor directives contain feature dependencies?*

To answer this question, we use the *number of methods with preprocessor directives (MDi)* and the *number of methods with feature dependencies (MDe)*. According to the results presented in Table 1, these metrics vary significantly across the product lines. Some product lines have few directives in their methods. For instance, only 2% of *irssi* methods have directives. On the other hand, this number is much bigger in other ones, like *python* (27.59%) and *mobile-rss* (27.05%). Following the convention "average ± standard deviation", our data reveal that 11.26% ± 7.13% of the methods use preprocessors.

Notice that the *MDe* metric is low in many product lines. However, we compute this metric with respect to all methods. Rather, if we take only methods with directives into consideration, we conclude that, when maintaining features—in other words, when maintaining code with preprocessor directives—the probability of finding dependencies increases a lot. Taking the *gnumeric* product line as an example, only 4.91% of its methods have directives and 2.24% have feature dependencies. Therefore, almost half of methods with directives (45.56%) have feature dependencies (see column *MDe/MDi* in Table 1, which stands for *MDe* divided by

MDi). Our data reveals that $65.92\% \pm 18.54\%$ of the methods with directives have dependencies. Therefore, the feature dependencies we consider in this paper are indeed common in the product lines we analyze.

5.2 Question 2

The second question is the following: *how feature dependencies impact on maintenance effort when using VSoC and emergent interfaces?*

To answer this question, we performed an evaluation with three replications. For each replication, we randomly select 122 methods from all product lines. As mentioned, we select all methods proportionally according to each particular product line to fit the two groups. Table 3 illustrates the number of product lines with their respective methods proportions according to each group. For example, in 13 product lines we select two methods of **Group 1** and one of **Group 2**. Only one product line (*sendmail*) has more methods of **Group 2**. This is consistent with our previous claim that methods of **Group 1** are more common.

Number of SPLs	Group 1	Group 2
23	1	1
13	2	1
3 (gimp, gnumeric, lampiro)	3	1
2 (parrot, linux)	4	1
1 (libxml2)	8	1
1 (sendmail)	1	5

Table 3. Number of SPLs with their respective methods proportions.

As mentioned, to estimate maintenance effort, we consider three metrics: *SLoC*, *NoFa*, and *NoFe*. We illustrate the results for each replication and each metric in Figure 7. Each bar summarizes one particular metric for all 122 methods. The idea is to *summarize* the effort of both approaches and then compare them. As can be seen, emergent interfaces reduced the effort in all replications and metrics. Taking the average of the three replications, when using emergent interfaces, developers would analyze 35% less fragments; 25% less features; and 35% less source lines of code.

We already expected that the effort reduction for features would be smaller when compared to the fragments reduction. Obviously, when developers, based on the interfaces information, discard fragments from their analyses to achieve a particular maintenance task, they also discard lines of code. However, this is not true for features, since we might have two fragments of the same feature, which means that discarding one fragment does not necessarily mean discarding the whole feature from the analysis.

When considering the number of methods, developers have less effort in 33% of methods for replication 1, in 34% for replication 2 and in 39% of methods for replication 3. However, this result is not interesting when analyzed in isolation. But when we cross these numbers with the number of product lines we achieve maintenance effort gains; we can see that these methods are scattered throughout the majority of the product lines we analyze. This indicates that emergent interfaces might indeed reduce maintenance effort in different situations such as product line domains, code sizes, languages, and so forth. Table 4 illustrates, for each replication, the number of product lines where emergent interfaces reduce the effort in at least one method.

Table 4 illustrates the total of methods in which emergent interfaces reduce the effort. Table 5 distributes these methods into the respective groups they belong to. As can be seen, the majority of the methods where emergent interfaces reduce effort are concentrated in **Group 2** (the one where methods have more than 2 fragments).

Rep.	Methods(Less effort)	SPLs(Less effort)
1	40 (33%)	34 (79%)
2	41 (34%)	36 (84%)
3	47 (39%)	36 (84%)

Table 4. Total of Methods and SPLs where emergent interfaces reduced effort.

Methods(Less effort)	Group 1	Group 2
40 (33%)	7	33
41 (34%)	7	34
47 (39%)	14	33

Table 5. Distribution of methods into their groups.

Previously, we mentioned we could favor emergent interfaces in case of selecting only methods with many fragments (in our case, only methods of **Group 2**). We believe this is true because when the number of fragments increases, the probability of finding at least one fragment with no feature dependency increases as well. In this case, the maintenance effort is smaller when compared to VSoC. The results presented in Table 5 suggest that our claim might be true.

Nevertheless, in order to further support this claim, we analyzed the methods of **Group 2** more deeply. Such a group has 47 methods for all replications and they have more than 2 fragments. According to Table 5, emergent interfaces reduce effort in 33, 34, and 33 methods for each replication. So, we achieve maintenance effort reduction in 70%, 72%, and 70% of the methods of this group. By analyzing our data, we can see that, in general, when the number of fragments increases, the percentage of methods in which we achieve maintenance effort reduction also increases (see Figure 8). For example, if we take only methods with more than 4 fragments into consideration, we have effort reduction in 83%, 82% and 84% of those methods.

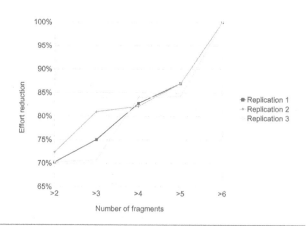

Figure 8. Estimating maintenance effort reduction when increasing the number of fragments.

Emergent interfaces achieve maintenance effort reduction in $35.25\% \pm 3.6\%$ of the randomly selected methods. The reduction happens in $82\% \pm 2.7\%$ of the SPLs we studied. Thus, our results suggest that the interfaces can reduce effort regarding simple SPL maintenance activities we focus on this paper, like when changing a single variable.

Now, we answer the **Question 2** for each approach.

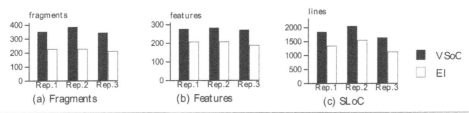

Figure 7. Fragments, features and *SLoC* that developers should analyze in the selected methods when using VSoC and emergent interfaces.

How feature dependencies impact on maintenance effort when using VSoC? Because VSoC does not provide any information about the existence or absence of feature dependencies, developers need to check this in the existing fragments and features. If we have many of them, the effort increases. However, notice that in 64.75% of the methods we analyze, the effort estimation is the same when compared to emergent interfaces. So, the negative impact on maintenance effort when using VSoC is not so common.

How feature dependencies impact on maintenance effort when using emergent interfaces? Based on our study, we can conclude that the more significative gains achieved by emergent interfaces can be observed specially in methods with many fragments. However, only 38% of the methods belongs to **Group 2**, so methods with many fragments occur occasionally. Nevertheless, although we neither evaluated nor focused on methods without dependencies, emergent interfaces also provide benefits in such cases. Figure 9 illustrates a method from *berkeley db*. The developer is supposed to change the value of the `pBt` variable and no feature uses it. Notice that when there is no dependency, the emergent interface is empty, so there is no need to check any fragment or feature. In contrast, VSoC does not provide this information, which may lead developers to analyze unnecessary code (features *black*, *white*, and *gray*).

Figure 9. Variable with no dependency.

5.3 Threats to validity

Metrics and effort estimation. Our study does not take the overhead to compute emergent interfaces into consideration. Also, the metrics we use are not sufficient to measure how much the maintenance effort reduces. Instead, they can estimate it. However, they are able to show differences between emergent interfaces and VSoC. Although not sufficient, the metrics are still useful to understand the benefits provided by emergent interfaces. Actually, we are aware of metrics that better measure effort (e.g., time). However, our effort estimation seems plausible since the time would be proportional to the number of artifacts (fragments, features, source lines of code) that the developer needs to analyze.

Unavailable feature models. We do not have access to the feature model of all SPLs, so the results of our three metrics (*SLoC*, *NoFa*, and *NoFe*) can change due to feature model constraints we are not aware of. Nevertheless, we believe that this fact changes our effort results only slightly, because the majority of methods we

use in our evaluation belongs to **Group 1** (methods with 1 or 2 fragments). Since the number of fragments is small in **Group 1**, it is difficult to find constraints between two features within a method.

Highlighting tools. When using preprocessors without the VSoC support, highlighting tools are helpful to identify variable usage. Hence, it is possible to find dependencies as well. However, besides losing the VSoC benefits (all features would be shown), highlighting tools are purely syntactical so it does not take flow and feature information into consideration. For example, we might select a variable in feature *A* and the tool highlights variable usage in feature *B*. Since they can be mutually exclusive due to a feature model constraint, the tool points out a false positive, which means that the dependency does not exist.

Dependencies. Our tool computes only *simple dependencies*, as showed in Figure 10(a). However, there are more dependencies neglected by our tool, such as *chain of assignments* (Figure 10(b)) and *interprocedural* (Figure 10(c)). In the first, we have a chain because if we change the *aper_size* value, its new value contributes to define the *iommu_size* value which, in turn, defines the value of *iommu_pages*. And we use this variable in another feature. Moreover, our tool does not consider interprocedural dependencies, as illustrated in Figure 10(c). Note we pass a variable as a method parameter and we use it in another feature in the target method. Since both kinds of dependencies are not present in our statistics, we believe that the real number of dependencies we present to answer **Question 1** is even higher. In this context, there is a risk when raising the number of dependencies: if one has to analyze all features and fragments, VSoC and emergent interfaces seem meaningless. In cases where hiding is not possible (there are feature dependencies in all fragments), we still have some benefits: tools that generate emergent interfaces can point exactly where the dependencies are. So, instead of analyzing a fragment with lots of *SLoC*, developers can focus on particular lines of code that indeed contain dependencies.

6. Related Work

In what follows, we present the related work.

6.1 Analyses on preprocessor-based SPLs

There is research on assessing the way developers use preprocessors in SPLs. Recently, researchers [13] created and computed many metrics to analyze the feature code scattering and tangling when using conditional compilation directives. To do so, they analyzed 40 software product lines implemented in C. They formulated research questions and answered them with the aid of a tool. We complement this work by taking feature dependencies into consideration. Also, we provide data in different product lines (the ones written in Java).

Researchers [14] examined the use of preprocessor-based code in systems written in C. Directives like `#ifdefs` are indeed powerful, so that programmers can make all kinds of annotations using them. Hence, developers can introduce subtle errors like annotating a closing bracket but not the opening one. This is an "undisci-

(a) Simple dependency.

```
public void computeLevel() {
  ...
  totalScore = ...
  ...
  #ifdef ARENA
  NetworkFacade.setScore(totalScore);
  #endif
}
```

(b) Chain of Assignments.

```
aper_size = info.aper_size * 1024 * 1024;
iommu_size = check(info.aper_base, aper_size);
iommu_pages = iommu_size >> PAGE_SHIFT;
...
#ifdef CONFIG_IOMMU_LEAK
...
... get_order(iommu_pages * sizeof(void *));
...
#endif
```

(c) Interprocedural.

```
public void play() {
  int soundIndex = ...;
  ...
  loadSounds(soundIndex);
}

private void loadSounds(int soundIndex) {
  #ifdef sound_api_nokia
  sounds[soundIndex] = ...;
  #endif
  ...
}
```

Figure 10. Dependencies from Best Lap, Linux kernel, and Juggling, respectively.

plined" annotation. Disciplined annotations hold properties useful for preprocessor-aware parsing tools so we can represent annotations as nodes in the AST. They found that the majority of the preprocessor usage are disciplined. Specifically, they found that the case studies have 84.4% of their annotations disciplined. We also analyzed several systems, but we focus on dependencies among features implemented with preprocessors.

Another study concerning preprocessor usage in C systems [4] points out that, despite their evident shortcomings, the controlled use of preprocessors can improve portability, performance, or even readability. They found that most systems analyzed make heavy use of preprocessor directives. Like our work, they compute the occurrence of conditional compilation directives as well. We did not find a lot of preprocessor usage. However, we focus only on methods. In contrast, they focus on the entire code (not only methods) and analyze many other kinds of preprocessors (like macros).

We complement these studies providing more data with respect to preprocessors usage. Besides, we estimate maintenance effort when using VSoC and emergent interfaces.

6.2 Safe composition

The scenarios we focus on this paper show behavioral problems that can arise when maintaining features in preprocessor-based SPLs. Among other possible scenarios, maintenance in a feature can also break compilation of another. Existing works detect such type errors; the safe composition problem. Safe composition relates to safe generation and verification of properties for SPL assets: i.e., providing guarantees that the derivation process generates products with properties that are obeyed [8, 9].

Safe composition is proposed for the Color Featherweight Java (CFJ) calculus [5]. This calculus establishes type rules to ensure that CFJ code only generates well-typed programs. TypeChef [9] is another type checker that aims at identifying errors in SPLs implemented with the C preprocessor. By using TypeChef, we do not need to generate all variants of the SPL. It relies on the concept of partial preprocessing where macros and file inclusions are processed while the directives that control the actual variability are not. The remaining code is then parsed. The generated AST contains information about the #ifdefs, in which reference analysis can be performed to then solve whether all variants are well typed or not.

Emergent interfaces can help in the sense of preventing type errors, since the interface would show the dependencies between the feature we are maintaining and the remaining ones. Nonetheless, safe composition approaches are complementary, since if the developer ignores the feature dependency showed by the interfaces and introduces a type error, these approaches catch them after the maintenance task.

6.3 Data-flow analysis for maintenance

Recent work [12] observed developers facing problems of understanding code during maintenance tasks. They found that a significant amount of a developer's work involves answering "reachability questions". This question is a search across the code for statements that match the search criteria. They observed that developers often inserted defects because they did not answer the reachability question successfully. Bringing to our context, we could search for dependencies. If we cannot answer where they are or which features they belong to, we can introduce errors in the SPL. Notice that this is similar to our scenarios and to the **late error detection** and **difficult navigation** problems.

During testing activities, there are features whose presence or absence do not influence some of the test outcomes, which makes many feature combinations unnecessary for a particular test, reducing the effort when testing SPL. This idea of selecting only relevant features for a given test case was proposed in a recent work [10]. The work uses data-flow analysis to recover a list of features we reach from a given test. Since the analysis yields only reachable features, we discard the other ones. Then, we use the reachable features as well as the feature model to discover the combinations we should test, reducing the number of combinations to test. In some sense, the data-flow analysis considers features (the reachable ones). But it is not completely feature-sensitive, since feature model information is not used during the data-flow analysis. In contrast, the data-flow analyses of our emergent approach are feature sensitive. They take feature and feature model information into consideration during the analyses. We detail these ideas elsewhere [17].

7. Concluding Remarks

In this paper, we presented an analysis on the impact of code level feature dependencies during maintenance of preprocessor-based SPLs. Firstly, we presented two scenarios that can introduce behavioral errors in product lines due to such dependencies. Then, we focused on two research questions. To answer them, we built a tool to collect data from 43 product lines of different domains, sizes, and languages. The data correspond to preprocessor usage and to what extent feature dependencies occur in practice. They reveal that $65.92\% \pm 18.54\%$ of the methods with directives have dependencies. So, the feature dependencies we consider in this paper are reasonably common in the product lines we studied.

Besides, we performed an empirical study to assess the impact of these feature dependencies on maintenance effort when using two approaches: VSoC and emergent interfaces. We estimated effort by using three metrics that essentially counts the number of artifacts that the developer can analyze during SPL maintenance tasks. We observed that emergent interfaces achieved effort reduction in $35.25\% \pm 3.6\%$ of the methods we studied. This way, our results suggest that emergent interfaces can reduce effort during the

SPL maintenance tasks we focus on this paper, like when changing a variable. Also, we found that the more significative reductions can be observed specially on the presence of methods with many fragments and features. However, it is important to note that these methods occur occasionally. So, in the majority of the analyzed methods (64.75%), the effort estimation is the same for both approaches. This way, the negative impact on maintenance effort when using VSoC is not so common.

Our data complement previous work on preprocessor usage. In addition, we present an evaluation that is helpful to understand to what extent emergent interfaces complement VSoC in the maintenance effort context.

8. Acknowledgments

We would like to thank CNPq, a Brazilian research funding agency, and National Institute of Science and Technology for Software Engineering (INES), funded by CNPq and FACEPE, grants 573964/2008-4 and APQ-1037-1.03/08, for partially supporting this work. Also, we thank SPG (http://www.cin.ufpe.br/spg) members for feedback and fruitful discussions about this paper.

References

[1] V. Alves. *Implementing Software Product Line Adoption Strategies*. PhD thesis, Federal University of Pernambuco, Recife, Brazil, March 2007.

[2] V. Alves, P. M. Jr., L. Cole, P. Borba, and G. Ramalho. Extracting and Evolving Mobile Games Product Lines. In *Proceedings of the 9th International Software Product Line Conference (SPLC'05)*, volume 3714 of *LNCS*, pages 70–81. Springer-Verlag, September 2005.

[3] P. Clements and L. Northrop. *Software Product Lines: Practices and Patterns*. Addison-Wesley, 2002.

[4] M. D. Ernst, G. J. Badros, and D. Notkin. An empirical analysis of c preprocessor use. *IEEE Transactions on Software Engineering*, 28:1146–1170, December 2002.

[5] C. Kästner and S. Apel. Type-checking software product lines - a formal approach. In *Proceedings of the 23rd International Conference on Automated Software Engineering (ASE'08)*, pages 258–267. IEEE Computer Society, September 2008.

[6] C. Kästner and S. Apel. Virtual separation of concerns - a second chance for preprocessors. *Journal of Object Technology*, 8(6):59–78, 2009.

[7] C. Kästner, S. Apel, and M. Kuhlemann. Granularity in Software Product Lines. In *Proceedings of the 30th International Conference on Software Engineering (ICSE'08)*, pages 311–320, New York, NY, USA, 2008. ACM.

[8] C. Kästner, S. Apel, T. Thüm, and G. Saake. Type checking annotation-based product lines. *ACM Transactions on Software Engineering and Methodology (TOSEM'11)*, 2011.

[9] A. Kenner, C. Kästner, S. Haase, and T. Leich. Typechef: toward type checking #ifdef variability in c. In *Proceedings of the 2nd International Workshop on Feature-Oriented Software Development (FOSD'10)*, pages 25–32, New York, NY, USA, 2010. ACM.

[10] C. H. Kim, D. Batory, and S. Khurshid. Reducing combinatorics in testing product lines. In *Proceeding of the 10th International Conference on Aspect Oriented Software Development (AOSD'11)*, New York, NY, USA, 2011. ACM. To appear.

[11] R. Kolb, D. Muthig, T. Patzke, and K. Yamauchi. A Case Study in Refactoring a Legacy Component for Reuse in a Product Line. In *Proceedings of the 21st International Conference on Software Maintenance (ICSM'05)*, pages 369–378, Washington, DC, USA, 2005. IEEE Computer Society.

[12] T. D. LaToza and B. A. Myers. Developers ask reachability questions. In *Proceedings of the 32nd ACM/IEEE International Conference on Software Engineering (ICSE '10)*, pages 185–194, New York, NY, USA, 2010. ACM.

[13] J. Liebig, S. Apel, C. Lengauer, C. Kästner, and M. Schulze. An analysis of the variability in forty preprocessor-based software product lines. In *Proceedings of the 32nd ACM/IEEE International Conference on Software Engineering (ICSE'10)*, pages 105–114, New York, NY, USA, 2010. ACM.

[14] J. Liebig, C. Kästner, and S. Apel. Analyzing the discipline of preprocessor annotations in 30 million lines of c code. In *Proceeding of the 10th International Conference on Aspect Oriented Software Development (AOSD'11)*, pages 191–202, New York, NY, USA, March 2011. ACM.

[15] D. L. Parnas. On the criteria to be used in decomposing systems into modules. *CACM*, 15(12):1053–1058, 1972.

[16] K. Pohl, G. Bockle, and F. J. van der Linden. *Software Product Line Engineering*. Springer, 2005.

[17] M. Ribeiro, H. Pacheco, L. Teixeira, and P. Borba. Emergent Feature Modularization. In *Onward! 2010, affiliated with ACM SIGPLAN International Conference on Systems, Programming, Languages and Applications: Software for Humanity (SPLASH'10)*, pages 11–18, New York, NY, USA, 2010. ACM.

[18] H. Spencer and G. Collyer. #ifdef considered harmful, or portability experience with C news. In *Proceedings of the Usenix Summer 1992 Technical Conference*, pages 185–198, Berkeley, CA, USA, June 1992. Usenix Association.

[19] S. Trujillo, D. Batory, and O. Diaz. Feature refactoring a multi-representation program into a product line. In *Proceedings of the 5th International Conference on Generative Programming and Component Engineering (GPCE'06)*, pages 191–200, New York, NY, USA, 2006. ACM.

A. Online Appendix

We invite researchers to replicate our study. All results are available at: http://www.cin.ufpe.br/~mmr3/gpce2011. *Best lap* and *juggling* product lines are commercial products. Hence, we cannot distribute their source code.

System	Version	Domain	Language	MDe	MDi	MDe/MDi	NoM
berkeley db	5.1.19	database system	C	7.66%	9.07%	84.46%	10636
cherokee	1.0.8	webserver	C	6.37%	8.91%	71.52%	1773
clamav	0.96.4	antivirus program	C	7%	9.35%	74.92%	3284
dia	0.97.1	diagramming software	C	1.94%	3.04%	63.75%	5262
emacs	23.2	text editor	C	2.45%	5.59%	43.8%	4333
freebsd	8.1.0	operating system	C	6.57%	8.98%	73.2%	130307
gcc	4.5.1	compiler framework	C	4.55%	5.95%	76.4%	50777
ghostscript	9.0	postscript interpreter	C	5.76%	7.25%	79.44%	17648
gimp	2.6.11	graphics editor	C	1.85%	2.87%	64.48%	16992
glibc	2.12.1	programming library	C	5.38%	10.03%	53.67%	7748
gnumeric	1.10.11	spreadsheet application	C	2.24%	4.91%	45.56%	8711
gnuplot	4.4.2	plotting tool	C	10.14%	15.41%	65.83%	1804
httpd (apache)	2.2.17	webserver	C	9.34%	12.19%	76.59%	4379
irssi	0.8.15	IRC client	C	1.44%	2%	71.93%	2843
linux (kernel)	2.6.36	operating system	C	3.68%	4.9%	75.09%	208047
libxml2	2.7.7	XML library	C	22.9%	26.92%	85.07%	5324
lighttpd	1.4.28	webserver	C	11.79%	16.73%	70.5%	831
lynx	2.8.7	web browser	C	15.03%	21.41%	70.18%	2349
minix	3.1.1	operating system	C	2.99%	4.53%	65.96%	3114
mplayer	1.0rc2	media player	C	8.82%	12%	73.51%	11730
openldap	2.4.23	LDAP directory service	C	9.91%	12.82%	77.33%	4026
openvpn	2.1.3	security application	C	14.7%	17.95%	81.91%	1694
parrot	2.9.1	virtual machine	C	1.38%	6.12%	22.52%	1813
php	5.3.3	program interpreter	C	8.89%	11.78%	75.51%	10436
pidgin	2.7.5	instant messenger	C	3.38%	5.26%	64.3%	10965
postgresql	8.4.5	database system	C	4.5%	6.33%	71.14%	13199
privoxy	3.0.16	proxy server	C	17.84%	20.95%	85.15%	482
python	2.7	program interpreter	C	5%	27.59%	18.14%	12590
sendmail	8.14.4	mail transfer agent	C	0.84%	4.52%	18.52%	1195
sqlite	3.7.3	database system	C	9.06%	10.64%	85.19%	3807
subversion	1.6.13	revision control system	C	2.66%	4.03%	65.99%	4894
sylpheed	3.0.3	e-mail client	C	5.15%	7.57%	68%	3634
tcl	8.5.9	program interpreter	C	8.4%	10.65%	78.91%	2761
vim	7.3	text editor	C	5.76%	11.05%	52.14%	6354
xfig	3.2.5b	vector graphics editor	C	2.37%	3.93%	60.24%	2112
xinelib	1.1.19	media library	C	6.91%	9.88%	70.01%	10501
xorgserver	1.7.1	X server	C	7.39%	10.15%	72.76%	11425
xterm	2.6.1	terminal emulator	C	20.46%	24.63%	83.08%	1080
bestlapcc	1.0	mobile game	Java	11.95%	20.7%	57.75%	343
juggling	1.0	mobile game	Java	11.14%	16.71%	66.67%	413
lampiro	10.4.1	mobile instant messenger	Java	0.33%	2.6%	12.5%	1538
mobilemedia	0.9	mobile application	Java	5.8%	7.97%	72.73%	276
mobile-rss	1.11.1	mobile feed application	Java	23.84%	27.05%	88.11%	902

Table 1. MDi: Methods with Directives; **MDe:** Methods with Dependencies; **NoM:** Number of Methods. We do not round the numbers to avoid cases where **MDe** = 0%.

Investigating the Safe Evolution of Software Product Lines

Laís Neves, Leopoldo Teixeira,
Paulo Borba

Informatics Center
Federal University of Pernambuco
50740-540, Recife – PE – Brazil
{lmn3, lmt, phmb}@cin.ufpe.br

Vander Alves

Computer Science Department
University of Brasília
70910-900, Brasília – DF – Brazil
valves@unb.br

Demóstenes Sena, Uirá Kulesza

Computing Department
Federal University of Rio Grande do
Norte
59072-970, Natal – RN – Brazil
demostenes.sena@ifrn.edu.br,
uira@dimap.ufrn.br

Abstract

The adoption of a product line strategy can bring significant productivity and time to market improvements. However, evolving a product line is risky because it might impact many products and their users. So when evolving a product line to introduce new features or to improve its design, it is important to make sure that the behavior of existing products is not affected. In fact, to preserve the behavior of existing products one usually has to analyze different artifacts, like feature models, configuration knowledge and the product line core assets. To better understand this process, in this paper we discover and analyze concrete product line evolution scenarios and, based on the results of this study, we describe a number of safe evolution templates that developers can use when working with product lines. For each template, we show examples of their use in existing product lines. We evaluate the templates by also analyzing the evolution history of two different product lines and demonstrating that they can express the corresponding modifications and then help to avoid the mistakes that we identified during our analysis.

Categories and Subject Descriptors D.2.7 [*Distribution, Maintenance, and Enhancement*]: Restructuring, reverse engineering, and reengineering; D.2.13 [*Reusable Software*]: Domain engineering

General Terms Design, Languages

Keywords Software Product Lines, Refinement, Product Line Safe Evolution

1. Introduction

A software product line (PL) is a set of related software products that are generated from reusable assets. Products are related in the sense that they share common functionality. This kind of reuse targeted at a specific set of products can bring significant productivity and time to market improvements [21, 25]. To obtain these benefits with reduced upfront investment and risks, previous work [2, 7, 18] proposes to minimize the initial product line (domain) analysis and development process by deriving a product line from an existing product. A similar process applies to evolving a product line, when

adding new products or improving the product line design requires extracting variations from previous parts shared by a set of products.

Manually extracting and changing different code parts when evolving a product line requires substantial effort, especially for checking necessary conditions to make sure the extraction is correctly performed. Moreover, this process is tedious and can also introduce defects, modifying the behavior of the products before the extraction process, and compromising the promised benefits on other dimensions of costs and risks.

To better understand this process, in this paper we discover and analyze concrete product line evolution scenarios and, based on the results of this study, we describe a number of safe evolution templates that developers can use when working with product lines. For this, we rely on a product line refinement notion that preserves the product line original products behavior [5]. This notion is important for safely evolving a product line by simply improving its design or even by adding new products while preserving existing ones, assuring safety for product line existing users. We use the definitions and suggestions from our group previous works [4], [5] to identify evolution scenarios and then generalize these scenarios to other situations through the templates.

These templates specify transformations that go beyond program refactoring notions [14, 22] by considering both sets of reusable assets that not necessarily correspond to valid programs, and extra artifacts, such as feature models (FM) [10, 15] and configuration knowledge (CK) [10], which are necessary for automatically generating products from assets. Previous work [1] from our group describes a set of product line refactorings regarding feature models. We extend this work describing now safe evolution templates that also deal with configuration knowledge and product line assets, in addition to feature model.

For each template, we show examples of their use in existing product lines. We evaluate the templates by also analyzing the evolution of two different product lines and demonstrating that they can express the corresponding modifications and then help to avoid the mistakes that we identified during our analysis.

This paper makes the following contributions:

- we discover and analyze product line evolution scenarios by mining part of a product line SVN history (Section 2);

- we identify and describe precisely a number of product line safe evolution templates that abstract, generalize and factorize the analyzed scenarios (Section 4);

- we show evidence that the identified templates can justify all evolution scenarios identified in the SVN history of two product lines and could avoid the mistakes that we found during our analysis. We also show the frequency of use for each template in the analyzed scenarios (Section 5);

Besides these sections, Section 6 lists the works related to our research and Section 7 presents the concluding remarks.

2. Motivating Example

In order to better illustrate the problems that might occur when manually evolving PLs, we present a maintenance scenario based on TaRGeT PL [12]. TaRGeT is a PL of automatic test generation tools and is implemented using Eclipse RCP plug-ins technology. TaRGeT has been developed since 2007 by our research group and its current version has 42 implemented features and counts approximately 32,000 LOC. The history track of 3 major releases and 10 minor releases is available in an SVN repository.

While analyzing TaRGeT's SVN history we have found several evolution steps that were supposed to be safe, such as a design improvement or the addition of new products, but actually introduced errors to the PL. **Scenario A** describes one of these cases, the implementation of the new *Component Keyword* text field in the *Test Case Preferences* window. Figure 1 shows the new field. This field should only appear when the *XLS STD* feature is selected. This feature is related to TaRGeT's output format and, when selected, generates test suites in a format compatible with Microsoft Excel.

With that in mind, Figure 2 describes changes applied to the FM, CK and source code artifacts in order to address this evolution scenario. The CK notion that we use here is represented as a table and maps feature expressions (in the left-hand side column) to asset names (in the right-hand side column). We use propositional formulae having feature names as atoms to represent feature expressions that represent presence conditions [11]. In this case, due to limited space, we only show fragments of CK and FM that are related to the example context. As TaRGeT has many features implemented, due to limited space it is not possible to show everything here. The tick signs indicate what changed.

In summary, to modify the PL, the developers first created the aspect *STDPreferencesAspect*, which is responsible for introducing the *Component Keyword* field. However, when updating the CK, they made a mistake and the aspect was associated to the *Output* feature instead of *XLS STD*. The developers then tested product with the *XLS STD* feature selected and saw that the new field was present in the window as expected. They also tested the products with other output formats but they only verified if the main features were correct. As a consequence, they thought that the products were working as expected and committed the modified code to make the changes effective. They did not notice that the new *Component Keyword* field became visible in all products, thus introducing a bug in the PL.

This example demonstrates that manually evolving a PL is error-prone, because in order to make sure that the behavior of existing products is not affected, one usually has to analyze different artifacts, like FMs, CK and the PL assets (such as classes, configuration files or aspects). In addition, the bugs that might be introduced during manual evolution of PL could be difficult to track because they are present only in certain product configurations and the configuration space normally increases.

Analyzing TaRGeT's evolution history through releases 4.0 to 6.0 (from January 2009 to January 2010), we identified a total of 20 evolution scenarios. We provide more details about how we identified these scenarios in Section 5. We verified that the minimum number of modified classes in these scenarios was 1 and the maximum was 54, and the average number of modified classes was 12.9. We also found that about 10% of these modifications introduced a defect in the PL. This shows that issues like the one just presented might happen often and demand special attention.

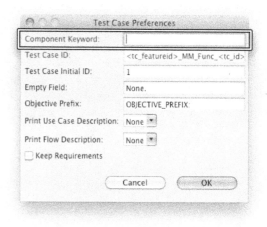

Figure 1. Scenario A - *Test Case Preferences* widow with the new *Component Keyword* field

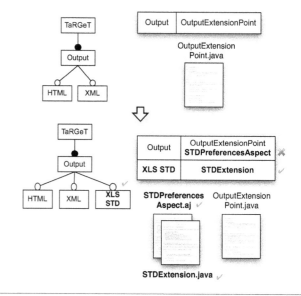

Figure 2. Scenario A - Adding the new optional feature *STD Output*

To better understand the problems that might occur with manual PL evolution, in following sections we explain how we discovered and analyzed concrete PL evolution scenarios and, based on the results of this study, we describe a number of safe evolution templates that developers can use when working with PLs.

3. Product Line Refinement and Safe Evolution

To guide our PL evolution analysis and help us to identify the evolution scenarios, we rely on a PL refinement notion [4, 5]. Such notation is based on a program refinement notion [5], which is useful for comparing assets with respect to behavior preservation. In this section we briefly introduce these necessary concepts to understand the PL safe evolution templates described in the next section.

The formal definition for PLs consists of a FM, a CK, and an asset mapping (AM) that jointly generate products, that is, well-formed asset sets in their target languages. The set of all valid product configurations corresponds to the semantics of a feature model and we represent it as $[\![F]\!]$. We represent the application of the semantics function to a configuration knowledge K, an asset mapping A, and a configuration c as $[\![K]\!]_c^A$. This function maps product configurations and AMs into finite sets of assets (products).

DEFINITION 1. ⟨Product line⟩
For a feature model F, an asset mapping A, and a configuration knowledge K, we say that tuple

$$(F, A, K)$$

is a product line when, for all $c \in [\![F]\!]$,

$$wf([\![K]\!]_c^A)$$

□

The wf represents the well-formedness constraint and is necessary because missing an entry on a CK might lead to asset sets that are missing some parts and thus are not valid products. Similarly, a mistake when writing a CK or AM entry might yield an invalid asset set due to conflicting assets. Here we demand PL elements to be coherent as explained.

Similar to program refinement, PL refinement preserves behavior. However, it goes beyond source code and other kinds of reusable assets, and might transform FM and CK as well. The notion of behavior is lifted from assets to PLs. In a PL refinement, the resulting PL should be able to generate products that behaviorally match the original PL products. So users of an original product cannot observe behavior differences when using the corresponding product of the new PL. This is exactly what guarantees safety when improving the design of a PL.

In most of PL refinement scenarios, however, many changes need to be applied to the code assets, FMs and configuration knowledge, which often [18] leads the refactored PL to generate more products than before. As long as it generates enough products to match the original PL, users have no reason to complain. The PL is extended, but not arbitrarily. It is extended in a safe way. This is illustrated by Figure 3, where we refine the simplified MobileMedia PL (detailed in Section 5) by adding the optional Copy feature. The new PL generates twice as many products as the original one, but what matters is that half of them – the ones that do not have feature Copy – behave exactly as the original products. This ensures that the transformation is safe; we extended the PL without impacting existing users.

We formalize these ideas in terms of asset set refinement. Basically, each program (valid asset set) generated by the original PL must be refined by some program of the new, improved, PL.

DEFINITION 2. ⟨Product line refinement⟩
For product lines (F, A, K) and (F', A', K'), the second refines the first, denoted

$$(F, A, K) \sqsubseteq (F', A', K')$$

whenever

$$\forall c \in [\![F]\!] \cdot \exists c' \in [\![F']\!] \cdot [\![K]\!]_c^A \sqsubseteq [\![K']\!]_{c'}^{A'}$$

□

Remember that, for a configuration c, a configuration knowledge K, and an asset mapping A related to a given product line, $[\![K]\!]_c^A$ is a well-formed set of assets. Thus $[\![K]\!]_c^A \sqsubseteq [\![K']\!]_{c'}^{A'}$ refers to asset set refinement. The definition just mentioned relates two PLs, therefore, all products in the target PL should be well-formed. The PL refinement definition is a pre-order, which allows us to

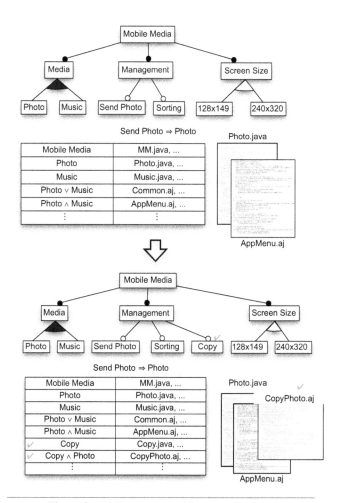

Figure 3. Adding an optional feature refinement

compose different safe evolution templates and also have a valid well-formed PL. The definition is also compositional, in the sense that refining one of FM, AM, or CK that are part of a valid PL yields a refined valid PL. Such a compositionality property is essential to guarantee independent development of these artifacts in a PL.

The $\sqsubseteq$ symbol is a relation that says when the transformation is safe. It does not mean functional equivalence because the PL refinement notion is a pre-order. It can reduce non-determinism, for example.

4. Safe Evolution Templates for PLs

Based on this notion of refinement, in this section, we describe how we discovered and analyzed concrete PL evolution scenarios and, from the results of this study, we present a number of safe evolution templates. The templates provide guidance on how to structure extracted variant parts and help to avoid problems that might occur when evolving PLs manually.

The templates are valid modifications that can be applied to a PL thereby improving its quality and preserving existing products' behavior. The PL transformations listed here involve artifacts like FMs, CK and core assets, which can be source files, aspects, configuration files and others. It is important to mention that the PL refinement notion that we rely on (see Section 3) is independent from the FM and CK [5] languages used. However, as the safe evolution templates describe operations using these artifacts, they are specific to the language used to define them.

To discover the safe evolution templates, we identified and analyzed different evolution scenarios from the TaRGeT PL between releases 4.0 to 5.0. During this time, we identified a total of 11 safe evolution scenarios, which means evolution steps according to the refinement notion that we rely on. After this step, we analyzed the changes performed in code assets, FM and CK. We also considered SVN commit comments and revision history annotations in the source files. Based on these results, we derived a set of safe evolution templates that abstract, generalize and factorize the analyzed scenarios and can be used in different contexts.

Regarding the used notation, each template described here shows the FM, AM and CK status before and after the transformation. FMs contain only the features that are necessary to understand the templates. These are the features that are involved or are affected by the template being described. If we want to say that a feature may contain other features related to it, this can be expressed by a trace above or below the feature.

We represent the CK with a two-column table, in which the left-hand column contains feature expressions, which represent presence conditions **??**, that are mapped to asset names, represented in the right-hand column. This representation is useful to separate asset information from its configuration. The ellipsis indicates other lines different from the one that is explicitly expressed. An asset mapping maps asset names into assets. It is useful to avoid conflicting assets names in the CK. Two curly braces represent the AM, grouping a mapping of asset names, on the left-hand side, to assets, on the right-hand side.

In the case that FM, AM or CK are not changed in the transformation, they are expressed in the template by the single letters F, A and K, respectively. Each template also declares meta-variables that abstractly represent the PL elements, for example an arbitrary feature expression or an arbitrary asset name. The letters F, A and K are also meta-variables. If a variable appears in both sides of a transformation, this means that it remains unchanged. On the bottom we express the pre-conditions to the transformation.

4.1 Template 1 – Split Asset

When analyzing evolution scenarios that changed a mandatory feature to optional, we observe that this type of operation usually involved tracking the code related to the feature and extracting it to other artifacts, like aspects, property files or Eclipse RCP plug-in extensions (in case of TaRGeT).

To generalize these cases, we derived Template 1, illustrated by Figure 4. This template indicates that it is possible to split an asset a into two other assets a' and a'' as long as the set of assets $a'a''$ refines asset a. The first restriction is necessary to guarantee that the behavior of the old asset a is preserved. We used the other restrictions to simplify CK and AM representation. When n appears in other CK lines, it is only necessary to change all occurrences for n, n'.

Another variation of this template is that n' can also represent an existing asset in the PL. We could discuss other variations too, but the focus here is on the basic template. The variations can often be derived from the basic template by composing it with other templates. We can say that Template 1 is a PL refinement because for each product that contained asset a in the source PL, there is now a corresponding refined one in the target PL that contains the composition of assets a' and a''. This specific transformation improves PL quality because it is possible to modularize feature behavior in different assets.

In our study, this template was used, in the scenario that appears in Figure 5, where developers want to extract the *Interruption* feature code that is scattered along three different Java classes (the

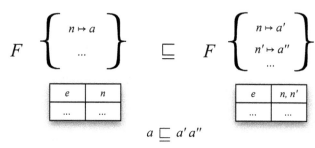

$$a \sqsubseteq a'a''$$

n and n' do not appear in other CK lines
n' is not used in other AM lines

Figure 4. Template 1 - Split asset

ones listed in the CK) to a new Aspect. For this, they applied the *Split Asset* template and its variations several times and extracted the feature code to the new aspect *PMInterruptionAspect*. The FM is not affected by the transformation. The source files in the figure represents the AM.

We decided to present the templates in details because we intend to provide tool support for them in the future. So, this details will be important when defining the tool requirements. We use a declarative approach to describe the templates because we believe this improves presentation and helps developers to better understand the templates. Traditional approaches like the used in Fowler's templates are imperative and difficult presentation.

The PL refinement notion that supports our templates is not limited to any specific kind of asset, which can be class files, aspects, configuration files, among others. That is why we can use them in different contexts from the ones we present in this work. However, some of our templates have restrictions associated to assets refinement, as for example in Template 1. In order to address these restrictions, the developer should choose a proper asset refinement notion that can be more or less restrictive, such as programming transformation laws or tests, according to his reality.

4.1.1 Split Asset – Code Transformations

In order to better explain the code transformations, such as in the example presented on Figure 5, we need transformations that deal specifically with code assets. This is necessary because the general abstract PL templates only establishes the refinement constraint. That is why we specify more precisely code transformations templates that complement the general templates for PL safe evolution. The existing refactorings in the Eclipse IDE are an example of these code transformations to refactor Java code assets.

For Template 1, there are many variation extraction mechanisms described in other works [2, 8] that could be classified as code transformation templates. However, we only mention here the ones that we observed in our analysis of TaRGeT PL. These code templates are helpful because they propose valid transformations that do not deteriorate the PL. So if a developer needs to maintain the PL, with the templates he reduces the possibility of introducing errors, increasing confidence.

In a practical scenario, like the one that appears in Figure 5, the developer first selects a PL template that makes the necessary transformation in the CK and FM, in this case the Split Asset template, and then selects the code transformation templates to actually implement the necessary changes in code assets. In the above mentioned example, we applied templates *Extract Resource to Aspect - after*, *Extract Method to Aspect*, *Extract Context* and *Extract After Block* to extract the feature code to the *PMInterruptionAspect*. These code templates first appeared in a catalog of refactoring tem-

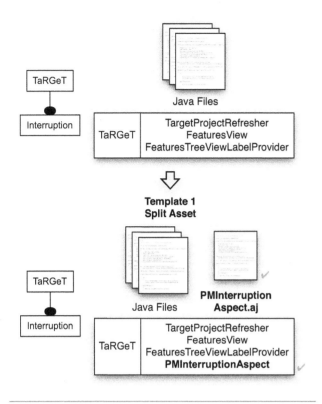

Figure 5. Split asset example

```
public void createFormContent(IManagedForm managedForm) {

    ScrolledForm form = managedForm.getForm();
    form.setText("Test Selection Page");

}
```

⇩

```
public void createFormContent(IManagedForm managedForm) {

    ScrolledForm form = managedForm.getForm();
    form.setText(properties.getProperty("test_selection_page"));

}
```

+

```
invalid_similarity_value = Invalid Similarity Value
test_purpose_creation = Test Purpose Creation
test_selection_page = Test Selection Page
```

Figure 6. Example of text extraction to properties file

plates to extract code from classes to aspects, using AspectJ [2]. The templates from this catalog rely on aspect oriented programming to modularize crosscutting concerns, which often occur in PLs.

Another code template that we identified during our analysis is useful to extract constants in the source code, usually user interface texts, to a properties file. We could define many other code templates to other types of values. This operation is commonly performed when there is the need to localize the user interface to support different languages, like in the example shown in Figure 6, where the form title text *"Test Selection Page"* is moved to a properties file. In this code template the original class is refined by the composition of the new refactored class with a call to the properties file, and the properties file itself.

Figure 7 shows the abstract transformation template. The notation used follows the representation of programming laws [6]. On the right-hand side, all occurrences of text *s* in *body* are replaced by a call to the property that contains its value. We denote the set of field declarations, method declarations and properties declarations by *fs*, *ms* and *ps*, respectively. We use *T* to represent the return type of method *m*. In class *C* constructor we place a call to a new method responsible to load the properties file. On the bottom we list the transformation restrictions.

In our study, we also identified code transformation scenarios that involved variation extraction to extension points. To capture that, we have a code template that represents this operation. This template uses Eclipse plug-ins extension point pattern and defines that it is possible to extract code within a class, create an extension point and replace the code in the class by a call to existing extensions that implement that new extension point. A new extension is then created with the extracted code. Due to limited space, we do not show the transformation details. As TaRGeT is an Eclipse RCP application, we observed that many variations are implemented

provided
- there is no atribute *p* in *fs*;
- there is no method *loadProperties* in *ms*
- there is no property *property_name* in *props*

Figure 7. Abstract template for text extraction to properties file

with the extension point mechanism and can be justified by this template.

4.2 Template 2 – Refine Asset

Another template that we propose based on the observations of our study is shown in Figure 8. This template defines that it is possible to modify an asset *a*, transforming it into asset *a'*, as long as the new asset *a'* refines the original asset *a*. The first restriction is related to asset set refinement. We assure PL refinement because the behavior of each product that contained asset *a* is preserved by a corresponding refined product that contains asset *a'*.

Template 2 also relies on code transformation templates. For example, we could use Template 2 combined with existing refactorings for object-oriented, aspect-oriented, and conditional compilation programs, for example Eclipse refactorings. In practice, we know that some of these code transformations might change other

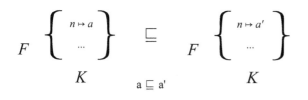

Figure 8. Template 2 - Refine asset

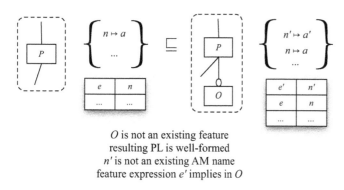

O is not an existing feature
resulting PL is well-formed
n' is not an existing AM name
feature expression *e'* implies in *O*

Figure 9. Template 3 - Add new optional feature

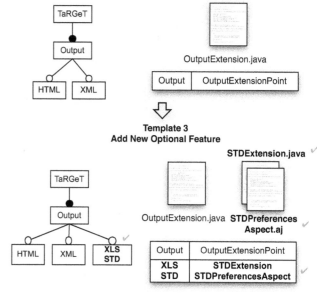

Figure 10. Add new optional feature example

code assets. For instance, if a class that is used by other classes is renamed (class-renaming refactoring), these classes need to be modified as well. We can have variations of Template 2 to deal with these cases that involve more than one asset.

4.3 Template 3 – Add New Optional Feature

Template 3 emerged when analyzing evolution scenarios like the one described in our motivating example, when a developer needs to introduce an optional feature to the PL. This template, presented in Figure 9, states that it is possible to introduce a new optional feature *O* and add a new asset *a* associated to a feature expression *e'* in the CK only if the restriction that says that selecting *e'* implies selecting *O* is respected. The restriction assures that the new assets are only present in products that have feature *O* selected and that products built without the new feature correspond exactly to the original PL products. The template also states that we can not have another feature named *O* in the FM nor another asset name *n'* in the AM, and that the resulting PL is well-formed. We assure refinement because the resulting PL has the same products that it had before in addition to products that contain feature *O*, and we improve the resulting PL quality by increasing its configurability.

In practice, the template implementation should be flexible enough to allow the association of more than one asset to the new optional feature in the CK. Figure 10 shows the application of Template 3 in the scenario that we describe in our motivating example. The new assets *STDExtension* and *STDPreferencesAspect* are correctly associated to the new *XLS STD* feature in the CK.

4.4 Template 4 – Add New Mandatory Feature

Template 4, represented in Figure 11, indicates that we can insert a new mandatory feature, represented by *M*, on a FM as long as we preserve the CK, represented by *K*, and the AM, represented by *A*. The template restricts that we can not have another feature named *M* in the FM. This transformation is a refinement because the AM and the CK do not change, so products before and after the transformation are still the same. It increases quality because it improves FM readability.

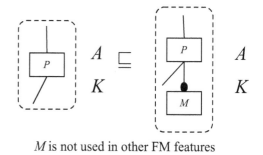

M is not used in other FM features

Figure 11. Template 4 - Add new mandatory feature

If we had added new assets and associated them with feature *M* in the CK, it would not be possible only with this template to ensure that these artifacts would not alter the behavior of existing products. Consequently, we could not assure that the transformation was a safe evolution step. It is possible to generalize even more the template considering that we can add any kind of feature to the FM (mandatory, optional, alternative, or) if we preserve code assets and CK.

Figure 12 illustrates the template utilization. In this example, developers inserted a new mandatory feature *Word* under the *Input* feature. This feature identifies the possible formats of use case documents that TaRGeT accepts as input. The *Word* feature represents the Microsoft Word format. This transformation is useful to improve FM readability and also to restructure the PL to receive new features, as demonstrated in Figures 12 and 14. Similarly to this operation, it is possible to add any kind of feature (optional, alternative, or) in the FM, as long as the CK and FM do not change.

We observed in our study that Template 4 is usually used together with other templates following it. We decided to divide this transformation into two steps to facilitate the automation and reuse of the templates, since it is possible to combine templates to derive

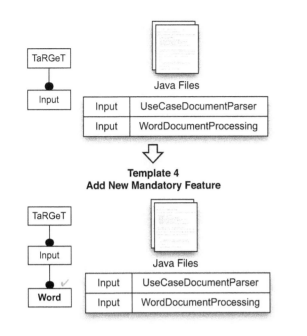

Figure 12. Add new mandatory feature example

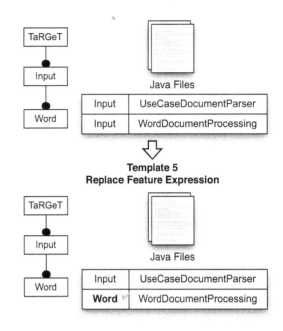

Figure 14. Template 5 - Replace feature expression example

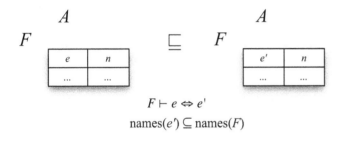

$$F \vdash e \Leftrightarrow e'$$

$$\text{names}(e') \subseteq \text{names}(F)$$

Figure 13. Template 5 - Replace feature expression

more complex transformations, due to the transitivity of the PL refinement notion.

4.5 Template 5 – Replace Feature Expression

Template 5 in Figure 13 expresses that it is possible to change the feature expression associated to an asset n in the CK from e to e', when these expressions are equivalent according to the FM. The restrictions specify that all product configurations from a feature model F lead to equivalent evaluation for the feature expressions in both e and e'. They also specify that the feature expression e' only references names from F. This template improves PL quality by enhancing CK readability.

We found many occurrences of this template combined with Template 4. Figure 14 illustrates how we can use Template 5 in the example described in Figure 12. In this example, the template changed the feature expression related to the *WordDocumentProcessing* asset from *Input* to *Word*. This is possible because as *Word* is a child of *Input*. Thus, selecting the first means that the second is also selected. This operation is useful because it improves CK readability, as it allows to associate asset names to more coherent feature expressions. It also helps to restructure PL existing features, like *Word* and *Input* in Figure 12 example.

4.6 Discussion

When deriving the templates we assured first that they complied with the refinement notion that we rely on. After deriving the preliminary versions, we realized that in some cases the restrictions associated to the templates were too strong and that they could not be used in other situations different from the ones we analyzed. So we decided to discard unnecessary conditions in order to make the templates more general and consequently more useful.

Besides, we found that we could divide some templates into more steps, which improved understanding and would help an automation process in the future in order to provide better support to developers. So we refactored and evolved these templates and new ones were derived.

We also observed that in some evolution scenarios that we analyzed, it was usually necessary to combine more than one template, for example, templates 4 and 5. This information can be useful when defining a strategy to compose the templates in an automated solution. The transitivity of the PL refinement notion allows the combination of different templates resulting in a well-formed PL.

A limitation of our templates it that they are not able to support preprocessor based annotations, which we can implement in Java using third party tools like Velocity. This is because the CK notation that we use here maps feature expressions to asset names, which are described in the AM. In order to support these annotations, it would be necessary to extend the CK notion, allowing mapping asset transformations into assets. We intend to this as future work.

Table 1 summarizes all templates proposed in this work. Templates 1 to 5 are detailed in this section. Template 3 was first mentioned in a previous work [4]. Template 6 defines transformations that occur in CK and AM when adding a new alternative feature in the FM. Similarly, Template 7 defines the same transformations to include an OR feature in the FM. Finally, Template 8 defines asset removal and contains the program transformation law for class elimination [6] defined as a code transformation template. We derived this template when analyzing another PL, which we describe

Table 1. Safe Evolution Templates for Product Lines

Template	Name
1	Split Asset
2	Refine Asset
3	Add New Optional Feature
4	Add New Mandatory Feature
5	Replace Feature Expression
6	Add New Alternative Feature
7	Add New OR Feature
8	Delete Asset

in more details in Section 5. The templates not detailed here can be found in our website.[1]

5. Analyzing Product Line Safe Evolution

This section describes how we investigated the evolution scenarios and presents an analysis on the expressivity of our safe evolution templates. We also show the frequency of use of each template in the evolution scenarios. Finally, we list the main threats to our study in the end of this section.

5.1 Data and Setup

To perform our study, we chose two different PLs. We first studied TaRGeT [12], which we previously mention in Section 2. We also analyzed MobileMedia [13], a PL for media (photo, video and audio) management on mobile devices. MobileMedia has been refactored and evolved to incorporate new features in order to address new scenarios and applications along many releases. It has been implemented in two different versions: (i) an object-oriented Java implementation that uses conditional compilation to implement variabilities; and (ii) an aspect-oriented Java implementation that uses AspectJ aspects to modularize the PL variabilities, which we used in this study. One of the authors was involved in TaRGeT development and one other author worked as a developer in MobileMedia AspectJ implementation.

We divided the analysis of TaRGeT in two different steps. First, we analyzed TaRGeT evolution from release 4.0 to release 5.0 (from January to July 2009) to derive the transformation templates that we presented in Section 4. Then, in the second step, we analyzed TaRGeT evolution between releases 5.0 and 6.0 (from July 2009 to January 2010) in order to verify if the templates that we had previously identified could address the changes performed during this period. As mentioned in Section 2, we identified 11 safe evolution scenarios between releases 4.0 and 5.0 and 9 safe evolution scenarios between releases 5.0 and 6.0. When analyzing Mobile-Media, we evaluated its evolution between releases 4 to 8 and we identified 8 safe evolution scenarios performed in the PL during this period.

For both PLs, we had the code of all releases and the evolution history available in SVN repositories. To identify the evolution scenarios, we first compared the FM and CK of each release to verify which features and assets were added, removed or modified from one release to another. Each of these operations (feature addition, removal or modification) corresponded to an evolution scenario. We then analyzed the scenarios and we discarded the ones that were not safe evolutions according to the PL refinement notion, for example, introduction of a mandatory feature or bug correction. Regarding the scenarios that involved assets modification, we also inspected the assets history in the SVN repository, comparing different versions of each of them to discover how the developers

implemented the changes. For this, we also relied on commit comments and revision history annotations present in source files that described the changes that developers executed.

5.2 Interpretation

In our study, we also examined whether our templates were sufficient to express the modifications implemented in the identified safe evolution scenarios. Table 2 lists the frequency of use for each template in TaRGeT and MobileMedia PLs. For each safe evolution scenario that we analyzed, we listed which templates would be necessary to address the modifications performed by the developers. For example, if the implementation required extracting parts of a class to an aspect, it would be necessary to apply the Split Asset template several times until all code was moved to the aspect. In these cases we only list the template once, even if it is used more than one time in the same scenario. This is because we want to verify if our set of templates was sufficient to express the safe evolution scenarios implementation, no matter how many times they were used.

According to Table 2, we observed that in the TaRGeT PL, Template 6 - Add New Alternative Feature was the most widely used in the analyzed safe evolution scenarios. We believe that this was due to the implementation of different formats for input use case documents (Word, XML, XLS) and output test suites (XML, HTML and XLS). On the other hand, we did not find any occurrence of Template 8 - Delete Asset.

Among MobileMedia safe evolution scenarios, we did not found any occurrence of Template 7 - Add New OR Feature because it does not have any OR feature. Template 1 - Split Asset and Template 2 - Refine Asset were the most used templates. The former was applied with code templates to extract subclass and to extract class member to aspect. The latter was applied in release 5 to introduce a new alternative feature in the PL, which was also relied on Template 6 - Add New Alternative Feature. Finally, Template 8 - Delete Asset was used once when an exception handling class became no longer useful.

Another fact that we have noticed when analyzing both PL history was that some operations usually involved a large number of modified classes. In TaRGeT PL, the average number of modified assets was 12.9 and in MobileMedia PL the average was 11 assets. This might indicate that if we implement the templates together with a development tool, we could also improve productivity. However, evaluate this is not the focus of our work.

In both cases we found that our transformation templates, in addition to the FM refactorings listed in previous work [1] were sufficient to address the modifications performed in the analyzed safe evolution scenarios, which reinforces the expressivity of our safe evolution templates. Besides, during our study, we identified 2 cases that actually introduced new bugs in the PL, in the second step of TaRGeT's analysis. We described one of these errors in Section 2. The other error was similar to this one and involved the incorrect association of a feature expression in the CK for assets related to a new alternative feature. We can avoid this error using Template 6 - Add new alternative feature.

In MobileMedia we found 4 cases that introduced errors in the PL. One of these cases involved extraction of class fields to an aspect that was associated to an incorrect feature expression in the CK. This problem could be avoided by using Template 1 - Split Asset. The other errors are about incorrect association of feature expressions in the CK, that could be avoided using Template 5 - Replace Feature Expression.

We also have proved soundness for all templates listed in Table 1 using the Prototype and Verification System (PVS) [20]. This formal proof is done in accordance with the general PL refinement

Table 2. Templates Frequence

Template	TaRGeT	MobileMedia
Split Asset	4 (13.79%)	6 (25%)
Refine Asset	5 (17.24%)	6 (25%)
Add New Optional Feature	5 (17.24%)	4 (16.66%)
Add New Mandatory Feature	3 (10.34%)	1 (4.16%)
Replace Feature Expression	3 (10.34%)	4 (16.66%)
Add New Alternative Feature	8 (27.58%)	2 (8,33%)
Add New OR Feature	1 (3.44%)	0 (0%)
Delete Asset	0 (0%)	1 (4,16%)

theory (See Section 3). The templates proof details are not in the scope of this work, but they can be retrieved in our website.[2]

It is important to mention that we only guarantee that the templates' application does not introduce errors in the PL if the developer follows exactly the steps described in the transformations, respecting the restrictions. We acknowledge that it would be ideal to have the templates semi-automated together with development tools in order to avoid possible mistakes developers might make when applying the templates manually. However, the templates are an useful guide to help developers to perform safe modifications in the PL.

These two aspects are important because together they address the problem of the likely chance of error in manual PL evolution; we assure that the templates do not introduce new bugs and also that the developer does not need to perform modifications that are not described by the templates.

5.3 Threats to Validity

Since we performed our analysis manually and we only verified the PL changes between the available releases, it is possible that some evolution scenarios have not been taken into consideration. In this case we may have missed evolution steps that could not be justified by our templates or scenarios that would enhance the expressivity of our set of templates. However, we believe that the evolution scenarios that we did not analyze are mostly related to code refactorings and we already have a template to deal with this kind of change, namely Template 2 – Refine Asset. We could missed some code transformation templates by not analyzing these refactorings, but we know that there are a great number of code templates that can be used with Template 2 and it is not our intention to list them all in this work.

Our approach is based on the fact that manually evolving PLs is error-prone. In this study we found evidences of this issue by identifying evolution scenarios that were supposed to preserve the behavior of existing products but in fact introduced errors in the PL. Despite this, it is also possible that we have overlooked errors introduced by the manual changes during PL evolution and that the number of errors is even bigger, which encourages us to continue with our research.

Another threat to our work is the fact that MobileMedia is a small system that was developed for educational purposes. However, we observed that the same categories of evolution scenarios that we identified in TaRGeT PL were present in MobileMedia, which indicates that these scenarios are relevant to our study.

We believe that the fact that we already knew the available templates when we were analyzing the two PLs evolution did not influenced our results, because first we listed the modifications the developers executed and then we tried to match these changes with the available templates. If none of the templates could be applied, we analyzed if it was necessary to modify some of them or to create a new template that could address the changes.

Because of the limited quantity of PLs analyzed, the quantitative results cannot be generalized with confidence. However, the qualitative results are an evidence that our set of safe evolution templates is quite expressive.

6. Related Work

The notion of PL refinement discussed here first appeared in a PL refactoring tutorial [4]. Besides covering PL and population refactoring, that tutorial illustrates different kinds of refactoring transformation templates that can be useful for deriving and evolving PLs. Another work [5] extended this initial formalization making clear the interfaces between the PL refinement theory and languages used to describe PL artifacts. In our work we use the existing definitions for PL refinement and the idea of safe evolution transformation templates, but we go further by proposing other new templates based on the analysis of a real PL and evaluating these templates in two other PLs.

Alves et al. [1] proposed a refactoring notion for PL relating FMs and described a catalog of FM refactorings. Our work is complementary to this one because the PL refinement notion that we rely on, and consequently our templates, supports other PL artifacts like CK and assets, in addition to FM.

Early work [9] on PL refactoring focus on Product Line Architectures (PLAs) described in terms of high-level components and connectors. This work presents metrics for diagnosing structural problems in a PLA, and introduces a set of architectural refactorings that can be used to resolve these problems. Besides being specific to architectural assets, this work does not deal with other PL artifacts such as FMs and CK, as do the safe evolution templates presented in our work. There is also no notion of behavior preservation for PLs.

Several approaches [16, 17, 19, 24] focus on refactoring a product into a PL, not exploring PL evolution in general, as we do here with our templates. First, Kolb et al. [17] discuss a case study in refactoring legacy code components into a PL implementation. They define a systematic process for refactoring products with the aim of obtaining PL assets. There is no discussion about FMs and CK. Similarly, Kastner et al. [16] focus only on transforming code assets, implicitly relying on refinement notions for aspect-oriented programs [8]. As discussed here and elsewhere [4] these are not adequate for justifying PL refinement. Trujillo et al. [24] go beyond code assets, but do not explicitly consider transformations to FM and CK as our templates do. They also do not consider behavior preservation; they indeed use the term "refinement", but in the quite different sense of overriding or adding extra behavior to assets.

Liu et al. [19] also focus on the process of decomposing a legacy application into features, but go further than the previously cited approaches by proposing a refactoring theory that explains how a feature can be automatically associated to a base asset (a code module, for instance) and related derivative assets, which contain feature declarations appropriate for different product configurations. Contrasting with the refinement notion that we rely on, this theory does not consider FM transformations and assumes an implicit notion of CK based on the idea of derivatives. So it does not consider explicit CK transformations as we do here. Their work is, however, complementary to ours since we abstract from specific asset transformation techniques such as the one supported by their theory. By proving that their technique can be mapped to the notion of asset refinement, both theories could be used together.

Thüm et al. [23] present and evaluate an algorithm to classify edits on FMs. They classify the edits in four categories: refactorings, when no new products are added and no existing products are removed; specialization, meaning that some existing products are removed and no new products are added; generalization, when new products are added and no existing products removed and arbitrary

---

[2] http://twiki.cin.ufpe.br/twiki/bin/view/SPG/TheorySPLRefinement

edits otherwise. In our work, we also analyzed edits in other artifacts like CK and code assets, in addition to FM. However, we are only interested in refactorings and generalization edits, not considering specialization and arbitrary edits.

7. Conclusions

In this paper we investigate the safe evolution of product lines and based on the results of this study we present and describe a set of safe evolution templates that can be used by developers in charge of maintaining product lines. The described templates abstract, generalize and factorize the analyzed scenarios and are in accordance with the refinement notion that we rely on. The templates express transformations in feature models and configuration knowledge. We abstract code assets modifications through code transformation templates, which are more precise transformations that deal with changes in code level. Some of our general product line templates might have a set of code transformation templates associated to them.

We also present the preliminary results of a study that we performed to evaluate the evolution of two product lines. We show evidence that the discovered templates can address the modifications performed in the safe evolution scenarios that we identified analyzing the SVN history of these two product lines. We present examples of how using our templates could avoid the mistakes that we found during our analysis and we show the frequency of occurrence of each template among the analyzed scenarios. These results, in addition to the templates formal proofs, intend to address the problem of the likely chance of errors in manual evolution in product lines.

We know that our results are limited by the context of the two product lines that we analyzed and that new templates (both general and specific for code assets) can be necessary to justify other transformations that we did not analyze in this paper. In order to complement these results, we intend to extend our study by analyzing other product lines from different domains.

Our results also show evidence that product line manual evolution can be time consuming, because it usually involves the analysis and modification of a great number of source code artifacts. We believe that the templates automation integrated with a development tool could address this issue. As future work, we intend to implement our templates integrated with FLiP [3], an existing product line refactoring tool developed by our group. We also plan to execute a controlled experiment to evaluate the time, and consequently, productivity gains when using our templates to evolve product lines.

Acknowledgments

We would like to thank CNPq, a Brazilian research funding agency, and National Institute of Science and Technology for Software Engineering (INES), funded by CNPq and FACEPE, grants 573964/2008-4 and APQ-1037-1.03/08, for partially supporting this work. Laís is supported by CNPq, grant 131499/2010-6. We also thank the anonymous reviewers for their detailed comments. In addition, we thank SPG[3] members for feedback and fruitful discussions about this paper.

References

[1] V. Alves, R. Gheyi, T. Massoni, U. Kulesza, P. Borba, and C. J. P. de Lucena. Refactoring product lines. In *GPCE 2006, Portland, Oregon, USA*, pages 201–210. ACM, 2006.

[2] V. Alves, P. Matos, L. Cole, A. Vasconcelos, P. Borba, and G. Ramalho. Extracting and evolving code in product lines with aspect-oriented programming. *Transactions on Aspect-Oriented Software Development*, 4:117–142, 2007.

[3] V. Alves, F. Calheiros, V. Nepomuceno, A. Menezes, S. Soares, and P. Borba. Flip: Managing software product line extraction and reaction with aspects. In *SPLC*, page 354, 2008.

[4] P. Borba. An introduction to software product line refactoring. In *GTTSE'09 Summer School*, Braga, Portugal, 2009.

[5] P. Borba, L. Teixeira, and R. Gheyi. A theory of software product line refinement. In *ICTAC'10*, pages 15–43, Berlin, Heidelberg, 2010. Springer-Verlag.

[6] A. Cavalcanti, P. Borba, A. Sampaio, and M. Cornelio. Algebraic reasoning for object-oriented programming. *Science of Computer Programming*, Jan. 2004.

[7] P. Clements and L. Northrop. *Software Product Lines: Practices and Patterns*. Addison-Wesley, 2001.

[8] L. Cole and P. Borba. Deriving refactorings for AspectJ. In *AOSD'05*, pages 123–134. ACM Press, 2005.

[9] M. Critchlow, K. Dodd, J. Chou, and A. van der Hoek. Refactoring product line architectures. In *1st International Workshop on Refactoring: Achievements, Challenges, and Effects*, pages 23–26, 2003.

[10] K. Czarnecki and U. Eisenecker. *Generative programming: methods, tools, and applications*. Addison-Wesley, 2000.

[11] K. Czarnecki and K. Pietroszek. Verifying feature-based model templates against well-formedness OCL constraints. In *GPCE 2006*, pages 211–220, 2006.

[12] F. Ferreira, L. Neves, M. Silva, and P. Borba. Target: a model based product line testing tool. In *Tools Session of CBSoft 2010*, Salvador, Brazil, 2010.

[13] E. Figueiredo, N. Cacho, C. Sant'Anna, M. Monteiro, U. Kulesza, A. Garcia, S. Soares, F. C. Ferrari, S. S. Khan, F. C. Filho, and F. Dantas. Evolving software product lines with aspects: an empirical study on design stability. In *ICSE*, pages 261–270. ACM, 2008.

[14] M. Fowler. *Refactoring: Improving the Design of Existing Code*. Addison-Wesley, Aug. 1999.

[15] K. Kang, S. Cohen, J. Hess, W. Novak, and A. S. Peterson. Feature-oriented domain analysis (FODA) feasibility study. Technical Report CMU/SEI-90-TR-21, SEI, CMU, 1990.

[16] C. Kastner, S. Apel, and D. Batory. A case study implementing features using AspectJ. In *SPLC*, pages 223–232, 2007.

[17] R. Kolb, D. Muthig, T. Patzke, and K. Yamauchi. A case study in refactoring a legacy component for reuse in a product line. In *21st ICSM*, pages 369–378. IEEE Computer Society, 2005.

[18] C. Krueger. Easing the transition to software mass customization. In *4th International Workshop on Software Product-Family Engineering*, volume 2290 of *LNCS*, pages 282–293. Springer-Verlag, 2002.

[19] J. Liu, D. Batory, and C. Lengauer. Feature oriented refactoring of legacy applications. In *ICSE'06*, pages 112–121. ACM, 2006.

[20] S. Owre, J. Rushby, and N. Shankar. Pvs: A prototype verification system. In *11th International Conference on Automated Deduction*, pages 748–752. Springer-Verlag, 1992. ISBN 3-540-55602-8.

[21] K. Pohl, G. Böckle, and F. van der Linden. *Software Product Line Engineering: Foundations, Principles and Techniques*. Springer, 2005.

[22] D. B. Roberts. *Practical Analysis for Refactoring*. PhD thesis, University of Illinois, 1999.

[23] T. Thüm, D. S. Batory, and C. Kästner. Reasoning about edits to feature models. In *ICSE*, pages 254–264. IEEE, 2009. ISBN 978-1-4244-3452-7.

[24] S. Trujillo, D. Batory, and O. Diaz. Feature refactoring a multi-representation program into a product line. In *GPCE'06*, pages 191–200. ACM, 2006.

[25] F. van der Linden, K. Schmid, and E. Rommes. *Software Product Lines in Action: the Best Industrial Practice in Product Line Engineering*. Springer, 2007.

---

[3] http://www.cin.ufpe.br/spg

Static Analysis of Aspect Interaction
and Composition in Component Models

Abdelhakim Hannousse

Ascola, INRIA, EMN & Aelos, LINA,
Nantes, France
abdel-hakim.hannousse@emn.fr

Rémi Douence

LINA & INRIA, Nantes, France
remi.douence@inria.fr

Gilles Ardourel

Aelos, Université de Nantes, LINA,
Nantes, France
ardourel-g@univ-nantes.fr

Abstract

Component based software engineering and aspect orientation are claimed to be two complementary approaches. While the former ensures the modularity and the reusability of software entities, the latter enables the modularity of crosscutting concerns that cannot be modularized as regular components. Nowadays, several approaches and frameworks are dedicated to integrate aspects into component models. However, when several aspects are woven, aspects may interact with each other which often results in undesirable behavior. The contribution of this paper is twofold. First, we show how aspectized component models can be formally modeled in UPPAAL model checker in order to detect negative interactions (*a.k.a.*, interferences) among aspects. Second, we provide an extendible catalog of composition operators used for aspect composition. We illustrate our general approach with an airport Internet service example.

Categories and Subject Descriptors D.2.11 [*Software Engineering*]: Software Architectures: Languages; D.2.4 [*Software/Program Verification*]: Model Checking

General Terms Languages, Verification

Keywords aspectized component models, Aspect Interaction Analysis, Aspect composition

1. Introduction

Component based software engineering, or CBSE in short [1], enables the modularization of concerns in terms of separate software entities called components. Each component provides a set of services and may require other services from other components. Components can be assembled in order to construct complex component systems. On the other hand, aspect oriented programming, or AOP in short [2], focuses on the modularization of scattered and tangled concerns that cannot be modularized using regular software entities. Crosscutting concerns are not related to a specific paradigm and CBSE is not an exception. Current works on CBSE focus only on the integration of aspects into component models missing the interactions among woven aspects. Aspects woven to the same system may interact with each other which may results in undesirable

behavior, this kind of interaction is also known as *interferences*. Moreover, aspect interferences detection and resolution is still a challenge for AOP. In this paper we contribute by analyzing aspect interactions on component models. In a previous work [3], we introduced a declarative pointcut language VIL for component models. VIL enables the composition of aspects scattered on the architecture by reconfiguring systems. The implementation of aspect composition for Fractal component model [4] is given in [5] with an introduction to aspect interferences. In this paper, we extend our work in [5] by providing an architectural description language (ADL) to describe both structural and behavioral properties of components and aspects (section 3). We show how to formalize component systems using a set of transformation rules from our ADL to networks of automata (section 4). We use UPPAAL model checker [6] to detect potential interferences among aspects in the result formal system (section 5). Finally, we present a catalog of composition operators to solve interferences (section 6). The catalog describes five binary operator templates that can be instantiated for aspect composition. Our proposal is illustrated with a running example: an airport wireless connection.

2. Motivation Example: Airport Internet Access

Our case study is a simplified version of that given in [7] (only flight ticket owner users are considered, users who create personal accounts and pay for their Internet access time are omitted, and some composite components, such as `FlightTicketManager`, are abstracted into primitive components). The example models an airport service for providing a wireless Internet connection for passengers. Free Internet access is granted to passengers owning valid flight tickets. A passenger uses his/her flight ticket number to login and access the network for an associated time to the ticket.

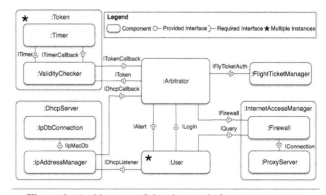

Figure 1. Architecture of the airport wireless access system

The component architecture of this application is depicted in Figure 1. The `User` component represents a passenger in the system. The `User`, first, requests an IP address from the `DhcpServer`, then it asks to login from the `Arbitrator`. Once connected, it sends queries to the `InternetAccessManager`. The `InternetAccessManager` forwards users' requests to the `Firewall` that blocks unauthorized Internet connections. The requests of users with enabled IP addresses are actually sent to the Net `ProxyServer`. The `User` component has multiple instances (one per customer) as noted with "⋆" in the figure. The `DhcpServer` delegates IP requests to the `IpAddressManager` that provides a dynamic allocation service of IP addresses. The allocated IP addresses are managed by the `IpDbConnection` component. The `Token` models a user session. When the `Arbitrator` receives a login request, it retrieves the authorized access time from the `FlightTicketManager`, orders the `InternetAccessManager` to enable communications for the user, and starts a new session by instantiating a `Token` and starting its `Timer` component. When session time elapses, the `Timer` informs the `ValidityChecker` which in turn informs the `Arbitrator`. The `Arbitrator` closes the session by calling the `InternetAccessManager` to disable the user communications, and the `DhcpServer` to disable its IP address.

We want to alter the above behavior by adding new features to the system. These features are non-modular and they cannot be added directly to the components when their source code is not available (*i.e.* black box based models). In such case, AOP [2] is the solution. Using AOP, the desired features are modeled as modular entities, called aspects, to be woven to the system, the feature behavior is modeled as advices that are executed whenever particular services are intercepted by a monitor. In this paper we introduce three aspects: `Bonus`, `Alert` and `NetOverloading`. The `Bonus` adds an additional free connection time to first class passengers. The `Alert` warns the connected passengers five minutes before the end of their sessions, and the `NetOverloading` blocks P2P connection queries when the number of connected passengers exceeds a given threshold number. In fact, other aspects are proposed and implemented for the example, but for space limitation only these three aspects and their interactions are presented. From the implementation point of view, since the source code of components may not be available to component users, aspects should be integrated in a transparent and a modular way. In [5] we extended Fractal component controllers to implement and compose such aspects.

For better understanding of aspect interactions and interferences in component systems, let us consider the original airport system, the `Bonus` and the `Alert` aspects. Let us also assume that the original session duration is 60 minutes, `Bonus` adds 10 minutes and `Alert` warns the user 5 minutes before the end of the session. When both aspects are bound to the system, we wish users to get a bonus time and be alerted exactly 5 minutes before the actual end of their sessions (*i.e.* alert at 65 minutes, end of session at 70 minutes).

In AOP [2], the aspect behavior defines a set of advices associated to pointcut expressions defining the join points where the aspect should interfere. Each advice executes extra code and implicitly/explicitly proceeds or skips the captured join points following the type of the advice (*i.e. before*, *after*, or *around*). Proceeded join points continue to the next advice if any, or continue their original path, while skipped join points are blocked. In our approach, we adopt the use of around-like advices where an extra-code is always executed before the join point access and the join point is explicitly proceeded or skipped. In addition, when two aspects intercept common join points (*i.e.* service calls), the advices of the two aspects on those services are executed sequentially, and the service call continues its original path (*i.e.* proceeded) only if at least one of the aspects decides to proceed the call, otherwise the call is skipped. This strategy is abstracted into a `Seq` operator. Figure 2 details

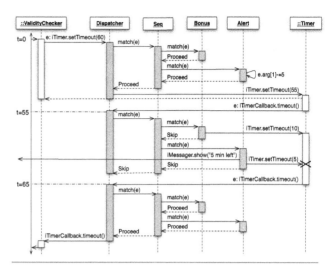

Figure 2. Seq(`Bonus`,`Alert`) scenario

the execution of the `Bonus` and the `Alert` behaviors sequentially (*i.e.* composed using `Seq`). At time 0, a user logs in for 60 minutes provided by his flight ticket. The message `setTimeout(60)` sent from a `ValidityChecker` to its `Timer` is intercepted and forwarded to the `Alert` aspect only (*i.e.* the `setTimeout(60)` is not of interest to `Bonus`). The `Alert` subtracts 5 minutes from 60 and proceeds the call with the new parameter value (55). As a result, a `timeout` service call is intercepted at time 55. The `timeout` is common intercepted service so that its call is forwarded to the `Bonus` first then to the `Alert`. The `Bonus` resets the `Timer` for 10 minutes and skips the call. Then, the call is sent to `Alert` that warns the user, resets the `Timer` for 5 minutes and skips the call. This violates the expected behavior: the alert is sent too early (at time 55 instead of the expected 65). Moreover, the `Timer` has been set twice with different values which does not conform with the current modelization of the `Timer` (see Figure 4) and hence it is inconsistent whatever happens next. This kind of interaction is called an interference since the desired behavior is not satisfied by the default sequential composition of aspects. To solve this interference, another composition strategy is needed: "*the first occurrence of `timeout` should only be managed by `Bonus` and the second occurrence should only be managed by `Alert`*". Within this new strategy, when a service of interest to both aspects is intercepted, its occurrences are passed in turn repeatedly (*i.e.* alternately) to the left and the right hand side aspects. When a service is of interest to one aspect only, the call is forwarded to its corresponding aspect. This strategy can be generalized and abstracted into a composition operator we call `Alt`. Figure 3 details the alternate execution of the `Bonus` and the `Alert` scenario (*i.e.* their composition using `Alt`). At time 0, a user logs in for 60 minutes provided by his flight ticket. The message `setTimeout(60)` sent from a `ValidityChecker` to its `Timer` is intercepted and forwarded to `Alert`. The `Alert` subtracts 5 minutes from 60 and proceeds the call. As a result the `setTimeout(55)` call is proceeded. At time 55, a `timeout` is intercepted which is a message of interest to both aspects. Here, the call is forwarded only to `Bonus` (first occurrence) that resets the `Timer` for 10 minutes and skips the message. Thus, the first `timeout` call is ignored. At time 65, a second `timeout` is intercepted. The call, this time, is forwarded only to `Alert` (second occurrence) that warns the user, resets the `Timer` for 5 minutes and skips the message. Thus, the `timeout` call is ignored again. At time 70, a third `timeout` call is intercepted and forwarded only to `Bonus` (third occurrence) that proceeds the call since the bonus

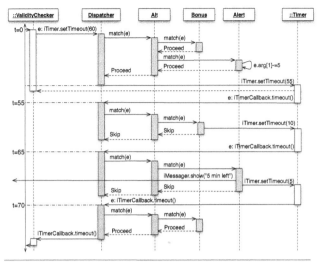

Figure 3. `Alt(Bonus,Alert)` scenario

Architecture	::=	**system** *id* ⟨*Interfaces*⟩ ⟨*Components*⟩ ⟨*Attachments*⟩ ⟨*Aspects*⟩ ⟨*Weavings*⟩
Interfaces	::=	**interface** *id* {(@(**sync** | **async**) *svId*)⁺}; ⟨*Interfaces*⟩*
Components	::=	⟨*Primitive*⟩ | ⟨*Composite*⟩ | ⟨*Components*⟩; ⟨*Components*⟩
Template	::=	[**attributes** (*t id*;)⁺] [**provides** (*itfId id*;)⁺] [**requires** (*itfId id*;)⁺]
Primitive	::=	**primitive** *id* [(*n* : ℕ⁺)] { ⟨*Template*⟩ **computation** ⟨*Behavior*⟩ }
Composite	::=	**composite** *id* [(*n* : ℕ⁺)] { ⟨*Template*⟩ **internals** *cId*⁺ }
Attachments	::=	(**client**=*cId₁.itfId₁* **server**=*cId₂.itfId₂*)*
Behavior	::=	**process** *id* { [(*t id*)*;] [**clock** *id**;] **state** *locId*⁺; **init** *locId*; **trans** ⟨*Transitions*⟩; }
Transitions	::=	(*locId* − > *locId* {[⟨*Guard*⟩] [⟨*Sync*⟩] [⟨*Assign*⟩]})⁺
Guard	::=	**guard** *bexp*
Sync	::=	**sync** [(**proceed** | **skip**).|[*asId*.]*itfId.svId* (! | ?)
Assign	::=	**assign** *exp*
Weavings	::=	(**weave** *asId* (*pctId*, *vexp*)⁺ | *opId* ⟨*Weavings*⟩⟨*Weavings*⟩))*
Aspects	::=	(**aspect** *id* ⟨*Behavior*⟩)*
Ops	::=	(**operator** *id* ⟨*Behavior*⟩)*

Table 1. An ADL for aspectized component systems

time is consumed. As a result, the `timeout` is proceeded. This ends the session and elaborates the desired behavior.

The above example confirms that the sequential composition of aspects is not sufficient to solve aspect interferences and other composition strategies are needed. One more example is the case when the airport manager decides to block P2P access when the network is overloaded. This also can be modeled as an aspect that interfere when calls to the `Firewall` and from the `IpAddressManager` are intercepted. The `NetOverloading` aspect requires the `IpAddressManager` for its `IIpMacDb` interface that defines `add(IP)` and `remove(IP)` services. Intercepting those services, the aspect is able to count the number of connected users. In addition, the aspect requires the `Firewall` component for its `IFirewall` interface that defines the `connect(IP)` service. Intercepting calls to this service enables the aspect to block calls to P2P addresses when the number of connected users exceeds a given threshold number. Now, if we want to prevent associating a bonus time to users when the system is overloaded, the `Bonus` and the `NetOverloading` aspects can be composed using a `Cond` operator. Within `Cond`, the `Bonus` behavior is not executed if the `NetOverloading` detects an overloading state of the system. In the following, we propose a formalization of component systems and aspects as a network of automata and we use UPPAAL model checker to check whether the system satisfies the desired behavior and whether the woven aspects interact safely (*i.e.* are interference-free). In addition, the composition strategies described above to solve aspect interferences are abstracted into binary composition operators that can be instantiated for arbitrary aspects. UPPAAL model checker is used to check whether an instantiated operator solves the interference.

3. ADL for Aspectized Component Systems

In this section we describe an ADL that enables the definition of both structural and behavioral properties of aspectized component systems. Our ADL is not a new language, instead, it enriches current ADL(s) such as Fractal-ADL [4] with explicit definition of aspects, aspect behaviors, aspect weaving rules, and aspect composition. Table 3 shows the BNF-like grammar of our ADL. In the table, *id* refers to general identifiers, *cId*, *itfId*, and *svId* refer to component, interface and service identifiers. In addition, *asId*, *pctId*, *opId*, and *locId* refer to aspect, pointcut, operator, and location identifiers, respectively, and we use *t* to refer to data types.

According to the above ADL specification, a component system is defined as a set of interfaces (*Interfaces*), components (*Components*), attachments (*Attachments*), aspects (*Aspects*), and a set of weaving rules (*Weavings*). Each interface is defined by an identifier and a set of service signatures, each of which is annotated with (@**sync** or @**async**) to indicate whether a service is synchronous or asynchronous, respectively. We distinguish two kinds of components: primitives and composites. A primitive component is defined with an identifier, a set of attributes, two sets of provided and required interfaces and a behavior indicated with the **computation** keyword. Compared with a primitive, a composite does not have a behavior, instead a set of its internal components are indicated within the **internals** keyword. Since different instances may exist in the component system configuration, an indication of the number of instances for each component is optionally indicated with a natural number (*n*) that follows the component name. The set of attachments defines the configuration of the system by setting down all the connections between components. Inspired from Fractal [4], a connection binds a component required interface (*i.e.* **client**) to a component provided interface (*i.e.* **server**). The weaving part of the ADL description, indicates which aspect should be woven to the system and how aspects are composed using binary composition operators. Both aspects and composition operators are defined with an identifier and an abstract behavior. By abstract behavior, aspect pointcuts are denoted with abstract names that should be replaced with concrete join points at the weaving stage (see section 4.6). To describe behaviors, we adopt UPPAAL XTA-like notation [9]. Accordingly, a behavior is indicated with a (**process**) keyword followed by potential declarations of local variables, clocks and a set of transitions. Each transition indicates the start and the end location, and a transition label. A transition label consists of a guard, a synchronization channel, and a sequence of assignments. A guard is a predicate (*i.e.* boolean expression *bexp*), its satisfaction enables the transition. For channel labels, we adopt the following notations in the ADL specification: concatenation of the interface and the service identifiers. In addition, a channel label can be prefixed with two predefined keywords (**proceed** or **skip**) to indicate the actions taken by an aspect. Assignments are a sequence of clock and/or variable assignments. Finally, for the weaving, an aspect is associated with a mapping (*pctId, vexp*) where: *pctId* is an abstract pointcut identifier used in the aspect behavior specification, and *vexp* is a VIL expression [3] used to define concrete join points for aspect instantiation.

```
1  system airportInternetAccess
2    interface ITimer {@sync setTimeout(int)}
3    interface ITimerCallback {@async timeout()}
4    interface IToken {@sync startToken()}
5    interface ITokenCallback {@async tokenInvalidated()}
6    // other interfaces
7    primitive Timer (n) {
8      provides ITimerCallback iTimerCallback;
9      requires ITimer iTimer;
10     // behavior (see section 4.1)
11   }
12   primitive ValidityChecker (n) {
13     provides ITimer iTimer, IToken iToken;
14     requires ITimerCallback iTimerCallback,
15             ITokenCallback iTokenCallback;
16     // behavior
17   }
18   composite Token (n) {
19     provides ITokenCallback iTokenCallback;
20     requires IToken iToken;
21     internals Timer, ValidityChecker;
22   }
23   client ValidityChecker.iTimer server Timer.iTimer;
24   // other attachments
25   aspect Bonus //Behavior
26   weave Bonus (pct, {(ValidityChecker,iTimer,timeout)});
```

Listing 1. An excerpt of the ADL of the airport system example

Listing 1 shows an excerpt of the ADL specification of the airport Internet access example. In the listing, four interfaces are declared with the signatures of their services (line 2-5). For example, the `ITimerCallback` interface defines only one asynchronous service named `timeout`. Two primitive components, the `Timer` and the `ValidityChecker`, are described (lines 7-11, 12-17, respectively) with their provided and required interfaces. The `Token` composite component is described (line 18-22) with its interfaces and internals. Since several tokens can be created, the component is parametrized with n (the maximum number of instances). The attachment description in (line 23) indicates that the `iTimer` interface of the `ValidityChecker` component is bound to the `iTimer` interface of the `Timer` component. The weaving declaration (line 26) indicates that the `Bonus` aspect (line 25) is bound to the system and its abstract pointcut `pct` should be replaced by the concrete join point (*e.g.*, the `timeout` service of the `iTimer` interface of the `ValidityChecker` component).

4. Aspectized Component Systems in UPPAAL

In this section we overview UPPAAL model checker and we describe the transformation scheme of our ADL to UPPAAL processes. The provided semantics of the woven system is not to be inspected but to be checked, this is similar to AspectJ where the woven code is not to be read.

4.1 Overview of UPPAAL

UPPAAL [6] is a toolbox, used to design, simulate and check CTL (Computation Tree Logic) [10] properties for systems that can be modeled as networks of timed automata. A timed automata is a regular finite state machine extended with local variables, data types, and clock variables. Each automaton in UPPAAL is called a *template* and each instance is called a *process*. A template can be parametrized with constants indicating how that template is instantiated (*e.g.*, how many instances are created). Template nodes are called *locations* while the edges are called *transitions*. For describing systems, UPPAAL provides both a graphical (XML format)

and a textual (XTA format) formalism. For better understanding of UPPAAL formalism, let us consider the behavior of the `Timer` component shown in Figure 4. The template can be read clockwise from the initial location. The initial location is distinguished with a double circle. The `Timer` waits for a `setTimeout` call with a parameter of type `TIME` (a user defined data type) declared at the top of the channel label (`time:TIME`). When it receives such event, it stores the time value in a local variable (`time:=t`), resets a clock variable `cl` to 0 and goes to the next location. Then, the `Timer` sends `E_..._setTimeout` indicating the end of the treatment of the `setTimeout` event (`setTimeout` is synchronous event) and goes to the next location. This latter is decorated with an invariant (`cl<=time`) to indicate that the process should not stay at that location when the invariant becomes false (`cl>time`). When that happens, the `Timer` enables the last transition by triggering a `timeout` event, resets the clock to 0 and returns to the initial location.

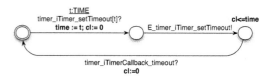

Figure 4. Formal Model for the `Timer` Component

Listing 2 shows the UPPAAL textual description (XTA) of the `Timer` component. Data types (*e.g.*, `TIME`) are declared first (line 1). Each template in UPPAAL is declared within the `process` keyword followed by the name of the template (`Timer` in this case) (line 2). Clock variables (`cl`) and local variables (`time`) are declared in the top of the declaration (line 3-4). Then the locations are listed (line 5), and the initial location is explicitly indicated (line 6). The transitions come last following the same syntax we adopted for behaviors specification (line 7-12).

```
1  typedef int[0,6] TIME;
2  process Timer() {
3  clock cl;
4  TIME time;
5  state l_0 {cl<=time}, l_1, l_2;
6  init l_0;
7  trans
8    l_0 -> l_1 {select t:TIME;
9                sync timer_iTimer_setTimeout[t]?;
10               assign time:=t, cl:=0;},
11   l_1 -> l_2 {sync E_timer_iTimer_setTimeout!;},
12   l_2 -> l_0 {sync timer_iTimerCallback_timeout!;};
13 }
```

Listing 2. UPPAAL-XTA description of the `Timer` component

UPPAAL also provides a simulator that enables the exhaustive examination of systems behaviors. Within the simulator, a user can interact with the system, execute the system step by step, decide which transition should be taken if many are enabled, and see how local variables and clocks values change during the execution. The UPPAAL model checker is designed to check reachability, safety and liveness properties expressed in a subset of CTL formulae [10]. When a particular property is violated, a counter example in terms of a diagnosis trace is automatically reported to the user. Thus, the user is given a feedback that helps on the detection of potential errors and how to correct them. The use of UPPAAL in our proposal is important because of its support of the following features: (1) template instantiation and (2) value passing which are intrinsic properties to component models, and (3) timing support which is important for our case study. In the following we describe how to transform the above ADL specification into UPPAAL processes.

4.2 Formalization of Primitive Components

Each primitive component is modeled as a UPPAAL process. Since primitive components come with their behavior specifications, those specifications should be transformed into compatible UPPAAL-XTA form. In our ADL, the behavior specification is chosen to be a subset of XTA description of templates in UPPAAL and hence minimum adaptations are needed. In particular, each channel label in the ADL specification consists of an interface identifier and a service signature which are sufficient for local behavior specification of components. In our formalization we adopt the following notation for channel labels: a concatenation of a component, an interface identifiers and a service signature separated with "_". This enables component bindings (see section 4.4). Accordingly, all the channel labels of a behavior specification should be prefixed by its correspondent component name. In addition, when several instances are required, channel labels are suffixed with "[id]" indicating the instance reference of each component; where id is a constant that ranges over [1..n] and n is the indicated number of instances for the underlying component specification. In UPPAAL-XTA, this number is modeled as a parameter to the template modeling the component. Listing 3 describes how to transform an ADL primitive component specification into a compatible UPPAAL-XTA template. The *clone()* function (line 5) makes a copy of a software entity behavior with a given fresh name *id*.

```
1 𝒫 : Primitive → UPPAALTemplate
2 𝒫⟦primitive cId { temp computation cpt }⟧ =
3        cpt[cId_itfId_svId / itfId.svId]
4 𝒫⟦primitive cId (n) { temp computation cpt }⟧ =
5        let p= clone(cpt,cId(const id : [1..n]))
6        in p[cId_itfId_svId[id] / itfId.svId]
```

Listing 3. primitive component transformation rule

4.3 Formalization of Composite Components

A composite is modeled as a set of UPPAAL processes, one for each bound interface. Each template of those processes has a central initial location and a set of directed cycles from and to that location. Each cycle describes one service. Asynchronous services are represented by cycles of two transitions: receives a call ($cId_1\_itfId_1\_s_i$?), then forwards it ($cId_2\_itfId_2\_s_i$!) (Listing 4 line 17-18). Synchronous services are represented by cycles of four transitions: receives a call ($cId_1\_itfId_1\_s_i$?), forwards it ($cId_2\_itfId_2\_s_i$!), waits for the reply ($E\_cId_2\_itfId_2\_s_i$?), and forwards the reply ($E\_cId_1\_itfId_1\_s_i$!) (Listing 4 line 12-15). When a composite has multiple instances, similar to a primitive, we suffix its channel labels in the specification with "[id]" (Listing 4 line 21-37). The following is the complete generation rule of a composite component from the ADL specification of composites where: *attachments()* function returns the set of attachments declared in the architecture, *type()* returns the definition of an interface in a given component architecture, *services()* returns the set of services defined in a given interface definition, *nbSync()* and *nbAsync()* return the number of synchronous and asynchronous services for a given interface definition, and *synchronous()* function checks whether a given service is synchronous in a given interface definition.

```
1 𝒞 : Composite → Architecture → UPPAALTemplate*
2 𝒞⟦composite cId₁ { temp internals cIds }⟧ a=
3   ∀itfId₁ ∈ interfaces(cId₁,a),
4   ∃(client= cId₁.itfId₁ server= cId₂.itfId₂) ∈ attachments(a):
5       process cId₁_itfId₁() {
6           state l₀,..,lₖ;
7           %k=nbSync(type(itfId₁,a))*3+nbAsync(type(itfId₁,a))
8           init l₀;
9           trans
10          ∀ sᵢ ∈ services(type(itfId₁,a)) {
11          if (synchronous(sᵢ)) {
12              l₀  -> l_{i₁} {sync cId₁_itfId₁_sᵢ?;} ,
```

```
13              l_{i₁}  -> l_{i₂} {sync cId₂_itfId₂_sᵢ!;} ,
14              l_{i₂}  -> l_{i₃} {sync E_cId₂_itfId₂_sᵢ?;} ,
15              l_{i₃}  -> l₀ {sync E_cId₁_itfId₁_sᵢ!;} ;
16          } else {
17              l₀  -> l_{i₁} {sync cId₁_itfId₁_sᵢ?;} ,
18              l_{i₁}  -> l₀ {sync cId₂_itfId₂_sᵢ!;} ;
19          }
20      };
21 𝒞⟦composite cId₁ (n) { temp internals cIds }⟧ a=
22   ∀(client= cId₁.itfId₁ server= cId₂.itfId₂) ∈ attachments(a)
23       process cId₁_itfId₁(const id : [1..n]) {
24           state l₀,..,lₖ;
25           %k=nbSync(type(itfId₁,a))*3+nbAsync(type(itfId₁,a))
26           init l₀;
27           trans
28           ∀ sᵢ ∈ services(itfId₁) {
29           if (synchronous(sᵢ)) {
30               l₀  -> l_{i₁} {sync cId₁_itfId₁_sᵢ[id]?;} ,
31               l_{i₁}  -> l_{i₂} {sync cId₂_itfId₂_sᵢ!;} ;
32               l_{i₂}  -> l_{i₃} {sync E_cId₂_itfId₂_sᵢ?;} ;
33               l_{i₃}  -> l₀ {sync E_cId₁_itfId₁_sᵢ[id]!;} ;
34           } else {
35               l₀  -> l_{i₁} {sync cId₁_itfId₁_sᵢ[id]?;} ,
36               l_{i₁}  -> l₀ {sync cId₂_itfId₂_sᵢ!;} ;
37           }
38       };
```

Listing 4. composite component generation rule

Let us consider the Token composite component. This component has two interfaces: iToken and iTokenCallback (see Listing 1 line 19-20). The interface iToken has one synchronous service: startToken (Listing 1 line 4) for starting a new session. This is modeled as a UPPAAL template with one cycle of four transitions (see Figure 5). The iTokenCallBack interface defines a single asynchronous service timeout (Listing 1 line 3) for signaling that a session time elapsed. This is modeled as a template with a single cycle of two transitions (see Figure 6).

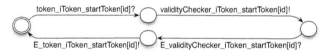

Figure 5. Formal Model for Token: iToken interface

Figure 6. Formal Model for Token: iTokenCallback interface

4.4 Formalization of Bindings

Component bindings can be modeled either as separate UPPAAL processes that receive channels from required interfaces and forward them to their bound provided interfaces, or by renaming. In our approach we adopt the second solution for minimum state number generation. By renaming, a bound interface $itfId_1$ of a component cId_1 to an interface $itfId_2$ of a component cId_2 is modeled by replacing each channel label occurrence $cId_1\_itfId_1\_s$ in the template of cId_1 by $cId_2\_itfId_2\_s$, for each service name s. This synchronizes the channels between the two bound components. Listing 5 describes the binding rule, where the *name()* function returns the name of a software entity (*e.g.,* component, interface, etc.).

```
1 ℬ : UPPAALTemplate → Architecture → UPPAALTemplate
2 ℬ⟦p⟧ a=
3   let cId₁= name(p)
```

```
4    in ∀ ( client= cId₁.itfId₁  server= cId₂.itfId₂ ) ∈
          attachments(a),
5      ∀s ∈ services(itfId₁) p[cId₂_itfId₂_s / cId₁_itfId₁_s];
```

Listing 5. components binding rule

Figure 7 depicts the `Timer` template after binding its required interface `iTimerCallback` to that provided by the `ValidityChecker` component (Listing 1 line 23). Thus, the `timer_iTimerCallback_timeout!` is replaced by `validityChecker_iTimerCallback_timeout!`.

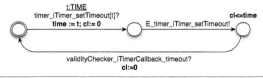

Figure 7. Formal model of the `Timer` component bound to the `validityChecker` component on the `iTimerCallback` interface

4.5 Formalization of component systems

A complete component system without aspects is modeled as the parallel composition of all the components of the architecture. The primitive components are adapted to follow the UPPAAL-XTA syntax and bound to each other using the binding rule, while composite templates are automatically generated from the ADL specification. Formally:

$$\mathcal{S}[\![a]\!] = \|_{\forall c \in primitives(a)} \mathcal{B}[\![\mathcal{P}[\![c]\!]]\!]a \ \|_{\forall t \in attachments(a)} \mathcal{C}[\![t]\!]a$$

The complete airport system example is modeled by 20 templates (9 for primitive components and 11 for composite components' interfaces).

4.6 Formalization of Aspects and Aspect weaving

The behavior of aspects is already described in the ADL specification following UPPAAL-XTA form. The aspect behavior defines a set of cycles from and to the initial location, each of which describes an advice behavior associated to an abstract pointcut *pctId*. The proceed and the skip actions taken by an aspect for each pointcut *pctId* are explicitly modeled by (*proceed_pctId!*) and (*skip_pctId!*) channels, respectively. Note that the behavior is abstract and should be instantiated for concrete join points. In our model, pointcuts are defined using VIL [3] in a declarative style. VIL interprets and transforms pointcut expressions into tuples of the form (*cId, itfId, svId*) (*i.e.* a component, an interface and a service identifiers). In the ADL specification of each aspect a mapping (*pctId,vexp*) from an abstract pointcut to an expression describing the concrete join points is given. In the instantiation process, for each mapping (*pctId,vexp*), we use VIL to interpret the expression *vexp* and returns a set of tuples of the form (*cId, itfId, svId*). For each tuple, we make a copy of the cycle denoting *pctId* in the aspect abstract behavior. Then, we replace each *pctId* occurrence, in the copy, by *cId_itfId_svId* from the tuple. Listing 6 describes this instantiation process. In the listing, the *behavior()* function returns the abstract behavior specification of a given software entity in a component architecture, *duplicateTransitions(b,pctId)*, as its name indicates, duplicates the set of transitions in the behavior specification *b* where *pctId* appears in the channel labels, $\mathcal{V}$ denotes VIL interpretation of pointcut expressions, and (union: $\oplus$, intersection: $\otimes$) are two VIL composition operators [3].

```
1 𝓘 : Weaving→Architecture→UPPAALTemplate*
2 𝓘[[weave asId map]] a= {
```

```
3    process asId {
4        // the declaration given in asId
5        trans
6            ∀(pctId, vexp) ∈ map :
7            let jps = 𝒱[[vexp]](a), b= behavior(asId,a)
8            in ∀(cId, itfId, svId) ∈ jps :
9                duplicateTransitions(b,pctId)[cId_itfId_svId / pctId]
10   }
11 𝓘[[weave w₁; w₂]] a= 𝓘[[weave w₁]] a ∪ 𝓘[[weave w₂]] a
12 𝓘[[weave opId w₁ w₂]] a=
13   let p=𝓘[[weave
         opId {(lhs, ⊕ₑw₁),(rhs, ⊕ₑw₂),(lrhs,(⊕ₑw₁) ⊗ (⊕ₑw₂))}]] a
14   in {𝓘[[w₁]] a ,𝓘[[w₂]] a ,p[name(w₁)/left; name(w₂)/right]}
```

Listing 6. Instantiation rule

In order to synchronize component processes with aspect ones (*i.e.* weaving aspects into the base system), a set of locations and transitions should be added to component specifications. This extension ensures that each intercepted service call is forwarded to the aspect process, which executes its behavior and returns either proceed or skip. In the former case, the extension ensures that the service call reaches its target and continues its original path. In the latter case, the extension ensures that the service call is skipped by returning to the initial location if the service is asynchronous. If the service is synchronous, all the actions between the begin and the end events of the service call are ignored. For instance, when the `Bonus` aspect is applied to the `ValidityChecker`, its corresponding template must be adapted as detailed in Figure 8. Part (a) shows an excerpt of the original `ValidityChecker` template and part (b) shows the same excerpt adapted. As a result, when `timeout` is received, it is forwarded to the `Bonus` aspect process. The `ValidityChecker` waits for either `skip` to return to the original location, or `proceed` to forward the `timeout` to the `Token` component. Listing 7 generalizes the process of aspect weaving.

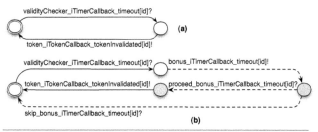

Figure 8. `ValidityChecker` template adaptation (a) original, (b) adapted

In Listing 7, the aspect process is instantiated first (line 3). Then for each concrete join point tuple, transitions and locations are added to the component process following the example shown in Figure 8. In the case of aspect composition, aspects are instantiated following the instantiation rule, then, the composition operator is instantiated. Finally, the components owning the join points are adapted so that all the services in the concrete join points are forwarded to the operator process. In the following we show how our modelization of aspectized component systems as UPPAAL processes serves for interferences detection.

```
1 𝒲 : Weavings → Architecture → UPPAALTemplate*
2 𝒲[[weave asId (ptcIdᵢ, vexpᵢ)⁺]] a=
3    𝓘[[weave asId (ptcIdᵢ, vexpᵢ)⁺]] a ∪
4    (∀vexpᵢ ∈ (ptcIdᵢ, vexpᵢ)⁺ :
5    let pts= 𝒱[[vexpᵢ]](a)
6    in ∀(cId, itfId, svId) ∈ pts :
7        let p = behavior(cId,a)
8        in
9        if synchronous(svId)
10           p|(
```

```
11              l_i -> l_{i1}: {X_1 sync cId_itfId_sId? X_2},
12              l_{i1} -> l_{i2}: {sync asId_itfId_svId!},
13              l_{i2} -> l_j: {sync proceed_asId_itfId_svId?},
14              l_{i2} -> l_k: {sync skip_asId_itfId_svId?},
15              l_k -> l_l: {Y_1 sync E_cId_itfId_svId! Y_1},
16              ) /
17              (
18              l_i -> l_j: {X_1 sync cId_itfId_svId? X_2},
19              l_k -> l_l: {Y_1 sync E_cId_itfId_s! Y_2},
20              )
21          ]
22     else
23          p|(
24              l_i -> l_{i1}: {X_1 sync cId_itfId_svId? X_2},
25              l_{i1} -> l_{i2}: {sync asId_itfId_svId!},
26              l_{i2} -> l_j: {sync proceed_asId_itfId_svId?},
27              l_{i2} -> l_0: {sync skip_asId_itfId_svId?},
28              ) /
29              (
30              l_i -> l_j: {X_1 sync cId_itfId_svId? X_2},
31              )
32          ])
33 W[[weave w_1; w_2]] a = W[[weave w_1]] a ∪ W[[weave w_2]] a
34 W[[weave opId w_1 w_2]] a = W[[weave
      opId {(lhs, ⊕e_{w_1}), (rhs, ⊕e_{w_2}), (lrhs, (⊕e_{w_1} ⊗ (⊕e_{w_2})))}]] a
```

Listing 7. weaving aspects to component systems

5. Interference Detection

For interference detection, we define a component system Γ as a pair $(a_\Gamma, \mathcal{P}_\Gamma)$ where, a_Γ is the ADL description of the component architecture of the system, and $\mathcal{P}_\Gamma$ is a set of CTL formulas describing the desired properties of the system. Our case study is defined as $(a_{airport}, \mathcal{P}_{airport})$. Where $\mathcal{P}_{airport}$ describes the set of properties the system ensures whenever it is executed. The system is designed to satisfy different (liveness, safety, and reachability) properties. These are given at the top of Table 2 ($\mathcal{P}_{airport}$). In particular, a user cannot stay connected forever (*Live 1*), the system is deadlock free (*Safe 1*), a user cannot stay connected more than the validity time indicated in his flight ticket (*Safe 2*), a user can connect to all the IP addresses when its access is enabled by the firewall (*Safe 3*), and several users can be connected at the same time (*Reach 1*). The formulas rely on different constants, variables and auxiliary functions: ID and IP denote the range for user identifiers and IP addresses, respectively, Connected and Disconnected are identifiers denoting particular locations on the user process, validity(id) is a global function that returns the authorized connection time of a user id, currentIp(id) returns the current IP address the user wants to connect, and enabled(id) checks whether a user id access is enabled by the firewall. The cl is a local clock associated to the user process, and the isConnected is a local variable in the user process that stores the firewall response of the user access to each IP address. The properties satisfaction indicates the well-definedness of component systems.

DEFINITION 5.1. *A component system $\Gamma = (a_\Gamma, \mathcal{P}_\Gamma)$ is well defined if the parallel composition of all the processes modelling the components of the system (see section 4.5) satisfies all the desired properties of such system:*

$$\mathcal{D}(\Gamma) \overset{\text{def}}{=} \mathcal{S}(a_\Gamma) \models \mathcal{P}_\Gamma$$

The intent of each aspect should also be given as a set of CTL formulas. The intent describes the set of properties the aspect ensures when it is woven to a system. The satisfaction of these properties when the aspect is woven determines the applicability of the aspect to the base system.

DEFINITION 5.2. *Given a component system $\Gamma = (a_\Gamma, \mathcal{P}_\Gamma)$, an aspect $\Lambda = (aId_\Lambda, map_\Lambda, \mathcal{P}_\Lambda)$, where $\mathcal{P}_\Lambda$ is the set of aspect intent*

properties, map_Λ is the mapping relation of the aspect abstract ponitcuts to concrete join points, and $\mathcal{P}_\Gamma^\Lambda \subseteq \mathcal{P}_\Gamma$ is the set of the base system properties that must be preserved after weaving Λ. An aspect is said to be correct with respect to a component system Γ if the following condition holds:

$$\mathcal{W}[[\textbf{weave } asId_\Lambda \ map_\Lambda]] \ a_\Gamma \models \mathcal{P}_\Gamma^\Lambda \wedge \mathcal{P}_\Lambda$$

Note that $\mathcal{P}_\Gamma^\Lambda$ must be determined by the user for each aspect. For instance, when the Bonus aspect is woven to the airport system, $\mathcal{P}_{airport}^{bonus}$ is defined as all the $\mathcal{P}_{airport}$ properties except (*Safe 3*), since Bonus allows the user to connect for more than the time indicated in his flight ticket (see *Safe 3'*). While in the case of Alert $\mathcal{P}_{airport}^{alert}$ is simply $\mathcal{P}_{airport}$ since the Alert adds a new feature to the system without altering its original behavior. The properties for Bonus ($\mathcal{P}_{bonus}$), Alert ($\mathcal{P}_{alert}$), and NetOverloading ($\mathcal{P}_{netOverloading}$) aspects are shown in the bottom part of Table 2. The Bonus aspect ensures that a user can stay connected a bonus time (BonusTime) after its authorized time elapses (*Safe 3'*). The Alert ensures that a user is always alerted before it is disconnected (*Live 2*) and the alert is intercepted exactly TimeAlert before the session time elapses (*Safe 4*). While the NetOverloading aspect ensures that a user is unable to access P2P addresses when the system is overloaded (*Safe 2'*). In the formulas, Alerted is an identifier denoting a particular location on the user process, isAlerted is a local boolean variable of the user indicating whether a user reached the Alerted location, BonusTime and AlertTime are constants denoting the bonus and the alert times, respectively. Finally, isP2P(ip) and isOverload() are two predicates defined in the NetOverloading aspect process to check whether an IP address is P2P and whether the server is overloaded, respectively.

Extending components with several aspects may give rise to interferences. Two aspects are interference-free with respect to a base program, when both aspects are woven to the system, the result system satisfies all the properties of the underlying aspects as well as the system properties to be preserved by both aspects. Formally:

DEFINITION 5.3. *Given a base system $\Gamma = (a_\Gamma, \mathcal{P}_\Gamma)$, two aspects $\Lambda_1 = (asId_{\Lambda_1}, map_{\Lambda_1}, \mathcal{P}_{\Lambda_1})$, $\Lambda_2 = (asId_{\Lambda_2}, map_{\Lambda_2}, \mathcal{P}_{\Lambda_2})$. Λ_1 and Λ_2 are interference-free if the following conditions hold:*

1. the base system is well defined: $\mathcal{D}(\Gamma)$

2. the composition is correct w.r.t Γ:

   (a) $map_{\Lambda_1} \cap map_{\Lambda_2} = \phi$:
$$\mathcal{W}[[\textbf{weave } (asId_{\Lambda_1} \ map_{\Lambda_1}); (asId_{\Lambda_1} \ map_{\Lambda_1})]] \ a_\Gamma \models \mathcal{P}_\Gamma^{\Lambda_1} \wedge \mathcal{P}_\Gamma^{\Lambda_2} \wedge \mathcal{P}_{\Lambda_1} \wedge \mathcal{P}_{\Lambda_2}$$

   (b) $map_{\Lambda_1} \cap map_{\Lambda_2} \neq \phi$:
$$\mathcal{W}[[\textbf{weave } Seq \ (asId_{\Lambda_1} \ map_{\Lambda_1}) \ (asId_{\Lambda_1} \ map_{\Lambda_2})]] \ a_\Gamma \models \mathcal{P}_\Gamma^{\Lambda_1} \wedge \mathcal{P}_\Gamma^{\Lambda_2} \wedge \mathcal{P}_{\Lambda_1} \wedge \mathcal{P}_{\Lambda_2}$$

Where $\mathcal{P}_\Gamma^{\Lambda_1}$ and $\mathcal{P}_\Gamma^{\Lambda_2}$ denote the set of base system properties to be preserved when Λ_1 and Λ_2 are woven to the system, respectively. In our case study, when both Bonus and Alert are woven to the system and composed using Seq, *Safe 3* and *Safe 4* properties are violated which reports an interference with a diagnostic trace similar to that given in Figure 2. The reported trace shows that both aspects reset the Timer for two different values and the Timer is not designed to accept such kind of behavior. In addition, the alert message is sent to the user early (*i.e.* before the consumption of bonus). Thus, we used the Alt operator that sets the Timer once for each intercepted timeout event, and ensures that the alert is sent to the user after consuming the bonus. The use of UPPAAL model checker this time shows that all the desired properties are satisfied which indicates that the interference is solved. In general, a composition operator solves an interference if when it is instantiated for two aspects and composed with the woven system, the interference disappears. Formally:

Properties for the Airport Base System ($\mathcal{P}_{airport}$)	
Live 1	`User(id).Connected --> User(id).Disconnected`
Safe 1	`A[] not deadlock`
Safe 2	`A[] ∀(id:ID),∀(ip:IP) (User(id).Connected ∧ currentIp(id)==ip ∧ Firewall.enabled(id)) ⇒ User(id).isConnected`
Safe 3	`A[] ∀(id:ID) User(id).Connected ⇒ User(id).cl<=validity(id)`
Reach 1	`E<> User(0).Connected ∧ (∀(id:ID) id!=0 ⇒ User(id).Connected)`
Properties for the Bonus aspect ($\mathcal{P}_{bonus}$)	
Safe 3'	`A[] ∀(id:ID) User(id).Connected ⇒ User(id).cl<=validity(id) + BonusTime`
Properties for the Alert aspect ($\mathcal{P}_{alert}$)	
Live 2	`Use(id).Connected --> User(id).Disconnected ∧ User(id).isAlerted`
Safe 4	`A[] ∀(id:ID) User(id).Alerted ⇒ User.cl== validity(id) - AlertTime`
Properties for the NetOverloading aspect ($\mathcal{P}_{netOverloading}$)	
Safe 2'	`A[] ∀(id:ID),∀(ip:IP) User(id).Connected ∧ currentIp(id)==ip ∧ NetOverloading.isP2P(ip) ∧ NetOverloading.isOverload()` `⇒ !User(id).isConnected`

Table 2. Properties of the airport wireless system and the intent of the aspects to be woven

DEFINITION 5.4. *Given a base system* $\Gamma = (a_\Gamma, \mathcal{P}_\Gamma)$ *and two interfering aspects* $\Lambda_1 = (asId_{\Lambda_1}, map_{\Lambda_1}, \mathcal{P}_{\Lambda_1})$ *and* $\Lambda_2 = (asId_{\Lambda_2}, map_{\Lambda_2}, \mathcal{P}_{\Lambda_2})$. *A composition operator* opId *solves the interferences among* Λ_1 *and* Λ_2 *if the following condition holds:*

$$\mathcal{W}[\![\mathbf{weave}\ opId\ (asId_{\Lambda_1}\ map_{\Lambda_1})\ (asId_{\Lambda_2}\ map_{\Lambda_2})]\!]\ a_\Gamma \models$$
$$\mathcal{P}_\Gamma^{\Lambda_1} \wedge \mathcal{P}_\Gamma^{\Lambda_2} \wedge \mathcal{P}_{\Lambda_1} \wedge \mathcal{P}_{\Lambda_2}$$

We should mention here that our example is a large case study. It is instantiated with three users for the base system and two users for the extended version with aspects. The instantiation of the system with more users leads to state explosion in UPPAAL. However, in our example, merely one user is sufficient to detect the interference of Bonus and Alert, and two users are sufficient to detect the interference between the Bonus and the NetOverloading aspects. Currently, we tackle state explosion by system abstraction. With abstraction, only the components affected by aspects are specified as shown above, the others are replaced with one or more simplified processes. However, this may reduce the precision of systems and it is error prone especially when abstractions are made manually.

6. Catalog of operators for aspect composition

In this section we provide five abstract composition operators modeled as UPPAAL templates. Those templates can be instantiated for two arbitrary aspects and a set of concrete join points in order to solve their potential interferences. Each presented operator is given with a short explanation of its applicability and a motivation example to help users to select the right composition strategy. This extendible set of operators is, of course, not complete but it forms a first step towards a catalog of patterns for aspect interaction resolution. For space limitation, we show the structure of the first operator only and we only describe the semantics for the rest of operators. The semantic of operators is presented as a table showing how an operator behaves according to the actions taken by its left-hand side (LHS) and right-hand side (RHS) aspects. In the table, (-) denotes that an aspect is not called for a given join point.

6.1 Sequential composition operator

The use of the Seq operator is restricted to aspects sharing at least one join point. The Seq ensures a precedence between aspects, it is common to several aspect-oriented languages such as AspectJ [8]. In our proposal we adopt the use of the Seq operator as a default composition strategy for aspects sharing join points. The Seq operator forwards a shared join point to both aspects and proceeds a join point when at least one of the aspects proceeds it, otherwise, the join point is skipped. In addition, non shard join points are forwarded to their corresponding aspects only. Figure 9 depicts

the template modeling the Seq operator. In the figure, the intercepted call by both aspects (`lrhs?`) is forwarded to the first aspect (`left_lrhs!`), the decision of this aspect is saved in a local variable (`fstAct`), then the call is forwarded to the second aspect (`right_lrhs!`). The call continues its original path when the second aspect returns proceed (`proceed_right_lrhs?`) or it returns skip (`skip_right_lrhs?`) while the first aspect returns proceed (`proceed_left_lrhs?`). Two other cycles are used to forward no shared join points to their corresponding aspects (cycles starting with `lhs?` and `rhs?`).

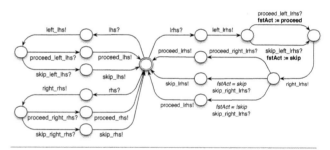

Figure 9. Seq template

6.2 Alternate composition operator

The Alt is used for two aspects that needed to be executed alternately on shared join points as shown between Bonus and Alert aspects. Thus for each shared join point, only one aspect is executed. This semantic is shown in Table 3, where `NbOcc(thisJP)` denotes the occurrence number of the current join point.

Pre	LHS	RHS	Alt(LHS,RHS)	Post
Shared join points				
NbOcc(thisJP)% 2=0	proceed	-	proceed	NbOcc(thisJP)++
	skip	-	skip	
NbOcc(thisJP)% 2=1	-	proceed	proceed	
	-	skip	skip	
LHS join points				
	proceed	-	proceed	
	skip	-	skip	
RHS join points				
	-	proceed	proceed	
	-	skip	skip	

Table 3. Alt operator semantic

Following the table, when a shared join point is captured, the number of occurrences of such join point is checked. If it is an odd number (resp. even number) the join point is forwarded to the LHS aspect (resp. RHS aspect), the number of occurrences of the join point is incremented and the action taken by the LHS aspect (resp. RHS aspect) is reported by the operator. No shared join points are forwarded to their corresponding aspects and their corresponding action is reported by the operator.

6.3 Conditional composition operator

The Cond operator is used for conditional dependency between aspects. That is the case where one aspect relies on state variables or any other effects generated from the execution of another aspect. In that case, both should be applied but the second is executed only when a predicate holds after the execution of the first aspect. One additional example of that previously presented above, is the case of a LegalAccess aspect that blocks the access to illegal IP addresses for minors. Since those addresses can be P2P, the manager may decide to apply the LegalAccess aspect behavior only for non first class customers. In that case, the Cond operator can be used between LegalAccess and NetOverloading aspects.

LHS	Post	Pre	RHS	Cond(p,LHS,RHS)
Shared join points				
proceed	maintain(p)	p	proceed	proceed
proceed	maintain(p)		skip	skip
skip	maintain(p)		-	skip
proceed	maintain(p)	!p	-	proceed
skip	maintain(p)		-	skip
LHS join points				
proceed			-	proceed
skip			-	skip
RHS join points				
-			proceed	proceed
-			skip	skip

Table 4. Cond operator semantic

The Cond operator (see Table 4) forwards each intercepted call to the first aspect and maintains a predicate "p" following the action taken by the aspect. According to the predicate, the call is forwarded to the second aspect or the action of the first aspect is directly taken. Another variant of this operator is designed to consider two aspects with no shared join points, it is shown in Table 5. In that variant, the predicate is maintained and stored when the action of the first aspect is taken on one join point and the predicate is evaluated later when another join point of interest of the second aspect is captured.

LHS	Post	Pre	RHS	Cond(p,LHS,RHS)
LHS join points				
proceed	maintain(p)		-	proceed
skip	maintain(p)		-	skip
RHS join points				
-		p	proceed	proceed
-			skip	skip
-		!p	-	proceed

Table 5. A variant of the Cond operator for no shared join points

6.4 Fst composition operator

The Fst operator can be used when two aspects implement two contradictory behaviors or two different algorithms for the same problem. The Fst can also be used for inclusion relation between aspects, this appears when all the properties of one aspect are satisfied when another aspect is applied. Take for example the case of another aspect that blocks P2P access for non first class customers when the system is overloaded. This property is satisfied by the NetOverloading aspect version presented in this paper and hence there is no reason to apply this new aspect when the former

is applicable. One more applicability case of the Fst operator is to hide some actions of aspects on specified join points.

LHS	RHS	Fst(LHS,RHS)
Shared join points / LHS join points		
proceed	-	proceed
skip	-	skip
RHS join points		
-	-	proceed

Table 6. Fst operator semantic

The Fst operator forwards to the first aspect all the intercepted shared join points and those of interest of the first aspect, and it proceeds all the join points of interest of the second aspect. Thus, only the first aspect is executed and the second aspect is never called. Table 6 shows the semantics associated to the Fst operator.

6.5 And composition operator

The And operator is used for the case where two aspects complement each other and should only be executed in a specific order otherwise an interference appears. Compared with Seq, the And operator proceeds a call only when it is proceeded by both aspects and skips a call when at least one of the aspects skips it (see Table 7). Consider for example the case of a LimitAccess aspect that counts the number of users being accessing to specific IP addresses and blocks the access to those addresses when a threshold number is reached. Since NetOverloading aspect blocks the access to P2P addresses when the system is overloaded, LimitedAccess must not count the skipped requests by NetOverloading aspect, otherwise the result number becomes erroneous.

LHS	RHS	And(LHS,RHS)
Shared join points		
proceed	proceed	proceed
proceed	skip	skip
skip	-	skip
LHS join points		
proceed	-	proceed
skip	-	skip
RHS join points		
-	proceed	proceed
-	skip	skip

Table 7. And operator semantic

7. Related Work

Interference detection and resolution is still a challenge for both features [11] and aspects [12]. However, few works are dedicated to analyze aspect interactions and composition in component models. In particular, JAsCo [13] is an aspectized component model and it provides an API to compose aspects in a programmatic way. But no interference detection support is provided. LEDA is a component framework and AspectLEDA [14] is its extension with aspects. Aspects in LEDA are represented by regular components and aspect execution is ordered following a predefined priority order.

Current works on features are focussing on domain specific interferences. In a recent work, Gouya et al. [15] propose an algorithm for feature interactions in IP multimedia subsystem (IMS). The algorithm uses a predefined interference rules based upon traces on service calls. Some of these interferences with their solutions are defined in a database, if the interference is not in the database, it is reported to the user. Several works are dedicated to aspect interference analysis in AOP. For example, Goldman et al. [16] model the base program, the aspects, and the woven system with state machines in order to formally check properties. Their weaving process is implemented by inlining the aspect state machine directly in the base system. Moreover, they focus on LTL and use two kinds of properties. First, they check if the base system satisfies aspect assumptions that enable their weaving. Second, they check if the woven system guarantees the expected behavior of aspects. The approach is limited to weave an aspect at a time and to only consider weakly invasive aspects. Moreover, when an interference is detected (*i.e.* a property is not satisfied) the programmer is responsible to fix it: they do not provide composition operators. Krishnamurthi et al. [17] also use state machines to model both aspects and base systems. However, the proposed approach defines a state machine for each advice. Moreover, the work is limited to treat aspects that do not modify data variables of base systems. Katz et al. [18] describe the expected behavior of aspects in LTL. In this work, a semi-automatic interactive process is proposed to define the assume-guarantee properties of aspects. Aspect interferences are checked independently of any base system by checking their guaranties properties. At the weaving stage, another check should be performed to show if the base system satisfies the assumptions of all the aspects to be woven. In [19] advices are annotated with assumptions about their composition. Interferences are detected by matching the assumptions of an advice and all the other advices. Finally, we should mention that our current proposal is a byproduct of our previous work on aspect interference detection and resolution [20] and formalization of aspects in a concurrent context [21]. The first work focuses on interferences at shared join points and introduces composition operators. The second models the woven system as FSP processes and checks properties with LTSA.

8. Conclusion

In this article, we have shown how to formally analyze aspect interferences in the context of component-based systems. First, a system is specified in an architecture description language (ADL) where primitive component behaviors and aspects are specified in UP-PAAL. Second, we have detailed a transformation scheme from ADL to UPPAAL generating a formal model of the complete system that can be model checked. This makes it possible to check whether the base system properties are violated by aspects and whether the desired properties of aspects are violated by aspect interferences. Third, our aspect advices explicitly return proceed or skip. This enables the definition of composition operators for aspects. We have proposed several operators and discussed how our approach makes it easy to define new ones. We have also formally modeled those operators which makes it possible to check whether a composition of aspects solves the interferences among them. In order to simplify and implement the ADL transformation to UP-PAAL network of automaton, we plan to use a model transformation framework such as Kermeta [23]. In addition, due to model checkers limitations and to avoid state explosion, we consider to provide a model transformer based on theorem provers such as B method [24]. Using B, each component and aspect can be modeled as machines that can be composed and checked using B tool. Another approach to prevent state explosion is to consider symbolic representation of states [25]. Note that our approach is not component model dependent. We have already shown how it can be applied to Fractal [5] and we plan to apply it to other models, this may require few adaptations. For example, Sofa [22] will require to extend our transformations in order to take into account component connectors for enabling several communication styles.

References

[1] C. Szyperski, D. Gruntz, and S. Murer, *Component Software: Beyond Object-Oriented Programming*, 2nd edition, ACM Press and Addison-Wesley, 2002.

[2] G. Kiczales and E. Hilsdale, "Aspect-oriented programming," in *ESEC-FSE*, p. 313, ACM, 2001.

[3] A. Hannousse, G. Ardourel, and R. Douence, "Views for aspectualizing component models," in *ACP4IS*, pp. 21–25, 2010.

[4] E. Bruneton, T. Coupaye, M. Leclercq, V. Quéma, and J.-B. Stefani, "The Fractal component model and its support in Java," *Software-Practice and Experience*, vol. 36, no. 11-12, pp. 1257–1284, 2006.

[5] A. Hannousse, R. Douence, and G. Ardourel, "Composable controllers in Fractal: Implementation and interference analysis," in *SEAA*, IEEE CS, to appear, 2011.

[6] G. Behrmann, A. David, and K. G. Larsen, "A tutorial on Uppaal," in *SFM-RT*, LNCS, vol. 3185, pp. 200–236, Springer-Verlag, 2004.

[7] O. Šery and F. Plášil, "Slicing of component behavior specification with respect to their composition," in *CBSE*, LNCS, vol. 4608, pp. 189–202, Springer, 2007.

[8] G. Kiczales, E. Hilsdale, J. Hugunin, M. Kersten, J. Palm, and W. G. Griswold, "An overview of AspectJ," in *ECOOP*, pp. 327–353, Springer-Verlag, 2001.

[9] K. G. Larsen, P. Pettersson, and W. Yi, "Uppaal in a nutshell," *International Journal on Software Tools for Technology Transfer*, vol. 1, pp. 134–152, 1997.

[10] T. Henzinger, X. Nicollin, J. Sifakis, and S. Yovine, "Symbolic model checking for real-time systems," *Information and Computation*, vol. 111, pp. 394 –406, 1992.

[11] M. Calder, M. Kolberg, E. H. Magill, and S. Reiff-Marganiec, "Feature interaction: a critical review and considered forecast," *Computer Networks*, vol. 41, no. 1, pp. 115 – 141, 2003.

[12] F. Sanen, E. Truyen, and W. Joosen, "Classifying and documenting aspect interactions," in *ACP4IS*, pp. 23–26, 2006.

[13] D. Suvée, W. Vanderperren, and V. Jonckers, "JAsCo: an aspect-oriented approach tailored for component based software development," in *AOSD*, pp. 21–29, ACM, 2003, .

[14] A. Navasa, M. A. Pérez-Toledano, and J. M. Murillo, "An ADL dealing with aspects at software architecture stage," *Information and Software Technology*, vol. 51, no. 2, pp. 306–324, 2009.

[15] A. Gouya and N. Crespi, "Detection and resolution of feature interactions in IP multimedia subsystem," *Int. J. Netw. Manag.*, vol. 19, pp. 315–337, 2009.

[16] M. Goldman, E. Katz, and S. Katz, "Maven: modular aspect verification and interference analysis," *Formal Methods in System Design*, vol. 37, pp. 61–92, 2010.

[17] S. Krishnamurthi and K. Fisler, "Foundations of incremental aspect model-checking," *ACM Transactions on Software Engineering and Methodology*, vol. 16, no. 2, pp. 1–39, 2007.

[18] E. Katz and S. Katz, "Incremental analysis of interference among aspects," in *FOAL*, pp. 29–38, ACM, 2008.

[19] A. Marot and R. Wuyts, "Detecting unanticipated aspect interferences at runtime with compositional intentions," in *RAM-SE*, pp. 31–35, ACM, 2009.

[20] R. Douence, P. Fradet, and M. Südhot, "Composition, reuse and interaction analysis of stateful aspects," in *AOSD*, pp. 141–150, ACM, 2004.

[21] R. Douence, D. L. Botlan, J. Noyé, and M. Südhot, "Concurrent aspects," in *GPCE*, pp. 79–88, ACM, 2006.

[22] T. Bures, P. Hnetynka, and F. Plasil, "Sofa 2.0: Balancing advanced features in a hierarchical component model," in *ICSER-MA*, pp. 40–48, IEEE CS, 2006.

[23] J.-M. Jézéquel, O. Barais, and F. Fleurey, "Model driven language engineering with Kermeta," in *GTTSE 3*, LNCS, vol. 6491, pp 201221. Springer Berlin/Heidelberg, 2011.

[24] D. Cansell, D. Mery, "Foundations of the B Method," *Journal of Computing and Informatics*, vol. 22, no. 3-4, pp. 221-256, 2003.

[25] A. Classen, P. Heymans, P.-Y. Schobbens, and A. Legay. "Symbolic model checking of software product lines", ICSE, ACM, 2011.

Infrastructure for Component-Based DDS Application Development *

William R. Otte, Aniruddha Gokhale, and
Douglas C. Schmidt

Dept of EECS, Vanderbilt University
{wotte,gokhale,schmidt}@dre.vanderbilt.edu

Johnny Willemsen

Remedy IT
jwillemsen@remedy.nl

Abstract

Enterprise distributed real-time and embedded (DRE) systems are increasingly being developed with the use of component-based software techniques. Unfortunately, commonly used component middleware platforms provide limited support for event-based publish/subscribe (pub/sub) mechanisms that meet both quality-of-service (QoS) and configurability requirements of DRE systems. On the other hand, although pub/sub technologies, such as OMG Data Distribution Service (DDS), support a wide range of QoS settings, the level of abstraction they provide make it hard to configure them due to the significant source-level configuration that must be hard-coded at compile time or tailored at run-time using proprietary, ad hoc configuration logic. Moreover, developers of applications using native pub/sub technologies must write large amounts of boilerplate "glue" code to support run-time configuration of QoS properties, which is tedious and error-prone. This paper describes a novel, generative approach that combines the strengths of QoS-enabled pub/sub middleware with component-based middleware technologies. In particular, this paper describes the design and implementation of DDS4CIAO which addresses a number of inherent and accidental complexities in the DDS4CCM standard. DDS4CIAO simplifies the development, deployment, and configuration of component-based DRE systems that leverage DDS's powerful QoS capabilities by provisioning DDS QoS policy settings and simplifying the development of DDS applications.

Categories and Subject Descriptors C.4 [*Computer Systems Organization*]: Performance of Systems—performance attributes; C.2.4 [*Software Engineering*]: Distributed Systems—components, deployment; D.2.11 [*Software Engineering*]: Software Architectures—domain-specific architectures

General Terms Software, Components, Deployment, Optimizations

* This work was supported in part by NSF CAREER 0845789 and CNS 0915976, and a contract from Northrop Grumman and AFRL GUTS. Any opinions, findings, and conclusions or recommendations expressed in this material are those of the author(s) and do not necessarily reflect the views of the National Science Foundation, AFRL, or NGC.

Keywords component-based real-time systems, predictable deployment

1. Introduction

The trend towards realizing enterprise distributed real-time and embedded (DRE) systems motivates the use of component-based middleware, such as the OMG's Lightweight CORBA Component Model (LwCCM) [11]. Component-based middleware offers DRE system developers significant flexibility in modularizing their system functionalities into reusable units, simplifies the deployment and configuration of the systems, and supports dynamic adaptation of system capabilities. Deployment and configuration standards, such as the OMG's Deployment and Configuration (D&C) specification [14], play a major role in realizing these capabilities.

Existing and planned enterprise DRE systems must increasingly support large data spaces generated by thousands of collaborating nodes, sensors, and actuators that must exchange information to detect changes in the operational environment, make sense of that information, and effect changes. These capabilities require scalable publish/subscribe (pub/sub) semantics [6] that support a range of QoS properties, that control properties, such as liveliness, latency, deadlines, timing, and reliability. Unfortunately, the conventional component technologies used to develop enterprise DRE systems either do not provide first class support for pub/sub semantics or do so in an ineffective manner that is not scalable and does not support real-time QoS properties.

A standardized, QoS-enabled pub/sub technology called the OMG Data Distribution Service (DDS) [12] has emerged as a promising pub/sub technology to support the requirements of enterprise DRE systems. DDS includes standard QoS policies and mechanisms to handle data (de)marshaling, node discovery and connection, and configuration. Middleware based on the DDS standard has been applied successfully in mission-critical domains, such as air traffic management systems [5] and tactical information systems [7].

While the DDS specification simplifies key implementation aspects of pub/sub application, these benefits come at price of increased complexity of configuration glue code that must be written and maintained. Moreover, this configuration boilerplate code tightly couples the QoS configuration of a DDS application at compile-time, unless application developers create ad hoc methods of specifying the middleware configuration at run-time. Analysis [1] has shown that as 80% percent of DDS-related code in a typical applications is associated with configuring the middleware. Likewise, over half of the DDS API that developers must learn is configuration-related.

Addressing these deployment and configuration requirements of modern DRE systems calls for component-based middleware, such as LwCCM, to provide first-class support for QoS-enabled, pub/-sub technologies, such as DDS. This need has been recognized and documented through the efforts of industry and academic collaborators in the OMG *DDS for Lightweight CCM* (DDS4CCM) [13] specification. Implementing this specification is hard, however, due to inherent and accidental complexities in integrating LwCCM and DDS. The inherent complexities stem from (1) differences in the language bindings and memory management strategies of the two middleware technologies, (2) incompatibilities between the various specifications, (3) deployment and configuration challenges to recognize DDS abstractions within LwCCM, and supporting variants of DDS in a single LwCCM implementation. The accidental complexities stem from (1) manual approaches to creating the deployment and configuration metadata for DDS elements within LwCCM, and (2) the need to minimize run-time overhead imposed by both the deployment and configuration metadata, and the additional abstraction atop native DDS.

This paper describes how we have integrated LwCCM and DDS to address the inherent and accidental complexities described above as follows:

1. We make systematic use of the extensible interface pattern in the form of mixins to extend existing interfaces as well as the deployment and configuration metadata to bridge the incompatibilities between the two technologies.

2. We describe a template-driven code generation approach that maximizes the potential for portability between various DDS implementations and maximizes maintainability.

3. We provide options to customize the integration, which ensures that the runtime footprint of the resulting system does not pay unwanted memory footprint penalties.

4. We support improvements to the D&C approach mandated by the DDS4CCM specification.

Our contributions enable the realization of a product-line of DDS4CCM systems where it is possible to vary the implementations of the DDS technology used as well as support a wide range of port types for the LwCCM component technology. Empirical evaluations of our approach demonstrate that our implementation of the DDS4CCM specification, which we call DDS4CIAO, substantially eases the development of DDS-based applications while providing performance almost identical to native DDS applications.

The remainder of this paper is organized as follows. Section 2 summarizes key challenges encountered when integrating DDS within LwCCM; Section 3 describes the design of DDS4CIAO that resolves the challenges described in Section 2.3; Section 4 examines the code generation of DDS4CIAO and analyzes the results of experiments that evaluate the performance of DDS4-CIAO; Section 5 compares DDS4CIAO with related work, and Section 6 presents concluding remarks.

2. Impediments to Integrating LwCCM and DDS

In this section we present both the inherent and accidental challenges in providing first class support for Data Distribution Service (DDS) within the Lightweight CORBA Component Model (Lw-CCM).[1] To better appreciate these challenges, we first provide an overview of LwCCM and DDS, and the deployment and configuration standard. Subsequently we elaborate on the challenges.

---

[1] The LwCCM is a subset of the OMG CORBA Component Model. In the rest of this paper we refer to LwCCM because of our focus on DRE systems but the issues apply equally well to CCM.

2.1 Overview of Relevant Middleware Technologies

This section provides an overview of OMG LwCCM and OMG DDS.

2.1.1 The Lightweight CORBA Component Model (LwCCM)

The OMG Lightweight CCM (LwCCM) [11] specification standardizes the development, configuration, and deployment of component-based applications. LwCCM uses CORBA's distributed object computing model as its underlying architecture, so applications are not tied to any particular language or platform for their implementations. *Components* in LwCCM are the implementation entities that export a set of interfaces usable by conventional middleware clients as well as other components. Components can also express their intent to collaborate with other components by defining *ports*, including (1) *facets*, which define an interface that accepts point-to-point method invocations from other components, (2) *receptacles*, which indicate a dependency on point-to-point method interface provided by another component, and (3) *event sources/sinks*, which indicate a willingness to exchange typed messages with one or more components.

Homes are factories that shield clients from the details of component creation strategies and subsequent queries to locate component instances. A container in LwCCM provides an operating environment that can be configured and shared by components requiring a common set of QoS policies and functional support.

2.1.2 The OMG Deployment and Configuration

The OMG Deployment and Configuration (D&C) specification [14] provides standard interchange formats for metadata used throughout the component application development lifecycle, as well as runtime interfaces used for packaging and planning. Figure 1 depicts an architectural overview of the OMG D&C model.

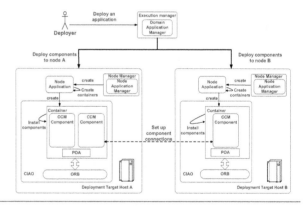

Figure 1. An Overview of OMG Deployment and Configuration Model

The runtime interfaces defined by the OMG D&C specification for deployment and configuration consists of the two-tier architecture comprising a set of global entities used to coordinate deployment and a set of node-level entities used to instantiate component instances and configure their connections and QoS properties. In addition to the runtime entities described above, the D&C specification also contains an extensive data model that is used to describe component applications throughout their deployment lifecycle. The D&C metadata defined by the data model contains a section where arbitrary configuration information may be included in the form of a sequence of name/value pairs, where the value may be an arbitrary data type. This configuration information is used to describe everything from basic configuration information (such as shared library entrypoints and component/container associations) to more complex configuration information (such as QoS properties or initialization of component attributes with user-defined data types).

2.1.3 Overview of the OMG Data Distribution Service (DDS)

The OMG DDS specification [12] defines a standard architecture for exchanging data in pub/sub systems. DDS provides a global data store in which publishers and subscribers write and read data, respectively. DDS provides flexibility and modular structure by decoupling: (1) *location*, via anonymous publish/subscribe, (2) *redundancy*, by allowing any numbers of readers and writers, (3) *time*, by providing asynchronous, time-independent data distribution, and (4) *platform*, by supporting a platform-independent model that can be mapped to different platform-specific models, such as C++ running on VxWorks or Java running on Real-time Linux.

DDS entities include *topics*, which describe the type of data to be written or read, *data readers*, which subscribe to the values or instances of particular topics, and *data writers*, which publish values or instances for particular topics. Moreover, *publishers* manage groups of data writers and *subscribers* manage groups of data readers.

Properties of these entities can be configured using combinations of DDS-supported QoS policies. Each QoS policy has ~2 parameters, with the bulk of the parameters having a large number of possible values, *e.g.*, a parameter of type long or character string. DDS provides a wide range of QoS capabilities that can be configured to meet the needs of topic-based distributed systems with diverse QoS requirements. DDS' flexible configurability, however, requires careful management of interactions between various QoS policies so that the system behaves as expected. It is incumbent upon the developer to use the QoS policies appropriately and judiciously.

2.2 Addressing Limitations in the LwCCM Port System via DDS4CCM

The OMG's DDS4CCM [13] specification was developed to overcome the following limitations in LwCCM and DDS while still preserving the inherent advantages of each technology.

Limitation 1: Support for event-based pub/sub communication in LwCCM is extremely limited. LwCCM does not specify a particular distribution middleware that must be used inside the container for communicating events. While this approach allows a substantial amount of flexibility on the part of implementation authors, allowing them to choose to implement this support using, for example, the CORBA Event Service or CORBA Notification Service, has two important drawbacks. First, the integration of new pub/sub middleware requires modification of not only the core container implementation, but potentially also the deployment and configuration infrastructure in order to properly operate. As a result, this is an extremely complex task, often requiring that the integrator be an expert in both the LwCCM implementation and the desired distribution middleware.

Second, in order to remain completely generic, the interface available to component developers for event-based communication consists of only two operations: 1) a single method per port that allows for a single event to be published at a time, and 2) a single callback operation that provides an event to the component as it arrives. This prevents the component from taking advantage of many features of pub/sub messaging middleware that provide for status notifications and per-message QoS adjustment.

Limitation 2: Grouping of related services must be done in an ad-hoc manner. In many cases, services offered by a component require more than one interface in order to provide correct operation. As a simple example, consider a scenario in which two components expect to cooperate via mutually connected interfaces. In this scenario, one component provides an interface "A" and requires an interface "B", while another component provides complementary ports (*i.e.,* provides "B" but requires "A"). In order for semantically correct operation, the connections for both "A" and "B" must go to the same component, but there exists no way in LwCCM to indicate this constraint on an interface level. To accomplish this goal, developers must rely on ad-hoc naming conventions and documentation. This approach has the unfortunate side effect of complicating the planning process and potentially causing subtle and pernicious run-time errors if connections are mis-configured.

The DDS4CCM specification addresses these limitations by enabling LwCCM to leverage the powerful pub/sub mechanisms of DDS. First, it provides a substantially simplified API to the application developer that completely removes the configuration of the DDS middleware from the scope of the application developer. Second, it provides a set of ready-to-use ports that hide the complexity and groups data writing/access API with the appropriate callback and status interfaces. Third, by providing integration with the LwCCM container, DDS applications are now able to take advantage of robust and mature deployment and configuration technologies that obviates the need to write boilerplate application startup code, run-time configuration of QoS policies, and coordinated startup and teardown of applications across multiple nodes.

In particular, DDS4CCM proposes two new constructs — *extended ports*, which allow for the grouping of related services, and *connectors*, which allow for flexible integration of new distribution middleware. These new entities are defined using an extension of the IDL language for components (IDL3) called IDL3+. It is possible to map each of these new IDL3+ language constructs back to basic IDL3 using simple mapping rules to enable inseparability with older CCM implementations. Next, we provide a brief overview of these enhancements.

Extended Ports: Extended ports provide a mechanism whereby component designers can group semantically related ports to create coherent services offered by a component. These extended ports, defined using a new IDL keyword `porttype`, are defined outside the scope of components. Extended ports are allowed to contain any number of standard LwCCM ports in either direction. While these ports are allowed in terms of the specification to contain standard LwCCM event ports, in practice this is highly unlikely due to the limitations outlined earlier. Moreover, in combination with connectors (described next), these extended port definitions could be used to recreate the behavior of the existing standard CCM event infrastructure.

Listing 1 shows IDL for an example extended port. In this example, we create a service whereby one component may notify another of data that is ready to be sent, and the destination component may optionally choose to pull that data from the source component. Since each of the interfaces `Data_Source` and `Notifier` are semantically linked, *i.e.*, operation of the component application would be fundamentally broken if these ports are not pairwise connected, they are grouped into a single `porttype`. This is an indication to both high level modeling tools and the component run-time that these ports must be connected as a pair, and can generate appropriate deployment plan meta-data to connect them at run-time. Extended ports are assigned to components using two new IDL3+ keywords. The `port` keyword indicates that the component supports the extended port *as described*. The `mirrorport` keyword indicates that the component *inverts* the direction of the extended port, *i.e.*, facets become receptacles.

Listing 1. Extended Port IDL

```
interface Data_Source {
  Data pull (in long uuid);
};
```

```
interface Notifier {
    void data_ready (in long uuid);
};
porttype NotifiedData {
    provides Data_Source data_source;
    uses Notifier data_ready;
};
component Sender {
    port NotifiedData data_out;
};
component Receiver {
    mirrorport NotifiedData data_in;
};
```

Some extended ports may vary only in the data type used as parameters. In order to avoid the necessity of re-defining an extended port for each new data type, IDL3+ offers a new template syntax that may be used to define services that are generic with respect to data type.

Connectors: While the extended port feature described above is quite useful, their power is most suited to providing novel communications mechanisms to components that provide/use those interfaces. In order for the extended ports to provide a coherent interface to a new distribution middleware, such as DDS or the CORBA Event Service, the business logic that supports that abstraction must be contained in some entity. This unit of business logic is called a *connector*. Connectors combine one or more extended ports to provide well-defined interfaces to new distribution middleware or communication techniques between components. In many cases, a single connector will support at least two extended ports, one intended for each "side" of the communications channel. By separating the core communications business logic, these connectors can then be used as COTS components across several applications without requiring modification of the core container code.

Connectors are defined similar to a component, using the new IDL3+ keyword `connector`. Connectors may contain, of course, one or more extended ports. In addition, they may also support attributes which are intended to be used to assist in runtime configuration, *i.e.* topic names, port numbers, QoS parameters, *etc.*. Finally, connectors also support inheritance which can be used to extend existing connectors with new capabilities. At runtime, instead of creating a new IDL type structure for the connector infrastructure, they are defined as components, deriving their interface from the same `CCMObject` used by regular components. Indeed, in the IDL3+ to IDL3 mapping, the `connector` keyword becomes `component`. This approach is much desirable in that no additional work is necessary in the D&C toolchain to support the deployment and configuration of connectors. Moreover, connector implementations can take advantage of the same Component Implementation Framework that is available to standard LwCCM components and thus can take advantage of advances in services offered by the container.

2.3 Challenges in Integrating LwCCM and DDS

Although the DDS4CCM specification attempts to address the limitations of individual technologies, realizing an implementation of the DDS4CCM specification is fraught with multiple inherent and accidental complexities explained below:

Challenge 1: Indicating that a connector implementation has been fully configured, and should be made ready for execution. After a connector implementation has received all necessary configuration information, it must proceed to create the underlying low-level DDS entities (*e.g.*, `DomainParticipant`, `DataWriter` and/or `DataReader`) that are necessary for correct operation. To accomplish this task, the specification mandates the use of an oper-

ation called `configuration_complete` on the external connector interface. This operation, however, is not delegated to the connector business logic and thus is insufficient to fully inform the connector implementation of completed configuration. Section 3.1 discusses our approach to resolve this challenge.

Challenge 2: Reducing D&C-related runtime memory footprint. The DDS4CCM specification mandates the use of LwCCM Homes (which nominally act as factories for component instances) as the primary vehicle for passing configuration information from the deployment plan to individual connector implementation during deployment. While this approach is certainly functional and sound (and in keeping with the spirit of the LwCCM specification), our experience developing component applications with LwCCM reveals that the home entity often adds very little value to the configuration of individual component, or in this case connector, instances. In most cases, the home implementation is little more than a simple factory that directly instantiates the component and nothing else. Meanwhile, the home instance carries a non-negligible amount of runtime footprint due to the CORBA interface and accompanying home-specific generated container code that is necessary. Section 3.2 discusses our approach to resolve this challenge.

Challenge 3: Reducing Connector-related runtime memory footprint. The decision to treat connectors for all intents and purposes as full LwCCM components greatly simplifies the implementation by substantially reducing the number of changes in the core container necessary to support the specification. A consequence of this decision, however, is that the runtime footprint of a LwCCM application using connectors could substantially increase. For example, assuming a deployment where each component instance has an associated connector instance, the number of actual "components" in the deployment is doubled. In memory-constrained DRE systems, this can be a significant impediment. Section 3.3 discusses our approach to resolve this challenge.

Challenge 4: Supporting Local Interfaces as Facets All of the extended ports contained in the DDS4CCM specification are defined as "local interfaces". Local interfaces are significantly different from standard CORBA interfaces due to the fact that they are not generated with any of the infrastructure necessary to support remote invocation. As a result, any invocation on these interfaces does not travel through the CORBA internal infrastructure and as such only incurs overhead nominally involved in a virtual method invocation. The problem this strategy causes with the deployment and configuration aspect of LwCCM is very subtle: since these local interfaces lack the necessary remoting code, it is impossible to pass references to these local objects through a standard CORBA interface. Indeed, this behavior is undefined; any attempt to do so will fail and cause an exception to be propagated to the caller. Unfortunately, all of the standard-defined connection methods, including the Component Navigation interfaces used by the D&C tooling to make connections between components rely on being able to retrieve object references to Facets over a standard CORBA interface and pass these references to the receptacle component over a similar interface. Not having an object reference for the extended port implies that the existing D&C tooling cannot be leveraged in a straightforward manner. Section 3.4 discusses our approach to resolve this challenge.

Challenge 5: Supporting Multiple DDS Implementations One significant benefit of writing DDS applications using the DDS4CCM API is that it potentially makes it substantially easier to switch between various DDS implementations. Prior work [16] has shown that differences in the architecture between these different implementations cause them to have different strengths depending on the architecture of the application and hardware environment. Moreover, due to the proprietary nature of most DDS implementations and the different licensing requirements of each implementation, the ability to quickly and easily switch the targeted implementation would greatly facilitate the development of COTS DDS components. While it is currently possible to target multiple DDS implementations *at compile time* due to the presence of a standard API, subtle differences in the implementations of these APIs can make this difficult to accomplish. Ideally, any implementation of the DDS4CCM specification would be architected in such a way that the core business logic of the connector is shielded from the differences between DDS implementations. In addition, the connector architecture could make it possible to delay the choice of DDS implementation from compile time to deployment time. Section 3.5 discusses our approach to resolve this challenge.

Challenge 6: Making it easy for users to define their own connectors The DDS4CCM specification provides for two connector types that correspond to common DDS usage patterns. The first provides for a state transfer pattern, and is intended to connect "Observable" components that publish state to other "Observer" components that consume that state. The second provides for event transfer connecting supplier components to consumer components. These two connectors, however, are not intended to be the only ones that are supported in the context of the specification. To that end, two "base" connectors are provided that collect the various configuration meta-data as attributes. It is intended that users be able to define their own connectors that are better suited to their usage cases. To support this capability, the code generation techniques should be extensible such that it is easy for users to create their own connectors without having to modify the code generators. Section 3.6 discusses our approach to resolve this challenge.

3. Resolving LwCCM and DDS Integration Challenges in DDS4CIAO

This section describes how we resolved the challenges in integrating LwCCM with DDS described in Section 2.3 by presenting the architectural and design choices made for DDS4CIAO, which is our implementation of the DDS for Lightweight CCM specification outlined in Section 2.2.

3.1 Accurate Indication of Successful Connector Configuration

The central difficulty outlined in **Challenge 1** from Section 2.3 revolves around the final configuration stage of the D&C process. In this case, there lies a crucial phase before the application is "activated", but after it is fully configured. In this portion of the D&C process, the connector business logic must make themselves ready for execution by, for example, instantiating various DDS entities. In Figure 2, which shows the lifecycle stages that connectors and components go through, this is represented by the "Passive" state. Unfortunately, the LwCCM specification currently provides no mechanism to communicate to the connector that it has entered this state; the only notification that is received when the component/connector becomes passive is when the prior state was "Active". To understand the reason for this, it is best to have a grasp of the layout of connectors and components at runtime.

Instantiated connectors consist of two primary pieces. First, there is a "Servant", which consists of the external CORBA interface and connector-specific container code. The Servant has two primary parts to its interface: (1) operations common to all connectors which come from the LwCCM specification (called the CCMObject interface), and (2) operations that result from the ports specified in the IDL declaration of the connector. Second is the "Executor", which contains the actual business logic that implements the connector. Operations on this interface result from two sources: (1) specification-defined lifecycle operations (called the

Figure 2. LwCCM Component and Connector Lifecycle Stages

SessionComponent interface), and (2) operations that result from the ports defined for the connector.

The configuration_complete operation mentioned in Section 2.3 is part of the CCMObject interface but is not, however, present on the SessionComponent interface so it cannot be directly delegated.[2] Unfortunately, the first lifecycle operation that is invoked on the Executor interface after its construction as defined by the LwCCM specification is ccm_activate. This lifecycle operation, however, must be disjoint from and occur later than configuration_complete.

One approach to work around this problem is to delay the creation of the DDS entities until the activation phase of the application lifecycle. This is problematic, however, because there exists no guarantee that a connector fragment will be activated *before* its connected component. If a component is activated before its connector and attempts to initiate outbound communication, that communication would naturally fail, potentially causing pernicious and difficult to reproduce errors. The ability for component business logic to receive a notification upon configuration completion but before activation has proven to be useful for components as well as connectors because connectors are anyway treated as components.

As a result, we have created a new interface that may be optionally used to extend the behavior of component executors to be able to receive these notifications. This interface, which we call ConfigurableComponent, uses a variation of the extension interface pattern to avoid changing the standard-defined SessionComponent interface. This new interface is intended to act as a mixin so that the component implementations wishing to receive configuration_complete will inherit from this in addition to the standard SessionComponent interface. The container, then, when it receives configuration_complete from the D&C tooling, will attempt a dynamic cast on the component implementation to determine if the operation should be delegated on a per-component basis.

3.2 Avoiding D&C-related Memory Footprint

Challenge 2, described in Section 2.3, deals with eliminating unnecessary footprint from the specification-defined deployment and configuration requirements of connectors. DDS4CCM connectors are configured via attributes present in the IDL interfaces defined by the specification, which allow for the fragment to be associated with a particular DDS domain and topic as well as the QoS policies.

Many hardware platforms commonly used for DRE systems remain extremely memory-constrained, so the additional run-time memory footprint imposed by the CCM home is at best undesirable. To avoid this additional overhead, DDS4CIAO provides the capability to install "un-homed" components and connectors. These un-homed components are allocated from simple factory functions exported from their implementation libraries in much the same manner that Homes are already constructed. Component-specific con-

---

[2] This artifact results from the standards specification.

tainer code, which is generated automatically from IDL, is then able to interpret the D&C plan meta-data and individually invoke the attribute setter methods on the component.

3.3 Reducing Connector-Related Memory Footprint

The solution **Challenge 3**, described in Section 2.3, attempts to reduce the runtime footprint of connector implementations. In order to accomplish this goal, we must determine which, if any services that a component requires that are not necessary for connector implementations. Given the limitations of the standard LwCCM event ports described in Section 2.2, it is highly unlikely that these inflexible port types would be used in the context of a connector — indeed, the extended port/connector infrastructure could be used to fabricate replacement infrastructure. Moreover, the DDS4CCM specification makes no use of the existing event infrastructure, making it an apt candidate for removal.

As a result, we sought to remove the event infrastructure from the connector infrastructure in such a way that it would still be present for standard components that may need to interface with legacy systems. In this case, there are two pieces to the event support in DDS4CIAO: (1) the base classes that provide support to the component-specific generated container code, and (2) the component-specific generated container code itself, which includes a component-specific context that provides services to the component business logic. The first portion of the event support — the base classes described above were split into two pieces — a *connector* base and a *component* base. The container base contains all necessary functionality for component and connectors minus the LwCCM event support. The necessary plumbing LwCCM event support is contained in the component base, which derives from the connector base. This way the code generation infrastructure can choose to omit support for the event infrastructure if desired by selecting a different base class for the generated code. Our approach makes this artifact configurable.

3.4 Supporting Local Facets

The solution to **Challenge 4** outlined in Section 2.3 is threefold. First, and most obviously, the Navigation and Introspection implementations generated for components with local facets and receptacles had to be modified to suppress any knowledge of these local ports. While this approach solves the issue of undefined behavior from trying to marshal one of these local object references, it also completely removes any standards-based mechanism by which a connection can be made by either the D&C tooling or any user attempting to use the Navigation interfaces. To address this undesired effect, a new connection API was created in the private interface to the CIAO container (which is our LwCCM implementation) that is used directly by the D&C tooling. This API accepts as arguments the string identifiers of two component endpoints as well as port names, and is able to use these to obtain references to the local Executor objects directly and create a connection without needing to marshal any local references over standard interfaces.

In order to make use of this new API, however, the D&C tooling needs an annotation on the connection meta-data so that it can be made aware that it should not attempt to use the standard Navigation API to make the connection. The data structure in the deployment plan that contains connection information encodes the type of connection (*e.g.*, Facet vs. Receptacle) as an enumerated value. While this enumeration could be extended to identify a new connection type (*i.e.*, LocalFacet), we endeavored to minimize changes to specification-defined types. The connection data structure does contain a section where requirements for deployments can be described using name/value pairs. This section would ordinarily be used to enumerate hardware capabilities or resources required by the connection. In this case, we require that any local facet con-

nected be annotated with a requirement on the container, namely that it provide support for local facets — when the D&C tooling encounters this annotation it assumes the connection to be local.

3.5 Ensuring Portability of DDS4CIAO Implementation

As described in **Challenge 5** from Section 2.3, we would like to ensure that the design of the infrastructure is maximally portable in order to easily support implementations from multiple DDS vendors. This goal is complicated by the fact that despite the presence of a standard C++ language mapping, there are subtle and pernicious differences between the actual implementations of these mappings. Moreover, there exist also subtle behavioral differences between implementations that complicate source-level compatibility, *i.e.*, generated type-specific constructs such as `DataWriters` and `DataReaders` may have different namespaces and naming conventions, and indeed the same may be true of the entire API.

We addressed this challenge by using three approaches. The first approach targets the API that we wrote the implementations of the DDS4CCM basic ports against. The DDS specification, in addition to the widely supported C/C++ language binding, also has a language binding that maps the API into IDL interface definitions. This language binding is not widely implemented, but provides a promising vehicle for implementing portable DDS business logic in the context of the DDS4CCM basic ports. Since we are using the same IDL code generator as with the rest of the CIAO infrastructure, we can ensure that the APIs we are using to implement these ports are consistent.

Much of the work for supporting different DDS implementations then can be accomplished by providing an implementation of this IDL language binding. At first glance, this may seem a daunting proposition — however, this binding consists of only about 36 interfaces, many of whose functions may be directly delegated to the native implementation. The remaining problem with using this IDL-based approach is reconciling the differences between the CORBA types that are part of the IDL language mapping and the data types used natively by the DDS implementation. While this conversion could be handled inside the vendor-specific implementation of the IDL language binding, this approach would incur potentially expensive data copies. Fortunately, many DDS implementations provide a CORBA compatibility layer that allows them to directly use types generated by the IDL compiler.

3.6 Connector Code Generation

Generating code for user-defined connectors is the focus of **Challenge 6** from Section 2.3. Our experience developing code generators for our CORBA and LwCCM implementations has shown us that it is eminently undesirable to embed large amounts of business logic in generated code. This is largely due to the difficulty of maintaining and extending the code generators themselves. If there is a bug, modification, or extension to be made, this effort often involves at least two engineers — one who is familiar with the middleware or problem at hand, and another who is familiar with the process of extending and modifying the code generator. In addition to the extra personnel requirements, it often substantially increases the amount of time to test these changes, as not only does the initial proposed modification needs to be tested (typically supplied to the code generation engineer as a handcrafted generated file), but also the final changes to the code generator and resulting modified output. For the same reason, this accidental complexity of the code generation process impedes the ability of users to create their own DDS4CCM connectors.

In order to avoid these accidental complexities, we designed the code generation infrastructure from the outset to contain zero DDS-4CCM business logic and to be extensible **without** the need to modify the code generator to add new connector implementations. The first, and most obvious step given the presence of parameterized modules from Section 2.2, was to leverage C++ templates for the implementations of the basic and extended DDS4CCM port types. Using C++ templates in this case allowed us to make generic two very important parts of the implementation − first, the core DDS-4CCM business logic contained in the basic and extended DDS-4CCM ports, but also the IDL wrapper (described in Section 3.5) around our target DDS implementation. These IDL wrappers require access to type-specific DDS entities (*e.g.* `DataWriters` and `Data Readers`) that are created by the code generation infrastructure that is part of the DDS implementation itself.

Connector implementations, then, are really a collection of template instantiations for the various basic and extended ports that are contained in their interface definition along with some configuration glue code. While we could certainly generate the source code for these connector implementations, that would still represent an obstacle to novel connector creation. Connectors themselves may contain a nontrivial amount of configuration business logic that interprets the values of attributes on the connector interface. As a result, if a user were to define a new connector with new configuration attributes, they would be required to modify the code generator to be able to use their new connector.

To address this concern, we elected to make connector implementations template classes as well. This allows the code generator for DDS4CCM to be extremely simple. In effect, the result of the code generation process is a header file that contains a set of C++ traits [10] which specify the properties necessary to use a particular IDL data type. These properties largely consist of the names of type-specific entities that are generated from the DDS infrastructure. These traits are then used to create concrete template instantiations of any required connector implementations. By default, we generate instantiations of the standard DDS4CCM connectors − the State and Event connectors described in Section 2.3. If a user defines their own connector in IDL, the code generator emits an include of a header file whose name derives from the name of the connector in IDL, and a concrete instantiation of a template class whose name is similarly derived. While the user must then provide an implementation of this template class, this is substantially less effort than would be required to modify the code generator.

4. Experimental Results

This section outlines two key empirical observations of the DDS4CIAO implementation described in Section 3 which cover two important goals outlined in Section 1. First, in Section 4.2, we quantify the impact that the code generation capabilities of DDS4CIAO have on the development and maintenance of DDS-enabled applications. Second, in Section 4.3, we characterize the overhead that DDS-enabled applications must pay in terms of latency when using the DDS4CIAO abstraction versus using the DDS API directly.

4.1 Experimental Scenario

All results described below were obtained using a simple "ping-pong" application. We chose a simple example since the business logic of the application is not important to evaluate the qualities of DDS4CIAO. Rather we are interested in understanding the overhead, if any, of the integration of LwCCM with DDS. In this application, an instance struct containing an octet sequence of a configured length and a sequence number would be written to the DDS data space by a "Sender". The instance would arrive at a "Receiver" entity, after which a new instance of the struct would be published on a separate topic with an identical sequence number but a zero length octet sequence. The "Sender", upon receipt of the second message, repeats the process with a new sequence number up to a specified number of iterations.

Two versions of this application were produced. The first uses the native C++ DDS API, with all customary error checking included. In the second version, the "Sender" and "Receiver" were each implemented as CIAO components and used DDS4CIAO to interface with the DDS middleware.

4.2 Evaluation of Code Generation

To evaluate the effectiveness of the code generation techniques described in Section 3.6, the implementation source files from the experimental scenario outlined in Section 4.1 were analyzed with the SLOCCount [15] tool. This is a program which counts physical Source Lines of Code (SLOC), and uses a number of heuristics to discard any whitespace and commenting present. For the purposes of this evaluation, only implementation source files were counted, discarding header files containing only class definitions. The reason for this is that header files for the DDS4CIAO implementation are largely generated automatically based on the class interfaces.

The results from this tool are summarized in Table 1. If only the total SLOC for the native programs and the component implementations are compared, DDS4CIAO shows only a nominal improvement over that of the native implementation. It is important to consider, however, that the DDS4CIAO implementation contains a large amount of generated class skeletons which are created from the IDL interface descriptions from the component automatically (SLOC for which is shown in the "DDS4CIAO Generated" column of the table). When these lines of code are subtracted from the total for the DDS4CIAO implementation, the improvement becomes substantially more dramatic. In the case of the Sender component, the improvement is on the order of 50%, and for the receiver the difference is an order of magnitude. The reason for this discrepancy is the Sender programs − both native and DDS4CIAO − contains a substantial amount of code in common to measure latencies and calculate/display results.

Table 1. Comparison of Source Lines of Code

Compo- nent	Native Lines	DDS4CIAO Total	DDS4CIAO Generated	DDS4CIAO Actual
Sender	643	560	211	349
Receiver	293	128	118	10

4.3 Evaluation of the Overhead of DDS4CIAO

To evaluate the overhead due to abstraction over the native DDS API introduced by the DDS4CIAO implementation, the experimental scenario described earlier in Section 4.1 was used to evaluate the latency performance using a recent commercial DDS implementation and DDS4CIAO 0.8.3. Each configuration was executed for 1,000 iterations each with payload sizes along powers 2, from 16 to 8192 bytes. Each experimental run was executed in two transport configurations: once using UDP and again using Shared Memory transport. The experimental testbed consisted of Dell Optiplex 755 computers, with an Intel E4400 CPU, 2GB of RAM, and gigabit network connections.

The results for the experimental runs with the UDP transport protocol are shown in Figure 3, which compares the average latency for each payload size, and Figure 4, which compares the minimum latency results for each payload size. These results show that for this transport protocol, the average latencies are nearly identical. Figure 5 shows the results from the experimental runs configured with the shared memory transport. This average latency result shows that the DDS4CIAO abstraction introduces approximately a four percent overhead over the native implementation for the shared memory transport. The best case results for the shared memory experiment are shown in Figure 6.

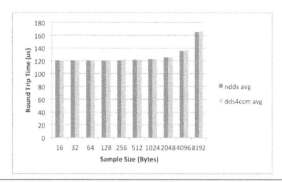

Figure 3. Ping Latency Average with UDP

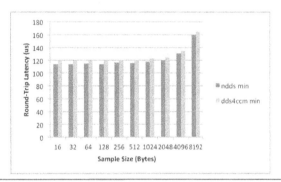

Figure 4. Ping Latency Minimum with UDP

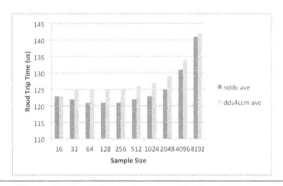

Figure 5. Ping Latency Average with Shared Memory

Table 2 summarizes the standard deviation of the experimental runs for both UDP and shared memory. These results show that the DDS4CIAO abstraction does not introduce additional jitter over the native implementation.

5. Related Work

This section compares our research on component-based DDS with related work.

PocoCapsule [8] is an Inversion of Control container based on the Dependency Injection (DI) design pattern. This component framework allows developers to use "Plain Old C++ Objects" (POCO) that have been decorated with PocoCapsule macros that allow the loading of these C++ classes into a PocoCapsule container. DDS4CCM and DDS4CIAO differ in several important aspects from PocoCapsule. First, DDS4CCM—and LwCCM in general—are industry standards that have language bindings defined for many programming languages. Second, PocoCapsule still requires some amount of low-level glue code in the component business

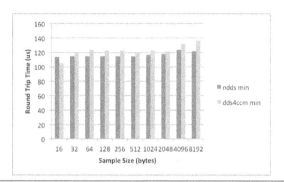

Figure 6. Ping Latency Minimum with Shared Memory

Table 2. Standard Deviation For All Experiments

Size	UDP	CIAO UDP	Shared	CIAO Shared
16	11.3	12.4	17.7	18.4
32	12.4	9.4	15	14.2
64	12.5	12.6	15.5	9.9
128	13.3	9.3	16	10.4
256	6.2	13.1	15.9	12.6
512	12.3	11.2	11.6	8.8
1024	14.7	8.1	15.7	12.1
2048	12.7	4.3	15.5	14.8
4096	7.1	13.7	15.3	10.8
8192	12.1	17.7	15.1	14.4

logic. Third, the DDS for PocoCapsule implementation currently only uses CORBA local interfaces to simulate small parts of the DDS API, and hence is not operable with standard-compliant DDS implementations.

Simple API for DDS (SimD) [2] uses C++ templates and template meta-programming to provide a simpler API for DDS that reduces the amount of infrastructure-related code required for DDS applications by an order of magnitude. Using SimD, a simple DDS application can be written in only 4 source hand-written lines of code, instead of dozens lines of code using the native API. While SimD reduces the complexity of the boilerplate code required for DDS applications, it differs substantially from DDS4CIAO in that it does not address run-time deployment and configuration capabilities provided by DDS4CIAO. Moreover, it has not yet been proposed as a standard.

Researchers at Real-Time Innovations, Inc [1] propose extensions to the DDS API to allow declarative configuration of DDS entities via an XML file that is interpreted at run-time. The application then queries the DDS middleware to obtain a particular `DataReader` or `DataWriter` that has been configured already with a domain and topic binding and QoS settings. While their work improves the state-of-the-practice in standards-based DDS application configuration, its capabilities are not as extensive as DDS4CCM and DDS4CIAO. First, our existing D&C tooling provides coordinated installation of application implementations and startup across multiple nodes. Second, the connector infrastructure developed for DDS4CIAO allows integration with other distribution middleware, such as CORBA, TENA, JMS, or even socket based network programs. Third, the decoupling provided by the DDS4CIAO implementation enables the selection of DDS implementation at deployment time.

SOFA [3, 4] is a component model with an integrated D&C framework that provides remote communication capabilities via a connector infrastructure similar in spirit to that which is part of the

DDS4CCM specification. SOFA, however, only provides connectors for CORBA and RMI distribution middleware. Our approach differs from that taken by SOFA in that the connectors implemented by DDS4CIAO are themselves lightweight components. The advantage of our approach is that any improvements to the QoS capabilities of the CIAO container can be automatically applied not only to all components deployed, but also connectors as well.

6. Concluding Remarks

This paper presents a novel generative approach for developing DDS-based component-oriented DRE systems. Our approach combines key advantages of the DDS middleware, such as low latency communication and extensive QoS policy support, with the strengths of a mature component model, such as simplified application composition and automatic deployment and configuration. We have prototyped and evaluated our approach via the DDS4CIAO middleware platform, which implements the Lightweight CCM (DDS4CCM) specification, while addressing a number of inherent and accidental complexities in integrating the DDS and LwCCM technologies. In particular, we have made extensive use of variants of the extensible interface pattern to extend the existing standard-defined LwCCM interface and deployment metadata to overcome incompatibilities between DDS and LwCCM and overcome oversights in the DDS4CCM specification. Additionally, we describe a template driven code generation technique that maximizes portability amongst DDS implementations while allowing users to extend DDS4CCM by defining their own connector types without having to modify the code generator.

Our experience developing applications with DDS4CIAO provided the basis for the following lessons learned:

Substantially reduced DDS application complexity. Tests and example applications developed with DDS4CIAO have shown that the simplified interface to the underlying DDS middleware, provided by the DDS4CCM specification, provides a platform that easier to write and develop DDS applications.

Automatic configuration of DDS middleware. By providing a strict separation of concerns between configuration-based aspects of DDS application development and configuration aspects, users can automatically configure the underlying middleware at deployment time using standards-based deployment plan descriptors already available with LwCCM.

Deployment-time binding of DDS implementation may ease application benchmarking. It is also possible that the DDS implementation used by the component application could be chosen at deployment time, rather than compile time. This enhancement will allow developers to evaluate the merits and performance characteristics of different DDS implementations rapidly.

Increased reliance on tooling. A consequence of developing with DDS4CIAO is the increased reliance on tooling, especially modeling tools. While writing the IDL and business logic for DDS-4CIAO components is straightforward, writing the deployment descriptors by hand is a difficult task that requires expert knowledge of the D&C specification. While the use of modeling tools — such as our CoSMIC toolsuite [9] or commercial tools that have emerged — can substantially ameliorate this concern, their use may not always be practical (CoSMIC, for example requires Windows while the commercial tools may be costly). A domain specific language (DSL) for describing deployments, configuration, and component packaging would substantially reduce the modeling requirement.

Applying connectors to the CCM CORBA infrastructure. The connector-based approach to integrating the DDS distribution middleware into CIAO has shown substantial promise. Unfortunately, however, the CORBA infrastructure that underlies CIAO/CCM still remains tightly integrated into the container implementation. A similar connector based approach could be used to convert Lw-

CCM into a "Common Component Model", which is completely agnostic to the underlying communications middleware, by moving all of the extant CORBA communications functions to connectors themselves. This approach has the advantage of not only being able to remove the CORBA infrastructure currently used for synchronous two-way communication, but also makes it possible to, for example, swap in an alternative non-CORBA based connector implementation, if desired.

CIAO, DAnCE, and DDS4CIAO are available in open-source format from download.dre.vanderbilt.edu.

References

[1] Alejandro de Campos Ruiz and Gerardo Pardo-Castellote and GianPiero Napoli and Fernando Crespo-Sanchez and Javier Sanchez Monedero. High-level Programming of DDS Systems. In *Proceedings of the OMG Annual Real-time and Embedded Systems Workshop (RTWS)*, Arlington, VA, Mar. 2011.

[2] Angelo Corsaro. Simple API for DDS. http://code.google.com/p/simd-cxx/.

[3] L. Bulej and T. Bures. A connector model suitable for automatic generation of connectors. Technical report, 2003.

[4] T. Bures, P. Hnetynka, and F. Plasil. Sofa 2.0: Balancing advanced features in a hierarchical component model. *Software Engineering Research, Management and Applications, ACIS International Conference on*, 0:40–48, 2006.

[5] C. Esposito and D. Cotroneo. Resilient and timely event dissemination in publish/subscribe middleware. *International Journal of Adaptive, Resilient and Autonomic Systems*, 1:1 – 20, 2010.

[6] P. T. Eugster, P. A. Felber, R. Guerraoui, and A.-M. Kermarrec. The Many Faces of Publish/Subscribe. *ACM Comput. Surv.*, 35(2):114–131, 2003.

[7] J. Hill, D. C. Schmidt, J. Slaby, and A. Porter. CiCUTS: Combining System Execution Modeling Tools with Continuous Integration Environments. In *Proceedings of the 15th Annual IEEE International Conference and Workshops on the Engineering of Computer Based Systems (ECBS)*, Belfast, Northern Ireland, Apr. 2008.

[8] Ke Jin. Component-Based CORBA+DDS Applications in PocoCapsule vs CCM. http://www.pocomatic.com/docs/whitepapers/corba/.

[9] T. Lu, E. Turkay, A. Gokhale, and D. C. Schmidt. CoSMIC: An MDA Tool suite for Application Deployment and Configuration. In *Proceedings of the OOPSLA 2003 Workshop on Generative Techniques in the Context of Model Driven Architecture*, Anaheim, CA, Oct. 2003. ACM.

[10] N. C. Myers. Traits: a new and useful template technique. *C++ Report*, June 1995.

[11] Object Management Group. *Lightweight CORBA Component Model RFP*, realtime/02-11-27 edition, Nov. 2002.

[12] Object Management Group. *Data Distribution Service for Real-time Systems Specification*, 1.2 edition, Jan. 2007.

[13] Object Management Group. *DDS for Lightweight CCM Version 1.0 Beta 2*. Object Management Group, OMG Document ptc/2009-10-25 edition, Oct. 2009.

[14] OMG. *Deployment and Configuration of Component-based Distributed Applications, v4.0*, Document formal/2006-04-02 edition, Apr. 2006.

[15] D. A. Wheeler. Sloccount, a set of tools for counting physical source lines of code, 2009.

[16] M. Xiong, J. Parsons, J. Edmondson, H. Nguyen, and D. C. Schmidt. Evaluating Technologies for Tactical Information Management in Net-Centric Systems. In *Proceedings of the Defense Transformation and Net-Centric Systems conference*, Orlando, Florida, Apr. 2007.

Generation of Geometric Programs Specified by Diagrams

Yulin Li

Amazon Inc., Seattle, WA.
stvliexp@gmail.com

Gordon S. Novak Jr.

University of Texas at Austin
novak@cs.utexas.edu

Abstract

The GeoGram system [21] generates programs for geometric computations by combining generic software components as specified by diagrams constructed using a graphical interface. The user specifies known and desired quantities. As diagrams are constructed, the system maintains symbolic geometric facts describing the construction. Inferences based on the diagram are used to derive new facts and to introduce new objects based on geometric reasoning, to filter choices presented to the user, to interpret the user's intention in ambiguous cases, to detect over-specification, and to generate the program. A knowledge base of descriptions of generic software components is used to prove that features of the geometry can be computed from known values. These local proofs are combined to guide generation of a program that computes the desired values from inputs. The library of generic geometric program components is used to generate both in-line code and specialized subroutines; partial evaluation improves the efficiency of the generated code. The resulting program is automatically translated into the desired language. The program can also be run interactively to simulate the geometry by generating graphical traces on the diagram as input quantities are varied.

Categories and Subject Descriptors I.2.2 [*Artificial Intelligence*]: Automatic Programming—Program synthesis; D.2.6 [*Software Engineering*]: Programming Environments—Graphical environments; D.2.2 [*Software Engineering*]: Design Tools and Techniques—Computer-aided software engineering (CASE)

General Terms Design, Languages, Algorithms, Human Factors, Verification

Keywords Program Generation, Software Components, Reusable Libraries, Geometry, Theorem Proving, Visual Programming, Model-Based Programming

1. Introduction

Geometric calculations are important in many areas of science and engineering, and in computer graphics. However, geometric programs are often difficult for humans to write. The equations involved quickly become difficult as the complexity of the geometry increases. Since there are many features of a geometry that could be computed and there may be multiple ways to compute them, there is a large search space to be explored in finding a sequence of computations that derives the desired values from the inputs. Geometry has many special cases and mathematical singularities that, if not properly tested, become program errors. In order to use libraries of geometric subroutines, a programmer must be familiar with the libraries and must conform to the programming language and data structures that library routines assume. An application is likely to involve some specialized geometry for which no subroutines exist, requiring some custom programming.

This paper describes a system that allows a user to generate a program to perform desired geometric calculations. The desired program is specified primarily by interactive construction of one or more diagrams using a graphical interface. As a diagram is constructed, the system maintains a set of symbolic facts about the geometry. Inference from these facts is used for several purposes, as we will describe. When the diagrams are complete, a program is generated from the facts by, in effect, proving that a certain combination of generic program components will calculate the desired outputs from the specified inputs, given the geometry; these components are then specialized to use the user's data structures, optimized by partial evaluation, and automatically translated into the desired programming language. From the user's point of view, a working program is generated automatically from the diagram. Since diagrams are relatively easy for the user to construct, the process of generating correct geometric programs from components has been simplified. The user states the problem in terms of the application domain, geometry, rather than programming in textual form.

Although the system described here is specialized to geometry, it exemplifies what we believe to be an important principle: the representation of a system in terms of domain components, with symbolic descriptions of the components and their properties and constraints, and the use of logical inference and constraint satisfaction to derive new properties, insert new components, simplify the user interface, check for errors, select methods of achieving goals, and guide the synthesis of a complete program from generic program components that correspond to the domain components.

2. Motivating Example

Consider the following example tug-of-war problem, from [34] p. 305, Fig. 1 and Fig. 2:

> Rope-pulling takes place in a large room, which contains a large round pillar of a certain radius. If two groups are on the opposite side of the pillar, their pulled rope cannot be a straight line. Given the position of the two groups, find out the minimum length of rope required to start rope-pulling.

Depending on the input data, there might be a straight-line path between the two groups that misses the pillar; otherwise, the path of the rope around one side of the pillar is likely to be shorter than the path around the other side. Although this seems like a simple problem, the on-line judge [31] reports that less than 11% of submissions of this problem (number 10180) to the judge are correct, and only 40% of users eventually get it right.

The GeoGram system [21] described in this paper allows the user to generate a correct program for geometric problems such as this by constructing a diagram that describes the geometry; constructing such a diagram using a graphical user interface is usually easier and faster than writing the equivalent code. The program for the above problem was synthesized using this system and submitted (in C) to the on-line judge; it was judged correct the first time. Although we did not make any efforts to improve the efficiency of the generated code, this first submission ranked in the top 13% of correct programs in speed of execution.

Although we have not done studies comparing the speed of programming and correctness between this system and ordinary programming, it seems clear to the authors that using this system would be faster and produce better programs. Simply put, most humans are not very good at geometric programming, and it is not hard to do better.

The rope example will be used in the following sections, as we describe the user interface, the symbolic representation of the geometry, logical inference that underlies many of the capabilities of the system, and the program synthesis process. A valuable feature is the ability to generate graphical traces of values on the geometric diagram as input values are varied. The system is illustrated using selected examples including the rope problem, a mechanical linkage, a geometry theorem, and calculation of a pattern for cutting sheet metal to form a truncated cone. Last are a description of related work and conclusion.

The system described here is specialized for geometry. In this approach, a geometry is modeled as a structure of domain components, and properties and relations of these components are inferred using geometric rules and propagated between components. We have used a similar approach to generate programs that solve physics problems [26] and to combine and specialize generic software components to form a variety of application programs [30]. Therefore, we believe that the approach described here generalizes to program generation from components in a variety of areas.

3. User Interface

The user interface is simple and utilitarian, but allows geometries to be constructed fairly easily. Many graphical interfaces for geometry exist (e.g., [17]), and most are more polished than this one. We do note cases where geometric reasoning allows the interface to be more convenient for the user.

3.1 Drawing Window and Example

The user interface is illustrated using the rope problem above. The interface uses a single drawing window with several attached command menus as shown in Fig. 1.

The **Draw** menu appears in the upper-right corner of Fig. 1; this menu contains symbols that specify drawing of points, horizontal line segments, general line segments, general triangles, isosceles triangles, circles, connected lines, and constructed figures (the "wheel" icon). At upper-left is the **Program** Menu, with commands Horizontal, Pin, Equal, Apply Op, Apply Pred, Input, Output, Setup, Program, Use Units, Test, Trace, and Untrace All. At lower-left is the **Control** Menu, with commands Done, Move, Show Facts, Show Equalities, Show Grid, Hide Geom, Unhide Geoms, Toggle Names, and Verbose. The effects of selected commands are described later.

In the diagram of Fig. 1, the user has begun the construction of geometry for the Rope problem. The two points P2 and P3 were made by clicking on the point icon (dot) on the Draw menu, then clicking at the desired location on the drawing area. The user can also specify that these are inputs by clicking on the Input entry of the Program menu; desired outputs are designated similarly. The circle was made by clicking on the circle icon, clicking the desired center point on the drawing, then expanding the circle with the mouse and clicking when it reached the desired size; the system added the center point P1 as an object automatically. The tangent lines were made by first clicking and highlighting one point and the circle, then clicking Construction (the wheel icon); this brings up a menu of possible constructions involving a point and a circle, "Line from a Point to the closest Point on a Circle" and "Line from a Point Tangent to a Circle". The user chose the Tangent option; since there are two possible tangents from a point to a circle, the system constructed a menu showing the actual slopes of the lines that could be constructed, so that the user could choose. The system then added the tangent line and the point of tangency. Finally, the user clicked both points of tangency and the circle, then the wheel icon to construct the arc along the circle between the two points.

By continuing the geometric construction in a similar manner, the user constructed a diagram as shown in Fig. 2; this diagram includes the necessary geometric constructions, including the two possible paths of the rope around the sides of the pillar and the straight-line path in case the rope misses the pillar.

The user has also added three simple equations, to express the total rope lengths along the two paths around the pillar and the minimum of those lengths, plus a test of whether the straight-line path between the two points intersects the pillar; this test is used in making a conditional expression in an equation (not shown here) that produces the final output.

3.2 Geometric Constructions

The response to a Construction command (the wheel icon) is determined dynamically based on declarative rules, each of which has the form shown in Fig. 3. Because constructors are described by a set of rules, new constructors can easily be added.

```
(method ?result = (<method> <arguments>)
    (pname <description string>)
    (sig <signature types>)
    (when <precondition clauses>)
    (test <test clause>) )
```

Figure 3. Construction Method Syntax

An example construction rule is shown in Fig. 4; the rules use Lisp syntax, which avoids having to parse them. Each rule gives the signature for a certain geometric construction, along with a descriptive string, a precondition for use of the construction, and a test that determines whether the construction is applicable in the current diagram. The rule of Fig. 4 describes a constructor `pline` for the line-segment from a given point perpendicular to a given

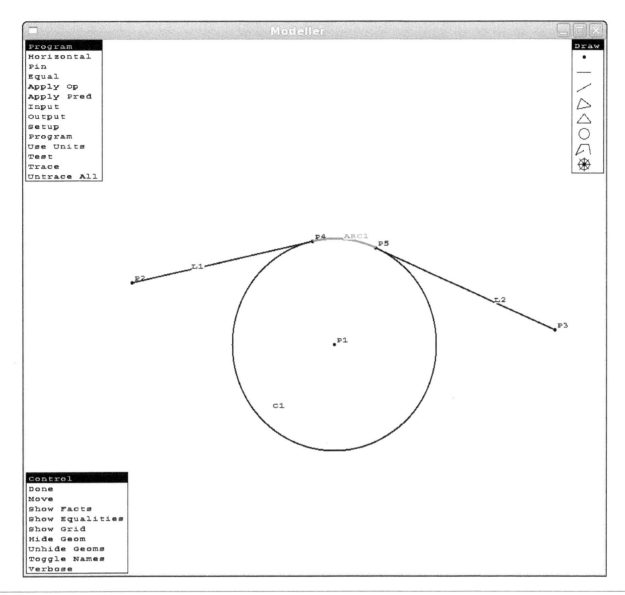

Figure 1. Modeler Window

```
(method  ?ls = (pline ?p1 ?ln)
  (pname "Perpendicular from Point to Line")
  (sig   (?ls line-seg)
         (?p1 point)
         (?ln line-seg))
  (test (not (gg-lineseg-throughp
                (value-from-diagram ?ln)
                (value-from-diagram ?p1)))) )
```

Figure 4. Construction Method Example

line-segment; the signature would be written conventionally as:

$$pline : point \times lineseg \rightarrow lineseg$$

This rule has a test, described below. Most clauses of the rule contain variables indicated by a ? prefix, such as ?p1; these become bound to objects in the diagram and are replaced by the bindings during evaluation of the clauses.

The Construction command is invoked by the user after several objects on the diagram have been highlighted by clicking on them. The first step is to examine all rules to find those whose signatures match the selected set of objects and whose test is satisfied. In the example of Fig. 4, the construction is only meaningful if the point is not on the line; this test is performed on the values in the current diagram that is being constructed. Using the test in this manner prevents meaningless choices from being presented to the user.

Once a set of feasible methods has been found, a menu of the possibilities is presented to the user for selection. If the result objects are of different types, a menu to select the desired result type is presented first; this keeps the menus small. After the user has selected the desired method, the method call is instantiated and executed to construct the desired object on the diagram. Both the constructed object and facts that are made true by the construction are added to the Geometric Model.

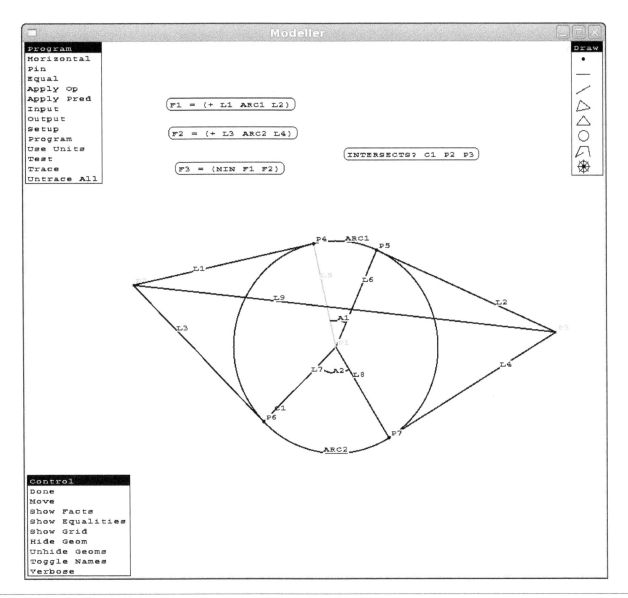

Figure 2. Rope Problem

4. Geometric Model

The major components of GeoGram are shown in Fig. 5. The geometric model, GeoFacts, is a collection of facts in symbolic form that describes the current geometric construction, including the types of objects and the relations between objects. New facts are added in response to additions to the geometric construction and by inference based on existing facts. Facts are used internally by the system; the user does not need to be aware of them.

The type of each object is stated as a type predicate in the form of a Lisp list, (tp <object> <type>), e.g. (tp C1 circle); in conventional logic notation this would be written as $Circle(c_1)$ or $Type(c_1, circle)$. The predicates used are outlined and briefly described in Fig. 6. Predicates are written as Lisp lists in prefix form; for example, (center c p) would be written in logic notation as $Center(c, p)$ and means "the center of c is p". The symbols with question marks in Fig. 6 indicate the types of the arguments of each predicate; these are replaced with symbols used in the drawing and geometric model when the predicates become instantiated. The set of predicates is open-ended, so more could easily be added.

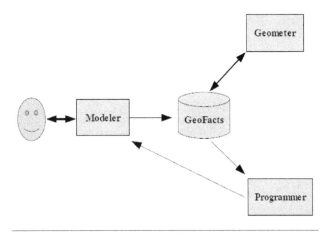

Figure 5. System Components

(angle-from ?lineseg1 ?ls2 ?an)	from 1 to 2 is ?an
(center ?circle ?point)	center is ?point
(concur-at ?line1 ?l2 ?l3 ?p)	all through ?p
(corner ?point ?triangle)	?point is a corner
(endpoint ?point ?curve)	end of lineseg/arc
(first ?point ?curve)	1st of lineseg/arc
(first-tangent-pt ?p ?c ?tan)	circle tan from ?p
(horizontal ?lineseg)	?lineseg is horiz
(intersect ?p1 ?p2 ?p3 ?p4 ?i)	lines 1-2, 3-4 at ?i
(last ?point ?curve)	last pt of lineseg/arc
(midpoint ?lineseg ?pt)	?pt is midpoint
(on ?pt ?curve)	?pt is on ?curve
(perpend ?lineseg1 ?lineseg2)	lines perpendicular
(radius ?lineseg ?circle)	?lineseg is radius
(second-tangent-pt ?p ?c ?tan)	2nd tan from ?p
(side ?lineseg ?triangle)	?lineseg is a side
(sweep-angle ?arc ?ang)	center ?ang of ?arc
(tp ?type ?g)	type of ?g is ?type
(vertex ?point ?angle)	?point is vertex

Figure 6. Geometric Predicates

Each kind of predicate has its own methods for storage and access; this facilitates rapid lookup that, in effect, includes simple inference. For example, parallelism is transitive, while perpendicularity is not; both are commutative. Lookup of $P(a, b)$ would succeed if P is commutative and $P(b, a)$ is known. A hash table is used to dispatch each kind of predicate to its appropriate manager. A query to the geometric model will typically contain some variables; the result gives sets of bindings (of variables to constants) that satisfy the query. For example, the query (perpend ?ls1 ?ls2), asking for all pairs of perpendicular line segments, might return a binding list ((?ls1 L3) (?ls2 L2)), i.e. the query is satisfied by the known predicate $Perpend(l_3, l_2)$.

Equalities are important for relating different views of a single object, such as orthographic views or the relation between a flat sheet metal pattern and the same material when bent into a 3-dimensional shape. Equalities are represented in a special way: rather than predicates, they are represented as equivalence classes that contain all the variables whose values are equal. This representation prevents rapid growth of the number of predicates and allows a fast test of equivalence. When two variables are declared equal (via the Equal button of the Program menu), their equivalence classes are merged.

Equations can be constructed by the user by clicking on diagram elements and selecting an operator (using the Apply Op menu command) to combine them; alternatively, they could be entered as text. In addition to equations entered by the user, the system has equations that represent geometric knowledge, such as the fact that the sum of interior angles of a triangle equals $180°$. Predicate (boolean test) values can be specified by clicking on diagram elements, then clicking Apply Pred to select a predicate involving those objects; the resulting predicate can then be used in constructing an if expression used in an equation.

5. Inference

Forward-chaining inference [33] is used to derive new facts from directly asserted facts and rules of geometry. In forward chaining, if facts a and b are known, and there is a rule $a \wedge b \rightarrow c$, the fact c would be asserted, i.e. added to the database of facts. This inference is run during diagram construction so that as many facts as possible are known at each point.

```
(and (tp circle ?cir)
     (tp line-seg ?d)
     (endpoint ?p ?d)
     (endpoint ?q ?d)
     (on ?p ?cir)
     (on ?q ?cir))
test (neq ?p ?q)
=>   (chord ?d ?cir)
```

Figure 7. Rule: Chord of a Circle

```
(and (tp point ?p1)
     (tp point ?p2)
     (tp point ?p3))
=> (tp triangle ?tri)
test (not (collinear
           (value-from-diagram ?p1)
           (value-from-diagram ?p2)
           (value-from-diagram ?p3)))
with ?tri = (new-triangle ?p1 ?p2 ?p3)
```

Figure 8. Rule: Triangle from Three Points

5.1 Rules

An inference rule has four parts: condition, assertion, a test, and possibly object definitions. The condition and assertion are as usual in logic: if the condition is true, the assertion must also be true. Variables in the condition become bound to objects in the geometric model by unification with predicates in the Geometric Model; there is an implicit "for all" quantification.

The test of a rule must also be satisfied before the rule can fire; while the condition is a conjunction of knowledge base predicates, a test is code that is executed immediately based on the present variable bindings. Tests are commonly used to rule out degenerate variable bindings, e.g. to require that two points must be distinct. Redundant firings of rules based on permutations of variable bindings (e.g., a line could be constructed through two points in either order) are prevented by a test that imposes a lexicographic ordering on the variable names; this allows one firing to succeed but causes others to fail. The rule of Fig. 7 states that a line-segment connecting two (distinct) points on a circle is a chord of the circle; in logic notation, this would be: $\forall c, d, p, q : Circle(c) \wedge Lineseg(d) \wedge Endpoint(p, d) \wedge Endpoint(q, d) \wedge On(p, c) \wedge On(q, c) \wedge p \neq q \rightarrow Chord(d, c)$. Since the $p \neq q$ is a test, the system executes it immediately to cause the trivial case where $p = q$ to fail.

The definition part of a rule allows new objects to be constructed, as shown in Fig. 8, where a triangle is constructed from three points. Notice that the test in this case is based on values from the current diagram rather than symbolic proof; the latter is unlikely to be possible. We assume that the diagram specified by the user represents a typical case for the inputs of the program; an assertion could be added to the generated program to verify that the condition is true at runtime, but this has not been implemented.

5.2 Forward Chaining

When a new fact is added to the geometric model, rules are examined to see which ones are satisfied (based on both precondition and test); this may produce multiple instances of rules and bindings. All satisfied rules are run at once, and their resulting assertions are added (when novel) to the geometric model. This process continues until a fixpoint is reached, i.e. no additional rules are triggered.

Continually updating the geometric model by adding new facts improves usability of the system, e.g. by reducing the amount of

```
(method ?pt = (intersection-pt ?L1 ?L2)
  (when
    (tp line-seg ?L1)
    (tp line-seg ?L2)
    (intersect-at ?L1 ?L2 ?pt))
  (test
    (string< (toString ?L1) (toString ?L2))) )
```

Figure 9. Construction Method Example

user input that is required. When the user constructs a line tangent to a circle from a given point, the system will automatically construct a radius line to the point of tangency and record that the tangent line and radius line are perpendicular. The system automatically displays only inferred objects that are closely related to a user input, as in this example; there is a Hide Geom command in the Control menu in case the user does not want to see the inferred object. Menus of construction possibilities that are presented to the user are filtered to contain only items that make sense, and this test depends on an up-to-date geometric model.

6. Program Generation

Once the diagram is complete, a program is generated upon command. The user has specified which variables are inputs and which are desired as outputs; the system must determine how to compute the outputs given the inputs. This is done by a process analogous to data flow or topological sort, in which the system determines what values can be computed by solver programs from the input variables, given the geometry; this process is repeated until output variables are reached. The code synthesized for the examples described in this paper is given in [21].

Computations are available from a library of solvers, which contains generic geometric subroutines written in Generic Lisp, GLISP [25]; these can be either short in-line code, subroutines to be compiled in-line, or closed subroutines. Code becomes specialized for the data structures, units of measurement, and output language used in the application by the GLISP compiler. Partial evaluation by the compiler allows computations on constants to be performed at compile time, including simplification of code for special cases by elimination of if statements when a test has a constant value.

Each solver is described symbolically by a method description; these are similar to the methods used in diagram construction, Fig. 3. Because solvers are described by a set of rules, new solvers can easily be added. An example solver rule is shown in Fig. 9.

This rule states that the method intersection-pt can be used to compute the intersection ?pt of two line-segments. The rule illustrates two features commonly seen in solver rules. First, the when clause is quite restrictive: this one requires that the intersection point of the two line segments be proved to exist via geometric reasoning. Line segments might cross accidentally on the diagram, but such a crossing might not exist for different input data. Second, the rule prevents combinatoric and redundant use of the solver (switching the order of arguments) by requiring a lexicographic ordering of arguments. Tests can also be used to infer the intentions of the user: in some cases, there are two symmetric solutions to a problem, e.g. determining the location of a point based on its distances from two other points. The tests of solver rules can be used to select the solution that is consistent with the existing diagram, under the assumption that the diagram represents the model intended by the user.

The use of rules causes the geometry of the problem to constrain the generation of the program: a solver can only be used if the geometry satisfies the when clause of its rule. Thus, the specified geometry and inferred geometric facts guide and constrain the program generation process.

Equations can also be used in the solution process. A simple equation solver can solve an equation for any of its variables, so an equation can be used as a solver for one variable given values for the others. The equation solver assumes that each variable occurs at most once in an equation. Given an initial equation (in Lisp syntax) for one variable in terms of others, the solver rewrites the equation to remove the top operator. For example, (= x (+ y z)) can be rewritten as (= (- x y) z) or as (= (- x z) y). This process, applied recursively, can solve an equation for any of its variables. For the program generation process, equations are expanded internally into solvers for each of their variables.

The solution is generated in a breadth-first search process [33] using dynamic programming. Initially, input variables are marked as being known. Solvers are identified that compute unknown variables using only known ones as input; when such a solver is found, a hyper-arc is added to a graph giving the solver method and its inputs for the result variable, and the result variable is marked as known. This process continues until fixpoint; it must terminate because the set of variables is finite (inference is finished and no new objects can be created at this point). When done, if the output variables are known, a program can be generated from the graph that was formed (if not, an error message is generated).

The above process produces a data-flow graph, showing source data flowing into solver routines, which produce results; the graph starts from input variables designated by the user and shows everything that can be computed from those inputs, given the geometry. Following the graph backwards from desired output variables eliminates computations that are not needed; the graph provides an ordering of computations that is followed in the generated code, so that values of variables are computed before they are used.

If there were multiple solvers available for some tasks, it would be possible to associate estimated runtime costs with solvers and find the minimum-cost solution; this has not been implemented. With a single output, a greedy algorithm similar to Dijkstra's shortest-path algorithm could be used; if solvers or the desired program had multiple outputs, the search would be more complex.

Calls to the solver programs that compute the desired output are generated as a program in GLISP [25], using an ordering that follows the solution graph and computes variables before they are used. The GLISP program is compiled into Lisp; this will also generate specialized versions of solver subroutines as needed [28] [29] to use the data structures and measurement units [27] of inputs and intermediate values.

The generic geometry subroutines are written in a form that produces a subset of Lisp that can be automatically translated to other languages, i.e. the routines do not use Lisp features such as cons (with garbage collection) that might not be available in other languages. There is a data structure access form that is emulated if executed in Lisp and can be translated to the proper form of structure access in other languages; this allows the user to specify the data representations to be used in the target language. With automatic translation, the system described here can produce output in the user's choice of C, C++, Java, or Pascal, as well as Lisp.

The program generation process is also used to detect redundant specification by the user. It is possible that the user may specify as an input a variable that can be determined from other input variables; this would be redundant and possibly contradictory. An attempt is made to generate a program for each input variable given the other inputs; if this succeeds, the variable is redundant, and an error message is generated.

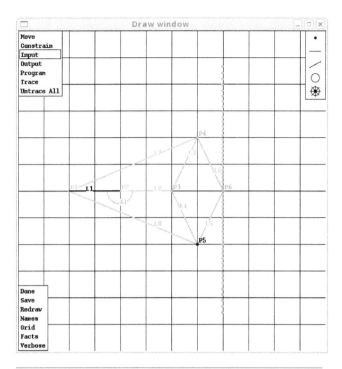

Figure 10. Peaucellier-Lipkin Linkage

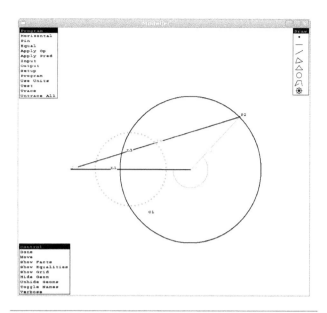

Figure 11. Circle Midpoint Theorem

7. Traces

A useful feature is the ability to generate a graphical trace of a variable on the diagram as an input is varied. The user specifies an input variable and range of variation and a variable to be traced. The Lisp version of the generated program is used to compute the value of the output variable from the inputs, with other inputs being taken directly from the diagram. The resulting values are shown on the diagram in a different color, allowing visualization of the results. If the user moves some entities on the diagram, the trace is rerun dynamically, so that the effects of changing the diagram can also be visualized.

Traces can be used for visualizing the motions of mechanical linkages, visualizing the results of geometry theorems, and generating patterns for cutting sheet metal to form desired shapes. These are illustrated with examples below.

The first example is a mechanical linkage, the Peaucellier-Lipkin Linkage [32]; this was the first planar linkage to generate perfect straight-line motion from rotational motion. The diagram and trace are shown in Fig. 10, with the angle A1 of the line-segment L1 being varied and the point P6 being traced; the trace confirms the straight-line motion produced by the linkage.

The next example visualizes a geometry theorem: the locus of midpoints of the line segment between a fixed point and a circle generates a circle of half the diameter of the original circle. The diagram and trace are shown in Fig. 11: a line segment connects a fixed point P3 at the left to a point P2 on the large circle C1; as the angle A1 of the point P2 is varied, the midpoint P4 of the line segment traces out a dotted circle of half the diameter of circle C1.

The final example shows the generation of a pattern for cutting sheet metal to form a truncated cone when the flat metal is bent into the three-dimensional shape. The diagram and trace are shown in Fig. 12. In this diagram, the large circle C1 is the flat piece of sheet metal prior to cutting; the radius of this circle equals the height of the cone along the diagonal. The triangle and smaller circle represent orthographic views of the constructed figure, the circle being on a horizontal plane at the bottom of the cone and the triangle a side view, perpendicular to the plane of truncation. Equations are used to state that variables in these different views are equal. The trace shows the cut line formed by point P17 (equivalent to P16 on the triangle) that is produced as angle A1 is varied until angle A2 reaches a stopping point; this cut would be used to produce the desired pattern.

This example was fun to test by printing the diagram from the screen, cutting out the pattern with scissors, and taping the ends together; the constructed cone exhibits a planar cut at the angle shown on the diagram.

8. Testing

The system described here has been tested on other examples, including the Watt Linkage [38], Burmester Linkage [8], finding the incircle of a triangle, computing a pattern for a doubly truncated cone, and visualizing other geometry theorems. Based on the range of examples that have been done, we believe that it can generate programs for a useful set of geometry problems that would pose some difficulty for human programmers.

The system was tested by submitting the code generated for the rope example of Fig. 2 to the on-line judge [31]. A handwritten driver program was used to perform input and output and call the generated subroutine. The programs described by Skiena and Revilla [34] and tested by the on-line judge are designed as practice problems for student programming contests, so they are problems that might take a human programmer on the order of an hour. As mentioned earlier, the generated program was judged correct on the first try, while only 11% of submissions overall are correct.

The generated program was judged as being in the top 13% of correct submitted programs in efficiency. We did not make any attempt to improve efficiency before submission. The process of translating the generated code to other languages generates new objects on the heap for structured variables such as vectors and lines; efficiency could be improved by eliminating these, either by rewriting the generic geometry routines to destructure intermediate variables or by improving the translation process to use stack variables for variables that are only used locally.

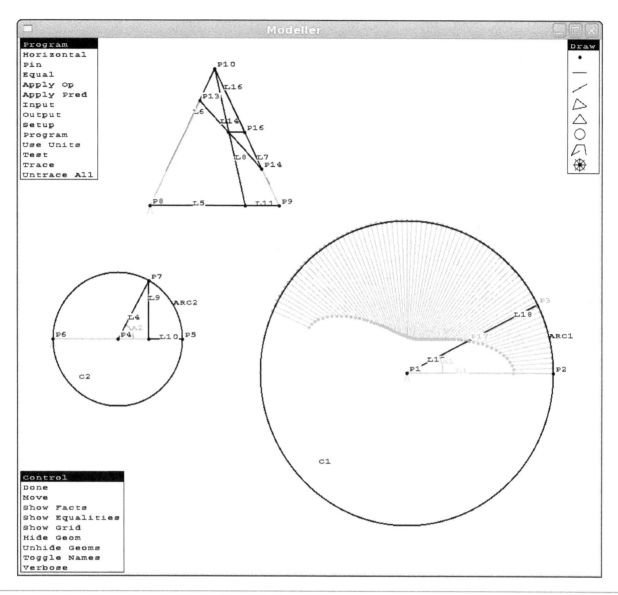

Figure 12. Pattern for Truncated Cone

9. Related Work

The system described in this paper touches on many different areas of research; we try to cover these areas briefly in this section. CAD systems and interactive geometry systems no doubt contain some reasoning about geometry that is equivalent to that in our system. To our knowledge, the system we describe is the first whose purpose is to generate usable program code for geometric calculations in multiple languages.

9.1 Domain-Specific Generators

Domain-specific program generators have been written for several areas. KIDS [35] and related systems generate programs that perform combinatoric search. SciNapse [1] generates simulations for systems of partial differential equations, such as the Black-Scholes equations used in analysis of derivative securities, from a relatively short domain-specific description. Bhansali and Hoar [6] synthesized programs to solve geometric constraint-satisfaction problems for the domain of mechanical CAD. The Amphion system [37] [22] synthesizes programs to solve astronomical computations based on calls to subroutines from a large library: the user specifies the desired computation as a network, which is converted to a theorem that is proved constructively; a program can then be extracted from the proof. Amphion allows a computation to be specified by a GUI that shows named components and relations expressed as links between component symbols; GeoGram's GUI is somewhat like Amphion's, but represents actual planar geometry. Solar-Lezama, Bodik, *et al.* describe a compiler [36] for *sketches*, which are integer or bit programs in a C-like `Sketch` language that allows use of ?? to designate a *hole* that must be filled with some expression to make the program correct; the compiler synthesizes the needed expression by search and correctness proofs using a SAT solver.

9.2 Component Reuse

There are many subroutine and component libraries, and most program generators use libraries in some form. Two issues that impede the use of libraries are the need for the user to know the contents of the library in order to use it, and the restrictions on language and data structures imposed by the library routines. In our approach, the system has the knowledge of the library (in the form of solver rules), and programs can be generated for the user's choice of language and data structures. Krueger [20] and Mili [23] discuss technical challenges and criteria for successful reuse. Ellman [13] describes a system that can synthesize programs to simulate and generate animations of a physics-based system using hybrid automata, which combine finite automata and differential equations. The simulation programs generated are impressive; the input is in terms of pre-defined schemas using a formal language similar to predicate calculus.

9.3 Graphical Programming

There are several approaches to graphical programming. LabVIEW [19] allows specification of programs by graphical connection of components with data-flow arcs. Systems such as Alice [2] embed a traditional object-oriented programming language in a graphical interface, removing from the user the need to learn syntax. The VIP system [26] generates programs from a graph that connects components representing physical and mathematical principles, with the connections representing equality of values.

9.4 Software Product Lines

Product lines are groups of related products, such as emergency communication radios, which have optional features that are selected and configured to form individual products. AHEAD [4] verifies the feasibility of a specification by checking against a grammar and design rules; it can also handle non-code artifacts such as makefiles and documentation. Refinements are implemented by inclusion of code sections and expressed by equations in terms of functional composition.

9.5 Transformational Systems

Czarnecki and Eisenecker [12] describe several systems for generating programs from more compact specifications by transforming the specifications to forms closer to implementation until executable code is reached. Baxter et al. [5] take a related approach with their Design Maintenance System, the idea being that programs should be maintained (modified) at the design level rather than code. Our system is transformational in the sense that generic component programs are specialized by the GLISP compiler so that they operate on the user's data structures and representations.

9.6 Geometry Systems

Borning's ThingLab [7] was an early system that allowed graphical specification of geometry and could simulate changes due to movement of elements by message-passing relaxation. There are many systems [39], including Geometer's Sketchpad [17], Cinderella [11], and Geometry Explorer [40], that allow interactive construction of geometric diagrams and that prove theorems and/or simulate visualizations. These clearly overlap what our system can do, but they do not appear to generate programs.

Chou [9] revolutionized geometry theorem proving; more recent systems by him and colleagues [10] [16] can also perform visualizations and can construct diagrams automatically. [15] surveys automatic diagram generation.

9.7 CAD Systems

Many Computer-Aided Design systems have geometric design as their primary goal, and thus they contain extensive facilities for geometric modeling and reasoning. Unfortunately, CAD systems are often proprietary, and hence many techniques they use are not published. Goel, Vattam, Wiltgen, and Helms [18] provide an excellent overview of the history of knowledge-based CAD and many references in their discussion of a next-generation CAD system. Freixas,

Joan-Arinyo, and Soto-Riera [14] discuss ways to handle the mathematical singularities that arise in dynamic geometry, especially in design of mechanisms.

10. Future Work and Insights

Geometry is plagued by singularities and special cases; for example, a circle can be constructed that passes through three points, but not when the points are collinear. One way of safeguarding against such cases is for the generic solver routines to incorporate error checks. Our system GeoGram generates code to protect against null values returned by solvers. It would be fairly easy to add to the description of each solver a precondition on values of arguments; these could then be translated into assertions if the target language permits. More generally, the techniques described in [14] might be adapted for generation of runtime checks.

Since both geometric facts and the generated program are created by inference using rules, it would be possible to use the rules to generate documentation that explains and justifies the program that is produced. We have implemented such justification for a physics problem solver [24].

It should be straightforward to extend the system to generate programs that produce animations. To animate, for example, a mechanical linkage, it would simply be necessary to calculate the values of all dependent variables in the diagram (which is being done already for the programs being generated), then call drawing programs to redraw the whole diagram. Animations would make it easier to visualize the operation of a complex linkage.

The system described here is useful in its own right as a generator of geometric programs. It also exemplifies a class of systems that use models of the underlying domain both to generate programs for that domain and to aid the user in specifying the design of the programs. We agree with Balzer [3] that a design in terms of domain components is a better form of "source code" than programs in traditional languages.

Older software systems, such as traditional compiled languages and operating systems such as Unix, require a user to present a fully detailed and precise program or command, issuing error messages but otherwise providing little help. The user must map from the application domain to the facilities provided by the language. Use of component libraries requires memorization of the components and their requirements, leading to balkanization of the profession into ".NET programmer" and other tribes.

It seems clearly better for programs to be generated from components that are closer to the domain of application than traditional languages. At the same time, the programming system should incorporate the knowledge of the components (rather than requiring that knowledge to be memorized) and should help with the programming process by:

- making inferences and obvious choices that follow from human decisions, so that not all details need to be explicitly stated
- propagating information, such as data types, between components that are interfaced and using that information to perform inferences and to constrain and specialize components
- presenting context-dependent choices for selection, so that the user does not have to memorize names
- generating specialized versions of components, so that a single set of generic components works for a variety of data structures, parameter choices, and languages.

11. Conclusion

This paper describes a system for generating geometric programs, an important class of applications, from generic software components. Compared to manual programming and the use of program libraries, we believe it improves both ease of use and accuracy:

- The system incorporates knowledge of geometry and knowledge about the library components, so that the user does not need to know these details.

- Correctness is improved by the use of domain-dependent proofs and checks that might be overlooked with manual programming and libraries:

  ▪ Preconditions of solver routines must be proved before the solvers can be used.

  ▪ Checks are made for redundant inputs.

- Simulation of a geometry using traces allows the user to visualize the problem and verify that the observed behavior is correct.

In addition to being important in its own right, this work provides techniques that are valuable for generation of programs from components in other domains, as well as for the science of design.

12. Acknowledgments

We thank Don Batory and the anonymous reviewers for their suggestions for improving this paper.

References

[1] Robert L. Akers, Elaine Kant, Curtis J. Randall, Stanly Steinberg, and Robert L. Young. Scinapse: A problem-solving environment for partial differential equations. *IEEE Computational Science and Engineering*, 4(3):32–42, July 1997. www.scicomp.com.

[2] Alice web site. www.alice.org.

[3] Robert Balzer. A 15 year perspective on automatic programming. *IEEE Trans. Software Engr.*, 11(11):1257–1267, November 1985.

[4] Don Batory, Jacob Sarvela, and Axel Rauschmayer. Scaling step-wise refinement. *IEEE Trans. Software Engr.*, 30(6):355–371, June 2004.

[5] Ira D. Baxter, Christopher Pidgeon, and Michael Mehlich. Dms: Program transformations for practical scalable software evolution. In *Proc. Intl. Conf. Software Engr.* IEEE Press, 2004.

[6] Sanjay Bhansali and Tim J. Hoar. Automated software synthesis: An application in mechanical cad. *IEEE Trans. Software Engr.*, 24(10):848–862, October 1998.

[7] Alan Borning. The programming language aspects of thinglab, a constraint-oriented simulation laboratory. *ACM Trans. Programming Languages and Systems*, 3(4):353–387, October 1981.

[8] Burmester link. gtrebaol.free.fr/doc/flash/four_bar/doc/.

[9] Shang-Ching Chou. *Mechanical Geometry Theorem Proving*. Kluwer Academic Publishers, 1987.

[10] Shang-Ching Chou, Xiao-Shan Gao, and Jing-Zhong Zhang. A deductive database approach to automated geometry theorem proving and discovering. *J. Automated Reasoning*, 25(3):219–246, 2000.

[11] Cinderella web site. www.cinderella.de/tiki-index.php.

[12] Krzysztof Czarnecki and Ulrich W. Eisenecker. *Generative Programming: Methods, Tools and Applications*. Addison-Wesley, 2000. www.generative-programming.org.

[13] Thomas Ellman. Specification and synthesis of hybrid automata for physics-based animation. *Automated Software Engineering*, 13(3), 395-418 2006.

[14] Marc Freixas, Robert Joan-Arinyo, and Antoni Soto-Riera. A constraint-based dynamic geometry system. *Computer-Aided Design*, 42(2):151–161, February 2010.

[15] Xiao-Shan Gao. Automated geometry diagram construction and engineering geometry. In *ADG-98, LNAI 1669*, pages 232–258. Springer, 1999.

[16] Xiao-Shan Gao and Qiang Lin. Mmp/geometer - a software package for automated geometric reasoning. In *ADG 2002, LNAI 2930*, pages 44–66. Springer, 2004.

[17] dynamicgeometry.com/.

[18] Ashok Goel, Swaroop Vattam, Bryan Wiltgen, and Michael Helms. Cognitive, collaborative, conceptual and creative – four characteristics of the next generation of knowledge-based cad systems: A study in biologically inspired design. *Computer-Aided Design*, 2011.

[19] National Instruments. www.ni.com/labview/.

[20] Charles W. Krueger. Software reuse. *ACM Computing Surveys*, 24(2):131–184, June 1992.

[21] Yulin Li. The diagrammatic specification and automatic generation of geometry subroutines. www.cs.utexas.edu/forms/tech_reports/reports/tr/TR-1991.pdf, May 2010.

[22] Michael Lowry, Andrew Philpot, Thomas Pressburger, and Ian Underwood. Amphion: Automatic programming for scientific subroutine libraries. In *Methodologies for Intelligent Systems, LNCS 869*, pages 326–335. Springer, 2004.

[23] Hafedh Mili, Fatma Mili, and Ali Mili. Reusing software: Issues and research directions. *IEEE Trans. Software Engr.*, 21(6):528–562, June 1995.

[24] www.cs.utexas.edu/users/novak/cgi/physdemo.cgi.

[25] Gordon S. Novak. Glisp: A lisp-based programming system with data abstraction. *AI Magazine*, 4(3):37–47, Fall 1983.

[26] Gordon S. Novak. Generating programs from connections of physical models. In *Proc. 10th Conf. Artificial Intelligence for Applications*, pages 224–230. IEEE CS Press, March 1994.

[27] Gordon S. Novak. Conversion of units of measurement. *IEEE Trans. Software Engineering*, 21(8):651–661, August 1995.

[28] Gordon S. Novak. Creation of views for reuse of software with different data representations. *IEEE Trans. Software Engineering*, 21(12):993–1005, December 1995.

[29] Gordon S. Novak. Software reuse by specialization of generic procedures through views. *IEEE Trans. Software Engineering*, 23(7):401–417, July 1997. www.cs.utexas.edu/users/novak/.

[30] Gordon S. Novak. Computer aided software design via inference and constraint propagation. *Integrated Computer-Aided Engineering*, 16(3):181–191, 2009.

[31] uva.onlinejudge.org.

[32] en.wikipedia.org/wiki/Peaucellier-Lipkin_linkage.

[33] Stuart Russell and Peter Norvig. *Artificial Intelligence: A Modern Approach*. Prentice-Hall, 2010.

[34] Steven S. Skiena and Miguel A. Revilla. *Programming Challenges*. Springer, 2003.

[35] Douglas R. Smith. Kids: A semiautomatic program development system. *IEEE Trans. Software Engr.*, 16(9):1024–1043, September 1990.

[36] Armando Solar-Lezama, Liviu Tancau, Rastislav Bodik, Vijay Saraswat, and Sanjit Seshia. Combinatorial sketching for finite programs. In *ASPLOS '06*. ACM, 2006.

[37] Mark Stickel, Richard Waldinger, Michael Lowry, Thomas Pressburger, and Ian Underwood. Deductive composition of astronomical software from subroutine libraries. In *12th Conf. on Automated Deduction, LNCS 814*. Springer, 1994.

[38] Watt linkage. en.wikipedia.org/wiki/Watt's_linkage.

[39] List of interactive geometry software. en.wikipedia.org/wiki/List_of_interactive_geometry_software.

[40] Sean Wilson and Jacques D. Fleuriot. Combining dynamic geometry, automated geometry theorem proving and diagrammatic proofs. In *Proc. European Joint Conf. on Theory and Practice of Software (ETAPS)*, page 151, 2005.

Model-Driven Engineering and Run-Time Model-Usage in Service Robotics

Andreas Steck, Alex Lotz and Christian Schlegel

University of Applied Sciences Ulm, Germany
Department of Computer Science
{steck,lotz,schlegel}@hs-ulm.de

Abstract

The development of service robots has gained more and more attention over the last years. A major challenge on the way towards industrial-strength service robotic systems is to make the step from code-driven to model-driven engineering. In this work we propose to put models into the focus of the whole life-cycle of robotic systems covering design-time as well as run-time. We describe how to explicate parameters, properties and resource information in the models at design-time and how to take these information into account by the run-time system of the robot to support its decision making process. We underpin our work by an exhaustive real-world example which is completely developed with our tools.

Categories and Subject Descriptors D.2.2 [*Software Engineering*]: Design Tools and Techniques

General Terms Experimentation

Keywords Component Based Software Engineering, Model-Driven Engineering, Run-Time Model Usage, Service Robotics

1. Introduction

Service robots are expected to fulfill complex tasks in unstructured everyday environments. Several robotic systems have already demonstrated promising capabilities like fetching beer from the refrigerator, playing pool, folding piles and performing interaction with humans. However, the implementation of those systems is still more of an art than a systematic engineering process. A systematic engineering process is essential to replace hand-crafted single-unit systems by systems composed out of matured and reusable components in order to decrease costs and time to market and to increase robustness.

Typically, in robotics software there is no separation between the roles of the component builder and the system integrator. This is however necessary to enable reuse and establish a market for robotics software components as is already available for hardware components (e.g. sensors, robot platforms, manipulators). The vision is a component shelf (fig. 1) where component builders provide their components for reuse by system integrators. A system integrator reuses existing solutions in form of components having

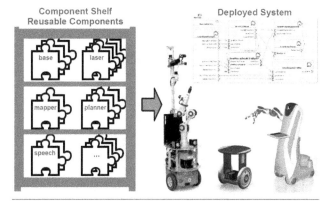

Figure 1. Building robotic systems by composing reusable components with assured services.

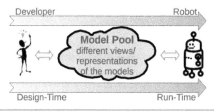

Figure 2. Models created at design-time are used and manipulated at run-time by the robot.

just a black-box view on them. That requires explication of parameters, properties and resource information of the components.

Furthermore, advanced robots which operate in complex open environments have to cope with many different situations and contingencies. At run-time, the robot has to manage a huge amount of different execution variants that can never be foreseen and completely pre-programmed and can thus not be analysed and checked entirely at design-time. Managing the sheer variety of different execution variants requires to specify variation points at design-time and to bind them at run-time depending on situation and context. Therefore, the robot control mechanism, which orchestrates the components of the whole system, has to carry out such analysis and checks before setting the configuration. To be able to check whether the desired configuration and parametrization of the components is valid and reasonable, explicated information about components is required and needs to be taken into account.

An effective way to explicate such information and making it accessible for further processing is to rely on models [34]. They provide the ability to abstract and generalize from experience. Models are widely used in different domains since they are computational and can be transformed into different representations that can be manipulated by humans, as well as computers (fig. 2). We believe that making the step from code-driven to model-driven engineering in robotics is one of the basic necessities to achieve both (i) separation of roles and (ii) managing run-time decisions.

This paper presents our approach of making the step towards model-centric robotic systems. The contributions are:

- making the step from code-driven to model-driven development of robotic systems by providing a robotics meta-model for robotic software components,

- providing levels of abstraction which allow to transform the models and generate code out of them,

- using the models of the robotics software components at design-time for simulation and analysis purposes, for example, relatime schedulability analysis of the relatime tasks,

- bridging between design-time models of robotics software components and their run-time representation,

- using models at run-time to support the decision making process of the robotic system by binding at run-time variation points that have been left-open purposefully at design-time,

- an exhaustive real-world example where the approach is applied.

2. Motivation

Software for autonomous robots is typically embedded, concurrent, real-time, distributed and data-intensive and must meet specific system requirements, such as safety, reliability, and fault tolerance. From this point of view robotic systems are similar to software systems in other domains, such as avionics, automotive, factory automation, telecommunication and even large scale information systems. The major differences that arise in robotics compared to other domains are *not* the huge amount of different sensors and actuators or the various hardware platforms. Instead, the huge amount of different system configurations changing even at run-time depending on current situation and context and a prioritized assignment of limited resources to activities are seen as robotic specific requirements. The resulting level of complexity goes beyond what is already handled in other domains. A complex robotic system can not be treated as a whole finalized system at design-time, for example, trying to analyse whether resource constraints are fulfilled.

The idea presented in this paper is to use models for the entire life-cycle of the system. Such a model-centric view puts the models into the focus at both design-time and run-time. Models are, for example, used from the very beginning in the development of the software components, they support the deployment of the components to compose the robot system and they are finally used at run-time to support the decision making process. Models allow to explicate parameters and resource information to make these accessible by different tools and mechanisms and, for example, to ensure resource awareness.

Models provide the ground for separation of roles as needed to make the step towards "able" industrial strength robots. They allow for components with explicitly stated properties. That is a prerequisite to compose systems out of reusable building blocks which provide assured and approved solutions. Models are a perfect mean to express the characteristics and structure of a *CBSE* approach [15]. In *CBSE* a complex system is split into independent units with well-formed interfaces. *CBSE* shifts the emphasis in system-building from traditional requirement analysis, system design and implementation to composing software systems out of a mixture of reusable off-the-shelf and custom-built components.

Although *CBSE* has been introduced into robotics, the missing abstraction of not using models to describe the components results in several drawbacks. Up to now, in most robotic systems fundamental properties of the software components are currently hidden in the source code of the components. In particular, *Non-Functional Properties (NFPs)* and *Quality of Service (QoS)* parameters are not explicated. Although such properties are considered being mandatory to compose complex systems out of reusable building blocks, they are not yet addressed in a systematic way by most robotic development processes. Consequently, these properties can not be taken into account neither at design-time, for example by analysis tools, nor at run-time by the robot control system.

Taking a look into current robotic systems, reuse of existing solutions is mostly limited to the level of libraries and does not take place at the system integration level. In most robotic systems the integration and reuse of existing solutions is more like plumbing and thus error-prone and time consuming. Existing solutions are mostly bound to specific robotic middleware hypes, which typically change too fast to adapt existing solutions to the new technologies.

Robotics so far circumvented the problem of a missing abstraction by not separating between the roles of the component builder and the system integrator. As long as both roles are carried out by the same persons, explicit descriptions which allow black-box reuse of existing solutions are not considered as essential. However, separation of roles is mandatory towards proper market structures and development of a robotics market. Composing complex robotic systems which are more mature and complex as current robots requires an established component market. Such a component market allows an integration of cutting edge solutions provided by different experts from different sites. Models allow to compete at the level of different implementations of components. They allow to collaborate at the model level of component interfaces and to collaborate at the system level.

Especially the run-time model usage and exploitation of the explicated properties and information is mandatory to manage the huge amount of different situations and contingencies of open environments in order to achieve robust task execution. The best matching between current situation and proper robot behavior becomes overwhelming even for the most skilled robot engineer. The sheer variety of execution variants does at design-time neither allow an optimal solution nor an exhaustive assignment of proper reactions to situations. Instead, robustness requires situation and context dependent selection of available skills and system configurations at run-time. Thus, at design-time the developer specifies variation points and corridors in which the robot can make decisions and operate at run-time [31]. Thereby, appropriate properties and resource information are to be taken into account, also to support the decision making process at run-time.

The relevance of making the step towards *MDSD* in robotics arises from multiple reasons and provides several benefits:

- abstracting from implementation details allows to express approved solutions and best-practices, as well as harmonizing and comparing different solutions independently of the implementation,

- being able to provide different implementations of the agreed abstract model allows competition at the level of implementations and collaboration at the system integration level,

- expressing *QoS* parameters, like response times, for example, to ensure collision avoidance,

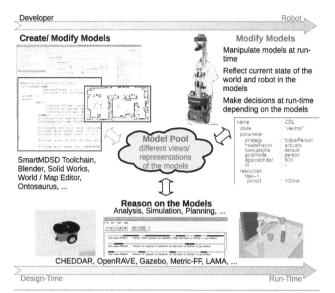

Figure 3. The system engineer, as well as the robot reason on and manipulate the same models, but with different representations and views.

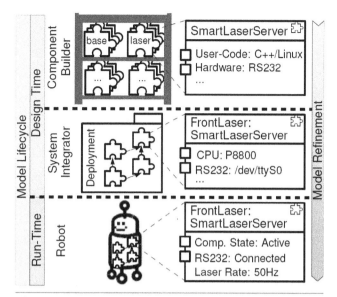

Figure 4. Model refinement by the example of software components covering design-time as well as run-time aspects.

- managing execution variants and system configurations at run-time by making the models accessible for the run-time system,

- and finally, generating other models and artifacts, like source code out of the models.

3. Model-Centric Robotic Systems

Several models covering different aspects (software components, mechanics, simulation, analysis, planning) of the overall system co-exist in parallel. The idea is not trying to harmonize the different models into one uniform representation. Rather, each model can have its specific representation according to the used tools (*CHEDDAR* [8], *OpenRAVE* [9], *Gazebo* [11], *Metric-FF* [16], etc.). This ensures that different and already existing tools and mechanisms can be used which depend on their proprietary model format. The model pool (fig. 3) can be seen as a container for the different heterogeneous models providing references to the models and maintaining meta information. It is a virtual construct to bundle the different models.

Several models which are created at design-time by the developer are used at run-time by the robot. Thus, both the system engineer and the robot reason on the parameters, constraints, properties and other information explicated in the same models. However, they access them through different representations. Knowledge of how to transform models between the different representations and which partial information has to be taken into account, what representation is required and how results can be incorporated back is encoded in the tools (design-time) and in the action-plots (run-time). To prevent inconsistencies between the different models, modifications are just carried out in the original model and not in the representations.

During the whole life-cycle the models are refined step by step until they finally get executable. The models comprise variation points which are bound during the development phase. Some variation points are bound by the component builder, while others are bound by the system integrator. The models also comprise variation points that are just bound during operation of the robot after specific context and situation dependent information is available. This way, variation points support separation of roles (e.g. component

builder, system integrator) and support run-time decisions based on design-time models.

The SMARTSOFT MDSD TOOLCHAIN (section 4) is one example of a tool covering design-time aspects of models of software components. SMARTTCL (section 5) provides mechanisms for run-time model usage. The current approach is to extract information out of the models and provide them in the desired representation to perform reasoning, analysis and simulation. As the models coexist in parallel and are not harmonized, they can be inconsistent. At design-time consistency of representations is achieved by the transformations encoded in the toolchain to generate the representation. Transformation rules encode what partial information to take from which model to end up with a consistent representation for that specific partial view. At run-time SMARTTCL action blocks represent valid queries and consistently aggregate the results in a precoded way for the particular context.

4. The SMARTSOFT TOOLCHAIN: Making the step towards MDSD in Robotics

This section illustrates how we made the step towards MDSD and introduces our SMARTSOFT MDSD TOOLCHAIN. The toolchain is based on the *Eclipse Modeling Project (EMP)* [10]. It is available for download on Sourceforge (`http://smart-robotics.sf.net`).

4.1 Identifying Stable Structures

Separating the roles of the component builder, system integrator and the robot requires to identify, specify and explicate stable structures as well as variation points each role can rely on. These stable structures and variation points build the ground for a model-based representation. Representing the structure of the component as meta-model enforces compliance of components with the meta-model via a MDSD-toolchain. We identified the component hull as the key structure to address the above challenges.

A component hull composed out of stable elements allows a component builder to provide his solutions with guarantee for system level conformance. At the same time it gives him as much freedom as possible to integrate his business logic inside the compo-

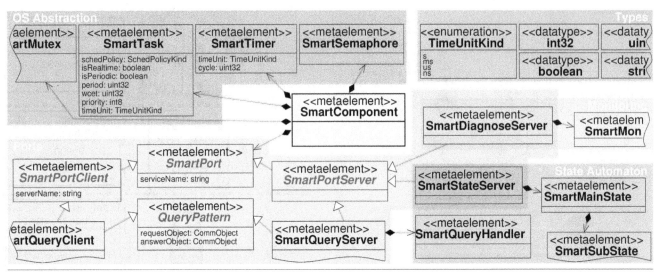

Figure 5. Excerpt of the SMARTMARS Meta-Model.

nent. The elements allow to explicate relevant information to ensure a black box view on the software components. The system integrator can then rely on the description of the component hulls to compose a system out of reusable blocks without inspecting the source files of each component. Since a component hull links the inner view and the outer view of a component, it has at least to comprise elements to explicate the communication ports and required resources (tasks, hardware dependencies), as well as access to component configurations (states, parameters).

Figure 4 illustrates how the different roles refine the model of the software components. The component builder creates a model which defines the provided/required services of the component, parameters and properties as well as constraints. First model refinements are performed and the model is enriched with the specifics of its purpose. The *SmartLaserServer*, for example, provides access to a laser range finder. The component contains two service ports: one to push the latest laser scan to subscribed clients and the other one to switch the component on and off. Furthermore, the model defines the constraints, that the user-code (business logic) of the component contains C++/Linux specific parts and that the component requires one serial port (RS232).

The system integrator picks the components out of the component shelf and deploys them onto the target system. The target system is specified by a *platform description model (PDM)* including information on the used processor type, provided hardware interfaces, the operating system and selected implementation of the SMARTSOFT framework. In this phase further variation points are bound. Constraints are checked, hardware requirements are matched with the target platform and *PDM* specific refinements on the model are performed. Such analysis, checks and simulations are based on the model of the components and their deployment.

At run-time the information explicated in the model is used to support the decision making process. The robot control system reasons and manipulates the model and reflects the adaptations in the models. The current configuration and state of the component is reflected in the run-time model representation. Using monitoring mechanisms, anomalies are detected and reported to the run-time system. The mechanisms that the robot uses to reason on the models might require specific representations depending on the mechanism. Therefore, the robot is able to transform between different representations at run-time.

Table 1. The set of patterns and services of SMARTMARS.

Pattern	Description	
send	one-way communication	
query	two-way request	
push newest	1-to-n distribution	patterns
push timed	1-to-n distribution	
event	asynchronous notification	
param	component configuration	
state	activate/deactivate component services	
wiring	dynamic component wiring	services
diagnose	introspection of components	

4.2 The SMARTMARS Meta-Model

Identifying stable structures lead to our component model which we express as the SMARTMARS (Modeling and Analysis of Robotic Systems) meta-model (fig. 5). SMARTMARS is independent of the modeling technology (*eCore, UML Profiles*). In the current version of our toolchain we implemented it as a *UML Profile* using *Papyrus UML*. That gives us a handy way to provide a graphical representation of the meta-model.

The instantiation of the SMARTMARS meta-model is the SMARTSOFT robotics framework. SMARTSOFT is independent of the implementation technology (middleware, programming language, operating system) and scales from 8-bit microcontrollers up to large scale systems [30]. Two open-source reference implementations are available. The first implementation is based on *CORBA* (*ACE/TAO*) and the second one on *ACE* [32] only.

The communication ports to handle inter-component communication are limited to a well defined set of services (table 1) with precisely defined semantics. The services are based on strictly enforced interaction patterns and are customized by the communication objects they transfer (e.g. laserscan, map). For user convenience further pre-configured services are provided (e.g. wiring, state) [29]. The services describe the outer view of a component, independent of its internal implementation. They decouple the sphere of influence and thus partition the overall complexity of the system. Internal characteristics can never span across components. The services provide stable interfaces towards the user code inside of the component and towards the other components independent of the underlying middleware structure. The interfaces can be used

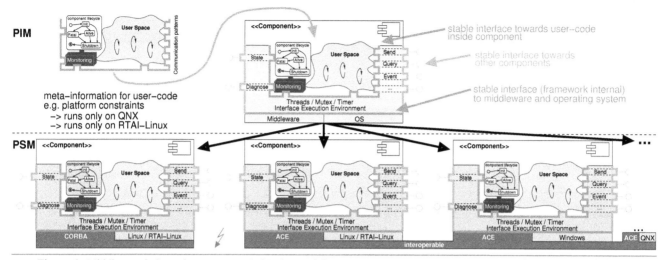

Figure 6. Middleware independence: user-code block *(top-left)* can be reused within different implementations of SMARTSOFT.

in completely different access modalities as they are not only forwarding method calls but are standalone entities. The *query* pattern, for example, provides both synchronous and asynchronous access modalities at the client side and a handler based interface at the server side. Interaction patterns are annotated with *QoS* parameters (e.g. cycle times for push timed pattern, timeouts for query and event pattern). This allows to build loosely coupled components which follow the principle of local responsibility.

The set of interaction patterns covers request/response and publish/subscribe communication as well as asynchronous notification. Dynamic reconfiguration of the components at run-time is supported by a *param* service to send name-value pairs to the components, a *state* service to activate/deactivate different behaviors of a component and *dynamic wiring* to change the connections between the components.

The *state service* is used by a component to manage transitions between service activations, to support housekeeping activities (entry/exit actions) and to hide details of private state relationships (appears as stateless interface to the outside). Inside of the components, the *state service* provides a state automaton with a generic and an individual part. The generic part provides a standardized life-cycle automaton for each component including the states: *Init*, *Alive*, *Shutdown* and *FatalError*. The individual part allows the component developer to add a component specific automaton as an extension into the Alive state of the generic automaton. [18]

Dynamic wiring is the basis for making both the control flow and the data flow configurable. This is required for situated and task dependent composition of skills to behaviors. The *wiring service* supports dynamic wiring of component services from outside (and inside) a component.It allows to connect service requesters to service providers dynamically at run time. A service requester is connected only to a compatible service provider (same pattern and communication object). Disconnecting a service requester automatically performs all housekeeping activities inside an interaction pattern to sort out not yet answered and pending calls, for example, by iterating through the affected state automatons (inside interaction patterns) and thus properly unblocking method calls that otherwise would never return. For example, the wiring mechanism already properly sorts out effects of a server being destroyed while clients are in the process of connecting to it. Of course, this relieves a component builder from a huge source of potential pitfalls.

Monitoring [18] provides a black box in a component to store different types of information from a component and to provide

this information as a generic service (*diagnose service*) to the outside of a component. This enables a system engineer, as well as the robot system itself, to gain insight into running components for the purpose of debugging, testing and monitoring. The information model of monitoring is based on *profiles*. Profiles allow to define different sources of information, individually in each component. Other components in a running system, as well as development tools, can use the *diagnose service* to request for particular information, which is currently of interest for monitoring.

4.3 Component Builder View on the Development of Components

The major steps to develop a SMARTSOFT component are depicted in fig. 6. The component builder develops the component in a platform independent representation using the meta-elements provided by the SMARTMARS meta-model. He focuses on the definition of the component hull – without any implementation details in mind. The component hull provides both a stable interface towards the user-code (inner view of component) and a stable interface towards the other components (outer view of component). These stable interfaces allow to reuse the user-code block (fig. 6 *top-left*) independent of the binding to a specific implementation of the SMARTSOFT concepts (*CORBA, ACE, Shared-Memory, etc.*). Due to the stable interface towards the user-code, algorithms and libraries can be integrated independent of any middleware structures. The integration is assisted and guided by the toolchain (e.g. *oAW recipes*). Tags on the user-code block are used to indicate constraints (e.g. runs only on *RTAI-Linux*). The stable interface towards the other components ensures replacement and rearrangement of components.

4.4 Model Transformation and Code Generation

The model transformation and code generation steps are implemented using *Xpand* and *Xtend* from the *Eclipse Modeling Project*. The transformation into the *PSM* is completely hidden from the component builder. For the component builder it looks like a one-step transformation from the *PIM* into the *PSI*. Taking a look behind the scenes the *PIM* is transformed into a *PSM* and afterwards the *PSI* is generated out of the *PSM*. The *PSI* is generated against the SMARTSOFT library. The user code is protected from modifications made by the code generator due to the *generation gap pattern* [36] which is based on inheritance.

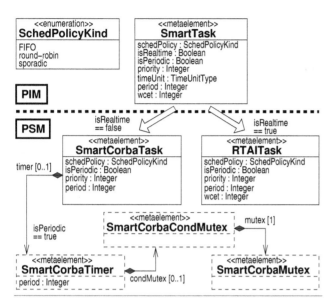

Figure 7. The transformation of the *PIM* and the *PSM* by means of the *SmartTask* meta-element.

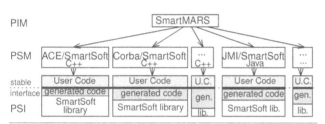

Figure 8. Generating different *PSIs*.

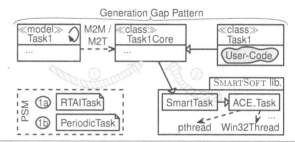

Figure 9. Gaps between desired (stable SMARTSOFT interface) and provided functionality (library) can be closed by the transformation steps (1) or by extending the library (2).

Figure 7 shows the transformation of the *PIM* and the *PSM* by the example of the *SmartTask* meta-element and the *CORBA (ACE/TAO)* based *PSM*. The *SmartTask* (*PIM*) comprises several parameters which are necessary to describe the task behavior and its characteristics independent of the implementation. Depending on the attribute `isRealtime` and the capabilities of the target platform (*PDM*) the *SmartTask* is either mapped onto an *RTAITask* or a non-realtime *SmartCorbaTask*[1]. If hard realtime capabilities are required and are not offered by the target platform, the toolchain reports this missing property. To perform realtime schedulability tests, the attributes `wcet` and `period` of the *RTAITasks* can be forwarded to appropriate analysis tools. In case the attributes specify a `non-realtime`, `periodic` *SmartTask*, the toolchain extends the *PSM* by the elements needed to emulate periodic tasks (as this feature is not covered by standard tasks). In each case the user integrates his algorithms and libraries into the stable interface provided by the `SmartTask` (user view) independent of the hidden internal mapping of the `SmartTask` (generated code).

Figure 8 illustrates how different implementations based on different middleware technologies are managed. The *PSI* consists of the SMARTSOFT library, the generated code and the user code. To be able to reuse a user-code block within different variants of SMARTSOFT, the stable interface of the user-code block needs to match with the interface generated by the transformation steps. This interface of the target platform is provided by the SMARTSOFT library and the generated code. It ensures that, for example,

a user-code block with C++ binding can be re-used within different C++ based SMARTSOFT implementations. These different implementations follow the exact same syntax and semantic. However, small gaps (if existent) between the different implementations can be closed by generating appropriate code fragments. For example, one implementation supports periodic tasks directly, while another one requires additional code fragments in the generated part of the *PSI* (cf. fig. 7).

Such gaps can be closed at least by the two ways illustrated in figure 9 by the example of the SMARTTASK: (1) Features, which are not covered by the library are added by the transformation steps into the generated code. This is either done by the M2M transformation as illustrated above by the example of making a standard task periodic, or directly in the M2T transformation step by providing suitable templates. This option has the advantage, that the library has not to be modified. (2) The missing functionality can also be integrated into the library. This option eases the transformation steps, but requires dedicated access for the framework/toolchain builder to the library. In our approach we provide the major part of the functionality within the library and thus keep the *PSM* very thin. Only small gaps are closed using the described option (1).

Furthermore, the deployment model and the models of the components can be transformed into analysis models. One example is the transformation into a *CHEDDAR* [8] specific analysis model to perform hard realtime schedulability tests. Therefore, the hard realtime tasks of the deployed components are taken into account. The parameters of the tasks which are explicated in the models are transformed into a representation which is specific to *CHEDDAR*. These transformation rules are encoded in the toolchain.

5. Exploiting Models at Run-Time

This section gives insights into the robot control system and how to use models at run-time. To support the decision making process, analysis tools are required for evaluation and balancing of different alternative plans or to check whether the desired system configuration is valid, before modifying the configuration of the robot. The concrete binding of variation points which were left open at design-time can be analysed at run-time to be able to decide for the most appropriate execution variant depending on current situation and context. In the same manner as analysis tools, simulators (e.g. physics simulators) are used to check pending execution steps with different parametrisation before the robot executes them.

The whole system from a *CBSE* point-of-view is illustrated in figure 10. To manage the huge amount of execution variants, a sequencing mechanism is used which supports the exploitation of models at run-time and thus allows to take advantage from the explicated parameters and properties. The task sequencing mechanisms are wrapped by a component hull and use thus the same communication infrastructure as the other components (skill components). The communication mechanisms between the sequencer

---

[1] Element names including *Corba*, indicate that the element belongs to the *CORBA* specific *PSM*.

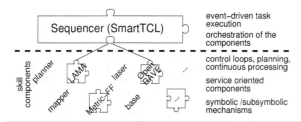

Figure 10. The sequencer coordinates the robot by orchestrating the components.

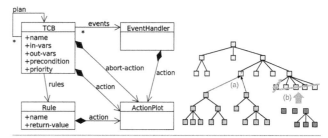

Figure 11. *left:* SMARTTCL meta-model. *right:* The SMARTTCL task-tree. (a) run-time decisions between execution variants; (b) contingency handling (*rules*) by replacing parts of the task-tree.

and the skill components are: (i) *param* to send commands and parameters by name-value pairs, (ii) *state* to activate/deactivate component internal behaviors, (iii) *query* to request information and (iv) *wiring* to change the data-flow between the components. The *event* mechanism, as well as the *diagnose* service are used by the skill components to signal notifications. The components have to follow the paradigm of local responsibility and cognizant failures [24], stating that systems should be designed to detect failures when they occur. Failures that can be handled locally inside of the component have to be handled there. Failures which can not be resolved inside the component have to be signaled (*events*) to the sequencer which provides appropriate recovery strategies. Due to the stable interfaces of the component, the different *events* which could be signaled are known at design-time and appropriate recovery strategies can be provided.

The sequencer has the control over the whole system. It performs dynamic on-line reconfigurations of the software components of the robot system. It parametrizes the components and switches different behaviors of the components on and off. The sequencer is the place to store procedural knowledge on how to configure skills to behaviors, when to use a symbolic planner or analysis tool and what kind of action plots are suitable to achieve certain goals. It bridges between continuous processing (motion control, path planning) and event driven task execution (discrete states). The sequencer directly interacts with the *Knowledge Base (KB)* to reflect, for example, the current world state, information about resources and the configuration of the software components. Furthermore, the *KB* contains information about the world, like object properties, persons and locations.

5.1 Bridging between Design-Time and Run-Time Models of Software Components

Software components are the major building blocks in almost every robotic system. They contain relevant parameters, properties and resource information which are required to be taken into account at run-time to support the decision-making process. This information can be used to perform analysis, validation, simulation and planning of different execution variants.

To take advantage of these models at run-time they are integrated into the robot control system. The *UML/XMI* representation is transformed at design-time by the toolchain into an ontology representation of the used *KB* system (e.g. *Knowledge Machine*, *PowerLOOM*). Thus a mapping of the meta-elements into the ontology concepts takes place. For example, in the meta-model a task is expressed by the meta-element `SmartTask` with attributes, like period, isPeriodic, wcet, and priority. In the ontology representation of *Knowledge Machine* the `SmartTask` is represented by the class `Task`, the attributes of the `SmartTask` are transformed to `slots` and the `composition` between the `SmartComponent` and the `SmartTask` is expressed by a `relation`.

In the deployment phase, the software components (executables), parameter files and the *KB* representation is loaded onto the

computer of the robot. At run-time, this ontology representation can then be accessed by the robot to reason on the parameters, for example, to check the resources, reflect the current state and activation of the components and the wiring between the components. This knowledge about the robot system allows for appropriate, approved and resource aware balancing between execution variants.

5.2 The Sequencer: SMARTTCL

The sequencer in the system is implemented with SMARTTCL [35]. The SMARTTCL meta-model is illustrated in figure 11 on the left. It supports hierarchical task decomposition and situation-driven task execution. At run-time a task-tree is dynamically created and modified depending on situation and context (fig. 11 *right*). SMARTTCL comprises three constructs: (i) *Task Coordination Blocks (TCB)*, (ii) *rules* for contingency handling and (iii) *event-handler* which are associated to events. Each construct comprises an action plot which contains the business logic.

The nodes of the task tree are instances of *Task Coordination Blocks (TCB)*. Each block comprises the action plot it executes and optionally a plan including references to other nodes (children). The *TCB*s are stored in the *KB* of the robot and instantiated at run-time just before execution. The concrete block is selected at run-time based on the *precondition* clause (fig. 11 *right* (a)). In SMARTTCL the reaction to failures is defined by *rules*. Whenever a *TCB* has finished, the *return message* is checked by the parent node and matched against the *rules* which are stored in the *KB*. The action plot of the matched rule is executed by the parent node, for example, to recover from a failure (fig. 11 *right* (b)). Therefore, the action plots can delete, replace or add nodes in the task tree or send commands and parameters to the components in the system. Each block is responsible to do its best trying to achieve the expected goal and state an error message (*return message*) if it fails. In such a situation only the parent which has spawned the child node "knows" about the purpose of the node in a wider context and can thus react to the failure. That hierarchical structure of responsibilities ensures a clear separation of concerns. The *rules* can be used to define a corridor in which the task execution and management of the nodes in the task tree have to remain.

In SMARTTCL a task-tree is specified at design-time. Several variation points are left open and bound at run-time: (i) selection for the exact *TCB* to execute (ii) the further expansion of a node is bound by a certain mechanism. An example for (ii) is the binding of variation points using a symbolic task planner (e.g. *Metric-FF*). At design-time just the action plot of the node calling the planner is specified. The action plot has encoded which partial information to extract out of the run-time model, how to transform it into the appropriate model representation of the symbolic task planner (e.g. *PDDL* [12]) and how to import the generated plan back into the SMARTTCL task-tree. As the generated plan is transformed into nodes of the tree, the execution is performed by the SMARTTCL

Figure 12. The clean-up scenario. (1) Kate approaches the table; (2/3) Kate stacks objects into each other; (4) Kate throws cups into the kitchen sink.

run-time system. Thus the mechanism of the *rules* is used to define how plan deviations are handled. Either the plan can be repaired locally, or a complete new plan has to be generated. This situation dependent knowledge is encoded in the action-plot of the *rules*.

6. Example

The work presented in this paper has been used to build and run several real-world scenarios, including the participation at the RoboCup@Home challenge. Our robot "Kate" can, for example, follow persons, deliver drinks, recognize persons and objects and interact with humans by gestures and speech. Different scenarios are built by composing already existing components (e.g. mapping, path planning, collision avoidance, laser ranger, robot-base, etc.) taken from the component shelf. The SMARTTCL sequencing mechanisms are also provided by a component taken from the shelf. Inside of this component the SMARTTCL model is refined to specify the desired robot behavior by adding new ones as well as reusing already existing ones. Thus, reuse takes place at the level of components as well as behaviors.

In the clean-up scenario [2] (fig. 12) the robot approaches a table, recognizes the objects which are placed on the table and cleans them either by throwing them into the trash bin or into the kitchen sink. The objects include cups, beverage cans and different types of crisp cans. The cups could be stacked into each other and have to be thrown into the kitchen sink. Beverage cans can be stacked into crisp cans and have to be thrown into the trash bin. Depending on the type of crisp can, one or two beverage cans can be stacked into. Furthermore, after throwing some of the objects into the correct destination the robot has to decide whether to drive back to the table to clean up the remaining objects (if existing) or to drive to the operator and announce the result of the cleaning task. The robot reports whether all objects on the table could be cleaned up or if any problems occurred, how many objects are still left. Already with just a few different objects to stack into each other and simple constraints on how to handle the objects, the amount of different execution variants to clean up a table gets overwhelming and can hardly be pre-program in fixed sequences of execution steps. Furthermore, contingencies, like no object could be found on the table, an object could not be grasped, no IK solution could be found to grasp an object and problems in the path-planning are handled. Almost every single step of such a sequence can fail for different reasons and requires appropriate recovery strategies. To bind the left open variation point (how to stack the objects) the node which

---

[2] http://youtu.be/xtLK-655v7k

is responsible to stack the recognized objects calls the symbolic task planner *Metric-FF*. The knowledge about recognized objects and the properties how to handle them are extracted from the *KB*, and transformed into a *PDDL* model representation, which is forwarded to the planner. The generated plan is then imported into the task-tree as child nodes. Several failures in the plan execution are handled – either the failure can be recovered locally in the task-tree or the plan has to be discarded and a complete new plan has to be generated. This recovery and re-planning strategies are managed by the parent node with the help of the *rules* and defines the corridor in which the generated plan has to remain. To further improve the robustness of the overall system the robot control system is additionally able to execute internal run-time diagnoses and to react on anomalies in the system. For example, a broken connection to the laser range finder device in the *SmartLaserServer* component is detected by monitoring and the sequencer can react on this failure and stop the robot navigation component and try to recover from that failure. Resources are managed by activating/ deactivating components (speech interaction, person tracking, localization, navigation, object recognition, *OpenRAVE*) depending on the current situation and task which is performed. For example to manipulate objects on the table, components for navigation are switched off to safe resources that can then be fully accessed by *OpenRAVE* for the trajectory planning of the manipulator. This management of the resources is performed by SMARTTCL taking information explicated in the models into account and reflecting modifications in their usage.

7. Gained Experience

In this section we describe the practical experience we gained by implementing the SMARTSOFT MDSD TOOLCHAIN. The following topics have been identified as missing in the current state, but are needed in our robotics use cases:

(1) Support for different roles (component builder, system integrator, robot) to refine the model are required to provide a clear separation between the roles. Each role should have different access policies individual for the model elements to specify and modify them. To illustrate: a component builder should, for example, be able to specify a range for a parameter, the system integrator then chooses a default value in this range and finally the robot modifies the parameter in the specified range according to the situation at run-time. The access policies should cover use cases like: (i) The component builder sets a value for a parameter that can not be changed either by the system integrator nor by the robot. (ii) The component builder models a parameter without specifying a default value. The parameter has to be bound by the system integrator, but can not be modified by the robot.

(2) Instances of components including dedicated parametrizations per instance are required by the system integrator to customize components individually for the use case and to model multiple executions of one component. For example, a robot with two laser scanners (front, rear) requires two instances of the same component. Each instance needs its individual parametrization, like different serial ports and different position offset values. The component builder should be able to specify which properties have to be bound by the system integrator during the deployment step. Instances and their individual parametrization is not adequately supported, for example, by *UML* and its extension mechanism *UML Profiles*.

(3) Mechanisms to express relations between model elements and their parameters should be included in the models. For example, we need to express that modifying the property "cycle time" of the navigation component directly changes the property "maximum allowed velocity" (e.g. linear relation). This is required that the system integrator can modify parameters in the model without knowing about their exact influence on other parameters. The relations between the model elements and their parameters should be modeled by the component builder.

(4) Binding and unbinding of model parameters. Modifying a specific parameter in the model may induce that depending parameters get unbound and have to be bound with respect to the new configuration. For example, changing the processor type invalidates all hard realtime worst-case execution times (*wcet*).

8. Related Work

In recent years, the *Model-Driven Engineering (MDE)* paradigm, has successfully been introduced in domains where systems are also highly complex, need a multi-disciplinary development approach, and require high reliability and robustness, such as: embedded systems, automotive and home automation.

For example, the *Artist2 Network of Excellence on Embedded Systems Design* [3] addresses highly relevant topics concerning realtime components and realtime execution platforms. The automotive industry is trying to establish the *AUTOSAR* standard [4] for software components and model-driven design of such components. *AUTOSAR* will provide a software infrastructure for automotive systems, based on standardized interfaces. Related to *AUTOSAR*, the ongoing *RT-Describe* project [28] addresses resource aspects. To adapt the system during run-time, *RT-Describe* relies on self-description of the components. Software components shall be enabled to autonomously reconfigure themselves, for example, by deactivating functions that are currently not needed. The *OMG MARTE* [25] activity provides a standard for modeling and analysis of realtime and embedded systems. They provide a huge number of non-functional properties (NFPs) to describe both the internals and externals of the system. Mappings to analysis models (*CHEDDAR, RapidRMA*) are available to perform scheduling analysis of *MARTE* models. This part of the *MARTE* profile is of interest to the robotics community.

In the *MOST* [23] project they are marrying ontology and software technology by integrating ontologies into *MDSD*. This is of interest for our work, as we are also dealing with both worlds. However, our focus is to reason on the models to support the decision making process of the robot at run-time.

The *DiVA* project [22] leverages models@runtime to support the design and execution of *Dynamic Software Product Lines (DSPL)* [14]. At design-time four views of a *DSPL* are described and used at run-time to drive the dynamic adaptation process. In [17], *DiVA* is used to address adaptations in robotics. The authors provide a case study to gain experience on advantages and drawbacks of applying *DiVA* to robotic systems. In their approach *DiVA* is used to adapt high-level models at run-time by the robot itself.

An introduction into robotics component-based software engineering (CBSE) can be found in [6, 7]. Several important design principles and implementation guidelines that enable the development of reusable and maintainable software building-blocks are motivated in detail. In robotics, models are currently mainly used at design-time to model single aspects like simulation, control and algorithms [20] [21]. For example, in *ROS* [27] the *Unified Robot Description Format (URDF)* is used to specify the model of the robot. This model can be used in *Gazebo* [11] (simulation) as well as in *Rviz* [27] (visualisation). Furthermore, models are used to define robotic software components. This allows to abstract from implementation and middleware details. The *Object Management Group (OMG)*, for example, has standardized a robotics component model [26]. Based on that standard several implementations [2, 13, 33] were developed. In [1] the *3-View Component Meta-Model (V3CMM)* is proposed to model component based systems independent of the execution platform. The *GenoM3* [19] project tries to harmonize different robotic frameworks by providing a generic component model and component templates that are spe-

cific for each framework. In these approaches they managed to identify stable structures and to provide them in the form of models. Thus, they can be re-used and compared. In the above mentioned approaches, models are used for documentation purposes, abstracting from implementation details, describing the components in an abstract representation and generating source code out of the models. These are already promising examples for what models can be used for, although they just cover small aspects. In comparison to those approaches, we additionally use the models to define variation points at design-time and bind them at run-time. Therefore, we take advantage of the parameters, properties and resource information which are made accessible in the models [31].

9. Conclusions and Future Work

In this paper we present the current state of our work to make the step towards model-driven engineering in robotics. We present first results of our overall goal to shift the emphasis towards a model-centric view on the whole system. Making the step from code-driven to model-driven engineering provides the ground for a component market, based on models and to provide a component shelf as described in this paper. Models encourage to separate between the roles of the component builder, system integrator and the robot. They allow to collaborate at the modelling level, and to compete at the level of implementations. That provides the freedom to choose whatever implementation technology is most adequate in a certain target domain. Furthermore, the at design-time in the models explicated information is used at run-time by the robot to support the decision making process. This is of importance to manage the huge amount of different situations and contingencies occurring in open real-world environments.

The presented work on the SMARTSOFT MDSD TOOLCHAIN provides promising results and reflects the state of the art of applying *MDSD* to the service robotics domain. The toolchain has successfully been used to build several robotic scenarios. The *MDSD* approach helped us to come up with running systems and to successfully master their overall complexity. Mastering the component hull with the help of a *MDSD* toolchain significantly improved the learning curve of developing proper robotics components. The component builder is guided by the toolchain and compliance with our component model is achieved by the meta-model. Students writing their thesis or doing an intern in our lab are able to build components without giving them to much explanations. We agree on the component hull and define the services the component should offer and they are free to implement the business logic according to their needs. The remaining component required to develop a whole scenario can be taken form our component shelf. Our robocup team, for example, which is driven by students from our university could reuse several of the already existing components without going through the source code of the components. A fixed component hull allows to implement components based on that hull but providing a different business logic inside the component. Consequently they can easily be replaced and thus compared against each other.

Providing stable structures in the form of meta-models proved to abstract from implementation details. The stable structures we identified and provide as our SMARTSOFT component model already demonstrate that different implementations can be provided. We have developed two reference implementations, one based on *ACE* (*messaging*) and the other one on *CORBA* (*ACE/TAO*). Furthermore, [5] is working on a *DDS* based implementation of SMARTSOFT.

In our toolchain the transformation currently relies on the two steps (i) *PIM* to *PSM* (M2M) and (ii) *PSM* to *PSI* (M2T). This strict two step transformation enforces a too narrow transformation workflow. Adding platform information is an important, but not the only step. The focus should be shifted towards a stepwise refinement of the model without any fixed number of steps. In such a refinement workflow, the target platform information, as well as results gained from analysis or simulations are incorporated step by step whenever new information is available or already available information has changed. Future work will deal with model refinement and its integrations into our toolchain. We will further extend the usage of the very same models during system development, deployment and at run-time. Especially the further integration of run-time simulation coordinated by the sequencer will be next steps for that the current results already provide a suitable foundation.

Acknowledgments

This work has been conducted within the *ZAFH Servicerobotik* (http://www.servicerobotik.de/). The authors gratefully acknowledge the research grants of state of Baden-Württemberg and the European Union. We thank Dennis Stampfer for his extraordinary support in implementing the SMARTSOFT MDSD TOOLCHAIN. We greatfully acknowledge the work of Jonas Brich, Siegfried Hochdorfer, Matthias Lutz and Manuel Wopfner for their contributions to the clean-up scenario described in the example section.

References

[1] D. Alonso, C. Vicente-Chicote, F. Ortiz, J. Pastor, and Álvarez B. V3CMM: a 3-View Component Meta-Model for Model-Driven Robotic Software Development. *Journal of Software Engineering for Robotics (JOSER)*, 2009.

[2] N. Ando, T. Suehiro, K. Kitagaki, T. Kotoku, and W. Yoon. RT-Component Object Model in RTMiddleware - Distributed Component Middleware for RT (Robot Technology). In *IEEE Int. Symposium on Computational Intelligence in Robotics and Automation (CIRA)*, 2005.

[3] ARTIST. Network of excellence on embedded system design. http://www.artist-embedded.org/, visited on May 15th 2011.

[4] AUTOSAR. Automotive open system architecture. http://www.autosar.org/, visited on May 15th 2011.

[5] J. Bandera, A. Romero-Garces, and J. Martinez. Towards a DDS-based Platform Specific Model for Robotics. In *6th Int. Workshop on Software Development and Integration in Robotics (SDIR VI) affiliated with ICRA 2011*, Shanghai, China, 2011.

[6] D. Brugali and P. Scandurra. Component-Based Robotic Engineering (Part I). *IEEE Robotics & Automation Magazine*, 16(4):84–96, Dezember 2009.

[7] D. Brugali and A. Shakhimardanov. Component-Based Robotic Engineering (Part II). *IEEE Robotics & Automation Magazine*, 17(1): 100–112, March 2010.

[8] Cheddar. a free real time scheduling analyzer, http://beru.univ-brest.fr/~singhoff/cheddar/, May 15th 2011.

[9] R. Diankov. *Automated Construction of Robotic Manipulation Programs*. PhD thesis, Carnegie Mellon University, Robotics Institute, August 2010.

[10] Eclipse Modeling Project. http://www.eclipse.org/modeling/, February 15th 2011.

[11] Gazebo. Gazebo - 3D multiple robot simulator with dynamics, 2006. http://playerstage.sourceforge.net/gazebo/gazebo.html, visited on May 15th 2011.

[12] M. Ghallab, C. K. Isi, S. Penberthy, D. E. Smith, Y. Sun, and D. Weld. PDDL - The Planning Domain Definition Language. Technical report, CVC TR-98-003/DCS TR-1165, Yale Center for Computational Vision and Control, 1998.

[13] Gostai RTC. http://www.gostai.com/products/rtc/, May 15th 2011.

[14] S. Hallsteinsen, M. Hinchey, S. Park, and K. Schmid. Dynamic Software Product Lines. *IEEE Computer*, 41(4):93–95, April 2008. ISSN 0018-9162.

[15] G. T. Heineman and W. T. Councill. *Component-Based Software Engineering: Putting the Pieces Together*. Addison-Wesley Professional, June 2001. ISBN 0201704854.

[16] J. Hoffmann and B. Nebel. The FF Planning System: Fast Plan Generation Through Heuristic Search. *Journal of Artificial Intelligence Research*, 14:253–302, 2001.

[17] J. F. Inglés-Romero, C. Vicente-Chicote, B. Morin, and B. Olivier. Using Models@Runtime for Designing Adaptive Robotics Software: an Experience Report. In *1st Int. workshop on Model Based Engineering for Robotics: RoSym'10 at (MODELS'10)*, Oslo, Norway, 2010.

[18] A. Lotz, A. Steck, and C. Schlegel. Runtime Monitoring of Robotics Software Components: Increasing Robustness of Service Robotic Systems. In *Int. Conf. on Advanced Robotics (ICAR)*, 2011.

[19] A. Mallet, C. Pasteur, M. Herrb, S. Lemaignan, and F. Ingrand. GenoM3: Building middleware-independent robotic components. In *IEEE Int. Conf. on Robotics and Automation (ICRA)*, 2010.

[20] Matlab / Simulink. http://www.mathworks.com/, May 15th 2011.

[21] MODELICA. http://www.modelica.org/, May 15th 2011.

[22] B. Morin, O. Barais, J.-M. Jézéquel, F. Fleurey, and A. Solberg. Models@Runtime to Support Dynamic Adaptation. *IEEE Computer*, pages 44–51, October 2009.

[23] MOST. Marrying Ontology and Software Technology. http://www.most-project.eu, visited on May 15th 2011.

[24] F. Noreils. Integrating error recovery in a mobile robot control system. In *Int. Conf. on Robotics and Automation (ICRA)*, pages 396–401, 1990.

[25] OMG MARTE. A UML Profile for MARTE: Modeling and Analysis of Real-Time Embedded systems, Beta 2, ptc/2008-06-08, June 2008.

[26] OMG RTC. Robotic Technology Component (RTC) Specification 1.0, 2008. http://www.omg.org/spec/RTC, May 15th 2011.

[27] M. Quigley, B. Gerkey, K. Conley, J. Faust, T. Foote, J. Leibs, E. Berger, R. Wheeler, and A. Ng. ROS: An open-source Robot Operating System. In *ICRA Workshop on OSS*, 2009.

[28] RT-Describe. Iterative Design Process for Self-Describing Real Time Embedded Software Components, 2010. http://www.esk.fraunhofer.de/en/projects/RT-Describe.html, visited on May 15th 2011.

[29] C. Schlegel. Communication Patterns as Key Towards Component-Based Robotics. *Int. Journal of Advanced Robotic Systems*, 3(1):49–54, 2006.

[30] C. Schlegel, T. Haßler, A. Lotz, and A. Steck. Robotic software systems: From code-driven to model-driven designs. In *Int. Conf. on Advanced Robotics (ICAR)*, June 2009.

[31] C. Schlegel, A. Steck, D. Brugali, and A. Knoll. Design Abstraction and Processes in Robotics: From Code-Driven to Model-Driven Engineering. In *Int. Conf. on Simulation, Modeling and Programming for Autonomous Robots (SIMPAR)*, volume 6472 of *LNCS*, pages 324–335. Springer, Darmstadt, Germany, 2010.

[32] D. Schmidt. The ADAPTIVE Communication Environment. http://www.cs.wustl.edu/~schmidt/, visited on May 15th 2011.

[33] B. Song, S. Jung, C. Jang, and S. Kim. An Introduction to Robot Component Model for OPRoS (Open Platform for Robotic Services). In *Workshop Proceedings of SIMPAR*, pages 592–603, 2008.

[34] T. Stahl and M. Völter. *Model-Driven Software Development: Technology, Engineering, Management*. Wiley, Chichester, UK, 2006. ISBN 978-0-470-02570-3.

[35] A. Steck and C. Schlegel. SmartTCL: An Execution Language for Conditional Reactive Task Execution in a Three Layer Architecture for Service Robots. In *Int. Workshop on DYnamic languages for RObotic and Sensors systems (DYROS/SIMPAR)*, pages 274–277. Springer, Darmstadt, Germany, 2010. ISBN 978-3-00-032863-3.

[36] J. Vlissides. Pattern Hatching – Generation Gap Pattern. http://researchweb.watson.ibm.com/designpatterns/pubs/gg.html, visited on May 15th 2011.

Generating Database Migrations for Evolving Web Applications

Sander D. Vermolen   Guido Wachsmuth   Eelco Visser

Delft University of Technology, The Netherlands

{s.d.vermolen, g.h.wachsmuth, e.visser}@tudelft.nl

Abstract

WebDSL is a domain-specific language for the implementation of
dynamic web applications with a rich data model. It provides developers with object-oriented data modeling concepts but abstracts
over implementation details for persisting application data in relational databases. When the underlying data model of an application
evolves, persisted application data has to be migrated. While implementing migration at the database level breaks the abstractions provided by WebDSL, an implementation at the data model level requires to intermingle migration with application code. In this paper,
we present a domain-specific language for the coupled evolution of
data models and application data. It allows to specify data model
evolution as a separate concern at the data model level and can be
compiled to migration code at the database level. Its linguistic integration with WebDSL enables static checks for evolution validity
and correctness.

Categories and Subject Descriptors   D.3.4 [*Programming Languages*]: Processors;   H.2.1 [*Database Management*]: Logical Design

General Terms   Languages

Keywords   Evolution, Domain Specific Language, Data Migration, Web Application

1. Introduction

WebDSL is a domain-specific language for the implementation
of dynamic web applications with a rich data model [16]. It provides developers with object-oriented data modeling concepts.
These concepts abstract over implementation details for persistence. These details are added in a two-step compilation process. In
the first step, the WebDSL compiler generates application code in
an object-oriented general purpose programming language, which
is Java. To achieve persistence, the generated code relies on the
Hibernate framework. This framework realizes an object-relational
mapping (ORM): Application data is kept in objects at runtime but
is persisted in a relational database. In the second step, the generated application code is compiled and the persistence framework
generates a relational database schema. When deploying the application, a relational database management system (RDBMS) generates an initial, empty database from this schema. The deployed
application will interact with the RDMBS to store and to retrieve
its data.

GPCE'11,   October 22–23, 2011, Portland, Oregon, USA.
Copyright © 2011 ACM 978-1-4503-0689-8/11/10... $10.00

Problem Statement.   As any other software, web applications and
their data models evolve. An evolved application has to be re-
compiled and redeployed. During recompilation, the persistence
framework generates a new database schema. Typically, the original database no longer complies with the new schema and original
application data cannot be accessed from the evolved application
anymore. During redeployment, the RDBMS instead generates a
new initial database from the new schema. But original application
data is a valuable asset. It needs to be migrated to co-evolve with
the application and its data model.

Implementing migrations at the database level breaks the abstractions provided by WebDSL. Developers have to be aware of
the persistence framework and its ORM to make sure that the migrated database complies with the new schema. They also have to
be aware of the RDBMS to provide details such as character set
definitions, collations, and storage engines.

To avoid breaking abstractions, migrations can be implemented
at the data model level in WebDSL. Since the generated code will
make extensive usage of the ORM, migration does not scale to large
amounts of data and is typically performed lazily. The application
migrates original data only when it needs to access this data. As
a consequence, the original data model has to remain part of the
evolving data model and application code is intermingled with
migration code. Maintenance of data model, application code, and
migration code becomes harder with every new evolution step.

Contribution.   In our previous work, we compiled an extensive
catalog of coupled operators for the evolution of object-oriented
data models [8]. These operators couple common evolution steps
at the data model level with their corresponding migrations at the
data level. In this paper, we focus on the implementation of these
operators in Acoda, a tool for the coupled evolution of WebDSL
data models and databases.

Acoda provides a domain-specific language for specifying data
model evolution as a separate concern at the data model level.
Its IDE offers static checks for evolution validity and correctness.
While evolution validity ensures that an evolution can be applied
to the original data model, evolution correctness secures that the
evolution yields the evolved data model.

Acoda implements coupled operators as a mapping from evolution steps to migration code in SQL. In this paper, we discuss this
mapping for particular operators in detail, including complex operators that work along the inheritance hierarchy or over references.
Thereby, we distinguish three kinds of migrations. First, *schema
modifications* change only the database schema. Second, *conservative migrations* rearrange data without data loss. Third, *lossy migration* supports potential data loss on purpose.

Outline.   We briefly introduce WebDSL's data modeling concepts
and its ORM in the next section. In Section 3, we discuss evolution
specification. In Sections 4 to 6, we address the generation of
migration code for selected operators in detail. We conclude the
paper with a discussion in Section 7.

2. WebDSL

WebDSL is a domain-specific language for the development of dynamic web applications that integrates data models, user interface models, actions, validation, access control, and workflow [16]. The WebDSL compiler verifies the consistency of web applications and generates complete implementations in Java. In this section, we focus on WebDSL's data modeling concepts and the ORM underlying the generated Java code.

Data modeling. A data model definition in WebDSL features *entity* declarations, which comprise a name and a set of properties. An entity declaration might inherit from another entity declaration, indicated with : . Each *property* has a name and a type. We distinguish two kinds of properties: Value properties, indicated with :: , and associations, indicated with → . For value properties, WebDSL supports basic data types such as `Bool` and `String`, but also domain-specific types such as `Email`, `Secret`, and `WikiText`, which all provide additional functionality. Associations refer either to entities declared in the data model (*single-valued*) or to a **Set** or **List** thereof (*multi-valued*).

Figure 1 (top) shows a data model for a publication management application similar to Researchr[1]. It models publications written by authors and a special type of publication, namely the published volume. Additionally, users can register and create personal bibliographies, which are collections of publications.

Object-relational Mapping. WebDSL's data modeling concepts abstract over implementation details for persistence. These details are added by the WebDSL compiler which addresses Hibernate as a persistence framework. At runtime, application data is kept in objects which are stored persistently in a relational database. There is a database table for each hierarchy of entities, named after the root entity declaration in a hierarchy. Throughout the paper, we will call these tables *hierarchy tables*. In the running example, there will be four tables `_User`, `_Bibliography`, `_Publication`, and `_Author`. Each of these tables has at least two columns: `id` stores object ids and acts as the primary key of the table while `DISCRIMINATOR` is used to distinguish which entity in the hierarchy is instantiated by an object. Object ids are implemented by universally unique identifiers (UUIDs) and are therefore database-wide (and beyond) unique.

Additional columns are added for each value property and for each single-valued association declared in one of the entities in an entity hierarchy. Since columns for single-valued associations will store the ID of a referred object, they act as implicit references. The implicit references are made explicit by a foreign key to the `id` column in the table corresponding to the type of an association. The RDBMS enforces foreign keys by preventing (or canceling) database operations that break integrity. The `_Bibliography` table will have three columns: `id` (primary key), `DISCRIMINATOR`, and `Bibliography_owner` (foreign key to `id` in `_User`).

Multi-valued associations are stored in separate *connection tables*. The names of these tables are composed from the names of the declaring entity, the association, and the association type. Each connection table has two columns to store pairs of object ids (referring and referred object). Both columns are foreign keys to the `id` column of the table corresponding to the declaring entity respectively the association type. A multi-valued association can either be a **Set** or a **List**. For sets, we place a primary key on the two columns, since we may not store a pair of objects twice. For lists, an additional index column is needed to persist order. Here we place a primary key on the combination of declaring entity reference and the index, since there can just be one reference per position

---

[1] Researchr is a web application for finding, collecting, sharing, and reviewing scientific publications: http://researchr.org.

```
─────────────────────── original data model ───────────────────────

entity Author {
    name :: String
}

entity User {
    email    :: Email
    password :: Secret
    public   :: Bool
}

entity Bibliography {
    owner        → User (not null)
    publications → Set<Publication>
}

entity Publication {
    key      :: String
    title    :: String
    abstract :: WikiText
    authors  → List<Author>
}

entity PublishedVolume : Publication {
    publisher :: String
}

─────────────────────── evolved data model ───────────────────────

entity Person {
    alias → Set<Alias> (not empty)
    email :: Email
}

entity Alias {
    name :: String (id)
}

entity User : Person {
    password :: Secret
}

entity Bibliography {
    public       :: Bool
    owner        → User (not null)
    publications → Set<Publication>
}

entity Publication {
    registrant → User
    key        :: String
    title      :: String
    abstract   :: WikiText
    authors    → List<Person>
}

entity PublishedVolume : Publication {
    editors   → List<Person>
    publisher :: String
}

─────────────────────── evolution model ───────────────────────

1 create Publication.registrant → User;
2 collect Bibliography.public over owner;

3 rename entity Author to Person;
4 create PublishedVolume.editors → List<Person>;
5 add super Person to User;
6 pull up Person.email;

7 extract entity Alias{name::String} from Person as alias;
8 make Alias.name id;
9 generalize Person.alias to Set;
```

Figure 1. Running example

in a list. For example, the association `Publication.authors` is stored in a connection table `Publication_authors_Author` with three columns `_Publication_id` (foreign key to `id` in `_Publication`), `Publicationauthorindex`, and `authors_id` (foreign key to `id` in `_Author`), where the first two columns act as the primary key.

3. Modeling Data Model Evolution

Typically, the evolution of a data model is only implicitly defined by its original and evolved version. For example, the middle part of Figure 1 shows an evolved version of the data model from the top of the figure. In this section, we discuss means to model this evolution explicitly.

Coupled Operators. Informally, the example evolution follows three stages: First, bibliography management is extended by allowing users to submit new publications, hence they are linked to publications as `registrant` and can now individually set bibliography visibility. This requires adding an association from `User` to `Publication` and a `public` property to bibliographies. The latter is collected from the `owner` of a bibliography as not to lose the user settings. Second, the system is refactored to support editors. This requires addition of an `editors` association, as well as renaming `Author` to a more general `Person`. Consequently, `User` can become a sub entity of `Person`, since they may also be editor or author of publications. The `email` of users is then generalized to be able to store email addresses for editors and authors. Third, the system is extended to support people (authors, editors, or users) to have different name aliases. Therefore, a person's `name` is extracted into a new entity, in which names are stored uniquely.

We can model this evolution as a sequence of coupled operator applications [8, 18]. At the data model level, coupled operators capture common evolution steps. Thereby, they go beyond simple creations, changes, and deletions of entities and properties. For example, the evolution model from the bottom part of Figure 1 includes the collection of a property over an association, the pull-up of a property into a parent entity, and the extraction of an entity. Each of these operators couples the evolution step at the data model level with a corresponding migration. This allows us to compile evolution models into migration code for the database level.

Linguistic Integration. The language for evolution models is linguistically integrated with WebDSL. It reuses WebDSL's data modeling concepts and parts of their syntax definition. For example, constructs for property and entity creation reuse the syntax for properties and entities. An evolution model includes references to the original and evolved data model. Static checks ensure evolution validity and correctness with respect to these data models. For evolution validity, preconditions for operator applications are checked in the context of the original data model [15]. These preconditions secure that the evolution can be applied to the original data model. For evolution correctness, it is checked whether the evolution maps the original data model to the evolved data model.

Migration. To migrate the original database, each operator application in an evolution model is compiled to its corresponding migration code. Thereby, the compiler follows the same ORM as the WebDSL compiler, namely Hibernate. This ensures that migrating the original database and generating an initial schema for the evolved data model will result in the same database schema. Furthermore, the compiler is aware of the RDMBS and generates details such as character set definitions, collations, and storage engines[2].

In the following sections, we discuss database migration for selected coupled operators. Thereby, we distinguish three kinds of migrations. Operators such as property and entity creation only require *schema modification*. Their corresponding migrations affect the database schema but not the stored data. We discuss such operators in Section 4. Many other operators such as entity renaming, entity extraction, super addition, or cardinality generalization allow for *conservative data migration*. Their corresponding migrations affect both the database schema and the stored data. But the

stored data is completely preserved during migration, no data is lost. We discuss such operators in Section 5. Only few operators such as property collection or property identification require *lossy migration*. Their corresponding migrations may not preserve the stored data completely. Some data may be lost intentionally during migration. We discuss such operators in Section 6.

4. Schema Modification

Schema modifying migrations change the database schema, but leave the persistent data untouched. They generally allow for more information to be stored and are thereby most commonly needed while extending application functionality.

4.1 Property Creation

In earlier work [8], we identified two coupled operators for property creation: one for value properties and one for associations. But in WebDSL and its Hibernate configuration, single-valued associations and multi-valued associations are dealt with differently. The first is stored inside the containing entity's table, the second is stored in its own connection table. Thus, Acoda provides three different coupled operators for property creation: one for value properties, one for single-valued associations, and one for multi-valued associations.

When we create a new value property in a data model, the original database schema is missing a column for this property. To be precise, the hierarchy table corresponding to the entity containing the new property is missing a column. We need to create the missing column in order to migrate the original database.

For the creation of a new single-valued association, the migration is similar. Again, the hierarchy table corresponding to the containing entity is missing a column for storing ids of the associated entity. Additionally, a foreign key needs to be created to enforce validity. This foreign key needs to point to the `id` column of the hierarchy table corresponding to the associated entity.

Example. Acoda generates the following migration for the creation of the `registrant` association in the running example:

```
1 create Publication.registrant → User;
```

```
ALTER TABLE _Publication
    ADD COLUMN `Publication_registrant`
        VARCHAR(32) default NULL,
    ADD CONSTRAINT f_Publication_registrant
        FOREIGN KEY `f_Publication_registrant`
            (Publication_registrant)
        REFERENCES _User (id);
```

It consists of a single SQL statement altering the `_Publication` table. First, it adds a new column `Publication_registrant` to store the association. Afterwards, it constrains this column with a foreign key to `id` in `_User`.

In contrast to single-valued references, multi-valued references are stored in separate connection tables. When we create a new multi-valued association in a data model, the original database schema is missing a table for this association. We need to create this table in order to migrate the original database.

Example. Acoda generates the following migration for the creation of the `editors` association:

```
4 create PublishedVolume.editors → List<Person>;
```

```
CREATE TABLE `PublishedVolume_editors_Person` (
    `_PublishedVolume_id` VARCHAR(32) default NULL,
    `_editors_id` VARCHAR(32) default NULL,
    `PublishedVolumeeditorsindex` integer,
    PRIMARY KEY (`_PublishedVolume_id`,
        `PublishedVolumeeditorsindex`),
    INDEX `forward_lookup`
```

---

[2] In the examples, we omit these details for readability.

```
        (_PublishedVolume_id(14)),
   CONSTRAINT `f_PublishedVolume_editors_b`
     FOREIGN KEY `f_PublishedVolume_editors_b`
       (_PublishedVolume_id)
     REFERENCES _Publication (id),
   CONSTRAINT `f_PublishedVolume_editors_f`
     FOREIGN KEY `f_PublishedVolume_editors_f`
       (_editors_id)
     REFERENCES _Person (id)
);
```

It comprises a single statement creating a table connecting `_PublishedVolume` to `_Person`. The table has three columns to store ids of published volumes, ids of persons, and list indices since order does matter. For a published volume and an index, the associated editor needs to be unique. Thus, the published volume and the index form the primary key of the table. Validity of the two columns which store ids is ensured by foreign keys. These point to the `id` columns in the connected tables. In order to support efficient use of the connection table, database indices are generated for the primary key, allowing efficient single editor lookup, and for the published volumes column, allowing efficient collection of the complete list of editors for a published volume.

4.2 Entity Creation

Similar to property creation, Acoda provides different coupled operators for the creation of a new entity: one for entities that do not extend another entity and one for entities that do.

When we create a new entity which does not extend another entity, the original database is missing a hierarchy table for this entity and connection tables for its multi-valued associations. We need to create these tables in order to migrate the original database. Since we explained the creation of connection tables already in the previous section, we only focus on the hierarchy table. Following Hibernate, this table needs to be named like the entity and needs to provide two columns `id` and `DISCRIMINATOR` as well as additional columns for value properties and single-valued associations. Columns for single-valued associations need to be constrained by foreign keys.

When we create a new entity which extends another entity, the original database is missing columns for its value properties and single-valued associations and connection tables for its multi-valued associations. The columns are missing in the hierarchy table of the extended entity. Thus, the migration is the same as for creating the properties of the new entity. Creating its value properties and single-valued associations will add the missing columns while creating its multi-valued associations will add the missing connection tables.

Figure 2 presents creation of an **entity** A:B with single- and multi-valued features `sf 1 .. sf n` and `mf 1 .. mf m` graphically. The figure above the dashed line shows the database before migration, the figure below the dashed line after migration. Each array denotes a table, each cell within an array a column. An open cell denotes columns which were already present before modification and remain unaltered. A solid double arrow denotes a uniqueness key, a dashed double arrow denotes a database index, and a single arrow denotes a foreign key. A* denotes the root entity in the hierarchy of entity A, t(a) denotes the target type of an association a. The id columns are always unique. We therefore omit the double solid uniqueness arrow on id columns.

5. Conservative Data Migration

Conservative migrations are needed when the domain of an application shifts or expands. They change the schema and rearrange data but do not lose information. Conservative migrations are most common in practice, yet tedious and error-prone to write manually.

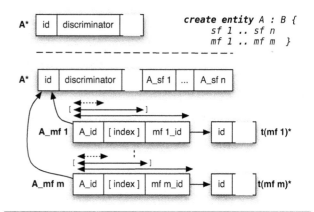

Figure 2. Database modification for entity creation.

5.1 Entity Renaming

In schema generation, entity names influence table and column names in hierarchy and connection tables as well as associated foreign keys. When an entity is renamed, these names need to be updated and foreign keys need to be recreated. More specifically, renaming entity A requires the following schema modifications:

1. Drop foreign keys for single- and multi-valued associations in A

2. Drop foreign keys for single- and multi-valued associations of type A

3. Rename the hierarchy table for A if A=A*

4. Rename columns for value properties and single-valued associations in A

5. Rename connection tables for multi-valued associations in A

6. Rename columns for multi-valued associations in A

7. Rename columns for multi-valued associations of type A

8. Create foreign keys for single- and multi-valued associations in A

9. Create foreign keys for single- and multi-valued associations of type A

However, entity names are also used as discriminator, distinguishing between different entities in a hierarchy. An entity rename therefore needs to migrate the data inside the hierarchy table for A, by replacing the old entity name in the `DISCRIMINATOR` column by the new entity name.

Example. Acoda generates the following migration for renaming `Author` to `Person`:

```
3 rename entity Author to Person;
```

```
ALTER TABLE Publication_authors_Author
  DROP FOREIGN KEY `f_Publication_authors_f`;
ALTER TABLE _Author
  RENAME _Person;
ALTER TABLE Publication_authors_Author
  RENAME Publication_authors_Person,
  ADD CONSTRAINT `f_Publication_authors_f`
    FOREIGN KEY `f_Publication_authors_f` (_authors_id)
    REFERENCES _Person (id),
UPDATE _Person
  SET DISCRIMINATOR = "Person"
  WHERE DISCRIMINATOR = "Author";
```

First, the foreign key for the `Publication.authors` association is dropped, after which the hierarchy table `_Author` can be renamed. Next, the connection table for the association is renamed and the dropped foreign key is recreated. Finally, the object discriminators are updated.

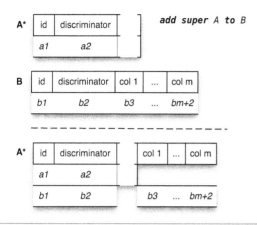

Figure 3. Database modification for super type addition.

5.2 Super Addition

When the original application models two inheritance-unrelated entities, separate tables are used to store the inheritance trees of both. When the application evolves by adding a super entity joining the two inheritance trees, the target application only uses a single table to store both entities. To support the new application, the original tables and associated data needs to be merged. The schema modifications are presented graphically in Figure 3. The migration of adding super entity A to entity B comprises the following steps:

1. Expand the table for A* by all single-valued properties in the inheritance tree of B (inh(B))

2. Create foreign keys for outward single-valued associations in inh(B)

3. Copy single-valued data from the old table for B to the table for A*

4. Drop foreign keys for outward (multi-valued and single-valued) associations in inh(B)

5. Create foreign keys for outward multi-valued associations in inh(B)

6. Drop foreign keys for inward associations to inh(B)

7. Create foreign keys for inward associations to inh(B)

8. Drop the old table for B

Step 1 creates the new space to store data for B and its sub entities inside the table, which was originally only used for A* and its sub entities. Step 2 creates foreign keys pointing away from the table of A*. Step 3 prevents any loss of data. Steps 5 and 7 create foreign keys pointing to the table of A*, which work on the copied data. Steps 4 and 6 drop all foreign keys, that point to the table for B, to prevent breaking the database integrity. Finally, step 8 deletes the old data. The order of steps is crucial, it targets to maximize the number of constraints at any point in migration: Foreign keys for outward single-valued associations are added before copying data, since they point away from the table for A* and thereby also hold on an incomplete (or empty) set of B records. Foreign keys for outward multi-valued associations and inward associations are created after copying, since they point to the table for A* and therefore require a complete data set. The foreign keys are dropped before the data is dropped to prevent them from breaking and the foreign keys are dropped before they are recreated to prevent name clashes. Note that except for their foreign keys, any connection table associated to inh(B) remains unaltered.

Example. In the running example, Person becomes super entity of User. Following the scheme outlined above: User has two single-valued properties email and password, which are added

to the Person table in step 1. Both these properties are attributes, hence step 2 can be omitted. Next, the user data is copied from the User table to the Person table in step 3. Step 4 can again be omitted. User has one inward association registrant from Publication, whose new foreign key is added in step 5 and whose old foreign key is dropped in step 7. Step 6 can again be omitted and step 8 drops the old user data. The steps are formalized in the following migration:

```
5 add super Person to User;
```

```
ALTER TABLE _Person
    ADD COLUMN `User_email` VARCHAR(255) DEFAULT '';
    ADD COLUMN `User_password` VARCHAR(255) DEFAULT '';
INSERT INTO _Person
    (id,DISCRIMINATOR, version_opt_lock,
        User_email, User_password)
    SELECT id,DISCRIMINATOR,
        version_opt_lock,_email,_password
    FROM _User;
ALTER TABLE _Publication
    DROP FOREIGN KEY `f_Publication_registrant`;
ALTER TABLE _Publication
    ADD CONSTRAINT `f_Publication_registrant`
    FOREIGN KEY `f_Publication_registrant`
    (Publication_registrant)
    REFERENCES _Person (id);
DROP TABLE _User;
```

5.3 Entity Extraction

To enrich a data model, an entity may need to be extracted from another entity. During entity extraction, a new entity is created using some or all of the properties of an existing source entity. A single-valued association is created to link objects of the two entities. An example entity extraction can be found in the running example, where Alias is extracted from Person, using a new association alias. We distinguish the following steps in a migration for extracting entity B from A as a:

1. Adapt the schema to store B

2. Add a column for a to the table for A*

3. Generate new identifiers in the column for a

4. Copy a as id and other single-valued columns in B from the table for A*

5. Create a foreign key for a

6. Drop the old columns in the table for A*

7. Move the data for multi-valued properties in B and update their ids using the mapping provided by a

Step 1 comprises a migration for creating an entity, as discussed in Section 4.2. Step 2 adds a column, but leaves out its foreign key. Step 3 generates new ids, which can be sequentially numbered, or as in our case UUIDs. Step 4 then performs the extraction for all single-valued data, by copying their columns including the newly generated ids and a discriminator ('B') to the new table. As the identifier duplication now validates the foreign key, it can be created in step 5. Step 6 then drops the old single-valued data from the table for A*. Finally, step 7 moves the multi-valued data to new connection tables, which were created in step 1. This data references A objects, whereas they should now be referencing B objects, therefore there links need to be updated using the mapping specified in the table for A* (id, A_a). After moving the multi-valued data, the old connection tables are dropped. Note that step 4 moves each property across association a to B. We could therefore have reused the migration generation for moving properties, yet this would yield an inefficient migration. Copying all data in one pass over the table for A* is more efficient then separate passes for each of the single-valued properties in B.

Figure 4 shows the database before and after migration. The data set identifiers are generated (step 3 above) and the data set for

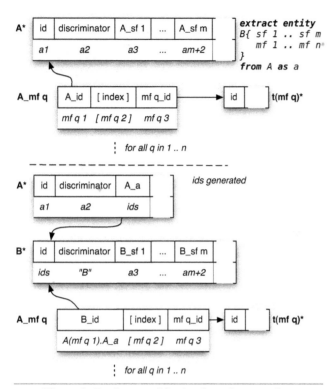

extract entity
B{ sf 1 .. sf m
   mf 1 .. mf n
}
from A as a

ids generated

for all q in 1 .. n

Figure 4. Database modification for entity extraction.

`B_id` is obtained by applying the mapping from `A` objects to `B` objects (step 7).

Example. In the running example, we extract entity `Alias` and its `name` property from `Person`, while creating an association `alias`. To adapt the database, we generate the migration shown below. Step 7 above is not represented, since `Alias` has no multi-valued properties.

```
7 extract entity Alias{name::String} from Person as alias;
```

```
CREATE TABLE IF NOT EXISTS `_Alias` (
    `DISCRIMINATOR` VARCHAR(255) default '',
    `id` VARCHAR(32) default NULL,
    `Alias_name` VARCHAR(255) default '',
    PRIMARY KEY (`id`)
);
ALTER TABLE _Person
    ADD COLUMN `Person_alias` VARCHAR(32)
        default NULL;
UPDATE _Person
    SET Person_alias = UUID();
INSERT INTO _Alias
    SELECT "Alias", Person_alias, Person_name
    FROM _Person;
ALTER TABLE _Person
    ADD CONSTRAINT `f_Person_alias`
    FOREIGN KEY `f_Person_alias` (Person_alias)
    REFERENCES _Alias (id);
ALTER TABLE _Person
    DROP COLUMN Person_name;
```

5.4 Maximum Cardinality Generalization

During the lifetime of an application, attributes often get generalized to expand the application's functionality. One type of property generalization is increasing its maximum cardinality. Any multi-valued cardinality uses the same database structure, its exact number is irrelevant. However, a single-valued association is represented as a column, whereas a multi-valued association as a connection table. In the running example, a person's alias is stored

within the `Person` table before step 7 and stored in a connection table afterwards. To support such generalization, we need to generate a migration, which first creates the connection table, then moves the data from the main table to the connection table and subsequently drops the old column.

Example. For generalizing the maximum `alias` cardinality in the running example, we generate the migration below. The first statement creates a connection table as discussed in Section 4.1. The second statement inserts the old data into the new connection table. The last two statements drop the old column by first dropping the foreign key and then dropping the column itself.

```
9 generalize Person.alias to Set;
```

```
CREATE TABLE IF NOT EXISTS `Person_alias_Alias` (
    `_Person_id` VARCHAR(32) default NULL,
    `_alias_id` VARCHAR(32) default NULL,
    INDEX `forward_lookup` (_Person_id(14)),
    CONSTRAINT `f_Person_alias_b`
        FOREIGN KEY `f_Person_alias_b` (_Person_id)
        REFERENCES _Person (id),
    CONSTRAINT `f_Person_alias_f`
        FOREIGN KEY `f_Person_alias_f` (_alias_id)
        REFERENCES _Alias (id)
);
INSERT INTO Person_alias_Alias
    SELECT id, Person_alias
    FROM _Person
    WHERE Person_alias IS NOT NULL;
ALTER TABLE _Person
    DROP FOREIGN KEY f_Person_alias;
ALTER TABLE _Person
    DROP Person_alias;
```

5.5 Property Pull-Up

For pulling up a property, Acoda provides different migrations for value properties, single-valued associations, and multi-valued associations. Value properties as well as single-valued associations are stored inside the inheritance hierarchy table. A property is pulled up from each of the sibling entities inside the hierarchy. The pulled up property is stored in one database column. During migration, the values for the different sibling columns need to be combined. This is achieved by creating the new column `A_f`, copying the data sets of each of the sibling properties separately and dropping the sibling properties afterwards. Figure 5 presents single-valued pull up. The pulled up data (`a12` to `an2`) is merged to form a new column `A_f`. When associations are pulled up, the old foreign keys are dropped (arrows in figure) and a single foreign key is created along with the new column `A_f`.

Example. In the running example, `email` is pulled up from `User` to `Person`. Email is a single-valued property and `User` has no sibling entities. Thus, for the example, we need to merge a single column with no foreign key, which amounts to creating a new column, copying the data and dropping the old column:

```
6 pull up Person.email;
```

```
ALTER TABLE _Person
    ADD COLUMN `Person_email`
    VARCHAR(255) DEFAULT '';
UPDATE _Person
    SET Person_email = User_email
    WHERE DISCRIMINATOR='User';
ALTER TABLE _Person
    DROP COLUMN `User_email`;
```

When pulling up a multi-valued association, the set of sibling associations is stored in a collection of connection tables. These need to be merged into a new table which has column names and foreign keys adapted to the new containing type. In contrast to single-valued associations, merging of multi-valued associations comprises a union of the sibling data sets and can thus be done in one SQL statement.

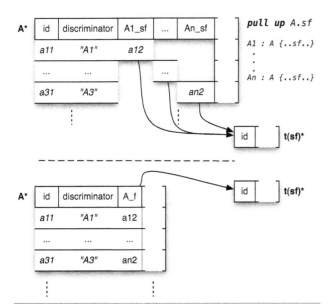

Figure 5. Database modification for single-valued property pull up.

6. Lossy Migration

Although data loss is generally not desirable, when correcting design flaws it can often not be avoided. Additionally, in many cases a migration may in theory potentially cause data loss, yet in practice for many databases this will not actually be the case.

6.1 Property Collection

It is common for properties to be repositioned during the life-span of an application. They can be repositioned across an inheritance relation (e.g. **pull up**), but can also be repositioned across an association. In WebDSL, associations are directed. When repositioning a property in the direction of the association, we speak of *moving* a property, when repositioning opposite to the association direction, we speak of *collecting* a property. When a property is repositioned across an association, we call the association a *bridge*.

There are two main reasons for collecting properties: First, the application may use numerous dereferences to access a property, in which case the dereference can be made permanent by collecting the property. Second, the property might no longer logically belong to the referred object but to the referring object. This is the case in our running example: We want to distinguish for each bibliography if it is public or not. In the original data model, the distinction is made only on a per user basis. Thus, the corresponding property `public` needs to be collected from `User` to `Bibliography`, using `owner` as a bridge.

Property collection may cause loss of data, since the bridge may not be surjective. There may be users who have set their public field but do not have a bibliography. To adapt a database to a collected single-valued property `f` in `A` from `B` across single-valued association `bridge`[3], we first create the new column to store `f`. Next, we join the tables for A* and B* (we compute their cross product) and filter the result on records where the bridge holds (`A.bridge = B.id`). Then we copy the old column for `f` to the new column for `f` in the cross product result. Finally we drop the old column for `f`. If `f` is an association, its new foreign key needs to be created along with creating its new column and its old foreign key needs to be dropped before dropping the old column.

---

[3] Note that A and B could be the same type

Figure 6. Database modification for property collection.

Note that the database index on the (primary) id column of the table for B ensures that the table join can be computed efficiently.

Figure 6 shows the process graphically, in which the middle stage represents the intermediate signature during update. During migration, data is typically duplicated: A user can have multiple bibliographies, each of which gets the same public value.

Example. To collect `public` from `User` to `Bibliography` in our running example, we generate the migration below. The first and last statement create and delete columns to store the `public` property. The second statement copies (and duplicates) the information by updating the `Bibliography` and `User` table joined together using `owner` as criterium.

```
collect Bibliography.public over owner;
```

```
ALTER TABLE _Bibliography
    ADD COLUMN 'Bibliography_public' BIT(1)
    DEFAULT FALSE;
UPDATE _Bibliography target, _User source
    SET target.Bibliography_public = source.User_public
    WHERE target.Bibliography_owner = source.id;
ALTER TABLE _User
    DROP User_public;
```

There are different migrations for collecting multi-valued properties and for collecting properties across a multi-valued bridge. In both cases, the migration is extended by including connection tables. When collecting a property across a multi-valued bridge, we need to extend the join above by the connection table representing the bridge. When collecting a multi-valued property, the property is represented as a connection table and we can thereby make a new connection table by rewriting the connection table's reference to B into a reference to A, using the bridge. To apply the rewriting efficiently, a database index on the bridge needs to be generated first.

6.2 Property Identification

When a property is kept unique by the application, yet is not modeled as such, it can be made unique to ensure correctness of the application logic. Also, when data is stored redundantly, it can be compacted by enforcing uniqueness of redundant properties. The latter is the case in the running example, where multiple aliases with the same name exist after entity extraction. By making an alias' name unique, only one object would be needed per name.

Although the schema generated for the new application would match the original schema, the application logic assumes property uniqueness, whereas this is not guaranteed by the database. The original database may contain duplicate values. Migration needs

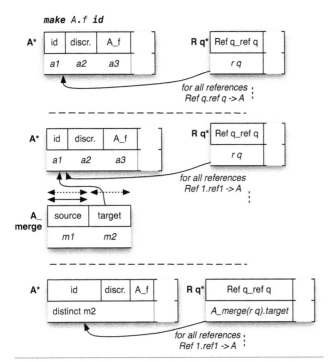

make A.f id

A* | id | discr. | A_f
a1 | a2 | a3

R q* | Ref q_ref q
r q

for all references
Ref q.ref q -> A

A* | id | discr. | A_f
a1 | a2 | a3

R q* | Ref q_ref q
r q

for all references
Ref 1.ref1 -> A

A_
merge | source | target
m1 | m2

A* | id | discr. | A_f
distinct m2

R q* | Ref q_ref q
A_merge(r q).target

for all references
Ref 1.ref1 -> A

Figure 7. Database modification for attribute identification.

to resolve these duplicates as to ensure uniqueness. There are two approaches to enforcing uniqueness: Either the identifying values are adapted to be unique, yet it is hard to provide a decent strategy to do so and in practice this is rarely desirable. Or the objects which contain duplicate values are merged. We use the latter. It may merge objects, which are not exactly the same, in which case information is lost.

Merging objects along an identifying property comprises two tasks: the objects need to be merged and all associations to these objects need to be updated to point to the merged objects. Both tasks make extensive use of a mapping from original objects to merged objects. As this mapping is computationally complex to derive, we compute it once and reuse the result. The schematical changes for making property `A.f` an identifier are shown in Figure 7. The top-most part shows the table for `A` and associations to this table, which may both be from single-valued associations (columns) as well as multi-valued associations (connection tables). The middle part shows the computed mapping from `A` object ids (source) to merged `A` object ids (target). Only the `target` column has a foreign key to `A*`. At the start of migration the source column also references `A` ids, yet after merge, `source` may point to no longer existing, merged objects. The bottom part shows the schema after migration.

For making `Alias.name` an identifier (step 8 in the running example), Acoda generates the following migration:

```
8 make Alias.name id;
```

```
CREATE TABLE Alias_merge
(   INDEX forward_lookup (source),
    INDEX reverse_lookup (target)   )
    CONSTRAINT `f_Alias_merge`
        FOREIGN KEY `f_Alias_merge`
        (target)
        REFERENCES _Alias (id)
    SELECT original.id AS source, target
    FROM
        _Alias AS original,
        (   SELECT min(id) AS target, Alias_name
            FROM _Alias
            GROUP BY Alias_name   ) AS merged
```

```
        WHERE original.Alias_name = merged.Alias_name;
UPDATE _Person AS ref, Alias_merge AS map
    SET ref.Person_alias = map.target
    WHERE ref.Person_alias = map.source;
DELETE FROM _Alias
    WHERE NOT EXISTS
    (   SELECT *
        FROM Alias_merge AS map
        WHERE map.target = id);
ALTER TABLE _Alias
    ADD CONSTRAINT `Alias_name_unique`
    UNIQUE (_name);
DROP TABLE MergeMap_Alias;
```

The first statement computes and stores the mapping form original aliases to merged aliases. It uses two indices for efficient lookup: a forward index to rewrite the associations and a backward index to update the alias table. The second statement updates the `alias` association from `Person`, which at this point in migration is still single-valued. The update joins the `Person` table and the map to update all associations efficiently. The third statement drops the old and redundant aliases, which can now safely be removed, since they are no longer in use. The fourth statement enforces uniqueness and the final statement removes the merge map.

7. Discussion

Related Work. Migration generation is common in software development. Evolving data models require data migration, evolving DTDs require XML migration, and evolving schema require database migration. Furthermore, migration is not restricted to data modeling. It also occurs where meta-models evolve, where domain-specific languages evolve [13], and where grammars evolve [14]. The coupled transformation problem is ubiquitous [11]. In this section, we relate our work to existing work on data model evolution and to work on coupled evolution in general.

Ruby on Rails offers support for migration of databases along an evolving web application[4]. The web applications use an ORM to persist data in a relational database. They offer support for versioning different databases running different versions of the same application. In contrast to our work, the Ruby on Rails migration support requires the developer to define database migrations himself in terms of the relational database. Ruby on Rails offers a set of SQL-like methods to alter a database, such as `create_table`, `add_column` and `remove_index`. They do not offer an evolution language at the application abstraction level.

In the area of data model evolution, most work focuses on evolving schema and migrating databases [2, 5, 6]. Schema describe structure of data storage, primarily focusing on storage techniques to improve query performance. Evolving schema requires the developer to be concerned with database implementation details. In our work, we bridge the ORM to allow the developer to define evolution in the application domain and abstract away from database details. From the application-level evolution specification, we generate schema evolution definitions (in SQL). We rely on the previous work on schema evolution to efficiently map the generated schema evolution onto a database migration. On the one hand, this allows the developer to reason in terms of application logic instead of database techniques. On the other hand, it allows us to introduce more advanced concepts into evolution specifications, such as inheritance, cardinalities, and associations.

Visser et al. formalize the more general coupled transformations [1, 4, 17]: Not only conforming artifacts are considered (such as a database or XML document), also dependent artifact transformations are formalized (such as query and constraint migration). The formalization makes use of data refinement theory and uses Haskell for presentation. Visser et al. do not offer concrete migrations in addition to the presented formalization. Although they

---

[4] http://guides.rubyonrails.org/migrations.html

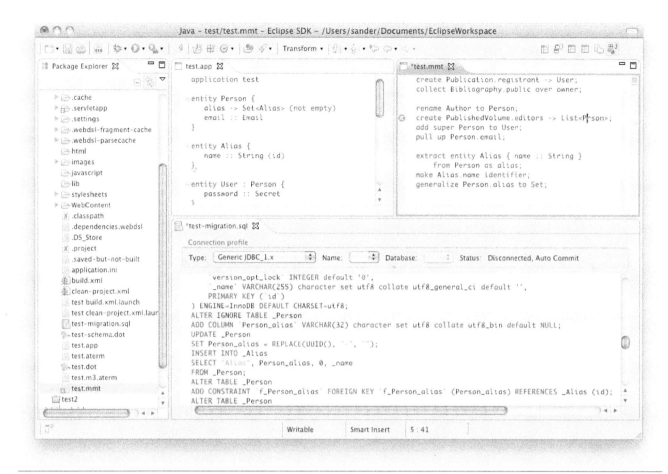

Figure 8. Screenshot of the Acoda Eclipse plugin. The left-most column shows the regular Eclipse project tree. The top-left editor displays a WebDSL data model. The top-right editor shows the evolution specification. The bottom editor shows the generated SQL migration.

consider flattening hierarchies and present a formalization of such, they do not consider inheritance, or a complete ORM. In their concluding remarks, they point out that inheritance would be useful to include, to extend the scope to object-oriented data models.

Lämmel and Lohmann discuss migration of XML data along evolving DTDs [12]. They formalize the migration concepts and distinguish two groups of evolution: refactorings and structure-extending and -reducing evolutions. They discuss higher-level evolutions, such as folding and generalization. Lämmel and Lohmann do not offer a language for describing evolution.

Similar to the application models considered in our work, meta-models are defined in terms of high-level concepts, such as inheritance and cardinalities. Meta-model evolution languages cover a high level of abstraction and are similar to evolution steps on object-oriented data models [3, 7, 9, 18]. We therefore reused the evolution steps defined on meta-models, which are outlined in previous work [8]. In contrast to our work, in meta-modeling, there is a close relationship between the data set structure and the data definition: models closely follow the structure defined in their meta-model. The relational structure of a RDBMS, does not closely follow the object-oriented structure of an application-level model. Thus, where model migration does not need to cover the gap between defined structure and implemented structure, our work covers the mapping between object domain and relational domain: the ORM.

Implementation.   The presented evolution modeling language is implemented as a part of Acoda[5]. To seamlessly integrate into regular development, Acoda offers an Eclipse plugin developed using Spoofax/IMP [10]. It operates in cooperation with the (already available) WebDSL plugin, which provides WebDSL application editing and compilation services. Acoda offers additional functionality around evolving WebDSL data models, such as comparison of original and evolved data model to yield an evolution model [15]; editor support for editing evolution models (such as syntax highlighting, instant error marking and content completion); generation of SQL migration code; and application of migrations to a database. The plugin can be used in the context of agile development, in which it supports a short development - migration - deployment - testing loop. For migration of production databases, Acoda also offers a stand alone version, which can be run on-site or remotely.

Figure 8 shows a screenshot of the plugin. The left-most column shows the regular Eclipse project tree. The top-left editor displays a WebDSL data model (the running example). This editor is provided by the WebDSL plugin. The top-right editor shows the evolution specification used throughout the paper, with a small typo to show evolution validity checking and corresponding error marking. This editor is provided by the Acoda plugin. The bottom editor shows the SQL migration generated by the plugin. Although this migration can be viewed and adapted by the developer, general practice is to apply the evolution specification directly, without examining

---

[5] http://swerl.tudelft.nl/bin/view/Acoda

91

SQL code. However, this still generates the SQL migration internally, which is then applied to the database.

Changing Persistence Implementation. WebDSL abstracts over implementation details for persistence. The presented migration generation is aligned to Hibernate. But the WebDSL compiler might change some of the parameters for Hibernate's ORM or might even address another persistence framework. Such changes would be transparent to evolution models, since Acoda abstracts over implementation details for migration and preserves WebDSL's data modeling abstractions. The Acoda compiler needs to reflect these changes and has to address the same ORM as the WebDSL compiler. These changes primarily amount to naming differences (of columns, tables, and keys) and a different type of inheritance representation (e.g. using separate tables for each entity, instead of hierarchy tables). To cope with naming differences, the naming in Acoda is pluggable and can be replaced by another naming scheme. To cope with a different inheritance representation, migration generations dealing with inheritance (e.g. the presented sub entity creation, property pull-up, and super addition) need to be adapted. Considering inheritance flattening is the more complex variant, adaptation will generally simplify migration generation.

Performance & Uptime. Databases serve live web applications. Database migration may cause application downtime. Good performance of migration is important to limit downtime.

Acoda constructs migrations from database operations. Efficiency of their implementation depends on the used RDBMS. Nevertheless, we optimize the usage of database operations at two levels: First, we combine evolution operators at the data model level to form more complex operators with a more efficient migration at the database level. For example, a class creation and a feature addition can be combined into a single class creation. Second, we combine SQL operations in the generated migrations at the database level. Acoda compiles a sequence of evolution operators into a sequence of SQL statement sequences. These sequences may overlap. For example, two changes on a table (e.g. a rename and a column addition) may be generated for different evolution operators, yet can be combined into a single `ALTER TABLE` statement, thus significantly improving performance. The two kinds of optimizations target to generate the most efficient migration script.

Furthermore, the generated migrations attempt to shorten the time in which the database is inaccessible as much as possible. For example, the super addition postpones data deletion to the last step, even though it could have been applied earlier. This allows the database to stay online in read-only mode while the more computation intensive steps are executed (such as copying data). Additionally, migrations generally only target a part of the database, remaining application data stays accessible (both readable and writable). In practice however, most migrations are short and can be executed while the application is updated. They cause little or no additional downtime on regular-sized (WebDSL) databases.

Acknowledgments

This research was supported by NWO/JACQUARD project 638. 001.610, *MoDSE: Model-Driven Software Evolution*.

References

[1] T. Alves, P. Silva, and J. Visser. Constraint-aware schema transformation. In *Ninth International Workshop on Rule-Based Programming*, 2008.

[2] P. Berdaguer, A. Cunha, H. Pacheco, and J. Visser. Coupled schema transformation and data conversion for XML and SQL. In *Practical Aspects of Declarative Languages (PADL 2007)*, volume 4354 of *LNCS*, pages 290–304. Springer, 2007.

[3] A. Cicchetti, D. D. Ruscio, R. Eramo, and A. Pierantonio. Automating co-evolution in model-driven engineering. In *Enterprise Distributed Object Computing Conference (EDOC 2008)*. IEEE, 2008.

[4] A. Cunha, J. Oliveira, and J. Visser. Type-safe two-level data transformation. In *Formal Methods Europe (FME 2006)*, volume 4085 of *LNCS*, pages 284–299. Springer, 2006.

[5] A. Gupta, I. S. Mumick, and V. S. Subrahmanian. Maintaining views incrementally. In *International conference on management of data (SIGMOD 1993)*, pages 157–166, New York, NY, USA, 1993. ACM.

[6] J.-L. Hainaut, C. Tonneau, M. Joris, and M. Chandelon. Schema transformation techniques for database reverse engineering. In *Proceedings of the 12th Intl. Conf. on the Entity-Relationship Approach (ER 1993)*, pages 364–375, London, UK, 1994. Springer-Verlag.

[7] M. Herrmannsdoerfer, S. Benz, and E. Juergens. COPE - automating coupled evolution of metamodels and models. In *ECOOP 2009 - Object-Oriented Programming*. Springer, 2009.

[8] M. Herrmannsdoerfer, S. D. Vermolen, and G. Wachsmuth. An extensive catalog of operators for the coupled evolution of metamodels and models. In *Software Language Engineering, Third International Conference (SLE 2010)*, LNCS. Springer, 2010.

[9] J. Hoßler, M. Soden, and H. Eichler. Coevolution of models, metamodels and transformations. In *Models and Human Reasoning*, pages 129–154, Berlin, 2005. Wissenschaft und Technik Verlag.

[10] L. C. L. Kats, K. T. Kalleberg, and E. Visser. Domain-specific languages for composable editor plugins. In *Proceedings of the Ninth Workshop on Language Descriptions, Tools, and Applications (LDTA 2009)*, Electronic Notes in Theoretical Computer Science. Elsevier Science Publishers, April 2009.

[11] R. Lämmel. Coupled software transformations (extended abstract). In *First International Workshop on Software Evolution Transformations*, Nov. 2004.

[12] R. Lämmel and W. Lohmann. Format evolution. In *RETIS 01: Proc. 7th International Conference on Reverse Engineering for Information Systems*, volume 155 of *books@ocg.at*, pages 113–134. OCG, 2001.

[13] M. Pizka and E. Juergens. Tool supported multi level language evolution. In *In Proceedings of SVM'07: Software and Services Variability Management Workshop Concepts, Models and Tools*, 2007.

[14] S. D. Vermolen and E. Visser. Heterogeneous coupled evolution of software languages. In *Model Driven Engineering Languages and Systems (Models 2008)*, volume 5301 of *LNCS*, pages 630–644. Springer, 2008.

[15] S. D. Vermolen, G. Wachsmuth, and E. Visser. Reconstructing complex metamodel evolution. In *Software Language Engineering, Fourth International Conference, SLE 2011, Braga, Portugal, Revised Selected Papers*, Lecture Notes in Computer Science. Springer Berlin / Heidelberg, 2012. To Appear.

[16] E. Visser. WebDSL: A case study in domain-specific language engineering. In *Generative and Transformational Techniques in Software Engineering (GTTSE 2007)*, volume 5235 of *LNCS*. Springer, 2008.

[17] J. Visser. Coupled transformation of schemas, documents, queries, and constraints. *Electron. Notes Theor. Comput. Sci.*, 200(3):3–23, 2008. ISSN 1571-0661.

[18] G. Wachsmuth. Metamodel adaptation and model co-adaptation. In *ECOOP 2007 - Object-Oriented Programming*, volume 4609 of *LNCS*, pages 600–624. Springer Berlin / Heidelberg, 2007.

Pragmatics for Formal Semantics

Olivier Danvy

Department of Computer Science, University of Aarhus *

danvy@cs.au.dk

Abstract

This tech talk describes how to write and how to inter-derive formal semantics for sequential programming languages. The progress reported here is (1) concrete guidelines to write each formal semantics to alleviate their proof obligations, and (2) simple calculational tools to obtain a formal semantics from another.

Categories and Subject Descriptors   D.1.1 [*Software*]: Programming Techniques—applicative (functional) programming; D.3.2 [*Programming Languages*]: Language Classifications—applicative (functional) languages; F.3.1 [*Logics and Meanings of Programs*]: Specifying and Verifying and Reasoning about Programs—Specification techniques; F.4.1 [*Mathematical Logic and Formal Languages*]: Mathematical Logic—Lambda calculus and related systems.

General Terms   Algorithms, Languages, Theory

Biosketch

Olivier Danvy is interested in all aspects of programming languages, including programming. His other mother is the Université Pierre et Marie Curie (Paris VI: PhD, 1986) and his other mother in law is Aarhus University (DSc, 2006), where he is currently supervising his 22nd PhD student.

References

[1] Olivier Danvy, Jacob Johannsen, and Ian Zerny. A walk in the semantic park. In Siau-Cheng Khoo and Jeremy Siek, editors, *Proceedings of the 2011 ACM SIGPLAN Workshop on Partial Evaluation and Semantics-Based Program Manipulation (PEPM 2011)*, pages 1–12, Austin, Texas, January 2011. ACM Press. Invited talk.

---

* Aabogade 34, DK-8200 Aarhus N, Denmark
http://users-cs.au.dk/danvy

GPCE'11,   October 22–23, 2011, Portland, Oregon, USA.
ACM 978-1-4503-0689-8/11/10.

Keynote

Application of Model Based Development to Flexible Code Generation

Gary Shubert
Lockheed Martin Space Systems
Denver, CO, USA
gary.j.shubert@lmco.com

Abstract

This address will present the author's views and perspectives on the past, present and future use of model based development techniques to enable the automated generation of source code and other forms of programming. This address will discuss past and present use of model based development and automated code generation at Lockheed Martin, with special emphasis on NASA's Orion Multi-Purpose Crew Vehicle Program. This address will discuss the advantages and disadvantages, associated with the current state of the practice techniques and tools, used to automatically generate source code from general purpose and domain specific models. This address will discuss the obstacles and enablers, associated with achieving the desired future state of complete and efficient automated generation of programming through transformation of general purpose and domain specific models.

Categories & Subject Descriptors: D.1.2 [**Automatic Programming (I.2.2)**]: Algorithms, Performance, Design, Standardization, Languages.

General Terms: Performance, Design, Reliability, Experimentation, Languages, Verification.

Bio

Gary Shubert is currently a Senior Software Manager for Lockheed Martin Space Systems Company and leads systems and software model based engineering process development and demonstration activities for the Military Support Program - System Evolution Test Bed and for the Space Vehicle Integration Laboratory. Gary joined Lockheed Martin in 1989 and has served in roles as an embedded flight software developer, flight software architect, and flight software manager, for launch vehicle, uncrewed and crewed spacecraft systems. Gary served as the software manager for the Orion proposal activities and as the flight software manager for the Orion development program. Gary has served as an avionics lead, software lead, and software architect, for the Space Based Radar, Reusable Space Transportation System, Evolved Expendable Launch Vehicle (Atlas V), and Space Common Data Link programs, and as a flight software engineer for the Titan IV and Advanced Interceptor Technologies programs. Gary has been a practitioner and a champion of model based software engineering and transformational automated code generation since 1989. He is the architect for three generations of Lockheed Martin developed automated code generators used on multiple production programs.

Gary is an instructor for Lockheed Martin's Object Centric Modeling and Ada programming language courses. His background prior to Lockheed Martin includes being a flight software engineer in the Control Systems Advanced Development department of Northrop Aircraft, and an independent verification and validation engineer and ground software engineer for the Mission Software department of TRW Defense Systems. He holds a bachelor's degree in Aeronautical/Astronautical Engineering from the University of Illinois, and a master's degree in Aeronautical/Astronautical Engineering from the University of Southern California.

Reflection in Direct Style

Kenichi Asai

Ochanomizu University
asai@is.ocha.ac.jp

Abstract

A reflective language enables us to access, inspect, and/or modify
the language semantics from within the same language framework.
Although the degree of semantics exposure differs from one language to another, the most powerful approach, referred to as the
behavioral reflection, exposes the entire language semantics (or the
language interpreter) that defines behavior of user programs for
user inspection/modification. In this paper, we deal with the behavioral reflection in the context of a functional language Scheme. In
particular, we show how to construct a reflective interpreter where
user programs are interpreted by the tower of metacircular interpreters and have the ability to change any parts of the interpreters
during execution. Its distinctive feature compared to the previous
work is that the metalevel interpreters observed by users are written in direct style. Based on the past attempt of the present author, the current work solves the level-shifting anomaly by defunctionalizing and inspecting the top of the continuation frames. The
resulting system enables us to freely go up and down the levels
and access/modify the direct-style metalevel interpreter. This is in
contrast to the previous system where metalevel interpreters were
written in continuation-passing style (CPS) and only CPS functions
could be exposed to users for modification.

Categories and Subject Descriptors D.3.3 [*Programming Languages*]: Language Constructs and Features—Control structures;
D.3.4 [*Programming Languages*]: Processors—Interpreters

General Terms Languages

Keywords Reflection, metacircular interpreter, metacontinuation,
continuation-passing style (CPS), direct style, partial evaluation

1. Introduction

A reflective language enables us to access, inspect, and/or modify
the language semantics from within the same language framework.
Originally, reflection was proposed by Smith in his pioneering work
on 3-LISP [15], where user programs were executed by an infinite
number of metacircular interpreters (called a reflective tower) and
had access to the expression, environment, and continuation of the
current computation. Since these pieces of information determine
the complete state of computation, user programs effectively have
control over how the state of computation is manipulated, in other
words, the language semantics itself. This kind of reflection is
called behavioral reflection.

The theoretical idea of 3-LISP was followed by two reflective
languages, Brown [6, 17] and Blond [5], which explained switching
of levels using metacontinuations and improved on the efficient
execution of programs under a tower of interpreters. The ability
to change the metalevel interpreter, as opposed to simply having
access to the state of computation, was added to these languages
by the present author in the reflective language Black [1, 2]. In this
language, the metalevel interpreter (or the operational semantics of
the language) is open to user programs as a collection of standard
functions and is subject to change at runtime. User programs have
not only access to the state of computation but also ability to change
the operational semantics directly.

The idea of reflection affected the design of programming languages in various ways. In the object-oriented language CLOS
(Common Lisp Object System), metaobject protocol [11] was used
to grant user programs access to metaobjects that define the semantics of baselevel objects as a kind of metacircular interpreter.
Similar idea was applied in the concurrent object-oriented language
ABCL/R3 [13] to tune and optimize the behavior of concurrent
objects. The idea of reflection was further developed into Aspect-
Oriented Programming [12], where various kinds of semantic aspects (among many cross-cutting concerns) are modularized and
made public for user control.

Although reflective capabilities are strong and useful, the reflective mechanisms provided in most languages are restricted, because
it is difficult to efficiently execute reflective programs, in particular
the ones that use behavioral reflection. For example, Java allows to
access various information via reflection, but does not allow radical
changes to the language semantics. On the other hand, it is difficult
to predict all the reflective capabilities that could be useful beforehand. Thus, whenever we need new reflective capabilities, we need
to modify the underlying language implementation.

To remedy this situation, the original approach to the behavioral
reflection using metacircular interpreters is gaining interest. Most
notably, Verwaest et al. [16] recently proposed a reflective system
which adopts Smalltalk-like object model with a tower of first-
class interpreters. Because the full language semantics is exposed
to user programs as a first-class interpreter, any modification to the
language semantics is possible.

To back up such work and provide its foundation, we deal with
the behavioral reflection in the context of a functional language
Scheme. In particular, we consider how to build a reflective system
in which the metalevel interpreter is written without any restriction. In our previous work [2], we have already proposed a general method to build a reflective system, but the method crucially
depended on the fact that the metalevel interpreter was written in
continuation-passing style (CPS). In this paper, we remove this restriction and allow for the metalevel interpreter to be written in the
ordinary direct style. In our past attempt [1], we have already constructed such a reflective system, but it was not quite right because
it suffered from the level-shifting anomaly. This paper clarifies why
the anomaly occurs and shows one possible method to avoid it. As

a result, the current system becomes the first such system without the anomaly.

The system is easier to use than before, since we do not have to program in CPS any more. We shall demonstrate a number of example executions in the paper. Theoretically, this paper clarifies how to build a reflective system where the metalevel interpreters are written in direct style. More practically, it gives a foundation upon which advanced features such as runtime specialization can be built for efficient execution of reflective programs.

2. Preliminaries: `shift` and `reset`

We will use the delimited control operators [4], `shift` and `reset`, in this paper. The `shift` operator captures and clears the current continuation up to the enclosing `reset` operator and binds it to its first argument before executing its second argument. For example, in the following expression

```
(+ 1 (reset (* 2 (shift k (k (k 3)))))))
```

the captured continuation bound to k is (* 2 □). It is applied twice in the body of `shift`, so the `shift` expression evaluates to 12. Since the captured continuation is cleared, it becomes the value of `reset` and the final answer becomes 13.

The `shift` operator is like `call-with-current-continuation`, but is different in that the captured continuation is delimited and thus composable, and that the captured continuation is cleared. We will use the delimited context as a representation of a level, and use `shift` to capture the continuation of the current level.

3. The reflective language Black

The reflective language we use in this paper is a Scheme-based language called Black [1, 2]. It is a standard Scheme interpreter with two new reflective constructs, EM and exit. The former stands for *Execute at Metalevel* and evaluates its argument at the metalevel, namely, at the level of the interpreter the current expression is evaluated. The latter is used to finish the current level and go up to the metalevel. The interaction between exit and the reflective framework in this paper will become one of the interesting topics of this paper.

To see how EM works, we demonstrate some example execution of Black.

```
> (black)
0-0: start
0-1> (* 2 (+ 1 4))
0-1: 10
0-2>
```

It is basically a standard Scheme interpreter. The first number 0 in the prompt indicates the current level. The second number indicates the number of iterations in the current level. To evaluate an expression at the metalevel, we use EM.

```
0-2> (EM (* 2 (+ 1 4)))
0-2: 10
0-3>
```

When EM is executed, its argument is sent as is to the metalevel for execution. At the metalevel, the expression (* 2 (+ 1 4)) is evaluated to 10 and the result is sent back to the current level.

We can observe the metalevel interpreter using EM.

```
0-3> (EM base-eval)
0-3: #<procedure #2 base-eval>
0-4>
```

The main function of the metalevel interpreter is called `base-eval`. We can even modify the definition of `base-eval` executing the

user programs. To do so, however, we need to know how the metalevel interpreter is written. Figure 1 shows the main parts of the metalevel interpreter. User programs are *supposed* to be executed by this interpreter. In other words, this is the interpreter observed by the user programs whenever they access it using EM. However, the actual Black interpreter is different from this user-observable interpreter. The Black interpreter executes user programs as though they are interpreted by the user-observable interpreter. It defines the API to access the metalevel, or the Metaobject Protocol, so to speak.

The user-observable interpreter is a standard eval/apply-style interpreter written in monadic style. Given an expression e and an environment r, the main function `base-eval` dispatches over e, and executes one of `eval-*` functions. We call these functions that comprise an interpreter *evaluator functions*. Lambda closures are represented as a tagged list, where the address (eq-ness) of `lambda-tag` is used to distinguish closures from other data.

The interpreter is standard except for three points. First, it includes `eval-EM` to interpret the EM construct. Its definition is (almost) metacircular: a special construct `primitive-EM` is used to interpret EM. The former is a primitive version of EM where the argument is evaluated before it is sent to the metalevel. The important point here is that the behavior of `eval-EM` cannot be described without the help of such a special construct. Since EM escapes the current level, its precise behavior can be described only in terms of the reflective tower. Thus, the user-observable interpreter can only include the definition of `eval-EM` that *magically* evaluates its argument at the metalevel.

Secondly, the definition of `my-error` in the user-observable interpreter is disappointing. It is supposed to print an error message and abort the current execution, but it is defined as returning 0 normally. Thus, if an error occurs (*e.g.*, by applying a boolean to an argument; see the else branch of `base-apply`), the result becomes 0 unconditionally and the execution continues which could result in further errors.

```
0-4> ((#t 3) 4)
(Not a function: #t)
(Not a function: 0)
0-4: 0
0-5>
```

In this example, (#t 3) results in an error and the corresponding error message is printed, but since its result becomes 0, it incurs further error at the outer application (0 4). Only the first error message is valid and the rest of the computation is completely bogus. For now, the user-observable interpreter is defined like this, because aborting the current execution requires special treatment, such as introduction of an error value or first-class continuation constructs. We will come back to this problem first in Section 4.4 and then more seriously in Section 5.

Finally, the user-observable interpreter is written in monadic style. It might first appear to contradict what this paper claims to achieve, because CPS is an instance of monadic style and the interpreter can be thought of as written in CPS rather than direct style. This is not the case, since the two monadic operators, unit and bind, in the user-observable interpreter do not have any special status. They are just other functions. The interpreter is written in direct style, because nested function calls are used. For example, in `eval-if`, the result of applying `base-eval` is passed to bind. We use monadic-style interpreter in this paper because we can change the language semantics in an interesting way by modifying unit and bind. Alternatively, we could have inlined the definition of unit and bind and started from a direct-style interpreter: all the rest of the story equally holds (except that we can no longer replace unit and bind because they would not exist any more).

```
(define (unit x) x)
(define (bind u v) (v u))
(define (base-eval e r)
  (cond ((number? e)         (unit e))
        ((boolean? e)        (unit e))
        ((symbol? e)         (eval-var e r))
        ((eq? (car e) 'if)   (eval-if e r))
        ((eq? (car e) 'set!) (eval-set! e r))
        ((eq? (car e) 'lambda) (eval-lambda e r))
        ((eq? (car e) 'EM)   (eval-EM e r))
        ((eq? (car e) 'exit) (eval-exit e r))
        ...
        (else (eval-application e r))))
(define (eval-var e r) (cdr (get e r)))
(define (eval-if e r) ; (if pred then else)
  (bind (base-eval (car (cdr e)) r)
    (lambda (pred)
      (if pred
        (base-eval (car (cdr (cdr e))) r)
        (base-eval (car (cdr (cdr (cdr e)))) r)))))
(define (eval-set! e r) ; (set! var body)
  (let ((var (car (cdr e)))
        (body (car (cdr (cdr e)))))
    (bind (base-eval body r)
      (lambda (data)
        (set-value! var data r)
        (unit var)))))
(define lambda-tag (cons 'lambda 'tag))
(define (eval-lambda e r) ; (lambda params body)
  (let ((params (car (cdr e)))
        (body (car (cdr (cdr e)))))
    (unit (list lambda-tag params body r))))
(define (eval-EM e r) ; (EM exp)
  (primitive-EM (car (cdr e))))
(define (eval-exit e r) ; (exit exp)
  (bind (base-eval (car (cdr exp)) r)
    (lambda (v) (my-error v r))))
(define (eval-application e r) ; (f a b c ...)
  (bind (eval-list e r)
    (lambda (l) (base-apply (car l) (cdr l) r))))
(define (eval-list e r)
  (if (null? e)
    (unit '())
    (bind (base-eval (car e) r)
      (lambda (val1)
        (bind (eval-list (cdr e) r)
          (lambda (val2)
            (unit (cons val1 val2))))))))
(define (base-apply op args r)
  (cond ((procedure? op)
          (unit (apply op args)))
        ((and (pair? op)
              (eq? (car op) lambda-tag))
          (let ((params (car (cdr op)))
                (body   (car (cdr (cdr op))))
                (env (car (cdr (cdr (cdr op))))))
            (base-eval body
              (extend env params args))))
        (else
          (my-error
            (list 'Not 'a 'function: op) r))))
(define (my-error e r)
  (write e) (newline) (unit 0))
```

Figure 1. The metalevel interpreter observed by users

Now that we know how the metalevel interpreter is written, we are ready to modify it. First, we save the original base-eval before modifying it.[1]

```
0-5> (EM (define old-eval base-eval))
0-5: old-eval
0-6>
```

The standard example is to change base-eval so that it prints the expression to be evaluated before actually evaluating it:

```
0-6> (EM (set! base-eval
          (lambda (e r)
            (write e) (newline) (old-eval e r))))
0-6: base-eval
0-7> (* 2 (+ 1 4))
(* 2 (+ 1 4))
*
2
(+ 1 4)
+
1
4
0-7: 10
0-8>
```

After replacing base-eval, the user program is interpreted by the modified interpreter. More examples will be shown in the subsequent sections.

4. How to construct Black

Given the user-observable interpreter in a metacircular way, it is not so difficult to construct a reflective tower by actually executing the interpreter on top of itself and handling reflective constructs specially. In fact, Jefferson and Friedman [8] implemented a simple reflective interpreter in this way. However, it suffers from at least two problems. First, the number of interpreters in the reflective tower has to be fixed beforehand. Secondly, the execution of user programs is extremely slow, due to the interpretive overhead. To make the metalevel interpreter modifiable, we need to interpret the metalevel interpreter using another interpreter. Thus, the user programs are interpreted by two interpreters. Usually, one more level of interpretation leads to order of magnitude slow down. This slow down is unavoidable, even if we do not use any reflective capabilities.

4.1 Interpreted vs. compiled code

To avoid the overhead of double interpretation, triple interpretation, etc., the Black system introduces distinction between interpreted code and compiled code. Interpreted code is sensitive to the redefinition of the metalevel interpreter because it is interpreted by it: after the metalevel interpreter is modified, the code will be executed under the modified interpreter. On the other hand, compiled code is insensitive to the redefinition of the metalevel interpreter because it is already compiled and is directly executed in machine code. Even if the metalevel interpreter is modified, the compiled code behaves the same as before.

By distinguishing two kinds of code, it becomes possible to achieve both the redefinability of metalevel interpreters and efficient execution. When Black is launched, all the functions in the metalevel interpreter are compiled code. Thus, the user programs are efficiently interpreted without requiring double interpretation.

---

[1] The metalevel interpreter in Figure 1 does not have define special form, but it is easy to support it. We will also use other standard special forms in the paper.

When user programs use reflection and modify a part of the interpreter, that modified part is replaced with an interpreted code. The point here is that until the metalevel interpreter is modified, user programs are interpreted efficiently, and even after it is modified, since only modified part is replaced with an inefficient interpreted code, most parts of the interpreter remain efficient compiled code.

With the introduction of compiled code, we no more have to fix the height of the reflective tower beforehand. When user programs use reflective capabilities and execute code at the metalevel, we lazily create the metametalevel interpreter to interpret the user code. If user goes up further (by a nested use of EM), more interpreters are created on demand.

Note that this design of a reflective tower does *not* keep all the power of reflection. Even if we go up two levels and modify the metametalevel interpreter, it does not affect the behavior of the metalevel interpreter because it is not interpreted. The introduction of compiled code means that we keep only the ability to *replace* the metalevel interpreter and abandon the ability to *modify inner workings* of the interpreter (without replacing it) in favor of efficient execution. More discussion on this point as well as the general method how to construct (CPS-based) reflective systems is found in [2].

4.2 Hook

The ability to replace the metalevel interpreter of Black is achieved by inserting *hooks* whenever a function is called. For example, eval-application makes three function calls, bind, eval-list, and base-apply (if we ignore the two calls to primitives):

```
(define (eval-application e r) ; (f a b c ...)
  (bind (eval-list e r)
    (lambda (l)
      (base-apply (car l) (cdr l) r))))
```

At each function call, we insert a call to meta-apply as follows:

```
(define (eval-application e r) ; (f a b c ...)
  (meta-apply 'bind
    (meta-apply 'eval-list e r)
    (lambda (l)
      (meta-apply 'base-apply (car l) (cdr l) r))))
```

The role of meta-apply is to check whether the called function is redefined or not and call an appropriate function. If it is not, meta-apply calls the default compiled code directly. If it is redefined to a user-defined (interpreted) function, on the other hand, meta-apply calls the interpreter one level above to interpret the redefined interpreted function. This way, meta-apply bridges a gap between compiled code and interpreted code. The exact definition of meta-apply is shown in the next section.

Where to insert meta-apply is arbitrary. If we insert it, the function call becomes sensitive to redefinition. If we do not insert it, the function call becomes insensitive to redefinition. In the current Black implementation, we hook all the evaluator functions and avoid hooking primitive functions and small environment manipulating functions.

4.3 Shifting levels

In Black, non-level-shifting functions are implemented simply by inserting meta-apply to appropriate places. The implementation of level-shifting functions, on the other hand, involves manipulation of levels. Before showing how level-shifting functions are implemented in Black, we first explain how levels are handled in Black.

To represent an infinite tower of interpreters, we use a *metacontinuation* stored in a global variable Mcont. A metacontinuation consists of a lazy stream containing a pair of an environment and a continuation for each level, starting from the current level. We use

cons-stream to create a lazy stream (whose tail part is delayed) and head and tail to extract head and tail parts of a stream (where the tail part is forced when extracted). Using a metacontinuation, shift up and down can be implemented as follows:

```
(define (shift-up code)
  (let ((meta-env (car (head Mcont)))
        (meta-cont (car (cdr (head Mcont))))
        (meta-Mcont (tail Mcont)))
    (set! Mcont meta-Mcont)
    (code meta-env meta-cont)))
(define-macro (shift-down code env cont)
  `(begin
     (set! Mcont (cons (list ,env ,cont) Mcont))
     ,code))
```

Shifting up a level is implemented as popping the environment and continuation at the top of Mcont and executing code at the metalevel with the popped values. Shifting down a level is implemented as pushing the environment and continuation to Mcont before executing code.[2] Note that shift-down is implemented as a macro, since the argument code has to be executed under the new Mcont.

To use these two functions, we somehow need to capture the current continuation to save it into the metacontinuation and install a continuation restored from the metacontinuation. The latter is easy: we just apply the continuation to a result. To accommodate the former, we use a control operator shift and maintain an invariant that the current level is delimited by reset.

Now, level-shifting functions are implemented as follows. See Figure 2. When meta-apply is called, it first captures and clears the current continuation using shift. It then shifts up one level and checks whether the called function is redefined or not by consulting the metalevel environment mr. If the called function is bound to a procedure, it means that it is a (default) compiled function. In this case, it is applied to the arguments in the original level under the original continuation. If the called function is not a procedure, it means that it is replaced with a user-defined closure. In this case, the closure is interpreted by the metalevel interpreter by calling base-apply at the metalevel. When the execution of the closure finishes, the result is passed to the original continuation at the original level.

Similarly, the execution of eval-EM proceeds by shifting up to the metalevel and executing the argument of EM by calling base-eval at the metalevel. When the execution finishes, the result is passed back to the original continuation at the original level.

Finally, base-apply requires level shifting. Although it is quite similar to base-apply in Figure 1 (except for the insertion of meta-apply), it has a new additional case where the applied function op is not a primitive procedure[3] but still a procedure (the second branch of cond). This is the case when the applied function is an evaluator function. In the user-observable interpreter (Figure 1), base-apply handles both a primitive and an evaluator function in the same way. In the actual interpreter, however, we need to distinguish them, because application of evaluator functions causes a level to shift down.

The shift down at base-apply can be understood as follows. The application of an evaluator function from a user program occurs in two cases: (1) when a user program calls an evaluator function explicitly, like (base-eval 3 '()), and (2) when a part of the metalevel interpreter is replaced with a user-defined closure,

---

[2] To push the environment and continuation, cons is used instead of cons-stream. This is because Mcont must refer to the current value of Mcont rather than the value when the tail part of the new Mcont is extracted.

[3] The function primitive-procedure? returns #t (true) if its argument is a primitive procedure, such as + and car.

```
(define (meta-apply proc-name . args)
  (shift k (shift-up (lambda (mr mk)
    (let ((op (cdr (get proc-name mr))))
      (if (procedure? op)
          (shift-down (k (apply op args))
                      mr mk)
          (let ((x (meta-apply 'base-apply
                               op args mr)))
            (shift-down (k x) mr mk)))))))))
(define (eval-EM e r) ; (EM exp)
  (shift k (shift-up (lambda (mr mk)
    (let ((x (meta-apply 'base-eval
                         (car (cdr e)) mr)))
      (shift-down (k x) mr mk)))))))
(define (base-apply op args r)
  (cond ((primitive-procedure? op)
         (meta-apply 'unit (apply op args)))
        ((procedure? op) ; evaluator functions
         (shift k
           (shift-down
             (go-up (apply op args))
             (get-global-env r) k)))
        ((and (pair? op)
              (eq? (car op) lambda-tag))
         ... similar to Figure 1 ... )
        (else
         (meta-apply 'my-error
           (list 'Not 'a 'function: op) r)))))
(define (go-up x)
  (shift-up (lambda (mr mk) (mk x))))
```

Figure 2. The Black interpreter (level-shifting functions)

and during the execution of that closure, a default compiled evaluator function is called, like the call to old-eval from the user-defined base-eval shown at the end of Section 3. In the former case, application of an evaluator function means launching a new interpreter below the current level. In the latter case, since the interpretation of the user-defined closure has finished and the execution resumes at the original level, the execution moves from the current level to the level below. In both cases, the level shifts down. To realize this shift down, base-apply first captures the current continuation in k and pushes it together with the current (global) environment into the metacontinuation (through shift-down). It then applies op to its argument at the level below. When the execution finishes, the result is returned back to the current level by passing it to go-up that returns its argument to the metalevel continuation (also shown in the figure).

4.4 Example

We can now execute the examples shown in the introduction. Here, we will demonstrate another example where we replace the two monadic operators unit and bind. Remember that the implementation of my-error (and hence the behavior of exit construct because eval-exit depends on my-error) was unsatisfactory. There are at least two approaches to remedy the situation. The first one is to introduce an error value and replace the identity monad with the error monad, which we demonstrate in this section. This solution has a benefit that it does not require modification of the Black system itself, but can be implemented within the ordinary user program. On the other hand, the system itself remains unsatisfactory and it leaves us a question whether it is possible at all to construct a reflective system in which abortion is handled more nicely. To address this question, the second solution uses the con-

trol operator shift to discard the current computation, which we will discuss in the next section.

The first solution is as follows:

```
> (black)
0-0: start
0-1> (EM (begin
        (define error-tag (cons 'error '()))
        (define (raise v) (cons error-tag v))
        (set! bind (lambda (v u)
          (if (and (pair? v)
                   (eq? (car v) error-tag))
              v
              (u v))))
        (set! my-error (lambda (e r) (raise e)))))
0-1: my-error
0-2>
```

We replace the bind operator with the one from an error monad and introduce a new monadic operator raise to raise an error. The address of the cons cell for error-tag is used to distinguish an error value from the ordinary value. If the first argument of bind turns out to be an error value, the second argument (continuation of bind) is discarded and the error value is returned. After this modification, we have the following interaction:

```
0-2> (* 2 (+ 1 4))
0-2: 10
0-3> ((#t 3) 4)
0-3: ((error) Not a function: #t)
0-4>
```

If the computation does not raise any error, we obtain the result as before. If an error occurs, on the other hand, all the rest of the computation (in the above example, application to 4) is discarded and the error value is returned.

This scenario is much better than the previous one. However, it is still not completely satisfactory.

```
0-4> (exit 0)
0-5: ((error) . 0)
0-6>
```

Even if we want to exit the current level, we can't, because exit is simply a variant of my-error. Instead of exiting the current level, it prints an error and stays in the same level. To actually exit the current level, we need to treat my-error as a level-shifting function.

5. Supporting exit

In this section, we consider how to finish the current level in my-error. Rather surprisingly, the problem turns out to be not so easy to solve.

5.1 Simple implementation

At first sight, it appears that we could simply and naturally define my-error as follows:

```
(define (my-error e r)
  (shift k (shift-up (lambda (mr mk)
    (set-value! 'old-env r mr)
    (set-value! 'old-cont k mr)
    (mk e)))))
```

To exit the current level, we store the current continuation in k, shift up one level, and execute the metalevel continuation mk. We can even memoise the values of r and k in the metalevel environment mr, so that after exiting to the level above, we can examine the value of r through the name old-env and resume the aborted computation by applying `old-cont`. We then have the following interaction:

```
> (black)
0-0: start
0-1> (exit 0)
1-0: 0
1-1> old-cont
1-1: #<procedure #2>
1-2>
```

The first number in the prompt indicates that we exit to the level 1. We see that the value `old-cont` is bound to a procedure. It contains the aborted baselevel computation. We can resume it by applying `old-cont` to a value.

```
1-2> (old-cont 10)
0-1: 10
0-2>
```

Because the execution is now back at the baselevel, the first number of the prompt is 0 again. Furthermore, the second number indicates that the value passed to `old-cont` becomes the value of `(exit 0)`.

This capability of exiting the current level and visiting the metalevel is particularly useful in the interpreter environment. Rather than issuing a sequence of expressions as an argument to EM, we can simply go up one level, modify the metalevel interpreter as we wish, and go back to the baselevel to see how the modified interpreter works. In fact, in our previous work [1], we treated `exit` as the main reflective construct.

So far, so good. However, the above definition of `my-error` leads to a rather subtle anomaly. The above scenario of going up and down works well only until the metalevel interpreter is modified. Suppose that we exit the baselevel again and install tracing into `base-eval` as we did in Section 3. We can do it without using EM, now:

```
0-2> (exit 0)
1-2: 0
1-3> (define old-eval base-eval)
1-3: old-eval
1-4> (set! base-eval
         (lambda (e r)
           (write e) (newline) (old-eval e r)))
1-4: base-eval
1-5>
```

After going back to the baselevel, a trace is displayed as expected.

```
1-5> (old-cont 0)
0-2: 0
0-3> (* 2 (+ 1 4))
(* 2 (+ 1 4))
*
2
(+ 1 4)
+
1
4
0-3: 10
0-4>
```

However, anomaly arises when we want to exit again.

```
0-4> (exit 0)
(exit 0)
0
0-4: 0
0-5>
```

We can no longer exit the level. Why does it happen?

5.2 Level-shifting anomaly

The level-shifting anomaly of not being able to exit the current level once we modify the metalevel interpreter stems from the fact that going up and down are not completely inverse of each other. Although it is easy to show that `shift-up` and `shift-down` are inverse of each other, their uses in `meta-apply` and `base-apply` are not. There are two cases to consider. First, whenever an evaluator function calls another compiled evaluator function via `meta-apply`, we make a round trip. Does this going up and down cause any problem? No. After coming back, the state is exactly the same as before, as we can confirm below. Assume that `proc-name` is bound to a compiled function `f`.

```
    (meta-apply proc-name . args)
-> (shift k (shift-up (lambda (mr mk)
     (shift-down (k (apply f args)) mr mk))))
-> (shift k (k (apply f args)))
-> (apply f args)
```

At the second step, shifting up followed by shifting down is canceled. At the last step, we used an axiom for `shift` [10]: `(shift k (k M))` is equal to M if k does not occur free in M. The details of the above derivation is not important. What we observe here is that a call to `meta-apply` reduces correctly to a call to the corresponding compiled function. In other words, the use of `meta-apply` in this setting is harmless.

The second case is more complicated. It happens when a compiled function calls a user-defined closure and after possible side-effects, the closure calls another compiled function as a tail call. The typical example is the tracing eval:

```
(set! base-eval
      (lambda (e r)
        (write e) (newline) (old-eval e r)))
```

Suppose that this user-defined `base-eval` is called from a compiled function, *e.g.*, a REP loop. When called, `base-eval` displays a trace and transfers control to `old-eval`. In this case, after printing of e is finished, we want the execution to continue at the current level as though `old-eval` was directly called from the original caller, *i.e.*, the REP loop. In other words, we want to cancel out going up and down needed to print traces.

However, in the current implementation, the original state is not completely recovered. Suppose that `proc-name` is bound to a user-defined closure op (such as `base-eval` above).

```
    (meta-apply proc-name . args)
-> (shift k (shift-up (lambda (mr mk)
     (let ((x (meta-apply 'base-apply op args mr)))
       (shift-down (k x) mr mk)))))
```

Assuming that `base-apply` is not redefined, the execution proceeds by interpreting the body of op. If the body of op calls a compiled function f (such as `old-eval` above) at the tail position, the execution eventually reaches the second branch of `base-apply`:

```
-> (shift k (shift-up (lambda (mr mk)
     (let ((x (shift k2
                (shift-down
                  (go-up (apply f args))
                  (get-global-env mr) k2))))
       (shift-down (k x) mr mk)))))
```

At this point, the continuation bound to k2 is `(shift-down (k □) mr mk)`, in other words, "go down and execute k." It is then stored in the metacontinuation by `shift-down`. As a result, the above expression reduces to:

```
(go-up (apply f args))
```

where the metalevel continuation (stored in the metacontinuation) contains additional frame "go down" at the top of its continuation.

Again, the details of this derivation is not important. The point is that the original call does not reduce to a call to f but it is wrapped with "go up" at the end of the current continuation, and the metacontinuation contains "go down" at the beginning. If the execution of f finishes normally, there arises no problem. The result is passed to the metalevel and is immediately sent back to the current level. However, if f aborts, a problem arises. Even if the current continuation is discarded and the control is transferred to the metalevel, the metalevel continuation contains superfluous frame "go down" at the front. Because of this frame, the execution immediately goes back to the baselevel, prohibiting exit.

5.3 Analysis

Both the "go down" frame in base-apply and the "go up" frame in meta-apply appear to be necessary. The former is required because the execution of (apply op args) in base-apply might finish and return a value (rather than calling another compiled function in tail position). To properly pass the result to the current level, the application has to be wrapped by the "go up" frame. The latter is required for a similar reason. If the execution of (meta-apply 'base-apply op args mr) in meta-apply at the metalevel finishes and returns a value, it has to be passed to the current level continuation k after going down.

However, closer inspection of these two functions reveals that going down in base-apply is split into two cases. One is when a new level is actually spawned (e.g., a user executes an evaluator function) and the other is when the execution called from the level below is finished and the computation goes back to the level below (e.g., the execution of redefined base-eval is finished and old-eval is called). The former requires the "go up" frame but the latter does not because it has the "go down" frame at the top, so we could instead cancel out the "go down" frame.

Unfortunately, to distinguish these two cases, we need to peek in the context to see if the closest frame is the "go down" frame. Such an operation is usually not permitted.

5.4 Solution

To avoid level-shifting anomaly, we need to examine the top frame of the system stack. The best way to achieve it would be to support *tail-reflection optimization* considered in [5], similar in spirit to tail-call optimization. However, directly supporting tail-reflection optimization requires modification of the underlying Scheme implementation. Since the optimization is specific to a reflective system, rather than modifying the Scheme implementation, we emulate the tail-reflection optimization in this paper by transforming the whole interpreter into CPS once and for all.

Converting the Black interpreter into CPS spoils some of our original benefits of having reflection in direct style. All the functions that are exposed for user modification have to be written in CPS. However, it appears to be the only solution under the environment where tail-reflection optimization is not supported. The good news is that we have to do it only once when we build a Black interpreter. Once it is done, we are able to reflect on the metalevel interpreter written in direct style.

The CPS transformation is mechanical. We use the following two monadic operators from the continuation monad:

```
(define (munit x) (lambda (k) (k x)))
(define (mbind u v)
  (lambda (k) (u (lambda (x) ((v x) k)))))
```

and expand all the (serious) nested calls using these operators. For example, the result of CPS transformation of eval-application is as follows:

```
(define (eval-application e r) ; (f a b c ...)
  (mbind (meta-apply 'eval-list e r)
    (lambda (l0)
      (meta-apply 'bind l0
        (lambda (l)
          (meta-apply 'base-apply
                      (car l) (cdr l) r)))))))
```

We are tempted to instantiate unit and bind to the ones from the continuation monad. We would then obtain a CPS interpreter immediately without modifying the interpreter (except for unit and bind). It is possible, but it results in a reflective interpreter where the metalevel interpreter is written in direct style but not in monadic style. Because unit and bind are given a special status, they are no longer visible from user programs. We will not take this approach in this paper to keep the ability to modify monadic operators.

Level-shifting functions are CPS transformed as in Figure 3. Because of the CPS transformation, we do not need shift any more, but the current continuation can be captured simply by lambda abstraction. Thus, (shift k ...) in Figure 2 is transformed to (lambda (k) ...) in Figure 3. Likewise, the context of a serious function call is transformed to an application of the call to its continuation. For example, in meta-apply, (k (apply op args)) is transformed to ((apply op args) k) and

```
(let ((x (meta-apply 'base-apply op args mr)))
  (shift-down (k x) mr mk))
```

is transformed to:

```
((meta-apply 'base-apply op args mr)
 (lambda (x) (shift-down (k x) mr mk)))
```

The CPS transformation of k in my-error is a bit complicated. It is basically a composition of k and k2, but shift-up and shift-down are inserted to properly adjust levels.

Because contexts are made explicit as continuations, we can now examine the top frame of a continuation by *defunctionalizing* [14] continuations. See Figure 4. We distinguish the frame "go down" (lambda (x) (shift-down (k x) mr mk)) by representing it as a list of its free variables (list k mr mk) (see the last line of meta-apply and eval-EM and the last part of my-error in Figure 4). Whenever a continuation is applied to a value x, we use an apply function (throw k x) as in munit and my-error. It checks whether the continuation is a list and if it is, it executes (shift-down (k x) mk mr). Similarly, mbind is changed to cope with this new frame.

By representing the "go down" frame as a list, it becomes possible to perform tail-reflection optimization. When we go down a level at the second branch of base-apply, we use a special operator shift-down/go-up. The role of this operator is to execute its first argument one level below with the "go up" continuation, but if the current continuation is the "go down" frame (list k2 mr mk), it cancels them out and installs k2 as the continuation of the level below.

With the above optimization, we can execute all the examples shown in this paper (except that the last (exit 0) in Section 5.1 is properly handled). We obtained a reflective language where the user-observable metalevel interpreter is written in direct style and which allows us to freely exit the current level.

6. Parser example

In this section, we show as a bigger example how a monadic parser [7] can be implemented by changing the metalevel interpreter.

The idea of a monadic parser is to interpret a context-free gram-

```
(define (meta-apply proc-name . args)
  (lambda (k) (shift-up (lambda (mr mk)
    (let ((op (cdr (get proc-name mr))))
      (if (procedure? op)
          (shift-down ((apply op args) k)
                      mr mk)
          ((meta-apply 'base-apply op args mr)
           (lambda (x)
             (shift-down (k x) mr mk)))))))))
(define (eval-EM e r) ; (EM exp)
  (lambda (k) (shift-up (lambda (mr mk)
    ((meta-apply 'base-eval (car (cdr e)) mr)
     (lambda (x) (shift-down (k x) mr mk)))))))
(define (base-apply op args r)
  (cond ((primitive-procedure? op)
         (meta-apply 'unit (apply op args)))
        ((procedure? op) ; evaluator functions
         (lambda (k)
           (shift-down
             ((apply op args) go-up)
             (get-global-env r) k)))
        ((and (pair? op)
              (eq? (car op) lambda-tag))
         (let ((params (car (cdr op)))
               (body   (car (cdr (cdr op))))
               (env (car (cdr (cdr (cdr op))))))
           (meta-apply 'eval-eval body
             (extend env params args))))
        (else
         (meta-apply 'my-error
           (list 'Not 'a 'function: op) r))))
(define (go-up x)
  (shift-up (lambda (mr mk) (mk x))))
(define (my-error e r)
  (lambda (k) (shift-up (lambda (mr mk)
    (set-value! 'old-env r mr)
    (set-value! 'old-cont
      (lambda (x) (lambda (k2)
        (shift-up (lambda (mr2 mk2)
          (shift-down (k x) mr2
            (lambda (x)
              (shift-down (k2 x) mr2 mk2)))))))
      mr)
    (mk e)))))
```

Figure 3. The Black interpreter in CPS (level-shifting functions)

```
(define (throw k x)
  (if (pair? k)
      (let ((k2 (car k))
            (mr (car (cdr k)))
            (mk (car (cdr (cdr k)))))
        (shift-down (throw k2 x) mr mk))
      (k x)))
(define (munit x) (lambda (k) (throw k x)))
(define (mbind u v) (lambda (k)
  (if (pair? k)
      (let ((k2 (car k))
            (mr (car (cdr k)))
            (mk (car (cdr k))))
        (u (list
             (lambda (x) (shift-up (lambda (mmr mmk)
               ((v x) (list k2 mmr mmk)))))
             mr mk)))
      (u (lambda (x) ((v x) k))))))
(define (meta-apply proc-name . args)
  (lambda (k) (shift-up (lambda (mr mk)
    (let ((op (cdr (get proc-name mr))))
      (if (procedure? op)
          (shift-down ((apply op args) k)
                      mr mk)
          ((meta-apply 'base-apply op args mr)
           (list k mr mk))))))))  ; pass a list
(define (eval-EM e r) ; (EM exp)
  (lambda (k) (shift-up (lambda (mr mk)
    ((meta-apply 'base-eval (car (cdr e)) mr)
     (list k mr mk))))))  ; pass a list
(define (base-apply op args r)
  (cond ((primitive-procedure? op)
         (meta-apply 'unit (apply op args)))
        ((procedure? op) ; evaluator functions
         (lambda (k)
           (shift-down/go-up ; optimize
             (apply op args)
             (get-global-env r) k)))
        ((and (pair? op)
              (eq? (car op) lambda-tag))
         ... the same as Figure 3 ... )
        (else
         (meta-apply 'my-error
           (list 'Not 'a 'function: op) r))))
(define (my-error e r)
  (lambda (k) (shift-up (lambda (mr mk)
    (set-value! 'old-env r mr)
    (set-value! 'old-cont
      (lambda (x) (lambda (k2)
        (shift-up (lambda (mr2 mk2)
          (shift-down (throw k x)
                      mr2 (list k2 mr2 mk2))))))
      mr)                    ; pass a list
    (mk e)))))
(define (shift-down/go-up code r k)
  (if (pair? k)
      (let ((k2 (car k))
            (mr (car (cdr k)))
            (mk (car (cdr (cdr k)))))
        (shift-down (code k2) mr mk))
      (shift-down (code go-up) r k)))
```

Figure 4. The defunctionalized Black interpreter with tail-reflection optimization

mar as a program. For example, consider the following grammar representing addition and multiplication over numbers.

$$
\begin{array}{llll}
E & ::= & T\,E' & \qquad T \ \ ::= \ N\,T' \\
E' & ::= & +\,T\,E' \mid \epsilon & \qquad T' ::= \ *\,N\,T' \mid \epsilon \\
&&& \qquad N \ ::= \ number
\end{array}
$$

Following this grammar, we write a parser program as in Figure 5. The functions e, e2, t, t2, and num correspond to the non-terminals E, E', T, T', and N, respectively. When called, these functions parse an input string (implicitly passed around as a state), and return all the possible parse trees together with the unparsed strings. Whether an input string is completely parsed by the grammar can be judged by checking the unparsed string: if it is an empty string, the input is completely parsed (see finish).

When defining these functions, we can use several monadic operators provided by the parser monad. The choice in the grammar is handled by amb. It tries to parse both the alternatives. When

104

```
(define (sat p)
  (let ((lst (read-state)))
    (cond ((null? lst) (none))
          ((p (car lst)) (write-state! (cdr lst))
                         (car lst))
          (else (none)))))
(define (item c) (sat (lambda (x) (eq? x c))))
(define (num) (sat number?))
(define (e)  ; E  = T E2
  (let* ((x (t)) (lst (e2)))
    (if (null? lst) x (cons '+ (cons x lst)))))
(define (e2) ; E2 = + T E2 | ε
  (amb (let* ((i (item '+)) (x (t)) (lst (e2)))
         (cons x lst))
       '()))
(define (t)  ; T  = Num T2
  (let* ((x (num)) (lst (t2)))
    (if (null? lst) x (cons '* (cons x lst)))))
(define (t2) ; T2 = * Num T2 | ε
  (amb (let* ((i (item '*)) (x (num)) (lst (t2)))
         (cons x lst))
       '()))

(define (finish result)
  (if (null? (read-state)) result (none)))
(define (parse grammar lst)
  (write-state! lst)
  (finish (grammar)))
```

Figure 5. Monadic parser (baselevel program)

```
(set! unit (lambda (x)
              (lambda (lst) (list (cons x lst)))))
(set! bind (lambda (u v) (lambda (lst)
  (apply append
    (map (lambda (p) ((v (car p)) (cdr p)))
         (u lst))))))
(set! start (lambda (x) (x '())))

(define (eval-read-state e r) ; (read-state)
  (lambda (lst) ((unit lst) lst)))
(define (eval-write-state! e r);(write-state! exp)
  (bind (base-eval (car (cdr e)) r)
        (lambda (v)
          (lambda (lst) ((unit #f) v)))))
(define (eval-amb e r) ; (amb e1 e2)
  (lambda (lst) (append
    ((base-eval (car (cdr e)) r) lst)
    ((base-eval (car (cdr (cdr e))) r) lst))))
(define (eval-none e r) ; (none)
  (lambda (lst) '()))
(define old-eval-application eval-application)
(set! eval-application (lambda (e r)
  (cond ((eq? (car e) 'read-state)
         (eval-read-state e r))
        ((eq? (car e) 'write-state!)
         (eval-write-state! e r))
        ((eq? (car e) 'amb)  (eval-amb e r))
        ((eq? (car e) 'none) (eval-none e r))
        (else (old-eval-application e r)))))
```

Figure 6. Monadic parser (metalevel modification/extension)

parsing fails, none is used. To obtain the input string, we use read-state, and the input string is initialized and updated (*e.g.*, parsed string is removed) by write-state!.

Compared to the standard monadic parsers, the parser presented here does not need monadic programming. Since the monadic operators are provided by changing the metalevel interpreter (to be explained soon), the ordinary constructs such as let* and if are interpreted in a monadic way. Thus, the surface program does not have to mention monads at all.

The monadic operators can be implemented easily. After exiting the current level, we load the program in Figure 6. We first replace unit and bind with the ones from the parser monad:

$$M \; A = String \rightarrow (A \times String) \; List$$

We represent the input string as a list of symbols. The start operator initiates the monadic computation by passing the initial string. It is used in the REP loop, whose user-observable definition is as follows:

```
(define (init-cont env level turn answer)
  (write level) (write '-) (write turn)
  (display ": ") (write answer) (newline)
  (write level) (write '-) (write (+ turn 1))
  (display "> ")
  (let ((ans (start (base-eval (read) env))))
    (init-cont env level (+ turn 1) ans)))
```

The evaluator functions for the new monadic operators follows in Figure 6. They are registered as special forms by inserting case branches before eval-application, in other words, before they are treated as ordinary function calls. We then launch the parser interpreter by calling init-cont, with "parser" as the name of the level. Suppose that the functions in Figure 5 and Figure 6 are saved in files "parser-meta.scm" and "parser.scm", respectively.

```
> (black)
0-0: start
0-1> (exit 0)
1-0: 0
1-1> (load "parser-meta.scm")
1-1: done
1-2> (init-cont init-env 'parser 0 'start)
parser-0: start
parser-1> (load "parser.scm")
parser-1: ((done))
parser-2> (parse e '(2 * 3 + 4 * 5 * 6 + 7))
parser-2: (((+ (* 2 3) (* 4 5 6) 7)))
parser-3> (exit 0)
1-2: 0
1-3>
```

The above grammar is unambiguous, but if we implement ambiguous grammar, we will obtain all the possible parse trees.

Although we launched a REP loop in the above example, more practical approach would be to call (start (base-eval exp init-env)) where exp is the baselevel parser program (Figure 5) followed by the main expression to initiate parsing (such as (parse e '(2 * 3 + 4 * 5 * 6 + 7)) above). We could then use the monadic parser whenever we need it, but stay in the ordinary interpreter otherwise. Furthermore, we could consider optimizing (start (base-eval exp init-env)) by specializing [9] (modified) base-eval with respect to exp, *i.e.*, compiling exp under the parser semantics defined by the modified base-eval. Because we could resolve the level-shifting anomaly and fix the basic framework of the reflective language, it becomes possible to think of such interesting optimization.

7. Discussion and future direction

7.1 EM vs. exit

In this paper, we have introduced two reflective constructs, EM and exit. If we used only EM, we would never encounter the level-shifting anomaly, because we cannot observe the superfluous "go up" and "go down" frames. Then, do we need exit at all? We believe yes at least for two reasons. The process of writing a reflective program consists of two parts: a metalevel program followed by a baselevel program. If exit was not provided, we have to wrap metalevel programs with EM all the time, which is quite cumbersome. Furthermore, we make mistakes. Proper handling of errors, which is realized by correct handling of the exit mechanism, is essential in programming in an interpreter environment.

7.2 Direct style vs. CPS

In the previous work [2], we have already shown how to build a reflective system where the metalevel interpreter is written in CPS. Because we can transform any program into CPS, all we can do with a direct-style Black can be done in the CPS Black. Then, do we really need a reflective system whose metalevel interpreter is written in direct style? We believe yes, because there is an important difference between the two systems. In CPS Black, we *must* write the metalevel interpreter in CPS. Otherwise, the exit mechanism breaks down. In CPS Black, exit is implemented as throwing away the current continuation. This is possible only when the metalevel interpreter is properly written in CPS. It does not work any more if we redefine evaluator functions in direct style. In other words, the behavior of exit in CPS Black depends on the user's writing CPS. In direct-style Black, such danger does not exist. To put differently, the DS Black makes it possible for the first time to perform exit at all times.

7.3 Interpreted code vs. compiled code

One of the motivations of this work is to establish a foundation for efficient implementation of reflective languages. This goal is not yet achieved. Rather, we have set up the basis on which efficient implementation is tried. In our previous work on CPS Black, we have already mentioned the compilation framework of reflective languages: converting interpreted code into compiled code via partial evaluation [9] of the metalevel interpreter with respect to baselevel program. Since the metalevel interpreter (the language semantics) is modifiable, we cannot construct a fixed compiler because it depends on the particular language semantics. However, we have not been able to tackle compilation, because so far we suffered from the level-shifting anomaly and the restriction that the metalevel interpreter has to be written in CPS. Now that we have solved these problems, we are ready to consider partial evaluation seriously. Another promising approach would be to try traced-based compilation framework successfully applied to the PyPy project [3] to reduce interpretive overhead.

8. Conclusion

In this paper, we described the reflective language Black whose metalevel interpreters are written in direct style. Implementation of the reflective construct EM was possible by the manipulation of metacontinuations, but implementation of seemingly simple construct exit turned out to require tail-reflection optimization. We have achieved the same effect by CPS transforming the metalevel interpreter once and for all. Although the Black interpreter is now written in CPS, the user-observable interpreter is in direct style. Thus, user programs can reflect on the direct-style metalevel interpreter. We hope that the resulting system can be a base platform for the efficient execution of reflective programs in the future.

Acknowledgments

Thanks to the anonymous reviewers for interesting comments. This work was partly supported by JSPS Grant-in-Aid for Scientific Research (C) 22500025.

References

[1] Asai, K. "Reflecting on the Metalevel Interpreter Written in Direct Style," Presented at the International Lisp Conference 2003 (ILC 2003), New York City, 12 pages (October 2003).

[2] Asai, K., S. Matsuoka, and A. Yonezawa "Duplication and Partial Evaluation — For a Better Understanding of Reflective Languages —," *Lisp and Symbolic Computation*, Vol. 9, Nos. 2/3, pp. 203–241, Kluwer Academic Publishers (May/June 1996).

[3] Bolz, C. F., A. Cuni, M. Fijalkowski, and A. Rigo "Tracing the Meta-Level: PyPy's Tracing JIT Compiler," *Proceedings of the 4th workshop on the Implementation, Compilation, Optimization of Object-Oriented Languages and Programming Systems*, pp. 18–25 (July 2009).

[4] Danvy, O., and A. Filinski "Abstracting Control," *Proceedings of the 1990 ACM Conference on Lisp and Functional Programming*, pp. 151–160 (June 1990).

[5] Danvy, O., and K. Malmkjær "Intensions and Extensions in a Reflective Tower," *Conference Record of the 1988 ACM Symposium on Lisp and Functional Programming*, pp. 327–341 (July 1988).

[6] Friedman, D. P., and M. Wand "Reification: Reflection without Metaphysics," *Conference Record of the 1984 ACM Symposium on Lisp and Functional Programming*, pp. 348–355 (August 1984).

[7] Hutton, G., and E. Meijer "Monadic Parsing in Haskell," *Journal of Functional Programming*, Vol. 8, No. 4, pp. 437–444, Cambridge University Press (July 1998).

[8] Jefferson, S., and D. P. Friedman "A Simple Reflective Interpreter," *Lisp and Symbolic Computation*, Vol. 9, Nos. 2/3, pp. 181–202, Kluwer Academic Publishers (May/June 1996).

[9] Jones, N. D., C. K. Gomard, and P. Sestoft *Partial Evaluation and Automatic Program Generation*, New York: Prentice-Hall (1993).

[10] Kameyama, Y., and M. Hasegawa "A Sound and Complete Axiomatization of Delimited Continuations," *Proceedings of the eighth ACM SIGPLAN International Conference on Functional Programming (ICFP'03)*, pp. 177–188 (August 2003).

[11] Kiczales, G., J. des Rivières, and D. G. Bobrow *The Art of the Metaobject Protocol*, Cambridge: MIT Press (1991).

[12] Kiczales, G., J. Lamping, A. Mendhekar, C. Maeda, C. Videira Lopes, J-M. Loingtier, and J. Irwin "Aspect-Oriented Programming," *Proceedings of the European Conference on Object-Oriented Programming (ECOOP'97)*, pp. 220–242 (1997).

[13] Masuhara, H., and A. Yonezawa "Design and Partial Evaluation of Meta-objects for a Concurrent Reflective Language," *Proceedings of the European Conference on Object-Oriented Programming (ECOOP'98), LNCS 1445*, pp. 418–439 (July 1998).

[14] Reynolds, J. C. "Definitional Interpreters for Higher-Order Programming Languages," *Proceedings of the ACM National Conference*, Vol. 2, pp. 717–740, (August 1972), reprinted in *Higher-Order and Symbolic Computation*, Vol. 11, No. 4, pp. 363–397, Kluwer Academic Publishers (December 1998).

[15] Smith, B. C. "Reflection and Semantics in Lisp," *Conference Record of the 14th Annual ACM Symposium on Principles of Programming Languages*, pp. 23–35 (January 1984).

[16] Verwaest, T., C. Bruni, D. Gurtner, A. Lienhard, and O. Niestrasz "PINOCCHIO: Bringing Reflection to Life with First-Class Interpreters," *Proceedings of the ACM International Conference on Object-Oriented Programming Systems, Languages, and Applications (OOPSLA '10)*, pp. 774–789, (October 2010).

[17] Wand, M., and D. P. Friedman "The Mystery of the Tower Revealed: A Non-Reflective Description of the Reflective Tower," *Conference Record of the 1986 ACM Symposium on Lisp and Functional Programming*, pp. 298–307 (August 1986).

Firepile: Run-time Compilation for GPUs in Scala

Nathaniel Nystrom

Faculty of Informatics
University of Lugano
Via Giuseppe Buffi 13
6904 Lugano, Switzerland
nate.nystrom@usi.ch

Derek White

CSE Department
University of Texas at Arlington
P.O. Box 19015
Arlington TX 76019-0015, USA
dwhite@uta.edu

Kishen Das

CSE Department
University of Texas at Arlington
P.O. Box 19015
Arlington TX 76019-0015, USA
kishen.das@gmail.com

Abstract

Recent advances have enabled GPUs to be used as general-purpose parallel processors on commodity hardware for little cost. However, the ability to program these devices has not kept up with their performance. The programming model for GPUs has a number of restrictions that make it difficult to program. For example, software running on the GPU cannot perform dynamic memory allocation, requiring the programmer to pre-allocate all memory the GPU might use. To achieve good performance, GPU programmers must also be aware of how data is moved between host and GPU memory and between the different levels of the GPU memory hierarchy.

We describe Firepile, a library for GPU programming in Scala. The library enables a subset of Scala to be executed on the GPU. Code trees can be created from run-time function values, which can then be analyzed and transformed to generate GPU code. A key property of this mechanism is that it is modular: unlike with other meta-programming constructs, the use of code trees need not be exposed in the library interface. Code trees are general and can be used by library writers in other application domains. Our experiments show Firepile users can achieve performance comparable to C code targeted to the GPU with shorter, simpler, and easier-to-understand code.

Categories and Subject Descriptors D.3.2 [*Language Classifications*]: Concurrent, distributed, and parallel languages, Object-oriented languages; D.3.4 [*Processors*]: Code generation, Compilers

General Terms Languages

Keywords GPU, Scala, OpenCL, run-time code generation

1. Introduction

Graphics processing units (GPUs) are increasingly being used to solve general-purpose computational problems. A single GPU can provide hundreds of processors at little cost. They are being used for scientific data analysis, financial applications, digital signal processing, cryptography and other applications Yet, programming these devices remains difficult. Languages such as OpenCL [22] and CUDA [23] allow data-parallel programming of GPUs at the

C (or C++) level of abstraction. However, the programming models of these languages are restrictive, prohibiting a number of standard features of object-oriented languages, e.g., recursion, dynamic memory allocation, and virtual method dispatch. In addition, programmers must explicitly manage the movement of data between the host memory and the device and between layers of the memory hierarchy on the device. Achieving optimal performance often relies on subtle details of the programming model. For example, misalignment of memory accesses can degrade performance by an order of magnitude [24].

This paper describes Firepile, a library for GPU programming in Scala. Firepile hides details of GPU programming within the library, allowing programmers to focus on the problem they wish to solve. The library performs facilities for managing devices and memory. Collections classes support data-parallel, functional operations. Performance of Firepile-generated code is comparable to C/C++ code. The library uses a novel approach of constructing code trees from function values at runtime. From these code trees, Firepile generates OpenCL kernels to run on the GPU. Kernel functions may be written in Scala and may use objects, higher-order functions, and virtual methods. The run-time compiler uses method specialization to translate these problematic constructs into the subset of C accepted by the OpenCL specification. The code tree mechanism provides advantages over explicit staging, as found in Lisp and other programming languages [3, 21, 29–31], that otherwise might require annotations, special types, or other extensions of standard Scala.

1.1 GPU programming

To help understand some of the challenges on GPU programming, we first sketch the architecture of a GPU and how one is programmed. We illustrate using NVIDIA's latest hardware architecture, Fermi [25] and the OpenCL programming model [22]; however, many of the same issues occur with other GPU architectures and other GPU programming models.

A Fermi GPU consists of up to 16 streaming multiprocessors (SM), each with 32 scalar processors, for a total of up to 512 cores. Threads are executed in groups of 32 called *warps*. All threads in a warp are executed using SIMD instructions on a single SM; that is, all threads execute the same instruction simultaneously. OpenCL abstracts threads and groups of threads into *work items* and *work groups*, respectively. The number of work items in a work group need not match the number of hardware threads in a warp.

A thread (work item) running on the GPU has access to multiple classes of memory. In addition to private, per-thread memory, all threads in a warp running on the same SM have access to shared, per-SM memory. Correspondingly, in OpenCL all work

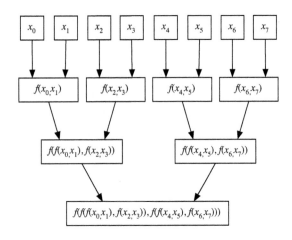

Figure 1. Performing a reduction in parallel. Operations in each row can be implemented independently. The output of the previous row is input to the next.

items in a work group have access to shared, *local* memory.[1] Finally, all threads running on the GPU have access to global GPU memory. Typical memory sizes are 64 KB for per-block memory and 256 MB up to 6 GB for global memory. In this architecture, communication between threads is limited. Threads running on the same SM can communicate through per-block memory. Threads running on different SMs could communicate through global memory, but global memory provides no synchronization guarantees: a write performed by a thread running on one SM will not be visible to a thread running at a different SM. OpenCL programmers must allocate date to work items and work groups with all of these restrictions in mind.

1.2 Example: reduce

To illustrate how the GPU architecture is utilized, consider a parallel reduction operation, a common building-block of many parallel algorithms. The reduce operation takes a non-empty input array with element type T and an associative function $f : (T, T) \rightarrow T$. The operation performs a reduction (or *fold*) on the array, computing a single value of type T for the entire array by applying f to pairs of elements. For instance, reducing an array of numbers with the + operation will sum the array, reducing with max will compute the maximum element of the array.

Because of the limited communication between threads on a GPU, a reduce operation cannot be written in the same way as it typically would be in a sequential program or in a parallel program to run on multicore processor with shared memory. The developer must keep in mind memory access limitations and the hierarchy of work items and work groups. Global data is partitioned among work groups, and each group can be allocated an area of per-group local memory for its work items to perform their task.

The reduce operation is implemented as a *kernel*. Each work item executes the kernel in parallel on a segment of the input array. The kernel uses work group and work item identifiers to calculate indices into global and local memory arrays. Using this approach, reduction of an array of length n can be computed in parallel $\log_2 n$ rounds, illustrated in Figure 1. First, f is applied to pairs

of elements, producing $n/2$ intermediate results. Then f is applied to pairs of these elements, halving the number of elements again. This process is repeated until one element remains.

To execute on a GPU, the array is first copied to GPU global memory. Then, in the first round, pairs of elements of the array are reduced and stored in a per-group local array. The remaining rounds read from this local array. All SMs thus run in parallel on their own data. Since each round depends on writes to the local memory performed by the previous round, a memory barrier is required to ensure these writes are visible to other threads running in that work group. In the end, each work group produces a single value.

Because writes at one SM are not visible to other SMs, the reduction of these intermediate per-group results cannot be completed on the GPU. Hence, the next step is to write each of the per-group results back to global memory. From here, the results, a much shorter array, are copied back to the host memory, and the reduction is completed on the CPU.

Using OpenCL, before invoking the kernel, the programmer must explicitly allocate storage on the GPU for the input, output, and local arrays. The programmer must also explicitly copy the input to the GPU's global memory and copy back the output. In addition, because C does not support first-class functions and because OpenCL does not allow dynamic dispatch, a new version of reduce must be written for each function f. This code duplication can be avoided by using the C preprocessor, but this is potentially error-prone.

1.3 Reduce in Firepile

Using Firepile's GPUArray class, to compute the sum of an array A via parallel reduction, one simply calls:

```
A.reduce(0)(_+_)
```

Figure 2 shows the implementation of reduce in the GPUArray class. The code is based on an example from the NVIDIA OpenCL SDK.[2] The implementation of reduce handles partitioning of the problem space and specifying how the operation should be parallelized. This implementation is built on top of a lower-level device library [6], handles the details of data movement to and from the GPU, and compiles Scala code into OpenCL kernels, as described in Section 3.

The reduce method starts by partitioning the problem space by rounding the input array size up to the next power of two and dividing it into blocks of equal length. Each work group will work on a different block, and each work item is responsible for computing a single output or intermediate result. Each work group thus accesses one segment of the array, performing a reduction into a local array.

The call to space.spawn invokes the reduce kernel on the GPU. The spawn method takes a call-by-name parameter. The block of code containing the kernel implementation is passed as a closure into spawn. The spawn method then compiles this block at run time into an OpenCL kernel.

Bytecode of the block passed to spawn is loaded into Soot for further examination. Case classes for Soot units representing bytecode expressions are matched for the generation of code trees that will later be translated into OpenCL C code for execution on the device.

The compiler has access to the environment of the block, allowing it to specialize the code based on the run-time values z and f. For instance, in the call to reduce above, the compiler can generate a specialized version of reduce using the + operator.

Although the GPU itself does not support dynamic memory allocation, the programmer can allocate memory within code passed

---

[1] CUDA and OpenCL use different names to refer to similar concepts. Per-thread memory is called *local* memory in CUDA, but *private* memory in OpenCL. Per-block memory is called *block* memory in CUDA, but *local* memory in OpenCL. We use the OpenCL terminology in this paper.

[2] http://developer.nvidia.com/opencl-sdk-code-samples.

to spawn. The compiler identifies array and object allocations within the kernel body and generates code to run *on the host* to allocate sufficient storage in GPU memory before the kernel is invoked. When the kernel is invoked, the input array is copied to the GPU. When the kernel completes, the output array is copied from the GPU into host memory. Unlike with the C API for OpenCL, the programmer does not need to specify the kind of memory (global, local, etc.) to allocate. Instead, the Firepile compiler analyzes the code to determine where a given buffer should be allocated. Movement of data between the host and GPU device are also handled by the library.

Developers can use the GPUArray library to program at a high-level or can implement their own kernels using the lower-level mechanisms provided by Firepile. Even at this lower level, tedious details of data movement and memory allocation are handled by the library rather than by the kernel developer.

1.4 Organization

The rest of the paper is organized as follows. Section 2 introduces the code tree mechanism used to translate Scala code into GPU kernels. Section 3 presents the Firepile library and compiler, including object and function translations and memory management. In Section 4, we describe our experiments and present our results. Related work is discussed in Section 5. Finally, in Section 6 we conclude and discuss of future work.

2. Code trees

In this section we describe the mechanism by which Firepile translates Scala code into OpenCL kernels to run on the GPU. The key idea is to create code trees from run-time function values. These trees can then be analyzed by the program and, in the case of Firepile, compiled into OpenCL C code.

The spawn method introduced in Section 1.3 serves as the entry point for the translation mechanism of Firepile. The method translates its argument, a function value, into an abstract syntax tree representing the function. These abstract syntax trees are implemented using tree classes based on the scala.reflect.generic.Tree subclasses in Scala standard library. The standard library classes were not used directly since using them requires implementing a large number of abstract classes and methods that were not needed.[3]

Code trees are constructed from function values by locating the JVM bytecode for the function, loading and parsing it, reconstructing Scala type and symbol information, and then finally creating the trees from the bytecode instructions.

The Scala compiler translates function values into anonymous Java objects with an apply method. This translation is illustrated for the function (x: Int) => x + a in Figure 3(a). Here, a is a local variable captured by the closure. Function invocation is translated into a call to the apply method. Variables captured by the function body are represented in bytecode as fields of the function object. Uses of these captured variables are translated into field accesses. In the example, the captured variable a is translated into the field a$1. The Scala compiler translates function creation into instantiation of the anonymous function object, passing the captured variables into the function object constructor, which initializes the fields.

The code tree constructed from the bytecode for (x: Int) => x + a is shown in Figure 3(b). The code tree nodes are instances of the case classes in Figure 4. By using Scala case classes, pattern matching can be done on code trees, making it easier to identify complex code sequences that need special handling in GPU code generation.

---

[3] http://github.com/dubochet/scala-reflection/wiki.

```
1  def reduce(z: A)(f: (A,A) => A)
2            (implicit dev: Device): A = {
3
4    val input = this.array
5
6    val n = input.length
7
8    // partition the problem by padding out to the next
9    // power of 2, and dividing into equal-length blocks
10   val space = dev.defaultPaddedBlockPartition(n)
11
12   // spawn the computation on the GPU, returning
13   // an array with one result per block
14   val results = space.spawn {
15     // allocate output in global storage
16     val output = Array.ofDim[A](space.groups.size)
17
18     // for each block, in parallel
19     for (g <- space.groups) {
20       // allocate temp in per-block storage
21       val temp = Array.ofDim[A](g.items.size)
22
23       // for each thread, in parallel
24       for (item <- g.items) {
25         val i = item.id
26         val j = g.id * (g.items.size * 2) + i
27
28         // do the first round of the reduction into
29         // per-block storage
30         temp(i) = if (j < n) input(j) else z
31
32         if (j + g.items.size < n)
33           temp(i) = f(temp(i), input(j + g.items.size))
34
35         // make sure subsequent rounds can see
36         // the writes to temp
37         g.barrier
38
39         // do the remaining log(n) rounds
40         var k = g.items.size / 2
41
42         while (k > 0) {
43           if (i < k)
44             temp(i) = f(temp(i), temp(i + k))
45           g.barrier
46           k /= 2
47         }
48
49         // copy the result back into global memory
50         if (i == 0)
51           output(g.id) = temp(0)
52       }
53     }
54
55     output
56   }
57
58   // finish the reduction on the CPU
59   results.reduceLeft(f)
60 }
```

Figure 2. Reduce in Firepile

2.1 Constructing code trees at run time

Loading the function bytecode The first step in constructing the code tree for a function is to locate the bytecode for the function. Given a function f, the java.lang.Class for f can be retrieved with f.getClass. Using the class object, the bytecode is loaded from the classpath into the Soot bytecode analysis framework [33]. The code for the function object's apply method is then located.

```
public final class A$$anonfun$m$1                    Function(List(LocalValue(_, x, scala.Int)),
  extends scala.runtime.AbstractFunction1               Apply(Select(Ident(LocalValue(_, x, _)),
{                                                                Method(scala.Int.$plus, scala.Int)),
  private final int a$1;                                   List(Select(Ident(ThisType(A$$anonfun$m$1), _),
  public int apply(int x) { return x + this.a$1; }             Field(a$1, scala.Int)))))
  public A$$anonfun$m$1(int a) { this.a$1 = a; }
}
```

   (a) Java translation of `(x:Int) => x+a` (simplified)   (b) Code tree for `(x:Int) => x+a`

Figure 3. Translation to Java and code tree for the function `(x:Int) => x+a` where a has been captured from the environment of the function. The Scala compiler generates JVM bytecode similar to the code generated for the Java code in (a). We use Java syntax rather than bytecode syntax since it is more readable. The Scala compiler generates additional methods in the function object, which we elide, to allow it to be used with generics and for type specialization. The code tree in (b) has been simplified to remove temporary variables. _ is used to elide symbols.

Tree class	Description
Function(formals,body)	Function tree containing list of formal parameter symbols and body tree.
ValDef(symbol,rhs)	Definition of a value represented by symbol with rhs tree for initialization.
Assign(lhs,rhs)	Assign rhs expression to lhs target.
Select(qual,symbol)	Selection of method or field symbol to be invoked on qual.
Apply(fun,args)	Apply a function fun to arguments list args.
Method(name,type)	Symbol for a method with name and return type type.
LocalValue(owner,name,type)	Symbol to represent a local value with owner, name, and type.
If(cond,tcase,fcase)	A conditional branch.
Literal(value)	A literal value.
Target(symbol,body)	A branch target with label symbol and body.
Goto(target)	Represents a jump to a target symbol target.
Block(stmts,type)	Represents a code block containing a tree of statements stmts with result type type.

Figure 4. Selected code tree classes

Type reconstruction One challenge with constructing code trees is that type information is lost in translation from Scala to JVM bytecode. Before building trees, an analysis is performed to reconstruct Scala types from the bytecode. Many Scala types are easily inferred due to the Scala compiler directly mapping these to appropriate JVM equivalents. For instance, primitive types such as `scala.Int` and `scala.Float` are compiled into their corresponding JVM types. `scala.Array[T]` is likewise mapped to a `T[]` array. However, many Scala types, e.g., structural types and type parameters of generic types, do not have a corresponding JVM equivalent. In addition, the types of local variables and operand stack temporaries are not represented directly in the bytecode.

The Scala compiler encodes signature information for each method and field as attributes in the class file. These give the Scala types of formal parameters and return types. Using the formal parameter types and the types of any fields and methods a method m accesses as a starting point, a simple forward flow analysis can be used to reconstruct the types of m's local variables and temporaries.

Tree construction Code trees are generated from the Soot representation of the method bytecode. The translation is mostly straightforward. Scala extractor objects are used to conveniently match various elements of Soot's bytecode representation. The function itself is represented by a `Function` object, shown in Figure 4. Most Scala expression or type forms have a corresponding `Tree` class. Branches are represented using `Goto` nodes; loops are not reconstructed.

Formal parameters and local variables are mapped to instances of the `LocalValue` class. `LocalValue(owner,name,type)` trees contain an owner `Symbol`, a parameter name `String`, and a `Type`. `Symbol` is an abstract class representing a class, type, method, variable, or similar declaration. The `Type` classes correspond to the various types constructors defined in the Scala specification [26].

In Scala, primitive operations such as + are actually method calls on values of the primitive classes (e.g., `scala.Int`), unary and binary bytecode instructions are therefore translated into method calls, represented by the `Apply` class. For example, the `iadd` bytecode instruction, which adds two integers a and b is translated into the node for `a.$plus(b)`:[4]

```
Apply(Select(Ident(LocalValue(_, a, _)),
            Method(scala.Int.$plus, scala.Int)),
      List(Ident(LocalValue(_, b, _))))
```

Figure 3(b) shows an example of the tree generated from the function `(x: Int) => x + a`, where a is a value captured from the environment of the function. The `Function` tree is generated containing a list of `LocalValues` for the parameters to the function. A method of type `scala.Int` representing + is then applied to the field a of class `ThisType(A$$anonfun$m$1)`, which is the type of the function itself.

3. The Firepile compiler

The Firepile library provides collections classes to perform data-parallel operations on a GPU. We expect most users to write programs that use these classes. However, to implement these collections classes, and to provide more control over GPU resources, the library also provides lower-level classes and methods for device and memory management, as well as a compiler for translating Scala functions into kernels to run on the GPU. In this section, we focus on the Firepile compiler and in particular how the code trees described in Section 2 are used to implement the compiler.

3.1 Writing a kernel

Consider again the `reduce` example from Figure 2 in Section 1.3. An input array of element type A is passed into the `reduce` method along with a reduction operation `f` and an initial value `z`. The method is written in an explicitly parallel style. The problem space is mapped onto a one-dimensional grid of work items, one for each element of the input array, padded out to the next power of two (line

---

[4] For conciseness, we elide some sub-expressions by writing _.

8). Each work item corresponds to a single thread on the GPU. The grid of work items is then partitioned into a set of work groups, each of which corresponds to a set of threads that execute on the same streaming multiprocessor (SM) on the GPU. All work items can access global memory. Each work group has its own local memory that can be used to share data between work items in the group.

The method then spawns a computation to run on the GPU (lines 14–56). On the GPU, an `output` array is allocated (line 16) into which the result will be written. In the generated code, the call to allocate memory on the GPU is actually performed on the CPU. Each work group will write to one element of `output`.

Next, each work group executes code in parallel with the other work groups (lines 19–53). Each group creates an array of the group size (line 21) in the local memory for that group. Again, in the generated code, the actual allocation runs on the CPU. This array will be used to share partial results between work items in the group. Next, each work item performs the same computation in parallel on different segments of the `input` array (lines 24–52). First, two elements of `input` are reduced into one element of the `temp` array. Then, $\log_2 |group|$ additional reduction operations are performed on the `temp` array. After each reduction operation, a barrier is executed to ensure that other work items in the group observe the writes to the array. Barriers on local memory are the only synchronization operation on the GPU supported by OpenCL. These operations put the reduced value for the work group's segment of the `input` array into `temp(0)`. The first work item in the group copies this partial result to the output array (lines 50–51), which is then returned to the CPU (line 55). Finally, the partial reduction results are reduced sequentially on the CPU (line 59).

The `spawn` function invokes the run-time compiler on the code block that is passed into it. It has the following signature:

```
def spawn(block: => Unit): Unit
```

The formal parameter type `=> Unit` indicates that `block` is a call-by-name argument of type `Unit`. Passing by name allows `spawn` to compile and run `block` as an OpenCL kernel rather than having `block` execute on the CPU. The block passed to `spawn` is responsible for assigning computation to the appropriate work items and work groups to be run on the GPU. In general, the block consists of one or more nested loops over work groups and work items. Any data declared in the scope of the group loop (line 19) but outside of the items loop (line 24) is treated as local memory to the work group and can be shared among the work items. Only array or variable declarations are expected in this code block since statements can only be executed by work items. The run-time compiler verifies that the code follows the expected pattern. The `spawn` method compiles the body of the work-item loop into a kernel. The kernel is specialized on function values captured by the block. The results of the compilation is memoized so that the next invocation of `spawn` on the same code block, with a compatible environment, does not recompile the code.

3.2 The run-time compiler

The Firepile compiler generates OpenCL kernels using code trees described in Section 2. The `spawn` function first constructs a code tree for its code block argument as outlined in Section 2. The trees are then compiled into C through a recursive translation function. The C code is, in turn, compiled by the JavaCL [6] library into a binary to be executed on the GPU.

Variables captured by the block passed to `spawn`—for instance the `input` array in Figure 2—are compiled into function parameters in the generated code. When the kernel is invoked, these parameters are initialized by copying data from the CPU into the GPU's global memory.

```
struct Object {            union Object_sub {
  int __id;                  int __id;
};                           struct Object _Object;
                             struct B _B;
struct A {                   struct A _A;
  struct Object _Object;   }
  int x;
};                         union A_sub {
                             int __id;
struct B {                   struct B _B;
  struct A _A;               struct A _A;
  int y;                   };
};
                           union B_sub {
                             int __id;
                             struct B _B;
                           };
```

Figure 5. Firepile class translation

The compiler assumes a closed world: any classes that will be used in the generated code are assumed to be available during compilation. Since the compiler is often invoked immediately before the kernel is run, this assumption usually holds. Any methods invoked by the kernel function being compiled are also compiled into native code. Any types referenced by the code block are also translated.

Built-in Scala data types are translated into C primitive types (e.g., `scala.Float` is translated into `float`). Arrays are translated into a two-word struct containing a field for the array length and a pointer to a buffer containing the array elements.

Because virtual dispatch is not supported by OpenCL, dispatch tables are not generated for each class; instead, objects are translated into a tagged union: that is, an object of class C is compiled into a struct containing a one-word type tag and a union of all possible subclasses of C. These tags will later be used to simulate virtual dispatch as described in Section 3.4. Methods are translated into C functions that take an explicit `this` parameter as their first argument.

Rather than treating first-class functions like regular Scala objects, they are instead handled specially. Since the compiler has access to the run-time environment of the code it is compiling, it can often identify the actual function values passed into a method and will then generate a specialized version of the method for that value. For instance, given the call `A.foldLeft(0)(_+_)` the compiler will generate a specialized version of `foldLeft` that returns the sum of the elements of `A`. If the function value has captured variables, the function's environment is translated into a C struct containing fields for each of the captured variables. This structure is passed into methods that take the function as an argument.

3.3 Class translation

Figure 5 illustrates how the following Scala classes are translated.

```
class A(val x: Int) { ... }
class B extends A(val y: Int) { ... }
```

Each class is translated into a struct and a union. The struct for class C represents an object of exactly that class. Each struct begins with the struct for its immediate superclass. The built-in `Object` class is translated into a struct with a type tag used to implement method dispatch, as described in the next section. The union generated for C is the union of the structs for all subclasses of C, plus the type tag. The union is used whenever a value that could be any subclass of C is needed. A source-language variable with type C is translated into a variable of the union type.

```
int A_m(A_sub* _this, int _arg0) { ... }
int B_m(B_sub* _this, int _arg0) { ... }

int dispatch_A_m(A_sub* _this, int _arg0) {
 switch (_this->__id) {
   case A_ID: {
     return A_m((A_sub*) _this, _arg0);
   }
   case B_ID: {
     return B_m((B_sub*) _this, _arg0);
   }
 }
}
```

Figure 6. Dispatch method for a method m with two possible implementing classes

3.4 Expression translation

When generating C code, the compiler performs pattern matching on the code trees. It first identifies certain known expressions that need to be handled specially on the GPU. These include accesses to the work group and work item identifiers, which are compiled into library calls in the generated kernel. Calls representing primitive operations like + are translated into the appropriate operation. The Firepile library also provides utility classes such as unsigned integers (useful when porting C code to Scala) and math operations analogous to those provided by the OpenCL math library. These are also handled specially by the compiler.

Since the GPU does not support virtual calls, these must be translated into nonvirtual calls. First, the compiler enumerates the possible receivers of the method to determine if it is monomorphic. This is done by first checking the modifiers of the class and the method for a final declaration. If the class and method are not final, the known subclasses are searched to determine if they override the method. If the method call is found to be monomorphic then the called method is recursively translated and a nonvirtual invocation is generated. If the call is not monomorphic, a call is generated to a dispatch method, which performs a switch on the object's type tag to invoke the appropriate method nonvirtually.

Consider a call to a non-monomorphic method m that could be implemented in either of classes A or B from Section 3.3.

```
val a: A = ...
a.m(10)
```

The call is translated into the following call to the dispatch function in Figure 6:

```
A_sub* a = ...;
dispatch_A_m(a, 10);
```

The types A_sub and B_sub used in the figure are defined in Figure 5.

A potential performance issue that can arise from simulating polymorphic calls is *warp divergence* when performing a method call over a collection of mixed types. Depending on the dynamic type of an item in a collection, a given method call may be dispatched to different functions in different threads executing within the same warp on an SM. Because of the SIMD execution model, the different execution paths will be serialized, resulting a slowdown. A possible optimization is to split the collection into separate arrays based on their run-time type, thus making the calls monomorphic and avoiding the warp divergence. Rearranging the collection to clustering elements of the same type would have a similar effect. We plan to support these optimizations in later versions of Firepile.

The compiler also handles array and object allocation specially. Since dynamic allocation cannot be performed on the GPU, all memory used by a kernel on the GPU must be pre-allocated before the kernel is invoked. Memory is allocated in one of the levels of the GPU memory hierarchy: global, local, and private. It must also be determined whether a given global array is to be used for input, output, or both. Most object allocation is simply rejected by the compiler. The kernel can only access objects passed into the compiler. The compiler identifies array allocations and based on their scope determines in which class of memory to allocate the array before the kernel is invoked. If the array does not escape the scope of the kernel's work-item loop, it is allocated in per-thread private memory; if it does not escape the scope of the kernel's work-group loop, it is allocated in per-group local memory. Otherwise, it is allocated in global memory. Since all memory used by the GPU must be pre-allocated before the kernel is invoked, allocation within loops that run on the GPU are prohibited. An allocation site in a given scope must dominate the exit of that scope. In addition, if the size of the array depends on a value computed by the kernel itself, the allocation is rejected. We plan to implement a more thorough memory analysis in the future, computing the memory requirements of the kernel as functions of the kernel's formal parameters.

Other expression types such as basic control constructs are translated in a straightforward manner. Exception throws are rejected by the compiler; exception handlers are simply elided from the generated code.

4. Experimental results

To evaluate the performance of Firepile, examples from the NVIDIA OpenCL SDK[5] were ported to Scala to use the library. The original examples are implemented in C++ with kernel code in the OpenCL subset of C with no optimizations beyond what is demonstrated in the example code added. The chosen examples are summarized in Figure 7. In addition to Reduce (similar to the code in Figure 2), Black-Scholes, matrix–vector multiplication (MVM), the discrete cosine transform (DCT8x8), and matrix transpose were ported. All benchmarks were run with four of the same problem sizes for each benchmark. Command-line options for problems sizes were added to the C++ versions when needed. For all benchmarks except MVM, problem sizes increase exponentially; the problem size for MVM increases linearly. The benchmarks were chosen to not exceed the capabilities of the current Firepile implementation. For instance, benchmarks with OpenCL vector operations were not ported since Firepile does not yet support these operations.

We compared Firepile against two C++ versions of each benchmark. In addition to the NVIDIA implementation of the benchmark, we constructed a hybrid version by replacing the NVIDIA kernel code with the Firepile-generated kernel. All other code, including the code to copy data to and from the GPU is identical to the original C++ version. This hybrid version is used to determine if performance differences between Firepile and the NVIDIA code can be attributed to the kernel translation or to differences in device initialization or data movement.

The three versions of each benchmark were run with the same data values and range of problem sizes. Experiments were performed on a system with a 3.0GHz Intel Core 2 Quad Q9650 CPU, 8GB RAM, and an NVIDIA GeForce 9800GT graphics card with 512MB of video memory, running Windows 7 Professional 64-bit. Firepile was compiled and run with Scala 2.9.0 and Java 1.6.0_24b07 using the HotSpot VM.

For each problem size and configuration tested, the benchmark was executed 30 times and the results averaged. To reduce inter-

---

[5] http://developer.nvidia.com/opencl-sdk-code-samples.

112

Benchmark	Sizes
Reduce	$2^{20}, 2^{21}, 2^{22}, 2^{23}$
Black-Scholes	2M, 4M, 8M, 16M
Matrix–vector multiplication (MVM)	12.1M, 13.2M, 14.3M, 15.4M
Discrete cosine transform (DCT8x8)	$2^{18}, 2^{19}, 2^{20}, 2^{21}$
Matrix-transpose	$2^{16}, 2^{18}, 2^{20}, 2^{22}$

Figure 7. Summary of benchmarks run for Firepile and C++

ference from the JIT compiler, each kernel execution consisted of a warm-up run followed by 16 repetitions. Warm-up runs were not included in the reported times. Results are shown in Figure 8. The hybrid configuration for Black-Scholes for a data size of 16M crashed the graphics card driver on our test system and times were not collected.

Firepile performance compares favorably to the NVIDIA implementation. For most benchmarks, run times for all three configurations were within 15%. The execution times for the hybrid configuration were between the times for the NVIDIA and Firepile configurations, as expected. With most benchmarks the NVIDIA C++ code outperformed Firepile, again as expected. The Firepile version of the Reduce benchmark performed as well as the NVIDIA and hybrid versions. The Firepile version of MVM was faster than the NVIDIA and hybrid versions. Firepile did not perform as well on DCT8x8, with execution times nearly double the NVIDIA version.

Execution time differences can be attributed to a variety of factors. First, there are differences between the generated kernel and the hand-written kernel. While the algorithms used were the same, Firepile generated kernels introduce additional temporary variables and use goto statements rather than structured control flow statements. In addition, placement and alignment of data differs from the C++ versions. In particular, arrays in the C++ version do not have a length field. The C++ versions of the code can also make use of pointer arithmetic, while Firepile generated kernels do not. The NVIDIA version of Matrix-transpose performed consistently better across all problem sizes. We attribute this difference to the heavy use of pointer arithmetic for data access into global arrays. The Black-Scholes benchmark generated the highest number of temporary variables of the benchmarks tested and performed slower than the NVIDIA example as expected. Additional temporaries can increase the memory footprint of a kernel by requiring it to use more private memory. A larger footprint can then reduce parallelism since the GPU can support only a fixed amount of private memory per SM.

There are also differences in data movement between the configurations. Because Firepile arrays have a length field, this additional data is copied to the GPU when the kernel is invoked. Array lengths are copied to the GPU in the hybrid configuration as well. For MVM, Firepile was 15% faster than both the NVIDIA and hybrid configurations, indicating that data copying times were faster. In contrast, the Firepile version of DCT8x8 was consistently slower than the other configurations.

Additional optimizations we have planned for later versions of the library should help to close the performance gap with the native versions of the kernels, while maintaining Firepile's ease of use.

5. Related work

5.1 Meta programming

Lisp [29] was the first language to introduce meta-programming features. Lisp supports *quasiquoting* [3], which allows programmers to construct code templates with "holes" that can be filled in

with concrete values. Various forms of quasiquoting are supported in many languages nowadays, including Scheme [15], Haskell [21], and C♯ [9]. MetaML [31] and MetaOCaml [30] support type-checking of quoted code. Scala has some experimental quasiquoting support in the class scala.reflect.Code. The Mnemonics [28] library uses this feature to generate bytecode from function values—the inverse of our code trees.

A key difference between our approach and quasiquoting is that our code trees are constructed at run time from function values. With quasiquoting, code trees are constructed statically by the programmer. By constructing trees statically, library writers who want access to the code of functions passed into the library must require that code trees, rather than functions, be passed into the library. Consider the reduce function from Figure 2. Rather than passing in a function of type (A,A) => A, the programmer would instead pass in a code tree, e.g., of type Code[(A,A) => A]. This exposes details of the implementation of the library to the caller. If the call to a function like reduce is hidden under a stack of other functions, then the use of code trees is exposed further.

Java [11] and other JVM languages also support code introspection or *reflection* features. These allow the programmer to inspect objects at run time and to access their members without having static knowledge. Firepile's code tree construction extends this feature by allowing introspection on the implementation of an object or function.

Bytecode instrumentation is an another approach we considered taking with Firepile. Java 6 supports *agents* in the java.lang.instrument package. Agents are loaded into the VM to intercept class loading and can rewrite classes as they are loaded. They can be used to implement new language features. For example, Deuce [17] adds software transactional memory support to Java through bytecode instrumentation. Our code trees differ from Java agents in that the program representation is at a higher level. Code trees are closer to the original Scala code than to Java bytecode. The Scala program itself, rather than an external entity, has control over when and how the trees are constructed.

Compiler plugins provide another way to extend the base programming language with new functionality. Compiler plugins extend the base compiler with new semantics by adding new compiler passes. For instance, the ScalaCL compiler plugin [7] transforms uses of the standard Scala collections library into OpenCL kernels. The ScalaQL plugin [10] extends Scala with database queries.

5.2 GPU programming

The two most widely used programming models for GPUs are CUDA [23] an OpenCL [22] Both provide similar abstractions and require explicit management of data movement to and from the GPU as well as between the different classes of memory on the GPU. Firepile generates OpenCL kernels. OpenCL kernels are written in an "extended subset" of C with no support for dynamic memory allocation, function pointers, or recursion. OpenCL C supports additional vector types not found in standard C. Firepile does not support these vector types. Wrappers for both CUDA and OpenCL exist for several languages, including Python [16, 19, 27] and Java [6, 14, 34].

CLyther [8] is an extension of Python with OpenCL support. CLyther provides access to OpenCL APIs like PyOpenCL, allows device memory management, and supports an emulation mode for OpenCL code. Similarly to Firepile, CLyther performs dynamic compilation of a subset of the base language (viz. Python) into OpenCL kernels.

An alternative for runtime code generation using Scala is to use the Scala compiler's plugin mechanism. The ScalaCL plugin [7] translates Scala code into corresponding kernel code, employing JavaCL wrappers for execution. Originally, ScalaCL allowed ker-

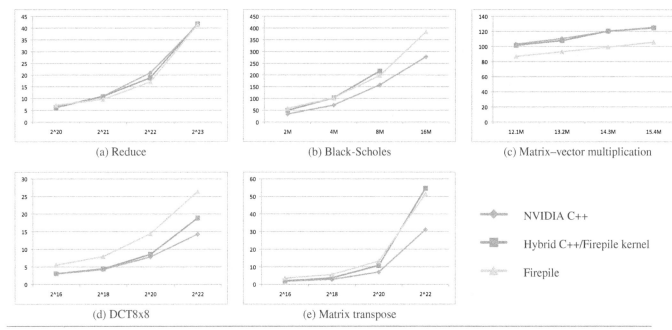

(a) Reduce

(b) Black-Scholes

(c) Matrix–vector multiplication

(d) DCT8x8

(e) Matrix transpose

- NVIDIA C++
- Hybrid C++/Firepile kernel
- Firepile

Figure 8. Total execution times in ms of each benchmark for different problem sizes.

nels to be written using an embedded DSL for specifying parallel computation on GPUs. The compiler plugin now identifies Scala loops that can be parallelized and transforms these to run on the GPU. The ScalaCL feature that performs translation is restricted to be used only with selected operations of its parallel collection library, whereas Firepile attempts to translate as much of Scala as possible and allows users to write root level kernel functions using Scala.

A hybrid compile time/runtime approach is taken by the commercial product from TidePowerd called GPU.NET [12]. GPU.NET enables GPU acceleration of .NET languages including C♯, F♯, and VB.NET. Methods must be annotated as kernels and kernel code generation from .NET bytecode (CIL) is performed behind the scenes and embedded inside assemblies. Memory transfers and scheduling are all performed in the background and programmers need not have any knowledge of the GPU architecture. Runtime plugins determine how the final assembly will be executed on available hardware, or executed on the CPU as a fallback option.

Accelerator [32] is a library for use with multicore CPUs and DX9 GPUs in order to increase performance of parallel code (array processing) execution. Intended for use with .NET, Accelerator programs are typically written in F♯ or C♯ 4.0, although using unmanaged C++ remains an option. Like GPU.NET, Accelerator supports multiple .NET languages.

Aparapi [1] is an API for AMD GPUs that allows the expression of data-parallel workloads in Java. Aparapi translates a subset of Java into OpenCL code. The subset is restricted to allow only primitive data types and one-dimensional arrays. In addition, primitive scalar fields are read only, static field support is limited, arrays cannot be passed as method arguments, nor can their lengths be accessed. Static methods, method overloading, recursion, and object allocation are all unsupported.

Chafi et al. [5] introduce Delite, a framework for parallelization of DSLs that can use Scala ASTs as their base. Delite performs parallel optimizations and data chunking, and allows for translation to C++ for execution on target systems. Delite includes classes that can be used to specify parallel execution patterns such as Map, Reduce, ZipWith, and Scan. Kernels can be generated from these

classes and an optimized execution graph that is executed by the Delite runtime.

Functional languages are a natural choice for data-parallel programming on (or off) GPUs. Nikola [20] is a first-order language for array computations that is embedded in Haskell and is compiled to CUDA. Low-level details such as data marshaling, size inference of buffers, management of memory, and loop parallelization are handled automatically. The quasiquoting feature of GHC [21] is used in translation to CUDA code and allows CUDA code to be written in as a Haskell program. Nikola supports both compile-time and run-time code generation.

Lee et al. [18] demonstrate GPU kernels embedded in Haskell as data-parallel array computations, mixing CPU and GPU computations while taking advantage of the type system to avoid some of the constraints associated with GPU architectures. The domain specific language used to write kernels is restricted to what can be compiled to CUDA. A run-time compiler `GPU.gen` translates the DSL into CUDA code and dynamically links it to the Haskell program using the Haskell plugins library.

There are several dedicated languages for GPUs and other accelerators. CUDA [23] supports GPU programming through an extension of C++. The Brook language [4] extends the C with data-parallel constructs for stream programming on GPUs. Kernels are mapped to Cg shaders by the source-to-source compiler and the Brook runtime handles kernel execution. The Liquid Metal system [2, 13] introduces the Lime programming language and runtime for acceleration designed to be executed across many architectures, including CPUs and FPGAs. Unlike Firepile, Liquid Metal requires the use of a special purpose language for programming accelerators in order to be more adaptable to data-parallel programming (functional, stream computing, bit-level processing, etc).

6. Conclusions

General-purpose computing on GPUs remains a difficult task. GPUs have a restricted programming model, disallowing features such as dynamic memory management and virtual methods. The Firepile library supports a richer programming model, allowing kernels to be written in Scala. Firepile works by translating function values at run time into code trees, from which GPU kernels can be generated. Performance of Firepile kernels is comparable to the performance of native C code.

Future plans for Firepile are to support more features of Scala—object allocation in particular—and to explore GPU-specific optimizations in the context of OO languages. Firepile currently supports only simple kernel where inputs are copied to the GPU, a kernel is run, and then outputs are copied back to the host. We wish to support more complex scenarios where multiple kernels are executed with minimal data movement between the host and GPU. We also plan to explore the use of run-time generated code trees to implement other domain-specific extensions of Scala.

Acknowledgments

The authors thank Gutemberg Guerra-Filho for generously allowing us the use of his lab and computers for running experiments.

References

[1] Aparapi: Java API for expressing GPU bound data parallel algorithms. http://developer.amd.com/zones/java/aparapi/Pages/default.aspx, 2011.

[2] Joshua Auerbach, David F. Bacon, Perry Cheng, and Rodric Rabbah. Lime: a Java-compatible and synthesizable language for heterogeneous architectures. In *Proceedings of the 25th ACM Conference on Object-Oriented Programming Systems, Languages and Applications (OOPSLA 2010)*, pages 89–108, 2010.

[3] Alan Bawden. Quasiquotation in Lisp. In *Partial Evaluation and Semantic-Based Program Manipulation*, pages 4–12, 1999.

[4] Ian Buck, Tim Foley, Daniel Horn, Jeremy Sugerman, Kayvon Fatahalian, Mike Houston, and Pat Hanrahan. Brook for GPUs: stream computing on graphics hardware. In *ACM SIGGRAPH 2004 Papers (SIGGRAPH '04)*, pages 777–786, 2004.

[5] Hassan Chafi, Zach DeVito, Adriaan Moors, Tiark Rompf, Arvind K. Sujeeth, Pat Hanrahan, Martin Odersky, and Kunle Olukotun. Language virtualization for heterogeneous parallel computing. In *Onward! '10: Proceedings of the ACM International Conference on Object Oriented Programming Systems Languages and Applications*, October 2010.

[6] Olivier Chafik. JavaCL: Java wrappers for OpenCL. http://code.google.com/p/javacl, 2011.

[7] Olivier Chafik. ScalaCL: Faster Scala: optimizing compiler plugin + GPU-based collections (OpenCL). http://code.google.com/p/scalacl, 2011.

[8] Clyther: Python language extension for OpenCL. http://clyther.sourceforge.net, 2011.

[9] ECMA. Standard ECMA-334: C♯ language specification (4th edition). http://www.ecma-international.org/publications/standards/Ecma-334.htm, June 2006.

[10] Miguel Garcia, Anastasia Izmaylova, and Sibylle Schupp. Extending Scala with database query capability. *Journal of Object Technology*, July 2010.

[11] James Gosling, Bill Joy, Guy Steele, and Gilad Bracha. *The Java Language Specification*. Addison Wesley, 3rd edition, 2005. ISBN 0321246780.

[12] GPU.NET: Library for developing GPU-accelerated applications with .NET. http://www.tidepowerd.com/product, 2011.

[13] Shan Shan Huang, Amir Hormati, David F. Bacon, and Rodric Rabbah. Liquid metal: Object-oriented programming across the hardware/software boundary. In *Proceedings of the 22nd European Conference on Object-Oriented Programming (ECOOP 2008)*, volume 5142 of *Lecture Notes in Computer Science*, pages 76–103, 2008.

[14] JOCL: Java bindings for OpenCL. http://www.jocl.org, 2011.

[15] Richard Kelsey, William Clinger, and Jonathan Rees (editors). Revised⁵ report on the algorithmic language Scheme. *ACM SIGPLAN Notices*, 33(9):26–76, October 1998.

[16] Andreas Klöckner, Nicolas Pinto, Yunsup Lee, Bryan C. Catanzaro, Paul Ivanov, and Ahmed Fasih. PyCUDA: GPU run-time code generation for high-performance computing. http://arxiv.org/abs/0911.3456, 2009. In submission.

[17] G. Korland, N. Shavit, and P. Felber. Noninvasive concurrency with Java STM. In *Third Workshop on Programmability Issues for Multi-Core Computers (MULTIPROG-3)*, January 2010.

[18] Sean Lee, Vinod Grover, Manuel M. T. Chakravarty, and Gabriele Keller. GPU kernels as data-parallel array computations in Haskell. In *Workshop on Exploiting Parallelism using GPUs and other Hardware-Assisted Methods (EPHAM)*, 2009.

[19] Calle Lejdfors and Lennart Ohlsson. Implementing an embedded gpu language by combining translation and generation. In *Proceedings of the 2006 ACM symposium on Applied computing (SAC '06)*, pages 1610–1614, 2006.

[20] Geoffrey Mainland and Greg Morrisett. Nikola: embedding compiled GPU functions in Haskell. In *Proceedings of the third ACM symposium on Haskell (Haskell '10)*, pages 67–78, 2010.

[21] Geoffrey B. Mainland. Why it's nice to be quoted: Quasiquoting for Haskell. In *Proceedings of the 2007 ACM symposium on Haskell (Haskell '07)*, 2007.

[22] A. Munshi and Khronos OpenCL Working Group. The OpenCL specification, 2009.

[23] NVIDIA. Compute unified device architecture programming guide. http://developer.download.nvidia.com/compute/cuda/1.0/NVIDIA_CUDA_Programming_Guide_1.0.pdf, 2008.

[24] NVIDIA. NVIDIA OpenCL best practices guide, version 1.0. http://www.nvidia.com/content/cudazone/CUDABrowser/downloads/papers/NVIDIA_OpenCL_BestPracticesGuide.pdf, 2009.

[25] NVIDIA. NVIDIA's next generation CUDA compute architecture: Fermi. http://www.nvidia.com/content/PDF/fermi_white_papers/NVIDIA_Fermi_Compute_Architecture_Whitepaper.pdf, 2010.

[26] Martin Odersky et al. The Scala language specification, 2006–2011.

[27] PyOpenCL: Python programming environment for OpenCL. http://mathema.tician.de/software/pyopencl, 2011.

[28] Johannes Rudolph and Peter Thiemann. Mnemonics: type-safe bytecode generation at run time. In *Proceedings of the 2010 ACM SIGPLAN workshop on Partial evaluation and program manipulation (PEPM)*, pages 15–24, 2010.

[29] Guy L. Steele, Jr. and Richard P. Gabriel. The evolution of Lisp. In *HOPL-II: The second ACM SIGPLAN conference on History of programming languages*, pages 231–270, New York, NY, USA, 1993. ACM.

[30] Walid Taha. A gentle introduction to multi-stage programming. In *Domain-Specific Program Generation*, pages 30–50, 2003.

[31] Walid Taha and Tim Sheard. Multi-stage programming with explicit annotations. In *Proceedings of the ACM-SIGPLAN Symposium on Partial Evaluation and semantic based program manipulations (PEPM)*, pages 203–217, 1997.

[32] David Tarditi, Sidd Puri, and Jose Oglesby. Accelerator: Using data parallelism to program GPUs for general-purpose uses. In *Proceedings of the 15th International Conference on Architectural Support for Programming Languages and Operating Systems (ASPLOS)*, October 2006.

[33] Raja Vallée-Rai, Phong Co, Etienne Gagnon, Laurie Hendren, Patrick Lam, and Vijay Vijay Sundaresan. Soot: A Java bytecode optimization framework. In *Proceedings of the 1999 conference of the Centre for Advanced Studies on Collaborative research (CASCON)*, 1999.

[34] Yonghong Yan, Max Grossman, and Vivek Sarkar. JCUDA: A programmer-friendly interface for accelerating Java programs with CUDA. In *Proceedings of the 15th International Euro-Par Conference on Parallel Processing (Euro-Par '09)*, pages 887–899, 2009.

Monitoring Aspects for the Customization of Automatically Generated Code for Big-Step Models

Shahram Esmaeilsabzali

Electronics and Computer Science
University of Southampton
se3@ecs.soton.ac.uk

Bernd Fischer

Electronics and Computer Science
University of Southampton
b.fischer@ecs.soton.ac.uk

Joanne M. Atlee

Cheriton School of Computer Science
University of Waterloo
jmatlee@cs.uwaterloo.ca

Abstract

The output of a code generator is assumed to be correct and not usually intended to be read or modified; yet programmers are often interested in this, e.g., to monitor a system property. Here, we consider code customization for a family of code generators associated with big-step executable modelling languages (e.g., statecharts). We introduce a customization language that allows us to express customization scenarios for the generated code independently of a specific big-step execution semantics. These customization scenarios are all different forms of runtime monitors, which lend themselves to a principled, uniform implementation for observation and code extension. A monitor is given in terms of the enabledness and execution of the transitions of a model and a reachability relation between two states of the execution of the model during a big step. For each monitor, we generate the aspect code that is incorporated into the output of a code generator to implement the monitor at the generated-code level. Thus, we provide means for code analysis through using the vocabulary of a model, rather than the detail of the generated code. Our technique not only requires the code generators to reveal only limited information about their code generation mechanisms, but also keeps the structure of the generated code intact. We demonstrate how various useful properties of a model, or a language, can be checked using our monitors.

Categories and Subject Descriptors D.2.2 [*Design Tools and Techniques*]: State diagrams; D.2.5 [*Testing and Debugging*]: Monitors; D.3.4 [*Processors*]: Code generation; I.2.2 [*Automatic Programming*]: Program transformation, Program modification; I.6.4 [*Simulation and Modelling*]: Model validation and analysis

General Terms Design, Languages

Keywords AspectJ, Semantics, Statecharts, MDE, AOP

1. Introduction

Automatic code generation from high-level models is a key technology to raise the abstraction level in software development, and so to increase productivity, and improve code reliability. While the output of a code generator is usually not meant to be read or modified by a programmer, it is often necessary to have a means to understand the behaviour of the code, for example, in order to integrate it into an existing code base or to inspect its correctness.

In this paper, we introduce a framework for automatic customization of generated code to enhance it with the capability to monitor a property at runtime. Our system receives a property-of–interest for the generated Java code of a model, and produces AspectJ [1] code that is woven to the generated code to monitor the property. Our system works with the output of a family of code generators [2] that each generates code for a behavioural model specified in a *big-step modelling language* (BSML) [3].

BSMLs are a widely used class of modeling languages, which includes statecharts [4] and its variants [5], among other formalisms. A BSML can be used to specify the behaviour of systems that interact with their environments; e.g., a banking machine or a microwave. In a BSML model, the reaction of a model to an input is described by a big step, which consists of a sequence of small steps, each of which is the execution of a set of transitions. There is a plethora of BSMLs, which can be essentially distinguished by their semantic variations [3, 6]. These variations specify the detail of how transitions become enabled and how they are executed.

In our framework, a monitoring property is specified in the *big-step monitoring language* (BML), which we introduce in this paper. A BML monitor uses the vocabulary of a BSML model, and *not* the often unreadable vocabulary of the generated code, to specify a property for the generated code of the model. As such, our framework raises the level of abstraction that a developer works at: a developer neither needs to know about the code generation mechanism, nor about the mechanism by which a model-level property is monitored at the generated-code level. A BML property can be considered as a kind of predicate-logic formula over the transitions of a model, together with a *reachability* (or an *unreachability*) operator that specifies whether a certain state of a big step can reach (must not reach) another state of the big step. Quantification can be used to specify a general property about a model; e.g., the *global consistency* [7] property asserts that a transition that is triggered with the absence of an event and a transition that generates the event cannot be executed in the same big step. A BML property is either an *invariant*, required to hold in all big steps, or is a *witness*, required to hold in at least one big step. A novelty in the design of our BML is that it can be uniformly used by different BSMLs.

We define the semantics of BML by adapting the temporal operators of LTL [8] to work in the scope of a big step. A key idea in our semantics is that the *enabledness* and *execution* information about the transitions are treated as *uninterpreted functions* [9]: the semantics of BML is independent of how transitions become enabled and how they are executed. As such, BML abstracts away from the particularities of the semantics of BSMLs, and thus, is uniformly adoptable by the family of BSMLs. This allows for adopting BML for the output of different code generators as well.

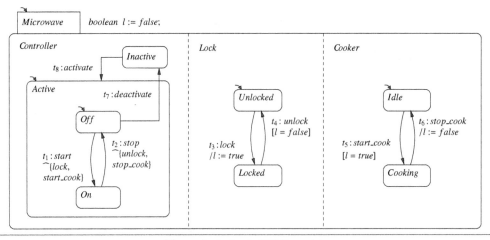

Figure 1. A simple BSML model.

We have implemented BML for a family of code generators [2] that generates code for a subset of BSMLs. We have developed a code generator that for each BML monitor generates the multi-threaded AspectJ code that collects the necessary information to interpret the monitor at runtime. Because of the design of our BML and the structure of the BSML-generated code, our generated aspects need to intercept the execution of only a few of methods of the BSML-generated code. To implement BML for a new code generator, we require the BSML-generated code to expose only limited programmatic means to inspect the execution of big steps.

Our contribution in this paper is threefold. First, we introduce a language that allows to specify monitors to analyze the behaviour of generated code by using the vocabulary of a model, rather than the detail of its generated code. Thus, we combine model analysis with code analysis, as advocated by others [10, 11], to decrease the gap between the model and the code. Second, we present a uniform, automatic approach to implement BML monitors for a family of code generators that support different BSML semantics. Finally, we present a non-intrusive, aspect-based technique to customize the generated code to analyze its behaviour. Our technique is comparable with other approaches that aim at improving the extensibility of object-oriented software via aspects [12, 13].

The remainder of the paper is organized as follows. Section 2 presents an overview of the syntax and semantics of BSMLs. Section 3 presents our BML and its example applications. Section 4 presents the semantics of BML. Section 5 presents our implementation of BML for a family of code generators. Section 6 discusses related work. Section 7 concludes the paper.

2. Background: Big-Step Modelling Languages

In this section, we present an overview of the family of big-step modelling languages (BSMLs), whose semantics we deconstructed and compared in our previous work [3, 6]. We begin with describing the common, normal form syntax that we have adopted for BSMLs. We then briefly describe the common semantics of BSMLs, together with some of their semantic variations. There are further semantic variations that are not considered in this paper; details can be found in our previous work [3, 6]. We use the BSML model in Figure 1 as our running example throughout the paper.

2.1 Normal Form Syntax

To provide a unifying semantic framework for BSMLs, we introduced a normal form syntax, which is similar to the syntax of original statecharts [4, 7]. A BSML model is a hierarchical, extended finite state machine that consists of: (i) a hierarchy tree of control states, and (ii) a set of transitions between these control states.

Control states. A *control state*, graphically represented by a rounded box, represents a noteworthy moment in the execution of a model. Each control state has a *type*, which is either *And*, *Or*, or *Basic*. The control states of a model form a *hierarchy tree*, where the leaves (and only they) have type *Basic*. A *child* of an *And*-state or *Or*-state is surrounded by the box representing its *parent*; the children of an *And*-state are separated from one another by dashed lines. The *ancestor* and *descendant* relations are defined with their usual meanings. As an example, the model in Figure 1 is a simplified BSML model for the software system that controls the operation of a microwave oven. Control state *Microwave* is an *And*-state that has three children, namely, *Controller*, *Lock*, and *Cooker*, which are all *Or*-states; note that the surrounding lines around these *Or*-states have been removed to simplify the graphical representation. Control state *Unlocked* is a *Basic*-state and a child of *Lock*. One of the children of an *Or*-state is its *default* control state, which is signified by an incoming arrow without a source. The *root* of the hierarchy tree must be an *Or*-state, which is not explicitly shown if it has only one child; e.g., as in the model in Figure 1. Each control state has a unique *name* that appears at its top, left corner.

Transitions. A *transition*, graphically represented by an arrow, specifies behaviour in a BSML model. Each transition, t, has a *source control state*, $src(t)$, and a *destination control state*, $dest(t)$, together with the following four optional elements: (i) a *guard condition*, $gc(t)$, which is a boolean expression over a set of variables, enclosed by a "[ ]"; (ii) a *triggering condition*, $trig(t)$, which is the conjunction of a set of events and negation of events; (iii) a set of *variable assignments*, $asn(t)$, which is prefixed by a "/", with at most one assignment to each variable; and (iv) a set of *generated events*, $gen(t)$, which is prefixed by a "^". Each transition name is followed by a ":". As an example, in the model in Figure 1, t_1 is a transition, with $src(t_1) = Off$, $dest(t_1) = On$, $gc(t_1) = true$, $asn(t_1) = \emptyset$, $trig(t_4) = start$, and $gen(t_4) = \{lock, start\_cook\}$. Transitions t_3, t_4, t_5, and t_6 use variables; e.g., $asn(t_3) = \{l := true\}$ and $gc(t_5) = [l = true]$. Variable l is used to disallow the situation where t_5 is executed before t_3 and t_4 is executed before t_6, to avoid microwave radiation while the door is unlocked. The *arena* of a transition t, denoted by $arena(t)$, is the lowest *Or*-state in the hierarchy tree such that the source and destination control states of the transition are its descendants. For example, in the model in Figure 1 $arena(t_7) = Controller$ and $arena(t_1) = Active$. For a model M, we denote the set of all its transitions as $Trans(M)$.

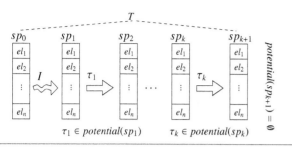

$$\tau_1 \in potential(sp_1) \qquad \tau_k \in potential(sp_k)$$

Figure 2. Structure of a big step.

2.2 Common Semantics and Semantic Variations

A BSML model specifies the behaviour of a system that interacts with its environment. An *environmental input* is a set of input events together with a set of assignments to input variables. The reaction of a BSML model to an environmental input is a *big step* that consists of a sequence of *small steps*, each of which can be the execution of a set of transitions.

2.2.1 Model Initialization

Initially, in a BSML model, all variables are assigned their initial values; all events are *absent* (i.e., their statuses are *false*); and the model resides in the default control state of its root. Furthermore, the following invariants always hold for a BSML model: (i) if the model resides in one of its *And*-states, it resides in all of its children; and (ii) if it resides in one of its *Or*-states, it resides in exactly one of its children. As an example, initially, the BSML model in Figure 1 resides in control states *Microwave, Controller, Lock, Cooker, Active, Off, Unlocked,* and *Idle.* Variable *l* is initialized with a *false* value. Events *start, stop, activate, deactivate* are environmental input events of the model (they are not generated by any transition). The model has no environmental input variables.

2.2.2 Structure of a Big Step

Figure 2, adopted from our previous work [6], depicts the structure of a big step, T. The execution of a big step is an alternating sequence of snapshots and small steps, in response to an environmental input I. A *snapshot* of a BSML model is a valuation of its *snapshot elements*, each dealing with an aspect of the semantics of a BSML. For example, there is a snapshot element that maintains the set of control states that a model resides in: upon the execution of a transition, its source control state is removed from the snapshot element and its destination control state is added to the snapshot element. Similarly, there are snapshot elements that maintain the values of variables, the statuses of events, *etc.* The number of snapshot elements of a BSML model depends on the semantics of the BSML. In the big step in Figure 2, there are $k+2$ snapshots, namely, $sp_0, sp_1, \cdots, sp_{k+1}$, and n snapshot elements, namely, $el_1, \cdots, el_n$. We call snapshot sp_0 and snapshot sp_{k+1} the *source snapshot* and the *destination snapshot*, respectively, of big step T. Snapshot sp_1, called the *beginning snapshot*, includes the effect of receiving input I at snapshot sp_0. Each tuple, $(sp_i, \tau_i, sp_{i+1}), (1 \le i \le k)$ is a small step of T. For each small step, (sp_i, τ_i, sp_{i+1}), sp_i and sp_{i+1} are its *source snapshot* and *destination snapshot*, respectively. The effect of the execution of a small step is stored in its destination snapshot. We refer to a big step through its sequence of small steps; e.g., we refer to big step $T = \langle sp_0, I, sp_1, \tau_1, sp_1, \cdots, \tau_k, sp_{k+1} \rangle$ as $\langle \tau_0, \cdots, \tau_k \rangle$. At each snapshot, there might be more than one set of transitions that can be executed as the next small step; we call each of these sets of transitions a *potential small step* of that snapshot. We denote the set of potential small steps of a model at a snapshot, sp, as $potential(sp)$. For a BSML model M, we denote the set of all its possible big steps as $bigsteps(M)$.

2.2.3 Common Semantics

The flowchart in Figure 3, adapted from our previous work [3], depicts the conceptual stages in executing a single big step. At the beginning of a big step, an environmental input is received from the environment. The next six stages of the flowchart specify the necessary stages in forming and executing a small step. The flowchart iterates until its big step becomes *maximal*, meaning that there is no more small steps to be executed, at which point the big step concludes and the flowchart reaches its end. In each iteration of the flowchart, if there are more than one potential small steps, stage 5 chooses one non-deterministically. As an example, when the BSML model in Figure 1 resides in its default control states, if environmental input event *start* is received at the beginning of a big step, transition t_1 can be taken as a small step. The execution of t_1 generates events *lock* and *start_cook*, which trigger transition t_3 to be taken as the second small step. However, if $gc(t_5)$ would have been *true* and the BSML semantics would have only allowed one transition per small step, then $\{t_3\}$ and $\{t_5\}$ each would have been a potential small step after the execution of t_1.

2.2.4 BSML Semantic Variations

Each of the six numbered stages of the flowchart in Figure 3 could be carried out differently in different BSMLs, and thus, is a semantic variation point for BSMLs. We call these semantic variation points the *semantic aspects* of BSMLs [3]. Each semantic aspect can be instantiated with a *semantic option* that specifies how the corresponding stage of the semantic aspect must be carried out [3]. We use the sans serif and SMALL CAPS fonts to refer to the name of a semantic aspect and a semantic option, respectively.

The feature diagram [14] in Figure 4 shows six semantics aspects together with a common set of semantic options for each of the semantic aspects. Since variables and events are optional in the syntax of BSMLs, their corresponding semantic aspects are optional features of the feature diagram. In this paper, we consider only a commonly used subset of the semantic aspects and semantic options, which are also supported by the family of code generators that we consider in our implementation.

The Event semantic aspect specifies the snapshots in which a generated event is present and can trigger a transition. Three common semantic options for the Event semantic aspect are that a generated event is: (i) present only in the destination snapshot of the small step that generates it (the NEXT SMALL STEP semantic option); (ii) present in the destination of the small step that generates it, and in all subsequent snapshots in the big step (the REMAINDER semantic option); or (iii) present throughout the next big step after the big step in which it is generated (the NEXT BIG STEP semantic option).

The GC Variable semantic aspect concerns the variable values used to evaluate guard conditions. Two common semantic options are: (i) to use variable values from the beginning of the current big step, according to the assignments in the previous big step (the GC BIG STEP semantic option); or (ii) to use variable values in the current snapshot, thus taking into account the assignments made in the current big step (the GC SMALL STEP semantic option). The semantic options for the RHS Variable semantic aspect are similar. As an example, in the model in Figure 1, when the model resides in its default control states and input event *start* is received, only employing the REMAINDER and GC SMALL STEP semantic options results in the expected behaviour: $\langle \{t_1\}, \{t_3\}, \{t_5\} \rangle$; e.g., if the GC BIG STEP semantic option is employed, t_5 is not executed.

The Concurrency and Priority semantic aspects deal with forming the set of potential small steps of a BSML model at each snapshot, using the set of enabled transitions determined by stages 1 and 2 of the flowchart in Figure 3. The Concurrency semantic aspect specifies whether exactly one (the SINGLE semantic option) or a maximal set of transitions that the lowest common ancestor of their

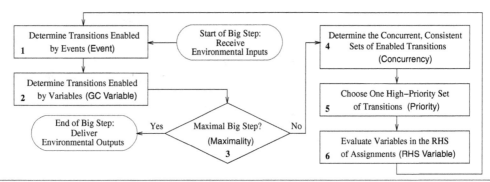

Figure 3. Operation of a big step and its semantic variation points.

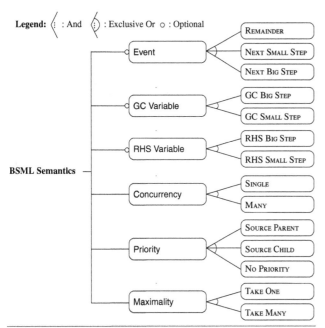

Figure 4. A set of common semantic aspects (in the sans serif font) and semantic options (in the SMALL CAP font) of BSMLs.

arenas is an *And*-state (the MANY semantic option) can be included in a small step. The Priority semantic aspect specifies whether a transition, t, has a higher priority than another transition, t', in which case if t can be included in a potential small step, then t' must not belong to any potential small step. Two common semantic options are that a transition with a higher source control state has a higher priority than a transition with a lower one (the SOURCE PARENT option) and vice versa (the SOURCE CHILD option).

The Maximality semantic aspect specifies when a big step becomes maximal. Two common semantic options are that: (i) once a transition, t, is taken by a small step, no other transition whose arena is an ancestor or descendant of *arena*(t) can be taken in that big step (the TAKE ONE semantic option); and (ii) a big step can continue until there is no more transitions whose trigger and guard condition are satisfied (the TAKE MANY semantic option).

3. A Monitoring Language for BSMLs

This section introduces our *big-step monitoring language* (BML). A BML *monitor* for a BSML model specifies a property of the modelled system. The evaluation of such a property amounts to a runtime monitor that observes the execution of the model at the big-step granularity for adherence to the specified property. Monitoring

at the big-step granularity is useful since it is compatible with the design philosophy of BSMLs that considers a big step (and not its constituent small steps) as a unit of execution. Section 4 describes the semantics of BML, which is oblivious to whether big steps of a BSML model are executed by the model itself or, for example, by the generated code for the model: it requires only information about the enabledness and execution of the transitions of the model. Similarly, this semantics is oblivious to the particularities of the plethora of BSML semantics: it treats the information about the enabledness and the execution of transition as uninterpreted boolean functions [9]. As such, BML provides a high-level means to specify properties about a BSML model that can be uniformly monitored both at the model and code level. In this paper, we are interested in monitoring only the behaviour of generated code. Section 5 presents our implementation of BML at the generated-code level.

The BNF in Figure 5 presents the abstract syntax of BML. As shown in the first line of the BNF, a monitor is either an *invariant*, which specifies a property that should hold for all big steps of the model, or a *witness*, which specifies a pattern that could happen in a big step of the model. An invariant monitor intercepts the execution of the model in order to find a *counterexample* for the property that it represents. A witness monitor intercepts the execution of the model in order to find a *witness example* of the property that it represents. A monitor is meant to execute as long as the model executes. An invariant monitor returns all counterexamples that it encounters during the execution of the model, and similarly, a witness monitor returns all witness examples.

Predicates. To specify monitors for a model, BML provides two basic unary predicates: *en* and *ex*, both of which operate over the transitions of the model. Predicate *en*(t) evaluates to *true* in a snapshot iff transition t is *enabled*, i.e., iff t belongs to a potential small step in that snapshot. Predicate *ex*(t) evaluates to *true* in a snapshot iff it is about to be *executed* by the next small step. By definition, if *ex*(t) is *true* at a snapshot, so is *en*(t). As an example, in the model in Figure 1, invariant monitor I: $\neg en(t_3) \lor \neg en(t_5)$ asserts that transitions t_3 and t_5 are never enabled together (i.e., there is no race between locking the microwave door and starting the radiation); and witness monitor W: $ex(t_7)$ asserts that transition t_7 is executed at least in one big step (i.e., microwave can be deactivated). Predicates *en* and *ex* do not have a snapshot parameter because such a parameter is implicit in the semantics of BML.

Reachability expressions. Besides a predicate-logic-like syntax, BML uses two operators that each can be used to specify a kind of reachability or unreachability relation between the snapshots of a big step. Binary operators, $\hookrightarrow$ and $\not\hookrightarrow$ are *reachability* and *unreachability* operators, respectively. We call an expression that uses a reachability operator or an unreachability operator a *reachability expression* or an *unreachability expression*, respectively. In a reachability (or an unreachability) expression, the left operand is called

Monitor	::=	**I:** Invar | **W:** Witness
Invar	::=	$ISpExp_1$ | $ISpExp_1 \hookrightarrow ISpExp_2$ |
		$ISpExp_1 \not\hookrightarrow ISpExp_2$
$ISpExp_1$	::=	BoolExp | $Quant_A$ BoolExp
$ISpExp_2$	::=	BoolExp | Quant BoolExp
Witness	::=	$WSpExp_1$ | $WSpExp_1 \hookrightarrow WSpExp_2$ |
		$WSpExp_1 \not\hookrightarrow WSpExp_2$
$WSpExp_1$	::=	BoolExp | $Quant_E$ BoolExp
$WSpExp_2$	::=	BoolExp | Quant BoolExp
BoolExp	::=	**en**(t) | **ex**(t) | ¬BoolExp |
		BoolExp ∧ BoolExp |
		BoolExp ∨ BoolExp
Quant	::=	$Quant_A$ | $Quant_E$
$Quant_A$	::=	∀ t_v ∈ Tr ·
$Quant_E$	::=	∃ t_v ∈ Tr ·
t	::=	t_v | t_c
t_v	::=	*A logical variable over transitions*
t_c	::=	*A transition of the model:* $t_c \in Trans(M)$
Tr	::=	*A subset of* $Trans(M)$; $Tr \in 2^{Trans(M)}$ |
		A function's value, $f: t \to 2^{Trans(M)}$

Figure 5. A BNF for the abstract syntax of BML.

the *source expression*, and the right operand is called the *destination expression*. The source expression specifies the snapshot(s) in a big step over which a reachability (or an unreachability) expression should be evaluated. The destination expression specifies the snapshot(s) that must be reached for the reachability to hold (or that must not be reached for the unreachability expression to hold). For example, $e_1 \hookrightarrow e_2$ specifies that from a snapshot of a big step that satisfies e_1, a future snapshot of the big step, including the current snapshot, can be reached in which e_2 is satisfied. An invariant monitor checks for a counterexample in which a reachability expression does not hold, while a witness monitor checks for an example in which a reachability expression holds. As an example, for the model in Figure 1, invariant $I: ex(t_3) \hookrightarrow ex(t_5)$ specifies that it is always the case that if transition t_3 is executed, then transition t_5 will also be executed in the same big step (i.e., if the microwave door is locked, then radiation eventually starts). The invariant $I: ex(t_5) \not\hookrightarrow ex(t_3)$ asserts that transition t_5 is not executed before or at the same time as t_3. Invariants $I: ex(t_5) \not\hookrightarrow ex(t_3)$ and $I: ex(t_5) \hookrightarrow \neg ex(t_3)$ are not the same: if $ex(t_5)$ is *true*, the latter invariant would hold when t_3 is not executed at least in one snapshot.

Quantification. To specify a monitor that applies to a range of transitions, the syntax of BML allows to quantify over a set of transitions of a model. For a monitor of a model that uses a (un)reachability[1] expression, each of its source and destination expressions can use a quantification. We assume the following two syntactic well-formedness conditions: (i) a monitor does not have any free variables; and (ii) its quantifiers use distinct logical variables. Invariants and witnesses use different kinds of *outer quantifications*, where an outer quantifier of a monitor is the quantifier that appears immediately after an "*I* :" or "*W* :". An invariant (a witness) could only use a universal (an existential) quantification as its outer quantifier. For example, invariant monitor $I: \forall t \in Trans(M) \cdot ex(t) \hookrightarrow \neg en(t)$ ensures that a transition of M cannot execute in all small steps of a big step, because it becomes disabled after it is executed. Witness monitor $W: \exists t \in Trans(M) \cdot ex(t)$ specifies that there exists a transition of M that is executed. The set of witness examples for this witness monitor at runtime could be used to animate the execution of M.

[1] "a (un)reachability" should be read "a reachability or an unreachability".

Range of quantification. The logical variable of a quantifier of an invariant ranges over a set of transitions. For a model, M, this range is either an explicit subset of the set of transitions of the model (i.e., a subset of $Tran(M)$) or a set that is determined by a syntactic function, f, where $f: t \to 2^{Trans(M)}$. For example, the invariant monitor, $I: \forall t \in Trans(M) \cdot ex(t) \not\hookrightarrow \exists t' \in samearena(t) \cdot ex(t')$, in effect, checks that the execution of M adheres to the TAKE ONE maximality semantics; function $samearena(t)$ returns the set of transitions, excluding t, whose arenas are the same as t's.

Implicit quantifications. The meaning of a monitor involves some implicit quantifications as well. An invariant monitor has two implicit universal quantifications that assert that the invariant holds for all big steps and for all of their snapshots. A witness monitor has two implicit existential quantifications that specify that there exists a big step and a snapshot of that big step such that the witness property holds for it. Also, in the meaning of a reachability expression, in an invariant or a witness, there is an implicit existential quantification that asserts that there exists a destination snapshot in which the reachability expression holds.

Checking semantic properties. A *semantic property* of a modelling language is a semantic attribute of the language that is common to all models specified in that language [15]. Using BML, we can specify an invariant monitor to check a semantic property of a BSML model. Such a monitor cannot be used to prove the presence of a semantic property at the language level, but it can be used, for example, to confirm one's understanding about a BSML semantics, or to gain confidence about the correctness of an implementation of a BSML semantics. Next, we present two such monitors.

In a *globally consistent* BSML semantics [7], if the negation of an event is used to trigger a transition in a big step, that event is not generated during the same big step. The following invariant asserts the global consistency property, for BSML model M,

$$I: \forall t \in Trans(M) \cdot ex(t) \not\hookrightarrow \exists t' \in neggen(t) \cdot ex(t'), \quad (1)$$

where $neggen(t)$ is the set of transitions in the model that each generates at least one of the negated literals in the trigger of t.

In a *quasi non-cancelling* BSML semantics, which is similar to a *non-cancelling* [15] BSML semantics, if a transition, t, becomes enabled in a big step, either t or one of its *neighbouring transitions* will be executed in that big step; two transitions are neighbours if they have the same source or destination control states. The following invariant asserts this property,

$$I: \forall t \in Trans(M) \cdot en(t) \hookrightarrow \exists t' \in neigh(t) \cdot ex(t') \lor ex(t), \quad (2)$$

where function $neigh(t)$ returns the neighbouring transitions of t.

As an example, in Figure 1, when the model resides in its default control states and environmental input event *start* is received, assuming that $gc(t_5) = [true]$, if the model employs the SINGLE and NEXT SMALL STEP semantic options, two big steps are possible: $\langle \{t_1\}, \{t_3\} \rangle$ (not executing t_5) and $\langle \{t_1\}, \{t_5\} \rangle$ (not executing t_3), which violate invariant (2). Employing the MANY concurrency semantics, which executes $\{t_3, t_5\}$, results in a quasi non-cancelling semantics.

A limitation. The non-cancelling semantic property [15][2] is a stronger property than the quasi non-cancelling property: in a non-cancelling semantics, an enabled transition, t, in the above monitor, cannot *become disabled* until the destination expression of the reachability expression becomes *true*. We cannot express the non-cancelling property in BML, because BML does not have a syntax to capture the notion of "becoming disabled"; we plan to include such a syntax in BML in the future; cf., Section 7.

[2] In previous work [15], we used the term "executable" with the same meaning as the term "enabled" here; we changed our terminology here to provide a clear distinction between en and ex predicates.

4. Semantics of BML

The meaning of a monitor is defined with respect to a BSML model and its big steps. Our semantics for BML assigns a boolean value to each monitor of a model. If an invariant monitor is assigned a *false* value, then there exists at least one counterexample big step that makes it *false*. If a witness monitor is assigned a *true* value, then there exists at least one witness-example big step that makes it *true*. The semantics of finding counterexamples and witness examples is implicit in the semantics of assigning truth value to a monitor.

We present the semantics of invariant and witness monitors separately. Except for the semantics of reachability and unreachability expressions, the semantics of BML is simply based on the semantics of predicate logic. We first consider the semantics of *ground* reachability and unreachability expressions, whose source and destination expression do not use any quantification. We then extend these semantics to the cases with quantification.

Notation. We use notation $[\![y]\!]$ to denote the meaning of a BML term y. We use a subscript to denote the big step under which y is evaluated; e.g., $[\![y]\!]_T$ is the meaning of y under big step T. To specify the semantics of reachability and unreachability, we adapt the "globally" ($\square$) and "finally" ($\diamond$) temporal operators of linear temporal logic (LTL) [8], to express temporal properties of individual big steps of a model. To evaluate an LTL formula l against a big step T, we write $[l]_T$. Within a big step, the $\square$ operator requires its operand to hold in all snapshots of the big step; the $\diamond$ operator requires its operand to hold at least in one of the snapshots of the big step, including the current snapshot. These temporal operators can be nested and combined with logical operators. For example, predicate $[\diamond(\square\neg en(t_1))]_T$ asserts that transition t_1 is finally disabled in big step T and henceforth remains disabled in T.

4.1 Semantics of Monitors without Quantification

Semantics of invariant monitors. Given a big step, T, the meaning of a ground invariant monitor that neither uses a reachability nor an unreachability expression is easy; e should always be *true*:

$$[\![I\colon e]\!]_T \equiv [\square e]_T$$

The meaning of a ground invariant monitor that uses a reachability expression is described by the following formula, which uses a request-response temporal pattern:

$$[\![I\colon e_1 \hookrightarrow e_2]\!]_T \equiv [\square(e_1 \Rightarrow (\diamond e_2))]_T.$$

Similarly, the meaning of a ground invariant monitor with an unreachability expression is described by the following formula:

$$[\![I\colon e_1 \not\hookrightarrow e_2]\!]_T \equiv [\square(e_1 \Rightarrow (\neg\diamond e_2))]_T.$$

As such, it can be observed that $[\![I\colon e_1 \not\hookrightarrow e_2]\!]_T \neq \neg([\![I\colon e_1 \hookrightarrow e_2]\!]_T)$, because, for example, if e_1 is always *false* in T, then both $[\![I\colon e_1 \not\hookrightarrow e_2]\!]_T$ and $[\![I\colon e_1 \hookrightarrow e_2]\!]_T$ are *true*.

Semantics of witness monitors. Given a big step T, the meaning of a ground witness monitor that neither uses a reachability nor an unreachability expression is easy; finally, e should become *true*:

$$[\![W\colon e]\!]_T \equiv [\diamond e]_T.$$

The meaning of a ground witness monitor that uses a reachability expression is described by the following formula:

$$[\![W\colon e_1 \hookrightarrow e_2]\!]_T \equiv [\diamond(e_1 \wedge \diamond e_2)]_T,$$

which asserts that e_1 becomes *true* in T, followed by e_2.

Similarly, the meaning of a ground witness monitor that uses an unreachability expression is described by the formula,

$$[\![W\colon e_1 \not\hookrightarrow e_2]\!]_T \equiv [\diamond(e_1 \wedge (\neg\diamond e_2))]_T.$$

4.2 Semantics of Quantification

To specify the semantics of a monitor that uses quantification, we expand the monitor to a set of ground monitors. A quantified boolean expression has exactly one quantifier, while a quantified reachability or an unreachability expression can have up to two quantifiers (one in the source and one in the destination expression). Thus, we use two expansion functions: one for each quantifier.

The first expansion function, exp_out, eliminates the outer quantifier of a monitor. For an invariant monitor, $i = I\colon \forall t \in T \cdot e$, $exp\_out(i) = \bigwedge_{t_c \in T}(I\colon e[t_c/t])$, where $e[t_c/t]$ means rewriting e by replacing the quantification variable t with transition t_c. Similarly, For a witness monitor, $w = W\colon \exists t \in T \cdot e$, $exp\_out(w) = \bigvee_{t_c \in T}(W\colon e[t_c/t])$. Each of the monitor terms $I\colon e[t_c/t]$ or $W\colon e[t_c/t]$ might use another quantification, if e is a (un)reachability expression with two quantifications. The second expansion function, exp_in, eliminates these inner quantifications in a standard way. Function exp_in, as opposed to exp_out, does not introduce any new ground monitors; it just expands a destination expression. The two functions are identity functions if their inputs do not have an expected quantifier.

We then define the semantics of invariant $I\colon e$ of model M as:

$$[\![I\colon e]\!] \equiv \forall T \in bigsteps(M) \cdot [\![exp\_in(exp\_out(I\colon e))]\!]_T,$$

where each of $[\![exp\_in(exp\_out(I\colon e))]\!]_T$ is the evaluation of the conjunction of a set of ground invariants.

Similarly, we define the semantics of witness $W\colon e$ as:

$$[\![W\colon e]\!] \equiv \exists T \in bigsteps(M) \cdot [\![exp\_in(exp\_out(W\colon e))]\!]_T,$$

where each of $[\![exp\_in(exp\_out(I\colon e))]\!]_T$ is the evaluation of the disjunction of a set of ground witnesses.

An invariant must hold in all big steps, and thus a universal quantification is used in its semantics; a witness needs to hold in at least one big step, and thus an existential quantification is used.

5. An Implementation of BML

We adopt the output of the family of code generators introduced by Prout, Atlee, Day, and Shaker [2] for our implementation of BML. These code generators themselves are generated, on the fly, by a parametric code generator generator (CGG) that, based upon the semantic parameter values that it receives, uses conditional compilation to act as a particular code generator. The normal form syntax, the semantic aspects, and the semantic options of BSMLs, as described in Section 2, can be modelled by the syntax and the semantic parameters of the CGG, as outlined below.

First, the CGG uses a syntax that is comparable to our normal form syntax in Section 2.1: while we use a notion of a hierarchy of control states, CGG uses a notion of *composition tree*. A composition tree consists of a hierarchy tree of *composition operators*, each of which specifies a policy in the execution of the transitions of its operands. The two needed composition operators to model our normal form syntax are the `Micro-Interleaving` and the `Micro-Parallel` composition operators, which provide the means to model the SINGLE and the MANY Concurrency semantics, respectively. The leaves of a composition tree, and only they, are *hierarchical transition systems* (HTSs), each of which can be considered as an *Or*-state without any *And*-state descendant. We assume that a model employs either only `Micro-Interleaving` composition or only `Micro-Parallel` composition. We call a model that satisfies this criterion a CGG-BSML model.

Second, the CGG provides a set of parameterized snapshot elements and predicates that each could be customized to model a semantic option. We call a CGG semantics that corresponds to a combination of our semantic options a CGG-BSML semantics.

Organization of the section. Section 5.1 describes the code generation mechanism of CGG. Section 5.2 presents our own code generation mechanism that customizes a piece of CGG-generated code with aspects to evaluate a BML monitor. Section 5.3 reports about our experiments and discusses issues related to our implementation.

5.1 Structure of Generated Code and its Execution Pattern

Our implementation of BML is based on knowledge about the high-level structure of the code generated by CGG. Similar knowledge is needed when implementing BML for a different code generator. Given a CGG-BSML semantics and a CGG-BSML model, CGG generates sequential Java code that implements the behaviour of the model; concurrency is simulated via sequential execution.

Structure of generated Code. The structure of the generated code is based on: (i) the structure of the composition tree of the model; and (ii) the snapshot elements specified through the input semantic parameter values. There is a Java class for each composition operator and a Java class for each HTS. Each model has m HTSs. We refer to the names of the classes that represent them as HTS_1, $\cdots$, and HTS_m. There is a class called EnvSensor that provides an interface to implement an environment for the generated code. There is a root class called GeneratedSystem that instantiates and manages all classes. In our implementation of BML, we need to deal only with the classes that represent the HTSs of a model (to obtain information about the enabledness and the execution of transitions) and the EnvSensor class (to obtain information about the scope of a big step). Table 1 enumerates the classes that we use in our implementation of BML, together with the list of a few of their methods, fields, and variables that we need. For convenience, we have specified a symbol to refer to the name of each method.

Execution pattern. The generated code for a CGG-BSML model, specified in a CGG-BSML semantics, follows the semantic structure of a big step in Figure 2. The start of a big step is signified by the execution of senseEnv. The set of potential small steps at a snapshot are identified by the execution of a sequence of enabled_trans methods of the HTS_is ($1 \leq i \leq m$). The set of transitions of a small step are executed by the execute methods of the HTS_is ($1 \leq i \leq m$). Thus, the execution of a small step by a piece of CGG generated code can be encoded by regular expression n^+x^+, where n and x are symbols representing the invocation of an enabled_trans and an executed method, respectively. The execution of a big step can be encoded as $v(n^+x^+)^*n^+$, where v represents the invocation of the senseEnv method; the last n^+ denotes that the big step is maximal. The ongoing execution of a BSML model can be modelled as a sequence of big steps: $(v(n^+x^+)^*n^+)^+$.

5.2 BML Code Generator (BML-CG)

We have implemented a prototype system, *BML code generator* (BML-CG), which given a CGG-BSML model and a monitor without quantification generates the multi-threaded AspectJ code that performs the runtime evaluation of the monitor against the execution of the CGG generated code of the model. Intuitively, the generated aspects follow the semantics of BML in Section 4. For example, for an invariant monitor with an unreachability expression, whenever the source of the expression becomes *true* in a big step, the system checks whether its destination expression could become *true* in that big step, in which case it produces a counterexample.

Two key insights about the generated code by BML-CG are that: (i) by using AspectJ, a monitor expression is evaluated without modifying the structure and the behaviour of the CGG generated code; and (ii) by using threads, the evaluation of a monitor that uses a (un)reachability expression is orthogonalized into units that each corresponds to a snapshot where the source expression of the (un)reachability expression becomes *true*. The latter property makes BML-CG readily amenable to support quantification, by evaluating the constituent ground monitors of a monitor orthog-

onally. Next, we describe the design of BML-CG, focusing mainly on our use of aspects and threads in the BML-CG generated code.

5.2.1 Aspect Code Generated by BML-CG

AspectJ provides a rich language to specify *point cuts*, *join points* and *advices* for a Java program [1]. In a BML-CG generated code, however, we only need to use *before* and *after* advices for join points in the execution of the methods listed in Table 1.

Figure 6 presents the three pointcuts together with five advices that we use in our generated code to implement a BML monitor. In our implementation of BML-CG, we distinguish between four types of monitors: (i) invariants with reachability operators; (ii) invariants with unreachability operators; (iii) witnesses with reachability operators; and (iv) witnesses with unreachability operators. (The monitors without a (un)reachability operator are special cases of one of the above four types.) The point cuts and advices in Figure 6 are the same for these four types of monitors, except for the advice invoked before an enabled_trans method, i.e., before() : HTSenJoin(Object p). This advice is specialized for each type of monitor. Next, we describe each advice in detail.

Before the execution of an enabled_trans method, its corresponding advice checks whether the source expression of the (un)reachability expression of the monitor, i.e., src_exp(en, ex), is *true*. Expression src_exp(en, ex) is evaluated with respect to the information about the enabledness and the execution of transitions stored in arrays en and ex, respectively; these information are updated as the execution of the CGG generated code continues. When src_exp(en, ex) is *true*, a new thread is forked that will check if the destination expression of the (un)reachability expression of the monitor could become *true*. The effect of the execution of a small step is evaluated at its destination snapshot, before checking for the enabledness of the transitions for the next small step. As such, it suffices to do the above evaluation only if the big step is not at the beginning snapshot and before the first n in the n^+x^+ sequence of the next small step; i.e., when !begSnapshot && firstEn is *true*. Once all threads evaluate the effect of the last small step, i.e., after waitForAllThreadsToReact() terminates, the information in arrays en and ex are reset for evaluating the new small step.

After the execution of an enabled_trans method, its corresponding advice collects the set of enabled transitions determined by the method in array en; similarly, after the execution of an execute method, its corresponding advice collects the enabled transition that is executed by the method in array ex. We use Java reflection mechanisms to collect these information from the enabled_transitions and trans fields, described in Table 1. (To use Java reflection, we had to change trans variables to become fields of their corresponding classes. This is the only change that we made to the CGG-generated code.) Both advices update the variables firstEn and firstEx, which determine whether the first n and the first x in the sequence of method executions of a small step n^+x^+ are encountered, respectively. The latter advice is also responsible: (i) to increment the index representing the current snapshot of a big step, to add an element to the vector that stores the counterexamples/witness examples; and (ii) to update the variable that determines the beginning snapshot of a big step.

Before the execution of the senseEnvJoin method, i.e., when a current big step ends and a new big step is about to start, its corresponding advice sets the endBigStep to *true*. Setting this variable to *true* signals all forked threads during the big step to terminate; function waitForAllThreadsToEnd() ensures that these threads terminate. After the execution of this method, the set of all counterexamples or witness examples could be inspected in variable result. After the execution of the senseEnvJoin method, at the beginning of a big step, its corresponding advice resets the variables of the system, preparing for a new big step.

Class	Method	Symbol	Role
EnvSensor	senseEnv(..)	v	This method simulates the behaviour of the environment by setting the environmental input events and variables.
HTS_1,···,HTS_m	enabled_trans(..)	n	For each HTS_i, $(1 \leq i \leq m)$, its method enabled_trans identifies the set of high-priority transitions whose arenas are in HTS_i and can be taken in the next small step; this set is stored in the field enabled_transitions of HTS_i.
HTS_1,···,HTS_m	execute(..)	x	For each HTS_i, $(1 \leq i \leq m)$, its method execute executes one of the transitions stored in the field enabled_transitions of HTS_i non-deterministically; variable trans in execute method stores the identifier of the executed transition.

Table 1. List of the methods, fields, and variables in the CGG generated code that are of interest for the implementation of BML.

```
/*Enabledness and execution information.*/
boolean[] en = new boolean[#TRANS];
boolean[] ex = new boolean[#TRANS];
/*Counterexamples or witnesses of a big step.*/
Vector<HashSet<Integer>> result = ⟨⟩;
boolean begSnapshot = true; /*sp_1 or not.*/
boolean endBigStep = false; /*sp_{k+1} or not.*/
/*First n and x in small step n⁺x⁺ or not.*/
boolean firstEn = true;
boolean firstEx = true;
int curSnapshot =0; /*Current snapshot.*/
pointcut HTSenJoin(Object p):
  execution(HTS*.enabled_trans(..));
pointcut HTSexJoin(Object p):
  execution(HTS*.execute(..));
pointcut senseEnvJoin(): execution(*.senseEnv(..));
before(): HTSenJoin(Object p) {
 if (!begSnapshot && firstEn) {
  /*Based on the type of a monitor, one is executed.*/
  if (src_exp(en,ex)) {
   new [I:s ↪ d]findCounter(curSp).start(); /*or*/
   new [I:s ↛ d]findCounter(curSp).start(); /*or*/
   new [W:s ↪ d]findWitness(curSp).start(); /*or*/
   new [W:s ↛ d]findWitness(curSp).start();
   waitForAllThreadsToReact();
   for(i=0 to #TRANS-1) {en[i] = false; ex[i] = false;}
  }
 }
}
after(): HTSenJoin(Object p) {
collectEnableds(p,en);
firstEx = true;
firstEn = false;
}
after(): HTSexJoin(Object p) {
collectExecuted(p,ex);
if (firstEx) {
 curSnapshot++; firstEx = false; firstEn = true;
 result.add(new HashSet());
}
if (begSnapshot) begSnapshot = false;
}
before(): senseEnvJoin() {
 endBigStep = true;
 waitForAllThreadsToEnd();
 /*Examine counterexamples and witness examples.*/
}
after(): senseEnvJoin() {
 for(i=0 to #TRANS-1) {en[i]= false; ex[i]=false;}
 result.clear();
 begSnapshot = firstEn = firstEx = true;
 endBigStep = false; curSnapshot = 0;
}
```

Figure 6. Point cuts and advices used in BML-CG generated code.

5.2.2 Multi-Threaded Code Generated by BML-CG

As mentioned earlier, the before() : HTSenJoin(Object p) advice, in the aspect in Figure 6, forks a thread when a snapshot of a big step is arrived at which the source expression of the (un)reachability expression of a monitor is *true*. Figure 7 shows these threads. Based on the type of a monitor, a thread is invoked to evaluate the monitor, through inspecting the value of the destination expression of the (un)reachability expression of the monitor, i.e., des_exp(en, ex). A thread terminates when the big step ends, i.e., when endBigStep becomes *true*. Functions addCounterExample and addWitnessExample store a counterexample and a witness example, respectively, in the last index of result.

We note that, for a witness monitor, once a thread is forked during a big step, no more subsequent threads needs to be forked because one witness example suffices; similarly, for an invariant monitor that uses an unreachability expression, one thread per big step is enough. However, in our implementation, we continue to fork new threads, in order to, (i) find all counterexamples and all witness examples; and (ii) to develop a multi-threaded implementation, with the necessary synchronization mechanisms, to provide the foundation to support: (a) monitors with quantification, each of which comprises of multiple ground BML terms; and (b) concurrent evaluation of multiple monitors. As a result of this design decision, the first and the fourth threads, as well as, the second and the third threads, in Figure 7, are symmetric.

5.3 Discussion

Experiments. Using BML-CG, we have experimented with the generated code of a few example BSML models. We ran various BML monitors against the CGG generated code for the example model in Figure 1 (and its variations). Using different BSML semantics, we checked that a BML monitor behaves as expected, and thereby, tested the correctness of CGG, BML-CG, and the model as a whole. For example, in the model in Figure 1, if input events *stop* and *deactivate* are received together at the beginning of a big step, when the model resides in its default control states, the expected behaviour would be non-deterministic: either big step $\langle\{t_1\}, \{t_3\}, \{t_5\}\rangle$ or big step $\langle\{t_7\}\rangle$ would execute. To confirm this behaviour, the following two properties should hold: $W: en(t_1) \wedge en(t_7)$ and $I: (en(t_1) \wedge en(t_7)) \hookrightarrow (ex(t_7) \vee ex(t_5))$. However, if the NEXT SMALL STEP event semantics is employed, the latter invariant would not hold because of counterexample big step $\langle\{t_1\}, \{t_3\}\rangle$. As another example, to eliminate the above non-determinism, we changed the source of t_7 to *Active*, and employed the SOURCE PARENT priority semantics, which assigns t_7 a higher priority than t_1; the model then satisfied invariant $I: \neg en(t_1) \vee \neg en(t_7)$. In our experiments, we ensured that we cover the range of possible monitors and the range of BSML semantic options. We did not find any unexpected behaviour. We also experimented with other example models, including the CGG generated code for a model of an elevator system of a three-story building. This system was specified in a notation

```
/*Used for monitors with reachability expressions*/
void [I:s ↪ d]findCounter(int sp) {
 int myLastSnapshot = sp-1;
 while(!endBigStep) {
  if (myLastSnapshot < curSnapshot) {
   if (des_exp(en,ex)) return;
   myLastSnapshot++;
  }
 }
 addCounterExample(result); }
/*Used for monitors with unreachability expressions*/
void [I:s ↛ d]findCounter(int sp) {
 int myLastSnapshot = sp-1;
 while(!endBigStep) {
  if (myLastSnapshot < curSnapshot) {
   if (des_exp(en,ex)) addCounterExample(result);
   myLastSnapshot++;
  }
 } }
/*Used for witnesses with reachability expressions*/
void [W:s ↪ d]findWitness(int sp) {
 int myLastSnapshot = sp-1;
 while(!endBigStep) {
  if (myLastSnapshot < curSnapshot) {
   if (des_exp(en,ex)) addWitnessExample(result);
   myLastSnapshot++;
  }
 } }
/*Used for witnesses with unreachability expressions*/
void [W:s ↛ d]findWitness(int sp) {
 int myLastSnapshot = sp-1;
 while(!endBigStep) {
  if (myLastSnapshot < curSnapshot) {
   if (des_exp(en,ex)) return;
   myLastSnapshot++;
  }
 }
 addWitnessExample(result); }
```

Figure 7. Different kinds of threads for evaluating monitors.

that uses asynchronous events, which is out of the current scope of BSMLs [3]. Our BML-CG, however, could deal with such a generated code. For example, we monitored that the three transitions that open the three doors of the elevator are never enabled together.

Cost of monitoring. The BML-CG generated code incurs a runtime cost to the execution of the CGG generated code. In terms of space, this cost is modest: we introduce only a few global variables and two boolean arrays, en and ex, whose sizes are the number of the transitions of the model. In terms of time, however, the cost is proportional to the number of running threads, which in the worst case – where at each snapshot of a big step, one thread is forked – is proportional to the length of a big step. This cost includes the computation time of the threads, the cost of their synchronization, and the overhead of aspects and Java reflection. The cost of the evaluation of a BML monitor is not related to the size of the monitor: the evaluation of the source and destination expression of a (un)reachability expression are constant-time boolean evaluations. The size of a model, however, could indirectly affect the cost of evaluation: a big model can produce a long big step. In our experiments, we did not notice a tangible slowdown in the execution time of the GCC-generated code. However, we observed the importance of building the right environment for checking a BML property, so to avoid executing irrelevant transitions in checking the property.

BML for other code generators. Our implementation of BML relies on knowledge about how to obtain the set of enabled and ex-

ecuting transitions of each small step, and how to determine the start and the end of a big step at runtime. Any code generator that somehow exposes these information could be enhanced with a BML monitoring capability. The more explicit these information are exposed, the more efficient an implementation could be. For example, if the CGG generated code would expose each of the set of enabled and executed transitions of a small step in a single field of a single class, then it would be possible to use only two join points to collect these sets, instead of twice as many as the number of HTSs. Such a saving could result in a significant performance improvement. Even better, if these fields would have been accessible via existing methods of the generated code, no Java reflection would have been needed. We chose to use CGG as is to demonstrate the relative independence of BML from a code generator.

6. Related Work

Our work is related to *runtime monitoring frameworks* (RMFs), such as Temporal Rover [16] and PathExplorer [17], which provide tool support for monitoring an input temporal property against the execution of a program. In an RMF, an input temporal property is usually an LTL formula that is encoded in an *input format* (IF). Our BML and the IF of a typical RMF are comparable: they are both used to specify monitoring properties. Our BML, however, is distinct in two main respects. First, BML uses the vocabulary of models, such as the names of transitions and their enabledness and execution information, to specify a monitoring property for generated code. The IF of an RMF, however, uses the vocabulary of programs, such as the names of variables, methods, segments of the code, etc. Second, BML, by virtue of being specialized for the family of BSMLs, is preequipped with abstraction constructs that facilitate the specification of properties. As such, using the IF of an RMF to specify a property that is equivalent to a BML property could be challenging. For example, specifying the equivalent property to BML property (2) in Section 3 could be a hard task; even articulating such a property in natural language through the vocabulary of the code can be very complicated. Of course, to evaluate a BML monitor at the code level, similar to an RMF property, the vocabulary of the code needs to be used. However, the abstraction constructs of BML provide guidelines not only about how to check these properties against the code, but also about how to generate/derive the code, in the first place, to facilitate such checks.

A class of RMFs, which we call *aspect-based* RMFs (AB-RMF), use aspects to specify and implement runtime monitors for programs [18–23]. The IFs of these RMFs and their implementation strategies are comparable to our BML and our BML-CG, respectively. While in our implementation of BML we use aspects, the syntax and the semantics of BML are independent of aspect technology. In an AB-RMF, however, its IF, its syntax, semantics, and implementation are all based on aspects, and thus based on the terminology of programs. While compared to a regular RMF, an AB-RMF provides a higher level of abstraction for property specification, it still uses a generic, program-level IF, as opposed to our BML, which is a specialized, model-level IF. Our use of aspects in the BML-CG generated aspects is comparable with the implementation of an AB-RMF: they both use the notion of execution join points to incrementally evaluate a property of the code at runtime. The difference is that we chose AspectJ simply because the output code of CGG naturally lends itself to be instrumented with aspects. Our regular-expression–like notation, in Section 5.1, is comparable to the IF of AB-RMF *Tracematches* [18].

Our work is comparable to frameworks that combine the aspect-oriented and generative programming paradigms [24–27]. Our work is distinct in that it focuses on a specific usage of generating aspects, as opposed to "general-purpose aspect languages", which are criticized for "losing their purposefulness" [28].

Our work is related to works that promote using aspects at the model level [12, 13], either to capture aspects during the modelling process [12], or to facilitate the extension of object-oriented code [13]. The point cuts in our implementation are model-based point cuts in that they originate from the vocabulary of a BSML model.

Hand-written aspects have been used to extend the functionality of a piece of generated code [29]. Our work is different in that BML works with model-level vocabulary of BSML models, and our implementation automatically generates aspect code.

Lastly, our work follows the goals of software development methodologies that advocate model-driven code analysis [10, 11].

7. Conclusion and Future Work

In this paper, we introduced a language for specifying runtime monitors that analyze the behaviour of a piece of generated code that is derived from a model specified in a big-step modelling language (BSML). Also, we introduced a customization mechanism that modifies the generated code to enhance it with a runtime monitoring capability. Our big-step monitoring language (BML) has a high-level syntax that uses the vocabulary of a model, rather than the detail of the generated code, to specify a runtime monitor. As such, our BML raises the level of abstraction that a developer works at when analyzing the generated code. A novelty in the design of our BML is that it abstracts away from the particularities of the syntax and semantics of the plethora of BSMLs, and thereby, lends itself to be adopted by a wide range of modelling languages and by the output of a wide range of code generators. We have implemented the core, quantified-free fragment of BML for a family of code generators. We have developed a non-intrusive code generation technique that customizes a piece of generated code with the AspectJ, multi-threaded code that monitors a property.

We plan to extend our implementation to support quantified BML monitors. As discussed in Section 3, we plan to extend BML with predicates that capture the notions of "becoming disabled", and "becoming enabled". Also, to specify a wider range of runtime monitors, we plan to extend BML to support *backward* reachability and unreachability operators, so that a monitor could refer to the past snapshots of a big step. Lastly, we are interested in introducing an *action* syntax to BML so that a BML term could not only monitor the behaviour of generated code, but also could modify it. As an example, using action *disable*(), which removes a transition from the set of enabled transitions, it is possible to enforce a globally-consistent behaviour, as specified in property (1) in Section 3, by disabling all transitions $t' \in neggen(t)$ in property (1).

Acknowledgements. We thank the reviewers for their helpful comments. The first and second authors were supported by EPSRC grant EP/F052669/1.

References

[1] G. Kiczales, E. Hilsdale, J. Hugunin, M. Kersten, J. Palm, and W. G. Griswold, "An overview of AspectJ," in *ECOOP'01*, no. 2072 in LNCS, pp. 327–353, Springer, 2001.

[2] A. Prout, J. M. Atlee, N. A. Day, and P. Shaker, "Semantically configurable code generation," in *MoDELS'08*, vol. 5301 of *LNCS*, pp. 705–720, 2008.

[3] S. Esmaeilsabzali, N. A. Day, J. M. Atlee, and J. Niu, "Deconstructing the semantics of big-step modelling languages," *Requirements Engineering*, vol. 15, no. 2, pp. 235–265, 2010.

[4] D. Harel, "Statecharts: A visual formalism for complex systems," *Science of Computer Programming*, vol. 8, no. 3, pp. 231–274, 1987.

[5] M. von der Beeck, "A comparison of Statecharts variants," in *FTRTFT'94*, vol. 863 of *LNCS*, pp. 128–148, Springer, 1994.

[6] S. Esmaeilsabzali and N. A. Day, "Prescriptive semantics for big-step modelling languages," in *FASE'10*, vol. 6013 of *LNCS*, pp. 158–172, Springer, 2010.

[7] A. Pnueli and M. Shalev, "What is in a step: On the semantics of statecharts," in *TACS*, vol. 526 of *LNCS*, pp. 244–264, 1991.

[8] A. Pnueli, "The temporal logic of programs," in *Proceedings of the 18th IEEE Symposium on the Foundations of Computer Science (FOCS-77)*, pp. 46–57, IEEE Computer Society Press, 1977.

[9] J. R. Burch and D. L. Dill, "Automatic verification of pipelined microprocessor control," in *CAV'94*, vol. 818 of *LNCS*, pp. 68–80, Springer, 1994.

[10] G. J. Holzmann, R. Joshi, and A. Groce, "Model driven code checking," *Automated Software Engineering*, vol. 15, no. 3-4, pp. 283–297, 2008.

[11] G. Holzmann, "Reliable software development: Analysis-aware design," in *TACAS'11*, vol. 6605 of *LNCS*, pp. 1–2, Springer, 2011.

[12] J. Gray, T. Bapty, S. Neema, D. C. Schmidt, A. S. Gokhale, and B. Natarajan, "An approach for supporting aspect-oriented domain modeling," in *GPCE'03*, vol. 2830 of *LNCS*, pp. 151–168, Springer, 2003.

[13] A. Kellens, K. Mens, J. Brichau, and K. Gybels, "Managing the evolution of aspect-oriented software with model-based pointcuts," in *ECOOP'06*, vol. 4067 of *LNCS*, pp. 501–525, Springer, 2006.

[14] K. C. Kang, S. G. Cohen, J. A. Hess, W. E. Novak, and A. S. Peterson, "Feature-oriented domain analysis (FODA) feasibility study," Tech. Rep. CMU/SEI-90-TR-21, SEI, Carnegie Mellon University, 1990.

[15] S. Esmaeilsabzali and N. A. Day, "Semantic quality attributes for big-step modelling languages," in *FASE'11*, vol. 6603 of *LNCS*, pp. 65–80, Springer, 2011.

[16] D. Drusinsky, "The temporal rover and the atg rover," in *SPIN Model Checking and Software Verification*, vol. 1885 of *LNCS*, pp. 323–330, Springer, 2000.

[17] K. Havelund and G. Roşu, "Monitoring Java programs with Java PathExplorer," in *RV'01*, vol. 55 of *Electronic Notes in Theoretical Computer Science*, pp. 1–18, Elsevier, 2001.

[18] C. Allan, P. Avgustinov, A. S. Christensen, L. Hendren, S. Kuzins, O. Lhoták, O. de Moor, D. Sereni, G. Sittampalam, and J. Tibble, "Adding trace matching with free variables to AspectJ," in *OOPSLA'05*, pp. 345–364, ACM Press, 2005.

[19] F. Chen and G. Rosu, "Mop: an efficient and generic runtime verification framework," in *OOPSLA'07*, pp. 569–588, ACM Press, 2007.

[20] V. Stolz and E. Bodden, "Temporal assertions using AspectJ," *Electronic Notes in Theoretical Computer Science*, vol. 144, no. 4, pp. 109 – 124, 2006. RV'05.

[21] E. Bodden, P. Lam, and L. Hendren, "Clara: A framework for partially evaluating finite-state runtime monitors ahead of time," in *RV'10*, vol. 6418 of *LNCS*, pp. 183–197, Springer, 2010.

[22] K. Havelund, "Runtime verification of C programs," in *TestCom/FATES'08*, vol. 5047 of *LNCS*, pp. 7–22, Springer, 2008.

[23] J. Seyster, K. Dixit, X. Huang, R. Grosu, K. Havelund, S. A. Smolka, S. D. Stoller, and E. Zadok, "Aspect-oriented instrumentation with GCC," in *RV'10*, vol. 6418 of *LNCS*, Springer, 2010.

[24] D. Zook, S. S. Huang, and Y. Smaragdakis, "Generating AspectJ programs with Meta-AspectJ," in *GPCE'04*, vol. 3286 of *LNCS*, pp. 1–18, Springer, 2004.

[25] D. Lohmann, G. Blaschke, and O. Spinczyk, "Generic advice: On the combination of AOP with generative programming in aspectC++," in *GPCE'04*, vol. 3286 of *LNCS*, pp. 55–74, Springer, 2004.

[26] D. R. Smith, "A generative approach to aspect-oriented programming," in *GPCE'04*, vol. 3286 of *LNCS*, pp. 39–54, Springer, 2004.

[27] U. Kulesza, A. F. Garcia, and C. J. P. de Lucena, "An aspect-oriented generative approach," in *OOPSLA'04 Companion*, pp. 166–167, ACM, 2004.

[28] T. Cleenewerck and J. Noyé, "Editorial domain specific aspect languages," *IET Software*, vol. 3, no. 3, pp. 165 –166, 2009.

[29] C. Henthorne and E. Tilevich, "Code generation on steroids: Enhancing cots code generators via generative aspects," in *Second International Workshop on Incorporating COTS Software into Software Systems: Tools and Techniques*, IEEE Computer Society, 2007.

Declaratively Defining Domain-Specific Language Debuggers

Ricky T. Lindeman   Lennart C. L. Kats   Eelco Visser

Delft University of Technology

r.t.lindeman@student.tudelft.nl, l.c.l.kats@tudelft.nl, visser@acm.org

Abstract

Tool support is vital to the effectiveness of domain-specific languages. With language workbenches, domain-specific languages and their tool support can be generated from a combined, high-level specification. This paper shows how such a specification can be extended to describe a debugger for a language. To realize this, we introduce a meta-language for coordinating the debugger that abstracts over the complexity of writing a debugger by hand. We describe the implementation of a language-parametric infrastructure for debuggers that can be instantiated based on this specification. The approach is implemented in the Spoofax language workbench and validated through realistic case studies with the Stratego transformation language and the WebDSL web programming language.

Categories and Subject Descriptors   D.2.3 [*Software Engineering*]: Coding Tools and Techniques; D.2.5 [*Software Engineering*]: Testing and Debugging—Debugging aids; D.2.6 [*Software Engineering*]: Programming Environments; D.3.4 [*Processors*]: Debuggers

General Terms   Languages

Keywords   Debugging, Domain-Specific Language, Language Workbench, Spoofax

1. Introduction

Domain-specific languages (DSLs) increase developer productivity by providing specialized syntax, semantics, and tooling for building software or writing specifications within a certain domain. They provide linguistic abstractions for common tasks in a domain, eliminating low-level implementation details and boilerplate code. DSLs are most effective when supported by specialized tooling including, but not limited to, an integrated development environment (IDE) with editors tailored for the language, a debugger, a test engine and a profiler [26].

The development of a new DSL without specialized tools is no easy undertaking. A compiler or interpreter for a new language requires a parser, data structures for abstract syntax trees, and likely traversals, transformations, type checkers, and so on. To increase the productivity of users of the DSL, IDE support should also be implemented. This entails the implementation of editor services ranging from syntactical services, such as syntax highlighting and an outline view, to semantic services such as content completion

and refactoring. In addition, a debugger can be built for the IDE, which further increases the productivity of DSL users by allowing them to spot runtime problems and providing insightful information regarding the runtime execution flow.

Program comprehension is vital to effectively debug applications during software maintenance [22]. DSLs improve program comprehension by using specialized notations and abstractions from the domain [15]. Thus, a DSL debugger will have a positive effect on the maintenance of DSL programs.

This paper focuses on the development of debuggers for DSLs. Although debugging is one of the most common tasks of software maintenance. DSL debuggers are often not available as the implementation effort of building a new debugger for a small language by hand is often prohibitive. First, the runtime system of the DSL must support stepping and state inspection, which is often not included in the initial DSL design. Second, the accidental complexity of the debugger IDE API makes it hard to integrate a DSL debugger into the IDE framework. Furthermore, the differences between DSL implementations make it difficult to reuse debug runtime components.

DSL engineering and language workbenches   DSL engineering software assists in the development of new DSLs. Examples include parser generators, meta-programming languages and frameworks, and tools and frameworks for building the IDE for a DSL. Language workbenches are a new breed of DSL engineering tools [7] that integrate software for most aspects of language engineering into a single development environment. Language workbenches make the development of new languages and their IDEs much more efficient, by *a)* providing full IDE support for language development tasks and *b)* integrating the development of the language compiler/interpreter and its IDE. Examples of language workbenches include MPS [25], MontiCore [16], Xtext [5], and our own Spoofax [12].

A key goal of DSL engineering software is to provide a layer of *abstraction* over general-purpose programming languages and APIs that makes language engineers more efficient in building DSLs. This abstraction can be provided by graphical user interfaces, such as wizards and configuration screens that are provided by most language workbenches. It can also be provided as a linguistic abstraction, by introducing a new high-level language for defining (some aspect of) a DSL. Language engineers can then write high level *language definitions* rather than handwrite every compiler, interpreter and IDE component. Particularly successful are parser generators, that can generate efficient parsers from declarative syntax definitions [13].

Generating a debugger from a language definition   Although the idea of generating a debugger from a language definition is not new [11], we developed a new, low-effort approach for the development of debuggers for DSLs. In this paper we propose a generic debugger generation framework for DSLs that abstracts over the complexity of writing a debugger by hand. The framework broadly consists of three components: First, a specialized, declarative specification language for coordinating debug events in a language-specific fashion. Second, a debug instrumentation tool that instruments DSL programs based on the specification. Third, a generic infrastructure for debuggers that is designed in four separate layers in order to maximize reusability between different DSL implementations.

The contributions of this paper are as follows:

- The introduction of a high level debugger specification language.

- The introduction of a four-layer infrastructure for integrating debuggers into an IDE while maximizing reuse.

- The implementation[1] of these components as part of the Spoofax Language Workbench [12] and the Eclipse IDE.

We validate our approach through two case studies on two languages that were previously defined for Spoofax. First, Stratego, a program transformation language [2], and second WebDSL, a DSL for modeling web applications with a rich data model [9].

Outline This paper is organized as follows. Section 2 describes the general architecture of a debugger and discusses different implementation techniques of DSLs and their debuggers. We then show how debuggers for DSLs can be specified as part of a language definition in Section 3, which can be used for a debug instrumentation processor, as described in Section 4. We describe the runtime architecture of our approach in Section 5. Case studies are described in Section 6. We we reflect on our work, compare it to related work, and provide concluding remarks in Sections 7 and 8.

2. Debuggers

Debuggers provide an important facility for code understanding and maintenance that is often considered to be a vital part of IDEs. Bugs in software are an unfortunate but inevitable part of software engineering reality. Locating (and trying to solve) bugs is an essential part of the development and maintenance process of software. Debuggers make this process more efficient. In this section we describe the general architecture of a debugger and the difficulties that arise when trying to create a debugger for a DSL.

2.1 General Architecture

Most debugger implementations consist of the following components:

- A *debugger front-end* that allows developers to control the execution flow and inspect the execution state.

- An *execution context* for the language, i.e. a certain position in the source code and usually a stack trace.

- An *execution state* for the language, i.e. some view of the program's state such as local variable values.

- *Debug events* that are fired as the debugged program reaches a certain state.

A debugger front-end interacts with the execution model of a language and is able to inspect the execution state of an application in different execution contexts during the execution of an application. A typical execution context for a language such as Java has the following scope hierarchy:

- *Application*: the top level scope.

- *Threads*: an application can be single threaded or multithreaded.

---

[1] Available with nightly builds of Spoofax 0.6.1 via http://www.spoofax.org/.

- *Stack frames*: for each subroutine or function call a new stack frame is created.

- *Instruction pointer*: the current active statement.

Debuggers can suspend the application at fixed points in the execution flow, as the application runtime fires an event indicating that it reached such a point. Using conditional and unconditional breakpoints the debugger can then decide to suspend the execution and allow developers to inspect the execution context and state.

The execution state can be inspected in terms of language-specific data structures. The availability and value of a variable is related to the previously defined scope in which the variable is defined and used.

To be able to inspect the execution context and state, a debugger has to know how the runtime state and the source code of a language are related. This means that a debugger depends on both the syntax and semantics of a language. Using debug information that contains relevant metadata (such as line number and filename) and a debug runtime library that matches the debug information to the runtime behavior of a program a debugger is able link the syntax and semantics.

2.2 Debuggers for DSLs

Debugger implementations must be specialized for the syntax and semantics of a language. Automating part of the implementation effort requires high-level specification of this variability in syntax and semantics. The remainder of this section discusses how differences in execution models, programming paradigm, and implementation approach of DSLs affect the implementation and architecture of debuggers.

2.2.1 Executability

A key design aspect relevant to debugging is the execution model of DSLs. Mernik et al. specify four kinds of executability [18]:

- DSL with well-defined execution semantics. A debugger for this kind of DSL is straightforward to implement.

- Input language of an application generator [4, 20].

- DSL not primarily meant to be executable but nevertheless useful for application generation.

- DSLs not meant to be executable [26].

As long as the semantics of the DSL are specified and the host language provides support for suspending the runtime execution, either via a debugger or emulated in the host language debug runtime library, it is possible to generate a debugger for a DSL that fits into one of the first three categories.

Non-executable DSLs are often used to formally describe domain-specific data structures. The semantics of the information is encoded in a domain-specific notation, also called jargon. Domain experts can use jargon to communicate in a non-ambiguous way. Debugging of data is not possible, but a graphical visualization (or perhaps multiple graphical visualizations) can help to comprehend the data structure.

2.2.2 Programming Paradigm

Related to the executability of a DSL is its programming paradigm. Imperative and declarative programming are two high-level contrasting paradigms that influence the implementation of a debugger. Imperative programming is a style of programming in which the programmer has to explicitly specify the computations that change a program state. In contrast, declarative programming only requires programmers to specify the logic of a computation without actually describing the control flow. DSLs often take elements from both paradigms.

A debugger for an imperative language is rather straightforward as the debugger should just follow the control flow. For declarative programs, the method of computations and the control flow are implicit, and whether or not to emit debug events that model the internal state of computations may depend on whether DSL users are assumed to have sufficient knowledge of the DSL implementation.

2.2.3 DSL Implementation Approach

The implementation approach of a DSL has a large impact on the DSL debugging capabilities. The effort required for debugger implementation is influenced by the availability of debugging capabilities of the runtime platform used, e.g. suspending the execution when demanded by the user and the ability to pass the execution state to the IDE. Therefore, in this section we will discuss various implementation approaches and the issues that arise when such an implementation technique is used.

DSLs can be classified as external and internal DSLs. External DSLs have their own syntax, whereas internal DSLs rely on the syntax of the host language [8]. For external DSLs, we can also distinguish DSLs relying on code generators, preprocessors, and interpretation. In this paper we focus on external DSLs, as they have their own specialized syntax and a translation step that makes it possible to provide a domain-specific debugger in a partially automated fashion. For completeness, we also discuss internal DSLs and the challenges in creating domain-specific debuggers for those languages.

Compiled DSLs Compiled DSLs are fully designed for and dedicated to a particular application domain. The DSL has its own syntax and is translated to a program in some target language by generating code for their host language, typically a general-purpose language such as Java. Implementing a debugger for these DSLs requires extending the generator with the generation of debugging metadata in the output code, as described in Section 2.1. When not directly supported by the runtime system of the host language, the generator should also generate additional code to fire events. It also requires the implementation of an actual debugger front-end that processes this information, shows it in the IDE, and allows IDE users to control the execution flow.

Domain-specific language extensions Domain-specific language extension is a technique that extends the host language with a domain-specific guest notation. The syntax of the host language can be extended by adding new syntactic constructs using macro-like extensions, by adding a preprocessing step that transforms the guest notation back to the host language, or by implementing a proper extension of the host language compiler.

Since language extensions are assimilated to their host language, one approach to debugging language extensions is to debug the program at the host language level. This can lead to problems as the execution context and state of the extension does not necessarily naturally align with the host language. Only by instrumenting the extension at the source level rather than at the target level it is projected, extensions can be debugged effectively.

Interpreted DSLs Interpreted DSLs have their own syntax and semantics. DSL programs are executed by a separately written interpreter that operates directly on the source code (or an abstract representation). Furthermore, interpreted DSL programs can be run on any platform as long as an interpreter is available. Calling an interpreter from a general purpose language is possible if they are written in the same language. Even interaction between the interpreter and the host language is possible but comes at the price of a more complicated interpreter implementation.

One of the advantages of an interpreter is that it directly operates on the program structure, this makes it easy to retrieve metadata at the DSL abstraction level. However, adding debug actions such as setting breakpoints and adding stepping supports requires extending the interpreter with an execution control component.

Internal DSLs and application frameworks Internal DSLs rely purely on the syntax and semantics provided by a general-purpose host language such as Ruby or Scala. They are distinguished from traditional libraries and application frameworks by their use of programming techniques such as fluent interfaces, operator overloading, and meta-programming capabilities provided by the host language such as template meta-programming and implicits. These features give the libraries a "language"-like feel to it, while still maintaining full integration and compatibility with the host language. Providing specialized, domain-specific tool support and statically checking internal DSLs is more difficult since these DSLs are really using general-purpose language constructs rather than specialized constructs.

For debugging, internal DSLs tend to fully rely on the debugger of their host language. While it is convenient to get a debugger for "free" with this approach, the debugger is not specific to the application domain. In particular, it does not show the execution flow and data structures in a domain-specific fashion. This would require analysis of the source code to determine the "DSL parts" and integration of specialized domain-specific debugging facilities with a general-purpose debugger, which is not trivial. First, it is hard to distinguish between GPL and DSL execution. Second, the data structures in the GPL may not match the domain data structures. And finally, although the DSL and the GPL can share the same syntax, the semantics may differ.

2.3 Summary

In theory, creating a debugger for a DSL does not differ much from generating a debugger for a traditional general purpose language. Just as with DSL programs, programs written in a general purpose language are translated to a lower level language. For instance, Java is translated to Java bytecode and C# to CIL. It is the task of the debugger to transform the low-level runtime state back to a suitable higher level representation.

Using the execution model, the programming paradigm and the implementation approach as a means to classify a DSL shows us that there is a great variety between them. Also, each classification has its own issues regarding the creation of a debugger. An automated approach to building debuggers should abstract over these issues in a language independent way.

The chosen implementation platform influences the amount of effort required and the approach to the implementation of a DSL debugger. However, not the distance between the DSL and the implementation platform is critical but rather the distance between the host language and DSL execution model.

3. Declarative Debugger Specification

We propose a language independent debugger implementation framework that abstracts over the issues raised in Section 2.2 regarding the executability, the programming paradigm and the implementation approach of a DSL. The framework broadly consists of three components: (1) a debugger specification language called SEL that uses the language definition to define the DSL debugging model, (2) a language-parametric debug instrumentation tool and (3) a generic debugger runtime infrastructure that communicates with IDE debug services.

As a basis for our approach we use an event-based debugging model to model DSL execution flow in a generic way. The SEL specification maps the language-specific syntax and semantics to this generic event-based debugging model. The instrumentation tool interprets the specification to augment DSL programs in executable form with debugging information. Augmented DSL programs interoperate with the generic debugger infrastructure, which provides the glue to connect an instrumented DSL program to the IDE debug services and changes the program model in reaction to the received debug events.

This section describes the event-based debugging model and the specification language (1) that describes the relation between the DSL program and debug events. Section 4 discusses the implementation of the debug information extraction and event generation used by the instrumentation tool (2). And in Section 5 the language independent debugger runtime infrastructure (3) is discussed. The infrastructure consists of the implementation of the host language dependent event-sending mechanism as well as the language independent debugger is discussed.

Debug event classes We use a set of four language-independent debug event classes to capture the runtime program behavior, following Auguston [1]. First, the `step` event models the execution order of DSL statements. However, a single statement does not have to be atomic, it can consist of multiple nested statements. For example, a call to a subroutine can generate multiple step events at a different level of granularity. Next, the `enter` and the `exit` event model this hierarchical relation between step events. The last event is the `var` event indicating a variable is declared at the current level in the hierarchy created by the `enter` and `exit` events.

The event-based approach eliminates the need to support the generation of DSL metadata in the actual code generator component. Writing the specification requires syntactic and semantic knowledge about the DSL as language independent debug events (`enter`, `exit`, `step`, `var`) have to be linked against matching syntax constructs.

Syntax event linking (SEL) While the debug events we use are the same across various DSLs, the actual instrumentation strategy differs per DSL implementation. We abstract over this implementation by specifying the relation between the semantic behavior (modeled with debug events) and the syntax constructs of a DSL. The syntax-event linking language (SEL) is used to describe this relation.

The SEL specification language describes where to inject a debug event, and transformation strategies that define how to generate debug events in DSL syntax and how to extract relevant debug information such as line number, filename and current method name from the DSL program.

An SEL specification consists of multiple event definitions. A single event definition is structured as follows:

```
event eventClass at pattern
            creates generator
            from extractor
```

A rule of this form specifies a pattern to match one or more syntactic constructs (`pattern`), used to inject one of the four debug events (`eventClass`). The actual injection is done using transformations that are specified in the Stratego transformation language [2], using the transformations indicated by the `generator` and `extractor` names. The generator is a transformation that generates a small DSL code fragment that represents a debug event, while the extractor extracts the debug information from the selected syntax construct. Multiple definitions can exist for the same `eventClass` as long as the patterns do not overlap. This section will continue with an example and a detailed explanation on the basic SEL syntax. We discuss the generation and extraction transformations in Section 4.

Syntax pattern matching To find specific AST nodes in a parsed program syntax construct patterns can match against a syntax construct in two ways: (1) using a syntactic category (sort) and (2) a specific AST node (constructor).

The syntax construct pattern is defined as follows:

```
Sort.Constructor
```

`Sort` and `Constructor` both point to existing identifiers in an SDF specification. Furthermore, either a `Sort` or `Constructor` can be ignored by using an underscore in the pattern. For example, `Statement._` matches against all constructors that are generated by the Statement sort, `Statement.VarDef` matches against all VarDef constructor generated by the Statement sort and `_.FunctionDecl` matches against all FunctionDecl constructors regardless of the sort.

An example SEL specification In Figure 1 a small DSL program with functions and statements is shown (left), together with its abstract syntax representation (right). Note that we show abstract syntax trees using a textual representation, using prefix constructor terms for tree nodes and indicating lists tree nodes with square brackets. Using graphical rectangles, the figure highlights function declarations and statements in the abstract syntax, marking the tree nodes that are important for the debugger.

Figure 2 shows SDF syntax definition rules[2] and a SEL specification mapping the functions and statements of Figure 2 to events. The dotted line shows how an enter debug event is matched against the `FunctionDecl` constructor using a syntax construct pattern with an explicit constructor. The solid line shows how a step debug event is matched against a category of syntactic constructs, containing the `FuncCall`, `VarAssign` and `Return` constructor using the `Statement` sort. `gen-func-enter` and `gen-stat-step` reference transformations that generate a debug event that fits into the DSL syntax. `extract-function-debug-info` and `extract-statement-debug-info` reference transformations that extract debug information from the matched syntax constructs.

4. DSL Program Instrumentation

One of the main tasks for runtime support of debugging is the incorporation of debugging information into executable DSL programs. This information can be incorporated by hand by adapting the translation step of DSLs, as outlined in Section 2.2. In this paper we use a reusable, language-parametric debug instrumentation tool instead, which uses the SEL specification to incorporate the necessary debug information.

Tool chain The debug instrumentation tool acts as a preprocessor that runs before the code generation or interpretation step of a DSL. Inspired by aspect-oriented programming, it weaves debugging information into DSL programs, again forming new, valid DSL programs. These can then be further processed by the standard code generator or interpreter used for the DSL.

Figure 3 shows the tool chain for DSL compilation or interpretation with debug information, based on the debug instrumentation tool. The first tool in the chain is the parser, which uses the syntax definition of the DSL to parse the input program. It produces an abstract syntax tree, which is used as the input of the instrumentation tool. The tool augments the abstract representation of the DSL program with debug information using the SEL specification. The result is used as the input for the standard processing pipeline of the language.

The normal processing pipeline of DSLs usually starts with a desugaring step that normalizes DSL constructs to their core form. It is important that the debug instrumentation is performed before this desugaring step, to allow the debugger to operate on the

---

[2] Note that in SDF, production rules take the form $p* \rightarrow sort$ `{cons(constructor)}`, indicating a pattern on the left-hand side and the syntactic category and abstract syntax constructor on the right [23].

Example program

```
module example

function main() {
      bar := 5 + 6;
      baz := baz(bar);
      result := baz + bar;
      print(result);
}

function baz(value) {
      bar := value + 22;
      return bar;
}
```

Parse →

Program in abstract syntax

```
Module(
  "example"
, [ FunctionDecl(
      "main"
    , []
    , [ VarAssign("bar", Add(Integer("5"), Integer("6")))
      , VarAssign("baz", FuncCall("baz", [VarUse("bar")]))
      , VarAssign("result", Add(VarUse("baz"), VarUse("bar")))
      , FuncCall("print", [VarUse("result")])
      ]
    )
  , FunctionDecl(
      "baz"
    , [ArgDef("value")]
    , [ VarAssign("bar", Add(VarUse("value"), Integer("22")))
      , Return(VarUse("bar"))
      ]
    )
  ]
)
```

Figure 1. An example DSL Program in concrete and abstract syntax.

SDF grammar example

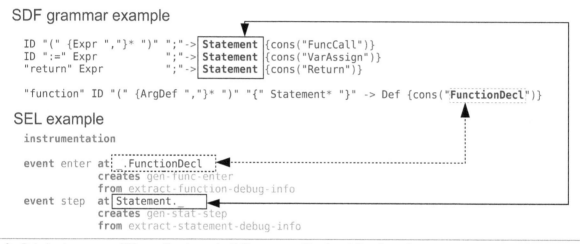

```
ID "(" {Expr ","}* ")" ";"-> Statement  {cons("FuncCall")}
ID ":=" Expr            ";"-> Statement  {cons("VarAssign")}
"return" Expr           ";"-> Statement  {cons("Return")}

"function" ID "(" {ArgDef ","}* ")" "{" Statement* "}" -> Def {cons("FunctionDecl")}
```

SEL example

```
instrumentation

event enter at  .FunctionDecl
         creates gen-func-enter
         from extract-function-debug-info
event step  at Statement.
         creates gen-stat-step
         from extract-statement-debug-info
```

Figure 2. Relation between an SEL specification and a DSL grammar. The dotted line shows how a constructor pattern is matched against one type of constructor. The solid line shows how a sort pattern is matched against a syntactic category (sort).

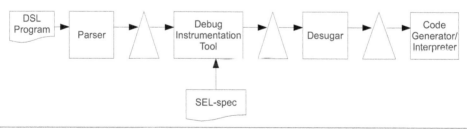

Figure 3. The tool chain for instrumentation and execution of DSL programs.

original source code without losing any syntactic sugar. Finally, after desugaring, the DSL program is used for code generation or interpretation.

Instrumentation by preprocessing The instrumentation tool processes DSL programs based on a bottom-up traversal over the abstract representation. If a constructor matches a pattern in the SEL specification then the matching extraction transformation is called to extract debug information. The extractor then returns a tuple containing debug information such as the name of a local variable dec-

laration and the line number[3] of a statement. Then the generator transformation is called with the event type and the debug information as its arguments and generates a debug event statement.

`step` events are inserted before the matched statement, `var` events are inserted after the matched statement and `enter` events are inserted at the start of the method body. Inserting `exit` events

---

[3] Note that we maintain position information in memory for the abstract representation, even though this is not shown in the textual rendition of Figure 1.

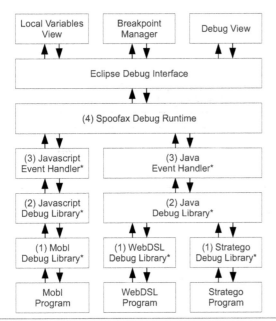

Figure 4. An overview of the integration of runtime components inside the Eclipse IDE, showing the components for the Mobl, WebDSL and Stratego DSLs. Components marked with an asterisk are specific to a DSL or DSL runtime platform.

is a bit more complicated when the DSL allows multiple return statements at non-fixed locations in a method body. The `exit` event cannot be inserted after the return statement, because the `exit` event will never be reached as the execution flow is already returned to the method caller. Also, just adding the `exit` event before the return statement would change the ordering of events because the return statement can contain an expression that calls another method. As an example, consider the following return statement:

```
return expression;
```

which should be transformed to something like this:

```
var temp := expression;
event(exit-event, debug-information);
return temp;
```

DSLs that support Java-like exceptions and try-finally blocks simplify the multiple exit points issue. To ensure that the `exit` event is always called for normal as well as exceptional exits the body of a method should be surrounded with a try-finally block and the `exit` event should be placed in the finally block.

Instrumenting code at the DSL level gives us the advantage that a DSL program instrumented with debug events can run on any back-end for which a native debug runtime library is implemented. The implementation of the native debug library and how the debugger receives the debug events are discussed in the next section.

5. Debugger Runtime Infrastructure

In this section we discuss our implementation architecture. The architecture consists of four layers: a DSL-level debug library (1), a platform-level debug library (2), a platform-level event handler library (3), and a shared, IDE-specific core library (4). These components and their integration with the Eclipse IDE and the DSL program are illustrated by Figure 4.

By splitting up the infrastructure components into four layers, we maximize reuse: when a new DSL is developed for a platform

that was previously targeted, only the DSL-level library has to be implemented (1). If a new platform is targeted, e.g. JavaScript, then the two, reusable platform-level libraries (2 and 3) should also be implemented. The common core library component (4) is neither language nor platform specific and does not require implementation unless a different IDE is used.

5.1 DSL-level Debug Library

The debug events that were added by the instrumentation tool of Section 4 are calls to the DSL debug library component. The functions in this library correspond to the four debugging event classes. They are implemented by simply forwarding the call to the platform-level debug library. The calls allow easy identification of the locations in the host locations that correspond to debug events, thus eliminating a reverse engineering step that maps fragments of generated code back to DSL code.

5.2 Platform-level Debug Library

The platform-level debug library is a lightweight library component that marshalls debug events to the platform-level event handler in the IDE. For example, for DSLs that are executed on the Java Virtual Machine (JVM), it forwards the event data from that JVM to the JVM in which the IDE runs. For DSLs that run on other platforms, or DSLs that are interpreted, a similar form of marshalling can be applied.

5.3 Platform-level Event Handler

The platform-level event handler is responsible for controlling the runtime system in which the DSL is executed. It also passes on events from the platform-level debug library to the IDE-level debug library.

Where the two previously discussed libraries are executed in the execution context of the DSL program, the platform-level event handler is a library component that operates as part of the IDE. As such, with Spoofax and Eclipse being based on Java, it is implemented in Java.

Most execution platforms provide native support for debugging. For example, the Java platform provides an API to control breakpoints and reflect over the execution state of a running Java application. This API can be used from the platform-level event handler to control the runtime of the running DSL program. For example, in our Java implementation of this library, we simply use the JVM API to set a breakpoint in the platform-level debug library to suspend it. The JVM API is also used to efficiently reflect over the runtime state, e.g. to inspect local variables.

For platforms that do not provide native debugging support, we can emulate the suspending behavior by using the platform-level debug library to pause until resumed by the IDE. Similarly, state can be inspected by manually marshalling it from the DSL level to the event handler.

5.4 IDE-level Debug Library

The IDE-level debug library is the largest component in our infrastructure, and can be shared between all DSLs and all DSL platforms. The component integrates with the Eclipse debug perspective UI, and reuses the Eclipse data structures that model the program state and the user interface elements that act has a graphical front-end for this model.

Each of the four debug event classes is processed and communicated to the Eclipse API. The `step` event is used to change the location of the instruction pointer in the top level stack frame. The `enter` event adds a new stack frame or introduces a new local scope, and the `exit` event removes the top stack frame or removes the current local scope. The `enter` and `exit` events also specify

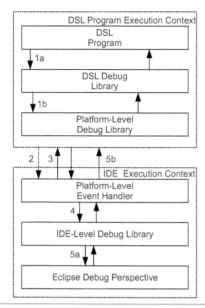

Figure 5. DSL program execution flow.

whether to push or pop a stack frame, or to only use a local scope. Finally, a `var` event declares a new variable in the current scope.

5.5 DSL Program Execution Flow

Figure 5 shows the control flow between the runtime components, the sequence is as follows:

1. (a) The DSL Program executes a debug-event sending statement, which (b) calls the matching method in the platform-level debug library.

2. A breakpoint is hit in the host language, DSL execution is suspended and the platform-level debug handler is notified of the event.

3. Using reflection, the debug information attached to the event is extracted from the suspended program.

4. The debug event is passed on to the IDE-level debug library and the DSL program state is updated. The program state is then used to compare it against the DSL breakpoints set by the user.

At this point two execution paths are possible:

5. (a) If a DSL breakpoint is hit, the DSL program stays suspended and the IDE jumps to the corresponding line in the DSL program and waits for the user to select the next action (which will be discussed in the next paragraph). (b) If no DSL breakpoint is hit, the DSL program execution is resumed.

When the DSL program is suspended the user can inspect the program state that was created and can take one of the following actions: *terminate*, *resume*, *step over*, *step into*, or *step out*. The implementation of the *terminate* and *resume* action is trivial. A *step* command will also resume the program execution but it will suspend the execution either when a breakpoint was hit (canceling the step request) or when the desired program state is hit. For a *step over* action, the execution is suspended once the next `step` event in the same stack frame is received or when the current stack frame is popped from the stack. For a *step into* action, the execution is suspended at the first step event that is received in the first child stack frame. For a *step out* action, the execution is suspended at the first step event originating from the parent stack frame.

6. Case Studies

We implemented our framework as part of the Spoofax language workbench [12]. To validate the implementation we performed two case studies. The first case study is performed with the Stratego transformation language and the second case study is performed with the WebDSL web programming language. A screenshot of the Stratego debugger is shown in Figure 6.

For each case study we will motivate why it was chosen and discuss the relevant issues raised in Section 2.2, followed by an overview of the components that have to be implemented in order to generate a fully working debugger.

6.1 Stratego

Stratego [2] is a transformation language used to transform program definitions using rewrite rules and traversal strategies. Stratego is actively used as a software analysis and generation tool in projects such as Spoofax [12], WebDSL [24] (a web programming DSL) and Mobl [10] (a DSL for mobile web application development).

By designing a debugger for Stratego, transformations written with the language can be stepped through and inspected. Since Stratego is also the basis for editor services in Spoofax [12], the same applies to editor services such as content completion.

Following to the categories specified in Section 2.2, we can identify Stratego as an imperative programming language with well defined execution semantics, which makes it relatively straightforward to recreate the program state during debugging with the proper debug information. When we consider the implementation approach, Stratego supports the compiled as well as the interpreted approach both available with a Java or C back-end, for this case study we focus on the compiled and the interpreted implementation approach with a Java back-end as it simplifies the implementation of the platform-level debug library and platform-level event handler. Adapting the Java code generator to support the generation of debug information is undesirable, due to the maturity and complexity of the Stratego compiler, making the debug instrumentation approach a viable solution to include debug information in Stratego programs.

Stratego debug events Stratego is a (non-pure) functional language based on the notion of strategy definitions and rules, which roughly correspond to functions in other languages, and strategy expressions, which roughly correspond to statements. Stratego also uses local variables that are assigned in match patterns. Together, these notions map naturally to the four debug events. Figure 7 provides an overview of the number of syntactic productions and their events.

Using the SEL language we can define the debug instrumentation preprocessor. First, we have to determine which syntax constructs correspond to which debug events. Second, we have to specify how we can extract the debug information from the abstract syntax tree. And finally, we have to determine how the debug information is stored.

Figure 8 shows a part of the SEL specification for the Stratego language. The `StrategyDef` sort is a syntax construct that corresponds to a strategy definition, these definitions will fire an `enter` event when called and fire an `exit` event when the execution returns to the caller. The `Strategy` sort captures all statements that will generate a `step` event. The `Strategy` sort can define new variables, but variables are also used as parameters in strategy signatures. Therefore, the `var` event has to be matched against the `Strategy` sort and the `StrategyDef` sort.

Figure 9 is an example of a Stratego rewrite rule that implements the `gen-strategy-enter` generation transformation referred to in Figure 8. Stratego rewrite rules have the form $r: p_1 \rightarrow p_2$

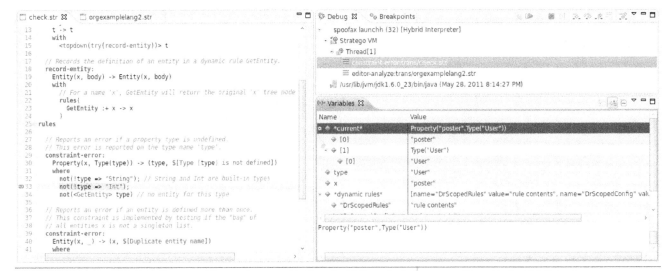

Figure 6. A screenshot of the Stratego debugger integrated in Spoofax/Eclipse. Left: Stratego editor with the highlighted current statement. Top right: Debug view showing the program state. Bottom right: Variables view showing the active variables.

Event class	Sort Category	Production Count
step	Strategy	58
enter/exit	RuleDef	3
enter/exit	StrategyDef	6
var	Strategy	58
var	RuleDef	3
var	StrategyDef	6

Figure 7. Syntax productions and events in Stratego.

```
instrumentation

event enter at StrategyDef._
           creates gen-strategy-enter
           from extract-strategy-debug-info
event exit  at StrategyDef._
           creates gen-strategy-exit
           from extract-strategy-debug-info
event step  at Strategy._
           creates gen-step
           from extract-step-debug-info
event var   at Strategy._
           creates gen-var
           from extract-var-info
event var   at StrategyDef._
           creates gen-strategy-var
           from extract-strategy-var-info
...
```

Figure 8. A part of the SEL specification for Stratego.

```
gen-strategy-enter:
  s -> Seq(SCallT("enter", ...), s)
```

Figure 9. Generation transformation for an enter event.

and rewrite a term pattern p_1 to a pattern p_2. This particular rule rewrites a strategy expression tree node to one that is preceded by an enter event.

Debugger runtime Stratego allows native method calls to Java which makes it possible to implement the DSL debug library which in turn calls a Java implementation of the platform-level debug library. For instance, the enter event of Figure 9 is implemented as

a call to an enter rule in the DSL debug library which in turn will call a Java method similar to enter(String name, ...) in the platform-level debug library.

Instrumentation Each debug event class requires a specific set of DSL program metadata to update the program state with meaningful information. To retrieve the location information, which is required for every event, Stratego programs can be parsed to an abstract syntax tree that includes source code locations annotations. This location information is made available in the extraction transformations to be included in the debug information for every event. Furthermore, the enter and exit events require the name of the rule or strategy and the var event requires the name of the variable as well as the value because Stratego does not allow variables to be redefined.

Rules and strategies usually have a single exit point, but if a rewrite rule fails the execution is returned to the caller just like a Java exception. Stratego supports a try-finally block using a different notation, thus the try-finally approach from Section 4 is used to make sure exit events are always fired.

Reflection This case studies show that it is possible to reconstruct the Stratego program state using debug events, but the actual event sending/receiving mechanism depends on the platform used by the DSL. Because we use the Java back-end version of Stratego we can reuse the Java debugger for suspending the runtime and inspecting the execution state. The Java Debug Runtime component then uses reflection to extract the debug information from the suspended Java program to change the program state. The program state is then used to determine if a Stratego breakpoint was hit using the strategy described in Section 5.4.

6.2 WebDSL

WebDSL is a DSL for web applications with a rich data model [9]. WebDSL is used as a subject to a case study because it contains imperative as well as declarative code. Defining a debugger for the imperative part of WebDSL is straightforward as it is based on the common execution model containing functions and statements. However, it is a much greater challenge to define a debugger for the declarative parts of the language. Therefore this case study will focus on defining a debugger for the declarative part of WebDSL.

WebDSL debug events WebDSL uses a declarative language for page definitions, with some support for control statements, to build the user interface of a webpage. WebDSL distinguishes page and template declarations, pages are complete page definitions while templates can be used to define reusable user interface components. Furthermore, template definitions can be locally redefined in a page or template definition only for the active definition.

During the evaluation of a page definition, the web page is outputted incrementally to a stream. These definitions can be debugged, but that would actually result in debugging the creation of the UI, not debugging the UI proper. Nevertheless, we use `enter`/`exit` events for page definitions and templates (parts of pages that can be included).

Template and page definitions are a mixture between control flow statements, basic user interface components and calls to template definitions. Not only do the debug events serve as actions that change the runtime state, a trace of debug events also show how a webpage is build. The `enter` event is fired as a new nested user interface element is created, while the `exit` event makes the current level final. The `step` event either models a control sequence, a call to a template that generates a subelement of the user interface or a call to generate a basic user interface element.

Debugger runtime WebDSL is implemented based on Java, which means we can reuse both the platform-specific event handler and the platform-specific debug library we also used for Stratego. A minor difference is that WebDSL applications are hosted in an Apache Tomcat environment, which must be configured before a debugger can be attached to it.

7. Discussion and Related Work

This paper presented a generic debugger generation framework for DSLs that abstracts over the complexity of writing a debugger by hand. Our work follows in a line of previous research aimed at more efficiently developing debuggers for custom languages [6, 11, 21, 27]. In this section we reflect over our work and highlight the differences to related work.

Applicability to different types of DSLs A key characteristic for debuggability of DSLs is their executability. Despite the fact that the relation between the executability of a language and the possible debugging capabilities is rather vague, it is possible to create a debugger as long as executable code is generated or code is executed by an interpreter.

Although the difference between a imperative and declarative programming language is precise, languages usually take elements from both paradigms. A debugger for a pure declarative language is hard to define as the execution model is hidden from the user. Nevertheless, the debugger can be used to show how the relationship between declarations is constructed improving program understanding.

We only evaluated our approach for interpreted and compiled DSLs. Debuggers for DSLs implemented as language extensions require special attention, as we only instrument the DSL parts and not the general-purpose parts of a program. Depending on the context in which the DSL extension is applied, additional effort is needed to integrate the debugger with a debugger for the host language.

While this paper focusses on debugging textual DSL programs, the same debugger generation approach can also be applied to domain-specific modeling languages (DSML). According to previous work DSML debuggers should debug both the synthesized artifacts and the model transformations [17]. First, our approach can be used when the synthesized artifacts are code and the model can be expressed as a textual DSL. For visual DSLs the instrumentation preprocessor and debugger runtime have to be modified to interact with the visual model. Secondly, the Stratego use case shows how our approach can be used to create a debugger for a transformation language. Furthermore, the instrumentation preprocessor can be used to link constructs at different levels of abstraction during a model transformation.

Performance Debugging incurs additional runtime overhead in both the program build process and the program execution. Debug instrumentation is a one time penalty during code generation, while the debug runtime introduces extra overhead during program execution. The overhead we experienced in our case studies was acceptable, but a general strategy to avoid the overhead can be to employ separate debug and release builds to minimize the overhead in deployed applications.

The debug instrumentation preprocessor has to traverse each input file only once to generate a debug instrumented DSL program. Therefore, the performance overhead is linear with respect to the size of the code base of a DSL program. The debug instrumentation overhead can be decreased significantly if the DSL supports separate compilation. A change to a single file does not have to result in a rebuild of the entire DSL program, because the preprocessor can operate on a single source file without being aware of the complete application code base.

The DSL program execution performance is affected by debug instrumentation because of the extra debug statements, adding extra method invocation overhead, and because the debugger has to inspect the program state with events. While our implementation architecture may incur larger performance overhead than common with debuggers natively supported on an execution platform, it is common to see a certain degradation in performance even in the most optimized natively supported debuggers.

Tools for building debuggers The Meta-Environment [14] was one of the first tools that supported the generation of language aware editors and debuggers for end-users. The debuggers were generated using a generic debugging framework called TIDE [21] which also used debug events to create the program state in the debugger. TIDE relies on the language developer to implement a single, handwritten debug adapter component to link the DSL runtime to the TIDE system. In contrast, we use a layered architecture in order to minimize the implementation effort. TIDE also requires the code generator or interpreter to be adapted by hand, where we provide the SEL language to weave in the required changes.

Wu et al. [27] describe a grammar-driven technique to build a debugging tool generation framework from existing DSL grammars. Similar to our approach, they allow language developers to link grammatical constructs to events using an aspect oriented approach. However, their approach is aimed at DSLs that are specified as ANTLR grammars with semantic actions for execution. Using a technique they call grammar weaving [19], they weave debug instrumentation into these semantic actions. In contrast, our approach relies on a separate debug instrumentation tool operating directly on the DSL program source code which does not dependent on the implementation approach of the DSL. Wu et al. also provide a debugging framework at the IDE level, but they lack the layered architecture that allows for further reuse across DSLs in our approach.

The Meta Programming System (MPS) [25] is a language workbench that uses projectional editing rather than free text editing. It is notable because of its built-in support for debugging for languages that are based on its Base Language (BL), a host language inspired by Java. Most DSLs in MPS are defined as extensions of BL. By mapping to BL statements and expressions, they can use the BL debugger. MPS does not currently provide an API or infrastructure for debugging based on other languages. In contrast, our approach is independent of a particular base language, and uses a preprocessor to maintain independence of the implementation technique of the language. We also provide a reusable infrastructure for implementing debuggers for other platforms.

Libraries for building debuggers Where we use a tool-centric approach to generate parts of a debugger implementation, there is also related work in the form of libraries for building debuggers in an efficient manner. The Eclipse platform itself provides the Language ToolKit (LTK) library, which provides a layer of abstraction over common language-oriented operations based on the tooling Eclipse provides for the Java language. A similar library provided for it is the Dynamic LTK (DLTK) library (eclipse.org/dltk), aimed at dynamic languages. The IDE Metatooling Platform (IMP) [3] is a combination of a library and a set of wizard for scaffolding. While these libraries provide a framework for debuggers that abstracts over the traditional low-level implementations and provide hooks for IDE integration, they do not offer the layered architecture that we apply for DSLs and still require manual implementation of instrumentation DSL programs.

8. Conclusions and Future Work

Debuggers are an important tool in modern software engineering practice. Full tool support with debugging facilities ensures optimal productivity of developers with DSLs. The debugging framework presented in this paper ensures that debugging support can be implemented for DSLs with a minimum of effort, by abstracting over the accidental complexity of standard debugging APIs and providing an infrastructure that maximizes reuse across multiple DSL implementations.

Future work is needed to further specialize debuggers for domain-specific languages. Directions include more sophisticated visualizations of domain-specific data structures, the addition of domain-specific event classes to match the execution model of some DSLs, and providing infrastructure for hot code replacement.

Acknowledgments

This research was supported by NWO project 612.063.512, *TFA: Transformations for Abstractions*.

References

[1] M. Auguston. Building program behavior models. In *ECAI Workshop on Spatial and Temporal Reasoning*, pages 19–26, 2007.

[2] M. Bravenboer, K. T. Kalleberg, R. Vermaas, and E. Visser. Strate-go/XT 0.17. A language and toolset for program transformation. *Science of Computer Programming*, 72(1-2):52–70, 2008.

[3] P. Charles, R. M. Fuhrer, S. M. S. Jr., E. Duesterwald, and J. Vinju. Accelerating the creation of customized, language-specific IDEs in eclipse. In S. Arora and G. T. Leavens, editors, *Object-Oriented Programming, Systems, Languages, and Applications, OOPSLA 2009*, 2009.

[4] J. C. Cleaveland. Building application generators. *Softw.*, 5(4), 1988.

[5] S. Efftinge and M. Voelter. oAW xText: A framework for textual DSLs. In *Workshop on Modeling Symposium at Eclipse Summit*, 2006.

[6] R. E. Faith, L. S. Nyland, and J. Prins. Khepera: A system for rapid implementation of domain specific languages. In *Conference on Domain-Specific Languages, October 15-17, 1997, Santa Barbara, California, USA*. USENIX, 1997.

[7] M. Fowler. Language workbenches: The killer-app for domain specific languages?
http://www.martinfowler.com/articles/languageWorkbench.html, 2005.

[8] M. Fowler. *Domain-Specific Languages*. Addison Wesley, 2011.

[9] D. M. Groenewegen, Z. Hemel, and E. Visser. Separation of concerns and linguistic integration in WebDSL. *Software*, 27(5), September/October 2010.

[10] Z. Hemel and E. Visser. Declaratively programming the mobile web with mobl. In *Object-Oriented Programming, Systems, Languages, and Applications, OOPSLA 2011*. ACM, 2011.

[11] P. Henriques, M. Pereira, M. Mernik, M. Lenic, J. Gray, and H. Wu. Automatic generation of language-based tools using the LISA system. *Software, IEE Proceedings -*, 152(2):54–69, april 2005.

[12] L. C. L. Kats and E. Visser. The Spoofax language workbench: rules for declarative specification of languages and IDEs. In W. R. Cook, S. Clarke, and M. C. Rinard, editors, *Object-Oriented Programming, Systems, Languages, and Applications, OOPSLA 2010*, pages 444–463. ACM, 2010.

[13] L. C. L. Kats, E. Visser, and G. Wachsmuth. Pure and declarative syntax definition: paradise lost and regained. In W. R. Cook, S. Clarke, and M. C. Rinard, editors, *Object-Oriented Programming, Systems, Languages, and Applications, OOPSLA 2010*, pages 918–932. ACM, 2010.

[14] P. Klint. A meta-environment for generating programming environments. *Transactions on Software Engineering Methodology*, 2(2):176–201, 1993.

[15] T. Kosar, N. Oliveira, M. Mernik, V. Pereira, M. Crepinsek, C. Da, and R. Henriques. Comparing general-purpose and domain-specific languages: An empirical study. *Computer Science and Information Systems*, 7(2):247–264, 2010.

[16] H. Krahn, B. Rumpe, and S. Völkel. Monticore: Modular development of textual domain specific languages. In R. F. Paige and B. Meyer, editors, *Objects, Components, Models and Patterns, TOOLS EUROPE 2008*, volume 11 of *LNBIP*, pages 297–315. Springer, 2008.

[17] R. Mannadiar and H. Vangheluwe. Debugging in domain-specific modelling. In *Software language engineering*, SLE'10, pages 276–285. Springer-Verlag, 2011.

[18] M. Mernik, J. Heering, and A. M. Sloane. When and how to develop domain-specific languages. *Computing Surveys*, 37(4):316–344, 2005.

[19] D. Rebernak, M. Mernik, H. Wu, and J. G. Gray. Domain-specific aspect languages for modularising crosscutting concerns in grammars. *IEE Proceedings - Software*, 3(3):184–200, 2009.

[20] Y. Smaragdakis and D. Batory. Application generators. *Encyclopedia of Electrical and Electronics Engineering*, 2000.

[21] M. van den Brand, B. Cornelissen, P. A. Olivier, and J. J. Vinju. TIDE: A generic debugging framework - tool demonstration. *ENTCS*, 141(4): 161–165, 2005.

[22] I. Vessey. Toward a theory of computer program bugs: An empirical test. *Int. Journal of Man-Machine Studies*, 30(1):23–46, 1989.

[23] E. Visser. *Syntax Definition for Language Prototyping*. PhD thesis, University of Amsterdam, September 1997.

[24] E. Visser. WebDSL: A case study in domain-specific language engineering. In R. Lämmel, J. Visser, and J. Saraiva, editors, *Generative and Transformational Techniques in Software Engineering II, Int. Summer School, GTTSE 2007*, volume 5235 of *LNCS*, pages 291–373. Springer, 2007.

[25] M. Voelter and K. Solomatov. Language modularization and composition with projectional language workbenches illustrated with MPS. In M. van den Brand, B. Malloy, and S. Staab, editors, *Software Language Engineering, SLE 2010*, LNCS. Springer, 2010.

[26] D. S. Wile. Supporting the DSL spectrum. *CIT. Journal of computing and information technology*, 9(4):263–287, 2001.

[27] H. Wu, J. Gray, and M. Mernik. Grammar-driven generation of domain-specific language debuggers. *Software: Practice and Experience*, 38(10):1073–1103, 2008.

Less is More: Unparser-completeness of Metalanguages for Template Engines

B.J. Arnoldus   M.G.J. van den Brand   A. Serebrenik

Technische Universiteit Eindhoven
Eindhoven, The Netherlands
B.J.Arnoldus@alumnus.tue.nl, {M.G.J.v.d.Brand, A.Serebrenik}@tue.nl

Abstract

A code generator is a program translating an input model into code. In this paper we focus on template-based code generators in the context of the model view controller architecture (MVC).

The language in which the code generator is written is known as a metalanguage in the code generation parlance. The metalanguage should be, on the one side, expressive enough to be of practical value, and, on the other side, restricted enough to enforce the separation between the view and the model, according to the MVC.

In this paper we advocate the notion of *unparser-complete metalanguages* as providing the right level of expressivity. An unparser-complete metalanguage is capable of expressing an unparser, a code generator that translates any legal abstract syntax tree into an equivalent sentence of the corresponding context-free language. A metalanguage not able to express an unparser will fail to produce all sentences belonging to the corresponding context-free language. A metalanguage able to express more than an unparser will also be able to implement code violating the model/view separation.

We further show that a metalanguage with the power of a linear deterministic tree-to-string transducer is unparser-complete. Moreover, this metalanguage has been successfully applied in a nontrivial case study where an existing code generator is refactored using templates.

Categories and Subject Descriptors   D.3.4 [*Programming Languages*]: Processors—Code generation; D.2.3 [*Software Engineering*]: Coding Tools and Techniques—Pretty printers

General Terms   Languages

Keywords   code generation, templates, unparser

1. Introduction

Code generators are programs translating input models to code. They can be seen as meta-programs since they manipulate code, i.e. code occurs both as data (object code) and as an executed artifact (meta-code). One traditionally distinguishes between *homogeneous* and *heterogeneous* code generators [24]. In homogeneous code generators the metalanguage and object language coincide. In heterogeneous code generators the metalanguage and the object

GPCE'11,   October 22–23, 2011, Portland, Oregon, USA.
Copyright © 2011 ACM 978-1-4503-0689-8/11/09... $10.00

```
<ul>
#foreach( $product in $allProducts )
    <li>$product</li>
#end
</ul>
```

Figure 1. HTML code for a list of products.

language may differ. A heterogeneous code generator can be implemented by means of, e.g., print statements, abstract syntax trees instantiation, term rewriting and templates [18, 21, 28]. In this paper we consider heterogeneous code generators, and more specifically, template-based code generators.

One of the most well-known applications of template-based code generation is the HTML generation in dynamic web applications, where each HTML page is generated on a user request. Templates can be also used in broader context, e.g., for generating data model classes and state machine pattern implementations. In general, templates can be seen as fragments of object code intermitted with holes, containing instructions expressed in the metalanguage. When a *template engine* processes a template it directly emits the object code to the output, and evaluates the instructions in the holes with respect to the input data. For example, the template in Figure 1, expressed in the Velocity Template Language [25], generates HTML code for a list of products given in the input data. Numerous template-based engines are available, including JSP [4], Velocity [25] and StringTemplate [21]. Every template engine has its own metalanguage and evaluation strategy. With the notable exception of the metalanguage of StringTemplates, most metalanguages lack a formal requirements definition.

The main contribution of this paper consists in formalizing the requirements for a metalanguage of a template engine in the context of the model view controller architecture. Intuitively, the metalanguage should be, on the one side, expressive enough to be useful for practical applications, and, on the other side, it should be restricted enough, to disallow, e.g., the view to modify the model. We claim that the right balance can be found by demanding from the metalanguage to be *unparser-complete*, i.e., to be able to express an *unparser* and not more than an unparser. Section 2 presents the intuition behind this claim. After introducing a number of preliminary notions in Section 3, in Section 4 we formalize the notion of an unparser and in Section 5 the related notion of the *desugar* function. Unparser-completeness is introduced in Section 6 closing the discussion of the theoretical framework.

A complementary task of showing practical power of unparser complete metalanguages, is the second contribution of this paper. We have designed our own metalanguage discussed in Section 7 and conducted a number of case studies. One of these case studies,

Figure 2. Two-stage architecture.

reimplementation of a finite-state machine generator `NunniFSMGen` is discussed in Section 8. Finally, related work is briefly reviewed in Section 9, and Section 10 concludes.

2. Requirements

In this section, we formulate the requirements for a template meta-language. We focus on the usage of templates in the context of the model view controller architecture (MVC) [19] and heterogeneous code generators. In MVC architecture, templates are commonly used to implement the *view* of the internal data of an application (*model*). A view can be rendering the HTML for a set of data from the database in case of web applications (cf. the code fragment in Section 1), or converting a given abstract syntax tree into code.

The MVC architecture decouples the models and its transformations from the view components, hereby reducing the complexity and increasing the flexibility of the system. This separation of concerns also allows different views for the same underlying model. We show in Section 8 the benefits of MVC in the context of a code generator. The same model is used for different target languages, resulting in less code-clones than the original implementation.

While in the original paper on MVC [19] the *view* was expected to send editing messages to the model, already in [7] this functionality was restricted to the *controller*, and the *view* was only allowed to receive the messages from the model to update the way the model is shown. This intuition was formalized in [21], where it has been argued that the view should neither alter the model nor perform calculations depending on the semantics of the model. Unfortunately, the separation of view and logic is not enforced in existing template engines, such as JSP, i.e., it is possible to write JSP templates with all logic in a single file. Typically, such a file will contain fragments in HTML, JSP-tags, Java, and SQL. Not only does this file violate the MVC architecture principle, because logic (model) and presentation (view) are not separated, but it is also hard to understand the file due to different escaping characters required to support multiple programming languages, executed at different stages.

Separation of model and view results in a two-stage architecture (see Figure 2). In a two-stage architecture, the template is solely responsible for instantiating a view based on the intermediate representation. i.e. the model. The input model is provided by the first stage that can implement calculations and transformations. This separation is not formalized in this article, however, intuitively its place is at the point where the code generator only has to handle target language specific issues. For example, in case of a web application the first stage implements the business logic responsible for fetching data from a database and preparing it for the actual HTML and/or PDF generation, while the HTML generation is carried out during the second stage and PDF generation using another implementation in the second stage. It is also possible to have an n-stage architecture, although, the n-stage architecture can be seen as a two-stage architecture, where the transformer and/or the code generator exist of multiple stages.

In order to enforce the two-stage architecture, the language of the templates should be restricted. For instance, it should not include constructs for performing calculations, in order to make sure that all calculations are carried out before the templates are evaluated, i.e., during the first stage. However, in order to be practical,

the language of the templates should be expressive enough. Indeed, a too restrictive metalanguage limits the applicability of the metalanguage, and thus of the template engine. Hence, we require the metalanguage to be able to implement code generators, which can produce *every* (correct) sentence of the output language. A code generator that can produce every sentence of the output language given an abstract syntax tree is called an *unparser*. The unparser is a special kind of code generator, transforming an abstract syntax tree to a concrete syntax, such that if the emitted concrete syntax is parsed then the input abstract syntax tree is obtained again, i.e. the semantics are not altered by the unparser. Unparsers are closely related to *pretty printers* [20] that in addition to producing every sentence of the output language given an abstract syntax tree take care of an appropriate layout.

3. Preliminaries

We start with a number of basic definitions and declarations of symbols used throughout this paper. We assume the reader to be familiar with the formal language theory and basics of the tree language theory [9, 15]. In this section we present the notation used and recall the most important definitions.

Integer variables are denoted k, i, j, p and r. Formal languages are sets of words, i.e., finite sequences of symbols derived from a finite set of symbols, known as an *alphabet* and denoted as Σ. The set of all words over Σ is denoted Σ^*. Every symbol c of Σ is associated with a unique non-negative integer, known as the *rank* of c and denoted r_c. The rank is equal to the number of children a node representing the symbol will have. We further use f to denote alphabet symbols with rank greater than 0. Σ_r for the set of symbols of rank r. X is a set of symbols called variables and we assume that the sets X and Σ_0 are disjoint. x is a variable $x \in X$ and is not used for integer values.

An important class of formal languages are the *context-free languages*, i.e., languages specified by a context-free grammar [15]:

Definition 3.1 (Context-free grammar and language). A context-free grammar (CFG) is a four-tuple $\langle \Sigma, N, S, Prods \rangle$, where Σ is the alphabet, N is a finite set such that $N \cap \Sigma = \emptyset$, $S \in N$ is the start symbol and $Prods$ is a finite set of production rules of the form $n \to z$ where $n \in N$ and $z \in (N \cup \Sigma)^*$. A context-free language $\mathcal{L}(G)$ is the set of words generated by the context-free grammar G. The set N is known as the set of *nonterminal symbols*.

For the sake of simplicity in this paper we focus on LALR grammars [10]. Our approach can be adapted to grammars with ambiguity by introducing ambiguity nodes and indicating the preferred derivations similarly to [26].

A *regular tree language* is a set of trees generated by a *regular tree grammar* [9]:

Definition 3.2. (Regular tree grammar). A regular tree grammar (RTG) is a four-tuple $\langle \Sigma, N, S, Prods \rangle$, where Σ is the alphabet; N is a finite set of nonterminal symbols with rank $r = 0$ and $N \cap \Sigma = \emptyset$; $S \in N$ is a start symbol; $Prods$ is a finite set of production rules of the form $n \to t$, where $n \in N$ and $t \in Tr(\Sigma \cup N)$, where $Tr(\Sigma \cup N)$ is the set of trees over Σ and N.

Example 3.3. Let G be $\langle \Sigma, N, S, Prods \rangle$, where $\Sigma = \{a, b\}$ with $r_a = 0$ and $r_b = 2$, $N = \{S\}$ and $Prods = \{S \to b(S, S), S \to a\}$. The grammar G is a regular tree grammar representing binary trees, and its language

$$\mathcal{L}(G) = \{a, b(a, a), b(b(a, a), a), b(a, b(a, a)), \dots\}$$

is a regular tree language. ∎

Next we introduce the notion of a linear tree homomorphism:

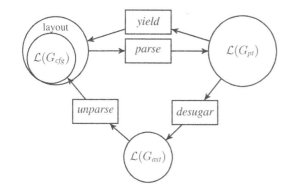

Figure 3. Relations between languages and their grammars.

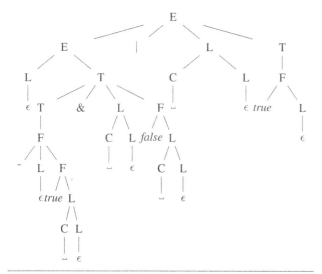

Figure 4. A parse tree of `~true & false | true` obtained with respect to the production rules of Example 4.1.

Definition 3.4. (Tree homomorphism) [9]. Let Σ and Σ' be two not necessarily disjoint ranked alphabets. For each $k > 0$ such that Σ contains a symbol of rank k, we define a set of variables $X_k = \{x_1, \ldots, x_k\}$ disjoint from Σ and Σ'.

Let h_Σ be a mapping which, with $c \in \Sigma$ of rank k, associates a term $t_c \in Tr(\Sigma', X_k)$. The tree homomorphism $h : Tr(\Sigma) \to Tr(\Sigma')$ is determined by h_Σ as follows:

$\diamond$ $h(a) = t_a \in Tr(\Sigma')$ for each $a \in \Sigma$ of rank 0,

$\diamond$ $h(c(t_1, \ldots, t_n)) = t_c\{x_1 \leftarrow h(t_1), \ldots, x_k \leftarrow h(t_k)\}$
where $t_c\{x_1 \leftarrow h(t_1), \ldots, x_k \leftarrow h(t_k)\}$ is the result of applying the substitution $\{x_1 \leftarrow h(t_1), \ldots, x_k \leftarrow h(t_k)\}$ to the term t_c.

h_Σ is called a *linear tree homomorphism* when no t_c contains two occurrences of the same x_k. Thus a linear tree homomorphism cannot duplicate trees.

Example 3.5. (Tree homomorphism) [9]. Let $\Sigma = \{g(,,), a, b\}$ and $\Sigma' = \{f(,), a, b\}$. Let us consider the tree homomorphism h determined by h_Σ defined by: $h_\Sigma(g) = f(x_1, f(x_2, x_3))$, $h_\Sigma(a) = a$, $h_\Sigma(b) = b$. For instance, we have: If $t = g(a, g(b, b, b), a)$, then $h(t) = f(a, f(f(b, f(b, b)), a))$.

4. Unparser

As already stated in Section 2, our expressivity requirements for metalanguages of template engines are based on the notion of the *unparser*. An unparser translates an abstract syntax tree representing a sentence into a textual representation of the sentence [6]. An unparser can be seen as a part of the "circle of code" shown in Figure 3, i.e. the circle from concrete syntax to parse tree to abstract syntax and back to concrete syntax. The textual representation of a program obeying a context-free grammar ($\mathcal{L}(G_{cfg})$ in Figure 3) can be *parsed* to obtain the corresponding parse tree ($\mathcal{L}(G_{pt})$). The set of parse trees of a context-free grammar is a regular tree language [9].

Since the parse tree contains exactly the same information as the textual representation, the textual representation can be restored using the parse tree. The corresponding mapping from $\mathcal{L}(G_{pt})$ to $\mathcal{L}(G_{cfg})$ is called *yield* [9]. Alternatively, one can *desugar* the parse tree, i.e., simplify it by removing the semantically-irrelevant layout information. In this way, an abstract syntax tree ($\mathcal{L}(G_{ast})$) is obtained. Finally, the *unparse* function closes the circle and maps elements of $\mathcal{L}(G_{ast})$ to $\mathcal{L}(G_{cfg})$.

Example 4.1. To illustrate the functions in Figure 3 consider the following set of production rules:

E → L T	F → "~" L F	L → C L
E → E "|" L T	F → "(" L E ")" L	L → ϵ
T → F	F → *true* L	C → "␣"
T → T "&" L F	F → *false* L	C → "\n"

The parse tree of `~true & false | true` with respect to these production rules is shown in Figure 4. In the running text we also write a parse tree as a term $n(s_1, t'_1, s_2, \ldots, s_r, t'_r, s_{r+1})$, where $t'_1 \ldots t'_r$ are sub parse trees with top nonterminals $n_1 \ldots n_r$ and strings $s_1 \ldots s_{r+1}$ are the terminals.

The sentence `~true & false | true` can be restored by applying *yield* to the tree in Figure 4. The *desugar* function provides a mapping of concrete syntax constructs (e.g., & and *true*) to abstract syntax constructs (*And* and *True*, respectively), applying the *desugar* function to the parse tree results in the abstract syntax tree $Or(And(Not(True), False), True)$. The abstract syntax tree can be unparsed to `~true&false|true`. Observe that while the application of *unparse∘desugar∘parse* produces a semantically equivalent sentence, layout preservation is not guaranteed. ∎

As suggested by the example, an abstract syntax tree corresponds to multiple semantically-equivalent textual representations, while *unparse* necessarily produces only one of these representations. This is why the set of context-free sentences is larger than the range of *unparse*, i.e.,

$$\mathcal{L}(G_{cfg}) \supseteq unparse(desugar(parse(\mathcal{L}(G_{cfg})))) \quad (1)$$

Moreover, the unparser is correct if and only if re-parsing its output sentences produce the same abstract syntax trees as the original inputs [22]. This correctness requirement means that the combination of *unparse* and *desugar* should not alter the meaning of the code represented by the concrete syntax or the abstract syntax:

$$\mathcal{L}(G_{ast}) = desugar(parse(unparse(\mathcal{L}(G_{ast})))) \quad (2)$$

Our intention is to derive the *unparse* function from the context-free grammar of the output language. However, in order to generate a textual representation from an abstract syntax tree the unparser should be aware of the mapping between concrete syntax constructs and abstract syntax constructs, akin to the one mentioned in Example 4.1. One possible way to construct the mapping is by means of heuristics [29]. However, this approach will introduce machine generated names for the abstract syntax tree nodes. In order to retain the full control of the abstract syntax constructs, we propose to integrate abstract syntax constructs (signature labels) in the production rules of a context-free grammar. Formally, a production rule in the augmented context-free grammar has the form $n \to z\{c\}$ where $n \in N$, $z \in (N \bigcup \Sigma)^*$ and c is an element of an alphabet Σ'. The set Σ' is the alphabet of the regular tree grammar belonging to the abstract syntax and is not necessarily disjoint from $N \bigcup \Sigma$. We furthermore require a signature label c to be used at most once. In order to remove the layout syntax and other superfluous syntax, it is allowed, under strict conditions, to have production rules without signature labels. These conditions are in the case of:

◇ **Layout syntax** - The nonterminals belonging to the layout syntax, such as whitespaces and comment, should not be defined with a signature label. The desugar function, as defined in Section 5, removes these syntax from the tree. It is mandatory, that the layout syntax includes the empty string ϵ, as the layout is not restored by the automatic derived unparser.

◇ **Chain rules** - It is allowed that production rules of the form $n_1 \to n_2$, are not accompanied with a signature label. The abstract syntax belonging to n_2 is propagated to n_1, which is allowed, since all signature labels are unique. Furthermore, it is allowed that n_2 is surrounded by layout nonterminals, as these layout syntaxes contain the empty string.

Example 4.2. (Augmented context-free grammar)

$E \to L\ T$	$F \to$ "~" $L\ F$ $\{Not\}$	$L \to C\ L$
$E \to E$ "|" $L\ T$ $\{Or\}$	$F \to$ "(" $L\ E$ ")" L $\{Br\}$	$L \to \epsilon$
$T \to F$	$F \to$ "$true$" L $\{True\}$	$C \to$ "␣"
$T \to T$ "&" $L\ F$ $\{And\}$	$F \to$ "$false$" L $\{False\}$	$C \to$ "\n"

The production rules above show the extension of a context-free grammar of Example 4.1 with signature labels. ∎

In presence of signature labels we further adapt the term notation for the parse trees and write $parse(s_1 \cdot s_1' \cdot s_2 \cdot \ldots \cdot s_r \cdot s_r' \cdot s_{r+1}) = <n, c> (s_1, t_1', s_2, \ldots, s_r, t_r', s_{r+1})$, where n is the top non-terminal, $t_1' \ldots t_r'$ are sub parse trees with top nonterminals $n_1 \ldots n_r$, strings $s_1 \ldots s_{r+1}$ are the terminals and c is the label associated with $n \to s_1, n_1, s_2, \ldots, s_r, n_r, s_{r+1}$. If there is no such label, $parse(s_1 \cdot s_1' \cdot s_2 \cdot \ldots \cdot s_r \cdot s_r' \cdot s_{r+1})$ is defined as $n(s_1, t_1', s_2, \ldots, s_r, t_r', s_{r+1})$. Furthermore, the function $parse$ used in this article is complete.

For a context-free grammar extended with signatures we can derive $unparse$. For each production rule in the context-free grammar there is a case in the definition of $unparse$, called an *action*, allowing $unparse$ to traverse the abstract syntax tree and to restore terminals whenever needed. For instance, in Example 4.1, given the production rule $T \to T$ "&" $L\ F$ $\{And\}$, the definition of the unparser should have an action for $unparse(And(x, y))$. In general, each action in $unparse$ has a left-hand side and a right-hand side, see Example 4.5. First, we provide the definition to derive an unparser from a given context-free grammar.

Definition 4.3. (Unparse). Let $G_{cfg} = \langle \Sigma, N, S, Prods \rangle$ be a context-free grammar augmented with signature labels, where N' is the set of non-terminals defined by the production rules with a signature label. Then, the corresponding function $unparse$ is defined by a set of actions $Actions$ such that for any $n \to z_1 \ldots z_k \{c\} \in Prods$

◇ either $mkLhs(z_1, \ldots, z_k, 1) \neq \epsilon$ and $unparse(c(mkLhs(z_1, \ldots, z_k, 1))) = mkRhs(z_1, \ldots, z_k, 1) \in Actions$,

◇ or $mkLhs(z_1, \ldots, z_k, 1) = \epsilon$ and $unparse(c) = mkRhs(z_1, \ldots, z_k, 1) \in Actions$,

where

$$mkLhs(i) = \epsilon$$
$$mkLhs(z_1, z_2, \ldots, z_j, i) =$$
$$\begin{cases} mkLhs(z_2, \ldots, z_j, i+1) & \text{if } z_1 \notin N' \\ x_i, mkLhs(z_2, \ldots, z_j, i+1) & \text{if } z_1 \in N' \text{ and} \\ & mkLhs(z_2, \ldots, z_j, i+1) \neq \epsilon \\ x_i & \text{otherwise} \end{cases}$$

and

$$mkRhs(i) = \epsilon$$
$$mkRhs(z_1, z_2 \ldots, z_j, i) =$$
$$\begin{cases} z_1 \cdot mkRhs(z_2, \ldots, z_j, i+1) & \text{if } z_1 \in \Sigma \\ unparse(x_i) \cdot mkRhs(z_2, \ldots, z_j, i+1) & \text{if } z_1 \in N' \\ mkRhs(z_2, \ldots, z_j, i+1) & \text{if } z_1 \notin (N' \cup \Sigma) \end{cases}$$

and $\cdot$ denotes the string concatenation operation.

Example 4.4. We illustrate Definition 4.3 with the production rule $T \to T$ "&" $L\ F$ $\{And\}$ from Example 4.2. Then, the set N' of non-terminals corresponding to production rules with signature information is $\{E, F, T\}$. Hence, "&" and L should be omitted from the left-hand side of the unparser action:

$$\begin{aligned} mkLhs(T, \text{"\&"}, L, F, 1) &= x_1, mkLhs(\text{"\&"}, L, F, 2) \\ &= x_1, mkLhs(L, F, 3) = \\ &= x_1, mkLhs(F, 4) = \\ &= x_1, x_4 \end{aligned}$$

since $mkLhs(5) = \epsilon$. Similarly, for the right-hand side of the action we ignore L:

$$\begin{aligned} mkRhs(T, \text{"\&"}, L, F, 1) &= unparse(x_1) \cdot mkRhs(\text{"\&"}, L, F, 2) = \\ & unparse(x_1) \cdot \text{"\&"} \cdot mkRhs(L, F, 3) = \\ & unparse(x_1) \cdot \text{"\&"} \cdot mkRhs(F, 4) = \\ & unparse(x_1) \cdot \text{"\&"} \cdot unparse(x_4) \cdot mkRhs(5) = \\ & unparse(x_1) \cdot \text{"\&"} \cdot unparse(x_4) \cdot \epsilon = \\ & unparse(x_1) \cdot \text{"\&"} \cdot unparse(x_4) \end{aligned}$$

Since $mkLhs(T, \text{"\&"}, L, F, 1) \neq \epsilon$, the action corresponding to $T \to T$ "&" $L\ F$ $\{And\}$ is $unparse(And(x_1, x_4)) = unparse(x_1) \cdot$ "&" $\cdot unparse(x_4)$. ∎

In general, the *left-hand side* matches on a node in the abstract syntax tree with the signature label c and the variables $x_1, \ldots, x_k$ are assigned to the subtrees belonging to the label c. Following the previous definition, the rank of c, i.e., the number of arguments of c created by $mkLhs$, is not necessarily equal to k: the rank of c is equal to the number of nonterminals in the pattern of the production rule labeled c in the augmented context-free grammar. Therefore, the variable x_i only exists in the action $unparse(c(\ldots)) = \ldots$ if a symbol at index i in the right-hand side of the corresponding production rule is a nonterminal $n \in N'$. The *right-hand side* constructs a string $s_1 \cdot \ldots \cdot s_k$. The number of strings k is equal to the number of symbols in the pattern of the corresponding production rule. Each s_i is either a string or a recursive unparser invocation. Specifically, s_i is a string, if a terminal is defined at index i in the production rule; an unparser invocation, if a nonterminal $n \in N'$ is defined at position i, and ϵ for the remaining case if $n_i \notin (N' \cup \Sigma)$.

Example 4.5. Example 4.4, continued. Given the aforementioned production rules, the following unparser is derived:

$unparse(Not(x_3))$	$=$	"~" $\cdot unparse(x_3)$
$unparse(And(x_1, x_4))$	$=$	$unparse(x_1) \cdot$ "&" $\cdot unparse(x_4)$
$unparse(Or(x_1, x_4))$	$=$	$unparse(x_1) \cdot$ "|" $\cdot unparse(x_4)$
$unparse(Br(x_3))$	$=$	"(" $\cdot unparse(x_3) \cdot$ ")"
$unparse(True)$	$=$	"true"
$unparse(False)$	$=$	"false"

∎

The unparser derived according to Definition 4.3 is linear and deterministic. We say that an unparser is *linear* if for each action in the unparser and every x_i in the action, x_i occurs not more than once in the action's right-hand side. The unparser is called *deterministic* if actions have incompatible left-hand sides, i.e., for every tree there exists only one applicable unparser action.

Theorem 4.6. The unparser derived according to Definition 4.3 is linear and deterministic.

Proof. Linearity follows from Definition 4.3: every variable appearing on the right hand side appears only once. Recall that a signature label c is used once in the augmented context-free tree grammar. A signature label c directly corresponds to one action in $unparse(c(x_1, \ldots, x_k))$. Since a signature label c is used for only one production rule, the left-hand sides of the unparser are unique and thus the unparser is deterministic. □

Definition 4.3 also ensures that *unparse* always terminates if its argument is a finite tree. Recall that $unparse(\ldots)$ for $n \rightarrow z_1 \ldots z_k \{c\}$ distinguishes between $mkLhs(z_1, \ldots, z_k, 1) = \epsilon$ and $mkLhs(z_1, \ldots, z_k, 1) \neq \epsilon$. However, $mkLhs(z_1, \ldots, z_k, 1) = \epsilon$ holds only if $z_i \in \Sigma$ for all i, $1 \leq i \leq k$. Therefore, the right-hand side expression $mkRhs(z_1, z_2 \ldots, z_k, 1) = z_1 \cdot \ldots \cdot z_k$ and *unparse* is defined as $unparse(c) = z_1 \cdot \ldots \cdot z_k$. Since the right-hand side of the latter equation does not contain calls to *unparse*, it cannot introduce non-termination. The remaining case we have to consider is $mkLhs(z_1, \ldots, z_k, 1) \neq \epsilon$. In this case *unparse* is defined as $unparse(c(mkLhs(z_1, \ldots, z_k, 1))) = mkRhs(z_1, \ldots, z_k, 1)$. Termination stems from the fact that every variable appearing on the right hand-side appears in the left-hand side, and from the reduction in the term size between the left-hand side and the right-hand side terms.

We cannot yet prove that the unparser of Definition 4.3 satisfies (1) and (2) as the *desugar* function is still to be defined.

5. Desugaring

The *desugar* function can be manually defined in the parser definition, like in parser implementations such as YACC [17]. These parsers allow to associate a *semantic action* with a production rule in the grammar, such that the semantic actions can directly instantiate an abstract syntax tree. A manually defined *desugar* function must define a linear tree homomorphism, as we argue later on, otherwise regularity of the abstract syntax tree is not guaranteed.

Having a context-free grammar with signature labels, the abstract syntax tree can be automatically instantiated from a parse tree. This is executed by the *desugar* function, which replaces the nodes in the parse tree with new nodes, which are labeled by signature labels. The rank of signature label c is equal to the number of nonterminals in the corresponding production rule of the context-free grammar. Nodes in the parse tree without a signature label are removed from the tree. This mechanism is responsible for removing the nodes that do not contain semantically significant information, such as chain rules and layout syntax.

Definition 5.1. (Desugar). The *desugar* function is defined by the following equations:

$$desugar(x) = \epsilon \qquad \text{if } x \in \Sigma$$
$$desugar(f(x_1, \ldots, x_k)) = dc(x_1, \ldots, x_k)$$
$$desugar(<f, c>(x_1, \ldots, x_k)) =$$
$$\begin{cases} c & \text{if } dc(x_1, \ldots, x_k) = \epsilon \\ c(dc(x_1, \ldots, x_k)) & \text{if } dc(x_1, x_2, \ldots, x_k) \neq \epsilon \end{cases}$$

and

$$dc() = \epsilon$$
$$dc(x_1, x_2, \ldots, x_k) =$$
$$\begin{cases} dc(x_2, \ldots, x_k) & \text{if } x_1 \in \Sigma \\ desugar(x_1), dc(x_2, \ldots, x_k) & \text{if } x_1 \notin \Sigma \text{ and} \\ & \quad dc(x_2, \ldots, x_k) \neq \epsilon \\ desugar(x_1) & \text{otherwise} \end{cases}$$

Example 5.2. (Desugar). Applying the *desugar* function to the parse tree t of `~true & false | true` using the grammar of Example 4.2 will result in the abstract syntax tree: $desugar(t) = Or(And(Not(True), False), True)$. ∎

Observe that Definition 5.1 ensures termination of *desugar* as long as its argument is a finite tree. Indeed, each subsequent call to *desugar* or dc reduces the size of the input argument either by removing the function symbol, e.g., $desugar(f(x_1, \ldots, x_k)) = dc(x_1, \ldots, x_k)$ or by reducing the number of arguments in the call, e.g., $dc(x_1, x_2, \ldots, x_k) = dc(x_2, \ldots, x_k)$.

Theorem 5.3. The abstract syntax tree obtained by applying the *desugar* function to a parse tree belongs to a regular tree language [8].

Proof. Recognizability of trees by finite tree automata is closed under linear tree homomorphism [11]. The *desugar* function is a linear tree homomorphism; subtrees are only removed and not duplicated. Since the abstract syntax tree is a linear tree homomorphism of the parse tree and the set of parse trees of a context-free language is a regular tree language [9], the abstract syntax tree belongs to a regular tree language. □

6. Unparser Completeness

We call a metalanguage capable to express unparsers *unparser-complete*. In this section we show that unparser-completeness is a *more* restricted notion than Turing-completeness. To establish this result we (1) show that the unparser as defined in Definition 4.3 can be expressed by a linear deterministic top-down tree-to-string transducer, and (2) recall that the top-down tree-to-string transducer is strictly less powerful than a Turing machine, i.e., top-down-tree-to-string transducers accept are a subset of the languages Turing machines can accept [27].

Definition 6.1. (Top-down tree-to-string transducer) [12]. A top-down tree-to-string transducer is a 5-tuple $M = \langle Q, \Sigma, \Sigma', q_0, R \rangle$, where Q is a finite set of states, Σ is the ranked input alphabet, Σ' is the output alphabet, $q_0 \in Q$ is the initial state, and R is a finite set of rules of the form:

$$q(\sigma(x_1, \ldots, x_k)) \rightarrow s_1 q_1(x_{i_1}) s_2 q_2(x_{i_2}) \ldots s_p q_p(x_{i_p}) s_{p+1}$$

with $k, p \geq 0$; $q, q_1, \ldots, q_p \in Q$; $\sigma \in \Sigma_k$; $s_1, \ldots, s_{p+1} \in \Sigma'^*$, and $1 \leq i_j \leq k$ for $1 \leq j \leq p$ (if $k = 0$ then the left-hand side is $q(c)$). M is called *deterministic* if different rules in R have different left-hand sides. M is called *linear* if, for each rule in R, no x_i occurs more than once in its right-hand side.

Example 6.2. Unparser in Example 4.5 can be seen as a top-down tree-to-string transducer $\langle Q, \Sigma, \Sigma', q_0, R \rangle$ such that the set of states $Q = \{unparse\}$, the input alphabet $\Sigma = \{Not, And, Or, Br, True, False\}$, the output alphabet $\Sigma' = \{$"~", "&", "|", "(", ")", "true", "false"$\}$ and the finite set of rules R is given by actions defining the unparser in Example 4.5.

Next we show that for each context-free grammar an unparser can be defined using a linear and deterministic top-down tree-to-string transducer. Furthermore, any unparser corresponding to Definition 4.3 can be mapped on a top-down tree-to-string transducer.

141

Theorem 6.3. An unparser based on a linear deterministic top-down tree-to-string transducer can be defined for every context-free grammar augmented with signature labels.

Proof. We show that $\mathcal{L}(G_{ast}) = desugar(parse(unparse(\mathcal{L}(G_{ast}))))$ for the production rules of the form $n \to s_1 n_1 s_2 \ldots s_r n_r s_{r+1} \{c\}$.

Every production rule in a context-free grammar can be projected on the form $n \to s_1 n_1 s_2 \ldots s_r n_r s_{r+1} \{c\}$, where $s_1, \ldots, s_{r+1}$ are strings and may be the empty string ϵ, and $n, n_1, \ldots, n_r$ are the nonterminals. In case the pattern $s_1 s_2$ occurs, the strings can be concatenated into a new string s_1'. We assume that the augmented grammar meets the requirements for augmenting a grammar with signature labels as sketched in Section 4. The abstract syntax tree belonging to this production rule $t_{ast} = c(t_1, \ldots, t_r)$, where $t_1, \ldots, t_r$ are the abstract syntax trees belonging to $n_1 \ldots n_r$. The corresponding tree-to-string transducer rule is: $q(c(x_1, \ldots, x_r)) \to s_1 q_1(x_1) s_2 \ldots s_r q_r(x_r) s_{r+1}$, where $q, q_1, \ldots, q_r$ are transducer states. Application of the transducer to the abstract syntax tree consists in *matching* the tree against the pattern $c(x_1, \ldots, x_r)$ and *replacing* it with a string originating from $s_1 q_1(x_1) s_2 \ldots s_r q_r(x_r) s_{r+1}$, where $q_1(x_1), \ldots, q_r(x_r)$ have been recursively applied to $t_1, \ldots, t_r$, i.e., $q(c(t_1, \ldots, t_r)) = s_1 \cdot s_1' \cdot s_2 \cdot \ldots \cdot s_r \cdot s_r' \cdot s_{r+1}$, where $s_1' = q_1(t_1) \ldots s_r' = q_r(t_r)$. In Section 7 this match-replace intuition will be used to define an eponymous construct in our unparser-complete metalanguage.

Parsing $s_1 \cdot s_1' \cdot s_2 \cdot \ldots \cdot s_r \cdot s_r' \cdot s_{r+1}$ produces a parse tree $parse(s_1 \cdot s_1' \cdot s_2 \cdot \ldots \cdot s_r \cdot s_r' \cdot s_{r+1}) = < n, c > (s_1, t_1', s_2, \ldots, s_r, t_r', s_{r+1})$, where $t_1' \ldots t_r'$ are sub parse trees with top nonterminals $n_1 \ldots n_r$ and strings $s_1 \ldots s_{r+1}$ are the terminals. The abstract syntax tree is $desugar(< n, c > (s_1, t_1', s_2, \ldots, s_r, t_r', s_{r+1})) = c(t_1 \ldots t_r)$, where $t_1 = desugar(t_1'), \ldots, t_r = desugar(t_r')$, which is equal to the original abstract syntax tree. Since this relation holds for every production rule in a context-free language, the unparser can be defined using a top-down tree-to-string transducer for every context-free language. $\square$

The proof that $\mathcal{L}(G_{cfg}) \supseteq unparse(desugar(parse(\mathcal{L}(G_{cfg}))))$ also holds is very similar to the proof of Theorem 6.3. One should take the string s as starting point instead of the abstract syntax tree. The superset relation is a result of the fact that layout is not available in the abstract syntax tree and as a result it cannot be literally restored during unparsing. The language produced by the unparser is thus always a sentence of $\mathcal{L}(G_{cfg})$, but the set of sentences of $\mathcal{L}(G_{cfg})$ is greater than the set of sentences the unparser can produce.

Theorem 6.4. The relation $\mathcal{L}(G_{cfg}) \supseteq unparse(desugar(parse(\mathcal{L}(G_{cfg}))))$ holds for the unparser.

Proof. First, similarly to the proof of Theorem 6.3, the relation

$$\mathcal{L}(G_{ast}) = desugar(parse(unparse(\mathcal{L}(G_{ast}))))$$

holds when using a context-free grammar without production rules for layout syntax. Next we extend $\mathcal{L}(G_{cfg})$ with layout syntax resulting in $\mathcal{L}(G_{cfg})'$, then $\mathcal{L}(G_{cfg})' \supset \mathcal{L}(G_{cfg})$, since every sentence without layout must be in $\mathcal{L}(G_{cfg})'$, otherwise the languages are not semantical equal. Thus every sentence the unparser produce must be at least in $\mathcal{L}(G_{cfg})$, otherwise the *unparse* function does not meet the requirement of the unparser to be semantically transparent. $\square$

The last step is that we show that the unparser is linear and deterministic.

Theorem 6.5. The unparser of Definition 4.3 is a linear and deterministic top-down tree-to-string transducer.

```
<: match :>
  <: Matchpattern =:> String
  ...
  <: Matchpattern =:> String
<: end :>
```

Figure 5. Match-replace construct.

Proof. The derivation of an unparser using Definition 4.3 can be mapped on a top-down tree-to-string transducer. Considering Definition 4.3 the unparser contains actions of the form:

$$unparse(c) = s$$
$$unparse(c(x_1, \ldots, x_k)) = s_1 \cdot unparse(x_1) \cdot \ldots \cdot s_k$$
$$\cdot unparse(x_k) \cdot s_{k+1}$$

The similarity with the top-down tree-to-string transducer is obvious. Substitute the occurrences of *unparse* by states named q and the unparser becomes a tree-to-string transducer.

The unparser is linear, since each x_i occurs once on the left-hand side and once on the right-hand side.

The unparser is also deterministic, since it is derived from a context-free grammar augmented with signature labels, where each signature label is only used for one production rule. $\square$

These theorems show that an unparser can be specified using a linear deterministic top-down tree-to-string transducer.

So far we have shown that the unparser as defined in Definition 4.3 can be expressed by a linear deterministic top-down tree-to-string transducer. Recall that the top-down tree-to-string transducer is strictly less powerful than the Turing machine, i.e., top-down-tree-to-string transducers accept a subset of the languages Turing machines can accept [27]. Indeed, the class of tree languages a top-down tree-to-string transducer can recognize is equal to its corresponding finite tree automaton [12]. Unlike a Turing machine, a top-down tree-to-string transducer cannot change the input tree on which it operates but only emit a string while processing the input tree. The class of languages the top-down tree-to-string transducer accepts is the class of *path-closed tree languages* [27], being a subset of regular tree languages [9]. One can show that the languages of abstract syntax trees of the augmented grammar are path-closed, since a signature label is only used for one production rule.

7. Metalanguage

To verify the usefulness of unparser-completeness metalanguages in practice, we have designed a metalanguage for templates and applied it in a number of case studies, including a redesign of a domain-specific language for web information systems, reimplementation of the Java-back end of a tree-like data structures manipulation library ApiGen [5], dynamic XHTML generation and reimplementation of the state-machine-based code generator NunniFSMGen. In the current section we focus on the metalanguage itself, while in Section 8 we present the NunniFSMGen case study, and discussion of other case studies can be found in [2]

The metalanguage provides three constructs: match-replace, subtemplate invocation and substitution. The *match-replace* (Figure 5) is a construct containing a set of match-rules with a tree pattern and an accompanying result string. The result string may contain metalanguage constructs, which are evaluated recursively.

The match-replace matches the match-patterns against the current input tree in the context. At the start of evaluation, this is the complete input tree. In case a match-pattern is valid, the match-replace starts evaluating the string belonging to the match-rule. In the match-pattern variables may be bound, which can be used while evaluating the string belonging to the match-rule. After the string is evaluated, the result is used to replace the match-replace. This construct enables tree-matching, like the left-hand side of the state rules of the tree-to-string transducer.

The second construct is *subtemplate invocation*. Subtemplates allows to divide a template in multiple smaller units, but more important for unparser-completeness, is that this construct enables recursion. Two constructs are necessary to implement subtemplates, namely the declaration of subtemplates and the subtemplate call. The concrete syntax of a subtemplate declaration is `IdCon[ String ]`, while the syntax of a subtemplate call is `<: IdCon( Expr ) :>`. For instance, Figure 6 contains a subtemplate declaration *unparse* [...] , Lines 1–10 and five recursive subtemplate calls, e.g., `<:unparse($x):>` in Line 3. The template evaluator selects the subtemplate based on the identifier and it replaces the subtemplate call with the string resulting from the evaluated subtemplate. The `Expr` is used to obtain a new input data context for evaluating the subtemplate. Subtemplates support metavariable lookups, that return either a subtree of the input data or a terminal, i.e. a string value. For usability reasons, the `Expr` supports more operations than necessary. The constructs of declaring string constants and string concatenations (||) do not allow to change the input data tree, and thus not break unparser-completeness. Note that the template engine preserves layout information defined in the string and no additional layout, other than specified in the string, is emitted to the output.

The match-replace and subtemplate constructs are sufficient to implement unparsers, and, hence, any metalanguage implementing these constructs is (at least) unparser-complete. Figure 6 shows an unparser for the running example language expressed in the given template metalanguage. For the ease of comprehension, in Figure 6 and the subsequent figures demonstrating code fragments in the template metalanguage, we adhere to the following typesetting convention. Structural elements of the metalanguage, such as match and `<:` are typeset in the boldface; names of subtemplates and variables are typeset in the italics; labels are underlined, and, finally, the terminals, i.e., elements being directly placed in the output are typeset in roman.

For usability reasons we also include in our metalanguage a *substitution* construct that allows one to insert data from the input directly into the template. The syntax of the substitution is `<: Expr :>`. Example of the substitution construct can be found, e.g., in Line 7 of Figure 11. This line is responsible for outputting the string "class " followed by the class name, that consists of the value of the variable *$state* and the word "State", i.e., the template evaluator first determines the value of the expression between `<:` and `:>` which must yield a string, and then replaces with this value the placeholder in the template. One can show that the substitution can be written as a combination of subtemplates and match-replaces [2] and, hence, it does not extend new functionality of the metalanguage. This combination of subtemplates and match-replaces is, however, very verbose and frequently used, so we decided to provide an explicit construct for the substitution construct.

8. Case Study: Reimplementation NunniFSMGen

In this section we show that the metalanguage introduced in Section 7 is indeed usable to specify a non-trivial code generator. As the case study we consider reimplementation of NunniFSMGen[1]. NunniFSMGen translates an abstract specification of a finite state machine into an implementation in Java, C or C++. It uses the state design pattern [13] to implement the state machine in the different output languages. The original implementation is a single stage

[1] http://sourceforge.net/projects/nunnifsmgen/ (accessed on May 5, 2011)

```
1   unparse[
2   <: match :>
3     <:Not( $x )        =:> ~<:unparse( $x ):>
4     <:And( $x1 , $x2 )=:> <:unparse( $x1 ):> & <:unparse( $x2 ):>
5     <:Or( $x1 , $x2 ) =:> <:unparse( $x1 ):> | <:unparse( $x2 ):>
6     <:Br( $x )        =:> ( <:unparse( $x ):> )
7     <:True            =:> true
8     <:False           =:> false
9   <: end :>
10  ]
```

Figure 6. Unparser for booleans expressed in template metalanguage.

STANDBY	activate	WARMINGUP	warmup
STANDBY	deactivate	–	–
STANDBY	hotenough	ERROR	!
STANDBY	maintenance	MAINTENANCE	maintenance
WARMINGUP	activate	–	–
WARMINGUP	deactivate	STANDBY	heateroff
WARMINGUP	hotenough	STANDBY	heateroff
WARMINGUP	maintenance	MAINTENANCE	heateroff
ERROR	activate	–	–
ERROR	deactivate	–	–
ERROR	hotenough	–	–
ERROR	maintenance	MAINTENANCE	–
MAINTENANCE	activate	STANDBY	initialize
MAINTENANCE	deactivate	–	–
MAINTENANCE	hotenough	–	–
MAINTENANCE	maintenance	–	–

Figure 7. Transition table for a central heating system.

code generator using print statements, while we reimplemented it using a parser, a model transformation and templates.

8.1 Functionality of NunniFSMGen

NunniFSMGen is an open source tool developed by the Swiss-based company NunniSoft. NunniFSMGen can translate an abstraction specification of a state machine, given as a transition table, to a corresponding implementation in Java, C or C++. The transition table is a set of transition rules of the form `startState event nextState action`: if a state machine residing in the `startState`, receives an `event`, then the `action` is executed and the state of the machine is changed to `nextState`.

In general, the `action` is implemented as a method invocation. If, however, – is specified as an `action`, then no action is required when the transition is executed. Similarly, if – is specified as a `nextState`, then a transition rule does not cause a change of state. Finally, the `action` can also contain an exclamation mark, `!`. The exclamation mark defines that the action must throw an exception and after that the state machine will go the `errorState`.

Example 8.1. Figure 7 shows the transition table of a central heating system example delivered with NunniFSMGen. Figure 8 presents a snippet of a parser used to obtain an abstract syntax tree representation of the state machine. The model transformation presented in Section 8.2 uses this abstract syntax tree as input.

8.2 State Machine Implementation

NunniFSMGen implements a variant of the state pattern using the transition table as input, where the events are handles and the states are implemented as concrete states. The transition table cannot be used directly for generating the code using our template metalanguage. The state pattern has a hierarchical structure, where each state implements handlers for each event, while the transition table is list of vectors pointing from the `startState` to the `nextState`.

```
rules ([
  transition ("STANDBY","activate",
    nextstate ("WARMINGUP"), action ("warmup")),
  ...
  transition ("MAINTENANCE","maintenance",
                    nonextstate , noaction )
])
```

Figure 8. Part of the abstract syntax tree of the transition table of the central heating system.

```
afsm (
  transitions ([
    transition ( "STANDBY", events ([
      event ("activate",
              nextstate ("WARMINGUP"), action ("warmup") ),
      event ("deactivate", nonextstate , noaction ),
      event ("hotenough", nextstate ("ERROR"),
                                  erroraction ),
      event ("maintenance", nextstate ("MAINTENANCE"),
                              action ("maintain") ) ])),
    ...
  ]),
  events ([ "activate", "deactivate",
            "hotenough", "maintenance" ]),
  actions ([ "warmup","maintain","heateroff",
                            "initialize" ])
)
```

Figure 9. Abstract implementation of the state design pattern of the heater transition table.

A model transformation is necessary to map the vector based transition table to the hierarchical based state design pattern. First, the transformation collects all unique events from the transition rules and stores them in the set `events`. Then, it collects all unique actions from the transition rules and stores them in the set `actions`. Finally, it creates a new `transition` rule for each state and adds for each event a triple with the `event`, the `nextState` and the `action`. Transition rules are collected in the set `transitions`.

Implementation of this model transformation is straight-forward. It contains seven equations based on 18 sub-equations. The abstract implementation of the state design pattern of the central heating system is shown in Figure 9. The square brackets denote list, an additional feature of the used tree format.

8.3 Original Code Generator

The original implementation of NunniFSMGen is a generator based on print statements written in Java. Its main class contains a simple parser for the input transition table, constructing a one-to-one in memory representation of the transition table.

For each output language a code generator class is implemented, containing the generator logic and object code fragments. Based on the selected output language a code generator class is instantiated and provided with the loaded input data.

We consider such a code generator class as a single-stage code generator, since the different code generator classes share a significant amount of code. The shared code is not factorized out in a model transformation. Furthermore, since it is a single-stage code generator, the model transformations are mostly entangled between object code artifacts. During the initialization of the code generator, only the set of events and the set of states are calculated.

To illustrate the adverse effects of the single-stage code generation used in NunniFSMGen consider the generation of the particular code for an event. Implementation of the required behavior is selected based on a set of conditions distinguishing

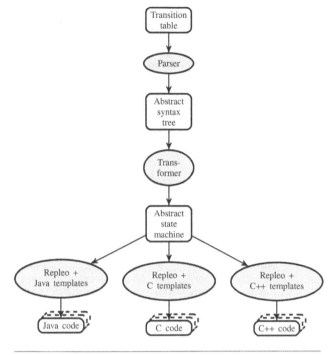

Figure 10. Architecture of the reimplemented NunniFSMGen.

between the following five kinds of events: no state change, no action (`startState event - -`); no state change, with action (`startState event - action`); state change, no action (`startState event nextState -`); state change, with action (`startState event nextState action`); state change to `error-State` with error action (`startState event errorState !`). Since NunniFSMGen exists of three almost independent single-stage code emitters for C, C++ and Java, the set of conditions corresponding to the choice of the implementation is cloned between the code emitters. Moreover, similarity between C++ and Java means that the code emitters for these languages are almost identical, except for the object code. In case of the code emitter for C, the meta code is almost the same, but the approach used to implement the exception handling in the object code differs from the C++ and Java implementations.

8.4 Reimplemented Code Generator

The reimplementation of NunniFSMGen is based on a two-stage architecture using a parser, a model transformation phase and templates. The previous discussed input model parser and model transformations are output language independent. The output is an abstract syntax of a state machine, which is still output language independent. The templates in the second stage contain the additional information in the object code to implement an output language specific instantiation of a state machine. In this case for output languages, C, C++ and Java, a set of templates is defined.

Code shared by the templates is limited to the meta code responsible for traversing the input data tree: while all templates use the same abstract representation of the state machine as input data, tailored model transformations are unnecessary for each one of the output languages. In this way the model transformation has been separated from the part of the code generator that depends on the output language. The architecture of the reimplemented NunniF-SMGen is shown in Figure 10. The templates are evaluated by Repleo [2]. Repleo is a template engine based on the unparser-complete metalanguage as defined in this article.

```
1   transitions[
2   <: match :>
3     <:[transition( $state , $events),
4          $transitions] =:>
5       template[
6          <: $state + "State.java" :>,
7          class <: $state + "State" :> extends State
8          {
9            ...
10         }
11     ]
12     <: transitions($transitions) :>
13   <: [] =:>
14   <: end :>
15  ]
```

Figure 11. Java snippet of the template implementation.

```
1   eventcode[
2   static int <: $state + "State" + $event :>
3       ( struct FSM *fsm ,
4         void * o ) {
5     int ret = 0;
6     ...
7     <: match $nextstate :>
8       <: nextstate($nextstatename) =:>
9        if ( ret < 0 )
10          fsm->changeState( fsm ,
11            &m_ErrorState );
12       else
13          fsm->changeState( fsm ,
14            &<: "m_" + $nextstatename
15              + "State" :> );
16     <: nonextstate =:>
17        if ( ret < 0 )
18          fsm->changeState( fsm ,
19            &m_ErrorState );
20     <: end :>
21     ...
22     return ret;
23  }
24  ]
```

Figure 12. C snippet of the template implementation.

Figures 11 and 12 show snippets of the reimplementation using templates in Java and C, respectively. For the sake of brevity we do not include the reimplementation in C++, which can be found in [2]. Observe the use of the built-in template *template* (e.g., Figure 11, Lines 5–11). The template engine evaluates the second argument of *template* and stores the result in a file with the name obtained by evaluating its first argument. So, if *$state* is STANDBY then, evaluation of Lines 5–11 of Figure 11 results in storing the Java code generated by Lines 7–10 in the file called STANDBYState.java.

8.5 Evaluation

The introduction of templates based on an unparser-complete metalanguage has improved the NunniFSMGen implementation. The new implementation uses a two-stage architecture, where the old implementation almost directly generates code from the transition table in a single-stage architecture. The two-stage architecture including the unparser-complete metalanguage enforced a clear separation between the model transformation and the code generation. The first stage parses and rewrites the transition table in order to get an abstract implementation of the state design pattern. The second stage is responsible for generating the concrete code for the different output languages.

We expect that the strict separation between the model transformation and the code generation reduces the implementation effort required to add a new output language. Furthermore, the original code generator contains code clones between emitters for the different output languages. Presence of clones might lead to diverging evolution of the emitters, i.e., a risk of inconsistent behavior of, e.g., Java and C implementations of the same state machine. By separating model transformation encapsulating the shared code from code generation depending on the target language, we successfully eliminate the cross-emitter clones. Clone elimination is also apparent in the counts of source lines of code in the original implementation vs. the reimplementation: 1430 vs. 738 source lines of code.

Clearly, while the templates foster reuse and help in eliminating of the cross-emitter clones, there is still the potential for cloned templates. No cloned templates were found in the reimplementation. In general, cloned templates are an indication of a non-optimal design.

9. Related work

Numerous template engines and associated metalanguages can be found both in the academia and the industry [4, 16, 21, 25]. Unfortunately, formal expressivity requirements of such languages have attracted less attention from the research community with [21] being the only notable exception we are aware of. Similarly to [21] we advocate the separation between the view and the model.

ERb [16] is a text template interpreter for the programming language Ruby. ERb introduces special syntax constructs to embed Ruby code in a text file. The metalanguage of ERb is Ruby and thus Turing-complete, as a result there is no restriction on the code ERb can generate. However, to implement an unparser, a developer should take into account that metavariables are globally accessible and writable. Hence, it is necessary to specify a stack mechanism in the meta-code explicitly.

JSP [4] is a template based system developed by Sun Microsystems. It is designed for generating dynamic web pages and XML messages in Java-based enterprise systems, where the evaluation is tuned for performance. The Java language is available as metalanguage in JSP pages, although special tag libraries are available to provide concise constructs. JSP supports variables and a `for` loop, and hence, JSP goes beyond the unparser-completeness. Moreover, it has the same problem with scoping of meta-variables as ERb. It is necessary to use different scopes for different variables, introducing unwanted boilerplate code.

Velocity [25] is a template evaluator for Java. It provides a basic template metalanguage, called Velocity Template Language, to reference Java objects. The metalanguage of Velocity is also Turing-complete, as it is possible to set variables. In case of implementing unparsers, Velocity has the same problem with the variable scopes as ERb and JSP. As a consequence temporary variables are necessary when a subtemplate is recursively called.

The main lessons learned from the related template engines is that not only the available constructs are important, but also the variable scope handling in the evaluator. Furthermore, the metalanguage should be powerful enough to handle all (path-closed) regular tree languages. For example, StringTemplate [21] is not capable of referring to the different children of a node if the children have the same label. An extra input data transformation is necessary to guarantee the input tree can be accepted by StringTemplate.

We have used the ideas of unparser-completeness to construct the new version of a metalanguage for our template engine Repleo [3]. Repleo supports syntax-safe template evaluation, i.e., it guarantees that the generator always instantiates a sentence belonging to the desired output language or in case it cannot produce such a sentence, that the evaluator terminates with an error message. The first version of Repleo [3] was based on a metalanguage inspired by ERb [16] and the ideas of [21]. Two major differences can be found between the first version of the metalanguage and the current one. First, the metalanguage of [3] provides a broader set of expressions, allowing the template designer to violate the separation of concerns principle, e.g., by defining mathematical operations on the input data. Second, the metalanguage of [3] did not support recursive template evaluation, which is necessary for unparser-completeness. The reimplementation of Repleo [2] is based on the notion of unparser-completeness, such as presented in this article.

Finally, *unparse* and *desugar ∘ parse* can be seen as inverse to each other. Such properties as linearity (cf. Theorem 4.6) are often assumed in studies of program inversion [14]. Furthermore, relation between parsers and unparsers (pretty printers) was studied in [1, 23]. We stress, however, that our goal is different: unlike [1, 23] we do not focus on finding a unified framework for parsers and unparsers but apply these interrelated notions to formalize the requirements for a metalanguage of a template engine in the context of the model view controller architecture.

10. Conclusions

In this paper, following the ideas of Parr [21], we have presented a formal notion of unparser-completeness. Unparser-completeness of a metalanguage provides the balance between expressivity and restrictiveness. On one hand, the metalanguage is expressive enough to implement an unparser, and, hence, can instantiate any semantically correct program in the object language. On the other hand, the metalanguage is restricted enough to enforce the model-view separation in terms of Parr [21].

Next, we showed that a linear deterministic top-down tree-to-string transducer is powerful enough to implement an unparser. Using the notion of the top-down tree-to-string transducer we have shown that unparser-completeness is a weaker notion than Turing completeness, i.e., unparser-complete meta-languages are not necessarily Turing-complete. The enforcement of separation of concerns is also met, as this transducer does not allow to express calculations or modify the model.

At the end, we showed that unparser-completeness is not only a theoretical framework. We reimplemented NunniFSMGen using templates based on an unparser-complete metalanguage. This metalanguage enforces us to use a two-stage architecture for the reimplementation, which resulted in an improved separation between model transformations and code emitting.

References

[1] A. Alimarine, S. Smetsers, A. van Weelden, M. C. J. D. van Eekelen, and M. J. Plasmeijer. There and back again: arrows for invertible programming. In *ACM SIGPLAN workshop on Haskell*, pages 86–97, New York, NY, USA, 2005. ACM.

[2] B. J. Arnoldus. *An Illumination of the Template Enigma: Software Code Generation with Templates*. PhD thesis, Technische Universiteit Eindhoven, 2010.

[3] B. J. Arnoldus, J. W. Bijpost, and M. G. J. van den Brand. Repleo: a Syntax-Safe Template Engine. In *GPCE '07*, pages 25–32, New York, NY, USA, 2007. ACM Press.

[4] H. Bergsten. *Javaserver Pages*. O'Reilly & Associates, Inc., Sebastopol, CA, USA, 2nd edition, 2002.

[5] M. G. J. van den Brand, P. E. Moreau, and J. J. Vinju. A generator of efficient strongly typed abstract syntax trees in Java. *IEE Proceedings Software*, 152(2):70–78, 2005.

[6] M. G. J. van den Brand and E. Visser. Generation of formatters for context-free languages. *ACM Transactions on Software Engineering and Methodology*, 5(1):1–41, 1996.

[7] S. Burbeck. Applications Programming in Smalltalk-80: How to use Model-View- Controller (MVC), 1992.

[8] L. G. W. A. Cleophas. Private communication, September 2009.

[9] H. Comon, M. Dauchet, R. Gilleron, C. Löding, F. Jacquemard, D. Lugiez, S. Tison, and M. Tommasi. Tree Automata Techniques and Applications. Available on: http://www.grappa.univ-lille3.fr/tata (accessed on November 30, 2010), 2008. release November, 18th 2008.

[10] F. L. Deremer. *Practical Translators for LR(k) languages*. PhD thesis, Massachusetts Institute of Technology, Cambridge, MA, USA, 1969.

[11] J. Engelfriet. Tree Automata and Tree Grammars. Manual written lecture notes, 1974.

[12] J. Engelfriet, G. Rozenberg, and G. Slutzki. Tree transducers, L systems, and two–way machines. *Journal of Computer and System Sciences*, 20(2):150–202, 1980.

[13] E. Gamma, R. Helm, R. Johnson, and J. Vlissides. *Design patterns: elements of reusable object-oriented software*. Addison-Wesley Longman Publishing Co., Boston, MA, USA, 1995.

[14] R. Glück and M. Kawabe. A program inverter for a functional language with equality and constructors. In A. Ohori, editor, *Programming Languages and Systems*, volume 2895 of *LNCS*, pages 246–264. Springer, 2003.

[15] J. Hartmanis. Context-free languages and Turing machine computations. In *Symposia in Applied Mathematics*, volume 19 of *Mathematical Aspects of Computer Science*, pages 42–51. Amer Mathematical Society, 1967.

[16] J. Herrington. *Code Generation in Action*. Manning Publications Co., Greenwich, CT, USA, 2003.

[17] S. C. Johnson. Yacc: Yet Another Compiler-Compiler. Technical Report 32, Bell Laboratories, Murray Hill, NJ, USA, 1975.

[18] P. Klint, T van der Storm, and J. J. Vinju. RASCAL: A Domain Specific Language for Source Code Analysis and Manipulation. In *SCAM '09*, pages 168–177, Los Alamitos, CA, USA, 2009. IEEE Computer Society Press.

[19] G. E. Krasner and S. T. Pope. A description of the model-view-controller user interface paradigm in the Smalltalk-80 system. *Journal of Object Oriented Programming*, 1(3):26–49, 1988.

[20] D. C. Oppen. Pretty printing. Technical Report STAN-CS-79-770, Computer Science Department, Stanford University, October 1979.

[21] T. J. Parr. Enforcing Strict Model-View Separation in Template Engines. In *WWW '04: International Conference on World Wide Web*, pages 224–233, New York, NY, USA, 2004. ACM Press.

[22] N. Ramsey. Unparsing expressions with prefix and postfix operators. *Software: Practice & Experience*, 28(12):1327–1356, 1998.

[23] T. Rendel and K. Ostermann. Invertible syntax descriptions: unifying parsing and pretty printing. In *ACM SIGPLAN Haskell symposium*, pages 1–12, New York, NY, USA, 2010. ACM.

[24] T. Sheard. Accomplishments and Research Challenges in Meta-programming. In *SAIG*, volume 2196 of *LNCS*, pages 2–44, London, UK, 2001. Springer.

[25] T. Sturm, J. von Voss, and M. Boger. Generating Code from UML with Velocity Templates. In J.-M. Jézéquel, H. Hußmann, and S. Cook, editors, *UML*, volume 2460 of *LNCS*, pages 150–161. Springer, 2002.

[26] M. G. J. van den Brand, J. S. Scheerder, J. J. Vinju, and E. Visser. Disambiguation filters for scannerless generalized LR parsers. In R. Horspool, editor, *Compiler Construction*, volume 2304 of *LNCS*, pages 21–44. Springer, 2002.

[27] J. Virágh. Deterministic ascending tree automata I. *Acta Cybernetica*, 5:33–42, 1981.

[28] E. Visser. Stratego: A language for Program Transformation based on Rewriting Strategies. System Description of Stratego 0.5. In *RTA '01*, volume 2051 of *LNCS*, pages 357–361, Berlin, Heidelberg, 2001. Springer.

[29] D. S. Wile. Abstract syntax from concrete syntax. In *ICSE*, pages 472–480, New York, NY, USA, 1997. ACM Press.

Towards Automatic Generation of Formal Specifications to Validate and Verify Reliable Distributed Systems

A Method Exemplified by an Industrial Case Study

Vidar Slåtten   Frank Alexander Kraemer   Peter Herrmann

Norwegian University of Science and Technology (NTNU),
Department of Telematics, N-7491 Trondheim, Norway.
{vidarsl, kraemer, herrmann}@item.ntnu.no

Abstract

The validation and verification of reliable systems is a difficult and complex task, mainly for two reasons: First, it is difficult to precisely state which formal properties a system needs to fulfil to be of high quality. Second, it is complex to automatically verify such properties, due to the size of the analysis state space which grows exponentially with the number of components. We tackle these problems by a tool-supported method which embeds application functionality in building blocks that use UML activities to describe their internal behaviour. To describe their externally visible behaviour, we use a combination of complementary interface contracts, so-called ESMs and EESMs. In this paper, we present an extension of the interface contracts, External Reliability Contracts (ERCs), that capture failure behaviour. This separation of different behavioural aspects in separate descriptions facilitates a two-step analysis, in which the first step is completely automated and the second step is facilitated by an automatic translation of the models to the input syntax of the model checker TLC. Further, the cascade of contracts is used to separate the work of domain and reliability experts. The concepts are proposed with the background of a real industry case, and we demonstrate how the use of interface contracts leads to significantly smaller state spaces in the analysis.

Categories and Subject Descriptors   C.0 [*General*]: Systems specification methodology;   C.2.4 [*Computer-Communication Networks*]: Distributed Systems—Distributed applications; D.2.2 [*Software Engineering*]: Design Tools and Techniques—Computer-aided software engineering (CASE);   D.2.4 [*Software Engineering*]: Software/Program Verification—Formal methods, Model checking, Reliability;   D.2.13 [*Software Engineering*]: Reusable Software

General Terms   Design, Reliability, Verification

Keywords   Model-driven engineering, reliable systems, fault tolerance, component contracts, compositional verification, model checking

1. Introduction

Since nearly half a century ago, theoretical computer scientists have developed a plethora of techniques to model and to verify software in a formal way. In spite of several outstanding results, however, formal methods are still not used that much in practise. A likely reason is the complexity of many methods which tend not only to be laborious but also require a considerable amount of expertise. Hence, to make the application of formal techniques more popular in software development, they must be much simpler and faster to use. An approach to achieve this is through model-driven engineering, for instance on the basis of UML or SDL. These languages can be effectively used to describe software in such a way that implementations can be automatically generated from them. Further, formal methods may be used to analyze them, as they often give an appropriate level of abstraction. In this way, models can be used as front-ends for formal tools, which leads to what Rushby [24] calls "disappearing formal methods."

Our method SPACE and its tool Arctis [14, 18] are designed with this strategy in mind and optimized for the development of reactive, distributed applications. System behaviour is modelled by UML activities that due to their token semantics similar to Petri-nets [16, 22] can be easily understood. The activities have been provided with a reactive formal semantics [16] such that both automatic code generation [14, 18] and formal analysis [18] are possible. Moreover, this modelling technique is scalable since activities can be composed using UML call behavior actions, which we refer to as *blocks*. A block may both embed an activity and be a part of another one. The interaction between the two activities is modelled by UML pins through which tokens flow when transferring from one activity to the other. The behaviour at this interface is modelled by contracts in the form of so-called External State Machines (ESMs, [15]) and an extended version of them (EESMs, [26]). This allows for storing blocks in libraries and re-using them in different software models (see [15]).

Arctis facilitates the formal analysis of system models for important, generally desirable software properties by using a model checker [18]. Since the model checker does its analysis by an exhaustive search of the reachable system states, it works fully automatically. Further, error traces can be animated on the UML activities such that the Arctis users do not need a deeper understanding of the formalism laying behind the analysis.

A disadvantage of model checking is that models of realistic systems often comprise too many system states to be checked in an acceptable amount of time. This is due to the combinatorial blow-up in the number of states when combining component behaviours, known as the state explosion problem. In Arctis, we mitigate this problem by compositional verification (see [18]). In particular, we use the interface contracts to reduce the system verification to a number of local verification runs each concerning only a single activity as well as a number of (E)ESMs. Thus, the number of states to be model checked grows linearly with the number of the activities in the system model instead of increasing exponentially.

However, while this strategy works to ensure that each building block is well-formed from a local point of view, for some systems we also need to check application-specific system properties. This holds especially for properties with respect to reliability, i.e., to check how a system reacts in the presence of communication and process failures. The need to consider the system with a larger scope and the presence of failures increases the complexity (and hence, the state space) drastically, simply because of the higher degree of concurrency. Furthermore, mechanisms to improve reliability often employ multiple instances of a given type for redundacy (see, for instance [19]). Here, one has to take also data that distinguishes the individual instances into account, which further escalates the state space to be checked.

This paper is devoted to demonstrating how compositional verification can mitigate the state explosion problem for reliable systems. To achieve that, we validate the concept of EESMs [26] by showing how they are applied in an industrial case study where we were contracted to add a fault-tolerant best-effort mutual exclusion protocol to an existing system of intelligent clothes lockers for hospitals (see Sect. 2). In Sect. 3, we describe our development method for reliable systems, extended from earlier work considering just message loss [27], and the specifications created for the case study. In addition, we show how the activities and contracts are transformed into TLA$^+$ [20], the input language of the TLC model checker [29]. In contrast to proofs of system functionality, not all theorems specifying the reliability properties to be verified can be automatically generated at the moment. Instead, we demonstrate the flexibility of the framework by showing how the best-effort mutual exclusion property can be expressed by an expert (see Sect. 3.2). Furthermore, in Sect. 4, we introduce a novel extension we call External Reliability Contracts (ERCs) as a way to handle the effects of process crashes and message loss in a compositional manner, while still being able to verify larger system sizes under failure-free semantics. We show that our variant of compositional verification gives significant savings over monolithic verification and discuss our findings, in Sect. 5 We survey some related work in Sect. 6 and conclude in Sect. 7.

2. Texi Case Study: Lockers that Read RFID

Texi AS is a company that delivers RFID-based logistics systems to organize work wear, typically for hospitals. All clothes have a small RFID tag sewn into the fabric, which is used to track the clothes during the entire usage cycle. Our case study focuses on the lockers in the hospital that store the clothes and make them available to the hospital staff. The lockers are equipped with antennas that can read the RFID tags, so that they know which clothes are stored in them.

When employees want new clothes, they swipe their employee card through a card reader. The locker then checks if the employee is allowed access to the locker. If the employee has access, the door is unlocked. After the clothes are removed and the door is closed again, the reading process is started to see which clothes have been removed by the employee.

A typical installation in a hospital has many lockers that stand next to each other, and the reading process of the antennas takes several seconds. For that reason it is likely that several employees access closely located lockers simultaneously. This can lead to wrong reading results, since the antennas may interfere once two or more lockers read at the same time.

For this reason, we introduced a solution that delays the reading within lockers so that only one locker may read at a time. Obvi-

ously, this can be achieved by introducing a central controller that takes the role of coordinator among all lockers that are in danger of interference. A locker then has to obtain permission before it may activate its antennas. Such a solution, however, introduces several single points of failure. If the central controller goes down, or if a locker does not release its read permission, all further reading requests from other lockers will not be answered and employees will not be able to get their work wear. For that reason, we had to develop a more robust solution, where a locker can carry on alone, if other parts of the system fail.

2.1 System Requirements

According to Texi, the requirements for the improved system are the following: If possible, only one locker shall read its contents at a time. However, availability should still have priority over this mutual exclusion property, since the possible inconsistencies due to concurrent reading can be manually corrected, but a blocked locker would hinder hospital work. Hence, we cannot use a mutual exclusion algorithm that blocks if a locker is unable to contact the central controller. Instead we create a protocol that attempts to provide mutual exclusion of locker reads, but does not necessarily provide it in the presence of process crashes and message loss.

While it is easy to express a mutual exclusion property, *"no two lockers should have permission to read their contents at the same time,"* it is not straightforward to express the kind of best-effort mutual exclusion property (in the following called *BEME* property) that our customer requests. For our protocol, the BEME property can be expressed as a mutual exclusion property that is conditional on the absence of message loss and process crashes. We note that message loss is indistinguishable from a long delay. Thus, such events can be explicitly modelled in the form of timeout events. The same goes for process crashes, which we can model as a transition to a state where no further events can take place in the crashed component of the system, except a restart event. With this in place, we might simply state the BEME property to be *"as long as no timeout or crash has occurred, the mutual exclusion property must hold."* However, this does not say anything about whether the system will recover from a faulty state and go back to providing the mutual exclusion property once a sufficiently long time has passed without further crashes or timeouts taking place. To include this, we can express the BEME property as *"if there is a time after which no further timeouts or crashes occur, then there will eventually be a time where the mutual exclusion property holds forever."* In addition to the BEME property, the customer naturally wants the system to be free from any deadlock scenarios and that all read requests are eventually granted.

Next, we will introduce our method and the specification of the case study before we revisit the BEME property in Sect. 3.2.

3. The Method for Reliable Systems

As explained above, the main specification element of the SPACE method are building blocks, expressed by UML activities and encapsulated by formal contracts. Within the method, we distinguish three levels of descriptions for the external contracts of a building block that have different significance with respect to the overall development workflow:

- External State Machines (ESMs, [15]) are UML state machines that describe the order in which parameter pins on the building blocks may be used. ESMs do not consider any data or sessions (multiple instances of a block), which in many cases is sufficient to explain how blocks are to be assembled correctly to more comprehensive applications. The complexity of the analysis is also limited, so that checking whether the blocks are correctly integrated can be performed in the background of the editing process, without interrupting the user.

- Extended ESMs (EESM, [26]) are an extension of ESMs that adds actions and guards on data variables. This is especially useful for mechanisms that increase the reliability of systems, since they often require multiple instances of the same block, i.e., sessions. Since session IDs are data, EESMs may capture relations of several sessions, or simply count how often a certain action has been executed. Thus, EESMs are more expressive than ESMs, but this comes at the cost that the verification with EESMs is more complex. This analysis is therefore carried out in an extra step with temporal logic as the basis (see Sect. 3.2).

- External Reliability Contracts (ERCs, introduced in this paper) add yet another layer to the contracts. They amend (E)ESMs by describing behaviour that results from communication and process failures. In principle, this behaviour could be directly expressed within the (E)ESMs. However, we have observed that this behaviour is often orthogonal to the original, purely functional behaviour described by (E)ESMs. It can therefore be expressed separately, much like an aspect in aspect-oriented programming. This also has the benefit that systems may be analyzed both with and without failures, as discussed later.

To make our method practical, we also take into account the level of expertise that is needed to fulfil a certain task. Therefore, we identify two groups of engineers:

- *Domain experts*, who are familiar with a certain application domain and relevant technologies, such as for example RFID and embedded systems. Domain experts have programming skills and may also model on the level of UML activities, but do not need the ability to formulate and verify temporal theorems, for instance.

- *Reliability experts*, who are familiar with reliability problems and possible solutions, and who are also familiar with the necessary formal methods to assure system quality with respect to reliability. To optimally utilize their expertise, we assume that reliability experts are hired on a case-by-case basis. Therefore the method should be optimized to keep their overhead regarding non-reliability related questions low, as we will discuss in the following.

Within a verification project [2], in which we apply our tool to industrial cases such as the one presented, we see that this categorization is quite to the point. With respect to these roles, we expect our method to be used in the following way, as illustrated in Fig. 1:

1. Domain experts create the main part of the application by composing building blocks. We have measured that up to 71% of blocks may be reused from libraries (see [15]). This may already include some building blocks provided by reliability experts, if their necessity is obvious or if the domain expert already knows these blocks from previous projects. For the domain expert it is often sufficient to look at the (simple) ESMs to integrate building blocks correctly into a system.

2. The basic analysis (A_1) is executed in the background, so that the resulting specification S is at least well-formed and describes consistent compositions of the building blocks, as far as the ESMs are concerned. This eases the job of the reliability expert, since many inconsistencies and ambiguities are already removed.

3. The consistent model S is handed over to a reliability expert, who performs an in-depth analysis A_2 using the model checker TLC [29]. TLA$^+$ [20], the input language of TLC, is generated automatically from the UML model, now also including

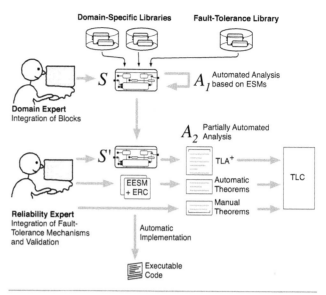

Figure 1. The development method

the variables, actions and guards contributed by EESMs. Some systems, such as the one presented in our case study, require also application-specific properties for which the reliability expert formulates the corresponding theorems, as explained in Sect. 3.2.

4. To verify properties also with realistic assumptions including faulty channels and crashing processes, the ERCs of the building blocks are taken into account, or, where necessary, introduced.

The results of A_2 may require that additional fault-tolerance mechanisms are introduced or given functionality is changed. Depending on the extent of the changes, these are either done by the reliability expert alone, or in cooperation with the domain expert. These decisions may also require feedback from the customer, when consequences of failures and remedies have to be taken into account. In our case study, for instance, Texi had to make the trade-off between data consistency and locker availability.

5. From a consistent specification, executable code can be generated by a model transformation from the UML activities to state machines and a subsequent code generation step. This step is completely automated, and we verified that the code generation preserves system constraints [14]. It is hence guaranteed that this code also fulfils the properties of the original specification.

Needless to say, this method is an idealized workflow that serves as an orientation rather than an inflexible corset. In practise, the separation between the experts may be less distinct than described. In addition, since building blocks may be checked back into the library, complete solutions that already take reliability concerns into account may be directly applied by domain experts. In [19], for instance, we developed a robust leader election protocol. Although the protocol is not trivial, the resulting building block is so easy to handle that it can be integrated by a domain expert without any trouble.

3.1 System Design in SPACE

In the following, we focus on the parts of the system that deal with mutual exclusion between lockers, and do not further detail

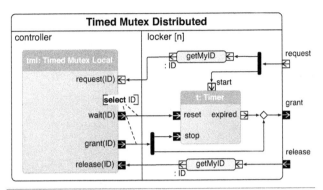

Figure 2. UML activity showing the mutual exclusion protocol

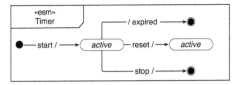

Figure 3. ESM of the Timer block

other functionality. We assume that steps 1 and 2 have already been carried out, and focus now on the work of the reliability expert.

Figure 2 shows the UML activity for the Timed Mutex Distributed building block that we created to implement the mutual exclusion protocol. Partitions represent separate components of the system that are physically distributed. They are named in the upper left corner, in this case *controller* and *locker*. The fact that there can be more than one locker is represented by *[n]* after the name of the locker partition. To distinguish the different lockers, each of them has a specific ID. In the implementation, we have chosen the IP address of each locker as its ID. The single controller partition contains a building block *Timed Mutex Local*, which implements the locally concentrated part of the protocol.

UML activities have a semantics based on token flows. For the building blocks, we use a *reactive* variant of them [16], in which tokens flow in run-to-completion steps (so-called *activity steps*), each of which are triggered by an observable event, either the expiration of a timer or the reception of a signal.

Each locker partition of the building block can receive a request for the read permission via the starting pin named *request*, through which a token enters the activity, travels along the edge to the fork node and is duplicated. One duplicate enters the Timer block via pin *start*. The other passes through operation *getMyID*, which retrieves the ID of the locker, and comes to rest at the partition border between the locker and the controller partition. All tokens rest between partitions, as message passing is asynchronous, meaning that the sending and receiving of a message are two different events.

Two activity steps are now enabled: One step is triggered by the token on the topmost edge arriving at its destination and entering the block Timed Mutex Local via pin *request(ID)*. Another possibility is for the timer to emit a token. To see why this can happen, we must consider the external contract of the Timer block.

The ESM of block *Timer* is shown in Fig. 3. It shows that once a token has passed via the *start* pin, the block may spontaneously emit a token via its *expired* pin and will also accept tokens via the pins *stop* and *reset*. Therefore, a possible next event is that the timer expires, releasing a token through the *expired* pin, via the merge node and on through the *grant* pin of the locker partition. Hence, this timer ensures that no locker is blocked from reading its contents by the controller crashing or a communications failure.

Figure 4 shows the EESM of the Timed Mutex Local block, and thus also the behaviour we can expect from it. EESMs are different from ESMs in that their state does not just consist of the control state like *active*, but also the values assigned to any variables they have (i.e., they are *extended* finite state machines [6]). Due to the extra variables, EESMs are initialized implicitly, as shown by the transition from the initial state, at the very left. That is, the initial transition is executed together with the startup of the component (modelled by a top-level partition) the building block is part of. In

the case of Timed Mutex Local, the EESM tracks two sets, the IDs that have been sent through pin *request* and the same for pin *grant*. An EESM also takes into account that a block can be instantiated as *multi-session*, which means that several instances of a block execute concurrently. Therefore, every variable of the EESM is an array in which each block instance has its own index, i. Note that in Fig. 2, only one instance of the Timed Mutex Local block is instantiated, so i is always 1.

The EESM only allows one request from each ID for each block instance at a time. To express this, the transition labelled *request(i, ID)* has a guard stating that for a *request(i, ID)* event to happen, that ID must not already be in the set *requests[i]*. Further, the transition has an operation, written in a lined rectangle, that specifies that the new ID is added to the set represented by *requests[i]*. A *wait(i, ID)* transition can only take place if the block has already received a request from that ID, but not yet sent out a grant. A *grant(i, ID)* transition has the exact same guard as *wait(i, ID)*, but has an additional operation to update the *grants* variable. The *release(i, ID)* transition is only enabled when ID has been granted. This transition resets the contract with respect to that ID by removing it from both the requests and grants set, allowing new requests with that ID.

Looking back at Fig. 2, we see that a token released from the *wait(ID)* pin of block *tml*, denoted *tml:wait(ID)*, will need to rest at the partition border before being received by the locker it is destined for. As there are several lockers, a select statement [17] is used to only send the message to the locker with the address given in the ID parameter of the token. Upon arrival at the locker, the token originating from *tml:wait(ID)* will enter the *reset* pin of the Timer block, hence delaying the expiration of the timer. If the timer has already expired when this happens, the semantics of the contract is that the token is discarded as it attempts to enter the block via a pin that the contract, in its current state, does not allow tokens to pass. During our analysis, such a scenario raises a warning so that the developer can make sure it is intentional.[1]

The events following a token being released via *tml:grant(ID)* are similar to the above, only here, the token is duplicated upon arrival at the locker to both stop the timer and pass through the *grant* pin of the Timed Mutex Distributed block itself. The EESM of Timed Mutex Distributed, shown in Fig. 5,[2] does not permit more than one grant without a release and request in-between, for that locker instance. If a grant has already happened, the token will be discarded when trying to leave the block via the grant pin, just like a token trying to enter a block at the wrong time. The EESM also tells us that a token can enter the Timed Mutex Distributed block via pin *release* if that locker instance has received

---

[1] Note that this filtering effect only applies when the contract can decide if a transition is enabled based solely on local information. An EESM transition with a guard that refers to a remote variable (e.g., another component instance being in a specific state) cannot filter out tokens, hence any violations are real errors.

[2] When an EESM does not use any data apart from session IDs and transitions do not reference other sessions, we present it in a simpler way that looks like an ESM except for the additional index *(i)* on every transition label [26].

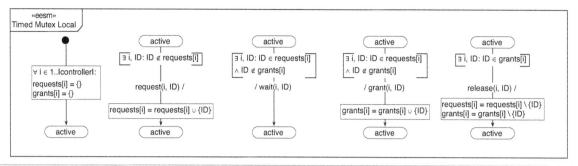

Figure 4. EESM of the Timed Mutex Local block

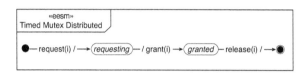

Figure 5. EESM of the Timed Mutex Distributed block

a grant. This will cause the token to be sent towards the controller component and received in a later step to enter *tml:release(ID)*, resetting its EESM with respect to that ID.

The activity of the Timed Mutex Local block is shown in Fig. 6. The protocol to ensure mutual exclusion is implemented by a combination of two blocks: The block of type Mutex ensures that only one locker is given read permission at a time and keeps track of the lockers that have requested permission. The Wait block is taking care of the notification towards each individual locker. It is instantiated as a multi-session block, which means that it is executed with several instances, one for each locker ID, signified by the additional shadow around it and the parameter *(n)*. This session pattern simplifies the modelling of concurrent behaviour, since each session instance only has to keep track of the protocol state of a single locker.

Due to space constraints, we do not show the contracts of Mutex and Wait, but give an informal overview of the behaviour of Timed Mutex Local: The first request is granted right away, whereas subsequent requests are queued at the Mutex block while the corresponding Wait block instances periodically send out tokens via their *keepWaiting* pins. This period is shorter than the duration of the Timer block in Fig. 2, to prevent its expiration under non-failure conditions. Once a previously granted locker sends a release, or the Wait block instance for this locker times out, the next ID in the Mutex queue is used to tell its Wait block instance to grant read permission. Hence, timeouts from the Wait block instances ensure that the protocol can continue even if the release of a read permission is never received.

As there is more than one instance of the Wait block, we have to use select statements when communicating with them. More importantly, since each Wait block instance is implemented as its own state machine, the run-time-support system treats messaging between the parent state machine (the controller) and the children state machines (the Wait block instances) in an asynchronous manner, but with the FIFO property.

3.2 Analysis A_2 of Timed Mutex Local

To verify more detailed properties of our specifications than analysis A_1 supports, we use a formalism based on temporal logic, the Temporal Logic of Actions (TLA, [20]). We can generate TLA$^+$, the language for TLA, automatically from the Arctis models [18],

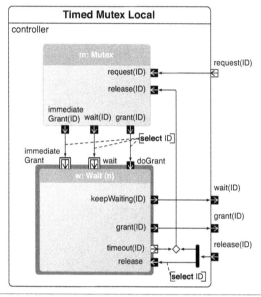

Figure 6. UML activity showing the part of the mutual exclusion protocol that is local to the controller

although not all features introduced in this paper are yet supported by the implementation.

Figure 7 shows an excerpt of the TLA$^+$ specification of the EESM, the activity and the consistency proof for Timed Mutex Local, focusing on the events related to a token passing through the *request(ID)* and *wait(ID)* pins. Each run-to-completion step of the activity, and each EESM transition, is represented as one TLA$^+$ action.[3] The TLA$^+$ actions for the EESM transitions are quite similar to the graphical representation. The main difference is that updates of variables are written in a different style and that variables that are not changed in a transition are explicitly marked as such. The activity part of Fig. 7 refers to contracts of inner blocks by ⟨*block name*⟩!⟨*(E)ESM transition*⟩ like *m!request_ wait(1, ID)*.[4] It also uses functions *sendToWait(⟨pin name⟩, ID)* and *receiveFromWait(⟨pin name⟩, ID)*, which are both functions we have defined to asynchronously send and receive tokens with the given ID via the named pins. From the part of the specifica-

---

[3] In TLA and TLA$^+$, an action is a predicate on a pair of system states, modelling the changes to the variables that are carried out in a system step.

[4] The index parameter of the Mutex block is hard coded as 1, since there is only one instance being used in the activity. All EESMs still have an index, so we can use the same TLA$^+$ segment to express them regardless of how many instances are actually used.

```
┌──────────── MODULE Excerpt_for_request_and_wait ────────────┐
  From the EESM
  request(i, ID) ≜
  ∧ ID ∉ requests[i]
  ∧ requests' = [requests EXCEPT ![i] = requests[i] ∪ {ID}]
  ∧ UNCHANGED ⟨grants⟩

  wait(i, ID) ≜
  ∧ ID ∈ requests[i]
  ∧ ID ∉ grants[i]
  ∧ UNCHANGED ⟨grants, requests⟩


  From the activity
  request_m_request_m_wait_w_wait(ID) ≜
  ∧ m ! request_wait(1, ID)
  ∧ sendToWait(waitPin, ID)
  ∧ UNCHANGED ⟨w_state, fromWait⟩

  request_m_request_m_immGrant_w_immGrant(ID) ≜
  ∧ m ! request_immediateGrant(1, ID)
  ∧ sendToWait(immediateGrantPin, ID)
  ∧ UNCHANGED ⟨w_state, fromWait⟩

  w_keepWaiting_wait(ID) ≜
  ∧ receiveFromWait(keepWaitingPin, ID)
  ∧ UNCHANGED ⟨w_state, m_queue, toWait⟩


  From the proof
  requestEvent(ID) ≜
  ∧ eesm ! request(1, ID)
  ∧
    ∨ act ! request_m_request_m_wait_w_wait(ID)
    ∨ act ! request_m_request_m_immGrant_w_immGrant(ID)

  waitEvent(ID) ≜
  ∧ act ! w_keepWaiting_wait(ID)
  ∧ IF ENABLED eesm ! wait(1, ID)
     THEN eesm ! wait(1, ID)
     ELSE UNCHANGED ⟨requests, grants⟩

  p1 ≜ □(∀ ID ∈ IDs :
  ENABLED eesm ! request(1, ID) ⇒
    (ENABLED act ! request_m_request_m_wait_w_wait(ID)
    ∨ ENABLED
      act ! request_m_request_m_immGrant_w_immGrant(ID)))

  p2 ≜ □(∀ ID ∈ IDs :
  ENABLED act ! w_keepWaiting_wait(ID) ⇒
    ENABLED eesm ! wait(1, ID))
└──────────────────────────────────────────────────────────┘
```

Figure 7. TLA$^+$ excerpt for the proof of the Timed Mutex Local block

tion headed by "From the proof", we see that the events of the EESM and the activity are connected so as to take place together in one atomic step. For example in the action *requestEvent(ID)*, whenever a *request(i, ID)* action takes place for the EESM, either a request *m_request_m_wait_w_wait(ID)* or *request_m_request_m_immGrant_w_immGrant(ID)* action must take place in the activity at the same time. In contrast, as modeled by *waitEvent(ID)*, when the activity wants to send a token through the wait pin, we may accept that the EESM does not allow it, due to the semantics of discarding tokens that attempt to travel via pins at the wrong time. This is expressed with the IF-THEN-ELSE construct.

Theorems that verify the consistency of the activity and its (E)ESM can be generated automatically. For example, to verify that a token accepted through pin *request* by the EESM is also accepted by the activity, we use the model checker TLC [29] to check the invariant *p1* from Fig. 7. The invariant states that whenever the EESM is ready to allow a token through the *request* pin (i.e., the

corresponding TLA$^+$ action is enabled), one of the corresponding transitions of the activity are also enabled. Invariant *p2* states the same thing for events where tokens pass through the outgoing wait pin. The difference is that any violation of this invariant is interpreted as just a warning, not something that necessarily has to be corrected. Instead, the developer should make sure that any scenarios where the activity can send a token through the pin, but the EESM does not allow it, are intentional. The scenarios are given automatically by the model checker in the form of an error trace that we can visualize in the Arctis models [18].

The design of Timed Mutex Local shown in Fig. 6 has a bug that can lead to a deadlock situation. When running TLC, it returns an error trace to show that the design allows the following scenario:

1. A request from locker L1 is received, granted and released, but the release only gets as far as being duplicated by the fork node so that one token reaches *m:release(ID)* to remove the request entry, while the other token has not yet been received by the Wait block through its *release* pin.

2. The Wait block for locker L1 emits a token through its timeout pin, which rests in the asynchronous channels from the Wait blocks to the controller.

3. Another request from locker L1 is received, an entry is added in the Mutex block and a token put in the queue to the corresponding Wait block via pin *immediateGrant*.

4. The timeout from the L1 instance of Wait is finally received by the controller and reaches *m:release(ID)*, which removes the new request from locker L1 instead of the original request.

This causes an inconsistency between the state of the Wait blocks and the state of Mutex that later on can deadlock the system. The chance of this sequence of events actually happening is very small, especially as the delay from the local, but asynchronous message passing between the Wait blocks and the rest of the controller partition is expected to be much shorter than the non-local message passing. However, these are the kind of subtle faults that could take down a system after years of operation and be very difficult to pinpoint when trying to figure out the reason for the failure.

One could solve the problem by changing the run-time-support system so that local messages always have priority over non-local ones, or we can insert a First block that ensure that either only the release or the timeout for a certain ID reaches Mutex, as shown in Fig. 8. The nice thing about this new version, is that the EESM is exactly the same as before, so the replacement does not trigger a need to redo any of the verification done already. Using the EESM of the Timed Mutex Local block, we just need to verify consistency of the EESM and activity for this new block.

Although we primarily want to prove the BEME property for the Timed Mutex Distributed block, we can also express it for the Timed Mutex Local block. This "BEME Local" property will then be *"if there are ever no more timeouts, then eventually the block will grant at most one read request at a time"*. This is a liveness property, meaning that it describes something that should happen. In our method, the theorems for these properties are formulated manually. To verify liveness properties, we need to add constraints to filter out behaviours that are unreasonable for a real system, such as a dice that is rolled infinitely many times yet never shows a "six". Typically this means constraining the behaviours to those where things that can always or infinitely often happen, do actually happen sometimes, known as *fairness* constraints [20]. To verify the BEME Local property, we also add a liveness constraint to the specification stating that eventually there will never be any more timeouts from any of the Wait block sessions, hence TLC only considers the part of the state space where this holds. We can then express the BEME local property in TLA$^+$

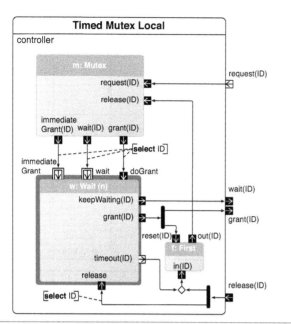

Figure 8. The new and improved activity of Timed Mutex Local

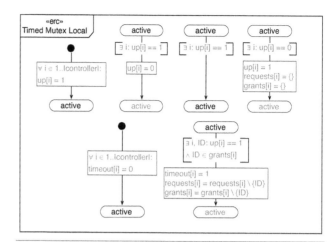

Figure 9. ERC of the Timed Mutex Local block

as $\Diamond\Box(Cardinality(grants[1]) \leq 1)$, which reads *"eventually always the cardinality of the set of granted IDs is at most one."*

Although advanced properties like this one, at least currently, have to be written manually, the reliability expert only has to add two lines to a TLA$^+$ specification of perhaps hundreds of lines to get TLC to check it. This shows that the automation provided by our method can also be very useful for the cases where some things have to be done manually.

We do not have the space to go in detail also about the verification of the Timed Mutex Distributed block. The only truly new property compared to the Timed Mutex Local block, is that we would like to verify that every request received from a locker is eventually responded to via a grant. Again, we will have to add fairness constraints to filter out unrealistic behaviours, and then we can express the property as *"always, for all lockers, a request from a given locker has been received implies that eventually a grant is sent to that locker."*

4. Modelling Realistic Semantics

Our interface contracts help developers to understand the behaviour of a block and facilitate compositional verification by describing only the events that are visible to the outside of the block. In order to do compositional verification under realistic semantics, the contracts must therefore describe the externally visible effects of process crashes and message loss, too. This could be done by writing a new ESM or EESM that includes extra transitions caused by these types of events, with the drawback of having to maintain two, partially overlapping, contracts, one for ideal semantics and another one for realistic semantics. To avoid this potential for inconsistency, we use an aspect-oriented notation to express what we call External Reliability Contracts (ERCs).

The ERC for the Timed Mutex Local block is shown in Fig. 9. In the following, we use the terminology of aspect-oriented programming, AspectJ in particular [1]. The part of the ERC in black is the *pointcut*, the pattern that must match in order to insert the *advice* given in blue colour. The first transition has a pointcut that looks for any transition that starts in an initial state and ends in a state called *active*. Looking at the EESM in Fig. 4, we see that there

is only one such transition. Hence, the ERC adds an extra variable *up* (an array, in case there is more than one instance of the block) to the EESM to denote the state of the process running the controller partition. The ERC transition to the right of this matches any state named *active* and adds a new transition with target state *active* so that every controller instance that is not crashed, i.e., up[i] = 1, can crash. The following transition matches any EESM transition that has state *active* as both its target and source. It adds an additional guard stating that the controller must be up in order for such an EESM transition to take place.

As shown in the top right corner, the ERC adds a transition from state *active* with *up* equal to 0 that restarts the controller. A transition with this guard tells us whether the existing state of the EESM is remembered after a crash or not. There is no persistent storage for the state of this block, so both the set of requests and grants are reset to the empty set upon restarting the component. Exchanging the Timed Mutex Local block and its ERC for an otherwise identical block that does use persistent storage, could alter the results of verification with realistic semantics. All local blocks have an ERC with at least these four transitions.

The timeout of a Wait block instance is not explicitly expressed in the EESM of Timed Mutex Local, as it does not trigger any tokens to traverse any external pins. However, the application-specific BEME property of Timed Mutex Distributed is conditional in timeouts eventually not happening anymore, so we want to export this event to the enclosing level through the ERC. As a result we include two more ERC transitions that are specific to exporting the timeout event, placed below the first row of transitions. More precisely, they export the activity step where a token arrives at the controller from *w:timeout(ID)* and reaches *m:release(ID)*, i.e., the event that can cause a new locker to be granted read permission before the previous holder has released it. The first transition adds a timeout variable to the contract, which is initialized to 0. The second transition states that a timeout for a given ID may happen when the component is not crashed and the ID is an element of the set of grants. It also removes the ID of the timed out Wait block instance from the contract sets, to allow new requests even if the release message is lost. Once the timeout event is explicit in the contract like this, we can use it to verify the BEME property for the Timed Mutex Distributed block.[5]

---

[5] We can also verify the BEME property compositionally under ideal semantics, by first verifying that Timed Mutex Local only gives two or more grants at the same time if a timeout has happened, and then we can refer to

Note that while the EESM is constructed independently from the ERC, the opposite is not true. The ERC is tailored to the existing EESM, and may have to change if the EESM changes.

We skip showing the ERC of Timed Mutex Distributed. Since each locker has a timer that effectively masks the effects of message loss or the controller crashing, the ERC is as simple as the first row of transitions from the ERC in Fig. 9. Not surprisingly, we find this pattern in other blocks as well: Blocks that are built to tolerate failures under realistic semantics have almost the same contract under ideal semantics; the ERC only adds that tokens cannot pass through pins of partitions that have crashed.

In principle, one can match different ERC transitions to the same (E)ESM transition, so that the application of one ERC transition un-matches others. Because of this, we currently demand that any ERC is expressed so as not to have conflicting aspect transitions, meaning that they can be applied in any order and get the same result. We also do not apply ERC transitions to (E)ESM transitions created by other ERC transitions, hence any such transitions must be self-contained, like the last transition in Fig. 9 that already includes "up[i] == 1" since this will not be added by the third ERC transition.

As seen in the next section, realistic semantics greatly increase the size of the state space. Having ERCs as aspects to (E)ESMs means that we always have access to a less complex specification with ideal semantics as well, easily trading details in the behaviour for verifying with more component instances when needed.

5. Discussion

To evaluate the usefulness of the EESMs and ERCs in terms of enabling compositional verification, we observed model checking runs of different specifications. Our hypothesis is that compositional verification will greatly reduce the verification effort, both when considering only ideal semantics (EESMs) and when checking with full realistic semantics (EESMs + ERCs). Table 1 gives the number of states found and the time it took to search through them for several variants of the Timed Mutex Distributed block and the Timed Mutex Local block.[6] The rows of the table are as follows:

TML gives the results for model checking the Timed Mutex Local block from Fig. 6 compositionally. That is, using the contracts of the inner blocks, Mutex and Wait, to abstract them.

TMD gives the results for model checking Timed Mutex Distributed from Fig. 2 when abstracting Timed Mutex Local by its contract.

TMD Comp. gives the aggregate results for compositional verification of Timed Mutex Distributed. This row is simply the sum of the results from the two rows above it. We use these number as a base line to compare the other numbers to.

TMD Direct represents monolithic verification and gives the results for model checking the Timed Mutex Distributed block and the Timed Mutex Local block at the same time. Here, we keep the EESM of Timed Mutex Local to filter out tokens traversing the boundaries of the block. This is to demonstrate the effect of analysing both parts at once, instead of separately. The numbers with unit x give how many times larger the number of states or seconds is compared to the base line of TMD Comp.

For one locker, TMD Direct has just over double the state space of TMD Comp., and for two lockers the monolithic verifica-

Number of lockers → Alternative ↓		1	2	3
Ideal Semantics				
TML	states	20	1 441	125 648
	time	0 sec	4 sec	56 sec
TMD	states	54	2 961	157 464
	time	0 sec	3 sec	44 sec
TMD Comp.	states	74	4 402	283 112
	time	0 sec	7 sec	100 sec
TMD Direct	states	166	388 018	> 80 M
	states, x TMD Comp	2.2 x	89 x	> 282 x
	time	3 sec	222 sec	> 16 hours
	time, x TMD Comp	-	32 x	> 576 x
TMDD NC	states	8 746	> 193 M	-
	states, x TMD Comp	118 x	> 44 296 x	-
	time	4 sec	> 29 hours	-
	time, x TMD Comp	-	> 14 914 x	-
Realistic Semantics				
TML	states	40	5 636	500 408
	time	1 sec	5 sec	359 sec
TMD	states	1 152	331 776	95 551 488
	time	3 sec	98 sec	64 101 sec
TMD Comp.	states	1 192	337 412	96 051 896
	time	4 sec	103 sec	64 460 sec
TMD Direct	states	1 920	25 970 688	-
	states, x TMD Comp	1.6 x	77 x	-
	time	4 sec	27 320 sec	-
	time, x TMD Comp	1 x	123 x	

Table 1. Number of states and time to find them using TLC

tion needs 89 times the state space and takes 32 times as long as compositional verification does. For three lockers, the difference is even greater: More than 282 times the state space and more than 576 times the time is used for monolithic verification. All numbers in the table prefixed by ">" are just an indication of the lower bound, as we terminated the model checking run at that point. Note that monolithic verification here only refers to removing one layer of abstraction, the Timed Mutex Local block, not replacing all blocks in Timed Mutex Distributed by their inner contents.

TMDD NC shows the results when attempting to model check the Timed Mutex Distributed block without any contract between it and the contents of the Timed Mutex Local block, i.e., simply adding the contents from the Timed Mutex Local block from Fig. 8 into Fig. 2. In this case, we do not have the contract of Timed Mutex Local to filter out behaviour between the part that came from Timed Mutex Local and the part from Timed Mutex Distributed. A comparison with the compositional case is thus not correct from the point of view of verification: Such a block not only needs to be verified in one run, but also passes more tokens between its parts, increasing the number of possible behaviours in each part. It is simply not the same specification. Nevertheless, we include it by the row TMDD NC (No Contract) to show the practical result of attempting to build the Timed Mutex Distributed block in this way. The results show that we can only model check the specification for one locker within reasonable time.

Considering realistic semantics means considering a much bigger state space, hence compositional verification is necessary even for small models. To do compositional verification in this case, we

---

whether the set of grants has had more than one element, instead of referring directly to whether a timeout has happened.

[6] We use the variant of Timed Mutex Local with the First block as that allows to search the whole state space without encountering a deadlock.

incorporate the ERCs into the contracts. The results of the model checking are as follows:

TML When analysing under realistic semantics, the state space of Timed Mutex Local almost quadruple for more than one locker. This is as expected since there are two new Boolean variables, *up* and *timeout*, to keep track of. We only track timeouts that allow another locker to get the read permission, hence this variable is never changed for the case with only one locker.

TMD It gets more complex for the Timed Muted Distributed block, as it contains message channels that can drop messages. Since it has more than one partition type and can have more than one instance of the locker partition, there are many combinations of crashes possible. Together with message loss, this greatly increases the state space under realistic semantics.

TMD Direct Just like with ideal semantics, we see an increase in the state space when model checking with both parts of the system at once with realistic semantics. The difference is that the numbers for the compositional verification are already much higher under realistic semantics, so the exponential blowup due to monolithic verification has a much greater effect in practise. This is especially so for the time taken to search the state space, as TLC tends to search fewer states per second for larger state spaces.

As we can see, the number of lockers contributes to the state space in an exponential manner, when not using any state space reduction techniques.[7] Hence, it is important to keep the starting numbers low, so that we can verify the specifications for a large enough number of lockers that we gain confidence in their correctness.[8] This is where the benefit of our compositional approach comes in: By analysing tightly coupled parts of the behaviour while abstracting the rest, we can avoid the exponential growth in the state space that stems from analysing too many parts of the behaviour at once. This in turn, allows us to reach further with respect to the number of instances of the same type the model checker can handle. To sum up, we see that compositional verification performs significantly better than monolithic verification with contracts, and that trying to build the system without contracts most likely would lead to a state space that is infeasible to model check at all with multiple lockers.

6. Related Work

The idea of compositional verification of temporal logic specifications, whether it is by manual proofs [13] or model checking [7], is not a new one. There are also several approaches that automate the compositional verification process. However, it is not trivial how a system is decomposed. Cobleigh et al. [9] use the L* learning algorithm coupled with a model checker for automatic assume–guarantee reasoning [8] about the properties of systems. They report that "the vast majority" of the 2-way decompositions found for each example system actually did not improve on monolithic verification. In fact, their results were not very promising: Only about half of the examples studied could be improved by assume–guarantee reasoning, and even in these cases the gains were mostly limited to expanding the model by one instance. However, later studies on the topic report better results [5, 23], although the improvements over monolithic verification are seldom by more than

factor 4. So why are our experimental results so different? Although these works and ours both deal with compositional verification, they are not directly comparable: First of all, we report on a single, albeit real, system. This is not enough to say anything precise about the performance. Further, these works find a new assumption for each property to verify, while we use a static contract for all properties. While they are looking for an assumption that perfectly abstracts the other part of the system for a given property, we take advantage of the fact that we control the resulting implementation and carry any extra constraints from the contracts into the actual implementation. Also, our development method naturally leads to tightly coupled clusters of behavioural logic with looser coupling between them, due to the inherent goal of creating reusable building blocks.

We use UML activities to model software components. There are other works giving UML activities a formal semantics [10, 11, 28], but these all omit contracts to enabled hierarchical activities. As pointed out in [4], we can only expect software components to be reused for critical systems if they come with clear instructions on how to be correctly reused and what guarantees they give under those conditions. UML already provides the concept of Protocol State Machines [22] to detail how a component can communicate with its environment. Mencl [21] proposes Port State Machines to improve on several shortcomings of Protocol State Machines, for example that they do no allow nesting or interleaving method calls, nor dependencies between a provided and required interface. His Port State Machines split method calls into atomic request and response events to allow for nesting and interleaving method calls, but they are restricted to pure control flow, as transition guards are not supported. Bauer and Hennicker [3] introduce a protocol description that is a hybrid of control flow and data state styles. However, this approach also lacks the ability to express dependencies between required and provided interfaces.

Like Port State Machines, our contracts have atomic interface events to allow for the expression of nesting and interleaving method calls. As they abstract both the block and its environment, they also express the provided and required interfaces in the same structure, hence allowing to express dependencies between them. In addition, our EESMs combine this with data variables so that we can more accurately express the behaviour of blocks with many instances [26] or blocks whose behaviour is otherwise strongly data dependent.

Sanders et al. [25] present semantic interfaces of service components, using finite state machine notation to describe both. Semantic interfaces can be used to find both complementary and implementing components, hence they support compositional verification. The main difference from our contracts is that semantic interfaces abstract local components that are asynchronously connected to remote or local components, while our contracts are mainly used internally in one process to connect sub-components, described as activity diagrams, synchronously together.[9] The fact that our contracts allow encapsulation of both local components and distributed collaborations between components, sets them apart from all the above.

7. Concluding Remarks

While we currently either analyse a specification under completely ideal or realistic semantics, we see an advantage in having more fine-grained control over the execution semantics of individual system parts. This could be achieved by extending our method and tool with a deployment model where one could easily alter which components and channels should have ideal or realistic semantics,

---

[7] We present data from unoptimized specifications, as the main point is to show the relationship between numbers of different rows.

[8] Model checking cannot prove properties of general models, only the model instances that are actually checked. Hence, there could be a number of lockers for which the properties do not hold. The best we can do is to check with a few instances for which most bugs will manifest themselves.

---

[9] As seen from the Wait blocks in Fig. 6, asynchronous coupling is also supported.

or even the ordering properties of a channel. For the scenario above, such a tool would enable faster analysis for one failure source at a time, but not reveal any problems caused by a combination of failure sources.

All ERCs written for this case study have been made manually. However, we could automate most of their construction for local blocks, which all have the three first transitions from Fig. 9 in common. If we enable developers to tag elements of the existing model with a ≪persistent≫ stereotype, we should be able to automatically generate the restart transition as well.

ERCs are used to export reliability-related events that are not directly visible as tokens passing through pins. It may be that other non-functional properties of our models can be described in the same manner, adding them as aspects to (E)ESMs. For example, there is work to analyse security aspects of SPACE models [12], and we can imagine a use for a concept like this to export security aspects from inside a block to a higher level.

If we are to apply several aspect-oriented contracts to each base contract, perhaps even created by different people, the problem of conflicting aspects transitions is likely to increase. In such a case, we might need to develop a conflict resolution mechanism to ensure that there is no ambiguity in the result of the aspect weaving.

In summary, we have shown that encapsulation using our contracts can reduce the state space to verify by at least factor 100 compared to monolithic verification. We have introduced ERCs to allow compositional verification also under realistic semantics. ERCs allow to easily switch between analysis under ideal or realistic semantics. Since the state space under realistic semantics is larger than under ideal semantics, this allows trading realistic behaviour descriptions for larger model sizes, when convenient.

References

[1] ApectJ web site. URL http://www.eclipse.org/aspectj. Last accessed May 2011.

[2] Arctis Verification Project. Norwegian Research Council, FORNY Project no. 199644.

[3] S. Bauer and R. Hennicker. Views on Behaviour Protocols and Their Semantic Foundation. In *Algebra and Coalgebra in Computer Science*, volume 5728 of *LNCS*, pages 367–382. Springer, 2009.

[4] A. Beugnard, J.-M. Jezequel, N. Plouzeau, and D. Watkins. Making Components Contract Aware. *Computer*, 32:38–45, 1999.

[5] Y.-F. Chen, E. M. Clarke, A. Farzan, F. He, M.-H. Tsai, Y.-K. Tsay, B.-Y. Wang, and L. Zhu. Comparing Learning Algorithms in Automated Assume-Guarantee Reasoning. In *Proc. of the 4th int. conf. on Leveraging applications of formal methods, verification, and validation - Volume Part I*, ISoLA'10, pages 643–657. Springer-Verlag, 2010.

[6] K. T. Cheng and A. S. Krishnakumar. Automatic Functional Test Generation using the Extended Finite State Machine Model. In *Proc. 30th Int. Design Automation Conf.*, DAC'93, pages 86–91. ACM, 1993.

[7] E. Clarke, D. Long, and K. McMillan. Compositional Model Checking. In *Proc. of the Fourth Annual Symposium on Logic in computer science*, pages 353–362. IEEE Press, 1989.

[8] J. M. Cobleigh, D. Giannakopoulou, and C. S. Păsăreanu. Learning Assumptions for Compositional Verification. In *Proc. of the 9th int. conf. on Tools and algorithms for the construction and analysis of systems*, TACAS'03, pages 331–346. Springer-Verlag, 2003.

[9] J. M. Cobleigh, G. S. Avrunin, and L. A. Clarke. Breaking Up is Hard to Do: An Investigation of Decomposition for Assume-Guarantee Reasoning. In *Proc. of the 2006 int. symposium on Software testing and analysis*, ISSTA '06, pages 97–108. ACM, 2006.

[10] R. Eshuis. Symbolic Model Checking of UML Activity Diagrams. *ACM Trans. Softw. Eng. Methodol.*, 15(1):1–38, 2006.

[11] N. Guelfi and A. Mammar. A Formal Semantics of Timed Activity Diagrams and its PROMELA Translation. In *Proc. 12th Asia-Pacific SE Conf.*, pages 283–290, 2005.

[12] L. Gunawan, F. Kraemer, and P. Herrmann. A Tool-Supported Method for the Design and Implementation of Secure Distributed Applications. In *Engineering Secure Software and Systems*, volume 6542 of *LNCS*, pages 142–155. Springer Berlin / Heidelberg, 2011.

[13] P. Herrmann and H. Krumm. A Framework for Modeling Transfer Protocols. *Computer Networks*, 34(2):317–337, 2000.

[14] F. A. Kraemer. *Engineering Reactive Systems: A Compositional and Model-Driven Method Based on Collaborative Building Blocks*. PhD thesis, Norwegian University of Science and Technology, 2008.

[15] F. A. Kraemer and P. Herrmann. Automated Encapsulation of UML Activities for Incremental Development and Verification. In *Proc. of the 12th Int. Conf. on Model Driven Engineering, Languages and Systems (Models)*, volume 5795 of *LNCS*, pages 571–585, 2009.

[16] F. A. Kraemer and P. Herrmann. Reactive Semantics for Distributed UML Activities. In *Formal Techniques for Distributed Systems*, volume 6117 of *LNCS*, pages 17–31, 2010.

[17] F. A. Kraemer, R. Bræk, and P. Herrmann. Synthesizing Components with Sessions from Collaboration-Oriented Service Specifications. In *Proc. 13th Int. SDL Forum Conf. on Design for Dependable Systems*, SDL'07, pages 166–185, 2007.

[18] F. A. Kraemer, V. Slåtten, and P. Herrmann. Tool Support for the Rapid Composition, Analysis and Implementation of Reactive Services. *Journal of Systems and Software*, 82(12):2068–2080, 2009.

[19] F. A. Kraemer, V. Slåtten, and P. Herrmann. Model-Driven Construction of Embedded Applications based on Reusable Building Blocks – An Example. In *SDL 2009*, volume 5719 of *LNCS*, pages 1–18. Springer-Verlag Berlin Heidelberg, 2009.

[20] L. Lamport. *Specifying Systems: The TLA+ Language and Tools for Hardware and Software Engineers*. Addison-Wesley Longman Publishing Co., Inc., 2002.

[21] V. Mencl. Specifying Component Behavior with Port State Machines. *Electronic Notes in Theoretical Computer Science*, 101:129–153, 2004.

[22] Object Management Group (OMG). Unified Modeling Language: Superstructure, Version 2.3, 2010.

[23] C. S. Păsăreanu, D. Giannakopoulou, M. G. Bobaru, J. M. Cobleigh, and H. Barringer. Learning to Divide and Conquer: Applying the L* Algorithm to Automate Assume-Guarantee Reasoning. *Form. Methods Syst. Des.*, 32:175–205, 2008.

[24] J. Rushby. Disappearing Formal Methods. In *High-Assurance Systems Engineering Symposium*, pages 95–96. ACM, 2000.

[25] R. T. Sanders, R. Bræk, G. von Bochmann, and D. Amyot. Service Discovery and Component Reuse with Semantic Interfaces. In *SDL 2005: Model Driven Systems Design*, volume 3530 of *LNCS*, chapter 6, pages 1244–1247. Springer, 2005.

[26] V. Slåtten and P. Herrmann. Contracts for Multi-instance UML Activities. In *Formal Techniques for Distributed Systems*, volume 6722 of *LNCS*, pages 304–318, 2011.

[27] V. Slåtten, F. A. Kraemer, and P. Herrmann. Towards a Model-Driven Method for Reliable Applications: From Ideal to Realistic Transmission Semantics. In *Proc. 2nd Int. Workshop on Software Engineering for Resilient Systems (SERENE 2010)*. ACM Digital Library, 2010.

[28] H. Störrle. Semantics and Verification of Data Flow in UML 2.0 Activities. *Electronic Notes in Theor. Comp. Sci.*, 127(4):35–52, 2005.

[29] Y. Yu, P. Manolios, and L. Lamport. Model Checking TLA+ Specifications. In *Proc. 10th IFIP WG 10.5 Adv. Research Working Conf. on Correct Hardware Design and Verification Methods (CHARME'99)*, volume 1703 of *LNCS*, pages 54–66, 1999.

Comparing Complexity of API Designs: An Exploratory Experiment on DSL-based Framework Integration

Stefan Sobernig

Institute for IS and New Media
WU Vienna, Vienna, Austria
stefan.sobernig@wu.ac.at

Patrick Gaubatz

Software Architecture Group
University of Vienna, Vienna, Austria
patrick.gaubatz@univie.ac.at

Mark Strembeck

Institute for IS and New Media
WU Vienna, Vienna, Austria
mark.strembeck@wu.ac.at

Uwe Zdun

Software Architecture Group
University of Vienna, Vienna, Austria
uwe.zdun@univie.ac.at

Abstract

Embedded, textual DSLs are often provided as an API wrapped around object-oriented application frameworks to ease framework integration. While literature presents claims that DSL-based application development is beneficial, empirical evidence for this is rare. We present the results of an experiment comparing the complexity of three different object-oriented framework APIs and an embedded, textual DSL. For this comparative experiment, we implemented the same, non-trivial application scenario using these four different APIs. Then, we performed an Object-Points (OP) analysis, yielding indicators for the API complexity specific to each API variant. The main observation for our experiment is that the embedded, textual DSL incurs the smallest API complexity. Although the results are exploratory, as well as limited to the given application scenario and a single embedded DSL, our findings can direct future empirical work. The experiment design is applicable for similar API design evaluations.

Categories and Subject Descriptors D.2.8 [*Metrics*]: Complexity measures; D.3.2 [*Language Classifications*]: Specialized application languages; D.1.5 [*Object-oriented Programming*]

General Terms Design, Experimentation, Measurement

Keywords Domain-Specific Language, Application Programming Interface, Complexity, Object Points

1. Introduction

Designing and implementing application programming interfaces (APIs) for reusable software components, such as class libraries, object-oriented (OO) application frameworks, or container frameworks, is a process of making critical decisions at the design level and at the implementation level. Decisions include, among

others [19], the adoption of certain architectural patterns (e.g., inversion-of-control layer), the choice between composition- or inheritance-based integration, and parametrization techniques (e.g., argument passing strategies). These decisions affect the quality attributes of applications constructed from the resulting APIs. This is because application engineers, who use APIs to help develop their applications, are influenced by the API's complexity (e.g., the levels of expressiveness in terms of program sorts supported) and the API's perceived usability (e.g., kinds of error prevention).

In this paper, we consider constructing APIs by providing an *embedded textual* domain-specific language (DSL, [13, 18]) on top of OO frameworks. DSLs are special-purpose programming languages engineered for a particular problem or application domain. An *embedded* (or internal) DSL extends and widely integrates with its host language (e.g., Java, Ruby, XOTcl) by reusing the host language's syntactic and behavioural models. Embedded DSLs as language extensions typically inherit those characteristics from their host languages [18]. Textual DSLs offer a textual concrete syntax to its users.

DSLs are claimed to enable domain experts to understand, test, co-develop, and maintain DSL programs. In its role as an API, a DSL targets domain experts as the API users. For them, a DSL-based API wraps framework functionality using domain abstractions. Depending on the DSL's language model, framework functionality is sometimes made composable through declarative specifications. A DSL might also provide alternative execution and parametrization modes, adding to or substituting those offered by the host language.

The use of DSLs as APIs is motivated by the belief that DSLs have, for the most part, a positive impact on the quality attributes of the resulting DSL programs. In particular, their comprehensibility, maintainability, communicability, and reusability are said to be positively affected (see, e.g., [7–9, 20]). To give an example, DSLs are commonly judged as more *expressive* than a general-purpose programming language. This augmented expressiveness [20] is explained by DSLs exposing a comparatively small number of high-level domain abstractions as first-class language elements. Expressiveness is also said to be positively influenced by providing a predominantly declarative concrete syntax, which is ideally extracted from the respective application domain (e.g., some DSLs use a tabular notation inspired by spreadsheets). This increased expressive-

GPCE'11, October 22–23, 2011, Portland, Oregon, USA.
Copyright © 2011 ACM 978-1-4503-0689-8/11/10... $10.00

ness is expected to facilitate developing and maintaining programs written in DSLs.

Despite such fundamental claims on the benefits of DSLs, empirical evidence is limited. To date, very few studies on DSLs have been conducted [8, 9]. As for qualitative approaches, most data sources are opinion statements and experience reports, collected from domain experts in terms of "industry case studies" (see, e.g., [14]) and from DSL prototype implementations [22]. Details about collecting and processing the evidence are often missing.

A first rigorous, survey-based effort [9] attempts to confirm conjectures about general success factors as perceived by a small developer population using a single DSL. However, these qualitative findings do not touch the issue of DSL-based API complexity. Besides, qualitative findings cannot be traced back to the structural properties of an API at the code level. The few quantitative studies exhibit several limitations: In particular, the research questions cover DSL aspects other than API complexity from the perspective of API users. Important examples are exploratory evaluations of the maintainability property of the DSL implementations themselves [10] and comparing different DSL implementation techniques [11]. Other studies look at domain-specific *modeling* [4, 12], rather then domain-specific programming languages. As for the measurement methods applied, some study designs fall short by primarily measuring source lines of code (LOC; see, e.g., [4, 12, 24]).

This situation motivated us to conduct an exploratory experiment to capture descriptive statistics as indicators of API complexity comparing four different approaches to API design, including an embedded DSL. Guided by the quantitative observations, a qualitative analysis explores the research question whether API users receive the advantage of a reduced API complexity when using a DSL-based API on top of an OO framework, as compared to using alternative APIs (i.e., a class library, an abstract-class, or a container framework). For this experiment, we created four programs realizing the same, predefined, and non-trivial application scenario. This application scenario describes a service provider component for a distributed single-sign-on infrastructure based on the Security Assertion Markup Language (SAML; [16]). Each program, however, is integrated with a different OO framework, with each framework API representing another API design approach. To obtain complexity indicators, we conducted an Object-Points (OP) analysis [17] for the four programs. The qualitative evaluation, based on the initial quantitative observations of this experiment, provides an indication for the potential of DSLs to reduce structural API complexity.

We report on our experiment as follows: In Section 2, we give an introduction to the experiment design. After having introduced important experimental units, the notion of *object points* as an indicator for API complexity is provided. Section 3 adds details about the experiment procedure, including an introduction to the technical domain of the experiment, federated identity management using SAML, and the selected application scenario. First quantitative observations of the experiment are reported in Section 4, before Section 5 critically revisits our findings. After a discussion of related work in Section 6, Section 7 concludes the paper.

2. Experiment Design

In this section, we introduce the necessary terminology (see Figure 1) and give some background on the Object-Points (OP) measurement method. The OP method is exemplified by applying it to a selected detail of our experimental code base.

2.1 Experiment Units

Application programming interface (API) – The interface of a software component to be used by the developers to access the functionality provided by the component. The corresponding function-

ality is commonly implemented by a set of sub-components. Thus, an API may bundle several component (or object) interfaces. The API provides an abstract view on the possible collaborations of these sub-components. While providing access to public functionality, the API discloses a protocol for integrating the API in client applications. This protocol gives the necessary details about the integration techniques adopted by the API design, e.g., template and hook classes, callback variants, dependency injection, as well as deployment and configuration descriptors. As a result, an API does not only consist of code units (e.g., classes, interfaces, methods), but also of behavioral protocols and of auxiliary data items (e.g., configuration files).

Program – The object-oriented software component which integrates and completes the OO framework (by means of the framework API) to realize the application scenario. In our experiment, we considered the program both in its source-code and language-dependent representation, as well as in a language-independent UML representation for comparing programs written in different programming languages (Java, XOTcl). The UML representation includes class and interaction models. For the actual measurement step, data was gathered on the syntactical structure of the programs in their UML representation. The program implementation sets a concise *working framework* [6], i.e., the feature chunk of the API needed to implement a specific application scenario. By capturing such a single working framework in terms of the program, the measurement results are eligible for an analysis comparing different APIs. For instance, the number and the types of working tasks are stable for a given application scenario.

Structural complexity – The notion of API complexity spans a considerable space of observable API design properties and the API's perceived usability [19] beyond the scope of a single, exploratory experiment. For example, an API's usability is affected by various cognitive components of various API stakeholders (developers, product users), including the abstraction level, learning style, and domain correspondence of API abstractions [6]. To allow observations on API complexity which can be directly linked to properties in the program structure, we limit ourselves to a working definition of structural, syntactic complexity observable from three properties of an object-oriented program [1]. First, the *size* of a program denotes the number of distinct entities (i.e., classes and objects) constituting the program. The interface size indicates the potential complexity resulting from all the possible object compositions used to implement the program. Second, the *interaction level* describes the permissive interactions between the entities (e.g., operation calls between objects). Third, the *parametric complexity* captures the complexity resulting from the number and the types of the members owned by each program entity (i.e., each class with the number of attributes and operation parameters having an object-type). To quantify these structural properties in an integrated measure construct, we apply an Object-Points analysis [17]. This working definition of structural API complexity implies a surrogate measurement: The API complexity is approximated by observing the above mentioned structural properties of a given program, constructed from a working framework of this API.

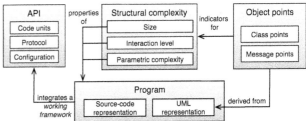

Figure 1: Overview of the Experiment Units

$$CP = \left(W_C \cdot |C| + \sum_{c \in C} |A_c| + W_{R_c} \cdot \sum_{c \in C} |R_c| + W_{O_c} \cdot \sum_{c \in C} |O_c|\right) \cdot \overline{N_C}$$

$$N_c = \prod_{s \in Super_c} \frac{|A_c| + |R_c| + |O_c|}{|A_c| + |R_c| + |O_c| + |A_s| + |R_s| + |O_s|}$$

$$MP = \left(W_{O_M} \cdot |O_M| + \sum_{o \in O_M} |P_o| + W_{S_o} \cdot \sum_{o \in O_M} |S_o| + W_{T_o} \cdot \sum_{o \in O_M} |T_o|\right) \cdot \overline{N_{O_M}}$$

$C, |C| \dots$	Set of classes. Class count
$|A_c| \dots$	Attribute count per class c, $c \in C$
$|O_c| \dots$	Operation count —"—
$|R_c| \dots$	Relation count —"—
$Super_c \dots$	Set of directly generalizing classes of class c: for all $s \in Super_c$, $s \in C$, $s \neq c$
$N_c \dots$	Novelty weight of class c, $c \in C$
$\overline{N_C}$	Avg. class novelty. $\frac{\sum_{c \in C} N_c}{|C|}$
$O_M \subset \bigcup_{c \in C} O_c \dots$	Set of called operations
$|O_M| \dots$	Called operation counts
$|P_o| \dots$	Parameter count of operation o, $o \in O_M$
$|S_o| \dots$	Source count —"—
$|T_o| \dots$	Target count —"—
$N_o \dots$	Novelty weight —"— $\in \{1, 0.5\}$
$\overline{N_{O_M}} \dots$	$\frac{\sum_{o \in O_M} N_o}{|O_M|}$

Table 1: Class- and Message-Points Measures

2.2 Object-Points Analysis

For our measurement and data analysis, the structural data gathered from the programs is processed using an Object-Points (OP) analysis. In particular, we apply the OP analysis by Sneed [17], not be confused with object-oriented variants of Function Points (see e.g. [2]). The OP analysis is applied for predicting the development effort (i.e., the program size) based on UML implementation models of a given program.

Note that, in our experiment, the Sneed OP analysis does *not* serve for estimating development effort. We adopted the Sneed OP method to compute indicator measures for reflecting selected structural properties of an object-oriented (OO) program. The objects (and object members) enter the analysis as *counts* (e.g., object counts, or counts of messages exchanged between two objects in a given interaction). Predefined *weights* are then assigned to these selected counts. For our experiment, the weight values are adopted as proposed by Sneed [17]. The weighted counts represent the actual OP value for a given program. See Table 2 for a list of used weights, their value loadings in our experiment, and their explanation. The OP value for a program results from the summation of two intermediate measure values, i.e., the *class* and the *message points*.

The class points (CP) of a program result from the counts and the weights representing the number of classes in the respective program, as well as the structure of these classes (i.e., their attributes, their operations, and their structural relations with other objects). Therefore, the CP measure reflects the program size and the parametric complexity of the analyzed program. In turn, the message points (MP) count the number, the structure, and the uses of operations provided by the objects (i.e., in terms of their signature interface) reflecting the interaction level property of a program. As the programs and the properties (size, interaction level, parametric complexity [1]) act as surrogates of API complexity for the scope of a specific working framework of the entire API, the OP indicators only represent indirect measure constructs of structural API complexity.

When compared to alternative approaches of OO complexity measurement [1], the Sneed OP analysis allows for comparing program structures in different languages. This is because intermediate UML models serve as the data source and weightings can compensate for language-specific statement sizes of code units (e.g., method bodies) while avoiding the methodical issues of LOC measurement. In addition, the Sneed measure constructs capture certain structural dependencies directly as a source of complexity. For example, the message points based on a UML interaction capture the static interaction level of a given application scenario. The Sneed measure constructs also present certain practical advantages. Most importantly, the constructs allow for direct traceability between program structures (e.g., a UML class's record of owned operations) and the indicator values (e.g., the CP value as size indicator) for qualitative evaluations.

Weight	Loading	Description
W_C	4	The value of 4 has been adopted from the standard weight of entities in the Data Points analysis; see [17].
W_{R_c}	2	Also adopted from the standard Data Points method; a weight of 2 reflects the fact that a single relation affects exactly two entities; see [17].
W_{O_c}	3	This weight reflects the average size of methods found for a representative code base in the programming language under investigation. The value 3 is the standard value proposed in [17], expressing a ratio of 15:5 between the avg. method statement size of more high-level (e.g. Smalltalk) and more low-level programming languages (e.g. C++).
W_{O_M}	2	Similarly to W_{R_c}, the weight 2 reflects that a single message occurence involves two entities – the sender and the receiver; taken from [17].
W_{S_o}	2	The standard value adopted from [17].
W_{T_o}	2	The standard value adopted from [17].

Table 2: Weights in the Sneed Object-Points analysis

Class points, CP – The CP measure is calculated from the UML class model. The measure is constructed as an adjusted summation of four summands, each being accompanied by a fixed weighting factor adopted from [17]. The summands are the class count $|C|$, the sum of attribute counts $|A_c|$, the sum of operation counts $|O_c|$, and the sum of relation counts $|R_c|$. The class count $|C|$ is the cardinality of the set of classes in the model and reflects the program size. The class count is corrected for the weight W_C. For each class $c \in C$, counts for owned attributes are established. Note that associations with neighbor classes are also counted as attributes (rather than relations). Depending on the navigability (unidirectional, bidirectional) of an association, it is recorded either for the non-navigable association end or both ends. The count of owned operations is then calculated, with the sum of operation counts for all classes being weighted by W_{O_c}. The weight corrects the count for its statement value, i.e., the average size of an operation implementation in terms of statements. The weighted operation count is therefore an indicator of class size.

The final summand is the sum of relation counts over all classes. In our experiment, relations mean generalization relations to one (or multiple) classes. Generalizations are counted for both the generalizing and the specializing ends, to reflect the two-way dependency introduced by this relationship (e.g., comprehending the feature set of by a specializing class requires the partial study of the generalizing class). The applied weighting factor W_{R_c} with a value of 2 accounts for the fact that a single relation affects exactly two entities.

The summation is then adjusted for the average class novelty $\overline{N_C}$. This factor computes from the product of novelty weights N_c per class (see Table 1). Provided that a class c is related to at least one generalizing class (which is reflected by a relation count $|R_c| > 0$), the novelty is calculated as the normalized ratio between the counts of attributes, operations, and relations *owned by* the specializing class and the total counts of both the specializing as well as the generalizing class. This novelty factor balances between the increased complexity caused by generalization relations (which is captured by a $|R_c| > 0$) and the locality of refinements in the specializing class, with the latter facilitating API elaboration. At the extremes, an N_c value of 0 represents a class without generalization relationships, without ownership of attributes and without operations. $N_c = 1$ means that a class c defines its entire record of attributes, operations, and relations in a freestanding manner; i.e., without inheriting any of these from a generalizing class.

Message points, MP – The MP measure is expressed over data drawn from both the UML class and the UML interaction model of the analyzed program. Most importantly, it is defined over a subset of all operations defined in the class model, i.e. the set of operations O_M actually used in the interaction. This corresponds to all operations referenced by the call events registered with message occurrences in the interaction.

As can be learned from Table 1, and similar to the CP measure, there are four summands based on weighted counts and a general novelty weight. The first summand is the number of operations referenced by message occurrences in the model, multiplied by W_{O_M}. The weight indicates that every message occurance involves two entities – the sender and the receiver. This called operations count $|O_M|$ indicates the *general* level of interaction between the collaborating objects.

The remaining summands are specific to each called operation o. First, the sum of parameter counts $|P_o|$ (including input and output parameters of an operation) is established. This reflects the parametric complexity at all operation call sites. Second, the sources and targets of each called operation in terms of the sending and receiving lifelines of the corresponding messages are collected. This yields the source counts $|S_o|$ and the target counts $|T_o|$, with each receiving a fixed weight (W_{S_o} and W_{T_o}). While the general operation count $|O_M|$ indicates the degree of interaction, the source and target counts stand for the intensity of the given object interactions. Complexity in the static program behavior is thus captured in terms of message occurrences.

For each of the called operations $o \in O_M$, a per-operation novelty weight N_o is applied. Called operations which combine with an operation provided by a generalizing class (also contained in the class model) are adjusted by a weight of 0.5. Replacing (overwriting) operations or newly defined ones enter the MP calculation with their full count values. The per-operation novelty compensates for the repeated inclusion of message points components when computed for two (or more) combinable operations along a generalization hierarchy. At the same time, any $N_o > 0$ reflects that each called operation, whether it refines another operation or not, adds another layer of complexity (e.g., parametric complexity with varying parameter sets). The actual weighting component of the MP measure is the average novelty weight over all called operations $\overline{N_{O_M}}$.

Object points, OP – The aggregate OP value results from summing the two partial results, i.e. the MP and the CP values. While the original definition of the OP measure [17] involves a third summand for expressing the Use Case (UC) complexity (e.g., based on a UML use case model of the underlying application scenario), we can omit this summand in our experiment. This is because in our comparative experiment based on a single application scenario, we take the UC complexity as a constant.

In our experiment, the OP score is used as an absolute value characteristic for each program structure. When contrasting the OP scores of different programs, the range of OP scores offers explicable thresholds for ordering the programs to each other. For instance, in such a range of data points, a relatively higher OP score points to an increased structural API complexity of a given program relative to the others.

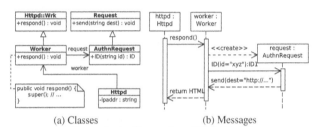

(a) Classes   (b) Messages

Figure 2: An Exemplary UML Model

2.3 Applying the Sneed OP Analysis

In the following, we give an overview of the Sneed Object-Points (OP) method by looking at an introductory example (see Figure 2). Consider a measurement applied to the simple UML model example given in Figures 2a and 2b. The input data for the actual OP measurement is given in Tables 3a and 3b.

The interaction model identifies three classes as the participants in the abstracted application scenario: `Httpd`, `Httpd::Wrk`, and `AuthnRequest`. As for the class-points (CP) calculation, these constitute the set C. In table 3a, the per-class counts of owned attributes, operations, and relations are depicted, collected from the class model. While data collection on attributes and operations is straightforward for this introductory example, we will now discuss the relationships between classes and the class novelty weightings.

First, table 3a records the generalization relations between `AuthnRequest` and `Request`, as well as `Worker` and `Httpd::Wrk`. The generalizations are marked for both the generalizing and the specializing ends. Second, the uni-directed association `worker` is counted as a second attribute on behalf of the non-navigable association end `Httpd`. Similarly, `request` is counted on behalf of `Worker`. Third, the generalization relations are also reflected in the class novelty ratios $N_{AuthnRequest}$ (0.5) and N_{Worker} (0.6). These weightings are computed as the ratio of non-inherited members of `AuthnRequest` to the total number of members owned by `AuthnRequest` and `Request`: $\frac{2}{4}$. This ratio indicates the extent to which `AuthnRequest`'s parametric complexity is explained by its member structure alone. Using the CP formula from Table 1, we compute the total CP score of our example model: $(4 \cdot 5 + 3 + 2 \cdot 3 + 3 \cdot 4) \cdot \frac{4.1}{5} = 33.62$.

Returning to Figure 2b, the data for deriving the message points (MP) value in Table 3b can be collected from the interaction model. The first observation is that the three message occurrences refer to a set O_M of three distinct operations being called. This simplifies the subsequent counting because all the source and target counts amount to 1. The generalization relationship between the classes `Worker` and `Httpd::Wrk` results in a novelty adjustment for `Worker.respond`, with the operation overloading the

`Httpd::Wrk.respond` operation (see Figure 2b). The total MP score results from the term $(2 \cdot 3 + 3 + 2 \cdot 3 + 2 \cdot 3) \cdot \frac{2.5}{3} = 17.5$. This yields a final OP score of our example model as the sum of the CP and MP values: $33.62 + 17.5 = 51.12$.

$c \in C$	$|A_c|$	$|R_c|$	$|O_c|$	$|N_c|$
Httpd	2	0	0	1
Httpd::Wrk	0	1	1	1
Worker	1	0	1	0.6
Request	0	1	1	1
AuthnRequest	0	1	1	0.5
20	3	6	12	0.82
CP		**33.62**		

$o \in O_M$	$|P_o|$	$|S_o|$	$|T_o|$	$|N_o|$
Worker.respond	0	1	1	0.5
AuthnRequest.ID	2	1	1	1
Request.send	1	1	1	1
6	3	6	6	0.833
MP		**17.5**		

(a) Class points (CP)   (b) Message points (MP)

Table 3: The CP and MP Scores of the Exemplary Model

3. Experiment Procedure

For the experiment, we selected an application domain and picked a single use case from this domain to be realized by the programs during the experiment (see Section 3.1). In a second step, we investigated existing software components in this application domain. We put special emphasis on adopting software components that provide different API designs (see Section 3.2). Having identified four characteristic software components, the actual experiment involved implementing four programs based on these reusable components (see Section 3.3). In a final step, the resulting programs were documented in terms of UML models (see Section 3.4). Based on these UML representations, the object points for each program were calculated.

3.1 Domain

In the context of computer network security, *digital identities* are created and assigned to *subjects* (e.g., human users). Thus, digital identities allow for identifying different subjects unambiguously. To prove the ownership of a digital identity, a subject has to authenticate. This authentication step involves presenting credentials, such as user name and password pairs. With each subject owning several digital identities (e.g., for different web sites), remembering and managing multiple credentials can becomes tedious task. A *Federated Identity Management* system provides the infrastructure for a so-called single sign-on (SSO) service. In an SSO-scenario, an *Identity Provider* issues a digital identity token for a particular subject. This token is then accepted by a number of *service providers* (also called *relying parties*). Thereby, the digital identity token provides the subject with a *federated identity* that can be used to access different services.

The Security Assertion Markup Language (SAML) [16] provides a well-established XML-based framework that supports creating and operating federated identity management environments. In SAML, different types of assertions can be expressed to provide a subject with corresponding digital tokens. The SAML standard defines a precise syntax for defining assertions and rules for exchanging them. SAML is defined as a flexible framework that can be extended and adapted for a range of use cases, including SSO. The SSO use case is directly supported by SAML's *Web Browser SSO Profile*. The programs realized during the experiment implemented SSO service providers using SAML's HTTP POST binding.

3.2 API Designs

For conducting the experiment, we selected three existing software artifacts for the technical domain of SAML: OpenSAML[1], simpleSAMLphp[2], and JAXB[3]. As we could not identify any prior DSL-

[1] OpenSAML: http://opensaml.org/

[2] simpleSAMLphp http://simplesamlphp.org/

[3] JAXB: http://jaxb.java.net/

based approach, we decided to develop a DSL on top of an underlying infrastructure for XML data binding: xoSAML[4]. Each of these software components realizes a predominant object-oriented API design, that is, a class library, an abstract class framework, a container framework, and an embedded textual DSL.

OpenSAML — This Java component provides a partial domain model for SAML (e.g., SAML messages, assertions), an XML data binding infrastructure tailored towards the needs of SAML (e.g., unmarshalling SAML documents into Java objects and vice versa), and utility classes for realizing SAML protocols (e.g., context objects, message en- and decoders, signature validators). With this, OpenSAML realizes a conventional reuse approach in terms of a *class library*. The classes are packaged into a library namespace, offering themselves for direct reuse (without instantiation protocol) in client programs. For an integration developer, navigating and picking from various concrete class hierarchies is necessary.

simpleSAMLphp — This component written in PHP does not aim at providing support for the entire protocol domain offered by SAML (such as OpenSAML), nor does it create means to generically map between object and XML document representations of SAML artifacts. Rather, simpleSAMLphp limits itself to helping realize preselected scenarios in the SAML/SSO use case. Its reuse strategy is that of a small-scale class library, without imposing any particular integration protocol (e.g., subclassing).

JAXB — The Java-based component delivers a reference implementation for the *Java Architecture for XML Binding* specification and, thus, embodies a generic XML-object binding framework. The XML/object mapping is based on a generator infrastructure, performing transformation from XML Schema descriptions to Java code models. For our experiment, we generated Java representations from the SAML schemas. JAXB also realizes a container framework based on Java beans, managing object lifecycles (e.g., bean factories) and component dependencies explicitly (e.g., dependency injection). In contrast to the other projects, JAXB does not provide any SAML utilities (e.g., message context objects, validators).

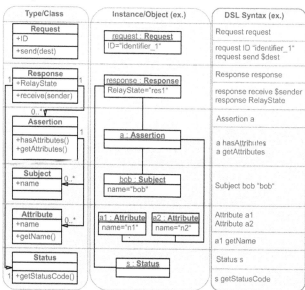

Figure 3: Core Language Model of xoSAML (simplified)

xoSAML — This component represents an embedded, textual DSL for specifying SAML assertions and corresponding SAML request and response messages. xoSAML is implemented in the host language *Extended Object Tcl* (XOTcl), a Tcl-based object-

[4] xoSAML: https://bitbucket.org/pgaubatz/xosaml

oriented scripting language [15]. xoSAML supports creating, manipulating, and exchanging SAML assertions and messages in a minimized, declarative textual notation. xoSAML integrates with a generator framework for mapping XML schemas to class structures; SAML entities are so provided as an XOTcl class library. Figure 3 depicts some examples that show the different abstraction layers of our DSL. In particular, it shows a (simplified) class diagram of the DSL's language elements and an excerpt of the object diagram for the SSO scenario. Corresponding DSL statements exemplify xoSAML's concrete syntax.

3.3 Application Scenario

Having identified the four reusable software components (OpenSAML, simpleSAMLphp, JAXB, and xoSAML), we continued by implementing the application scenario. We obtained four different implementations of a single-sign-on (SSO) service provider (SP). The actual application scenario is illustrated by Figure 5 in terms of a simplified UML sequence diagram. The sequence diagram shows the messages exchanged for a single SAML authentication request. Initiated by the browser side, a request for accessing a web resource is received by the SP. The SP returns an authentication request which is redirected to the authoritative identity provider. The identity provider verifies the credentials and returns an authentication response. The response contains assertions to be evaluated by the SP to decide about the authorization state and about granting access to resources. The SP implementations, therefore, covers handling the authorization request and evaluating the assertions.

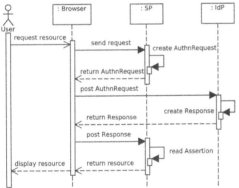

Figure 5: SSO in a Web Context

3.4 UML Implementation Models

The code bases of the resulting programs reflect various API designs and disparate programming languages (i.e., Java, PHP, XOTcl) as well as abstraction levels (e.g., general-purpose vs. domain-specific languages). To obtain language-independent representations of the four programs, each program was documented via UML sequence and UML class diagrams. The UML models were created in a manual design review after having completed the implementation task.

To collect structural data from the relevant working framework [6] of the API examined, we applied selection criteria for establishing the UML models. As for the class model, we selected classes defined by the reused software components (e.g., OpenSAML, xoSAML) which were refined or instantiated by the program. In addition, those declared in the scope of client programs were incorporated. Based on this initial set of classes, we further included classes by traversing the generalization relationships. The traversal was terminated when having collected all the classes that provide a feature accessed by the program (e.g., an attribute or a called operation). By documenting all relevant operation calls, the

UML sequences served for identifying the list of classes to consider.

4. Quantitative Analysis

In our experiment, two data sets were created. The first describes the underlying code bases and the intermediate UML representations (see Table 4). The second represents the OP measure computations (see Table 5).[5]

To begin with, the programs realized during the experiment are limited in code size: None of them exceeds 150 *lines of source code* (LOC). The four programs differ in terms of their LOC, as stated by SLOCCount [21]. While the OpenSAML-based implementation amounts to more than 151 lines of Java code, the programs interfacing with xoSAML and JAXB come at a LOC size of 144 and 120 lines, respectively. The smallest code base could be realized using simpleSAMLphp (see Table 4).

Inspecting the UML packages using SDMetrics [23], we learn that the code base complexity is not directly reflected by the program structure. From this structural viewpoint, OpenSAML exhibits the most extensive structural composition. The OpenSAML-based program is built using more than 30 classes with more than 8 operations each, in average. As a package JAXB is slightly smaller, yet structurally comparable with 20 classes and, in average, 11 operations each. xoSAML and simpleSAMLphp fall into a category in terms of class sizes. However, the two programs differ by the amount of operations per class. simpleSAMLphp reports relatively large operation records per class, with each counting an average of 28 operations.

As for inter-class relations $|R|$, the programs built from OpenSAML and from JAXB are characterized by a relatively high number of realized relations (e.g., attributes types, parameter types of owned operations, associations, dependencies). However, in average, each class in JAXB is connected to more neighbor classes (1.45) than an average class in OpenSAML (1). Similarly, the xoSAML and the simpleSAMLphp programs exhibit nearly the same relation counts, however, an average simpleSAMLphp class is linked to one class more than the average xoSAML class (see Table 4).

Program using...	OpenSAML	JAXB	simpleSAMLphp	xoSAML
LOC	151	120	48	144
# classes $|C|$	31	20	8	15
# operations $|O|$	254	222	110	37
# relations $|R|$	30	28	15	14
Cohesion $H = \dfrac{|R|+1}{|C|}$	1	1.45	2	1

Table 4: Descriptive Statistics on the Code and Model Representations [21, 23]

Table 5 shows the class- (CP), the message- (MP) and the object-points (OP) scores calculated for the four programs examined according to the OP procedure introduced in Section 2.2. The data rows representing each program are sorted by their ascending OP value. Within brackets, the normalized OP scores, adjusted to the lowest OP value, are given. We can make the following observations:

- The program constructed from the xoSAML DSL features the *lowest* OP score.
- The program sizes expressed in LOC (see Table 4), and the LOC-based ranking of the programs, do not relate to the order by OP value.

[5] The XMI representations of the UML models and the preprocessed data collection for the Object-Points analysis are available from http://swa.univie.ac.at/~patrick/op.zip. The programs' source code is maintained at https://bitbucket.org/pgaubatz/xosaml (see directory examples/ServiceProvider/).

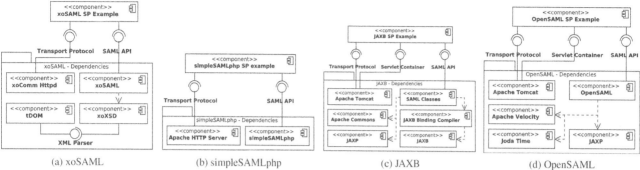

(a) xoSAML   (b) simpleSAMLphp   (c) JAXB   (d) OpenSAML

Figure 4: An Overview of Required Components

- The program sizes in terms of the total number of classes $|C|$ and operations $|O|$ follow the pattern of the OP values.
- Despite its OP-based top rank, the xoSAML program does not have the smallest code base.
- The simpleSAMLphp program accounts for an MP value smaller than xoSAML's, while still having a higher OP score.
- The simpleSAMLphp program has a higher OP score than its xoSAML equivalent, while having a code base which is three times smaller than xoSAML's.
- JAXB and OpenSAML have comparably high OP values, with a consistent structure of the CP and MP summands.
- The OP scores of the high-OP programs JAXB/OpenSAML is 3.5 to 4 times the OP value of xoSAML.

	CP ($\overline{N_C}$)	MP ($\overline{N_{O_M}}$)	OP
1. xoSAML	179.76 (≈ 0.79)	87 (1)	266.76
2. simpleSAMLphp	270.53 (≈ 0.64)	85.81 (0.89)	356.34
($\triangle$ xoSAML)	*(1.51)*	*(0.99)*	*(1.34)*
3. JAXB	755.46 (≈ 0.98)	188 (1)	943.46
($\triangle$ xoSAML)	*(4.2)*	*(2.1)*	*(3.54)*
4. OpenSAML	860.75 (≈ 0.84)	224 (1)	1084.75
($\triangle$ xoSAML)	*(4.79)*	*(2.57)*	*(4.07)*

Table 5: The OP Analysis Scores

5. Qualitative Analysis

In this section, we revisit our research question about whether API users benefit from a lowered complexity when using an API based on an embedded, textual DSL on top of an OO framework. For this, we review the quantitative observations documented in Section 4. We also point out relations to related work and its limitations. As already stated, the quantitative and qualitative observations below are first and tentative results; no firm recommendations can be derived therefrom.

5.1 Observations

API Complexity and the xoSAML DSL – The embedded, textual DSL (xoSAML) examined for the selected application scenario (SAML service provider) results in the most favorable OP score (266.76) among the API designs compared. This comparatively low OP score reflects that an API user is only exposed to an API feature chunk of low structural complexity for the DSL-based integration: The chunk's size is limited in terms of participating classes ($|C| = 15$) and the smallest number of operations per class ($35/15 \approx 2.5$). The xoSAML API chunk shows a relatively weak connectedness of classes ($H = 1$), resulting from the small number of associations and generalizations between the classes. While this reduced connectedness decreases the level of novelty, xoSAML's average novelty factor $\overline{N_C} = 0.79$ indicates that the API chunk implements a considerable share of the functionality

(i.e., operation implementations) used in the application scenario. Taking into account all these components, and given the humble API chunk size in terms of classes, we obtain the smallest class-points (CP) score in the experiment.

This CP score even compensates for a relatively higher object interaction level compared to simpleSAMLphp's one, as hinted at by a message points (MP) score of $87 > 85.51$. The comparable MP scores reflect the structural similarity of the two APIs interaction design in terms of called operation counts $|O_M|$ and the operation's parameter counts ($|P_O|$, max. 2). Besides, xoSAML and simpleSAMLphp, offer a programming model requiring step-by-step calls to clearly separated query-or-command operations (referred to as *command-query APIs* in [7]). This is reflected by source $|S_O|$ and target counts $|T_O|$ of 1 (i.e., there is mostly one message occurrence of a given operation in the call sequence). The slight difference in the OP scores is explained by deviating novelty factors $\overline{N_{O_M}}$ of 1 and 0.89, respectively.

xoSAML DSL vs. PHP Class Library – We would have expected a more substantial OP score difference between the DSL-based program (xoSAML) and the one based on the PHP class library (simpleSAMLphp). However, tracing back the OP scores to the simpleSAMLphp program's structure reveals that simpleSAMLphp, in contrast to the other frameworks, does not require any HTTP-related processing as part of the API feature chunk used. Instead, transport handling is purely delegated to the Apache HTTP request processor. This translates into a comparatively lower OP score for simpleSAMLphp. In addition, the simpleSAMLphp's average class novelty factor balances the high per-class operation counts, with $\overline{N_C} = 0.64$ the lowest in the experiment indicating a larger share of operations than in xoSAML being implemented outside the API chunk.

xoSAML DSL vs. Java OO Frameworks – While the OP analysis indicates that the DSL-based program incurs the least API complexity as approximated by the Sneed OP values, we did not expect the considerable difference of 250% and 300%, respectively, between the DSL-based implementation and the two Java-based programs. The structural complexity of the OpenSAML- and JAXB-based programs results from the multitude of classes (i.e., class counts $|C|$ of 20 and 31, respectively) in the API feature chunk. The class counts reflect that the SAML/XML artifacts are provided as Java classes in a direct mapping. The average size of per-class operation records (with approx. 8 operations each) and the two highest average class novelty factors ($\overline{N_C}$ of 0.84 and 0.98, respectively) also contribute to the considerably higher CP scores (860.75 and 755.46). In addition, there is a parametrization overhead resulting from container and beans management (factories), especially for JAXB.

Expressiveness and API Complexity – Expressiveness is a key dimension of API design [19]. DSL literature considers DSLs beneficial in terms of tailoring the expressiveness for the domain experts as API users. By tailoring, literature often refers to a DSL exposing only a *reduced* set of domain abstractions [20] at a higher abstraction level as compared to the underlying host language abstractions [10]. While our experiment design does not cover the issue of abstraction level, which entails aspects such as domain correspondence [6], some observations hint at a refined notion of expressiveness. While a naive reading might relate expressiveness to the mere number of distinct domain abstractions (e.g., the class count $|C|$), our experiment shows that this is not sufficient. For example, the simpleSAMLphp API chunk with only 8 classes is yet parametrically complex due to the relatively high number of operation counts per class (e.g., an API user must acquaint herself with a complex signature interface). This and similar effects are reflected by the CP measure construct, reporting a higher CP score for simpleSAMLphp (270.53) than for xoSAML (179.76) with 14 classes as domain abstractions.

A related observation is that the JAXB program shows a lower CP score (755.46) than the OpenSAML-based program (860.75). JAXB is a container framework directly operating on SAML/XML artifacts through a generic XML-object mapping infrastructure, while OpenSAML introduces intermediate and aggregating abstractions in terms of a SAML domain model. Hence, we would have expected JAXB to exhibit a CP score higher than the OpenSAML's one. This, however, is not the case (see Table 5). Instead, we found that for the OpenSAML implementation 31 classes were needed (compared to 20 for JAXB). This gives rise to the conjecture that designing a domain model (plus utility classes), rather than providing direct access to the SAML/XML protocol and assertion entities, can be detrimental to the framework integration effort.

LOC Measurement – Related quantitative approaches for comparing DSL and non-DSL programs are based on LOC measurement [4, 12, 24]. The known limitations include a lack of standardized rules for data collection (especially in a multi-language setting), an inverse relationship to notions of labor productivity [5], and major threats to construct validity. For instance, structural complexity (e.g., interaction level) and change locality cannot be captured by LOC-based measures alone.

When contrasting the LOC-based program sizes (see Table 4) and the OP scores of the programs in our experiment (see Table 5), there is no correspondence between the two resulting complexity rankings. In fact, the OP measurement reports the lowest OP score for xoSAML (266.76), while, at the same time, the corresponding LOC size (144) compares to the those of the high-OP programs JAXB (120) and OpenSAML (155). This indication, albeit our experiment design being limited, supports a critique of LOC-based measurement.

5.2 Threats to Validity

This exploratory experiment and its design pose several threats to construct validity, to internal validity, and to external validity. The threats have the potential of making wrong quantitative and qualitative observations.

Construct validity – The Object-Points (OP) measure constructs impose threats to our experiment's validity. This is because a) the Sneed OP approach per se is not used in its originating analysis context, b) the measure constructs (class and message points) have not been confirmed as appropriate means for approximating API complexity by prior empirical work, and c) the choice of weight loadings opens a range of methodical issues.

The Sneed OP analysis was originally calibrated for estimating development effort of large-scale software projects by predicting program sizes from UML models and statement size estimators, established by prior empirical mining in existing code bases (e.g., average method sizes in terms of language statements). Consequently, the comparatively small sizes of our programs might introduce a bias towards an over- or underestimation of structural properties (e.g., the weighted interface size). However, as we compare projects of comparable size in our experiment, the OP measurement for each project would be similarly affected; effectively voiding the negative effects for the comparative analysis. That being said, we cannot rule out that the OP analysis produces distorted results when applied to our small-scale projects of not more than 150 LOC and 30 UML classes.

Closely related to the above threat are the characteristic Object-Points (OP) component weights and the issue of deciding on their value loading for an experiment (e.g., the class W_C, source W_{S_O}, and target weights W_{T_O}; see Section 2.2). In the original application context of the Sneed OP analysis, the weight values are either adopted from closely related measurement instruments (e.g., the Data Points analysis) and/or are mined for a target programming language to establish an empirical predictor, e.g., for the average method size specific to a given language. For our experiment, we adopted the standard values documented for the Sneed OP analysis [17]. While this has practical advantages (e.g., reusing default values established over multiple multi-language projects), it bears the risk of underestimating observations, if the weights are too small, or of overestimating them in the inverse case. As for the standard W_{O_C} value, reflecting the average method size in terms of statements, this caused us a particular tension: Sneed [17] states that this weight should be based on the average size of methods (in terms of language statements) for a particular programming language. For an experiment design, this requires to perform a calibration (i.e. the estimation of the average size of methods). This, however, assumes the availability of a critical number of code bases in the targeted language; a condition not satisfiable for the xoSAML DSL. Hence, we reverted to the default value of 3. To mitigate this general threat, we consulted the available literature on OP to investigate the origin of the standard values. In addition, we exchanged emails with Harry M. Sneed to clarify their justifications. Alas, for W_{S_o} and W_{T_o}, we were not able to recover details about the choice of 2. This undermines attempts of qualitatively evaluating observations based on message points (MP) scores.

Internal validity – The experiment design might have caused our observations not to follow directly from the data collected, i.e., the program structures implemented and processed. The base artifacts of the experiment were four different APIs and four resulting programs, implementing the single sign-on use case. While these four implementations realize the same application scenario (SSO service provider), the power and the completeness of their functionality differ with respect to framework and language specifics. We so risk having compared different functionality, resulting in a misleading measurement. To mitigate this risk, we took care to define a precise application scenario, based upon which the API feature chunk was extracted. In addition, the program implementations, while developed by one author alone, were reviewed by a second repeatedly. Given the small program sizes (i.e., 48-151 LOC), we considered this sufficient, at least for avoiding obvious design and implementation mistakes. Also, when relying on a single developer, there is the risk of introducing a bias due to a continued learning effect between one implementation and another. We strove for containing this threat by developing the four programs in parallel.

A key decision when designing the experiment was that of a surrogate measurement: For the analysis, data is gathered on the syntactical structure of the programs constructed from a specific API. The analyzed program sets a concise *working framework* [6], i.e., the feature chunk of the API needed to implement a specific application scenario. Considering programs integrating a given API chunk as measurement proxy bears a considerable risk, e.g., by the requirement to limit the program to the API chunk and the application scenario. Analyzing the entire API, however could equally introduce a bias because each API varies in terms of the provided features (turning, e.g., into a comparatively increased interface size and a greater interaction level). By observing the interface as used to construct a given program, the resulting measurement is more eligible for a comparative analysis. Most importantly, some factors influencing the perceived complexity [6] can be considered constant. For instance, the number and the type of working tasks to complete is specific to a given scenario.

An important risk follows from the choice of surrogate-based measurement of API complexity over a program structure implementing a concise API feature chunk (i.e., a working framework [6]). This requires the program code to be strictly limited to assembling and configuring services offered by the framework APIs, without introducing code and structural noise due to implementation deficiencies etc. To minimize this threat, we took the following actions. First, API protocol steps (authorization request, assertion handling) were implemented in terms of single operation declarations; or, alternatively, a single method with a switch-threaded control flow. Second, declaring new classes and new operations for the scope of the program was to be limited to a minimum. Ideally, the programs as pure assembly and configuration components should be implemented by a single operation. Exceptions were the requirement to derive final from abstract classes, when expected by the framework API protocol, or implementing operations from required interfaces. While the simpleSAMLphp program did not require a single class declaration, the API design of OpenSAML and JAXB made it necessary to define new classes.

The need for UML representation of the analyzed programs is a further source of possible distortion: On the one hand, the selective inclusion of UML model elements into the OP analysis (see Section 3.4), required to capture the chosen API feature chunk, might result in a inappropriate mapping of source code to model structures. On the other hand, bridging between language and UML abstractions involved critical decisions. For example, in xoSAML's host language XOTcl the equivalent for attributes can be considered both UML operations and UML attributes. The transformation rules, while applied uniformly to all projects, might have introduced an unwanted bias.

Another concern is that one of the four framework APIs, the xoSAML DSL, was designed and implemented by one of the authors because no DSL-based API implementation for the SAML domain had existed to our knowledge. Although we put a lot of effort in implementing a generic facility, the risk remains that we were biased towards a research prototype known to be explored in our experiment.

For the same reason, we might have been biased when evaluating and selecting the Object-Point method for our experiment design, adopting a measurement approach leaning itself towards our DSL implementation. For this initial experiment, we avoided this threat by selecting a standard variant of the OP analysis documented in literature [17]. The Sneed OP variant was picked by senior researchers unaware of the DSL implementation details. The selection criteria were the suitability for measuring diverse API designs, written in different OO languages (XOTcl, Java), and the fit for approximating our working notion of API complexity.

External validity – The generalizability of the experiment results is constrained. Our experiment is limited in its scope and exploratory in nature. As for the scope, the initial findings were drawn from experiences with a single application scenario and with a single embedded, textual DSL. xoSAML is not representative for the considerable variety of embedded DSLs available. While xoSAML shares some common characteristics of embedded DSLs (e.g., a

command-query style, use of a method chaining operator) and exposes many general-purpose features of the hosting OO scripting language XOTcl [15], these similarities are not sufficient for the criterion of representativeness. In addition, and as already stated, our working notion of complexity does not cover many relevant dimensions of API complexity. Nevertheless, the experiment is repeatable for DSL-based APIs in other domains.

6. Related Work

In this section, we discuss related work on predominantly quantitative evaluation approaches for DSL-based software projects.

Bettin [4] documents a quantitative study on measuring the potential of domain-specific modeling (DSML) techniques. Using a small-scale example application, Bettin compares different software development approaches: the traditional (without any abstract modeling), the UML-based and the DSML-based approach. Bettin implemented the same example application using every single development approach and compared the development efforts needed. The efforts are measured by counting Lines of Code (LOC) and necessary input cues called Atomic Model Elements (AME; e.g., mouse operations or keyboard strokes). The findings are that the DSML-based approach required the least effort, with the UML-based approach ranking second and so preceding manual modeling.

Zeng et al. [24] introduce the AG DSL for generating dataflow analyzers. Their evaluation approach examines manual and generated creation of AG and corresponding C++ programs, by comparing the program sizes in terms of LOC and by contrasting the execution times. The evaluation results suggest for a single application scenario that the manually-written DSL code is more than ten times smaller than its C++ equivalent.

Merilinna et al. [12] describe an assessment framework for comparing different software development approaches (e.g., DSL-based vs. manual coding). The framework is also applied to DSMLs. The primary unit of measurement in this framework is time; for example, the amount of time needed to learn the DSML, or, the time to implement a specific use case. The approach therefore does not directly cover program structure as source of API complexity.

A DSL-based refactoring of an existing simulator software in the domain of army fire support is presented by Batory et al. [3]. Similarly to our approach, they conducted a quantitative evaluation using class complexity measurement. Therein, the class complexity is quantified by the number of methods, the number of LOC, and the number of tokens/symbols per class. By comparing the class complexities of both the original and the new DSL-based implementation, they state their DSL's positive impact on the program complexity, by reducing it approximately by a factor of two.

Kosar et al. [11] compare ten DSL implementation approaches by looking at indicators of implementation and end-user effort. In contrast to our work, Kosar et al. focus on technical options for DSL implementation, such as source-to-source transformations, macro processing, interpreting vs. compiling generators etc. Kosar et al. address a different aspect than our experiment, namely the DSL implementation itself.

In the direction of evaluating DSL implementation techniques, Klint et al. [10] investigate whether development toolkits for external DSLs (e.g., ANTLR or OMeta) have an observable impact on the maintainability of the resulting DSL implementations. Their study reports on assessing the maintainability of six alternative implementations of the same DSL using different host languages and DSL toolkits. Based on this DSL portfolio, a quantitative measurement is performed to compute an array of structural complexity indicators: volume (number of modules, module members, and module sizes in LOC), cyclomatic complexity, and code duplication ratios. Klint et al. conclude by stating that using DSL toolkits does not necessarily reduce structural complexity (that is, increases a DSL's maintainability), yet DSL generators decrease the need for boilerplate code.

7. Conclusion

Based on a literature review on domain-specific languages (DSLs), as well as our own experiences in building DSLs, we identified the need for exploring quantitative measurement approaches, capable of relating code-level properties of APIs to alleged effects of DSLs on selected quality attributes. Available empirical evidence appears too limited, particularly when expanded into statements on process and business performance: For example, experience reports hint at considerably reduced development times for DSL-based software products, an improved time-to-market, and substantial reductions in development and delivery costs (e.g., for developer or customer trainings; see e.g. [3, 4, 24]).

In this paper, we report first quantitative observations on the structural complexity of programs constructed from different types of APIs, obtained from an exploratory experiment in the domain of federated identity management. We adopted the Sneed Object-Points (OP) analysis [17] for quantifying API complexity specific to different programming interface designs. The OP scores derived from our experiment point towards a reduced API complexity when providing an embedded, textual DSLs as an API. If one accepts the working definition of structural API complexity in this paper and the Sneed OP measure constructs as adequate indicators, this observation is a clear direction for follow-up, confirmatory studies. By thoroughly reporting our experiment design, as well as by providing our raw data[5], this paper enables the reader to reproduce our results and to adopt the experiment procedure for such follow-up experiments.

As future work, we will address the identified threats to validity. That is, we will further explore the usefulness of the OP analysis to evaluate different API design approaches by refining its measure constructs. For this, we will also review alternative measure constructs (as offered by OO complexity measurement [1]) to complement an OP analysis.

Acknowledgments

We gratefully thank Jurgen Vinju for helping improve the paper as a report of empirical research; and Harry M. Sneed for clarifying details about the Object-Points analysis in private communication. Thanks are also due to the anonymous reviewers for their helpful and detailed comments.

References

[1] R. K. Bandi, V. K. Vaishnavi, and D. E. Turk. Predicting Maintenance Performance Using Object-Oriented Design Complexity Metrics. *IEEE Transactions on Software Engineering*, 29:77–87, 2003.

[2] R. D. Banker, R. J. Kauffman, and R. Kumar. An Empirical Test of Object-Based Output Measurement Metrics in a Computer Aided Software Engineering (CASE) Environment. *Journal of Management Information Systems*, 8(3):127–150, 1992.

[3] D. Batory, C. Johnson, B. MacDonald, and D. von Heeder. Achieving Extensibility through Product-Lines and Domain-Specific Languages: A Case Study. *ACM Trans. Softw. Eng. Methodol.*, 11(2):191–214, 2002.

[4] J. Bettin. Measuring the Potential of Domain-Specific Modelling Techniques. In *Proceedings of the 2nd Domain-Specific Modelling Languages Workshop (OOPSLA), Seattle, Washington, USA*, pages 39–44, 2002.

[5] J. Capers. *Applied Software Measurement: Global Analysis of Productivity and Quality*. McGraw-Hill, 3rd edition, 2008.

[6] S. Clarke and C. Becker. Using the Cognitive Dimensions Framework to evaluate the usability of a class library. In *Proceedings of the 15h Workshop of the Psychology of Programming Interest Group (PPIG 2003), Keele, UK*, pages 359–336, 2003.

[7] M. Fowler. *Domain Specific Languages*. The Addison-Wesley Signature Series. Addison-Wesley Professional, 1st edition, 2010.

[8] P. Gabriel, M. Goulão, and V. Amaral. Do Software Languages Engineers Evaluate their Languages? In *Proceedings of the XIII Congreso Iberoamericano en "Software Engineering"*, 2010.

[9] F. Hermans, M. Pinzger, and A. van Deursen. Domain-Specific Languages in Practice: A User Study on the Success Factors. In *Proceedings of the 12th International Conference Model Driven Engineering Languages and Systems (MODELS 2009) Denver, CO, USA, October 4-9, 2009*, volume 5795 of *Lecture Notes in Computer Science*, pages 423–437. Springer, 2009.

[10] P. Klint, T. van der Storm, and J. Vinju. On the Impact of DSL Tools on the Maintainability of Language Implementations. In C. Brabrand and P.-E. Moreau, editors, *Proceedings of Workshop on Language Descriptions, Tools and Applications 2010 (LDTA'10)*, pages 10:1–10:9. ACM, 2010.

[11] T. Kosar, P. M. López, P. Barrientos, and M. Mernik. A preliminary study on various implementation approaches of domain-specific languages. *Information and Software Technology*, 50(5):390–405, 2008.

[12] J. Merilinna and J. Pärssinen. Comparison Between Different Abstraction Level Programming: Experiment Definition and Initial Results. In *Proceedings of the 7th OOPSLA Workshop on Domain-Specific Modeling (DSM'07), Montréal, Candada*, number TR-38 in Technical Report, Finland, 2007. University of Jyväskylä.

[13] M. Mernik, J. Heering, and A. Sloane. When and How to Develop Domain-Specific Languages. *ACM Computing Surveys*, 37(4):316–344, 2005.

[14] MetaCase. Nokia Case Study. Industry experience report, MetaCase, 2007.

[15] G. Neumann and U. Zdun. XOTcl, an Object-Oriented Scripting Language. In *Proceedings of Tcl2k: The 7th USENIX Tcl/Tk Conference*, Austin, Texas, USA, 2000.

[16] OASIS. Security Assertion Markup Language (SAML) V2.0 Technical Overview. http://docs.oasis-open.org/security/saml/Post2.0/sstc-saml-tech-overview-2.0-cd-02.pdf, 2008.

[17] H. M. Sneed. Estimating the costs of software maintenance tasks. In *Proceedings of the International Conference on Software Maintenance (ICSM'95), Opio (Nice), France, October 17-20, 1995*, pages 168–181. IEEE Computer Society, 1995.

[18] M. Strembeck and U. Zdun. An Approach for the Systematic Development of Domain-Specific Languages. *Software: Practice and Experience*, 39(15):1253–1292, 2009.

[19] J. Stylos and B. A. Myers. Mapping the Space of API Design Decisions. In *2007 IEEE Symposium on Visual Languages and Human-Centric Computing (VL/HCC 2007), 23-27 September 2007, Coeur d'Alene, Idaho, USA*, pages 50–60. IEEE Computer Society, 2007.

[20] A. van Deursen and P. Klint. Little languages: Little Maintenance? *Journal of Software Maintenance*, 10(2):75–92, 1998.

[21] D. A. Wheeler. SLOCCount. http://www.dwheeler.com/sloccount/, last accessed: October 14, 2008.

[22] D. Wile. Lessons learned from real DSL experiments. *Science of Computer Programming*, 51(3):265–290, 2004.

[23] J. Wüst. SDMetrics. http://sdmetrics.com/, last accessed: May 27, 2011, 2011.

[24] J. Zeng, C. Mitchell, and S. A. Edwards. A Domain-Specific Language for Generating Dataflow Analyzers. *Electronic Notes in Theoretical Computer Science*, 164(2):103–119, 2006.

Growing a Language Environment with Editor Libraries

Sebastian Erdweg*   Lennart C. L. Kats†   Tillmann Rendel*
Christian Kästner*   Klaus Ostermann*   Eelco Visser†

* University of Marburg
† Delft University of Technology

Abstract

Large software projects consist of code written in a multitude of different (possibly domain-specific) languages, which are often deeply interspersed even in single files. While many proposals exist on how to integrate languages semantically and syntactically, the question of how to support this scenario in integrated development environments (IDEs) remains open: How can standard IDE services, such as syntax highlighting, outlining, or reference resolving, be provided in an extensible and compositional way, such that an open mix of languages is supported in a single file?

Based on our library-based syntactic extension language for Java, SugarJ, we propose to make IDEs extensible by organizing editor services in *editor libraries*. Editor libraries are libraries written in the object language, SugarJ, and hence activated and composed through regular import statements on a file-by-file basis. We have implemented an IDE for editor libraries on top of SugarJ and the Eclipse-based Spoofax language workbench. We have validated editor libraries by evolving this IDE into a fully-fledged and schema-aware XML editor as well as an extensible LaTeX editor, which we used for writing this paper.

Categories and Subject Descriptors D.2.6 [*Programming Environments*]; D.2.13 [*Reusable Software*]; D.3.2 [*Language Classifications*]: Extensible languages

General Terms Languages

Keywords language extensibility, library, DSL embedding, language workbench

1. Introduction

Programming language extensibility is an old research topic that has gained new relevance by the trend toward domain-specific languages and the vision of language-oriented programming [6, 32]. Researchers have proposed a variety of different approaches to extend the syntax and semantics of languages and to embed languages in other languages, such as libraries [9, 14], extensible compilers [8, 21, 28], macro systems [1, 3, 24, 25], and meta-object protocols [22, 23]. However, while languages themselves have gained flexibility, tool support in the form of integrated development environments (IDEs) cannot keep up with the rapid development and composition of new languages.

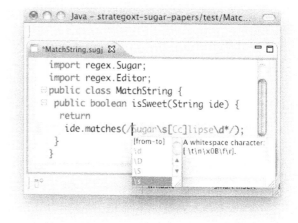

Figure 1. regex.Sugar provides a syntactic extension for regular expressions; regex.Editor provides the according IDE extension.

IDEs assist programmers, who spend a significant amount of time reading, navigating, adapting and writing source code. They provide *editor services* that improve a program's layout and support programmers in performing changes to the code, including syntax highlighting, code folding, outlining, reference resolving, error marking, quick fix proposals, code completion, and many more. The quality of IDE support for a language is hence a significant factor for the productivity of developers in that language. It is therefore desirable to provide the same level of tool support for extended and domain-specific languages that programmers are familiar with from mainstream programming languages.

However, as our own and the experience of others show, developing tool support for a new or extended language requires significant effort [5, 16, 20]. Although there are several advances to generate tool support from declarative specifications [7, 17], generation has to be repeated for every combination of language extensions because the generated editor services neither compose nor grow with the language.

Composable and growable editor services are especially important in the context of growable languages that support flexible and composable extensions, e.g., for the embedding of multiple domain-specific languages. In prior work, we developed *SugarJ*, a variant of Java which is extensible via sugar libraries [9]. A sugar library can export, in addition to ordinary types and methods, a syntactic extension and a transformation from the extended syntax back into the syntax of the base language. Sugar libraries are imported via the usual import mechanism of the base language. Multiple syntactic extensions can be composed by importing them into the same file, allowing a local mix of multiple embedded languages.

In this paper, we propose *editor libraries* to further generalize library-based extensibility towards IDEs. Editor libraries compose: When multiple languages are mixed within the same file (such as XML, SQL and regular expressions within Java), we import and thereby combine all corresponding editor services. Editor libraries (as other libraries) are self-applicable, that is, editor libraries can be used to develop other editor libraries. Furthermore, editor libraries encourage a generative approach through *staging*: We generate editor services from high-level specifications (yet another domain-specific language) at one stage and use the generated services at a later stage. Staging enables the coordination of editor services that span several source files or languages.

We have developed an Eclipse-based IDE with support for editor libraries called *Sugarclipse*. For each file, Sugarclipse considers all editor libraries in scope, interprets the associated editor services and presents the decorated source code and editing facilities to the programmer. Sugarclipse is based on the *Spoofax* language workbench [17], which supports the generation and dynamic reloading of Eclipse-based language-specific editors from declarative editor configurations. In Figure 1, we illustrate an example usage of Sugarclipse: The import of regex.Sugar activates a syntactic extension for regular expressions, which integrates regular expression syntax into the surrounding Java syntax (instead of the usual string encoding). The import of the editor library regex.Editor enables corresponding editor services for regular expressions such as syntax coloring and code completion. Sugarclipse automatically composes the editor services of the host language, here Java, and of the extension, here regular expressions, to provide uniform IDE support to the programmer. While in Sugarclipse and in this paper, we focus on editor libraries for SugarJ, the concept of editor libraries is similarly useful for embedded languages in syntactically less flexible languages (cf. Section 7).

With several case studies, we demonstrate the practicality of editor libraries and the power of their composition. Beyond small editor libraries such as regular expressions illustrated above, we implemented fully-fledged editor libraries for XML (including XML Schema) and Latex. We used the latter for writing this paper.

In summary, we make the following contributions:

- We introduce the novel concept of *editor libraries* for organizing IDE extensions in libraries of the object language, in particular, to provide IDE support for embedded DSLs.

- Editor libraries are activated using the host language's standard import mechanism, and editor libraries *compose* to support multiple DSLs and the base language in a single file.

- We describe a pattern of *editor library staging* to generate editor services from high-level specifications and to coordinate editor services between several source files or languages.

- We present *Sugarclipse*, an extensible IDE for SugarJ based on the Spoofax language workbench. Our growable IDE complements the syntactic extensibility of SugarJ with the capability of providing domain-specific editor services that conform to the embedded DSLs.

- We validate our approach through realistic *case studies* of fully-fledged editors for XML and Latex. We demonstrate how our IDE supports domain-specific and programmer-defined editor configuration languages as well as deriving editor services from language specifications.

Sugarclipse is an open source project that is publicly available at http://sugarj.org/editor. Our case studies and, in particular, the source of this paper are available at the same location.

2. An overview of Sugarclipse

Sugarclipse, as shown in Figure 2, consists of an editor that features services such as syntax coloring, error marking and code completion. Sugarclipse has built-in support for Java syntax only, but all of Sugarclipse's editor services are user-extensible: Additional syntax and editor services can be imported from libraries.

2.1 Using Sugarclipse

A Sugarclipse user activates editor support for an additional language by importing a corresponding library. For example, in Figure 2, the sugar library xml.Sugar provides a grammar for embedded XML documents, and the editor library xml.Editor provides editor services for XML. This editor library specifies syntax colouring, outlining, folding etc., for embedded XML documents without invalidating the built-in services for Java. For example, the resulting editor contains code folding and outlining for both Java and XML combined. The additional editor support only affects the XML part of the document and leaves the remaining editor support intact, most visible in Figure 2 from syntax highlighting (including correct highlighting of quoted Java code nested inside XML).

We can extend the XML example by requiring that the embedded XML should conform to a specific schema. Knowing that schema, Sugarclipse provides even more tailored editor support for the embedded XML, including content completion providing a list of all valid tags and error reporting for validation errors. To activate the additional editor support, the user imports the editor library xml.schema.BookSchema derived from the schema.

2.2 Editor services

A Sugarclipse user can also assume the role of editor-service developer, because editor services are specified declaratively within Sugarclipse. This is more expressive than setting options in the Eclipse menu and significantly easier than manually extending Eclipse by writing a corresponding plugin. In addition to error marking, Sugarclipse lifts and extends eight different editor services from Spoofax [17]. Each service can be declaratively specified in a domain-specific language.

- *Syntax coloring* highlights source code using a colored, bold or italic font.

- *Code folding* supports collapsing part of the source code to hide its details.

- *Outlining* gives a hierarchical overview over the current document and enables fast navigation.

- *Content completion* provides proposals for complementing the current source code.

- *Reference resolving* resolves a construct (typically a name) to its declaration and provides facilities to navigate to the declaration directly ("CTRL-click").

- *Hover help* displays documentation as a tooltip when hovering over a documented entity with the mouse.

- A *refactoring or projection* applies a transformation to (parts of) the source code and writes the result either in the original or a separate file.

- *Parentheses matching* marks matching parentheses in the source code and adds closing parentheses automatically. This service is also essential for *automatic indentation* after line breaks.

Conceptually, editor services can be understood as procedures that decorate syntax trees, for example, with coloring information. Sugarclipse then interprets these decorated trees and maps the decorations to the original source code or other means of visualization such as a separate outline window or a completion proposal viewer.

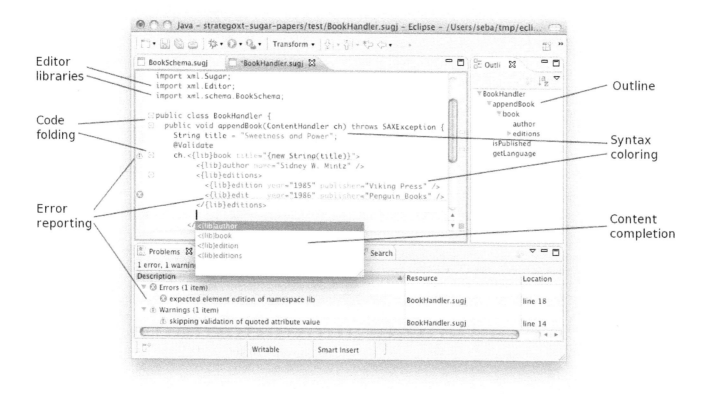

Editor libraries

Code folding

Error reporting

Outline

Syntax coloring

Content completion

Figure 2. Sugarclipse extended through the imported editor libraries. The quoted Java expression **new** String(title) is highlighted using the typical Java coloring, while the surrounding XML code uses an XML-specific coloring service.

```
package xml;

import editor.Colors;
import xml.XmlSyntax;

public editor services Editor {
    colorer
        ElemName : blue (recursive)
        AttrName : darkorange (recursive)
        AttValue : darkred (recursive)
        CharData : black (recursive)

    folding
        Element

    outliner
        Element
}
```

Figure 3. Editor library for coloring, folding and outlining of XML code.

Since editor services are mere tree decorators, their definitions are fairly simple in most cases (the definition of refactorings and projections being an exception). To reflect this simplicity in editor service implementations, we use an extended version of the declarative editor service configuration language provided by Spoofax [17].

Developers can bundle multiple editor-service specification in an editor library (declared with **public editor services**). For example, the xml.Editor library shown in Figure 3 provides editor ser-

vices for coloring, folding and outlining XML documents using declarative tree decoration rules. Each tree decoration rule specifies a syntax tree pattern to match against and the decoration to apply to matched trees. For example, the XML coloring rules match on trees of the kind ElemName, AttrName, AttValue and CharData, that is, trees derived from these non-terminal sorts as defined by the imported sugar library xml.XmlSyntax. The coloring rules thus declare that XML element names are shown in a blue font, XML attribute names in a dark orange font, etc., and that the coloring recursively applies to all nodes in the matched trees. Similarly, the folding and outlining services declare that XML elements are foldable and XML documents show up in the outline of source files.

We specifically support the development of editor libraries by providing, bundled with Sugarclipse, an editor library for writing editor libraries. In similar fashion, we encourage other developers of language embeddings to accompany their embeddings with editor support in the form of editor libraries.

3. Editor libraries

The basic use of editor libraries, as described in the previous section, is to serve as containers for editor service specifications. Before discussing the composability of editor libraries in detail, we describe a number of advanced usage patterns for editor libraries in SugarJ.

3.1 Domain-specific editor configuration languages

SugarJ supports syntactic abstraction over all of its ingredients, that is, Java code, syntactic sugar, static analysis specifications and, now as well, editor configurations. This design enables the

```
import xml.schema.XmlSchema;

public xmlschema BookSchema {
  <xsd:schema targetNamespace="lib">
    <xsd:element name="book" type="Book" />

    <xsd:complexType name="Book">
      <xsd:choice maxOccurs="unbounded">
        <xsd:element name="author" type="Person" />
        <xsd:element name="editions" type="Editions" />
      </xsd:choice>
      <xsd:attribute name="title" type="string" />
    </xsd:complexType>
  </xsd:schema>
}
```

Figure 4. An excerpt of the Book XML Schema. The xml.schema.XmlSchema library provides validation and editor services for XML schemas themselves.

development of customized and potentially domain-specific editor service configuration languages. For example, we have applied SugarJ's syntactic extensibility to provide an XML-specific editor service configuration syntax in the style of Cascading Style Sheets (CSS):

```
import editor.Colors;
import xml.CSS;
import xml.XmlSyntax;

public css CSSEditor {
  Element { folding; outlining }
  ElemName { rec-color : blue }
  AttrName { rec-color : darkorange }
  AttValue { rec-color : darkred }
  CharData { rec-color : black }
}
```

This CSS-style editor configuration corresponds and, in fact, desugars to the editor configuration in standard editor service syntax shown in Figure 3; CSS is just another syntax for configuring editor services.

3.2 Staged editor libraries

Many editor services are not static, but rather depend on the contents of the file being edited and imported files. For example, hover help for non-local Java methods depends on the method definitions in other files and code completion for XML elements depends on the corresponding schema. Hand-written IDEs support such editor services by managing a set of files as a project, explicitly coordinating between the information retrieved from each file. Unfortunately, neither SugarJ nor Spoofax have a notion of projects: In Spoofax, editor services for different files are independent, and in SugarJ, files are processed one after another. Sugarclipse, however, supports separate *generation and application stages* for editor libraries from different source files, which enables rich patterns of interaction between editor services of individual source files.

The central idea of our *staging pattern* is to first generate editor services from domain-specific declarations in one file and to later use them in another file. The generated editor services may well be of auxiliary nature such as a mapping from method names to the documentation of these methods, which a hover help editor service can query to display documentation of a method as a tooltip. In general, Sugarclipse employs the transformation language Stratego [29] for auxiliary editor services, and an import statement brings the generated editor services into scope.

For example, we applied the staging pattern to promote XML schemas as domain-specific declarations for XML editor services

that are specific to an XML dialect. Such editor services include XML validation and tag completion. Figure 4 shows an excerpt of the Book XML schema, which declares a dialect of XML for describing books. From this schema, we generate the definition of a static analysis as well as code completion. For the former, we desugar an XML schema into a set of Stratego rules that traverse a given XML document to check whether this document conforms to the schema. In other words, we generate a type checker for each XML schema. The result of applying the XML Book type checker is shown in Figure 2, where quoted Java expressions within an XML document are marked but ignored otherwise. Furthermore, our XML Schema embedding desugars each schema into a set of schema-specific completion templates. For instance, the following completion template results from desugaring the above Book schema.

```
completion template : Content =
  "<{lib}book title=\"" <string> "\">"
  "</{lib}book>"
```

Accordingly, when importing the Book schema, Sugarclipse recognizes the accompanying editor services and provides code completion to the programmer as shown in Figure 2.

As this case study illustrates, Sugarclipse supports the implementation of editor services that involve multiple files using a generative approach; the staging pattern effectively facilitates data flow from one source file to another.

3.3 Self-applicability

Like conventional libraries, editor libraries are self-applicable, that is, editor services can be used during the development of other editor libraries. For example, we have implemented code completion for the code completion editor service using an editor library:

```
public editor services Editor {
  completions
    completion template : EditorServiceCompletionRule =
      "completion template" " : " <Sort> " =\n\t"
      "\"" <prefix> "\" <" <placeholder> ">"
}
```

This template provides content completion for completion templates themselves. Completion templates are represented as sequences of strings and placeholders such as <Sort>, which Sugarclipse marks for the user to replace. The above completion template expands into the following code on selection, where the underlined fragments are placeholders:

```
completion template : Sort =
  "prefix" <placeholder>
```

More generally, we provide full editor support for writing editor libraries in Sugarclipse using editor libraries.

4. Editor composition

A key feature of Sugarclipse is the ability to compose editor libraries. For example, we can import support for regular expressions and XML in the same document. The editor then supports both language extensions with corresponding syntax highlighting, and other facilities. Editor libraries cooperate to present a coherent user interface even though their respective authors might not have planned for their editor library to be used in that exact combination of editor libraries.

We can compose editor libraries developed independently, such as regular expressions and XML, but we can also develop editor libraries that extend other libraries and editor libraries that explicitly interact with other editor libraries through extension points. Let us illustrate such interaction with an example from the domain of text documents (which we will describe in more detail in Sec. 6.2): We express a bibliography database in one language (e.g., Bibtex-like) and write the text with references to bibliography items in another language (e.g, Latex-like). When composing both languages, we would like to add editor services to navigate from bibliography references to their definitions, to suggest available references with content completion, to provide hover help, and so forth. These editor services need to bridge elements in different files and from different languages.

Although different kinds of interactions and even conflicts between editor services are possible, we argue that editor services are largely independent and have local effects. In addition, for many services, interactions can be implicitly resolved using generic strategies. Finally, for intended interactions as in the bibliography example, we apply the staging pattern for explicitly coordinating editor services.

4.1 Local variation and global consistency

Editor libraries extend the *local* behavior of the SugarJ editor. There are different notions of locality:

- Editor libraries affect only files that import them explicitly. In these files, only the part after the import is affected.

- Editor libraries that extend distinct editor services compose naturally. For example an editor library defining syntax coloring will not conflict with another editor service providing content completion.

- Editor libraries usually reason about small and local subtrees of the abstract syntax tree. For example, an editor library typically defines syntax highlighting for specific syntactic forms, not for the overall program, and editor libraries that accompany a DSL embedding reason over tree fragments of that DSL only. Editor libraries that act on different parts of the abstract syntax tree naturally compose. For example, the XML editor library shown in Figure 3 only decorates XML fragments of the syntax tree and does not affect Java fragments.

The *global* behavior of the SugarJ editor, however, is fixed and cannot be extended by editor libraries. For example, the SugarJ editor supports a fixed set of editor services such as syntax highlighting, reference resolving, hover help, etc. as discussed in Section 2.2. The SugarJ editor presents a coherent user interface to access these editor services. For example, key bindings or the visual appearance of error markers are defined by the SugarJ editor directly and are therefore consistent across error libraries.

Together, global consistency and local variation go a long way ensuring that Sugarclipse supports arbitrary languages while still providing a coherent user interface. Some interactions between editor libraries cannot be resolved by locality, however, and require implicit or explicit coordination between editor libraries.

4.2 Implicit coordination

Although most editor libraries work locally, their results can conflict or overlap. For most editor services, conflicts can be resolved implicitly following generic strategies: aggregation and closest match.

For most editor services, aggregating results of different editor libraries is sufficient. For example, in our XML embedding, both Java and XML code completion services would respond to a prefix ch., which could be followed by a Java method name or an XML element. Sugarclipse simply shows all completion proposals. Aggregation works similarly for code folding, outlining and error marking.

For some other services, primarily syntax highlighting and hover help, simple heuristics can resolve conflicts implicitly. For example, when one editor library specifies that all tokens in assignments should be blue, whereas another editor library specifies that all tokens in while loops should be red, Sugarclipse needs to coordinate between these editor libraries and decide in which color to display tokens in an assignment nested within a while loop. As heuristic, we propose a closest-match rule, as used for style sheets in HTML: Color information, hover help, and other specifications on an AST node overrule corresponding specifications of the parent node; always the most specific information is used for presentation. For our example above, the closest-match rule displays the assignment blue, because the match on assignments is more specific (closer to the tokens in question) than the match on the while loop.

Aggregation and the closed-match rule resolve most conflicts implicitly in a natural way. Explicit coordination is usually necessary only for intended interactions.

4.3 Explicit coordination

Not all editor libraries are supposed to be independent. Editor libraries might explicitly extend the behavior of other libraries or interact with them in controlled ways.

An editor library can add additional editor-service specifications to another library. For example, the XML-Schema library builds on top of the XML library and extends it with code completion and error checking. In addition, different editor libraries can interact explicitly through the staging pattern to share data and coordinate editor services. The staging pattern, described in Section 3.2, enables communication from one editor library to another through the generation of auxiliary editor services. In our example, the bibliography database shares information about all known entries by generating an auxiliary editor service (technically: Stratego rules) that maps entry names to their definitions:

```
bibtex−entry : "Hudak98" −>
  BibtexEntryStm("@inproceedings",
    BibtexEntryName("Hudak98"), ...)
```

Any other editor library can use this information to integrate with the bibliography editor library. For example, our Latex editor library supplies hover help and content completion for citations (\cite{...}), and checks for undefined references.

4.4 Limitations

Although editor-library composition is usually straightforward in practice, there are limitations. Most significantly, we cannot provide modular guarantees about editor services in hostile environments.

Editor services use a global namespace without hiding. In principle, editor libraries could access (auxiliary) services of all other imported editor libraries and extend them. We discourage uncontrolled sharing and use naming conventions (similar to fully qualified names in Java) to avoid accidental name clashes. The staging-based communication between editor libraries relies on conventions and implementation patterns; there is no explicit scoping concept for staged services yet.

Furthermore, editor services should make little assumptions about the global structure of the AST. Editor services are used in a context where the AST of a file typically contains structures from different languages. For example, navigating from an AST element to its direct parent should be avoided, instead one should search for a direct or indirect parent of the expected type. Such strategies make editor libraries more robust against additional language extensions. However, Sugarclipse currently does not enforce locality and cannot detect violations modularly.

Building a module system to provide explicit namespaces and checked interfaces for Sugarclipse and the underlying SugarJ is an

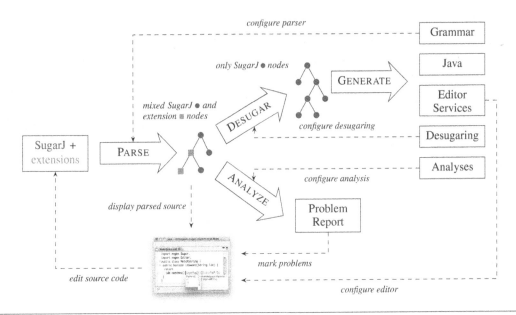

Figure 5. Data flow in Sugarclipse. The results of the processing pipeline (⟹) are used to configure (- -→) the earlier stages.

interesting avenue for future work. Such a module system should prevent name clashes and control what kind of information (technically: which Stratego rules) can be shared between editor libraries. To a large degree this seems to be a straightforward adoption of concepts from other module systems, such as the compilation manager in Standard ML [2]. On top, semantic interfaces could enable modular detection of conflicts between two editor libraries, so we would report an error when importing both of them.

In our experience, conflicts between editor libraries are rare and patterns for explicit coordination are easy to implement when required. Naming conventions and implementation patterns seem sufficient to avoid conflicts in practice. Hostile environments (deliberate attacks against editor libraries) are currently not a practical concern for editor extensions. Sugarclipse appears useful for many practical tasks, even without modular guarantees. Nevertheless, more experience in a broader set of applications is necessary to assess the difficulty of editor library composition.

5. Technical realization

In Sugarclipse, we combine the sugar libraries of SugarJ [9] with the IDE foundation of Spoofax [17] to support editor libraries for growing an IDE. SugarJ parses a file incrementally, because each declaration can extend the grammar of the rest of the file, and like in Spoofax, we use a generic editor component which can be configured to support different languages. Sugarclipse adds editor libraries into the mix: sugar libraries can desugar source code into editor libraries, and editor libraries in scope reconfigure the editor while a source file is edited. Together, these components enable to grow the IDE with editor libraries.

5.1 Architecture

Source code documents are often processed in many stages, compile-time and run-time being traditionally the most well-known. A library can affect several of these stages. For example, a Java class library contains, among other things, type definitions and method bodies. Clients of the library are type-checked against the type definitions in the library at compile-time, but method calls to method definitions in the library are executed at run-time. In our previous work on sugar libraries in SugarJ, we have broadened the

applicability of libraries by considering additional stages: parsing, desugaring and analysis. Sugar libraries contain grammar or desugaring rules to affect these stages of the SugarJ implementation. In the present work on editor libraries, we consider an integrated development environment as an integral part of the language implementation, that is, we consider an additional editor stage, which can be affected by editor libraries.

The interaction of these stages in Sugarclipse is shown in Figure 5. The editor stage is depicted by the Sugarclipse screenshot, all other stages are depicted as block arrows (⟹). The parsing stage transforms a source code document into an heterogeneous abstract syntax tree with nodes from different language extensions. The desugaring stage expands all nodes corresponding to language extensions into nodes of the base language, and the generation stage transforms the resulting homogeneous abstract syntax tree into separate source code artefacts containing grammar extensions, desugaring rules, editor services and so on. At the same time, the analysis stage checks the heterogeneous abstract syntax tree and produces a problem report listing all found errors and warnings.

The results of compilation can configure earlier stages as depicted with dashed arrows (- -→) in Figure 5. For example, generated grammars configure the parsing stage for clients of a sugar library and the generated analyses are applied in the analysis stage. In addition to these stages, the results of compilation also configure the editor, as we detail in the following subsections. In particular, the editor displays the input file's content with syntax highlighting according to the parsed source code, marks problems found by the analysis stage and behaves according to the editor services currently in scope. When the programmer changes code in the editor, the processing pipeline is run again to produce updated grammars, desugarings, etc., and any changes in these artifacts are reflected in the various stages.

5.2 Incremental parsing

Sugarclipse supports languages with extendible syntax by relying on SugarJ for incremental parsing. Parsing with SugarJ is an incremental process because import declarations and syntax definitions can change the syntax for the rest of the file. To this end, SugarJ repeatedly parses a single top-level entity (e.g., import or class declaration) followed by the remainder of the file as a string. For each such parse, SugarJ extends the grammar according to the parsed entitiy before continuing to parse the remainder of the file.

In the context of Sugarclipse, two additional concerns arise. First, the parser must associate every node of the abstract syntax tree with position information which the editor needs for marking errors, moving the cursor for reference resolving or outline view navigation, and so on. Second, the parser must associate some nodes of the abstract syntax tree with tokens that are used for syntax highlighting.

To reconcile incremental parsing of SugarJ with creating tokens and collecting position information, we use the same tokenizer for each parse. After each parse, we partially retract the tokenizer to ignore all tokens after the top-level entity and to reset the parser position accordingly. After parsing, we combine the trees of all top-level entities and ensure that the tree nodes have pointers to corresponding tokens and position information.

5.3 Dynamic loading of editor services

Sugarclipse supports editor libraries by relying on Spoofax to provide a generic Eclipse-based editor which can dynamically load and reload editor services. Although Spoofax still distinguishes the building and loading of editor services into separate phases, its dynamic loading capability forms the basis for editor services that are transparently built and loaded with library imports in Sugarclipse.

In the context of Sugarclipse, two additional concerns arise. First, parse tables and editor services need to be adapted on-the-fly whenever the corresponding language or editor libraries change. This is accomplished by running the full processing pipeline whenever a file has been changed and needs to be reparsed. The editor then dynamically reloads the possibly regenerated editor services. To ensure optimal responsiveness of the editor, generation and reloading happens in a background thread. Any services that were already loaded and parse tables that were already built are cached. Second, in Sugarclipse, each file determines the required language components and editor components by means of library imports. Sugarclipse therefore needs to maintain a separate set of editor services for each file. In contrast, Spoofax normally uses a language-level factory class. We subclass that factory with a specialized implementation that loads editor services in a file-specific fashion.

To conclude, in the present section we presented Sugarclipse's architecture, which augments SugarJ's processing pipeline with an additional editor stage that can be configured via editor libraries. The editor stage connects to the processing pipeline through presenting the parsed syntax tree, marking errors and loading the (possibly staged) editor services. The following section reports on our experiments with this realization of Sugarclipse.

6. Case studies

We applied our Sugarclipse implementation to demonstrate the practicability of editor libraries. We have developed editor libraries for a small number of simple language extensions such as regular expressions, where editor services only act locally and no explicit coordination is necessary. These simple editor services compose with the basic SugarJ editor services and other simple editor services through implicit coordination. For example, our regular expression editor library would compose easily with an editor library for SQL to provide editor services for regular expressions nested within SQL statements, because each library acts on syntax tree of the respective DSL only.

In addition to these simple editor libraries, we have conducted two realistic case studies to evaluate the practicability and composability of editor libraries for larger languages: XML and LᴬTEX. In both case studies, we demonstrate Sugarclipse's support for the

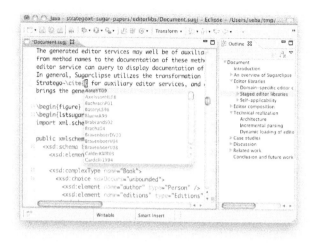

Figure 6. Editor services for Latex in Sugarclipse: outline, nested syntax coloring, citation completion, reference checking, code folding.

staging of editor services, and in the Latex case study we additionally apply explicit coordination to compose editor libraries.

6.1 Growing an XML IDE

XML and XML Schema demonstrate many interesting facets of editor libraries, including domain-specific editor configuration languages and editor library staging as described in Section 3. Although the XML Schema editor library extends the editor library for XML with schema-specific tag completion and validation, both libraries compose with editor services such as Java or SQL. This composability is based on locality and implicit coordination in the form of aggregation and the closest match rule (cf. Section 4).

In summary, we have grown Sugarclipse through the use of syntactic extensions and editor libraries into an XML-aware IDE that features coloring, folding, outlining, schema-specific tag completion and XML validation. Several potential editor services have not been implemented so far, but qualify as future student projects, for example, reference resolving according to XML Schema references or hover help to display documentation from the schema within the XML document.

6.2 Growing a Latex IDE

Language extensions such as XML or regular expressions extend the Java fragment of SugarJ and provide editor services that compose with Java services. Compared to Java, these language extensions are relatively small and do not cross-cut Java programs too much. Therefore, we also wanted to gain experience with incrementally growing a language from scratch by composing multiple sublanguages and their editor services into one unified language. To this end, we grew Sugarclipse into a Latex IDE by composing a Latex core with libraries for mathematical formulas, listings of (parsed and IDE-supported) source code and Bibtex bibliographies and citations. However, we only provide an IDE frontend for the Latex language and its libraries: Latex code in Sugarclipse compiles to regular Latex files, which use regular Latex libraries. In Figure 6, we show a screenshot of our Latex IDE.

The basic Latex language consists of macro calls \emph{arg}, environments \begin{abstract}...\end{abstract}, structure declarations \section{A}, \paragraph{B}, and so forth, and of course text. We support these concepts in our core Latex syntax definition and editor library, which, for example, highlights section headers in a bold, blue font, proposes code completions for macro calls, or provides a structural document outline.

In separate libraries, we define the syntax and editor support for various extensions of the Latex core:

First, the math library introduces a new language construct for formulas $n \to n + 1$ and according editor services (e.g., highlighting). These services act locally and thus compose with other Latex extensions.

Second, the listings library supports source code listings in a document. Typically, such source code listings are unparsed, unchecked and, often enough, erroneous. Within the code listing, all language-specific editor services are available, if the corresponding editor libraries are in scope. This way, we compose the Latex editor services with editor services for Java, services for editor libraries and services for language extensions such as XML Schema. For example, while writing this paper, Sugarclipse provided us syntax coloring and error checking for the schema in Figure 4, as shown in the screenshot of Figure 6.

Third, we separately implemented a syntactic extension and editor library for Bibtex, which, for instance, provides reference resolving and hover help for string constants within a bibliography. Bibtex and Latex interact via citations \cite{...} that occur in a Latex document and refer to Bibtex entries. However, the according editor services do not compose automatically in a meaningfully way; explicit coordination is necessary to provide code completion, hover help or checking for undefined references. We provide these editor services for citations by generating and explicitly coordinating services as described in Section 4.3.

The key feature of our Latex IDE is its extensibility: users can extend the IDE through syntax definitions and editor libraries to support, for instance, vector-graphics libraries. Staging and explicit coordination of editor services provides the conceptual means for implementing a wide range of powerful IDE extensions.

7. Discussion

In this paper, we have focused on the integration of editor libraries into a syntactically extensible object language such as SugarJ. In this section, we point out a number of further application scenarios for editor libraries and discuss whether it is sensible at all to organize editor services as part of source files.

7.1 Language embedding

There are several approaches to embed domain-specific languages, even when the host language is not syntactically extensible. Typical examples are string-based embeddings and embedding a language with constructs of the host language, known as pure embedding [14]. The latter works even better if the host language has a flexible syntax, as in Scala. In Figure 7, we illustrate three typical embeddings: embedding regular expressions as plain strings in Java, embedding XML as API calls in C#, and embedding LINQ-style queries in Scala.

Even for DSL embeddings in a nonextensible language, we want to add domain-specific IDE support. Even if regular expressions are embedded as strings or XML is embedded as API calls, we want to provide domain-specific editor services such as syntax coloring and content completion. Using editor libraries, DSL implementers can accompany their DSL embeddings with editor services to support programmers.

In the case of string-based embedding, Sugarclipse attempts to parse the document in more detail than the host language. In the pure-embedding scenario, we provide editor-service declarations that reason about more complex syntactic structures, for example nesting of XAttribute instantiation inside XElement instantiation. The general library mechanism works equivalently for languages that are syntactically extensible or not.

```
s.matches("a\\.*[0−9]")
```
(a) String-based embedding of regular expressions in Java.

```
new XElement("book",
    new XAttribute("title", new String(title)),
    new XElement("author", new XAttribute("name", "Mintz"))))
```
(b) Pure embedding of XML in C#.

```
from(books)(b => where(b.isPublished) select(b.title))
```
(c) Pure embedding of SQL in Scala.

Figure 7. Typical DSL embeddings in Java, C# and Scala.

7.2 Library-based pluggable type systems

The notion of pluggable type systems was first proposed by Bracha and describes type systems that accept extensions (plugins) to enforce additional static analyses on demand [4]. Programmers can configure a pluggable type system by selecting a set of extensions to activate. Due to Sugarclipse's support for marking user-defined errors and warnings visually in the source file and problems view, Sugarclipse is especially well-suited for the application of library-based pluggable type systems. In a library-based pluggable type system, type system extensions are organized in libraries and activated through usual import statements.

Pluggable type systems enable the definition of specialized language subsets for various purposes: pedagogical language subsets prohibit the use of certain language constructs, convention-based language subsets enforce the compliance with code style or author guide lines, language subsets for a particular platform (e.g., Java targeting Google Web Toolkit) often support part of the standard library only. However, more sophisticated language restrictions are possible as well. For instance, we implemented XML validation as a library-based type system plugin.

7.3 Are editor libraries a good idea?

Sugarclipse raises the question whether it is a good idea to have editor definitions as part of the sources of a program. One could argue that such metadata should be kept separate, because they are not part of the program semantics and they potentially couple the sources to a specific IDE. Our answer to this objection is twofold: First, SugarJ and Sugarclipse are attempts to tear down stratifications into base and metalevel. This enables self-applicability and the use of the same mechanisms for abstraction, versioning, deployment, evolution and so forth at all metalevels. Second, we tried to reduce the conceptual coupling to a specific IDE by making the editor definitions as abstract as possible, such that Sugarclipse-like functionality can be adopted for many IDEs. While more experience is necessary for the final word on editor libraries, we believe that the positive evidence we collected makes further research worthwhile.

8. Related work

Our work follows in a line of previous work on extensible and customizable code editors, IDEs, and language workbenches. We provide an overview and compare these works to Sugarclipse.

Extensibility of code editors and IDEs. Notable early examples of extensible code editors are Emacs and Vim. They support extensibility by means of plugins, written in dynamic languages such as Lisp and Vim Script. Using APIs and hooks to coordinate actions in the editor, these plugins can introduce syntax highlighting and shortcuts or commands specific to a language. Plugins that introduce more advanced features, such as inline error markers are rare for these editors.

Modern IDEs distinguish themselves from the traditional code editors and programming environments by combining a rich set of programmer utilities such as version management with a variety of sophisticated language-specific editor services [12]. These IDEs parse the source code as it is typed, rather than treating it as text with regular-expression-based syntax highlighting. The parsed abstract syntax tree is used for semantic editor services such as inline error marking and content completion. Examples of these IDEs are Eclipse, IntelliJ IDEA, and Visual Studio. Each provides extensibility by means of plugins, written in general-purpose languages such as Java or C#, for which APIs and hooks are provided to customize the IDE experience.

Extensible code editors and IDEs use a plugin model for the organization and distribution of editor components. In contrast to our library-based approach, plugins are not part of the object language but are externally implemented and integrate into an editor's architecture directly. This has a number of significant implications. First, editor libraries can be activated through object language imports on a *per-file basis*, whereas plugins require external activation instead, for example, on a per-editor mode or per-language basis. Second, independent editor libraries typically *compose* based on locality and implicit coordination, whereas plugins have to be designed for composition a priori. Third, editor libraries are *declarative* and describe how to perform editor services, rather than imperatively changing the editor execution. Finally, while IDEs such as Eclipse or Visual Studio require the environment to be restarted whenever the implementation of editor service changes, editor libraries ensure a transparent compilation model.

Customizability of code editors and IDEs. IDEs usually provide some adaptability through configurations such as custom coloring schemes or user-defined code templates. However, these facilities are often coarse-grained and hard to deploy or share. For instance, Eclipse's standard Java plugin JDT defines a fixed set of colorable entities (decimal and hexadecimal numbers must look the same), requires completion templates to apply either to Java statements or type members only, or to complete Java (no completion templates for expressions only) and does not support an import and export mechanism for all editor configurations. In contrast, editor libraries are deployable just like usual Java libraries and enable precise configuration of editor services based on the language's full syntactic structure. Furthermore, since editor libraries are part of the object language, it is possible to package them with conventional programming libraries. This enables library-specific editor services such as code completion templates for typical use cases of an API or warnings for depreciated uses.

Language workbenches. Language workbenches are tools that integrate traditional language engineering tools such as parser generators and transformation systems and tools to develop IDE support [11]. By combining these tools and by providing IDE support for these metaprogramming tasks, language workbenches enable developers to efficiently create new languages with IDE support.

Language workbenches based on free text editing and parsing include EMFText [13], MontiCore [19], Rascal [27], Spoofax [17], TCS [15] and Xtext [7]. These workbenches provide modern editor service facilities such as content completion, following in a line of work on extensible IDEs with metaprogramming facilities, such as the Meta-Environment [18, 26]. Similar to our work, these workbenches provide support for developing and using editor services. However, they strictly separate metaprogramming and programming. Languages and editor services are deployed together in such a way that they apply to a certain file extension. Any changes to the language or editor service can only be applied at language-definition level. In contrast, in our work editor services can be freely imported and composed as editor libraries across any number of metalevels, which enables the self-application of editor services.

In addition to language workbenches designed to implement arbitrary textual languages, there are also tools that are based on a fixed host language. Examples include Helvetia [22], a Smalltalk-based environment, and DrRacket [10], aimed at the Racket programming language (formerly known as Scheme). Helvetia supports syntactic extensibility and custom syntax highlighting for extensions through a dynamic meta-object protocol, but has no support for more sophisticated editor services such as reference resolving, content completion, or static checks. DrRacket does not provide the same syntactic flexibility as Helvetia or Sugarclipse, but does provide autogenerated reference resolving editor services. In Helvetia, language definitions can be loaded for a Smalltalk image and activated in parts of the application. In DrRacket a language definition can only be selected at file level using the `#lang` directive. Both tools are highly tied to their respective host languages, using dedicated metaprogramming systems. For instance, reference resolving in DrRacket demands that new constructs for binding identifiers are defined in terms of predefined binding constructs of the Racket language. In contrast, our editor libraries approach is language-agnostic as our Java-independent case study for Latex shows.

MPS is a language workbench based on projectional editing rather than free text editing [30, 31], notable for its support for compositionality of languages. It allows language extensions to be activated in a specific parts of an application, but does not organize them as true libraries. MPS strictly separates metaprogramming and programming by providing fixed templates for syntactic and semantic customization of language components.

In summary, while current language workbenches integrate metaprogramming and programming into a single IDE environment, they still strictly separate language definitions and language uses into two different worlds. They do not support composition of extensions as libraries, although MPS allows project-level configuration of the set of languages that is supported. Unlike our editor libraries they cannot import and compose editor services. They also provide limited support for self-applicability and abstraction over editor service definitions. Our work, which is based on the Spoofax [17] language workbench, shares properties such as providing IDE support for language development, but does away with the restrictions of the two-world approach of current language workbenches.

9. Conclusion and future work

Our main idea in Sugarclipse is the application of libraries for organizing IDE extensions as reusable units. As our case studies show, editor libraries are particularly beneficial in combination with syntactically extensible programming languages such as SugarJ and represent an important step towards our ultimate goal of *language libraries*. Language libraries enable the implementation of all aspects of a language as a library. Currently, we support the library-based adaptation of parsing, desugaring, analyzing and editor presentation, but lack library-based extensibility for implementing the semantics of a language extension. In our future work, we would like to support the configuration of builder services that declare the semantics of embedded languages and integrate into Sugarclipse naturally. Builder services should replace traditional build scripts completely and specify the order as well as the tool used to build a set of source files.

In addition, we would like to further investigate the modularity and composability of editor libraries. In particular, we would like to explore scoping mechanisms for editor libraries that retain composability while providing clearer interfaces for explicitly coordinating services with staged editor libraries. We also plan to conduct a large-scale case study to evaluate the composability of editor libraries more accurately, namely Java Server Pages. Java Server Pages brings together a number of languages such as HTML, Java, JavaScript and CSS. We plan to provide editor libraries for each of these language separately and to compose the resulting editor libraries to form an editor library for Server Pages. While conducting this case study, we would furthermore like to explore new declarative means for explicitly coordinating editor libraries.

Acknowledgments

This work is supported in part by the European Research Council, grant No. 203099, and NWO/EW Open Competition project 612.063.512, *TFA: Transformations for Abstractions*.

References

[1] J. Bachrach and K. Playford. The Java syntactic extender (JSE). In *Proceedings of Conference on Object-Oriented Programming, Systems, Languages, and Applications (OOPSLA)*, pages 31–42. ACM, 2001.

[2] M. Blume and A. W. Appel. Hierarchical modularity. *Transactions on Programming Languages and Systems (TOPLAS)*, 21:813–847, 1999.

[3] C. Brabrand and M. I. Schwartzbach. Growing languages with metamorphic syntax macros. In *Proceedings of Workshop on Partial Evaluation and Program Manipulation (PEPM)*, pages 31–40. ACM, 2002.

[4] G. Bracha. Pluggable type systems. In *OOPSLA Workshop on Revival of Dynamic Languages*, 2004.

[5] M. Chapman. Extending JDT to support Java-like languages. Invited Talk at EclipseCon'06, 2006.

[6] S. Dmitriev. Language oriented programming: The next programming paradigm. Available at http://www.jetbrains.com/mps/docs/Language_Oriented_Programming.pdf., 2004.

[7] S. Efftinge and M. Voelter. oAW xText: A framework for textual DSLs. In *Workshop on Modeling Symposium at Eclipse Summit*, 2006.

[8] T. Ekman and G. Hedin. The JastAdd extensible Java compiler. In *Proceedings of Conference on Object-Oriented Programming, Systems, Languages, and Applications (OOPSLA)*, pages 1–18. ACM, 2007.

[9] S. Erdweg, T. Rendel, C. Kästner, and K. Ostermann. SugarJ: Library-based syntactic language extensibility. In *Proceedings of Conference on Object-Oriented Programming, Systems, Languages, and Applications (OOPSLA)*. ACM, 2011.

[10] R. B. Findler, J. Clements, C. Flanagan, M. Flatt, S. Krishnamurthi, P. Steckler, and M. Felleisen. DrScheme: A programming environment for scheme. *Journal of Functional Programming*, 12(2):159–182, 2002.

[11] M. Fowler. Language workbenches: The killer-app for domain specific languages? Available at http://martinfowler.com/articles/languageWorkbench.html, 2005.

[12] M. Fowler. PostIntelliJ. Available at http://martinfowler.com/bliki/PostIntelliJ.html, 2005.

[13] F. Heidenreich, J. Johannes, S. Karol, M. Seifert, and C. Wende. Derivation and refinement of textual syntax for models. In *Proceedings of European Conference on Model Driven Architecture – Foundations and Applications (ECMDA-FA)*, volume 5562 of *LNCS*, pages 114–129. Springer, 2009.

[14] P. Hudak. Modular domain specific languages and tools. In *Proceedings of International Conference on Software Reuse (ICSR)*, pages 134–142. IEEE, 1998.

[15] F. Jouault, J. Bézivin, and I. Kurtev. TCS: A DSL for the specification of textual concrete syntaxes in model engineering. In *Proceedings of Conference on Generative Programming and Component Engineering (GPCE)*, pages 249–254. ACM, 2006.

[16] C. Kästner, T. Thüm, G. Saake, J. Feigenspan, T. Leich, F. Wielgorz, and S. Apel. FeatureIDE: Tool framework for feature-oriented software development. In *Proceedings of International Conference on Software Engineering (ICSE)*, pages 611–614. IEEE, 2009.

[17] L. C. L. Kats and E. Visser. The Spoofax language workbench: Rules for declarative specification of languages and IDEs. In *Proceedings of Conference on Object-Oriented Programming, Systems, Languages, and Applications (OOPSLA)*, pages 444–463. ACM, 2010.

[18] P. Klint. A meta-environment for generating programming environments. *Transactions on Software Engineering Methodology (TOSEM)*, 2(2):176–201, 1993.

[19] H. Krahn, B. Rumpe, and S. Völkel. Monticore: Modular development of textual domain specific languages. In *Proceedings of Technology of Object-oriented Languages and Systems (TOOLS)*, pages 297–315. Springer, 2008.

[20] S. McDirmid and M. Odersky. The Scala plugin for Eclipse. In *Proceedings of Workshop on Eclipse Technology eXchange (ETX)*, 2006. published online http://atlanmod.emn.fr/www/papers/eTX2006/.

[21] N. Nystrom, M. R. Clarkson, and A. C. Myers. Polyglot: An extensible compiler framework for Java. In *Proceedings of Conference on Compiler Construction (CC)*, pages 138–152. Springer, 2003.

[22] L. Renggli, T. Gîrba, and O. Nierstrasz. Embedding languages without breaking tools. In *Proceedings of European Conference on Object-Oriented Programming (ECOOP)*, LNCS, pages 380–404. Springer, 2010.

[23] M. Tatsubori, S. Chiba, M.-O. Killijian, and K. Itano. OpenJava: A class-based macro system for Java. In *Proceedings of Workshop on Reflection and Software Engineering*, volume 1826 of *LNCS*, pages 117–133. Springer, 2000.

[24] S. Tobin-Hochstadt, V. St-Amour, R. Culpepper, M. Flatt, and M. Felleisen. Languages as libraries. In *Proceedings of Conference on Programming Language Design and Implementation (PLDI)*. ACM, 2011.

[25] L. Tratt. Domain specific language implementation via compile-time meta-programming. *Transactions on Programming Languages and Systems (TOPLAS)*, 30(6):1–40, 2008.

[26] M. Van den Brand, A. Van Deursen, J. Heering, H. De Jong, et al. The Asf+Sdf Meta-Environment: A component-based language development environment. In *Proceedings of Conference on Compiler Construction (CC)*, volume 2027 of *LNCS*, pages 365–370. Springer, 2001.

[27] T. van der Storm. The Rascal language workbench. Submitted to Language Workbench Competition 2011, available at http://www.languageworkbenches.net/lwc11rascal.pdf., 2011.

[28] E. Van Wyk, L. Krishnan, D. Bodin, and A. Schwerdfeger. Attribute grammar-based language extensions for Java. In *Proceedings of European Conference on Object-Oriented Programming (ECOOP)*, LNCS, pages 575–599. Springer, 2007.

[29] E. Visser. Stratego: A language for program transformation based on rewriting strategies. In *Proceedings of Conference on Rewriting Techniques and Applications (RTA)*, LNCS, pages 357–362. Springer, 2001.

[30] M. Voelter. Embedded software development with projectional language workbenches. In *Proceedings of Conference on Model Driven Engineering Languages and Systems (MoDELS)*, volume 6395 of *LNCS*, pages 32–46. Springer, 2010.

[31] M. Voelter and K. Solomatov. Language modularization and composition with projectional language workbenches illustrated with MPS. http://voelter.de/data/pub/VoelterSolomatov_SLE2010_LanguageModularizationAndCompositionLWBs.pdf, 2010.

[32] M. P. Ward. Language-oriented programming. *Software – Concepts and Tools*, 15:147–161, 1995.

Helping Programmers Help Users

John Freeman
Texas A&M University
jfreeman@cse.tamu.edu

Jaakko Järvi
Texas A&M University
jarvi@cse.tamu.edu

Wonseok Kim
Texas A&M University
guruwons@cse.tamu.edu

Mat Marcus
Canyonlands Software Design
mmarcus@emarcus.org

Sean Parent
Adobe Systems, Inc.
sparent@adobe.com

Abstract

User interfaces exhibit a wide range of features that are designed to assist users. Interaction with one widget may trigger value changes, disabling, or other behaviors in other widgets. Such automatic behavior may be confusing or disruptive to users. Research literature on user interfaces offers a number of solutions, including interface features for explaining or controlling these behaviors. To help programmers help users, the implementation costs of these features need to be much lower. Ideally, they could be generated for "free." This paper shows how several help and control mechanisms can be implemented as algorithms and reused across interfaces, making the cost of their adoption negligible. Specifically, we describe generic help mechanisms for visualizing data flow and explaining command deactivation, and a mechanism for controlling the flow of data. A reusable implementation of these features is enabled by our property model framework, where the data manipulated through a user interface is modeled as a constraint system.

Categories and Subject Descriptors H.2.2 [*Software Engineering*]: Design Tools and Techniques—user interfaces

General Terms Algorithms

Keywords user interfaces, software reuse, constraint systems, software architecture

1. Introduction

The dull, run-of-the-mill user interfaces—dialogs, forms, and such—do not get much attention from the software research community, but they collectively require a lot of attention from the programmer community. User interfaces abound, and they are laborious to develop and difficult to get correct. As an attempt to reduce the cost of constructing user interfaces, we have introduced *property models*, a declarative approach to programming user interfaces [8, 9]. The long term goal of this work is to reach a point where most (maybe all) of the functionality that we have come to expect from a high quality user interface would come from reusable

algorithms or components in a software library, parametrized by a specification of the data manipulated by the user interface. In particular, we have described reusable implementations for the propagation of values between user interface elements, the enablement and disablement of user interface widgets, and the activation and deactivation of widgets that launch commands.

This paper describes our work to direct these advances to the improvement of user interfaces. One purpose of a user interface is to provide the user with an easily interpreted view of a conceptual model for the internal states of the application and the interface itself. To the extent that the interface fails to do this, there exists a *gulf of evaluation* [7]. The gulf of evaluation exacerbates the cognitive effort required to understand and use an application, and can lead to user frustration.

This paper shows that with the power of components, generativity, and reuse we can go beyond merely implementing existing behavior more economically. If a user interface behavior can be successfully packaged into a reusable component, then we should explore more functionality for assisting users and closing the gulf of evaluation. We should aim for more consistent user interfaces with less surprising behavior, more explanations of why a user interface behaves the way it does, and more abilities to change the behavior of a user interface "on the fly" to better serve users' goals. In sum, we should aim for more features that *help* users in their interactions with an interface.

This paper describes several generic realizations of help and convenience features that could be provided as standard features of dialogs and forms. In particular, we focus on (1) visualizing how data flows in a user interface, (2) providing help messages for commands that are deactivated, and (3) providing the user with means to control the direction of the flow of data. We emphasize that the main contributions of the paper are the algorithms and the software architecture that enable implementing these features in a reusable manner, applicable to a large class of user interfaces with negligible programming effort. The realizations of these algorithms build on the property models approach, in which the data that a user interface manipulates and the dependencies within this data are modeled explicitly as a constraint system. Reusable user interface algorithms are thus algorithms that inspect and manipulate this constraint system.

We are at an early stage in our effort. To not overstate our contribution, we note that we have not conducted user studies, and we have not applied the proposed tools and algorithms to a large collection of user interfaces drawn from existing software. The computer-human interaction (CHI) research community, however, has devised many help and support features for user interfaces and

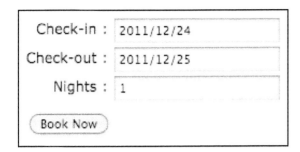

Figure 1. A dialog for reserving a hotel room.

argued for their usefulness [5, 13, 14]. We believe in these results, and wish to employ the science of software libraries, components, and generative programming to make implementing such features affordable, so that they become ubiquitous, liberated from their lonely existence in a handful of research systems.

We are working on a library that implements the property models approach in JavaScript, so that it can be run entirely within a web browser. The library is under active development, and its core is already publicly available [4].

2. Background

In the property models approach, the behavior of a user interface is completely derived from three specifications: the model of the data manipulated through the user interface, the visual elements and layout, and the connections between the visual elements and the data. We call these three specifications the *property model*, *layout*, and *bindings*, respectively:

1. The property model is essentially a constraint system: a set of variables and a set of relations that should hold true for those variables. We provide a declarative domain-specific language for specifying property models.

2. A layout is just that: a set of widgets provided by a graphical user interface (GUI) library and their positions. We provide a simple declarative language for specifying layouts, but a layout could just as well be created through calls to a GUI library API or by using a GUI design tool.

3. A binding connects one or more widgets with one or more variables in the property model, and can be one of two kinds: a *view binding*, where a widget is set to display the current value of a variable, or a *control binding*, where user interactions with a widget are translated to requests to change the value of a variable. Often a widget is bound to a variable via both types of bindings; this would be the case, for example, when a textbox that a user can edit is bound to a variable. In our current system, the specifications of bindings are embedded in the layout specification.

To demonstrate how these specifications give rise to a user interface, consider a simple dialog for reserving a hotel room, like the one that appears in Figure 1. The property model for this dialog is shown in Figure 2 and the layout and bindings in Figure 3. The core of these specification languages is described in [9], and we elaborate on extensions in the rest of the paper.

Launching a user interface merely requires passing the above three specifications to a function provided by the property models library, with a call that, omitting some details, looks roughly like this:

```
open_dialog(model, initial_values, layout);
```

```
model {
  interface: {
    checkin : today();
    nights: 1;
    checkout;
  }
  logic: {
    relate {
      checkout <== add_days(checkin, nights);
      checkin <== remove_days(checkout, nights);
      nights <== day_difference(checkin, checkout);
    }
  }
  invariant: {
    @description("Check−in date should not be in the past.")
    not_in_the_past <== check_checkin(checkin);

    @description("The Check−in date must come before
      the Check−out date.")
    at_least_one_night <== nights > 0;
  }
  output: {
    result <== { checkin: checkin, checkout: checkout };
  }
}
```

Figure 2. The model specification for the dialog in Figure 1. The expressions have access to JavaScript functions available in the runtime environment, e.g., those for manipulating dates.

```
layout {
  text (label : "Check−in", value : checkin);
  text (label : "Check−out", value : checkout);
  text (label : "Nights", value : nights);

  errors ();

  commandButton (label : "Book Now", value : result);
}
```

Figure 3. The layout and bindings specifications for the dialog in Figure 1.

Initial values in our system are dictionaries of labeled values, and they are used to initialize the variables in the property model.

We draw attention to the complete absence of event handling logic. All of it is delegated to algorithms in a software library. We have explained how we can generically support value propagation, script recording and playback, widget enablement and disablement, and command activation features [8, 9]. Our prior publications also contain a more introductory explanation of the property models approach. Here, we briefly summarize the approach, so that we can explain how the help features proposed in this paper can be implemented as reusable algorithms.

2.1 Property Model Constraint System

We represent property models as *hierarchical multi-way dataflow constraint systems* [16]. As mentioned above, a constraint system consists of variables and constraints. Abstractly, constraints represent relations among subsets of those variables; *solving* a constraint system means finding a valuation for the system's variables so that all relations in the system are satisfied. A hierarchical constraint system is one where constraints may have different strengths. If not all constraints can be satisfied, partial solutions to hierarchical constraint systems prefer to ignore weaker constraints in favor of enforcing stronger ones.

Formally, a multi-way dataflow constraint system is a tuple $\langle V, C \rangle$, where V is a set of variables and C is a set of constraints. Each constraint in C is a tuple $\langle R, r, M_C \rangle$, where $R \subseteq V$, r is some n-ary relation among variables in R ($n = |R|$), and M_C is a set of *constraint satisfaction methods*, or just *methods*. If the values of variables in R satisfy r, we say that the constraint is *satisfied*. Each method in M_C computes values for some subset of R using another subset of R as inputs. In the constraint systems of property models, all variables of R appear as an input or output of each method in M_C, and no two methods in M_C may share the same set of outputs. The programmer must ensure that executing any method of M_C will *enforce* the constraint, that is, satisfy the relation r.

The constraint satisfaction problem for a constraint system $S = \langle V, C \rangle$ is to find a valuation of the variables in V such that each constraint in C is satisfied. One such valuation is obtained if exactly one method from each constraint in C is executed, such that no variable is assigned a value by two methods; and the methods are executed in an order where no variable is assigned a value after another method has already used it as an input. A way to obtain such a valuation is thus characterized by a sequence of methods, often called a *plan*.

A multi-way dataflow constraint system can be represented as an *oriented*, *bipartite* graph $G_c = \langle V + M, E \rangle$. The vertex sets V and M correspond, respectively, to the variables and methods of the system, and the edges in E connect each method to its input and output variables: if $v, u \in V$ and $m \in M$, then edge (v, m) indicates that the variable v is an input of the method m, and (m, u) that m outputs to the variable u. We call the graph of a constraint system formed this way the *constraint graph*.

A plan can also be represented as a graph. Let $G_c = \langle V + M, E \rangle$ be a constraint graph and $M' \subseteq M$ the set of methods in the plan. The *solution graph* of the plan is $G_s = G_c[V + M']$, the vertex-induced subgraph of G_c. A solution graph is acyclic and the in-degree of all variable nodes is at most one. A plan corresponds to a topological ordering of the method nodes of a solution graph.

A third graph that is relevant for our purposes is the *evaluation graph*. It is obtained by observing which of its input variables a method needs in order to compute its result—methods use "by-name" parameter passing. If in computing the value of the method m, the value of one of its inputs v is needed, then the edge (v, m) of the solution graph is said to be *relevant*. Otherwise the edge is not relevant. Evaluating every method in a solution graph induces a partition of edges into relevant and not relevant. Assuming a solution graph $G_s = \langle V + M, E_V + E_M \rangle$, where E_V are the edges whose target vertex is in V, and E_M the edges whose target vertex is in M, the evaluation graph G_e is the subgraph of G_s induced by the edges $E_V + E_r$ where $E_r \subseteq E_M$ are the relevant edges. That is, $G_e = \langle V + M, E_V + E_r \rangle$.

The algorithm that guides how a user interface responds to user interaction is essentially that of maintaining the property model in a state where all constraints are satisfied. When a user changes the value of a user interface element, such as a textbox, and that element is bound to one of a property model's variables, a request to change the value of the variable is sent to the model. When the variable's value changes, some constraints may be no longer satisfied. The system is brought back to a satisfied state by computing a new solution graph, followed by evaluating the constraint satisfaction methods in this graph in a topological order. New values of changed variables are reflected back to the user interface elements bound to those variables.

It is usually the case that the constraint system of a property model is underconstrained. That is, many different solution graphs exist, and each solution graph corresponds to a different direction of flowing data in a user interface. For example, in the dialog for selecting dates for a hotel stay, data could flow from the start date

and end date fields to the field showing the number of nights; or it could flow from the start date and the number of nights fields to the field showing the end date.

To select among the many possible plans, we assign a "priority" to each variable, based on the order of updates to the property model's variables. Every time a variable is updated by a client, it is assigned the highest priority among all variables. Priorities are totally ordered. The flow that tends to follow the principle of least surprise for the user is the one that preserves as many of the values of the variables that have been updated most recently, that is, variables with high priorities. We can express an ordering between plans precisely in terms of solution graphs: a solution graph A is better than B if, of those variables that are sources[1] in exactly one of the graphs, the variable with the highest priority is a source in A. This definition induces a total ordering on solution graphs; the best solution graph according to this order is the one selected.

To compute the solution graph, we map the priorities of the variables to *stay constraints* in the underlying constraint system. When enforced, a stay constraint keeps a variable's value unchanged. We give these constraints strengths that respect the priority order of the variables they were derived from. With this mapping, we can apply Zanden's Quickplan algorithm [16] to produce a new solution graph.

The three graphs described above—the constraint graph, solution graph, and evaluation graph—have the following interpretations: the constraint graph represents the dependencies that could be in effect at some point during interaction with a user interface; the solution graph represents the dependencies that could be in effect with the current order of updates to the variables of a property model, for some values of those variables; and the evaluation graph represents the dependencies that are currently in effect for the current order of updates to the variables, for their current values.

Besides the algorithm outlined above for propagating values within user interfaces, other algorithms guide aspects of a user interface's functionality in our system. These algorithms enable and disable widgets and activate and deactivate commands. All these functionalities are based on queries to the three graphs described above. The information that enables the reusable implementations of the help functionalities described in this paper are similarly derived from those three graphs.

3. Dataflow Visualization

There are often dependencies among different values displayed in a user interface. When a value changes, the interface may try to satisfy certain relations in order to preserve the consistency of the data that is displayed. It will react to user edits by changing the values of other widgets, yielding a dataflow. In many cases, values may need to be propagated in different, even opposite directions, depending on what has changed and when. In determining the dataflow, user interfaces should strive for complying with the "principle of least surprise." As explained in Section 2, this means, for example, that the values that the user just finished editing should not be overwritten.

When an edit of one value triggers changes in other values, it can be unclear to the user which values are changing and for what reasons: changes may happen too quickly or inconspicuously to notice; it may appear that they are all directly related to the edited value, which could be misleading; or values may change in ways unexpected by the user. Each of these complications contributes to a gulf of evaluation with respect to value propagation.

Consider a simple dialog for image scaling, such as what appears in Figure 4. It provides two ways of editing the image dimensions—either absolutely, in pixels, or relatively, in

---

[1] In graph terminology, a vertex with no incoming edges is called a *source*.

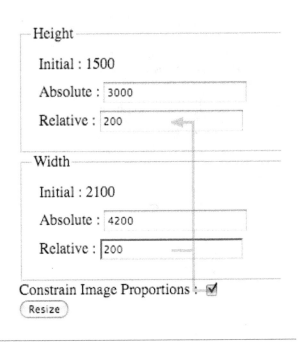

Figure 4. A dialog for resizing an image. The arrow is a visualization of a functional dependency in the dialog's property model.

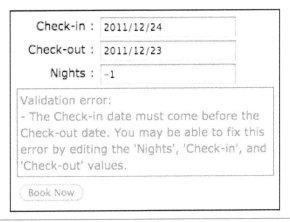

Figure 5. A dialog for reserving a hotel room, with a disabled command widget and accompanying help text.

percentages—with the option to preserve the ratio between the image's height and width. The values of all four textboxes and the checkbox are tied together in a complex, multi-way relationship. If the user edits one of the numeric values, the other three could change. To understand this behavior, a user will need to know which values currently affect which others.

In the context of property models, this information is contained in the evaluation graph: a variable's value is affected by its ancestors and affects its descendants. What is needed is an effective means—such as visualization—of communicating this information to the user.

In our implementation, we animated the flow of data among values in the model. For each method in the evaluation graph, an arrow is drawn connecting the widgets bound to its inputs and outputs. (Consequently, this means the arrow might have multiple heads or multiple tails or both.) To prevent confusion, an arrow is drawn only if the outputs had changed as a result of the most recent evaluation. These arrows are displayed, one at a time, according to the order of the methods' evaluation. To avoid interrupting casual use of the interface, the dataflow illustration is triggered only upon the explicit request of the user, indicated by clicking a button.

Now, the animation makes the relationships behind the interface explicit and clear, and thus fosters understanding in the user. Further, this behavior works for all interfaces built with property models for no additional cost.

We realize that our first attempt is rudimentary, and after seeing it in action, we identified some potential improvements. In one way, the animation seemed to play too quickly. The time an individual relationship was displayed seemed too short for digesting the information the visualization was trying to convey. In another way, the animation seemed to play too slowly. If we wanted to focus on one particular relationship, which was often the case, then we would have to wait for the animation to get to that point, and then wait for it to complete before we could see it again. The animation could have conformed better to how we wanted to consume the relation-

ship information—typically we were interested in just one or two relationships out of the whole graph.

Consequently, a more desirable alternative to animation may be to allow the user to glance at individual relationships separately and at their own pace. Contextual information for a field would include arrows connecting it to the the fields from which it was computed, and to the fields computed from it. This contextual information could be displayed, say, along with existing menus upon right-clicking a field. By displaying the network of dependencies in localized chunks, we avoid presenting too much information at once and cluttering the interface.

Finally, a more sophisticated layout algorithm could be used to produce more visually appealing arrows.

In the bigger picture, however, the prototype implementation suffices to demonstrate that our framework enables a data flow visualization to be described and implemented in a generic, reusable manner, and thus make it worth the while to invest more on improving the visualization, to eventually benefit a large class of user interfaces.

4. Explaining Command Availability

Whenever a user interface command is unavailable in the current context, most rich user interfaces will prohibit its execution by deactivating the corresponding command widget that invokes it. Visually, deactivation can take several forms, including "graying out" or hiding the widget. Human interface guidelines for several popular platforms recommend this behavior and alternatively describe widgets that are not enabled as "dimmed" [1], "disabled" [3, 11], or "insensitive" [6].

We have previously published an algorithm for property models that can automatically determine when a command widget should be deactivated according to the above guidelines [9]. A command becomes unavailable only in certain contexts, and to describe those contexts is to describe preconditions for the command. In a property model, the preconditions for a command are defined by the programmer with the help of *invariants*. Each of these special variables hold the result of a boolean expression that is true when the precondition is satisfied and false otherwise. Returning to our earlier example, a command that reserves a hotel room may require a positive number of nights, as in Figure 5. This precondition is expressed in the at_least_one_night invariant in the property model in Figure 2.

Continuing, a command widget launches some command in the program, and takes the command's parameters from the variable to which it is bound. In our example dialog, the specification in

Figure 3 binds the Book Now widget to the result variable. The value of this variable is derived from the two variables checkin and checkout, as can be seen from the model specification in Figure 2.

When an invariant variable evaluates to false, i.e., when a precondition fails, then the variables that contributed to that violation are marked, or "blamed," for being responsible. If any blamed variable is also used to evaluate a command's parameters, i.e., if in the evaluation graph a failed precondition and a command share a common dependency, then the command is deactivated.

From the perspective of the user, a couple of issues surround the behavior described above. First, a user may not understand why a particular command widget is deactivated. As stated above, programmers can express these reasons through invariants in the property model. However, since they appear only in the user interface code, the user may not know what they are and, consequently, have a limited understanding why a command widget is deactivated. A recent experience of one of the authors illustrates this case. In trying to change a password to a web system, an error message kept repeating simply that the new password entered did not satisfy the requirements of a valid password. The requirements were mostly revealed through trial and error. We can reasonably expect that a large portion of the users of that system will not succeed in the same task on the first, second, or even third try.

To alleviate the above problem, we can automatically generate help text that describes the reasons why a command widget is deactivated. If the programmer adds a natural language description of the precondition to the invariant variable, then we can present it to the user as an explanation for a deactivated command widget. Examples of such annotations are the @description strings in the property model specification of Figure 2. The explanation could be included with other contextual information, such as the dataflow visualization described in Section 3.

The second problem is that even after reading an explanation, a user may not know the actions necessary to re-activate a command widget. Using the property model, we can find which variables are responsible (to varying degrees) for the failed precondition. We can then direct the user to the widgets bound to those variables and expect that they can deduce how to interact with them to satisfy the precondition. In our hotel reservation example from Figure 5, we inform the user that changing any of the check-in, check-out, or nights values may be able to resolve the error. To determine the responsible variables, we look at the invariant representing the failed precondition and take its ancestors in the evaluation graph, i.e., the variables that contributed to its false value. We find the interactive widgets that are bound to those variables, then reference their labels in the help text.

A user interface is not limited to just this implementation, however. To varying degrees, other variables could be considered responsible. We chose to look at only variables that reach the invariant in the evaluation graph, but this might not include all variables that can reach it in the constraint graph. In some cases, such variables could be edited to affect the invariant's value, providing an alternative means to satisfy the precondition. Additionally, instead of just listing the interesting widgets in the explanation, we could highlight them when the user hovers over each name. This should resolve situations where it may not be clear to the user which widgets are being referenced.

The dependencies exhibited in the hotel dialog are simple, and a user likely does not have trouble finding ways to satisfy the command's preconditions. We use that example to explain the mechanism of generating help texts, rather than to advocate its usefulness. In larger dialogs and forms, dependencies easily get more complicated, and thus accurate help text are of greater importance. Figure 6 shows a (still relatively simple) survey form with more dependencies, implemented with our system. Many preconditions are

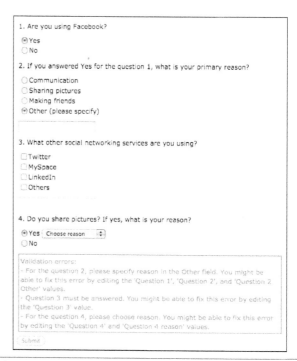

Figure 6. A user survey form demonstrating preconditions alongside more complex value relationships.

violated, and the generated help messages accurately identify the variables responsible for each violation.

It is important to note that the generation of help text is completely orthogonal to and works in harmony with the dataflow visualization described in Section 3. After marking values that are violating the precondition, the user can see the network of relationships among them to better determine a root cause.

5. Pinning

As is evident by now, a rich user interface may automatically, without consent from the user, change values in order to enforce relationships among them. Even though reasonable heuristics are applied, the behavior may be unexpected to the user. In our running example, the hotel reservation dialog from Figure 1, consider this sequence of user actions:

1. The user enters a check-in date.

2. The user enters a check out date.

3. The user realizes he did not mean to stay for the calculated number of nights, so he changes the number of nights value.

The user's expectations may or may not agree with the heuristic that our system follows. If the user is editing the nights in order to correct his last edit to the check-out date, then he might expect the check-out date to change accordingly. However, since the check-out date was edited more recently, our system assumes that the user would rather preserve that value, so it changes the oldest value: the check-in date.

In a more complicated interface with more relationships, we can imagine that such a turn counter to user's expectations could lead to the undoing of a larger portion of the user's work. We should note that no rule can be "correct" in all cases, as in some cases there is no single possible unsurprising dataflow. The expectation of the user interface's most natural behavior may, for different users (or even for the same user) in identical situations, be different. A

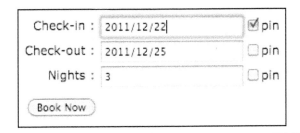

Figure 7. A dialog for reserving a hotel room, with a pinned value.

user interface should thus provide means to the user to control the preferred dataflow.

We provide a feature that allows the user to "protect," or *pin*, certain values as he moves along. Pinning does not prevent the user from further editing the value. It simply guarantees that the system will not automatically change the pinned value as a reaction to the user changing some other value. Figure 7 shows how pinning is offered in our system for the familiar hotel reservation example.

Implementing pinning translates naturally to property models. As we explained in Section 2, a stay constraint keeps a variable's value unchanged. The desired effect is thus attained if the stay constraint of the pinned variable is promoted to the same strength as that of the programmer-defined constraints. This guarantees that the stay constraint will be enforced in all solution graphs, and thus the pinned variable is not overwritten by any method.

Pinning is not without complications, though. Pinning a variable expands the set of constraints that must be enforced in each plan by adding the variable's stay constraint. If enough variables are pinned, the property model could become overconstrained, leaving it unsolvable. To prevent this, we can disable the pinning option for widgets bound to variables that, if pinned, would result in an overconstrained system. Identifying a variable as "pinnable" is straightforward: a single run of the constraint solver suffices to determine if the system can still be solved after a particular variable is pinned. Furthermore, after pinning a variable, it may be that some other variables are *derived* in all possible plans. Any user edits to such values will be overwritten. To prevent confusion, widgets bound to such variables should be disabled. We can identify these variables as well: after removing from constraints any methods that write to pinned variables, any variables written by a method in a constraint with no other methods will be derived in all solutions.

6. Role of Property Models in Implementation

We emphasize that the visual presentations of the three features discussed above are divorced from their underlying implementations. User interface developers are free to integrate them with existing interfaces however they see fit. For example, instead of using checkboxes labeled "pin", which may suggest to some users that pinning will "lock in" a value, protecting it even from user edits, a more user-friendly presentation could be to use a star-shaped checkbox, suggesting that pinning simply indicates high-priority, "favorite" values. Developers can experiment to find which visualization methods work best. Our intent is merely to provide the non-trivial framework to support them.

7. Related work

Features related to the three help mechanisms we have presented have been incorporated into various systems developed by the CHI community. We discuss a few representatives below. We are not aware of other work, however, where the main focus is on a generic

mechanism that supports implementing a large selection of such features alongside each other.

UIDE [5, 14] and HUMANOID [12] use preconditions on commands to disable widgets and to generate helpful explanations. UIDE also uses postconditions to explain how to enable a command widget [2, 13, 15]. The authors acknowledge that their system is not prepared to handle situations with complex, multi-way dependencies among actions and widgets; such dependencies are supported in an interface built on property models. Unlike UIDE, our generated help text does not attempt to provide a precise sequence of interactions for re-activating a command widget (in some cases, there may be many sequences to choose from), and we have not investigated its (in)feasibility. Further, we try not to burden the programmer with specifying postconditions for user interactions. We believe that the information available in a property model is enough to provide sufficient help.

The Heracles system supported pinning of its controls [10]. In Heracles, not all constraints are enforced after each user edit, and multi-way constraints are not supported. Thus, some of the issues facing pinning in property models are avoided. Heracles also opts to pin a variable automatically upon user edit, whereas we pin a variable upon explicit request only. The authors of Heracles, like us, cite potentially unclear dataflow and overwritten values as motivations for pinning.

8. Conclusion

This paper explains how three different user interface features, aimed at improving the user's experience when interacting with a computer, can be implemented generically—to provide any or all of the features within some user interface requires no code specific to the user interface. The adoption cost of these features is thus very small.

To emphasize the importance of the low cost of adoption, we concentrate on one of the three features. In Section 4 we describe the automatic generation of helpful explanations for why a command widget in a user interface is deactivated. We gave an example where a user had to, through trial and error, "fight" a system in accomplishing a password change task that would have been trivial had the system given adequate error diagnostics. The account holders of that in-house system are counted in thousands, and each has to go through the procedure periodically. Hence, collectively the time wasted by the users likely far surpasses the time it would have taken for the developer to program that help feature. Still the economics of programming did not make it worthwhile to do so. That particular help feature likely was not key during specifying the requirements or defining the deliverables, and at development time, the programmer(s) may have had other feature requests with higher priorities. On the other hand, we as users shrug off small frustrations with computer systems, once we find a way around them, and do not think twice about it. It is of no user's interest to spend much time to find out how one could get a small defect fixed or missing feature added.

We want to cast blame on neither the user nor the programmer—the incentives to take action to rectify the state of affairs is too small for both. The property models approach scales the incentives to cover a significantly larger class of user interfaces.

References

[1] Apple. Apple human interface guidelines. http://developer. apple.com/library/mac/documentation/UserExperience/ Conceptual/AppleHIGuidelines/index.html, May 2011.

[2] J. J. de Graaff, P. Sukaviriya, and C. van der Mast. Automatic generation of context-sensitive textual help. Technical Report GIT-GVU-93-11, Georgia Institute of Technology, Apr. 1993.

[3] Eclipse. User interface guidelines. http://wiki.eclipse.org/User_Interface_Guidelines, May 2011.

[4] J. Freeman, W. Kim, and J. Järvi. Hotdrink. URL http://code.google.com/p/hotdrink/.

[5] D. F. Gieskens and J. D. Foley. Controlling user interface objects through pre- and postconditions. In *Proceedings of the SIGCHI conference on Human factors in computing systems*, CHI '92, pages 189–194, New York, NY, USA, 1992. ACM. ISBN 0-89791-513-5.

[6] GNOME. GNOME human interface guidelines. http://developer.gnome.org/hig-book/stable/, May 2011.

[7] E. L. Hutchins, J. D. Hollan, and D. A. Norman. Direct manipulation interfaces. *Human-Computer Interaction*, 1:311–338, December 1985. ISSN 0737-0024.

[8] J. Järvi, M. Marcus, S. Parent, J. Freeman, and J. N. Smith. Property models: from incidental algorithms to reusable components. In *Proceedings of the 7th international conference on Generative programming and component engineering*, GPCE '08, pages 89–98, New York, NY, USA, 2008. ACM. ISBN 978-1-60558-267-2.

[9] J. Järvi, M. Marcus, S. Parent, J. Freeman, and J. N. Smith. Algorithms for user interfaces. In *Proceedings of the eighth international conference on Generative programming and component engineering*, GPCE '09, pages 147–156, New York, NY, USA, 2009. ACM. ISBN 978-1-60558-494-2.

[10] C. A. Knoblock, S. Minton, J. L. Ambite, M. Muslea, J. Oh, and M. Frank. Mixed-initiative, multi-source information assistants. In *Proceedings of the 10th international conference on World Wide Web*, WWW '01, pages 697–707, New York, NY, USA, 2001. ACM. ISBN 1-58113-348-0.

[11] Microsoft. Windows user experience interaction guidelines. http://msdn2.microsoft.com/en-us/library/aa511258.aspx, May 2011.

[12] R. Moriyon, P. Szekely, and R. Neches. Automatic generation of help from interface design models. In *Proceedings of the SIGCHI conference on Human factors in computing systems: celebrating interdependence*, CHI '94, pages 225–231, New York, NY, USA, 1994. ACM. ISBN 0-89791-650-6.

[13] P. Sukaviriya and J. J. de Graaff. Automatic generation of context-sensitive "show and tell" help. Technical Report GIT-GVU-92-18, Georgia Institute of Technology, July 1992.

[14] P. Sukaviriya and J. D. Foley. Coupling a UI framework with automatic generation of context-sensitive animated help. In *Proceedings of the 3rd annual ACM SIGGRAPH symposium on User interface software and technology*, UIST '90, pages 152–166, New York, NY, USA, 1990. ACM. ISBN 0-89791-410-4.

[15] P. N. Sukaviriya, J. Muthukumarasamy, A. Spaans, and H. J. J. de Graaff. Automatic generation of textual, audio, and animated help in uide: the user interface design. In *Proceedings of the workshop on Advanced visual interfaces*, AVI '94, pages 44–52, New York, NY, USA, 1994. ACM. ISBN 0-89791-733-2.

[16] B. V. Zanden. An incremental algorithm for satisfying hierarchies of multiway dataflow constraints. *ACM Trans. Program. Lang. Syst.*, 18(1):30–72, 1996.

Theorem-based Circuit Derivation in Cryptol

John Launchbury

Galois, Inc.

john@galois.com

Abstract

Even though step-by-step refinement has long been seen as desirable, it is hard to find compelling industrial applications of the technique. In theory, transforming a high-level specification into a high-performance implementation is an ideal means of producing a correct design, but in practice it is hard to make it work, and even harder to make it worthwhile. This talk describes an exception.

We introduce the domain-specific language, Cryptol, and work up to a design experience in which theorem-based refinement played a crucial role in producing an industrial quality FPGA encryptor and decryptor for AES. Quite simply, we are unlikely to have succeeded without the technique.

The Cryptol specification language was designed by Galois for the NSA as a public standard for specifying cryptographic algorithms. A Cryptol reference specification can serve as the formal documentation for a cryptographic module, eliminating the need for separate and voluminous English descriptions. Cryptol is fully executable, allowing designers to experiment with their programs incrementally as their designs evolve. Cryptol compilers can generate C, C++, and Haskell software implementations, and VHDL or Verilog HDL hardware implementations. These generators can significantly reduce overall life-cycle costs of cryptographic solutions. For example, Cryptol allows engineers and mathematicians to program cryptographic algorithms on FPGAs as if they were writing software.

The design experience we describe runs as follows: we begin with a specification for AES written in Cryptol, and over a series of five design stages we produce an industrial grade encrypt core. In each stage, we state theorems which relate the component behaviors in one stage with the corresponding behaviors in the refinement. The resulting cores, running at 350Mhz-440Mhz depending on the FPGA part, bear little relationship to the original, except that the step-by-step theorems ensured we had not gone astray.

We then repeat the pattern in generating a circuit for AES decrypt. While there are many similarities between encrypt and decrypt in AES, there are some crucial differences with regard to high performance. First concerns the generation of key material. The AES key is used as a seed for a specific pseudo-random number generator which produces key material for use in each of the AES rounds. For encrypt, the key-generator runs in sync with the action of encryption, so may be scheduled alongside it. For decrypt, they run counter to one-another, creating a major

challenge to be overcome. Second, the generated key material has an additional transformation applied to it, which occurs deep in the middle of the high performing core.

Using theorems as stepping stones along the way, we redesign the key expansion algorithm so that it will run in sync with the decryption. We then trace parallel steps to the derivation of encrypt, establishing a series of commuting diagrams along the way. Whenever we confronted bugs in the development process, we produced many theorems to isolate the bugs, using theorems as a principled kind of printf. When the bugs were found and eradicated, we elided many of the temporary theorems, leaving behind those that provided important insights into the behavior of the code.

This talk is a story of the journey with demonstrations of the tool at work. Its ultimate message is to highlight the value of including a theorem facility within purely functional domain-specific languages.

Categories and Subject Descriptors D.3.2 [*Language Classifications*]: Applicative (functional) languages; D.3.2 [*Language Classifications*]: Specialized application languages

General Terms Algorithms, Design, Languages, Performance, Verification

Keywords cryptography, functional programming, domain-specific language, FPGA, AES, theorem-based refinement

Bio

Dr. John Launchbury is Chief Scientist of Galois, Inc. John founded Galois in 1999 to address challenges in Information Assurance through the application of Functional Programming and Formal Methods. Under his leadership, formerly as CEO, the company has grown strongly, successfully winning and delivering on multiple contract awards for more than a decade. John continues to lead Galois' growing stature for its thought leadership in high assurance technology development.

Prior to founding Galois, John was a full professor in Computer Science and Engineering at the Oregon Graduate Institute School of Science and Engineering at OHSU. His instruction style earned him several awards for outstanding teaching, and he is internationally recognized for his work on the analysis and semantics of programming languages, and on the Haskell programming language in particular. John received First Class Honors in Mathematics from Oxford University in 1985. He holds a Ph.D. in Computing Science from University of Glasgow and won the British Computer Society's distinguished dissertation prize. In 2010, John was inducted as a Fellow of the Association for Computing Machinery (ACM)

GPCE'11, October 22–23, 2011, Portland, Oregon, USA.
ACM 978-1-4503-0689-8/11/10.

Author Index

Alves, Vander 33

Apel, Sven 3

Ardourel, Gilles 43

Arnoldus, B. J. 137

Asai, Kenichi 97

Atlee, Joanne M. 117

Batory, Don 13

Borba, Paulo 23, 33

Brabrand, Claus 23

Danvy, Olivier 93

Das, Kishen 107

Douence, Rémi 43

Erdweg, Sebastian 167

Esmaeilsabzali, Shahram 117

Felleisen, Matthias 1

Fischer, Bernd 117

Freeman, John 177

Gaubatz, Patrick 157

Gokhale, Aniruddha 53

Hannousse, Abdelhakim 43

Herrmann, Peter 147

Höfner, Peter 13

Järvi, Jaakko 177

Kästner, Christian 167

Kats, Lennart C. L. 127, 167

Kim, Jongwook 13

Kim, Wonseok 177

Kraemer, Frank Alexander 147

Kulezsa, Uirá 33

Launchbury, John 185

Li, Yulin 63

Lindeman, Ricky T. 127

Lotz, Alex 73

Marcus, Mat 177

Neves, Laís 33

Novak, Jr., Gordon S. 63

Nystrom, Nathaniel 107

Ostermann, Klaus 167

Otte, William R. 53

Parent, Sean 177

Pukall, Mario 3

Queiroz, Felipe 23

Rendel, Tillmann 167

Ribeiro, Márcio 23

Rosenmüller, Marko 3

Schlegel, Christian 73

Schmidt, Douglas C. 53

Sena, Demóstenes 33

Serebrenik, A. 137

Shubert, Gary 95

Siegmund, Norbert 3

Slåtten, Vidar 147

Soares, Sérgio 23

Sobernig, Stefan 157

Steck, Andreas 73

Strembeck, Mark 157

Teixeira, Leopoldo 33

Tolêdo, Társis 23

van den Brand, M. G. J. 137

Vermolen, Sander D. 83

Visser, Eelco 83, 127, 167

Wachsmuth, Guido 83

White, Derek 107

Willemsen, Johnny 53

Zdun, Uwe 157

join today!
SIGPLAN & ACM

www.acm.org/sigplan

www.acm.org

The **ACM Special Interest Group on Programming Languages** (SIGPLAN) explores programming language concepts and tools, focusing on design, implementation, and efficient use. Its members are programming language users, developers, theoreticians, researchers, and educators. The monthly newsletter, ACM SIGPLAN Notices, publishes several conference proceedings issues, regular columns and technical correspondence (available in electronic or hardcopy versions). Members also receive a CD containing the prior year conference proceedings and newsletter issues. SIGPLAN sponsors several annual conferences including OOPSLA, PLDI, POPL and ICFP, plus a number of other conferences and workshops.

The **Association for Computing Machinery** (ACM) is an educational and scientific computing society which works to advance computing as a science and a profession. Benefits include subscriptions to *Communications of the ACM*, *MemberNet*, *TechNews* and *CareerNews*, plus full access to the *Guide to Computing Literature*, full and unlimited access to thousands of online courses and books, discounts on conferences and the option to subscribe to the ACM Digital Library.

- ❏ SIGPLAN Print (ACM Member or Non-ACM Member) .... $ 110
- ❏ SIGPLAN Print (ACM Student Member)... $ 85
- ❏ SIGPLAN Online (ACM Member or Non-ACM Member) .... $ 25
- ❏ SIGPLAN Online (ACM Student Member).. $ 15
- ❏ ACM Professional Membership ($99) & SIGPLAN Print ($110).. $209
- ❏ ACM Professional Membership ($99) & SIGPLAN Print ($110) & ACM Digital Library ($99) $308
- ❏ ACM Professional Membership ($99) & SIGPLAN Online ($25).. $124
- ❏ ACM Professional Membership ($99) & SIGPLAN Online ($25) & ACM Digital Library ($99)........ $223
- ❏ ACM Student Membership ($19) & SIGPLAN Print ($85)... $ 104
- ❏ ACM Student Membership ($19) & SIGPLAN Online ($15)... $ 34
- ❏ *SIGPLAN Notices* only (available in electronic or hardcopy versions) .... $ 75
- ❏ *SIGPLAN Notices* Expedited Air (outside N. America) .... $ 55
- ❏ *FORTRAN Forum* (ACM or SIGPLAN Member) .... $ 16
- ❏ *FORTRAN Forum* (ACM Student Member).. $ 16
- ❏ *FORTRAN Forum* only .... $ 16
- ❏ Expedited Air for *FORTRAN Forum* (outside N. America).. $ 8
- ❏ Expedited Air for *Communications of the ACM* (outside N. America)....................................... $ 50

payment information

Name _____

ACM Member # _____

Mailing Address _____

_____

City/State/Province _____

ZIP/Postal Code/Country_____

Email _____

Mobile Phone_____

Fax _____

Mailing List Restriction
ACM occasionally makes its mailing list available to computer-related organizations, educational institutions and sister societies. All email addresses remain strictly confidential. Check one of the following if you wish to restrict the use of your name:

- ❏ ACM announcements only
- ❏ ACM and other sister society announcements
- ❏ ACM subscription and renewal notices only

Credit Card Type:　　❏ AMEX　　　❏ VISA　　　❏ MC

Credit Card # _____

Exp. Date _____

Signature_____

Make check or money order payable to ACM, Inc

ACM accepts U.S. dollars or equivalent in foreign currency. Prices include surface delivery charge. Expedited Air Service, which is a partial air freight delivery service, is available outside North America. Contact ACM for more information.

Questions? Contact:
ACM Headquarters
2 Penn Plaza, Suite 701
New York, NY 10121-0701
voice: 212-626-0500
fax: 212-944-1318
email: acmhelp@acm.org

Remit to:
ACM
General Post Office
P.O. Box 30777
New York, NY 10087-0777

SIGAPP11

www.acm.org/joinsigs

Association for
Computing Machinery

Advancing Computing as a Science & Profession

NOTES

www.ingramcontent.com/pod-product-compliance
Lightning Source LLC
Chambersburg PA
CBHW080412060326
40689CB00019B/4214